READINGS IN KINSHIP AND SOCIAL STRUCTURE

READINGS IN KINSHIP AND SOCIAL STRUCTURE

Nelson Graburn

University of California, Berkeley

HARPER & ROW, PUBLISHERS
New York, Evanston, San Francisco, London

CONTENTS

PREFACE AND ACKNOWLEDGEMENTS

This volume attempts to bring together some of the most important papers, past and present, in the anthropology of kinship and social structure. Though the collection is fairly comprehensive with respect to both subject matter and historical periods, limitations of size obviously prevent the volume from being as inclusive as one would wish. Many of the essays considered had to be omitted because of such factors as length, duplication of ideas, and the difficulties connected with tracking down copyright holders. The book, therefore, does not claim to evenly represent all authorities or points of view. Those selections included center around some of the major concerns of social anthropologists, and some of the more esoteric topics were consciously excluded. Each chapter covers a topic or a historical period, contains two to six papers, and has, in addition, an introductory section and a bibliography that relate the selected papers to other works and other authors. These references were important at the time that the chapter deals with or in the development of the subject under consideration.

The compilation of this volume was an enormous task and the editor feels indebted to a large number of people. My initial debt is to my former teachers at the University of Chicago, particularly Professors Fred Eggan and David Schneider, and to those anthropologists at the University of California, Berkeley, who have contributed to my further education and understanding and who were extremely helpful in the writing and editing of this work. I am also particularly thankful for the cogent and critical comments of Professors David Schneider and Robin Fox, who examined the earlier selections and original materials. The final work, however, differs somewhat from their suggestions, and the responsibility is entirely mine.

Over the past few years graduate and undergraduate anthropology students at Berkeley have been most helpful in their discussions both within and outside coursework, and they, too, influenced my choice of selections and presentation. Dr. Lilyan Brudner and Mr. Stephen Strong, of the Department of Anthropology at Berkeley, have both worked closely with me at different stages in the processes of making selections and preparing the volume. Their professional advice on matters both large and small was extremely valuable. A number of assistants and typists were particularly helpful to me in the organization and preparation of the manuscript as well as the extensive research and correspondance connected with it. I would particularly like to thank Patricia Sarr, whose hard work and encouragement helped speed the project through its most difficult stages.

I would also like to thank those editors and others who granted their permission to reproduce many of the included works, especially the American Anthropological Association and the Royal Anthropological Institute and, of course, those many authors who responded favorably to my requests. The staff of Harper & Row, particularly Mr. Walter Lippincott, have been most supportive and patient during this project, and I hope that the results will bear out their faith in me.

Nelson Graburn
Berkeley, California
May 1970

READINGS
IN
KINSHIP
AND
SOCIAL
STRUCTURE

INTRODUCTION

THE NATURE OF KINSHIP AND SOCIAL STRUCTURE

Kinship is only one aspect of social structure, but it is the aspect that has received the most attention from anthropologists. It is difficult to provide a simple definition of kinship that is adequate for cross-cultural research because, in most societies, kinship systems are inextricably bound up with other aspects of social structure and, moreover, because notions of what constitutes kinship vary greatly from society to society.

Most anthropologists would agree, however, that any investigation of kinship should begin with the ideas related to the nature of kinship in our own society and the writings of previous anthropologists. Basically we are concerned with the "family system" and, because of our own models, we might well begin with the nuclear family, (i.e., parents and their children). (See Chapter XV.) In our own society, we see a strong connection between kinship relationships and presumed biological relationships. Therefore, the majority of anthropologists have used the "grid" of biological relationships as the basis for their ideas on the nature of kinship groups and systems. It is true, of course, that in the many studies of kinship around the world we have discovered that biological relationships are not always the most fundamental to some other societies' kinship systems (see Chapter XII).

In our examination of the subject of kinship, we find that we must also investigate how each culture perceives the nature of biological relationships. For instance, the group that we may call the nuclear family may well include a father who is not the genitor of the children and, in many cases, this group tends to feel more real kinship than does one that is based on purely biological relationships.

We are also concerned with the rules that particular societies make concerning the ascription of individuals into families and into larger "kinship" groupings. By larger kinship groupings we mean those social groups whose members belong, by virtue of their kinship relationships, to other members. The simplest example would be the nuclear family into which one is born (or which one may form by marriage). The larger groups—the extended family, lineage, clan, moiety, and so on —are all nuclear families related through *descent* (i.e., the members trace their descent from a common ancestor with parent-child links between every generation). In some societies—our own, for example—we say that we are related to someone if we can trace common descent from any ancestor—this is called nonunilineal or bilateral descent (see Chapter X). Most of the world's societies, however, only trace their descent through one of the parent-child intergenerational links, for example, from father to son (as our surname system indicates), in which case we call it *patrilineal* descent, or from mother to daughter (or mother's brother to sister's son) which is *matrilineal* descent. A few societies have both types of unilineal descent systems, and we call the combination double descent. It is through being born into such groups that individuals are given a position in the social world.

These large, kin-based unilineal descent groups form the major segments of many of the societies studied by anthropologists, especially in Africa and Australia (Fortes, "The Structure of Unilineal Descent Groups," 1953c). Generally speaking lineages are descent groups leading back to a known ancestor, whereas clans are groups descending from a common *mythical* ancestor. Both types of groups are usually exogamous—that is, the members must find their mates from some other group. These types of relationships through parents and children, and also between brothers and sisters, are often called *blood* relationships, though we should be careful to remember that the use of the term implies *our* concept and may have nothing to do with "blood" or even biologically real relationships.

Apart from socially defined "blood" relationships, all kinship systems also involve marital (affinal) ties that link families and larger kin-based groups together and knit the segments into a whole. The relative strength or importance of blood versus affinal relationships in integrating the members and nuclear families of societies has formed the basis of the controversy between "alliance" and "descent" theorists (see Chapters XI and XV). All human societies have kinship relationships and groupings although the boundaries and distinctions between these aspects of social structure and the many other aspects may be very difficult to draw.

One essential component of all the world's kinship systems is the incest taboo, which may be used to help us define at least part of the kinship group. These are rules which are supposed to prevent people from having sexual and marital relationships with certain other people—usually the ones who are believed to be biologically related (see Chapter XIV).

There have been many uses of the term social structure in the history of anthropology and, in this introduction, we will not consider some of the more esoteric arguments (see Chapters VI, IX, and XI). All human societies exhibit some form of structure. Social structure is basically a "map" that places a society's many individuals into certain categories and, thereby, gives them expectations about how they will be treated and a set of rules guiding them in their behavior toward other persons (see Chapters IV, V, and VI). These categories are usually labeled, and we call the system of names the terminology system. Societies structure people into categories or positions according to a number of principles. One of the most important of these principles is kinship. In all societies, therefore, the many people to whom any one person might be related are grouped into a number of categories. This breakdown determines an individual's behavior toward these particular kinsmen. For example, there might be 10 or 20 people who stand in the relationship of "uncle" to one person. Generally speaking, however, the fact that they are all placed in the "uncle" category may mean that the individual who calls them "uncle" will act toward them in the same general manner and that, conversely, the individual may expect these "uncles" to act toward him in the same kind of way. These expectations of behavior are known as roles (see Chapter XIII). The categories or positions into which people are put by social structural maps or models are sometimes known as statuses.

Thus, on one level, social structure is the totality of culturally typical dyadic relationships in a society (see Chapters VI and IX). On an equally important level, all societies are composed of social groups large and small, villages or nuclear families, for example. So the study of social structure includes the elucidation of the nature and principles of grouping in any society and the examination of the relationships between groups as well as those between persons. The common principles of grouping and categorization in social structure include kinship, residence, economics, politics, religion, age, shared interests, sex, and occupation. Social structure, therefore, includes the study of the organization of social groups by all these principles and the types of ideal and real behavior between these organized groups or between persons or statuses.

Kinship is a major organizing principle for the social structure of a very large proportion of the world's societies. In all societies the local kinship group, often the nuclear family or the extended family, is the essential group for the early socialization of children. In addition these small kinship groups are very often the units of residence, production and consumption, social control, and mutual aid. As social structure is the map for the categorization of people according to social roles and groups, kinship is very often the major organizing principle for many of the important categorizations of groups and relationships in society. In most of the smaller scale societies in the world, kinship-based groups perform some of the major functions that are essential to the maintenance of any society. For example, in all societies the majority of the people are expected to get married and kinship-based groups are usually those that guide the choice of a marriage partner, even in the negative sense. In our own society one has to marry *outside* the nuclear family. In other societies one's choice of a partner may be more limited, for one has to marry outside one's clan or moiety, and these large kin-based groups may form a large part of any one society. On the other hand, the group in which one must look for a marriage partner may, in some societies, be defined as some other kinship group. For example, one may have to marry into clan X or Y because of its particular kinship relationship to one's own clan (see Chapter XI).

Large kin-based groups, such as lineages and clans also represent, very often, territorial and political groupings. When this is the case, one's legal and residential status with respect to any other person in the society will be based on one's membership in a particular kinship group. Kinsmen are often expected to cooperate in economic matters either by helping each other at work or in the distribution of the products of their work. This may occur at the level of dyadic interpersonal relationships (e.g., the exchange of gifts within a household family at Christmas), or it may occur between large kin-based groups. An example of the latter might involve the exchange of marriage payments between exogamous (outmarrying) groups such as lineages and clans. In some societies, such as traditional China or the Tallensi of West Africa, kin groupings form the basis of religion, especially when the ancestors become deified and have to be worshipped or placated.

Most of the functions that we have mentioned for kinship groups can—and often are—performed by other types of social grouping. In a few societies, the determination of whom one may or has to marry may be determined by rules other than those of incest and exogamy. For example, in India one must marry within one's caste and although caste groups may also be kinship groups, they are also the basis of important occupational, territorial, and ritual groupings. In nearly all societies the basic principles of the organization of groups are age and sex. The study of grouping by age and sex has to some extent been neglected by anthropologists (Lowie 1920; Chapter V). In some societies, peer groups or age mates may perform important functions in socialization, economic cooperation, and social control. In nearly all societies, certain occupations and expected kinds of behavior are determined by sex. Thus the society-organizing aspects of social structure may be thought of as essentially a matter of "division of labor." In all societies, people are divided into categories to perform certain tasks that have to be done and, at the same time, all these tasks contribute in their own ways to the running of society; this we may call social integration. The study of social structure, therefore, is the examination and analysis of social division of labor and social integration.

THE IMPORTANCE OF KINSHIP IN THE STUDY OF SOCIETY

A large proportion of all the work done in social anthropology has been concerned with the study of kinship systems. The reasons for this are more than accidental.

1. Kinship systems are universal.
2. Kinship systems are always important, though in differing degrees, in the structure of all human societies.
3. In the majority of societies traditionally studied by anthropologists, kinship has been the one—if not the major—organizing principle.
4. Kinship systems are relatively easy to identify and lend themselves to fairly simple analyses.
5. In the history of anthropology, the discovery of

societies in which kinship was so overwhelmingly important, and so different from our own structures, provided the stimulus for much investigation.

6. Many other aspects of the nature of society had been examined at some length by other social theorists before anthropology became a well-formulated social science—thus, it can be said that anthropologists have concentrated on a subject that other social scientists had tended to neglect.

As anthropology is the study of man, the important universal features of human society form a common bond of concern for the majority of anthropologists. The traditions of anthropological training have emphasized the study of society and kinship systems because of the history of anthropology and the universality of these systems and their importance in all social structures.

Partly because of historical accident and other factors mentioned above, many of the approaches and much of the theory of modern anthropology were first worked out in the study of kinship systems. The nature of social groupings, social categories, roles, statuses, social terminology systems, economic exchange and cooperation, and so on are examples of areas that were first studied with the use of data obtained from studying kin-based societies. Even as anthropology has grown and diversified, it remains true that these classic works (many of which are included in this book) form a common core of the culture of social anthropology and although our interests are now often very diverse, many of the older authorities may be thought of as our "ancestors." They therefore form a common bond between us.

THE AIMS OF THIS BOOK

The aims of this book are to present some of the most important writings of these "intellectual ancestors" as well as some of the writing dealing with our current concerns in the topics of kinship and social structure that have formed so much of the core of anthropological theory. This book is organized according to historical development as well as by topic for a number of important reasons. The order of the selected readings demonstrates the "logic" of the theoretical growth of the topic. This "logic" is only partially related to the scientific development of the subject itself. Anthropologists, as human beings with particular interests and backgrounds, have pushed the development of theory in directions that have often depended on their particular personalities and their relationships to their seniors as much as on their "search for the truth." Thus it is often as important to know where a particular anthropologist was trained, who was in his peer group, and when he was writing, as it is to know his logical contributions to the progress of theory. In fact, an examination of the contents of this book will show that particular topics tended to command the attention of anthropologists at particular times and that not all subjects have been dealt with in a smooth scientific progression during the last 100 years. Particular personalities became important in stimulating their colleagues' interest in some topic whose popularity lasted until other personalities and topics arose to provide new interests. Very often, one might say that anthropologists have reacted against the approaches and the topical interests of their teachers in ways that parallel intergenerational conflicts in families (see, especially, Chapters III and VI).

The history of theoretical development in anthropology has not always been determined by the internal concerns of the discipline. If one looks at the history of interests and developments in anthropology, one can easily see that anthropologists have often followed styles and concerns current in other scientific disciplines. One might cite the common concern—permeating all of the social and biological sciences—with evolution in the nineteenth century. In the early twentieth century, the emphasis was shifted to functionalism, following similar developments in such diverse fields as architecture, design, and behaviorist psychology. At the present time, there is the rise and interest in mathematical methods and computer techniques, borrowed from the scientific milieu around us. Many of the most successful theoretical models used in anthropology have been used in the other sciences, such as componential and formal analyses (see Chapter XII) that use concepts developed in logic and linguistics.

★ Each chapter of this book contains important

selections from the major authorities on a particular topic written during one major period of anthropological history. The book is designed to introduce the student to the more important topics of continuing concern in anthropology and make him familiar with some of the past and present leading authorities on these topics. The readings have been selected on two bases: as introductions to major topics and the development of topical theory at particular points in time and, secondly, as examples of how major authorities have approached and shaped these topics.

Each chapter is introduced by a short section that attempts to show how the authorities selected were related to each other intellectually and socially and to place them in the general framework of anthropological history. These introductions summarize the major points in the issues discussed in each chapter and attempt to relate these issues to the subjects of the adjacent chapters. In addition to discussing the major authorities whose works are included here, these introductions also try to provide brief discussions relating the selected works to those of other authorities important in the development of the topic.

At the end of each chapter are Selected Readings. The first portion in the Selected Readings refers to the works of other authorities who have commented on or criticized the ideas in the selections in that chapter so that the student may become familiar with diverse views on each topic. The second portion presents a list of the more important original sources bearing upon either the topic or the historical period with which the chapter is concerned. The Bibliography at the end of the book contains all references, including those that are mentioned by the authors of the Selected Readings which I have not found necessary to include in the more topical bibliographies following each chapter. The final Bibliography, for example, lists references to particular ethnographic sources or more obscure works.

DIRECTIONS IN THE STUDY OF SOCIAL STRUCTURES

Anthropologists have, by no means, been concerned with all social phenomena that might be included in the topics kinship and social structure. Partly because of the paucity of anthropologists and the large number of societies in the world, certain types of societies have received more emphasis than others and certain topics have been neglected almost entirely. As I mentioned above, certain topics have, in a way, been preempted by social scientists in other disciplines. The detailed study of interpersonal relationships within our own society is an example of a task that sociologists have been performing, often because they are concerned with pathological rather than normative relationships. Other sociologists have done considerable research into the nature and functioning of bureaucracies in large-scale societies. On the other hand, it may be said that anthropologists are the world's experts on the nature of kinship groups and personal relationships in the world's smaller-scale societies.

Furthermore it should be borne in mind that those societies studied by anthropologists are not a random sample and were often, in fact, groups existing under a severe disadvantage. The nineteenth century colonialization of most of the Third World preceded the majority of anthropological studies. Most of the societies studied were at the time under some kind of colonial domination; therefore, the individuals in it were, to some degree, no longer "free agents." These circumstances may possibly have seriously modified the groups' social behavior and cultural beliefs and some anthropologists have, perhaps, not discovered or mentioned the degree to which changes had taken place even within the kinship structures that they were describing. It is obvious that such changes as the advent of a cash economy or decimation through previously unknown diseases should have produced considerable modification of family life and interpersonal relations.

Anthropologists themselves are rarely members of the Third World and practically never come from the peoples studied; they therefore represent "the outside" or even the colonial society or national government to these peoples. As sensitive and careful as they might be, this situation has sometimes created barriers that have prevented full disclosure of important facts and feelings and, in some instances, has caused the anthropologist to view the peoples studied from an administrator's point of view. Even in post-colonial societies and in enclave or reservation situations, the facts of political and economic pluralism in both new and old nations may still be a hindrance to successful rapport and research. Some anthropological accounts describe the kinship and social structure as if the societies were holistically functional and independant; these accounts should, perhaps, be examined more critically than those whose authors show themselves to be aware of the total situation and the possible changes that the society may have been forced to undergo.

What Lowie told us in 1920 (*Primitive Society*) still holds true today: Even within our range of studies we have neglected the study of nonkinship-based social structures. While anthropologists have certainly studied the nature of the division of labour by sex and age in many societies, for example, our work on age-based or occupationally based groups is still very sketchy. The best that we have been able to do is to apply what we have learned about kin-based social behavior to relationships based on other social structural principles. There is still, then, plenty of work to be done in this area of investigation.

The probable future of the field can be found, in fact, in a list of the past and present neglects mentioned above. Anthropology in general, and social structural studies in particular, have tended to neglect the ongoing, everyday behavior of human relationships. This is partly understandable because of the very nature of social structure—the cultural guide to normative or "ideal" behavior. We have rarely tackled social pathology or conflict in any systematic way, though increased understanding of these phenomena might not only help make for a better world but would also, almost certainly, increase our understanding of normative processes. Real behavior, as opposed to normative expectations, involves such variety and often seems so arbitrary that we have concentrated on the "should" rather than the actual. Furthermore, the masses of actual events might be more amenable to statistical analyses—a type that has found less favor among anthropologists than sociologists. The very detailed study of personal interactions and the content of roles has only recently gained ground. This achievement has been due, mainly, to the work of social scientists outside of anthropology and/or those using multidisciplinary approaches involving anthropology, sociology, and psychology (see Chapter XIII).

If anthropology is "what anthropologists do" we might say that anthropology has been up until recently the study of non-Western societies. One of the rationales offered for this state of affairs has been that anthropologists can best study the patterns of human societies by examining them in their simpler forms, that is, in small-scale societies. This has not proved to be true for two reasons: (1) individuals and their behavior in small non-Western societies are by no means simple and (2) the theory has not worked, that is, the insights gained from less complex societies have given us very little insight into most aspects of the industrial complex civilizations that, more and more, are dominating the world. Furthermore social anthropology has tended to swing between the two extremes of abstract "grand theory" and detailed empiricism; few have achieved the balance that C. Wright Mills (The Sociological Imagination, 1959: 124–131) has shown to be the necessary ingredient of "classic work" in the social sciences.

In the anthropological study of complex societies it is, again, kinship studies that have led the way. The works of Firth, Bott, Schneider, and others (see Chapter XVI) have shown us that anthropologists need not be afraid to approach the complex societies in which we live. It is hoped that more anthropologists will strike out and study non-kin based groupings such as firms, governments, unions, churches, and so on so that they may add to the insights already gained by different approaches in other disciplines.

Another frequent criticism of social anthropology is that we have shown ourselves incapable of building adequate models for the study of changing societies. In spite of the few excellent contributions that deal mainly with changing kinship terminologies (see Chapter VII), this criticism is justified. Yet we live in a changing world and "static" studies are becoming less and less relevant. Change is a universal process and, as Herskovits once stated (1948), it is the stability in the world to be wondered at, not the constant flux! The study of change is the cutting edge that may illustrate what, in fact, holds society together and where the limits of these structural mechanisms lie. As the abnormal may define the normal, boundaries define structures and change may define stability.

It is sometimes wondered what contributions can be expected from such a dry and esoteric subject as kinship and social structure as anthropologists have pursued it. This is a legitimate concern. Naturally most anthropologists try to examine topics in which they are interested and, secondarily, in which their predecessors and contemporaries are interested. This is fine up to a point but can lead to a very specialized and incestuous discipline, or, as Robin Fox has put it: "Some talk only to each other, and others only to God" (1967: 10). The relevance of our studies does not have to be immediate and, in fact, we can never know what will be considered relevant in decades to come. Who, for instance, would have thought that the research of the obscure railroad lawyer, Lewis Henry Morgan, which dealt mainly with the kinship terminology systems of exotic peoples, would have found a place in the sociopolitical works of Marx and Engels (1884), and would have, moreover, contributed to the formulation and implementation of the communist movement. Nevertheless, one can hope that some insights into the nature of human behavior might prove useful to a world that needs all the help it can get.

The major theoretical directions of social anthropology are almost impossible to predict or even suggest. As noted above, many of our most valuable tools and methods have been developed outside of our discipline, so one might say, without being too facetious, that the smart young anthropologist should look at the newest developments in other fields for possible application. But anthropology itself is no longer such a young and minute discipline. One can hope that we might add to the concepts and methods of other social sciences, as we have already done with such concepts as culture and such methods as participant observation and genealogy. Present trends indicate that we shall use more sophisticated mathematical tools such as systems analysis or surface topography to illuminate our studies of more complex societies and problems. At the same time, however, the world is also moving in the opposite direction, toward openness and simplicity in human relationships, toward increasing leisure time with greater popular involvement in the social processes that affect us all, and toward more humanism in our machine-dominated world. Perhaps it is in this area that anthropologists may be able to make their larger contributions, through the study of the maintainance and integration of human relationships and groups.

II

SOCIAL EVOLUTIONARY THEORY AND THE RISE OF KINSHIP STUDIES

In our consideration of the early history of this subject, we are as concerned with the general question: Where did anthropology come from? as with specific contributions that could be labeled kinship or social structure. Many, if not most, of the ideas that came to the fore in the eighteenth and the nineteenth centuries were hardly new; often, in fact, they dated back as far as the writings of the classical Greek philosophers. We can separate three main sets of factors that were responsible for what came to be known as "anthropology."

1. The ideas of the social-moral-political philosophers, whose major goals were to explain, justify, or reform society as they knew it.
2. The ideas of progress and "science" growing out of the Renaissance, often combined with (1) but leading, eventually, to the idea of evolution.
3. The new sources of data with which to work—first, the rediscovered writings of classical antiquity, mainly Roman and Greek—and, since the fifteenth century, the many discoveries of the "new worlds" of primitive peoples that were a consequence of exploration, trade, and missionary activity.

The first two streams developed partially as a reaction to the preceding theological (and theocratic) ideas about the nature of the social (and physical) world. These ideas were breaking down and new "philosophies" were being created to replace them in both explanatory and "political" functions in the sixteenth to nineteenth centuries.

The idea of a science of society came out of the French school of thought, extending from the writings of Montesquieu through those of Saint Simon to Comte. Evolutionary ideas, particularly the unilineal "simple to complex" continuum, were first proclaimed forcefully in the works of Spencer, along with the idea of "survival of the fittest." While Spencer saw these ideas as applying to everything in the natural and social universe, we may separate evolution into its social and natural forms and concentrate on the former. In the early nineteenth century, biological evolutionary discoveries (e.g., Lyell, Boucher de Perthes, Darwin, and Wallace) gave added impetus to the social theories but did not precede them.

Social evolutionary theory may be divided into two major types:

A. Two-stage evolution, emphasizing civilized versus others, that may be subdivided as follows:
1. Civilized versus "natural man." The latter concept is derived from the "Law of Nations," an important Roman legal concept that emphasized "man" in the state of nature, that is, without law, or political and social institutions, and so on, and was sometimes confused with concepts of primitive man by such men as Rousseau.
2. Civilized versus ancient or primitive man. (The latter two were, invariably, equated.) This second type of theory had more explanatory/scientific goals, especially in the nineteenth century, than had the former (1) whose goals were more moral/political. The works of Maine and Durkheim are good examples (of 2). (See Chapters II and III.)
B. Multistage evolution, as described in the works of Bachofen, McLennan, and Morgan (see Chapter II). This concept developed out of the theory of the type (A, 2) and had similar explanatory/historical goals.

Theories of both types (A and B) were *unilineal* and all of them had underlying *functionalist* ideas. They showed that each stage of their schemes represented integrated societies based on an analogy with organisms. This latter idea developed out of the notion that societies are natural systems, a scheme well represented in earlier works, such as those of Montesquieu, Adam Smith, Hume, Locke, and so on.

In addition to the basic ideas cited above—evolution, functionalism, and comparative social science—some of the more specific and basically anthropological ideas came out of this period. Among them we should mention: the legal system and the corporate group, status versus contract (i.e., ascription versus achievement), kin versus territorial-based societies (Maine, *Ancient Law*, 1861), exogamy and endogamy (McLennan, *Primitive Marriage*, 1865), the distinction between structure and process (Comte, 1831). The discovery or renewed emphasis on such phenomena as patriliny versus matriliny—confused with patriarchy and matriarchy (Bachofen, *Das Mutterecht*, 1861; Fustel de Coulange, *The Ancient City*, 1864)—the couvade, totemism, polygamy, marriage rules, and various forms of "the family" are also noteworthy here. It is pertinent to note that the idea of "survival of the fittest" took hold in biology, but was neglected in social theories of the nineteenth century save for the works of Edmund Spencer.

By the middle of the nineteenth century, it was almost impossible to write any sociological treatises without taking evolution into account, as well as a functionalist view of society and most of the other ideas of previous writers. The intellectual milieu was such that "the present" was always seen as the peak of evolution as opposed to the past and primitive cultures of any time. In sociology, the Victorian family and other institutions were seen as the end point of a progressive continuum. What was changing, though, was the amount of knowledge of other societies, primitive and eastern, both in America (the Indians) and the rest of the world that became available with the great expansion of trade and exploration.

The greatest anthropologist of this period, and for many decades to come, was Lewis Henry Morgan (see Chapter II). His work represents, perhaps, the maximum flowering of social evolutionary theory. He introduced the idea that kinship and kinship terminologies were important bases and indications of the level of a society. He also thought that kinship terminology systems could not diffuse, but might represent evidence of former social stages. He constructed an elaborate multistage scheme of evolution (*Ancient Society*, 1877) in which each stage was a functionally integrated sociocultural system, and he held that all societies must (have) pass(ed) through this unilineal series of stages. He classified family systems as classificatory and descriptive and subdivided these into still smaller stages. He carried the idea of comparative studies to its logical extreme and was the first to rely mainly on data from primitive societies. In that his scheme was the most explicit, compared with those of, for example, Spencer and Rousseau, Morgan was the most easily attacked. The attacks on his unilineal theories became more successful as more data became available from non-Western societies (e.g., Westermarck, *History of Human Marriage*, 1891; Boas, "The Limitations of the Comparative Method in Anthropology," 1896). With the collapse of unilineal evolution, Morgan's ideas on kinship and social structure also became suspect and few people made advances in this field until Rivers revived the most important ideas (1907; *Kinship and Social Organization*, 1914a).

Edmund Tylor was less grandiose in his conjectural reconstructions and less of an adherent of unilineal evolution. Tylor was among the first to take seriously the investigation of diffusion as a major explanatory/reconstructive tool. Diffusionist ideas were also present in the works of, for example, Waitz, Ratzel, and Pitt-Rivers, and were later carried to extremes by the Heliolithicists in England and the Kulturkreislehre in Germany. These diffusionist ideas had considerable influence upon the American anthropologists of the early twentieth century. Tylor carved out the subject of anthropology as "Culture" (*Primitive Culture*, 1871) and put our discipline, as distinct from sociology and history, on the map. Although not a field worker, Tylor emphasized the great care that must be taken in interpreting data from exotic peoples and was the first to try to apply statistical methods (1888–1889). In order to assess both the reliability of data and the likelihood of conjectural reconstructions, Tylor followed Morgan in a refined but more limited expression of social evolution and, in particular, in the use of "survivals" as explanatory tools.

There were many other writers of this period who upheld part or all of Morgan's schemes (e.g., Lubbock, Wake, Engels, etc.), while others concentrated on the development of sociological theories (e.g., Stark, Kohler, Robertson Smith, McGee, etc.). Their works, however, have been considered less original or influential.

During the nineteenth century, the discipline of anthropology and the subtopics of kinship and social organization came into their own. Many of the ideas and definitions of modern anthropology were added to the literature: types of kinship terminology systems, refinements of descent group concepts, the functional integration of exogamy with these, and the rise of diffusion as an explanatory tool. Perhaps the most important advances were made in the area of method, particularly the assessment of the validity of data and the concentration on fieldwork and first-hand ethnographic accounts of living peoples.

THE PRIMITIVE FAMILY AND THE CORPORATION
Henry S. Maine

I repeat the definition of a primitive society given before. It has for its units, not individuals, but groups of men united by the reality or the fiction of blood-relationship.

It is in the peculiarities of an undeveloped society that we seize the first trace of a universal succession. Contrasted with the organisation of a modern state, the commonwealths of primitive times may be fairly described as consisting of a number of little despotic governments, each perfectly distinct from the rest, each absolutely controlled by the prerogative of a single monarch. But though the Patriarch, for we must not yet call him the Pater-familias, had rights thus extensive, it is impossible to doubt that he lay under an equal amplitude of obligations. If he governed the family, it was for its behoof. If he was lord of its possessions, he held them as trustee for his children and kindred. He had no privilege or position distinct from that conferred on him by his relation to the petty commonwealth which he

From Sir Henry Maine, *Ancient Law*, rev. ed. (London: Oxford University Press, 1931), pp. 178–181. Reprinted in 1959. Originally published in 1861.

governed. The Family, in fact, was a Corporation; and he was its representative or, we might almost say, its Public officer. He enjoyed rights and stood under duties, but the rights and duties were, in the contemplation of his fellow-citizens and in the eye of the law, quite as much those of the collective body as his own. Let us consider for a moment the effect which would be produced by the death of such a representative. In the eye of the law, in the view of the civil magistrate, the demise of the domestic authority would be a perfectly immaterial event. The person representing the collective body of the family and primarily responsible to municipal jurisdiction would bear a different name; and that would be all. The rights and obligations which attached to the deceased head of the house would attach, without breach of continuity, to his successor; for, in point of fact, they would be the rights and obligations of the family, and the family had the distinctive characteristic of a corporation—that it never died. Creditors would have the same remedies against the new chieftain as against the old, for the liability being that of the still existing family would be absolutely unchanged. All rights available to the family would be as available after the demise of the headship as before it—except that the Corporation would be obliged—if indeed language so precise and technical can be properly used of these early times—would be obliged to *sue* under a slightly modified name.

The history of jurisprudence must be followed in its whole course, if we are to understand how gradually and tardily society dissolved itself into the component atoms of which it is now constituted—by what insensible gradations the relation of man to man substituted itself for the relation of the individual to his family and of families to each other. The point now to be attended to is that even when the revolution had apparently quite accomplished itself, even when the magistrate had in great measure assumed the place of Pater-familias, and the civil tribunal substituted itself for the domestic forum, nevertheless the whole scheme of rights and duties administered by the judicial authorities remained shaped by the influence of the obsolete privileges and coloured in every part by their reflections. There seems little question that the devolution of the Universitas Juris, so strenuously insisted upon by the Roman Law as the first condition of a testamentary or intestate succession, was a feature of the older form of society which men's minds had been unable to dissociate from the new, though with that newer phase it had no true or proper connection. It seems, in truth, that the prolongation of a man's legal existence in his heir, or in a group of co-heirs, is neither more nor less than a characteristic of *the family* transferred by a fiction to *the individual*. Succession in corporations is necessarily universal, and the family was a corporation. Corporations never die. The decease of individual members makes no difference to the collective existence of the aggregate body, and does not in any way affect its legal incidents, its faculties or liabilities. Now in the idea of a Roman universal succession all these qualities of a corporation seem to have been transferred to the individual citizen. His physical death is allowed to exercise no effect on the legal position which he filled, apparently on the principle that that position is to be adjusted as closely as possible to the analogies of a family, which in its corporate character was not of course liable to physical extinction.

THE COMPARATIVE STUDY OF FAMILY SYSTEMS

Lewis H. Morgan

pub. 1870

In the systems of relationship of the great families of mankind some of the oldest memorials of human thought and experience are deposited and preserved. They have been handed down as transmitted systems, through the channels of the blood, from the earliest ages of man's existence upon the earth; but revealing certain definite and progressive changes with the growth of man's experience in the ages of barbarism. To such conclusions the evidence, drawn from a comparison of the forms which now prevail in different families, appears to tend.

All the forms thus far discovered resolve themselves, in a comprehensive sense, into two, the *descriptive* and the *classificatory*, which are the reverse of each other in their fundamental conceptions. As systems of consanguinity each contains a plan, for the description and classification of kindred, the formation of which was an act of

From Lewis H. Morgan, *Systems of Consanguinity and Affinity in the Human Family*, Smithsonian Institution—Contributions to Knowledge, 17, v–vii, 3–4, 10–15. Reprinted by permission of the Smithsonian Institution Press. Originally published 1870.

intelligence and knowledge. They ascend by the chain of derivation to a remote antiquity, from which, as defined and indurated forms, their propagation commenced. Whether as organic forms they are capable of crossing the line of demarcation which separates one family from another, and of yielding evidence of the ethnic connection of such families, will depend upon the stability of these forms, and their power of self-perpetuation in the streams of the blood through indefinite periods of time. For the purpose of determining, by ample tests, whether these systems possess such attributes, the investigation has been extended over a field sufficiently wide to embrace four-fifths and upwards, numerically, of the entire human family. . . .

A comparison of these systems, and a careful study of the slight but clearly marked changes through which they have passed, have led, most unexpectedly, to the recovery, conjecturally at least, of the great series or sequence of customs and institutions which mark the pathway of man's progress through the ages of barbarism; and by means of which he raised himself from a state of promiscuous intercourse to final civilization. The general reader may be startled by the principal inference drawn from the classificatory system of relationship, namely, that it originated in the intermarriage of brothers and sisters in a communal family, and that this was the normal state of marriage, as well as of the family, in the early part of the unmeasured ages of barbarism. But the evidence in support of this conclusion seems to be decisive. Although it is difficult to conceive of the extremity of barbarism, which such a custom presupposes, it is a reasonable presumption that progress through and out from it was by successive stages of advancement, and through great reformatory movements. Indeed, it seems probable that the progress of mankind was greater in degree, and in the extent of its range, in the ages of barbarism than it has been since in the ages of civilization; and that it was a harder, more doubtful, and more intense struggle to reach the threshold of the latter, than it has been since to reach its present status. Civilization must be regarded as the fruit, the final reward, of the vast and varied experience of mankind in the barbarous ages. The experience of the two conditions are successive links of a common chain of which one cannot be interpreted without the other. This system of relationship, instead of revolting the mind, discloses with sensible clearness, "the hold of the pit whence [we have been] digged" by the good providence of God.

INTRODUCTION

As far back as the year 1846, while collecting materials illustrative of the institutions of the Iroquois, I found among them, in daily use, a system of relationship for the designation and classification of kindred, both unique and extraordinary in its character, and wholly unlike any with which we are familiar. In the year 1851 (*League of the Iroquois*, p. 85) I published a brief account of this singular system, which I then supposed to be of their own invention, and regarded as remarkable chiefly for its novelty. Afterwards, in 1857 (Pt. II, p. 132), I had occasion to reexamine the subject, when the idea of its possible prevalence among other Indian nations suggested itself, together with its uses, in that event, for ethnological purposes. In the following summer, while on the south shore of Lake Superior, I ascertained the system of the Ojibwa Indians; and, although prepared in some measure for the result, it was with some degree of surprise that I found among them the same elaborate and complicated system which then existed among the Iroquois. Every term of relationship was radically different from the corresponding term in the Iroquois; but the classification of kindred was the same. It was manifest that the two systems were identical in their fundamental characteristics. It seemed probable, also, that both were derived from a common source, since it was not supposable that two peoples, speaking dialects of stock-languages as widely separated as the Algonkin and Iroquois, could simultaneously have invented the same system, or derived it by borrowing one from the other.

From this fact of identity several inferences at once suggested themselves. As its prevalence among the Seneca-Iroquois rendered probable its like prevalence among other nations speaking dialects of the Iroquois stock-language, so its existence and use among the Ojibwas rendered equally probable its existence and use among the remaining nations speaking dialects of the Algonkin speech. If investigation should establish the affirmative of these propositions it would give to the system a wider distribution. In the second place, its prevalence among these nations would render probable its like prevalence among the residue of the American aborigines. If, then, it should be found to be universal among them, it would follow that the system was coeval, in point of time, with the commencement of their dispersion over the American continent; and also that, as a system transmitted with the blood, it might contain the necessary evidence to establish their unity of origin. And in the third place, if the Indian family came, in fact, from Asia, it would seem that they must have brought the system with them from that continent, and have left it behind them among the people from whom they separated; further than this, that its perpetuation upon this continent would render probable its like perpetuation upon the Asiatic, where it might still be found; and, finally, that it might possibly furnish some evidence upon the question of the Asiatic origin of the Indian family.

This series of presumptions and inferences was very naturally suggested by the discovery of the same system of consanguinity and affinity in nations speaking dialects of two stock-languages. It was not an extravagant series of speculations upon the given basis, as will be more fully understood when the Seneca and Ojibwa systems are examined and compared. On this simple and obvious line of thought I determined to follow up the subject until it was ascertained whether the system was universal among the American aborigines; and, should it become reasonably probable that such was the fact, then to pursue the inquiry upon the Eastern Continent, and among the islands of the Pacific.

. . .

GENERAL OBSERVATIONS UPON SYSTEMS OF RELATIONSHIPS

Marriage the basis of the Family Relationships —Systems of Consanguinity and Affinity—Each Person the Centre of a Group of Kindred—The System of Nature Numerical—Not necessarily adopted—Every System embodies Definite Ideas —It is a Domestic Institution—Two Radical Forms—The Descriptive, and the Classificatory —Aryan, Semitic, and Uralian Families have the former—Turanian, American Indian, and Malayan the latter—Divergence of Collateral Lines from Lineal, Characteristic of the First—Mergence of Collateral Lines in the Lineal, of the Second—Uses of these Systems depend upon the Permanence of their Radical Forms—Evidence of their Modification—Direction of the Change —Causes which tend to the Stability of their Radical Features.

In considering the elements of a system of consanguinity the existence of marriage between single pairs must be assumed. Marriage forms the basis of relationships. In the progress of the inquiry it may become necessary to consider a system with this basis fluctuating, and, perhaps, altogether wanting. The alternative assumption of each may be essential to include all the elements of the subject in its practical relations. The natural and necessary connection of consanguinei with each other would be the same in both cases; but with this difference, that in the former the lines of descent from parent to child would be known, while in the latter they would, to a greater or less extent, be incapable of ascertainment. These considerations might affect the form of the system of consanguinity.

The family relationships are as ancient as the *family*. They exist in virtue of the law of derivation, which is expressed by the perpetuation of the species through the marriage relation. A system of consanguinity, which is founded upon a community of blood, is but the formal expression and recognition of these relationships. Around every person there is a circle or group of kindred of which such person is the centre, the *Ego*, from whom the degree of the relationship is reckoned, and to whom the relationship itself returns. Above him are his father and his mother and their ascendants, below him are his children and their descendants; while upon either side are his brothers and sisters and their descendants, and the brothers and sisters of his father and of his mother and their descendants, as well as a much greater number of collateral relatives descended from common ancestors still more remote. To him they are nearer in degree than other individuals of the nation at large. A formal arrangement of the more immediate blood kindred into lines of descent, with the adoption of some method to distinguish one relative from another, and to express the value of the relationship, would be one of the earliest acts of human intelligence.

Should the inquiry be made how far nature suggests a uniform method or plan for the discrimination of the several relationships, and for the arrangement of kindred into distinct lines of descent, the answer would be difficult, unless it was first assumed that marriage between single pairs had always existed, thus rendering definite the lines of parentage. With this point established, or assumed, a natural system, numerical in its character, will be found underlying any form which man may contrive; and which, resting upon an ordinance of nature, is both universal and unchangeable. All of the descendants of an original pair, through intermediate pairs, stand to each other in fixed degrees of proximity, the nearness or remoteness of which is a mere matter of computation. If we ascend from ancestor to ancestor in the lineal line, and again descend through the several collateral lines until the widening circle of kindred circumscribes millions of the living and the dead, all of these individuals, in virtue of their descent from common ancestors, are bound to the *"Ego"* by the chain of consanguinity.

The blood relationships, to which specific terms have been assigned, under the system of the Aryan family, are few in number. They are grandfather and grandmother, father and mother, brother and sister, son and daughter, grandson and granddaughter, uncle and aunt, nephew and niece, and cousin. Those more remote in degree are described either by an augmentation or by a combination of these terms. After these are the affineal or marriage relationships, which are husband and wife, father-in-law and mother-in-law, son-in-law and daughter-in-law, brother-in-law and sister-in-law, step-father and step-mother, step-son and step-daughter, and step-brother and step-sister; together with such

of the husbands and wives of blood relatives as receive the corresponding designation by courtesy. These terms are barely sufficient to indicate specifically the nearest relationships, leaving much the largest number to be described by a combination of terms.

So familiar are these ancient household words, and the relationships which they indicate, that a classification of kindred by means of them, according to their degrees of nearness, would seem to be not only a simple undertaking, but, when completed, to contain nothing of interest beyond its adaptation to answer a necessary want. But, since these specific terms are entirely inadequate to designate a person's kindred, they contain in themselves only the minor part of the system. An arrangement into lines, with descriptive phrases to designate such relatives as fall without the specific terms, becomes necessary to its completion. In the mode of arrangement and of description diversities may exist. Every system of consanguinity must be able to ascend and descend in the lineal line through several degrees from any given person, and to specify the relationship of each to *Ego;* and also from the lineal, to enter the several collateral lines and follow and describe the collateral relatives through several generations. When spread out in detail and examined, every scheme of consanguinity and affinity will be found to rest upon definite ideas, and to be framed, so far as it contains any plan, with reference to particular ends. In fine, a system of relationship, originating in necessity, is a domestic institution, which serves to organize a family by the bond of consanguinity. As such it possesses a degree of vitality and a power of self-perpetuation commensurate with its nearness to the primary wants of man.

In a general sense, as has elsewhere been stated, there are but two radically distinct forms of consanguinity among the nations represented in the tables. One of these is descriptive and the other classificatory. The first, which is that of the Aryan, Semitic, and Uralian families, rejecting the classification of kindred, except so far as it is in accordance with the numerical system, describes collateral consanguinei, for the most part, by an augmentation or combination of the primary terms of relationship. These terms, which are those for husband and wife, father and mother, brother and sister, and son and daughter, to which must be added, in such languages as possess them, grandfather and grandmother, and grandson and granddaughter, are thus restricted to the primary sense in which they are here employed. All other terms are secondary. Each relationship is thus made independent and distinct from every other. But the second, which is that of the Turanian, American Indian, and Malayan families, rejecting descriptive phrases in every instance, and reducing consanguinei to great classes by a series of apparently arbitrary generalizations, applies the same terms to all the members of the same class. It thus confounds relationships, which, under the descriptive system, are distinct, and enlarges the signification both of the primary and secondary terms beyond their seemingly appropriate sense.

Although a limited number of generalizations have been developed in the system of the first-named families, which are followed by the introduction of additional special terms to express in the concrete the relationships thus specialized, yet the system is properly characterized as descriptive, and was such originally. It will be seen in the sequel that the partial classification of kindred which it now contains is in harmony with the principles of the descriptive form, and arises from it legitimately to the extent to which it is carried; and that it is founded upon conceptions entirely dissimilar from those which govern in the classificatory form. These generalizations, in some cases, are imperfect when logically considered; but they were designed to realize in the concrete the precise relationships which the descriptive phrases suggest by implication. In the Erse, for example, there are no terms for uncle or aunt, nephew or niece, or cousin; but they were described as *father's brother, mother's brother, brother's son,* and so on. These forms of the Celtic are, therefore, purely descriptive. In most of the Aryan languages terms for these relationships exist. My father's brothers and my mother's brothers, in English, are generalized into one class, and the term *uncle* is employed to express the relationship. The relationships to *Ego* of the

two classes of persons are equal in their degree of nearness, but not the same in kind; wherefore, the Roman method is preferable, which employed *patruus* to express the former, and *avunculus* to indicate the latter. The phrase "father's brother" describes a person, but it likewise implies a bond of connection which *patruus* expresses in the concrete. In like manner, my father's brother's son, my father's sister's son, my mother's brother's son, and my mother's sister's son are placed upon an equality by a similar generalization, and the relationship is expressed by the term *cousin.* They stand to me in the same degree of nearness, but they are related to me in four different ways. The use of these terms, however, does not invade the principles of the descriptive system, but attempts to realize the relationships in a simpler manner. On the other hand, in the system of the last-named families, while corresponding terms exist, their application to particular persons is founded upon very different generalizations, and they are used in an apparently arbitrary manner. In Seneca-Iroquois, for example, my father's brother is my father. Under the system he stands to me in that relationship and no other. I address him by the same term, *Hä-nih',* which I apply to my own father. My mother's brother, on the contrary, is my uncle, *Hoc-no'-seh,* to whom, of the two, this relationship is restricted. Again, with myself a male, my brother's son is my son, *Ha-ah'-wuk,* the same as my own son; while my sister's son is my nephew, *Ha-yä'-wan-da;* but with myself a female, these relationships are reversed. My brother's son is then my nephew; while my sister's son is my son. Advancing to the second collateral line, my father's brother's son and my mother's sister's son are my brothers, and they severally stand to me in the same relationship as my own brother; but my father's sister's son and my mother's brother's son are my cousins. The same relationships are recognized under the two forms, but the generalizations upon which they rest are different.

In the system of relationship of the Aryan, Semitic, and Uralian families, the collateral lines are maintained distinct and perpetually divergent from the lineal, which results, theoretically as well as practically, in a dispersion of the blood.

The value of the relationships of collateral consanguinei is depreciated and finally lost under the burdensomeness of the descriptive method. This divergence is one of the characteristics of the descriptive system. On the contrary, in that of the Turanian, American Indian, and Malayan families, the several collateral lines, near and remote, are finally brought into, and merged in the lineal line, thus theoretically, if not practically, preventing a dispersion of the blood. The relationships of collaterals by this means is both appreciated and preserved. This mergence is, in like manner, one of the characteristics of the classificatory system.

How these two forms of consanguinity, so diverse in their fundamental conceptions and so dissimilar in their structure, came into existence it may be wholly impossible to explain. The first question to be considered relates to the nature of these forms and their ethnic distribution, after the ascertainment of which their probable origin may be made a subject of investigation. While the existence of two radically distinct forms appears to separate the human family, so far as it is represented in the tables, into two great divisions, the Indo-European and the Indo-American, the same testimony seems to draw closer together the several families of which these divisions are composed, without forbidding the supposition that a common point of departure between the two may yet be discovered. If the evidence deposited in these systems of relationship tends, in reality, to consolidate the families named into two great divisions, it is a tendency in the direction of unity of origin of no inconsiderable importance.

After the several forms of consanguinity and affinity, which now prevail in the different families of mankind, have been presented and discussed, the important question will present itself, how far these forms become changed with the progressive changes of society. The uses of systems of relationship to establish the genetic connection of nations will depend, first, upon the structure of the system, and, secondly, upon the stability of its radical forms. In form and feature they must be found able, when once established, to perpetuate themselves through indefinite periods of time. The question of their use must turn

upon that of the stability of their radical features. Development and modification, to a very considerable extent, are revealed in the tables in which the comparison of forms is made upon an extended scale; but it will be observed, on further examination, that these changes are further developments of the fundamental conceptions which lie, respectively, at the foundation of the two original systems.

There is one powerful motive which might, under certain circumstances, tend to the overthrow of the classificatory form and the substitution of the descriptive, but it would arise after the attainment of civilization. This is the inheritance of estates. It may be premised that the bond of kindred, among uncivilized nations, is a strong influence for the mutual protection of related persons. Among nomadic stocks, especially, the respectability of the individual was measured, in no small degree, by the number of his kinsmen. The wider the circle of kindred the greater the assurance of safety, since they were the natural guardians of his rights and the avengers of his wrongs. Whether designedly or otherwise, the Turanian form of consanguinity organized the family upon the largest scale of numbers. On the other hand, a gradual change from a nomadic to a civilized condition would prove the severest test to which a system of consanguinity could be subjected. The protection of the law, or of the State, would become substituted for that of kinsmen; but with more effective power the rights of property might influence the system of relationship. This last consideration, which would not arise until after a people had emerged from barbarism, would be adequate beyond any other known cause to effect a radical change in a pre-existing system, if this recognized relationships which would defeat natural justice in the inheritance of property. In Tamilian society, where my brother's son and my cousin's son are both my sons, a useful purpose may have been subserved by drawing closer, in this manner, the kindred bond; but in a civilized sense it would be manifestly unjust to place either of these collateral sons upon an equality with my own son for the inheritance of my estate. Hence the growth of property and the settlement of its distribution might be expected to lead a more precise discrimination of the several degrees of consanguinity if they were confounded by the previous system.

Where the original system, anterior to civilization, was descriptive, the tendency to modification, under the influence of refinement, would be in the direction of a more rigorous separation of the several lines of descent, and of a more systematic description of the persons or relationships in each. It would not necessarily lead to the abandonment of old terms nor to the invention of new. This latter belongs, usually, to the formative period of a language. When that is passed, compound terms are resorted to if the descriptive phrases are felt to be inconvenient. Wherever these compounds are found it will be known at once that they are modern in the language. The old terms are not necessarily radical, but they have become so worn down by long-continued use as to render the identification of their component parts impossible. While the growth of nomenclatures of relationship tends to show the direction in which existing systems have been modified, it seems to be incapable of throwing any light upon the question whether a classificatory form ever becomes changed into a descriptive, or the reverse. It is more difficult, where the primitive system was classificatory, to ascertain the probable direction of the change. The uncivilized nations have remained substantially stationary in their condition through all the centuries of their existence, a circumstance eminently favorable to the permanency of their domestic institutions. It is not supposable, however, that they have resisted all modifications of their system of consanguinity. The opulence of the nomenclature of relationships, which is characteristic of the greater portion of the nations whose form is classificatory, may tend to show that, if it changed materially, it would be in the direction of a greater complexity of classification. It is extremely difficult to arrive at any general conclusions upon this question with reference to either form. But it may be affirmed that if an original system changes materially, after it has been adopted into use, it is certain to be done in harmony with the ideas and conceptions which it embodies, of which the changes will be further and logical developments.

It should not be inferred that forms of consanguinity and affinity are either adopted, modified, or laid aside at pleasure. . . . When a system has once come into practical use, with its nomenclature adopted, and its method of description or of classification settled, it would, from the nature of the case, be very slow to change. Each person, as has elsewhere been observed, is the centre around whom a group of consanguinei is arranged. It is my father, my mother, my brother, my son, my uncle, my cousin, with each and every human being; and, therefore, each one is compelled to understand, as well as to use, the prevailing system. It is an actual necessity to all alike, since each relationship is personal to *Ego*. A change of any of these relationships, or a subversion of any of the terms invented to express them, would be extremely difficult if not impossible; and it would be scarcely less difficult to enlarge or contract the established use of the terms themselves. The possibility of this permanence is increased by the circumstance that these systems exist by usage rather than legal enactment, and therefore the motive to change must be as universal as the usage. Their use and preservation are intrusted to every person who speaks the common language, and their channel of transmission is the blood. Hence it is that, in addition to the natural stability of domestic institutions, there are special reasons which contribute to their permanence, by means of which it is rendered not improbable that they might survive changes of social condition sufficiently radical to overthrow the primary ideas in which they originated.

. . .

ON A METHOD OF INVESTIGATING THE DEVELOPMENT OF INSTITUTIONS; APPLIED TO LAWS OF MARRIAGE AND DESCENT

Edward B. Tylor

For years past it has become evident that the great need of anthropology is that its methods should be strengthened and systematised. The world has not been unjust to the growing science, far from it. Wherever anthropologists have been able to show definite evidence and inference, for instance, in the development series of arts in the Pitt-Rivers Museum, at Oxford, not only specialists but the educated world generally are ready to receive the results and assimilate them into public opinion. Strict method has however, as yet only been introduced over part of the anthropological field. There has still to be overcome a certain not unkindly hesitancy on the part of men engaged in the precise operations of mathematics, physics, chemistry, biology, to admit that the problems of anthropology are amenable to scientific treatment. It is my aim to show that the development of institutions may be investigated on a basis of tabulation and classification. For this end I have taken up a subject of the utmost real as well as theoretical interest, the formation of laws of marriage and descent, as to which during many years I have been collecting the evidence found among between three and four hundred peoples, ranging from insignificant savage hordes to great cultured nations. The particular rules have been scheduled out into tables, so as to ascertain what may be called the "adhesions" of each custom, showing which peoples have the same custom, and what other customs accompany it or lie apart from it. From the recurrence or absence of these customs it will be our business to infer their dependence on causes acting over the whole range of mankind.

Years since, long before my collection of data

Reprinted by permission of the Royal Anthropological Institute of Great Britain and Ireland from the *Journal of the Royal Anthropological Institute*, Vol. 18 (1889), pp. 245–256, 261–269.

approached its present bulk, and could be classified into the elaborate tables now presented, I became naturally anxious to know whether my labour has been thrown away, or whether this social arithmetic would do something to disclose the course of social history. The question was how to make the trial. I remembered a story I had once heard of Horace Vernet, that a friend asked him how he planned out his huge battle-pieces. The painter took the inquirer into his studio and began a picture for him by first touching in a bayonet in one corner of his canvas, then drawing the arm and sabre of the trooper slashing over the bayonet-thrust, and so on from one overlapping figure to the next till he reached the central group. It seemed to me that it would be well to begin thus in one corner of the field. The point I chose was a quaint and somewhat comic custom as to the barbaric etiquette between husbands and their wives' relatives, and *vice versa*: they may not look at one another, much less speak, and they even avoid mentioning one another's names. Thus, in America, John Tanner, the adopted Ojibwa, describes his being taken by a friendly Assineboin into his lodge, and seeing how at his companion's entry the old father and mother-in-law covered up their heads in their blankets till their son-in-law got into the compartment reserved for him, where his wife brought him his food. So in Australia, Mr. Howitt relates how he inadvertently told a native to call his mother-in-law, who was passing at some little distance; but the blackfellow sent the order round by a third party, saying reproachfully to Mr. Howitt, "You know I could not speak to that old woman." Absurd as this custom may appear to Europeans, it is not the outcome of mere local fancy, as appears on reckoning up the peoples practising it in various regions of the world, who are found to be about sixty-six in number, that is, more than one-sixth of the whole number of peoples catalogued, which is roughly three-hundred and fifty. Thus:—

AVOIDANCE.

Between H. and W.'s Rel.	Mutual	Between W. and H.'s Rel.
45	8	13

Now, on looking out from the schedules the adhesions of this avoidance-custom, a relation appears between it and the customs of the world as to residence after marriage. This is seen in the following computation of the people's whose habit is for the husband to take up his abode with the wife's family permanently, or to do so temporarily and eventually to remove with her to his own family or home (the reverse of this does not occur), or for the husband at once to take home the wife.

RESIDENCE.

H. to W.	Removal	W. to H.
65	76	141

Now, if the customs of residence and the customs of avoidance were independent, or nearly so, we should expect to find their coincidence following the ordinary law of chance distribution. In the tribes where the husband permanently lives with his wife's family (sixty-five out of three-hundred and fifty), we should estimate that ceremonial avoidance between him and them might appear in nine cases, whereas it actually appears in fourteen cases. On the other hand, peoples where the husband at marriage takes his wife to his home (one-hundred and forty-one out of three-hundred and fifty), would rateably correspond with avoidance between him and her family in eighteen cases, whereas it actually appears in nine cases only. Also, if the thirteen cases of avoidance between the wife and the husband's family were divided rateably among the different modes of residence, two or three cases should come among the peoples where the husband lives with the wife's family, but there are no such

cases. On the other hand, five cases should be found among the peoples where the wife lives in the husband's home or family, but actually there are eight. Thus there is a well marked preponderance indicating that ceremonial avoidance by the husband of the wife's family is in some way connected with his living with them and *vice versa* as to the wife and the husband's family. Hereupon, it has to be enquired whether the facts suggest a reason for this connexion. Such a reason readily presents itself, inasmuch as the ceremony of not speaking to and pretending not to see some well-known person close by, is familiar to ourselves in the social rite which we call "cutting." This, indeed with us implies aversion, and the implication comes out even more strongly in objection to utter the name ("we never mention her," as the song has it). It is different, however, in the barbaric custom we are considering, for here the husband is none the less on friendly terms with his wife's people because they may not take any notice of one another. In fact, the explanation of this ceremonial cutting may be simpler and more direct than in civilised Europe. As the husband has intruded himself among a family which is not his own, and into a house where he has no right, it seems not difficult to understand their marking the difference between him and themselves by treating him formally as a stranger. So like is the working of the human mind in all stages of civilisation, that our own language conveys in a familiar idiom the same train of thought; in describing the already mentioned case of the Assineboin marrying and taking up his abode with his wife's parents who pretend not to see him when he comes in, we have only to say that they do not *recognise* him, and we shall have condensed the whole proceeding into a single word. In this first example, it is to be noticed that the argument of a causal connexion of some kind between two groups of phenomena brings into view, so far at least as the data prove sound, a scientific fact. But we pass on to less solid ground in assigning for this connexion a reason which may be only analogous to the real reason, or only indirectly corresponding with it, or only partly expressing it, as its correlation with other connexions may eventually show. This important reservation, once stated, may be taken as understood through the rest of the enquiry.

Let us now turn to another custom, not less quaint-seeming than the last to the European mind. This is the practice of naming the parent from the child. When Moffat, the missionary, was in Africa among the Bechuana, he was spoken to and of, according to native usage, as Ra-Mary = father of Mary. On the other side of the world, among the Kasias of India, Colonel Yule mentions the like rule; for instance, there being a boy named Bobon, his father was known as Pabobon. In fact there are above thirty peoples spread over the earth who thus name the father, and, though less often, the mother. They may be called, coining a name for them, *teknonymous* peoples. When beginning to notice the wide distribution of this custom of *teknonymy*, and setting myself to reckon its adhesions, I confess to have been fairly taken by surprise to find it lying in close connection with the custom of the husband's residence in the wife's family, the two coinciding twenty-two times, where accident might fairly have given eleven. It proved to be still more closely attached to the practice of ceremonial avoidance by the husband of the wife's relatives, occurring fourteen times, where accident might have given four. The combination is shown on the diagram, fig. 1, the (approximate) numbers on which give the means of estimating the probable closeness of causal connection. Were the three customs so distantly connected as to be practically independent, the product of the corresponding fractions 132/350 × 53/350 × 31/350, multiplied into the three hundred and fifty peoples would show that their concurrence might be expected to happen between once and twice in the list of peoples of the world. In fact it is found eleven times. Thus, we have their common causation vouched for by the heavy odds of six to one. Many of the firmest beliefs of mankind rest, I fear, on a less solid basis. In tracing out the origin of the group of customs in conformity with these conditions, it is not necessary to invent a hypothesis, as an account of the proceedings of the Cree Indians will serve as a "luminous instance" to clear up the whole situation. Among these Indians the young husband, coming to live with his wife's parents, must turn his back on them, not speaking to them (especially not to his mother-in-law), being thus treated as a stranger till his first child is born; whereupon he takes its name, and is called "father of So-and-so," and thenceforth attaches himself to his parents-in-law rather than to his own parents. That is to say, he is ceremonially treated as a stranger till his child, being born a member of the family, gives him status as father of a member of the family, whereupon they consistently leave off the farce of not recognising him. When I brought this argument to the knowledge of Dr. G. A. Wilken, of Leyden, he pointed out to me that in his series of papers on "Primitive Forms of Marriage," where he gives instance of the naming of fathers from children, he had stated this practice to be an assertion of paternity. Undoubtedly it is so on the father's part, and its being so is quite compatible with its being a recognition of him by the wife's kinsfolk, the two aspects belonging to one social fact.

Taking the connection between residence and ceremonial avoidance to be substantiated by their relative adhesions, it is necessary to notice that there are cases where the husband, although he carries the wife away from the home of her parents, nevertheless goes through the form of avoiding them. This, under the circumstances, seems a motiveless proceeding, but is intelligible as a survival from a time when he would have

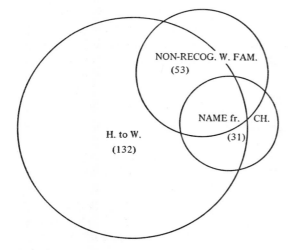

NON-RECOG. W. FAM.
(53)

NAME fr. CH.
(31)

H. to W.
(132)

Figure 1.

lived with them. These cases belong mainly to the Malay District and to Australia. In the Malay District the habit of residence in the wife's family is still a notable institution of the country, though being fast superseded by householding on the Arab and European models. In Australia, the native custom is described as being that the husband takes his wife to his own home, while at the same time he carries out the etiquette of cutting his mother-in-law to a ludicrous extreme, with slight traces of the avoidance of the father-in-law. It appeared to me that on the present explanation this must indicate a recent habit of residence on the wife's side, and reference showed a law of the Kurnai tribe of Gippsland, (Fison and Howitt, "Kamilaroi and Kurnai," p. 207.) that when a native kills game, certain parts of the meat (of a kangaru, the head, neck and part of the back) are the allotted share of the wife's parents. As the duty of supplying game to the wife's household when the husband lives there is one of the best-marked points of matriarchal law, I wrote to Mr. Howitt, as the leading authority on Australian anthropology, suggesting that further enquiry would probably disclose evidence hitherto unnoticed as to the maternal stage of society subsisting in Australia. After examination made, Mr. Howitt replied:—"I am now satisfied that your surmises are quite correct," and therewith he sent details bearing on the question, especially an account by Mr. Aldridge, of Maryborough, Queensland, as to the practice of the tribes in his neighbourhood. This I will quote, as being a strongly marked case of residence on the wife's side. "When a man marries a woman from a distant locality, he goes to her tribelet and identifies himself with her people. This is a rule with very few exceptions. Of course, I speak of them as they were in their wild state. He becomes part of and one of the family. In the event of a war expedition, the daughter's husband acts as a blood-relation, and will fight and kill his own blood-relations if blows are struck by his wife's relations. I have seen a father and son fighting under these circumstances, and the son would most certainly have killed his father if others had not interfered."

The relative positions of the two groups of customs, residence and avoidance, may now be more completely shown, by the aid of the diagram, fig. 2.

Here the space representing residence is divided into three sections, viz., residence on the wife's side; the transitional stage of removal (where the couple begin married life in the wife's house, but eventually move); residence on the husband's side. According to the previous arguments, the ceremonial avoidance between the husband and the wife's family is taken to have arisen within the periods when he and they lived permanently or temporarily in contact, and to have continued by survival into the period after this co-residence had ceased. There next appear[s] the small group of eight cases of mutual avoidance, at once between the husband and the wife's family, and the wife and the husband's family. These consistently are found in the removal stage, where both kinds of residence meet, surviving into the stage of residence on the husband's side. Avoidance between the wife and the husband's family has the same range, but here the conditions producing it belong to both stages of residence, and there is no question of survival.

From this distribution of the avoidance-customs, it appears that in the parts of the world open to the present inspection, the three stages of residence have tended to succeed one another in the upward order of the diagram. Residence on the wife's side appears earliest, after this the removal stage, and latest, residence on the husband's side. For if it be supposed that the course of society was in the reverse direction, as would be represented by turning the diagram upside down, avoidance between the husband and the wife's family would be represented as arising in the stage when the husband lived away from it, while avoidance between the wife and the husband's family, which ought on this supposition to continue by survival into the stage of residence on the wife's side, is not found there. The avoidance-customs, though practically so trifling, are thus signals showing the direction of a movement, of which we shall more fully see the importance, namely, the shifting of habitual residence from the wife's family to the husband's.

Let us now proceed to apply a similar method

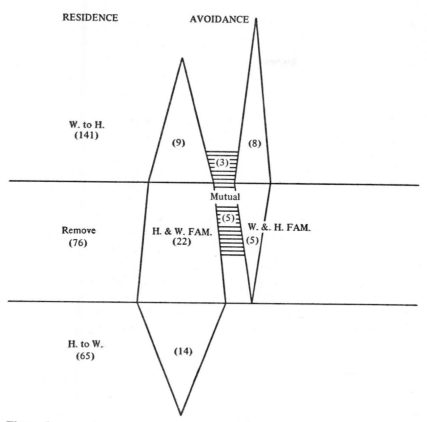

RESIDENCE   AVOIDANCE

W. to H.
(141)
                    (9)   (8)
                          (3)

                         Mutual

Remove   H. & W. FAM.   W. &. H. FAM.
(76)   (22)   (5)
                          (5)

H. to W.
(65)   (14)

Figure 2.

to the investigation of the great division of society into matriarchal and patriarchal. In the matriarchal system, descent in the family or clan is reckoned from the mother; authority is mainly on her side, the mother's brother being habitually guardian of the children; succession to rank and office, and inheritance of property, follow the same line passing to the brother or to the sister's son. In the patriarchal system descent is from the father; he has the power over wife and children; succession and inheritance are from him to his offspring. Between these extreme stages lies an intermediate or transitional stage in which their characteristics are variously combined. The terms partriarchal and matriarchal not being quite appropriate, I shall use in preference for the three stages the terms maternal, maternal-paternal, and paternal. The classification is necessarily somewhat vague, but I think will be found to have sufficient precision for the problem of determin-

ing the direction in which mankind has tended to move from one of the stages to another. In dealing with this problem certain customs relating to mothers-in-law will be used as indicators.

Among a large proportion of the nations of the world up to the middle levels of culture, the remarriage of widows is arranged, and more or less enforced, but the regulations are framed on two distinct principles. On the first principle the widow becomes the wife of her husband's brother, or near kinsman, according to some recognized order of precedence of claim. The word "levirate," from *levir* = husband's brother, has become the accepted term for this institution, but its sense must in most cases be extended to take in a series of kinsmen, among whom the brother-in-law only ranks first. Unfortunately, it has seldom been thought worth while to ascertain this precise order, which might throw light on family structure, as in an account drawn up by Mr. Howitt of the practice in Australian tribes where any man is eligible to succeed to the widow, if he stands in the relation of elder or younger brother to the deceased, beginning with actual brothers on the male or female side, according to the rule of descent in the tribe, and extending to tribal brothers who are in our terminology cousins, more or less near. The levirate appears in its various forms among one hundred and twenty peoples in my list, or about one in three in the world. On taking out its adhesions it seems sufficiently accounted for as a custom of substitution, belonging to the period, when marriage is a compact not so much between two individuals as between two families, often made when the couple are infants unable to understand it, in fact sometimes before their birth. That the levirate forms part of this family transaction is consistent with other customs more or less associated with it, viz., that when a wife dies or turns out ill her family are bound to replace her by another, a rule which sometimes even holds out for betrothal, and that the widow is not allowed to marry out of her husband's family unless by leave of his kinsmen, who have the choice of keeping her, or parting with her, usually for a price. The social distribution of the levirate is shown in fig. 3 to extend through all three social stages. It is in the maternal-paternal stage that it comes into competition with the second principle, unknown in the maternal stage, in which the father's widows pass by inheritance to his sons, especially the eldest son taking his stepmothers. A small but important group of cases forms a bridge between the two principles of levirate and filial succession, combining both in the same nation. This combination is well shown in Africa, where on a chief's death the head wife will pass by levirate to his brother, while her son, the new chief, will inherit a crowd of stepmothers, a less onerous legacy indeed than may seem, as they are practically slaves who hoe and grind corn for their own living. Looking at

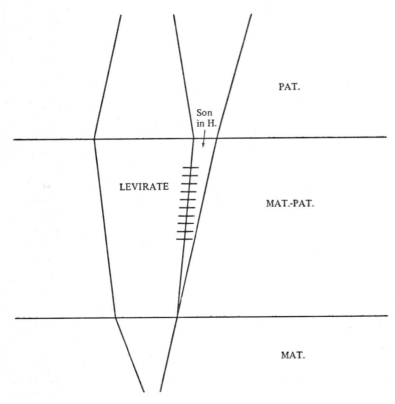

Figure 3.

the distribution of these groups of customs, it is seen to be only compatible with the view that the paternal rule followed the maternal, bringing with it even while its prevalence was but partial, the principle of paternal widow-inheritance.

The quaint custom of the couvade has now to be considered from the same point of view. In this the father, on the birth of his child, makes a ceremonial pretence of being the mother, being nursed and taken care of, and performing other rites such as fasting and abstaining from certain kinds of food or occupation, lest the new-born should suffer thereby. This custom is known in the four quarters of the globe. How sincerely it is still accepted appears in a story of Mr. Im Thurn, who on a forest journey in British Guiana noticed that one of his Indians refused to help haul the canoes, and on enquiry found that the man's objection was that a child must have been born to him at home about this time, and he must not exert himself so as to hurt the infant. In the Mediterranean district it is not only mentioned by ancient writers, but in Spain and France, in or near the Basque country, it went on into modern times; Zamacola, in 1818, mentions, as but a little time ago, that the mother used to get up and the father take the child to bed. Knowing the tenacity of these customs, I should not be surprised if traces of couvade might be found in that district still. Now examining the distribution of the couvade by the diagram, Fig. 4, we see that the farcical proceeding does not appear in the maternal stage, but arising in the maternal-paternal, at once takes its strongest development of twenty cases; in the paternal the number falls to eight cases, leading to the inference that here it is only kept up in dwindling survival.

Looking at this position, I must now argue that the original interpretation of the couvade given by Bachofen in his great treatise [1] in 1861, and

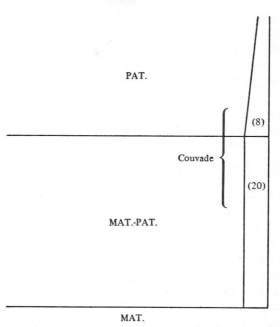

Figure 4.

supported by Giraud-Teulon, fits substantially with the facts, and is justified by them. He takes it to belong to the turning-point of society when the tie of parentage, till then recognised in maternity, was extended to take in paternity, this being done by the fiction of representing the father as a second mother. He compares the couvade with the symbolic pretences of birth which in the classical world were performed as rites of adoption. To his significant examples may be added the fact that among certain tribes the couvade is the legal form by which the father recognizes a child as his. Thus this apparently absurd custom, which for twenty centuries has been the laughing-stock of mankind, proves to be not merely incidentally an indicator of the tendency of society from maternal to paternal, but the very sign and record of that vast change.

· · ·

[1] J. J. Bachofen, "Das Mutterrecht," pp. 17, 255; Giraud-Teulon, "Les Origines du Marriage," p. 138. In my account of the couvade, "Early History of Mankind," Chap. X, I have laid stress on the magical-sympathetic nature of a large class of couvade rites as implying a physical bond between parent and child; thus an Abipone would not take snuff lest his sneezing might hurt his newborn baby, and a Carib father must abstain from eating sea-cow lest his infant get little round eyes like it. This motive, which is explicitly or implicitly recognised by the savages themselves, certainly forms part of the explanation of the couvade. It is, however, secondary, being due to the connexion considered as subsisting between parent and child, so that these sympathetic prohibitions may be interpreted as originally practised by the mother only, and afterwards adopted by the father also.

At this point it will be convenient to examine two institutions of early marriage law, namely, exogamy and classificatory relationship. The principle of exogamy was brought prominently into view fifty years ago, by Sir George Grey, (1841, vol II, p. 225) when he described the native Australian rule for a man not to marry a woman of the same family name or bearing the same animal-crest or kobong as himself; and called attention to the coincidence of this with the North American system of clans named from totem animals, a man being bound to marry outside his own totem or clan. Mr. J. F. McLennan (*Primitive Marriage*, 1865, pp. 48, 130) gave these customs the name of exogamy or "marry-out," and showed them to belong to "a most widely prevailing principle of marriage law among primitive races." Much information has since then come in, with the result of showing that exogamy has hardly to do with the capture of wives in war between alien nations, but rather with the regulation of marriages within groups of clans or tribes who have connubium; such clans or tribes may be more or less at strife, but they acknowledge ties of kindred and are usually allied by language. It is now also understood that a people may at once practice endogamy or "marry-in" within its borders, and exogamy or "marry-out" of its clans with one another. The situation may be understood among the Hindus, where a man must marry in his caste, but within that caste must not marry in his own gotra or clan. The effect of an exogamic rule is similar whether clanship follows the female or male line of descent. Next, as to the principle of classificatory relationship, an early mention of this is by Father Lafitau, ("Moeurs des Sauvages Ameriquains," 1724, Vol. I, p. 552) above one hundred and fifty years ago, who states that

> . . . among the Iroquois and Hurons all the children of a cabin regard all their mother's sisters as their mothers, and all their mother's brothers as their uncles, and for the same reason they give the name of fathers to all their father's brothers, and aunts to all their father's sisters. All the children on the side of the mother and her sisters, and of the father and his brothers, regard each other mutually as brothers and sisters, but as regards the children of their uncles and aunts, that is, of their mother's brothers and father's sisters, they only treat them on the footing of cousins. . . . In the third generation this changes, the great uncles and great aunts become again grandfathers and grandmothers of the children of those whom they called nephews and nieces. This continues always in the descending line according to the same rule.

In our own time, Lewis H. Morgan, living among the Iroquois as an adopted Indian, was struck with this system of relationships, so unlike what he had been brought up among, and which he at first thought to be a peculiar invention of his Iroquois. But finding, on enquiry, that it extended to other North American tribes, he eventually by circulating interrogatories succeeded in collecting a great series of systems of relationship, in which he established the wide prevalence of classificatory systems as he called them from the relatives being grouped in classes ("Systems of Consanguinity and Affinity of the Human Family," 1870). Under the term classificatory systems, Mr. Morgan included not only those approximating to the Iroquois type, but a much simpler and ruder plan prevalent in Polynesia; it is, however, convenient for me to confine my remarks here to the former group only. This system, as found among the American Indians, Mr. Morgan showed to be closely analogous to that of the Dravidian nations of Southern Hindustan. This latter is a well-known source of perplexity to a newly appointed English civilian, who may be told by a witness that his father was sitting in the house, but presently the same witness mentions his father as coming in from the field; the native is sharply reproved by the judge for contradicting himself, whereupon he explains, it was my "little father," by which he means his father's younger brother.

I am placing together the two institutions, exogamy and classificatory relationship, inasmuch as they are really connected, being in fact two sides of one institution. This was made out eight years ago, by the Rev. Lorimer Fison, in the work on the Kamilaroi and Kurnai tribes of Australia by him and Mr. Howitt (*op. cit* p. 76). This important explanation is still scarcely known to anthropologists, nor indeed, have I much right to reproach others with neglecting it, for I reviewed Fison and Howitt's book without distinctly realising the bearing of this argument on the theory of exogamy, which only came round to me lately in a way which I had better now describe, as it will enable me to explain shortly and plainly the whole problem. In tabulating the nations of the world, I found a group of twenty-one peoples whose custom as to the marriage of first cousins seemed remarkable; it is that the children of two brothers may not marry, nor the children of two sisters, but the child of the brother may marry the child of the sister. It seemed obvious that this "cross-cousin marriage," as it may be called, must be the direct result of the simplest form of exogamy, where a population is divided into two classes or sections, with the law that a man who belongs to Class A can only take a wife of Class B. Such a division, for instance, is familiar in Melanesia. Dr. R. H. Codrington describes it in the Banks Islands, where the natives have two families, called *veve*-mother, which implies that descent follows the mother's side, and a man must marry a wife of the other mother from himself, or as they say, not on his own side of the house but on the other. Thus, taking A, a, B, b, as males and females of the class A and B, and bearing in mind that the mother's children are of her class, but the father's children of the opposite class to his, we have [as shown in Figure 5, the following] :—

His
  father's brother's child
    or } is (tribal) brother or sister,
  mother's sister's child
therefore
  father's brother is (tribal) father,
  mother's sister is (tribal) mother,

His
  father's sister's child
    or } is tribal (cousin).
  mother's brother's child
Therefore
  father's sister is (tribal) aunt
  mother's brother is (tribal) uncle.

Figure 6.

Turanian classificatory system, as Morgan calls that including the above mentioned systems of North America and India, with others. Figure 6 puts concisely the main features of the argument as to a man's kin.

Though not proposing to enter fully into the deduction of classificatory relationships in all their varieties from the rule of exogamy, it is necessary to point out that the form of exogamy here contemplated is the simplest or dual form, in which a people is divided into two intermarrying classes. Systems of exogamy which are dual in their nature, that is, consisting of two classes or groups of classes, stand in direct connection with cross-cousin marriage and classificatory relation-

Two sisters, a, a, their : : Children, A, a, are of	Two brothers, A, A, their : : Children B, b, are of	Brother and sister, A, a, their : : Children B, a, are of
same class = tribal brother and sister = unmarriageable.	same class = tribal brother and sister = unmarriageable.	different class = tribal cousins = marriageable.

Figure 5.

Having come to this point, it seemed to me that I had seen something like it elsewhere, and on looking back to "Kamilaroi and Kurnai" I found that Fison had thus worked out the origin of the

ship. But if the number of exogamic divisions is not dual, if there are for instance three clans, and a man of one clan may take a wife of either of the two other clans, it is readily seen that the argument of Fig. 5 breaks down. Although at present only prepared to deal with exogamy and classificatory relationship in their dual form, I may notice that the treatment of the problem by the method of adhesions strengthens the view, not wanting in other evidence, that the dual form of exogamy may be considered the original form. In reckoning from the present schedules the number of peoples who use relationship names more or less corresponding to the classificatory systems here considered, they are found to be fifty-three, and the estimated number of these which might coincide accidentally with exogamy were there no close connexion between them, would be about twelve. But in fact the number of peoples who have both exogamy and classification is thirty-three, this strong coincidence being the measure of the close causal connexion subsisting between the two institutions. The adherence is even stronger as to cross-cousin marriage, of which twenty-one cases appear in the schedules, no less than fifteen of the peoples practising it being also known as exogamous. Here, indeed, the relation is not one of derivation, but of identity, the cross-cousin rule being actually a partial form or imperfect statement of the law of exogamy itself. Such adhesions between two or more customs have already been recognised as proving the existence of causal connexion, but it has now to be pointed out that they serve another purpose. The connexion, when proved, reacts on the evidence by which it was proved. When once it has been shown that cross-cousin marriage is part and parcel of exogamy, it may be argued that all the twenty-one peoples practising cross-cousin marriage are to be set down as exogamous. Now as only fifteen of them are expressly recorded to be so, the list of exogamous nations of the world has to be increased by six. So, classificatory relationship being evidence that the peoples practising it are or have been exogamous, this will add some twenty more to the list of nations among whom further investigation will probably disclose record that exogamic society once prevailed or still prevails. Even if no direct record is forthcoming, the indirect proof may with due caution be sufficient for placing them in the exogamous group, which may thus number above one hun-

dred peoples out of the three hundred and fifty of the world. Those who remember the sharp discussion between McLennan and Morgan years ago, and the view that the classificatory relationships were a mere system of addresses, will be struck with the way in which the controversy is likely to end. For myself I hardly know whether I feel more glad or sorry that my old friend McLennan to the day of his death never knew that Morgan and he, who believed themselves adversaries, were all the while allies pushing forward the same doctrine from different sides.

It thus appears that the number of nations who have the system of intermarrying clans is larger than has been known. But even this by no means measures the full importance of exogamy as a factor in the constitution of society. Anthropologists have long had before them the problem of determining how far clan-exogamy may have been the origin of the prohibited degrees in matrimony so variously defined in the laws of nations. The yet larger problem has been opened, how far laws of permission and prohibition of marriage may have led nations to define relationships and give them names, distinguishing for instance uncles from fathers, and cousins from brothers. It may, I think, conduce to the solution of these problems to notice two ways in which the collation of the present tables bears on the meaning and origin of exogamy.

There are conditions of society under which exogamy is found side by side with wife-capture, so that a barbaric marriage often involves both in one and the same act, as when a Tatar and a party of his friends, all armed to the teeth, ride off to the tents of a distant clan, and thence with simulated or even real violence carry off a bride. But on reckoning up the peoples among whom this combination of capture and exogamy is found, the number, though enough to show that they co-exist freely, falls short of what would justify the inference that they are cause and effect. Moreover, it appears that this co-existence belongs especially to the paternal stage of society, and to the maternal-paternal, in which paternal influence is partly established. This is intelligible enough from what has been already said as to the effect of capture in setting on foot paternal institutions, from its very outset, by bringing the wife into the husband's hands and home. We are thus led to a more fundamental test of the position of exogamy, by enquiring whether it existed in that earliest known stage of the maternal system of society, where the husband lives in the wife's family. The schedules show that there are in different parts of the world twelve or thirteen well-marked exogamous peoples whose habit of residence is for the husband to join the wife's family. This state of things seems to me to prevent our regarding exogamy as a result of capture, it being plain that the warrior who has carried a wife captive from a hostile tribe does not take up his abode in her family. If capture leads to any form of exogamy, this must, I think, be a paternal form, and if it be admitted that the maternal form is earlier, then it follows that capture is inadmissible as the primary cause of exogamy.

More than twenty years ago, in compiling a list of nations practising this custom of marrying out of the tribe or kin, I noticed that in any full discussion of the subject would have to be considered the wish to bind different tribes together in friendship by intermarriage. ("Early History of Mankind," 1865, p. 286.) Compiling the present tables has brought together observations to this effect.

. . .

On looking at the distinction between endogamy and exogamy from this point of view, it will be seen that there is a period in the growth of society when it is a political question of the first importance. While the vast forest or prairie still affords abundant food for a scanty population, small hordes may wander, or groups of households may be set up, each little tribe or settlement cut off from the rest, and marrying within its own border. But when tribes begin to adjoin and press on one another and quarrel, then the difference between marrying-in and marrying-out becomes patent. Endogamy is a policy of isolation, cutting off a horde or village, even from the parent-stock whence it separated, if only a generation or two back. Among tribes of low culture there is but one means known of keeping up permanent alliance, and that means is inter-

marriage. Exogamy, enabling a growing tribe to keep itself compact by constant unions between its spreading clans, enables it to overmatch any number of small intermarrying groups, isolated and helpless. Again and again in the world's history, savage tribes must have had plainly before their minds the simple practical alternative between marrying-out and being killed out. Even far on in culture, the political value of intermarriage remains. "Matrimonial alliances increase friendship more than aught else," is a maxim of Mohammed. "Then will we give our daughters unto you, and we will take your daughters to us, and we will dwell with you, and we will become one people," is a well known passage of Israelite history.

Exogamy lies far back in the history of man, and perhaps no observer has ever seen it come into existence, nor have the precise conditions of its origin yet been clearly inferred. Even the historical relation between exogamy and the system of classes known as totemism is not fully cleared up; whether as Prof. Robertson Smith takes it ("Kinship and Marriage in Early Arabia," 1885, p. 184), totemism supplied the necessary machinery for working a law of exogamy, or whether exogamy itself led to totemism. But as to the law of exogamy itself, the evidence shows it in operation over a great part of the human race as a factor of political prosperity. It cannot be claimed as absolutely preventing strife and bloodshed, indeed, it has been remarked of some peoples, such as the Khonds and the Banks Islanders, that the intermarrying clans do nevertheless quarrel and fight. Still by binding together a whole community with ties of kinship and affinity, and especially by the peacemaking of the women who hold to one clan as sisters and to another as wives, it tends to keep down feuds and to heal them when they arise, so as at critical moments to hold together a tribe which under endogamous conditions would have split up. Exogamy thus shows itself as an institution which resists the tendency of uncultured populations to disintegrate, cementing them into nations capable of living together in peace and holding together in war, till they reach the period of high military and political organisation. Seen from this point of view, the remarkable fact is more easily understood that exogamy, passing on from the maternal to the paternal stage of society, shifts its prohibitions from the female to the male line of descent, now allowing marriages which it treated formerly as incestuous, while prohibiting others which it formerly allowed without scruple. This transformation has been taking place within recent times among Malay and American tribes, and seems to be even going on still, it making no difference politically whether kinship follows the female or male line, if only marrying-out causes the requisite intermixture of the clans. In this connexion it is worth while to notice that there are a number of peoples in different parts of the world, who have a rule of exogamy not depending on kinship at all. For instance, Piedrahita relates of the Panches of Bogota, that those of one town did not marry any woman thereof, as all held themselves brothers, and the impediment of kinship was sacred to them, but such was their ignorance that if a sister were born in a different town from her brother, he was not prevented from marrying her. An anthropologist, with the list before him of the peoples who prohibit a man from marrying in his own village, might explain this not as a result of ignorance, but as an extreme case of what may be called "local exogamy."

The results here brought forward make no approach to exhausting the possible inferences to be drawn from the tables. These need not even be confined to working out the development of customs found in existence somewhere on the globe, but may in some measure restore the knowledge of forms of society now extinct. Interesting, however, as these problems are, I am more anxious to bring under discussion the method by which they are here treated, how imperfectly I am well aware. The interpretations offered will have to be corrected, the tabulated material improved in quantity and quality, and the principles it involves brought out more justly, yet at any rate it will remain clear that the rules of human conduct are amenable to classification in compact masses, so as to show by strict numerical treatment their relations to one another. It is only at this point that speculative explanation must begin, at once guided in its course and strictly limited in its

range by well-marked lines of fact to which it must conform. The key of the position is, as that veteran anthropologist, Prof. Bastian, of the Berlin Museum, is never weary of repeating, that in statistical investigation the future of anthropology lies. As soon as this is systematically applied, principles of social development become visible. Even the diagrams of this paper may suffice to show that the institutions of man are as distinctly stratified as the earth on which he lives. They succeed each other in series substantially uniform over the globe, independent of what seem the comparatively superficial differences of race and language, but shaped by similar human nature acting through successively changed conditions in savage, barbaric, and civilised life.

The treatment of social phenomena by numerical classification will, it must be added, react on the statistical material to which the method is applied. It is in classifying the records of tribes and nations that one becomes fully aware of their imperfect and even fragmentary state. The descriptions happily tend to correct one another's errors, but the great difficulty is blank want of information. As for extinct tribes, and those whose native culture has been re-modelled, there is nothing to be done. But there are still a hundred or more peoples in the world, among whom a prompt and minute investigation would save some fast vanishing memory of their social laws and customs. The quest might be followed up internationally, each civilised nation taking in hand the barbaric tribes within its purview. The future will, doubtless, be able to take care of itself as to most branches of knowledge, but there is certain work which if it is to be done at all, must be done by the present.

SELECTED READINGS*

A. Commentaries and Critiques

Buchler, Ira R. and Henry A. Selby
    1968 *Kinship and social organization.* New York: Macmillan, pp. 1–4.
Eggan, Fred
    1960 Lewis Henry Morgan in kinship perspec-

* A complete bibliography listing all of the references mentioned in this book begins on p. 415.

tive. In G. E. Dole and R. L. Carneiro (eds.), *Essays in the science of culture in honor of Leslie White*. New York: Crowell, pp. 179–201.

Evans-Pritchard, Edward Evan
1951a *Social Anthropology*. London: Cohen & West, chs. II–III.

Fox, Robin
1967 *Kinship and marriage*. London: Penguin Books, pp. 16–24.

Harris, Marvin
1968 *The rise of anthropological theory: A history of theories of culture*. New York: Crowell, pp. 8–249.

Kardiner, Abram and Edward Preble
1961 *They studied man*. New York: World, ch. III.

Lowie, Robert H.
1915 Exogamy and the classificatory systems of relationship. *American Anthropologist*, 17:223–239.
————1937 *The history of ethnological theory*. New York: Holt, Rinehart & Winston, chs. VI–VIII.
————1955 Lewis Henry Morgan in historical perspective. In E. A. Hoebel (ed.), *Readings in Anthropology*. New York: McGraw-Hill.

White, Leslie A.
1948a Lewis H. Morgan: Pioneer in the theory of social evolution. In H. E. Barnes (ed.), *An introduction to the history of sociology*. Chicago: University of Chicago Press, pp. 138–54.

B. Original Works

Engels, Friedrich
1884 *Origin of the family, private property and the state*. New York: International Publishers, 1942.

Fustel De Coulanges, Numa Denis
1864 *The ancient city*. Later translated by Willard Small. New York: Doubleday, 1956.

Lubbock, Sir John
1871 On the development of relationships. *Journal of the Royal Anthropological Institute*, 1:1–29.

Maine, Sir Henry
1861 *Ancient law*. London: Oxford University Press.

McGee, W. J.
1896 The beginning of marriage. *American Anthropologist*, 9:371–383.

McLennan, J. F.
1865 *Primitive marriage*. Edinburgh: A. C. Black.

Morgan, Lewis Henry
1870 *Systems of consanguinity and affinity of the human family*. Washington, D.C.: Smithsonian Institution Contributions to Knowledge No. 17.
————1877 *Ancient society*. New York: Rinehart & Winston. (1907)

Smith, William Robertson
1885 *Kinship and marriage in early Arabia*. Cambridge: Cambridge University Press.

Tylor, Edward B.
1865 *Researches into the early history of mankind*. London: J. Murray.
————1871 *Primitive culture*. London: J. Murray.
————1881 *Anthropology: An introduction to the study of man and civilization*. New York: Appleton-Century-Crofts.
————1889 On a method of investigating the development of institutions applied to laws of marriage and descent. *Journal of the Royal Anthropological Institute*, 18:245–272.

Wake, Charles S.
1879 The primitive human family *Journal of the Royal Anthropological Institute*, 9:3–19.

Westermarck, Edward
1891 *The history of human marriage*. London: Macmillan, 1921.

III

PSYCHOLOGICAL, ETHNOLOGICAL, AND SOCIOLOGICAL APPROACHES

The social sciences were in turmoil around the turn of the century. There were two major reasons: (1) unilineal evolutionary theory had been successfully attacked and was by then fast crumbling, and (2) a vast amount of fieldwork data—the collection of which had often been stimulated by evolutionary theories—was pouring in. "Anthropology" had begun as the science of the history of man up to and including what we classify as civilization. When the (evolutionary) prop under the grand scheme began to fall and the continuum ceased to exist, the future direction of the discipline became cloudy—appetites for the social sciences had been whetted, and basic science—rather than political goals—were the order of the day, especially since the publication of Tylor's 1871 book.

While evolutionary thinking continued to occupy some of the more eminent social scientists of this period, a search for other—and more fundamental—explanatory mechanisms was also in progress. In Europe it appeared in the independent works of Frazer (1890, 1910) whose thinking was based on both evolution and psychology (then called primitive mentality and morality). Freud (*Totem and Taboo*, 1918) extended his fundamental discoveries about psychic processes in middle-class Victorian Europe to all cultures. Though Frazer was widely respected in his day, his works have not stood the test of time. Freud's efforts were attacked and scorned when they appeared (Malinowski, 1927a and b), but had lasting effects on the later development of cultural anthropology, particularly in North America.

In Europe Emile Durkheim was the outstanding social scientist; he followed the French rationalist traditions of Montesquieu and Comte. Although Durkheim was a "two-stage evolutionist" (*The Division of Labour in Society*, 1893; *The Elementary Forms of the Religious Life*, 1912), his main concerns and contributions lay in (1) his redefinition of social science as a discipline separate from psychology (*The Rules of the Sociological Method*, 1895), (2) his declaration that the nature of society and social solidarity was the major subject matter of the social sciences (1895; *Suicide*, 1897; 1912), and (3) his demonstration of the usefulness of the statistical method in his monumental work on suicide (1897). Durkheim was an ardent functionalist and advanced the works of Maine (1861) and Tönnies (*Community and Society*, 1887) in differentiating the integrating mechanisms of primitive and complex societies. He, in turn, refounded the French school whose works have had the greatest influence on social anthropology (Mauss, *The Gift*, 1925; Lévi-Strauss, *The Elementary Structures of Kinship;* 1949 etc.).

In America the ghost of Morgan weighed heavily on the immigrant shoulders of Boas, Kroeber, and Lowie. First Boas (1896) and then Swanton ("The Social Organization of American Tribes," 1905; 1917) and others, having produced some outstanding ethnographic work themselves, used their data to attack the—then current

—"grand schemes." Boas' overt caution led to a negative attitude toward most theories, even though he did admit that ethnology was, eventually, to lead to the discovery of general laws through comparative theory. Ethnology, to Boas and many of his followers, was the study of the history of cultures and, in their opinion, the bases of such studies lay in extremely detailed field work in small areas. Although members of the Boas "school" provided some good enthnographic data on kinship and social organization, they made few advances (see Chapters IV and V) because (1) they were too eclectic in gathering data and they gave equal importance to all ethnographic detail, and (2) their data were often presented as distributions of traits or elements that seemed to prevent them from seeing the all important syntheses of social and cultural integration. They were more partial to diffusionist explanations than to any others; this preference can, perhaps, be explained by the fact that they were greatly influenced by the German diffusionist school, which had its roots in geography and its ultimate scientific exegesis in *Kulturkreislehre*.

Thus progress was being made along a number of different theoretical lines although the early attempts were often naive or nihilistic. The fruits of this "revolution" were to be reaped by those who followed these pioneers.

THE SOCIAL ORGANIZATION OF AMERICAN TRIBES

John R. Swanton

The majority of works published during the last thirty years that attempt to deal with the social organization of "primitive people" have been dominated by the totemic clan theory, i.e., the theory that in the earliest period of their development all tribes consisted of certain divisions or clans which practically took the place of families, and the members of each of which were compelled to marry into some other. This theory furthermore supposes that the offspring of such marriages always belonged to the clan of the mother, and that where we find the reverse condition it is a later development. An important adjunct of the clan is the totem—an animal, plant, or other object from which each clan derived its name and many of the members their personal names, and to which the members were supposed to stand in some mystic relation indicated usually by prohibitions or tabus.

It has been especially advocated by students who hold that the monogamous family was not a primitive institution but has been evolved from a stage in which sexual relations were more or less promiscuous, the line of ascent leading through stages in which a group of men were married to a group of women (group marriage), in which one woman was married to several men (polyandry), in which one man was married to several women (polygamy), in which one man and one woman paired for a certain period (the pairing family), until finally the true monogamous family was reached. But although this theory of marriage has been very successfully assailed by Westermarck and later writers, the totemic clan theory itself has effected such a lodgment in popular favor that it is now referred to casually as to one of the well-established principles of modern science. Constantly there are let fall such expressions as "traces of maternal descent," "relics of a previous maternal state of society," "customs showing the change from a maternal to a paternal condition," as if nothing were better recognized.

In the present paper I shall endeavor to determine how far the organization of American tribes

Reproduced by permission of the American Anthropological Association from *American Anthropologist*, Vol. 7, 1905, pp. 663–673.

north of Mexico, so far as we know it, bears out this theory, not pretending to pass final judgment on it as a whole. I am especially moved to this by the fact that the theory is thought to have been confirmed through material brought from this very quarter by an American ethnologist, Lewis H. Morgan, and all the more that no specific objection to his conclusions has appeared in print. The material for such a paper is so readily available, however, that no special credit is involved in merely assembling it. It should be said in the first place, with reference to Mr. Morgan's work, that data were so much more scanty in his time, especially from that very region which confirms the clan theory least, that his conclusions are not altogether surprising. Had he begun by studying western instead of eastern tribes they might have been different.

While seemingly simple, the question of the truth or falsity of the hypothesis under consideration is found to contain several subordinate questions, all of which need not be answered in the same way. Thus we can conceive of descent reckoned through the mother without the existence of clans, of a clan system in which the clans are without totems, and of one in which, while totems exist, there are no special tabus, names, or rites accompanying them.

Conforming in some measure to the type of organization assumed in the maternal clan theory are the five tribes of the Iroquois confederacy, the Tuscarora, Wyandot, Cherokee, Delaware, Mohegan, Tutelo, the Muskhogean tribes so far as known, Timucua, Yuchi, Natchez, Bilozi, tribes of the Caddoan confederacy, the Pueblos, Navaho, Apache, Haida, Tlingit, Tsimshian, Heiltsuk, Takulli, Tahltan, Knaiakhotana, and Kutchin.

This number would probably be considerably increased if we had accurate information concerning many tribes which are now extinct. Thus it is a fair inference that the remaining Iroquoian tribes—the Erie, Neutral Nation, Susquehannock, and Nottoway—were organized like those that are known to us, and that the remaining eastern Siouan tribes were organized like the Tutelo. Our knowledge of the latter depends mainly on the statements of two or three survivors of the Tutelo interviewed by Hale and Dorsey, after the rem-

nant of their tribe had been living for years with the Iroquois, whose strong clan system is well known. The main fact, however, is confirmed by Lederer in the following words:

> From four women, viz., Pash, Sepoy, Askari and Marskarin, they derive the race of mankind, which they, therefore, divide into four tribes, distinguished under those several names. They very religiously observe the degrees of marriage, which they limit not to distance of kindred, but difference of tribe, which are continued in the issue of the females: now for two of the same tribe to match, is abhorred as incest and punished with great severity. (Lederer, *Discoveries*, 1672, p. 8.)

At the same time it would seem as if totems were wanting.

On the authority of a Narrangset woman living in Kansas and the supposed relationship of the Narranganset to the Mohegan, Morgan (1877, pp. 173, 174) assumes that the tribes of southern New England were organized similarly; and from another single statement, attributed to Powhatan, regarding the descent of the chieftainship which he held, it is supposed that the same was true of the Algonquin tribes of eastern Virginia. These suppositions also have probability in their favor, but the small ground on which they stand should be kept in mind.

On the other hand the social organization of several of these tribes does not altogether square with the clan formula. Thus the Delaware consisted of three exogamic divisions called by Morgan Wolf, Turkey, and Turtle, but properly known as Munsee, Unami, and Unalachtigo, names which signify, respectively, "people of the stony country" or "mountaineers," "people down the river," and "people who live near the ocean." Commenting on this fact, Brinton says:

> These three divisions of the Lenape were neither 'gentes' nor 'phratries,' though Mr. Morgan has endeavored to force them into his system by stating that they were 'of the nature of phratries.' Each was divided into twelve families bearing female names, and hence probably referring to some unexplained matriarchal system. They were, as I have called them, subtribes. In their own orations they referred to each

other as 'playmates' (Heckewelder). (*The Lenape and Their Legends*, 1885, p. 40.)

The twelve subdivisions of each major section in later years are said to have taken on the character of clans, but it is to be noted that they lack totemic names, and this fact, together with the geographical character of the three main divisions, differentiates the tribe very strongly from the Iroquoians and Muskhogeans. This same local character is noted by Matthews and Bourke for the clans of the Navaho and Apache, respectively, and by Boas and the writer regarding all the minor divisions of the Haida, Tlingit, and Tsimshian.

Du Pratz, our only authority on the Natchez, informs us that their exogamous divisions corresponding to clans were different social strata and therefore really castes, and they appear to have been without totemic names. An analogy to this state of affairs is furnished, very curiously, by an Athapascan tribe, the Kutchin, living on Yukon and Porcupine rivers, Alaska. They are said to consist of three exogamous bands or camps which occupy different sections of country and differ in rank, the children always belonging to the band of the mother; but the divisions lack totemic names. Of the other Athapascan tribes of the far north we have the very best authority, that of Morice, for the statement that the Carriers and Tahltan (or western Nahane) have adopted their clan systems from the coast, and the reported clan system of the Knaiakhotana, from the description given of it, would seem to have arisen similarly. In the same way Boas indicates that the Heiltsuk, now in the maternal stage, have adopted their present organization from their northern neighbors. Even the three most pronounced maternal tribes of the north Pacific coast—the Haida, Tlingit, and Tsimshian—present anomalies in the fact that their larger totemic divisions extend into nearly all the towns occupied by each tribe and rather correspond to the phratries of other tribes than to clans proper, while the smaller divisions are, as I have said, rather to be considered as geographical groups.

Yet even among tribes which present this organization in its most typical form it would appear that the authority of the clan has been greatly exaggerated and the power and importance of the father's clan placed at a too low value. Thus, according to information kindly furnished by Mrs. Matilda Coxe Stevenson, among the Zuñi land is owned by families, not by clans. With the same people a man is practically prohibited from marrying into his father's clan as well as into that of his mother; he is known as the "child" of his father's clan, and certain offices are always held by the "child" of a special clan, thus bringing about a rude kind of paternal descent. The same abhorrence to marriage into the clan of one's father exists among the Navaho according to Matthews (1904, p. 758), and among the Iroquois according to Hewitt.

Organized on the basis of gentes, i.e., exogamic divisions with descent through the father, are the Abnaki, Ottawa, Potawatomi, Chippewa, Menominee, Sauk and Foxes, Miami, Shawnee, Kickapoo, Blackfeet, Omaha, Ponca, Winnebago, Iowa, Oto, Missouri, Osage, Kansa, Quapa, Yuman tribes, and Kwakiutl. It has been asserted that traces of a previous maternal condition are found in many of these, especially the tribes of Algonquian lineage, and a change such as that implied is of course quite possible; but the arguments that Morgan adduces in proof are too fragmentary to be conclusive, and for the Siouan tribes it is a pure assumption. The only western Siouan tribes claimed as possessing clans with maternal descent are the Mandan, Hidatsa, and Crows, and I think that the real state of affairs among those tribes has been misunderstood. In the first place the subdivisions of these three tribes are not totemic and should evidently be regarded as bands rather than clans. Secondly, it was customary among very many American tribes, no matter how each was organized internally, for a man marrying outside to live with his wife's people, and in such cases his children would remain with her. At the same time he might equally marry inside of his tribe or band and be succeeded by his son in whatever position he had attained. This Hewitt ascertained from some Crow Indians to be the state of affairs in that tribe, and, since they have separated from the Hidatsa in comparatively modern times, it may be assumed for the latter also. Nor is there good reason for thinking that the organization of the Mandan was different. Through mistakes of this kind many tribes have been assigned to a clan or gentile stage when the subdivisions which they possess are neither clans nor gentes; and for this reason it is preferable to accept the authority of Mooney (1892–1893, p. 956) regarding the social organization of the Cheyenne rather than that of Grinnell (1902, pp. 135–146). Of the subdivisions of this tribe only two present features at all suggestive of totemic clans, while one, the Sutayu, is known to have been formerly an independent tribe, and it would be absurd to suppose that it was then exogamic. In the case of the Blackfeet, Grinnell is our best authority, and I have followed him, but, inasmuch as he states that marriages now take place within the "gens," I am inclined to question whether they did not in ancient times as well. At all events these divisions are evidently not totemic, and the same is true of the Kwakiutl gentes, which are called after reputed ancestors or else by some grandiloquent term referring to their power and wealth.

In discussing the organization of the Mandan, Hidatsa, and Crows I have indicated a type of organization in which, while there may be tribal subdivisions, these are not exogamic, lack totems, and hence cannot be called either clans or gentes. In this type the family, although it may be a polygamous one, is the basis of the state, and property, authority, and emoluments either descend or tend to descend from father to son. In this category may be placed the Shoshonean, Salishan, and eastern Athapascan peoples, the Kutenai, the Nootka, the rest of the people of Washington, Oregon, and California excepting the Yuman tribes already referred to, the Arapaho, Kiowa, Crows, Cheyenne, and the tribes of the Caddoan stock outside of the Caddo confederacy. To these may be added the Eskimo and Aleut, and probably the Cree, the Algonquian bands east of Hudson Bay, the Khotana of the lower Yukon, and the Pima tribes. In the extent of country which it covers and the importance of some of the stocks involved, it will be seen that this system—or lack of system—compares very favorably with either of those already considered.

Thus on purely quantitative grounds a study of the tribes north of Mexico lends no overwhelming support to the theory of a primitively universal maternal clan system. But when we come to compare the tribes in which a clan system exists individually with those which are without it, the tenuous character of its foundations becomes painfully manifest. For, granting its truth, we are compelled to assume the inferiority of the tribes constituting the Iroquois and Creek confederacies, the Timucua of Florida, and the Natchez of Louisiana and Mississippi to the Cree and Eskimo, of the Pueblos and Navaho to the Paiute and tribes of California; and of the Haida, Tlingit, and Tsimshian to the Salishan and eastern Athapascan tribes.

Instead of being primitive, a study of the north Pacific area convinces one that the maternal clan system is itself evolved, for there is every indication that it there grew up in one small area at the mouths of the Nass and Skeena rivers and was spreading northward, southward, and inland at the time these tribes first came to the notice of Europeans. That an evolution has taken place in the Southwest is indicated by Fewkes' study of Hopi clans, as well as by everything that we have learned of the relation of Navaho culture to that of the Pueblos. It is also evident that the type of the social organization has some relation to environment, typical clan systems being found usually in the maize country, although the north Pacific coast presents an exception, while the loose type is found principally in cold northern regions and the barren western plateau where food is scarce. Yet here again California and the coast region of Oregon, Washington, and southern British Columbia must be excepted.

An interesting point to be noted is the position of gentile areas relative to two others. Unless we except the Blackfeet it will be seen that each of these touches on regions occupied by tribes in the two remaining categories. Thus the Sioux-Algonquian area lies between the Iroquois and Muskhogean tribes on one side and the Shoshonean, Salishan, and eastern Athapascan tribes on the other; the Yuman tribes lie between the Navaho and the Piman and Shoshonean tribes; and the Kwakiutl are between the maternally organized Heiltsuk and Nootka and Salish. This association suggests at once whether the evolution of the gentile system and the evolution of the clan system have borne any peculiar relation to each other. In the case of the Kwakiutl we know that the organization contains elements probably borrowed from their northern neighbors, and it is believed that their relatives on the north, the Heiltsuk, have changed to a maternal form of organization through the influence of the maternally organized Tsimshian and Haida. Supposing the same influence to continue, we might expect that the Kwakiutl, in time, would also have reached a maternal stage. In other words, the curious phenomenon here presents itself of a loosely organized tribe changing to a gentile and afterward to a clan system. At the same time the Kwakiutl gentile system can hardly be regarded as typical, and I should be inclined to doubt whether a gentile system that had attained the perfection of that of the Omaha, for instance, would pass over naturally into a clan system. This possibility ought to be reckoned with, however, in dealing with those "traces of a maternal stage" that we hear so much about. It might put quite a different interpretation on several conclusions arrived at by Morgan.

A thorough investigation of this problem demands an examination of certain tendencies among tribes in the last category. The relative proportion of cases in which a man goes to live with his wife's people to those in which a woman goes to live with those of her husband ought to be noted, also the attitude of the members of a band toward marriage within and marriage outside, and toward marriage among foreign tribes. The treatment of tribes or bands adopted into others or becoming allied to others ought also to be examined, as well as tendencies of a band or tribe to segregate, and the attitude of these parts toward each other and of other bands toward all.

The totemic side of the question, on the other hand, requires close investigation of the religious beliefs of primitive people and especially of the related phenomena presented by the personal manitu, the crest of the Northwest coast, the so-called "suliaism" of Salish tribes, and the heraldry of the tribes of the plains. It appears to be rather a badge or "medicine" affixed to bands which have become differentiated regardless of it than an essential element of clan or gentile organization.

More care should be exercised by sociologists in picking out "vestigial characters" [survivals]. Doubtless such exist, but in determining what they are we must first be certain that they have no meaning or function for the present generation, and secondly that, instead of vestiges, they are not rather tendencies toward something still in the future. Thus the application of the term "wife" to a wife's sister, or of "husband" to a sister's husband is not a "vestigial character" as has been maintained, but indicates the potential relationship in which the parties stand, a man having a prior claim on his wife's sister in case of his wife's death. Other so-called "vestigial characters" are of much the same order.

While this field presents abundant opportunities for future investigation, it would seem to the writer, from the evidence already adduced, that the primitive nature of the maternal clan is not substantiated by a study of the American tribes north of Mexico, and can be proved only by presenting more abundant proof from other quarters of the globe.

THE SOCIOLOGICAL METHOD

Emile Durkheim

WHAT IS A SOCIAL FACT?

Before inquiring into the method suited to the study of social facts, it is important to know which facts are commonly called "social." This information is all the more necessary since the designation "social" is used with little precision. It is currently employed for practically all phenomena generally diffused within society, however small their social interest. But on that basis, there are, as it were, no human events that may not be called social. Each individual drinks, sleeps, eats, reasons; and it is to society's interest that these functions be exercised in an orderly manner. If, then, all these facts are counted as "social" facts, sociology would have no subject matter exclusively its own, and its domain would be confused with that of biology and psychology.

But in reality there is in every society a certain group of phenomena which may be differentiated from those studied by the other natural sciences. When I fulfill my obligations as brother, husband, or citizen, when I execute my contracts, I perform duties which are defined, externally to myself and my acts, in law and in custom. Even if they conform to my own sentiments and I feel their reality subjectively, such reality is still objective, for I did not create them; I merely inherited them through my education. How many times it happens, moreover, that we are ignorant of the details of the obligations incumbent upon us, and that in order to acquaint ourselves with them we must consult the law and its authorized interpreters! Similarly, the church-member finds the beliefs and practices of his religious life ready-made at birth; their existence prior to his own implies their existence outside of himself. The system of signs I use to express my thought, the system of currency I employ to pay my debts, the instruments of credit I utilize in my commercial relations, the practices followed in my profession, etc., function independently of my own use of them. And these statements can be repeated for each member of society. Here, then, are ways of acting, thinking, and feeling that present the noteworthy property of existing outside the individual consciousness.

These types of conduct or thought are not only external to the individual but are, moreover, endowed with coercive power, by virtue of which they impose themselves upon him, independent of his individual will. Of course, when I fully consent and conform to them, this constraint is felt only slightly, if at all, and is therefore unnecessary. But it is, nonetheless, an intrinsic characteristic of these facts, the proof thereof being that it asserts itself as soon as I attempt to resist it. If I attempt to violate the law, it reacts against me so as to prevent my act before its accomplishment, or to nullify my violation by restoring the damage, if it is accomplished and reparable, or to make me expiate it if it cannot be compensated for otherwise.

In the case of purely moral maxims, the public conscience exercises a check on every act which offends it by means of the surveillance it exercises over the conduct of citizens, and the appropriate penalties at its disposal. In many cases the constraint is less violent, but nevertheless it always exists. If I do not submit to the conventions of society, if in my dress I do not conform to the customs observed in my country and in my class, the ridicule I provoke, the social isolation in which I am kept, produce, although in an attenuated form, the same effects as a punishment in the strict sense of the word. The constraint is nonetheless efficacious for being indirect. I am not obliged to speak French with my fellow-countrymen nor to use the legal currency, but I cannot possibly do otherwise. If I tried to escape this

Reprinted with permission of The Macmillan Company from *The Rules of the Sociological Method* by Emile Durkheim. George E. G. Catlin (translator). Copyright 1938 by George E. G. Catlin, renewed 1966 by Sarah A. Solovay, John H. Mueller and George E. G. Catlin. Pp. 1–5, 10–13, 110–112.

necessity, my attempt would fail miserably. As an industrialist, I am free to apply the technical methods of former centuries; but by doing so, I should invite certain ruin. Even when I free myself from these rules and violate them successfully, I am always compelled to struggle with them. When finally overcome, they make their constraining power sufficiently felt by the resistance they offer. The enterprises of all innovators, including successful ones, come up against resistance of this kind.

Here, then, is a category of facts with very distinctive characteristics: it consists of ways of acting, thinking, and feeling, external to the individual, and endowed with a power of coercion, by reason of which they control him. These ways of thinking could not be confused with biological phenomena, since they consist of representations and of actions; nor with psychological phenomena, which exist only in the individual consciousness and through it. They constitute, thus, a new variety of phenomena; and it is to them exclusively that the term "social" ought to be applied. And this term fits them quite well, for it is clear that, since their source is not in the individual, their substratum can be no other than society, either the political society as a whole or some one of the partial groups it includes, such as religious denominations, political, literary, and occupational associations, etc. On the other hand, this term "social" applies to them exclusively, for it has a distinct meaning only if it designates exclusively the phenomena which are not included in any of the categories of facts that have already been established and classified. These ways of thinking and acting therefore constitute the proper domain of sociology. It is true that, when we define them with this word "constraint," we risk shocking the zealous partisans of absolute individualism. For those who profess the complete autonomy of the individual, man's dignity is diminished whenever he is made to feel that he is not completely self-determinant. It is generally accepted today, however, that most of our ideas and our tendencies are not developed by ourselves but come to us from without. How can they become a part of us except by imposing themselves upon us? This is the whole meaning of our definition. And it is generally accepted, moreover, that social constraint is not necessarily incompatible with the individual personality. (We do not intend to imply, however, that all constraint is normal. We shall return to this point later.)

Since the examples that we have just cited (legal and moral regulations, religious faiths, financial systems, etc.) all consist of established beliefs and practices, one might be led to believe that social facts exist only where there is some social organization. But there are other facts without such crystallized form which have the same objectivity and the same ascendency over the individual. These are called "social currents." Thus the great movements of enthusiasm, indignation, and pity in a crowd do not originate in any one of the particular individual consciousnesses. They come to each one of us from without and can carry us away in spite of ourselves. Of course, it may happen that, in abandoning myself to them unreservedly, I do not feel the pressure they exert upon me. But it is revealed as soon as I try to resist them. Let an individual attempt to oppose one of these collective manifestations, and the emotions that he denies will turn against him. Now, if this power of external coercion asserts itself so clearly in cases of resistance, it must exist also in the first-mentioned cases, although we are unconscious of it. We are then victims of the illusion of having ourselves created that which actually forced itself from without. If the complacency with which we permit ourselves to be carried along conceals the pressure undergone, nevertheless it does not abolish it. Thus, air is no less heavy because we do not detect its weight. So, even if we ourselves have spontaneously contributed to the production of the common emotion, the impression we have received differs markedly from that we would have experienced if we had been alone. Also, once the crowd has dispersed, that is, once these social influences have ceased to act upon us and we are alone again, the emotions which have passed through the mind appear strange to us, and we no longer recognize them as ours. We realize that these feelings have been impressed upon us to a much greater extent than they were created by us. It may even happen that they horrify us, so much were they contrary to our nature. Thus, a group of individuals, most of whom are perfectly inoffensive, may, when gathered in a crowd, be drawn into acts of atrocity. And what we say of these transitory outbursts applies similarly to those more permanent currents of opinion on religious, political, literary, or artistic matters which are constantly being formed around us, whether in society as a whole of in more limited circles.

. . .

We thus arrive at the point where we can formulate and delimit in a precise way the domain of sociology. It comprises only a limited group of phenomena. A social fact is to be recognized by the power of external coercion which it exercises or is capable of exercising over individuals, and the presence of this power may be recognized in its turn either by the existence of some specific sanction or by the resistance offered against every individual effort that tends to violate it. One can, however, define it also by its diffusion within the group, provided that, in conformity with our previous remarks, one takes care to add as a second and essential characteristic that its own existence is independent of the individual forms it assumes in its diffusion. This last criterion is perhaps, in certain cases, easier to apply than the previous one. In fact, the constraint is easy to ascertain when it expresses itself externally by some direct reaction of society, as is the case in law, morals, beliefs, customs, and even fashions. But when it is only indirect, like the constraint which an economic organization exercises, it cannot always be so easily detected. Generality combined with externality may, then, be easier to establish. Moreover, this second definition is but another form of the first; for if a mode of behavior whose existence is external to individual consciousnesses becomes general, this can only be brought about by its being imposed upon them.

But these several phenomena present the same characteristic by which we defined the others. These "ways of existing" are imposed on the individual precisely in the same fashion as the "ways of acting" of which we have spoken. Indeed, when we wish to know how a society is divided politically, of what these divisions themselves are composed, and how complete is the fusion existing between them, we shall not achieve our purposes by physical inspection and by geographical observations; for these phenomena are social, even when they have some basis in physical nature. It is only by a study of public law that a comprehension of this organization is possible, for it is this law that determines the organization, as it equally determines our domestic and civil relations. This political organization is, then, no less obligatory than the social facts mentioned above. If the population crowds into our cities instead of scattering into the country, this is due to a trend of public opinion, a collective drive that imposes this concentration upon the individuals. We can no more choose the style of our houses than of our clothing—at least, both are equally obligatory. The channels of communication prescribe the direction of internal migrations and commerce, etc., and even their extent. Consequently, at the very most, it should be necessary to add to the list of phenomena which we have enumerated as presenting the distinctive criterion of a social fact only one additional category, "ways of existing"; and, as this enumeration was not meant to be rigorously exhaustive, the addition would not be absolutely necessary.

Such an addition is perhaps not necessary, for these "ways of existing" are only crystallized "ways of acting." The political structure of a society is merely the way in which its component segments have become accustomed to live with one another. If their relations are traditionally intimate, the segments tend to fuse with one another, or, in the contrary case, to retain their identity. The type of habitation imposed upon us is merely the way in which our contemporaries and our ancestors have been accustomed to construct their houses. The methods of communication are merely the channels which the regular currents of commerce and migrations have dug, by flowing in the same direction. To be sure, if the phenomena of a structural character alone presented this permanence, one might believe that they constituted a distinct species. A legal regulation is an arrangement no less permanent than a type of architecture, and yet the regulation is a "physiological" fact. A simple moral maxim is assuredly somewhat more malleable, but it is much more rigid than a simple professional custom or a fashion. There is thus a whole series of degrees without a break in continuity between the facts of the most articulated structure and those free currents of social life which are not yet definitely molded. The differences between them are, therefore, only differences in the degree of consolidation they present. Both are simply life, more or less crystallized. No doubt, it may be of some advantage to reserve the term "morphological" for those social facts which concern the social substratum, but only on condition of not overlooking the fact that they are of the same nature as the others. Our definition will then include the whole relevant range of facts if we say: *A social fact is every way of acting, fixed or not, capable of exercising on the individual an external constraint;* or again, *every way of acting which is general throughout a given society, while at the same time existing in its own right independent of its individual manifestations.*

. . .

We arrive, therefore, at the following principle: *The determining cause of a social fact should be sought among the social facts preceding it and not among the states of the individual consciousness.* Moreover, we see quite readily that all the foregoing applies to the determination of the function as well as the cause of social phenomena. The function of a social fact cannot but be social, i.e., it consists of the production of socially useful effects. To be sure, it may and does happen that it also serves the individual. But this happy result is not its immediate cause. We can then complete the preceding proposition by saying: *The function of a social fact ought always to be sought in its relation to some social end.*

Since sociologists have often misinterpreted this rule and have considered social phenomena from a too psychological point of view, to many their theories seem too vague and shifting and too far removed from the distinctive nature of the things they are intended to explain. Historians who treat social reality directly and in detail have not failed to remark how powerless these too general interpretations are to show the relation between the facts; and their mistrust of sociology

has been, no doubt, partly produced by this circumstance. We do not mean to say, of course, that the study of psychological facts is not indispensable to the sociologist. If collective life is not derived from individual life, the two are nevertheless closely related; if the latter cannot explain the former, it can at least facilitate its explanation. First, as we have shown, it is indisputable that social facts are produced by action on psychological factors. In addition, this very action is similar to that which takes place in each individual consciousness and by which are transformed the primary elements (sensations, reflexes, instincts) of which it is originally constituted. Not without reason has it been said that the self is itself a society, by the same right as the organism, although in another way; and long ago psychologists showed the great importance of the factor of association in the explanation of mental activity.

Psychological training, more than biological training, constitutes, then, a valuable lesson for the sociologist; but it will not be useful to him except on condition that he emancipates himself from it after having received profit from its lessons, and then goes beyond it by special sociological training. He must abandon psychology as the center of his operations, as the point of departure for his excursions into the sociological world to which they must always return. He must establish himself in the very heart of social facts, in order to observe them directly, while asking the science of the individual mind for a general preparation only and, when needed, for useful suggestions.

Psychological phenomena can have only social consequences when they are so intimately united to social phenomena that the action of the psychological and of the social phenomena is necessarily fused. This is the case with certain sociopsychological facts. Thus, a public official is a social force, but he is at the same time an individual. As a result, he can turn his social energy in a direction determined by his individual nature, and thereby he can have an influence on the constitution of society. Such is the case with statesmen and, more generally, with men of genius. The latter, even when they do not fill a social function, draw from the collective sentiments of which they are the object an authority which is also a social force, and which they can put, in a certain measure, at the service of personal ideas. But we see that these cases are due to individual accidents and, consequently, cannot affect the constitutive traits of the social species which, alone, is the object of science. The restriction on the principle enunciated above is not, then, of great importance for the sociologist.

THE DIVISION OF LABOR IN SOCIETY

Emile Durkheim

The requirements of our subject [an examination of the functions of the division of labor] have obliged us to classify moral rules and to review the principal types. We are thus in a better position than we were in the beginning to see, or at least to conjecture, not only upon the external sign, but also upon the internal character which is common to all of them and which can serve to define them. We have put them into two groups: rules with repressive sanctions, which may be diffuse or organized, and rules with restitutive sanctions. We have seen that the first of these express the conditions of the solidarity, *sui generis*, which comes from resemblances, and to which we have given the name mechanical; the second, the conditions of negative solidarity and organic solidarity. We can thus say that, in general, the characteristic of moral rules is that they enunciate the fundamental conditions of social solidarity. Law and morality are the totality of ties which bind each of us to society, which make a unitary, coherent aggregate of the mass of individuals. Everything which is a source of solidarity is moral, everything which forces man to take account of other men is moral, everything which forces him to regulate his conduct through something other than the striving of his ego is moral, and morality is as solid as these ties are numerous and strong. We can see how inexact it is to define it, as is often done, through liberty.

It rather consists in a state of dependence. Far from serving to emancipate the individual, or disengaging him from the environment which surrounds him, it has, on the contrary, the function of making him an integral part of a whole, and, consequently, of depriving him of some liberty of movement. We sometimes, it is true, come across people not without nobility who find the idea of such dependence intolerable. But that is because they do not perceive the source from which their own morality flows, since these sources are very deep. Conscience is a bad judge of what goes on in the depths of a person, because it does not penetrate to them.

Society is not, then, as has often been thought, a stranger to the moral world, or something which has only secondary repercussions upon it. It is, on the contrary, the necessary condition of its existence. It is not a simple juxtaposition of individuals who bring an intrinsic morality with them, but rather man is a moral being only because he lives in society, since morality consists in being solidary with a group and varying with this solidarity. Let all social life disappear, and moral life will disappear with it, since it would no longer have any objective. The state of nature of the philosophers of the eighteenth century, if not immoral, is, at least, *amoral*. Rousseau himself recognized this.

. . .

But not only does the division of labor present the character by which we have defined morality; it more and more tends to become the essential condition of social solidarity. As we advance in the evolutionary scale, the ties which bind the individual to his family, to his native soil, to traditions which the past has given to him, to collective group usages, become loose. More mobile, he changes his environment more easily, leaves his people to go elsewhere to live a more autonomous existence, to a greater extent forms his own ideas and sentiments. Of course, the whole common conscience does not, on this account, pass out of existence. At least there will always remain this cult of personality, of individual dignity of which we have just been speaking, and which, today, is the rallying-point of so many people. But how little a thing it is when one contemplates the ever increasing extent of social life, and, consequently, of individual consciences! For, as they become more voluminous, as intelligence becomes richer, activity more varied, in order for morality to remain constant, that is to say, in order for the individual to remain attached to the group with a force equal to that of yesterday, the ties which bind him to it must become stronger and more numerous. If, then, he formed no others than those which come from resemblances, the effacement of the segmental type would be accompanied by a systematic debasement of morality. Man would no longer be sufficiently obligated; he would no longer feel about and above him this salutary pressure of society which moderates his egoism and makes him a moral being. This is what gives moral value to the division of labor. Through it, the individual becomes cognizant of his dependence upon society; from it come the forces which keep him in check and restrain him. In short, since the division of labor becomes the chief source of social solidarity, it becomes, at the same time, the foundation of the moral order.

. . .

But if the division of labor produces solidarity, it is not only because it makes each individual an *exchangist,* as the economists say; it is because it creates among men an entire system of rights and duties which link them together in a durable way. Just as social similitudes give rise to a law and a morality which protect them, so the division of labor gives rise to rules which assure pacific and regular concourse of divided functions. If economists have believed that it would bring forth an abiding solidarity, in some manner of its own making, and if, accordingly, they have held that human societies could and would resolve themselves into purely economic associations, that is because they believed that it affected only individual, temporary interests. Consequently, to estimate the interests in conflict and the way in which they ought to equilibrate, that is to say, to determine the conditions under which exchange ought to take place, is solely a matter of individual competence; and, since these interests are in a perpetual state of becoming, there is no place for any permanent regulation. But such a conception is, in all ways, inadequate for the facts. The division of labor does not present individuals to one another, but social functions. And society is interested in the play of the latter; in so far as they regularly concur, or do not concur, it will be healthy or ill. Its existence thus depends upon them, and the more they are divided the greater its dependence. That is why it cannot leave them in a state of indetermination. In addition to this, they are determined by themselves. Thus are formed those rules whose number grows as labor is divided, and whose absence makes organic solidarity either impossible or imperfect.

But it is not enough that there be rules; they must be just, and for that it is necessary for the external conditions of competition to be equal. If, moreover, we remember that the collective conscience is becoming more and more a cult of the individual, we shall see that what characterizes the morality or organized societies, compared to that of segmental societies, is that there is something more human, therefore more rational, about them. It does not direct our activities to ends which do not immediately concern us; it does not make us servants of ideal powers of a nature other than our own, which follow their directions without occupying themselves with the interests of men. It only asks that we be thoughtful of our fellows and that we be just, that we fulfill our duty, that we work at the function we can best execute, and receive the just reward for our services. The rules which constitute it do not have a constraining force which snuffs out free thought; but, because they are rather made for us and, in a certain sense, by us, we are free. We wish to understand them; we do not fear to change them. We must, however, guard against finding such an ideal inadequate on the pretext that it is too earthly and too much to our liking. An ideal is not more elevated because more transcendent, but because it leads us to vaster perspectives. What is important is not that it tower high above us, until it becomes a stranger to our lives, but that it open to our activity a large enough field. This is far from being on the verge of realization. We know only too well what a laborious work it is to erect this society where each individual will have the place he merits, will be rewarded as he deserves, where everybody, accordingly, will spontaneously work for the good of all and of each. Indeed, a moral code is not above another because it commands in a drier and more authoritarian manner, or because it is more sheltered from reflection. Of course, it must attach us to something besides ourselves but it is not necessary for it to chain us to it with impregnable bonds.

It has been said with justice that morality— and by that must be understood, not only moral doctrines, but customs—is going through a real crisis. What precedes can help us to understand the nature and causes of this sick condition. Profound changes have been produced in the structure of our societies in a very short time; they have been freed from the segmental type with a rapidity and in proportions such as have never before been seen in history. Accordingly, the morality which corresponds to this social type has regressed, but without another developing quickly enough to fill the ground that the first left vacant in our consciences. Our faith has been troubled; tradition has lost its sway; individual judgment has been freed from collective judgment. But, on the other hand, the functions which have been disrupted in the course of the upheaval

have not had the time to adjust themselves to one another; the new life which has emerged so suddenly has not been able to be completely organized, and above all, it has not been organized in a way to satisfy the need for justice which has grown more ardent in our hearts. If this be so, the remedy for the evil is not to seek to resuscitate traditions and practices which, no longer responding to present conditions of society, can only live an artificial, false existence. What we must do to relieve this anomy is to discover the means for making the organs which are still wasting themselves in discordant movements harmoniously concur by introducing into their relations more justice by more and more extenuating the external inequalities which are the source of the evil. Our illness is not, then, as has often been believed, of an intellectual sort; it has more profound causes. We shall not suffer because we no longer know on what theoretical notion to base the morality we have been practicing, but because, in certain of its parts, this morality is irremediably shattered, and that which is necessary to us is only in process of formation. Our anxiety does not arise because the criticism of scholars has broken down the traditional explanation we use to give to our duties; consequently, it is not a new philosophical system which will relieve the situation. Because certain of our duties are no longer founded in the reality of things, a breakdown has resulted which will be repaired only in so far as a new discipline is established and consolidated. In short, our first duty is to make a moral code for ourselves. Such a work cannot be improvised in the silence of the study; it can arise only through itself, little by little, under the pressure of internal causes which make it necessary. But the service that thought can and must render is in fixing the goal that we must attain. That is what we have tried to do.

NOTES ON DURKHEIM'S EPISTEMOLOGY

Abram Kardiner and Edward Preble

A major contribution of *Elementary Forms of Religious Life*, one that is generally neglected by anthropologists, is in epistemology. As a philosopher, Durkheim was acquainted with the subtle problems of the theory of knowledge. This was Kant's major problem, and Durkheim had read and studied Kant's work with great interest, although with considerable suspicion. Specifically, Durkheim was interested in the so-called categories of the understanding: the ideas of time, space, number, substance, cause, and so on. Are these categories, through which we experience and understand the world, prior to all experience and an inherent part of the human mind, or are they constructed by the mind after sense experience of the objects of the external world? This is the classic argument between the rationalists and the empiricists. Durkheim can accept neither position. The universality and the external constraint of the categories argue against the empiricist position, for if these ideas are constructed by the individual, they can be changed at the whim of the individual. Empiricism here can result only in irrationalism. The rationalists, on the other hand, presume an objective reality for the logical life but can offer no explanation for the transcendent categories, except to say that they are "inborn" or that they emanate from a "divine reason"; explanations which cannot, in principle, be verified.

Only by admitting the social origins of the categories of the understanding can this unacceptable alternative be avoided, according to Durkheim. If the categories are collective representations, the objections to the classical positions can be overcome. As social ideas, they are imposed upon the individual and he is constrained to accept them without proof or persuasion. They are "necessary" in that a contact of minds would be impossible without them and human life would cease to exist. Logical conformity as well as moral conformity is a prerequisite of social existence. This explanation also does justice to the positive aspects of the empirical tradition because it relates the categories to observable phenomena: the realities of social life. In Australia, for example, some societies conceive of space as a great circle which is divided up just as the tribal circle is divided in their camp. Space, for them, is the image of the physical arrangement of the camp. The imitative rites of certain primitive peoples are based on the idea that like produces like; a definite conception of "cause." It may be assumed that the more sophisticated principle of causality is also a social product. Durkheim finds this true of all the rest of the categories of human thought.

This, in brief, is Durkheim's extension of assumptions, which were to all of human thought and experience formulated as early as the *Division of Labor*. Such a great and daring project necessarily involved him in contradictions and difficulties, but he was a stubborn man who could not be stopped from working out the most diverse and subtle implications of a central insight. He uncovered enough problems here to keep social scientists busy for a long time.

THE ORIGIN OF
THE INCEST TABOO

Sigmund Freud

THE SAVAGE'S DREAD OF INCEST

Primitive man is known to us by the stages of development through which he has passed: that is, through the inanimate monuments and implements which he has left behind for us, through our knowledge of his art, his religion and his attitude towards life, which we have received either directly or through the medium of legends, myths and fairy tales; and through the remnants of his ways of thinking that survive in our own manners and customs. Moreover, in a certain sense he is still our contemporary: there are people whom we still consider more closely related to primitive man than to ourselves, in whom we therefore recognize the direct descendants and representatives of earlier man. We can thus judge the so-called savage and semi-savage races; their psychic life assumes a peculiar interest for us, for we can recognize in their psychic life a well-preserved, early stage of our own development.

* * *

If this assumption is correct, a comparison of the "Psychology of Primitive Races" as taught by folklore, with the psychology of the neurotic as it has become known through psychoanalysis, will reveal numerous points of correspondence and throw new light on subjects that are more or less familiar to us.

For outer as well as inner reasons, I am choosing for this comparison those tribes which have been described by ethnographists as being most backward and wretched: the aborigines of the youngest continent, namely Australia, whose fauna has also preserved for us so much that is archaic and no longer to be found elsewhere.

* * *

Almost everywhere [in Australia] the totem prevails there also exists the law that *the members of the same totem are not allowed to enter into sexual relations with each other; that is, that they cannot marry each other.* This represents the *exogamy* which is associated with the totem.

This sternly maintained prohibition is very remarkable. There is nothing to account for it in anything that we have hitherto learned from the conception of the totem or from any of its attributes; that is, we do not understand how it happened to enter the system of totemism. We are therefore not astonished if some investigators simply assume that at first exogamy—both as to its origin and to its meaning—had nothing to do with totemism, but that it was added to it at some time without any deeper association, when marriage restrictions proved necessary. However that may be, the association of totemism and exogamy exists, and proves to be very strong.

* * *

The Darwinian conception of the primal horde does not, of course, allow for the beginning of totemism. There is only a violent, jealous father who keeps all the females for himself and drives away the growing sons. This primal state of society has nowhere been observed. The most primitive organization we know, which today is still in force with certain tribes, is *associations of men* consisting of members with equal rights, subject to the restrictions of the totemic system, and founded on matriarchy, or descent through the mother. Can the one have resulted from the other, and how was this possible?

By basing our argument upon the celebration of the totem we are in a position to give an answer:

One day [1] the expelled brothers joined forces, slew and ate the father, and thus put an end to

[1] The reader will avoid the erroneous impression which this exposition may call forth by taking into consideration the concluding sentence of the subsequent chapter.

the father horde. Together they dared and accomplished what would have remained impossible for them singly. Perhaps some advance in culture, like the use of a new weapon, had given them the feeling of superiority. Of course these cannibalistic savages ate their victim. This violent primal father had surely been the envied and feared model for each of the brothers. Now they accomplished their identification with him by devouring him and each acquired a part of his strength. The totem feast, which is perhaps mankind's first celebration, would be the repetition and commemoration of this memorable, criminal act with which so many things began, social organization, moral restrictions and religion.[2]

[2] The seemingly monstrous assumption that the tyrannical father was overcome and slain by a combination of the expelled sons has also been accepted by Atkinson as a direct result of the conditions of the Darwinian primal horde. "A youthful band of brothers living together in forced celibacy, or at least in polyandrous relation with some single female captive. A horde as yet weak in their impubescence they are, but they would, when strength was gained with time, inevitably wrench by combined attacks, renewed again and again, both wife and life from the paternal tyrant" (*Primal Law*, pp. 220-1). Atkinson, who spent his life in New Caledonia and had unusual opportunities to study the natives, also refers to the fact that the conditions of the primal horde which Darwin assumes can easily be observed among herds of wild cattle and horses and regularly lead to the killing of the father animal. He then assumes further that a disintegration of the horde took place after the removal of the father through embittered fighting among the victorious sons, which thus precluded the origin or a new organization of society; "An ever recurring violent succession to the solitary paternal tyrant by sons, whose parricidal hands were so soon again clenched in fratricidal strife" (p. 228). Atkinson, who did not have the suggestions of psychoanalysis at his command and did not know the studies of Robertson Smith, finds a less violent transition from the primal horde to the next social stage in which many men live together in peaceful accord. He attributes it to maternal love that at first only the youngest sons and later others too remain in the horde, who in return for this toleration acknowledge the sexual prerogative of the father by the restraint which they practise towards the mother and towards their sisters.

So much for the very remarkable theory of Atkinson, its essential correspondence with the theory here expounded, and its point of departure which makes it necessary to relinquish so much else.

I must ascribe the indefiniteness, the disregard of time

In order to find these results acceptable, quite aside from our supposition, we need only assume that the group of brothers banded together were dominated by the same contradictory feelings towards the father which we can demonstrate as the content of ambivalence of the father complex in all our children and in neurotics. They hated the father who stood so powerfully in the way of their sexual demands and their desire for power, but they also loved and admired him. After they had satisfied their hate by his removal and had carried out their wish for identification with him, the suppressed tender impulses had to assert themselves.[3] This took place in the form of remorse, a sense of guilt was formed which coincided here with the remorse generally felt. The dead now became stronger than the living had been, even as we observe it to-day in the destinies of men. What the father's presence had formerly prevented they themselves now prohibited in the psychic situation of "subsequent obedience" which we know so well from psychoanalysis. They undid their deed by declaring that the killing of the father substitute, the totem, was not allowed, and renounced the fruits of their deed by denying themselves the liberated women. Thus they created two fundamental taboos of totemism out of the *sense of guilt of the son*, and for this very reason these had to correspond with the two represented wishes of the Œdipus complex. Whoever disobeyed became guilty of the two only crimes which troubled primitive society.[4]

interval, and the crowding of the material in the above exposition to a restraint which the nature of the subject demands. It would be just as meaningless to strive for exactness in this material as it would be unfair to demand certainty here.

[3] This new emotional attitude must also have been responsible for the fact that the deed could not bring full satisfaction to any of the perpetrators. In a certain sense it had been in vain. For none of the sons could carry out his original wish of taking the place of the father. But failure is, as we know, much more favourable to moral reaction than success.

[4] "Murder and incest, or offences of like kind against the sacred law of blood are in primitive society the only crimes of which the community as such takes cognizance . . ." [Smith, W. R., 1889], *Religion of the Semites*, p. 419.

The two taboos of totemism with which the morality of man begins are psychologically not of equal value. One of them, the sparing of the totem animal, rests entirely upon emotional motives; the father had been removed and nothing in reality could make up for this. But the other, the incest prohibition, had, besides, a strong practical foundation. Sexual need does not unite men; it separates them. Though the brothers had joined forces in order to overcome the father, each was the other's rival among the women. Each one wanted to have them all to himself like the father, and in the fight of each against the other the new organization would have perished. For there was no longer any one stronger than all the rest who could have successfully assumed the role of the father. Thus there was nothing left for the brothers, if they wanted to live together, but to erect the incest prohibition—perhaps after many difficult experiences—through which they all equally renounced the women whom they desired, and on account of whom they had removed the father in the first place. Thus they saved the organization which had made them strong and which could be based upon the homo-sexual feelings and activities which probably manifested themselves among them during the time of their banishment. Perhaps this situation also formed the germ of the institution of the mother right discovered by Bachofen, which was then abrogated by that patriarchal family arrangement.

SELECTED READINGS

A. Commentaries and Critiques

Alpert, Harry
1961 *Emile Durkheim and his sociology.* New York: Russell and Russell.

Fortes, Meyer
1953b *Social anthropology at Cambridge since 1900.* Cambridge: Cambridge University Press.

Harris, Marvin
1968 *The rise of anthropological theory: A history of theories of culture.* New York: Crowell, pp. 250–318, 422–27, 464–82.

Kardiner, Abram, and Edward Preble
1961 *They studied man.* New York: World, chs. IV, V, VI.

Lowie, Robert H.
1937 *The history of ethnological theory.* New York: Holt, Rinehart & Winston, chs. VIII, IX, XII.

Maybury-Lewis, David A.
1965 Durkheim on relationship systems. *Journal for the Scientific Study of Religion,* 4:253–260.

Schneider, David M.
1965a Some muddles in the models: or, how the system really works. In M. Banton (ed.), *The relevance of models for social anthropology.* Association of Social Anthropologists of the Commonwealth, Monograph No. 1. London: Tavistock.

Tax, Sol
1937c From Lafitau to Radcliffe-Brown. In F. Eggan (ed.), *Social anthropology of the North American tribes.* Chicago: University of Chicago Press.

White, Leslie A.
1966 The social organization of ethnological theory. In *Rice University studies 52:4* Houston: Rice University Press, pp. 1–28.

B. Original Works

Boas, Franz
1896 The limitations of the comparative method in anthropology. *Science,* 4:901–908.

Durkheim, Emile
1893 *The division of labor in society.* Later translated by G. Simpson. N.Y.: Free Press, 1949.

————1895 *The rules of the sociological method.* Later translated by Solovay and J. Mueller and edited by George E. G. Catlin. N.Y.: Free Press, 1951.

————1897 *Suicide.* Later translated by J. Spaulding and G. Simpson. N.Y.: Free Press, 1951.

————1912 *Elementary forms of religious life.* Later translated by J. W. Swain. N.Y.: Free Press, 1954.

Frazer, Sir James George
1890 *The golden bough.* vol. 1. 1st ed. London: Macmillan.

————1910 *Totemism and exogamy.* 4 vols. London: Macmillan.

————1911–1915 *The golden bough.* 12 vols. 3rd ed. London: Macmillan.

Freud, Sigmund

1918 *Totem and taboo.* Later translated by A. A. Brill, M.D. New York: Vintage, 1946.

Swanton, John
1905 The social organization of American tribes. *American Anthropologist,* 7:663–673.
———1917 Some anthropological misconcep-
tions. *American Anthropologist,* 19:459–470.

Tönnies, Ferdinand
1887 *Gemeinshaft und gesellschaft.* Later translated by C. P. Loomis. *Community and society.* East Lansing: Michigan State Press, 1957.

IV

RIVERS AND KROEBER AND THE NATURE OF KINSHIP

During the early part of this century, Rivers in England and Kroeber in the United States both became interested in kinship terminology and social organization. Both had had extensive field-work experiences, but antithetical approaches. Rivers was an evolutionist with a sociological bent, whereas Kroeber had a "psychological" (or mental) view of culture despite his antitheoretical training under Boas.

Rivers in 1907 ("On the Origin of the Classificatory Systems of Relationships") tried to revive social evolutionary studies à la Morgan. Two of his major points were (1) that kinship terminology was an important indicator of social relationships in both present and former ages, and (2) that social systems, therefore, could be classified according to their types of kinship terminology system. Rivers and Kroeber also disagreed about the scientific aims of ethnology—over whether it was, in fact, a science of man working towards general laws. Kroeber avowed that the aims of ethnology could not be scientific at all. Kroeber ("Classificatory Systems of Relationships," 1909) attacked Rivers' views on the grounds that (1) the classification of terminology systems was invalid because they were not in fact systems, and (2) that, in many cases, terminologies do not reflect social institutions, for, in his opinion, they were, in fact, "psychological" in nature and origin. His own experience with California Indians had shown him that various types of kinship terminologies could be associated with a number of diverse social systems. Kroeber went on to show that terminologies could be "meas-

ured" according to the presence or absence of eight basic (universal) criteria for the merging or differentiation of categories of kinsmen. These criteria were geneological in content (e.g., generation, lineal versus collateral, etc.), but their distribution within a system reflected the mental processes of the people; Kroeber admitted that these mental processes could also explain the patterns of social relationships. Kroeber was perhaps right in stating that terminologies could not be used as indicators of *former* social institutions such as marriage practices. However, in various parts of the world these institutions have definitely been found to reflect *present* social practices, and Rivers and others had found this to be so.

Rivers at first ignored Kroeber's attack but demonstrated the usefulness of the "geneological method" (1910) of fieldwork. This method showed the influence of Tylor (1889) in making use of "statistical" statements of data. Thus Rivers was able to show the exact relationship between spoken norms and actual behavior in many spheres of activity, most importantly for kin-based behavior. In 1914a (*Kinship and Social Organization*) Rivers asserted his sociological interpretations of kinship terminology and social institutions as well as their use in conjectural history (*The History of Melanesian Society*, 1914b). In the former work, and its later edition *Social Organization*, (1924), Rivers presented a sound and textbook-like introduction to the modern study of social organization. Apart from his historical conjectures, the book is as good an introduction to the subject as any that has appeared since.

Kroeber answered Rivers' "reply" (1914a) with his major work on California kinship terminologies (1917a). He again rejected Rivers' assertions, declared that ethnology was not an explaining science, and continued to analyze and classify kinship terminology systems in terms of culture area and linguistic distribution, as well as "psychological" features. Kroeber's latter efforts were the first attempts at *formal* analysis of terminology systems. In this method of formal analysis, the system is analyzed according to its own internal features rather than any interpretive, sociological meanings. The formal features that Kroeber used were genealogical characteristics which, he felt, were *universal* measures. Kroeber's distributional work was continued by his colleague Gifford, but his formal analyses were not taken up again until 1937 when Davis and Warner published their work, and the formal and "componential" analysts (see Chapter XII) further pursued the subject, as shown in their recent works.

THE GENEALOGICAL METHOD

W. H. R. Rivers

It is a familiar fact that many peoples preserve long pedigrees of their ancestors, going back for many generations and often shading off into the mythical. It is perhaps not so well known that most people of low culture preserve orally their pedigrees for several generations in all the collateral lines so that they can give in genealogical form all the descendants of the great-grandfather or of the great-great-grandfather and therefore know fully all those whom we should call second or third cousins and sometimes their memories go even farther back. It is this latter kind of genealogy which is used in the method I propose to consider in this paper.

I begin with the method of collecting the pedigrees which furnish the basis of the method. The first point to be attended to is that, owing to the great difference between the systems of relationship of savage and civilised peoples, it is desirable to use as few terms denoting kinship as possible, and complete pedigrees can be obtained when the terms are limited to the following:—father, mother, child, husband and wife. The small pedigree which is given as a sample was obtained in

Reprinted by permission of the American Sociological Review from the *Sociological Review*, Vol. 3 (1910), pp. 1–11.

Guadalcanar in the Eastern Solomon Islands, and in this case I began the inquiry by asking my informant, Kurka or Arthur, the name of his father and mother, making it clear that I wanted the names of his real parents and not of any other people whom he would call such by virtue of the classificatory system of relationship. After ascertaining that Kulini had only one wife and Kusua only one husband, I obtained the names of their children in order of age and inquired into the marriages of offspring of each. Thus was obtained the small group consisting of the descendants of Arthur's parents. Guadalcanar being an island whose social system is characterised by matrilineal descent, Arthur knew the pedigree of his mother better than that of his father. I obtained the names of her parents, ascertaining as before that each had only been once married, and then asked the names of their children and obtained the marriages and descendants of each. Arthur was a man who had been away for a long time in Queensland and was not able to go beyond his grandparents, but if he had had more extensive knowledge, I should have inquired into the parentage of Sinei and Koniava, and obtained the descendants of their parents in exactly the same manner, and should proceed till the genealogical

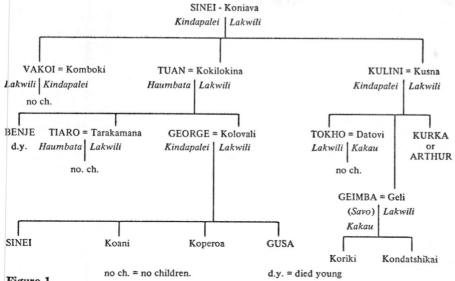

Figure 1.

no ch. = no children.   d.y. = died young

knowledge of his family possessed by my informant was completely exhausted. In collecting the pedigrees the descendants in both the male and female lines are obtained, but in writing them out in order to use them for the purposes to be considered in this paper, it is well to record on one sheet only the descendants in one line with cross-references to other sheets for the descendants in the other line.[1]

The exact method of arranging the names is a matter of no great importance, but I have found it convenient to record the names of males in capital letters and those of females in ordinary type, and I always put the name of the husband to the left of that of the wife. In polygynous or polyandrous marriages I include the names of the wives or husbands in square brackets.

A most important feature of the method is to record as far as possible the social condition of each person included in the pedigrees. The locality to which each person belongs should be obtained, and often it is necessary to record not only the district but also the name of some smaller territorial group, whether village or hamlet. If the people have a totemic organisation, the names of the totem or totems of each person

should be recorded, or if there are non-totemic clans or other social divisions, these should be given in the same way. In the same pedigree from Guadalcanar the names under those of the persons refer to exogamous clans which probably have a totemic nature.

In beginning work in a new place it is well to record any other facts about each person which may possibly have any social significance, and later the inquiry can be limited to those which are found to be important. Especial care should be taken to record the localities of those who have married into the community from other tribes or places. If adoption exists, the adopted children will almost certainly be included among those given as real children unless especial attention is devoted to the point, and in cases where it is possible, both real and adoptive parentage should be recorded.

In this collection of the material for the application of the genealogical method difficulties and sources of error are often encountered. One difficulty which I have met is the existence of a taboo on the names of the dead, and this can sometimes only be overcome with difficulty. In my own experience I have been compelled in consequence of this taboo to obtain the pedigrees in secret and from persons not of the family in question. Other sources of error and confusion are the practices of adoption and of exchanging names, and doubt-

[1] For the method of arrangement of a large mass of genealogical material the reader must be referred to "The Todas," London, 1906, and the Reports of the Cambridge Expedition to Torres Straits, Vols. v. and vi.

less new sources of difficulty may be found by those who seek to obtain pedigrees in new places.

In order that the pedigrees may be used in the ways I propose to describe it is necessary to be satisfied that they are trustworthy. In collecting the pedigrees of a whole community, there will be much overlapping; people who belong to the paternal stock of one informant will come in the maternal stock of another, and in the wife's ancestry of a third, and there will thus be ample opportunity of testing the agreement of the accounts of different informants. In nearly every community in which I have worked I have found that there are people with especial genealogical knowledge, and it is well to make use of these as much as possible. In my experience it is very dangerous to trust young men who nearly everywhere are no longer taking the trouble to learn the pedigrees from their elders, but if obtained from the latter, I have always found the pedigrees to be extraordinarily accurate when tested by the agreement of different accounts and by the general coherence of the complete genealogical record of the community.

Having now briefly described the method of recording the pedigrees and guaranteeing their accuracy I can proceed to detail the uses to which they may be put.

The first and most obvious use is in working out the systems of relationship. In nearly all people of lower culture these differ so widely from our own that there is the greatest danger of falling into error if one merely attempts to obtain the equivalents of our own terms by the ordinary method of question and answer. My procedure is to ask my informant the terms which he would apply to the different members of his pedigree, and reciprocally the terms which they would apply to him. Thus in the case of the pedigree from Guadalcanar which I have given as a sample, I asked Arthur what he called Tokho which gave the equivalent of "elder brother" when a man is speaking, while the name given by Tokho to Arthur gave the corresponding equivalent of "younger brother." The terms applied to one another by Vakoi and Arthur gave the equivalents of sister's son and mother's brother respectively, and the relationship of Komboki to Arthur gave the terms for mother's brother's wife and

husband's sister's son, and the other relationships on the mother's side were obtained in the same manner. For the names of relationships on the father's side the pedigree of Kulini, Arthur's father, would be used. It is as a matter of fact only exceptionally that a complete set of terms of relationship can be obtained from a single pedigree, but even if this were possible it is not advisable to do so, for there is always the chance of the occurrence of some double relationship, perhaps one by consanguinity and another by marriage, which may mislead, and I am never wholly content with a kinship system unless each of the relationships has been obtained from three separate pedigrees.

The following list of terms of relationship should be obtained:

Father	son
Mother	daughter
Elder brother (m.s.) *	younger brother (m.s.)
Elder brother (w.s.) **	younger sister (m.s.)
Elder sister (m.s.)	younger brother (w.s.)
Elder sister (w.s.)	younger sister (w.s.)
Father's brother	brother's child (m.s.)
Father's brother's wife	husband's brother's child
Father's brother's child	
Father's sister	brother's child (w.s.)
Father's sister's husband	wife's brother's child
Father's sister's child	
Mother's brother	sister's child (m.s.)
Mother's brother's wife	husband's sister's child
Mother's brother's child	
Mother's sister	sister's child (w.s.)
Mother's sister's husband	wife's sister's child
Mother's sister's child	
Father's father	son's child (m.s.)
Father's mother	son's child (w.s.)
Mother's father	daughter's child (m.s.)
Mother's mother	daughter's child (w.s.)
Husband	wife
Wife's father	daughter's husband (m.s.)
Wife's mother	daughter's husband (w.s.)
Husband's father	son's wife (m.s.)
Husband's mother	son's wife (w.s.)
Wife's brother	sister's husband (m.s.)
Wife's sister	sister's husband (w.s.)
Husband's brother	brother's wife (m.s.)
Husband's sister	brother's wife (w.s.)
Wife's sister's husband	
Husband's brother's wife	
Son's wife's parents	

* m.s. = man speaking.   ** w.s. = woman speaking.

They are arranged in two columns, those opposite to one another being reciprocals, so that if the terms are obtained by the genealogical method the name given by a man to any given relative would be entered in one column and the name given by the relative to him would have its place opposite to it. In the case of many relationships two forms are used, one when addressing a relative and the other when speaking of him, and both of these should be obtained. In many parts of the world different terms of relationship are used by people of different sexes, and the terms are also affected by the respective ages of the two parties to the relationship. In the list all the important differences according to sex have been included by specifying whether the term is being used by a man (m.s.) or a woman (w.s.), but the age distinctions have only been given in the cases of brothers and sisters. If, as often happens, elder and younger brothers of the father are distinguished these terms should also be obtained, and similar distinctions should be inquired into in the case of other relationships. Sometimes the distinctions according to age go even further, and there may be a distinctive term for each member of a family of three, four, five or more. If sons are distinguished from daughters in nomenclature, the terms should be given in each case in the list where the word "child" occurs.

The terms used for definite relationships by blood or marriage are also often applied to others with whom no such ties can be traced. I am in the habit of supplementing the genealogical method by asking for a list of all the people to whom a given man applies a term of relationship. On analysis it will usually be found that these fall into four classes: (1) relationships which can be traced in the pedigrees; (2) relationships by blood or marriage which cannot be so traced in the pedigrees available but which have nevertheless a genealogical basis, thus, in connection with the sample pedigree Arthur might say that he called a man *nianggu* or 'my mother's brother', because he was the *tasina* or 'brother' of Kusua; (3) relationships dependent on membership of a social division, thus Arthur might call a man

kukuanggu or 'my grandfather' because the latter was a Lakwili man of the same generation as Koniava; (4) relationships dependent on some artificial tie set up by the user of the term or even by his father or grandfather, such artificial relationships being sometimes transmitted from father to son.

The terms given in the list are sufficient to determine the general character of a system, but it will be well to obtain a certain number of terms for more distant relationships such as the father's father's brother and sister together with their children and grandchildren. Among these more distant relationships the sister's son's wife and sister's daughter's husband and their children are sometimes of special interest.

The next use of the pedigrees is in the study of the regulation of marriage. If the pedigrees of the whole of a population are collected as I have been able to do in several cases, we have in them a register of the marriages which have taken place in the community, reaching back perhaps for a hundred and fifty years. This register is preserved in the minds of the people and by its means we are able to study the laws regulating marriage just as in a civilised community one can make use of the records of a marriage registry office. We can see not only what marriages have been allowed or enjoined and what marriages have been prohibited, but we can express statistically the frequency of the different kinds. In many peoples of low culture there seems to be in progress a gradual transition from a condition in which marriage is regulated chiefly or entirely by means of a mechanism of clans or phratries or other social grouping to one in which the regulation of marriage depends on actual consanguinity, and the exact nature of the transitional stage of any given people can only be satisfactorily determined by such a concrete method as is provided by the study of a genealogical record. Further where marriage is regulated mainly by some social grouping the method enables us to discover any special tendencies for the people of certain divisions to intermarry, tendencies which may perhaps not have been noticed by the people themselves. The method renders possible the exact study of such forms of marriage as polygyny and polyandry, the Levirate and cross-cousin marriage. These institutions have many variations which easily escape attention by the ordinary methods of inquiry but which become perfectly clear when their nature is worked out in detail from the pedigrees. Further, the method enables us to detect how far the marriage regulations of a people are being actually followed in practice, and a study of the marriages in successive generations may reveal a progressive change in the strictness with which any given regulation has been observed. It is indeed possible to work out the most complex problems concerned in the regulation of marriage without ever having asked a direct question on the matter, though it is not desirable to do this, for one of the most interesting features of the genealogical method is furnished by the comparison of the results gained by the genealogical method with those derived from direct inquiry. If there are discrepancies between the two the investigation of these may not only give the clue to new points of view but much light may be thrown on the linguistic or psychological peculiarities which have been the cause of the misunderstanding.

The sample pedigree from Guadalcanar is too small to furnish a good example of the application of the method, but it will be noticed that in no case have two people of the same clan married and that out of a total of eight marriages, four have taken place between members of the Kindapalei and Lakwili clans, a fact which is probably explained by the existence of the cross-cousin marriage in that island. It also furnished one example of marriage with a member of another community, viz., with a native of the neighbouring island of Savo, the clans of which correspond closely to those of Guadalcanar.

The next line of application of the method is in the investigation of the laws regulating descent and the inheritance of property. Thus in the sample pedigree it will be seen that each person belongs to the clan of his mother, thus illustrating the matrilineal descent of this part of the Solomon Islands. The mode of succession of chiefs can be exactly studied in the same manner, while the method is especially important in the study of the inheritance of property. Thus it is possible to take a given piece of land and inquire into its history, perhaps from the time when it was first cultivated. The history of its divisions and subdivisions on various occasions may be minutely followed, and a case of ownership which would seem hopelessly complicated becomes perfectly simple and intelligible in the light of its history, and an insight is given into the real working of the laws concerning property which could never be obtained by any less concrete method.

Another line of application which is occasionally of great value is in the study of migrations. Thus in many parts of Melanesia there has taken place during the last fifty years a change from life in the bush to life on the sea-coast, and the information given by the localities of successive generations may throw much light on the nature of such a migration.

The uses so far considered are concerned with the study of social organisation, but the method is not without its uses in the study of magic and religion. In most of the people studied by myself it has been found that very definite functions in ceremonial are assigned to people who stand in certain relationships either to the performer of the ceremony or to the person on whose behalf it is being carried out. I believe that the exact inquiry rendered possible by the genealogical method would show that these functions connected with relationship are far more general than current anthropological literature would lead us to suppose, and further that the duties or privileges of kin discovered in this manner can be much more closely defined. The method enables one also to investigate ceremonial much more concretely than would be otherwise possible. When I am working at this subject I have my book of pedigrees by my side, and as I obtain the names of the various participants I look them out and see how they are related to the performer or subject of the ceremony, and at the same time there is the advantage that these become real personages to me although I may never have seen them, and the whole investigation proceeds in a manner which interests both me and my informants far more than if the personages in the account had been X, Y, and Z.

Still another large group of uses to which the method can be put is in the study of many problems which, though they are primarily biological, are yet of great sociological importance. I refer to such matters as the proportion of the sexes, the size of the family, the sex of the first-born child, the proportion of children who grow up and marry to the total number born, and other similar subjects which can be studied statistically by the genealogical method. We have in the pedigrees a large mass of data of the utmost value for the exact study of various demographic problems, but in this connection it is necesary to utter a note of warning. In my experience the memories of the people are less trustworthy in regard to the children of past generations who have died young or before marriage than in the case of those who have married and had offspring. It is obvious that the latter will have gained social importance which has made the preservation of their names natural, while it is less to be expected that those who have died young or unmarried should be so perpetuated. It has often been surprising to me that the latter are remembered as well as they are, but there can be little doubt that some must be forgotten, and that statistics concerning these more biological matters are less complete than those dealing with the more strictly social problems.

Still another most important use of the method is as an aid to physical anthropology. As an example of this I cannot do better than give the instance of an island visited by Mr. Hocart and myself last year where there are two constant sources of inter-mixture, in both cases with people whose physical characters are decidedly different from those of the general mass of the inhabitants. The measurement of the population of that island by the ordinary methods can hardly have had any definite result, but by means of the genealogical method we were able to discover the immediate ancestry of each person we measured. Further the combination of physical measurement with the use of genealogical method pro-

vides a mass of material for the study of problems in heredity. The method also makes it possible to work out very completely the mode of inheritance of such conditions as colour-blindness and albinism which are present in varying proportion in most parts of the world.

Some incidental advantages of the genealogical method may be briefly mentioned. Much information may be gained concerning transmission of names, and in the sample pedigree it will be noticed that a child has been given the name of his great-grandfather. Further, the name of some dead person, perhaps one who may have lived a century ago, will recall the story of the old life of the people which would possibly otherwise not have been obtained, and chance remarks thrown out in connection with the names of ancestors in this way often furnish most valuable suggestions for inquiry. Further, the mere collection of names provided in the pedigrees forms a storehouse of linguistic material which would be of great value if it were not for the fact that we have too little knowledge of the more living parts of the language to enable it to be utilised.

Having now considered the more detailed lines of inquiry in which genealogical method is useful or essential, I proceed to sum up briefly some of its advantages in more general terms. In the first place I would mention its concreteness. Everyone who knows people of low culture must recognize the difficulty which besets the study of an abstract question, not so much because the savage does not possess abstract ideas as that he has no words of his own to express them, while he certainly cannot be expected to appreciate properly the abstract terms of the language of his visitor or of any other foreign language which serves as the means of communication. The genealogical method makes it possible to investigate abstract problems on a purely concrete basis. It is even possible by its means to formulate laws regulating the lives of people which they have probably never formulated themselves, certainly not with the clearness and definiteness which they have to the mind trained by a more complex civilisation. Endless misunderstandings are avoided which are liable to arise between people from such different spheres, misunderstandings which have their source in differences of outlook and in the lack of appreciation on one side or other of the niceties of the language, whether European or native, which is serving as the means of communication. The method cannot do away with the difficulties which beset the interpretation of the social conditions of the savage by the visitor from another civilisation, but it gives a mass of definite and indubitable facts to be interpreted.

From this point of view the method is more particularly useful to those who, like myself, are only able to visit savage or barbarous peoples for comparatively short times, times wholly insufficient to acquire that degree of mastery over the native language to enable it to be used as the instrument of intercourse. To such the method is essential if there is to be any hope of getting facts of real value about the more complex features of social organisation. By means of the genealogical method it is possible, with no knowledge of the language and with very inferior interpreters, to work out with the utmost accuracy systems of kinship so complicated that Europeans who have spent their whole lives among the people have never been able to grasp them. It is not an exaggeration to say that in such a matter as this or in that of the regulation of marriage, it is possible by this method to obtain more definite and exact knowledge than is possible without it to a man who has lived for many years among the people and has obtained as full a knowledge as is ever acquired by a European of the language of a savage or barbarous people.

Another great general advantage of the method is that it gives one the means of testing the accuracy of one's witnesses. Among savages just as among ourselves there are the greatest differences between persons in the accuracy with which they can give an account of a ceremony or describe the history of a person or course of events. The genealogical method gives one a ready means of testing this accuracy. I do not mean merely that a person who remembers pedigrees accurately will probably have an accurate memory on other subjects, but that the concrete method of inquiry which the genealogical method renders possible enables one to detect careless-ness and inaccuracy so much more readily than is possible by the more ordinary methods of inquiry. It is not an unimportant point that the knowledge that the facts are accurate gives one a sense of comfort in one's work which is no small asset in the trying conditions, climatic and otherwise, in which most anthropological work has to be done. Further, the genealogical method not only gives one confidence in one's witnesses but it has an effect perhaps quite as important in giving the savage confidence in his questioner. Everyone knows the old statement that the chief characteristic of the savage is that he will tell you whatever you want to know. When he does this it is because it seems to him the easiest way of getting through a task in which he takes no interest, often because he does not understand the real nature of the questions, but I believe often because he recognizes that his questioner does not himself understand them. What seem to be the most simple questions to the uninstructed European may as a matter of fact be quite incapable of a straightforward answer, and it is not surprising that the puzzled child of nature should take the easiest way of ending the matter. I believe that the genealogical method puts the European inquirer on much the same footing as the native himself. It is quite certain that people of low culture would not preserve their pedigrees with the minuteness which is found to be the case if they were not of great practical importance in their lives, and the familiarity of his questioner with the instrument which he uses himself gives the savage confidence and interest in the inquiry which are of inestimable importance in getting information of real value. Further, the mutual confidence which is engendered by the use of the genealogical method in working out social organisation extends to other departments of anthropology, and is not merely limited in its effects to the former.

Another very valuable feature of the genealogical method to which I have already referred is the help it gives in enabling us to understand those features of savage psychology which give anthropological work its difficulties. I am always in the habit of inquiring into matters both by the genealogical method and by the ordinary method of question and answer. There will often be discrepancies, and the investigation of these discrepancies often gives the most valuable insight into the mental peculiarities which have been the cause of the misunderstanding.

In conclusion there are two advantages of the method which are of so much importance that they would, to my mind, be sufficient to make its use essential even if there were no others.

It is almost impossible at the present time to find a people whose culture, beliefs and practices are not suffering from the effects of European influence, an influence which has been especially active during the last fifty years. To my mind the greatest merit of the genealogical method is that it often takes us back to a time before this influence had reached the people. It may give us records of marriage and descent and other features of social organisation one hundred and fifty years ago, while events a century old may be obtained in abundance in all the communities with whom I have myself worked, and I believe that with proper care they could be obtained from nearly every people. Further, the course of the pedigrees is itself sometimes sufficient to demonstrate the gradual effect of the new influences which have affected the people.

The other pre-eminent merit of the method is that it gives us the means of not merely obtaining information but of demonstrating the truth of this information. Up till recently ethnology has been an amateur science. The facts on which the science has been based have been collected by people who have usually had no scientific training, and they have been imparted to the world with nothing to guarantee their accuracy or their completeness. It is a striking tribute to the essential veracity of the savage that these records are as good as they are, but anyone who has examined critically the records of any people must have found enormous diversities of evidence, and must have recognised that the records give in themselves no criteria which enable him to distinguish the false from the true. By means of the genealogical method it is possible to demonstrate the facts of social organisation so that they carry conviction to the reader with as much definiteness as is possible in any biological science. The genealogical and other similar methods which render such demonstration possible will go far towards putting ethnology on a level with other sciences.

CLASSIFICATORY SYSTEMS OF RELATIONSHIP

A. L. Kroeber

The distinction between classificatory and descriptive systems of relationship has been widely accepted, and has found its way into handbooks and general literature. According to the prevalent belief the systems of certain nations or languages group together distinct relationships and call them by one name, and are therefore classifying. Other systems of consanguinity are said to indi-

Reprinted by permission of the Royal Anthropological Institute of Great Britain and Ireland from the *Journal of the Royal Anthropological Institute*, Vol. 39 (1909), pp. 77–84.

cate secondary differences of relationship by descriptive epithets added to their primary terms, and to be therefore descriptive.

Nothing can be more fallacious than this common view. A moment's reflection is sufficient to show that every language groups together under single designations many distinct degrees and kinds of relationship. Our word brother includes both the older and the younger brother and the brother of a man and of a woman. It therefore embraces or classifies four relationships. The English word cousin denotes both men and women cousins; cousins on the father's or on the mother's side; cousins descended from the parent's brother or the parent's sister; cousins respectively older or younger than one's self, or whose parents are respectively older or younger than the speaker's parents; and cousins of men or women. Thirty-two different relationships are therefore denoted by this one English word. If the term is not strictly limited to the significance of first cousin, the number of distinct ideas that it is capable of expressing is many times thirty-two. Since then it is not only primitive people that classify or fail to distinguish relationships, the suspicion is justified that the current distinction between the two classes or systems of indicating relationship is subjective, and has its origin in the point of view of investigators, who, on approaching foreign languages, have been impressed with their failure to discriminate certain relationships between which the languages of civilized Europe distinguish, and who, in the enthusiasm of formulating general theories from such facts, have forgotten that their own languages are filled with entirely analogous groupings or classifications which custom has made so familiar and natural that they are not felt as such.

The total number of different relationships which can be distinguished is very large, and reaches at least many hundred. No language possesses different terms for all of these or even for any considerable proportion of them. In one sense it is obvious that a language must be classificatory as the number of its terms of relationship is smaller. The number of theoretically possible relationships remaining constant, there must be more ideas grouped under one term in proportion as the number of terms is less. Following the accepted understanding of what constitutes classificatory consanguinity, English, with its twenty terms of relationship, must be not less but more classificatory than the languages of all primitive people who happen to possess twenty-five, thirty, or more terms.

It is clear that if the phrase classificatory consanguinity is to have any meaning it must be sought in some more discriminating way. The single fact that another people group together various relationships which our language distinguishes does not make their system classificatory.

If there is a general and fundamental difference between the systems of relationship of civilized and uncivilized people, its basis must be looked for in something more exact than the rough and ready expressions of subjective point of view that have been customary.

It is apparent that what we should try to deal with is not the hundreds or thousands of slightly varying relationships that are expressed or can be expressed by the various languages of man, but the principles or categories of relationship which underlie these. Eight such categories are discernible.

1. *The difference between persons of the same and of separate generations.*—The distinctions between father and grandfather, between uncle and cousin, and between a person and his father, involve the recognition of this category.

2. *The difference between lineal and collateral relationship.*—When the father and the father's brother are distinguished, this category is operative. When only one term is employed for brother and cousin, it is inoperative.

3. *Difference of age within one generation.*—The frequent distinction between the older and the younger brother is an instance. In English this category is not operative.

4. *The sex of the relative.*—This distinction is carried out so consistently by the English, the one exception being the foreign word cousin, that the discrimination is likely to appear self-evident. By many people, however, many relationships are not distinguished for sex. Grandmother and grandfather, brother-in-law and sister-in-law, father-in-law and mother-in-law, and even such close relationships as son and daughter, are expressed respectively by single words.

5. *The sex of the speaker.*—Unrepresented in English and most European languages, this category is well known to be of importance in many other languages. The father, mother, brother, sister and more distant relatives may receive one designation from a man and another from his sister.

6. *The sex of the person through whom relationship exists.*—English does not express this category. In sequence we frequently find it necessary to explain whether an uncle is a father's

or a mother's brother, and whether a grandmother is paternal or maternal.

7. *The distinction of blood relatives from connections by marriage.*—While this distinction is commonly expressed by most languages, there are occasional lapses; just as in familiar English speech the father-in-law is often spoken of as father. Not strictly within the domain of relationship, but analogous to the occasional failure to express this category, is the frequent ignoring on the part of primitive people of the difference between actual relatives and fictitious clan or tribal relatives.

8. *The condition of life of the person through whom relationship exists.*—The relationship may be either of blood or by marriage; the person serving as the bond of relationship may be alive or dead, married or no longer married. Many North American Indians refrain from using such terms as father-in-law and mother-in-law after the wife's death or separation. Some go so far as to possess terms restricted to such severed relationship. It is natural that the uncle's relation to his orphaned nephew should tend to be somewhat different from his relation to the same boy while his natural protector, his father, was living. Distinct terms are therefore sometimes found for relatives of the uncle and aunt group after the death of a parent.

The subjoined table indicates the representation of the eight categories, and the degree to which they find expression, respectively in English and in several of the Indian languages of North America.

It appears that English gives expression to only four categories. With the exception, however, of the one and foreign word cousin, every term in English involves the recognition of each of these four categories. All the Indian languages express from six to eight categories. Almost all of them recognize seven. But in all the Indian languages the majority of the categories occurring are expressed in only part of the terms of relationship found in the language. There are even Indian languages, such as Pawnee and Mohave, in which not a single one of the seven or eight categories finds expression in every term. While in English the degree of recognition which is accorded the represented categories is indicable by a percentage of 100 in all cases but one, when it is 95, in Pawnee corresponding percentages range variously from about 10 to 90, and in

Table 1.

	ENGLISH.	N.A. INDIAN.					CALIFORNIA INDIAN.						
		ARAPAHO.	DAKOTA.	PAWNEE.	SKOKOMISH.	CHINOOK	YUKI.	POMO	WASHO.	MIWOK.	YOKUTS.	LUISEÑO.	MOHAVE.
No. of terms	21 [1]	20	31	19	18	28	24	27	28	24	28	34	35
Generation	21	20	31	11	13	23	24	21	27	24	22	30	26
Blood or marriage	21	19	31	17	18	26	24	27	28	24	28	32	34
Lineal or collateral	21	10	20	5	11	25	24	21	28	18	26	34	28
Sex of relative	20	18	29	17	2	12	16	21	20	20	17	18	22
Sex of connecting relative	0	6	6	2	0	20	13	13	14	10	14	19	21
Sex of speaker	0	3	18	4	0	15	3	3	10	2	12	10	14
Age in generation	0	3	7	2	2	2	3	4	4	4	4	12	8
Condition of connecting relative	0	0	0	0	8	1	0	0	0	0	[2]	0	1

[1] All terms are omitted, such as great grandfather, great-uncle, and second-cousin, which are not generally used in ordinary speech and exist principally as a reserve available for specific discrimination on occasion.

[2] Terms denoting relatives by marriage undergo a vocalic change to indicate the death of the connecting relative

Mohave from 5 to 95. All the other Indian languages, as compared with English, closely approach the condition of Pawnee and Mohave.

It is clear that this difference is real and fundamental. English is simple, consistent, and, so far as it goes, complete. The Indian systems of relationship all start from a more elaborate basis, but carry out their scheme less completely. This is inevitable from the fact that the total number of terms of relationship employed by them is approximately the same as in English. The addition of only one category to those found in English normally doubles the number of terms required to give full expression to the system; and the presence of three additional categories multiplies the possible total by about eight. As the number of terms occurring in any of the Indian languages under consideration is not much more than half greater than in English, and sometimes is not greater of all, it is clear that at least some of their categories must find only very partial expression.

In short, as far as the expression of possible categories is concerned, English is less complete than any of the Indian languages; but as regards the giving of expression to the categories which it recognizes, English is more complete. In potentiality, the English scheme is poorer and simpler; but from its own point of view it is both more complete and more consistent. As English may evidently be taken as representative of European languages, it is in this point that the real difference is to be found between the systems that have been called classificatory and those that have been called descriptive.

The so-called descriptive systems express a small number of categories of relationship completely; the wrongly-named classificatory systems express a larger number of categories with less regularity. Judged from its own point of view, English is the less classificatory; looked at from the Indian point of view it is the more classificatory, inasmuch as in every one of its terms it fails to recognize certain distinctions often made in other languages; regarded from a general and comparative point of view, neither system is more or less classificatory.

In short, the prevalent idea of the classificatory

system breaks down entirely under analysis. And in so far as there is a fundamental difference between the languages of European and of less civilized peoples in the method of denoting relationship, the difference can be determined only on the basis of the categories described and can be best expressed in terms of the categories.[1]

The categories also serve to indicate the leading characteristics of systems of the same general order. It is obvious, for instance, that the most important difference between Dakota and Arapaho is the strong tendency of the former to recognize the sex of the speaker. Chinook is notable for laying more stress on the sex of the speaker and of the connecting relation than on

---

[1] A tendency toward reciprocal expression is sometimes of importance and may influence the degree to which categories are given expression. Reciprocal terms are such that all the persons included in the relationship expressed by one term call by one name all the persons who apply this term to them. In the most extreme form of reciprocity the two groups of relatives use the same term. The paternal grandparents call their sons' children, whether boys or girls, by the same term which these children, both boys and girls, apply to their fathers' parents. Nevertheless, the reciprocal relation is just as clear, though less strikingly expressed, when each of the groups uses a different term for the other. Our English words father and child, or brother and sister, are not reciprocal, for the term child is employed also by the mother, and brother is used by the brother as well as by the sister. In fact the only reciprocal term in English is cousin. The tendency toward reciprocal expression is developed in many Indian languages. It is particularly strong in California. In some languages this tendency has brought it about that different categories are involved in the terms applied to a pair of mutual relationships. The term father's sister indicates the sex of the relative but not of the speaker. The exact reciprocal of father's sister is woman's brother's child. This term, however, does not recognize the sex of the relative indicated, but does imply the sex of the speaker. The two reciprocal terms therefore each involve a category which the other does not express. If the same categories were represented in the two terms, brother's daughter would correspond to father's sister and exact reciprocity would be impossible. When, therefore, the terms found are father's sister and woman's brother's child, it is clear that the tendency toward the establishment of exactly reciprocal terms has been stronger than the feeling favoring the consistent use or neglect of certain categories; in other words, the extent to which certain categories are expressed has been determined by the vigor of the reciprocal tendency.

the sex of the relative.[2] General differences such as naturally occur between the languages of one region and of another can also be expressed in terms of the categories. All the California systems, for instance, lay much more stress upon the sex of the connecting relative than do any of the Plains languages examined. The Plains systems are conspicuous for their weak development of the distinction between lineal and collateral relationship, this finding expression in two-thirds of all cases in Dakota, half in Arapaho, one-fourth in Pawnee. In seven California languages the corresponding values lie between three-fourths and complete expression. The method can be applied successfully even in the case of smaller and contiguous geographical areas. Of the seven California languages Luiseño and Mohave are spoken in southern California. Their systems show a unity as compared with the systems of the five languages from northern and central California. Both the southern California languages have a greater number of terms; both are stronger in the expression of the categories of the sex of the connecting relative and of age within the same generation; and both are weaker in the category of sex of the relative, than the others. Again, Chinook and Skokomish, both of the North Pacific Coast, are alike in indicating the condition of the connecting relative and in failing, on account of the possession of grammatical sex gender, to distinguish the sex of relatives themselves in many terms of relationship. There is a very deep-going difference between them, however, in the fact that Skokomish is as free as English from recognizing the sex of the speaker and of connecting relatives, while Chinook generally expresses both categories. In short, the categories present a means of comparing systems of terms of relationship along the basic lines of their structure and of expressing their similarities and differences without reference to individual terms or details.

The reason why the vague and unsatisfactory idea of a classificatory system of consanguinity has found such wide acceptance is not to be sought in any primary interest in designations of relationship as such, but in the fact that terms of relationship have usually been regarded principally as material from which conclusions as to the organization of society and conditions of marriage could be inferred. If it has been more clearly recognized that terms of relationship are determined primarily by linguistic factors, and are only occasionally, and then indirectly, affected by social circumstances, it would probably long ago have been generally realized that the difference between descriptive and classificatory systems is subjective and superficial. Nothing is more precarious than the common method of deducing the recent existence of social or marital institutions from a designation of relationship. Even when the social condition agrees perfectly with expressions of relationship, it is unsafe to conclude without corroborative evidence that these expressions are a direct reflection or result of the condition.

In the Dakota language, according to Riggs, there is only one word for grandfather and father-in-law. Following the mode of reasoning sometimes employed, it might be deduced from this that these two relationships were once identical. Worked out to its implications, the absurd conclusion would be that marriage with the mother was once customary among the Sioux.

In the same language the words for woman's male cousin and for woman's brother-in-law have the same radical, differing only in a suffix. Similar reasoning would induce in this case that marriage of cousins was or had been the rule among the Sioux, a social condition utterly opposed to the basic principles of almost all Indian society.

The use of such identical or similar terms for distinct relationships is due to a considerable similarity between the relationships. A woman's male cousin and her brother-in-law are alike in sex, are both of opposite sex from the speaker, are of the same generation as herself, and are both collateral, so that they are similar under four categories. In view of the comparative paucity of terms as compared with possible relationships, it is entirely natural that the same word, or the same stem, should at times be used to denote two

[2] No doubt, as has been pointed out, owing to the fact that the sex of the relative is indicable by purely grammatical means in this and certain other languages.

relationships having as much in common as these two.

No one would assume that the colloquial habit in modern English of speaking of the brother-in-law as brother implies anything as to form of marriage, for logically the use of the term could only be an indication of sister marriage. It is easily conceivable that in the future development of English the more cumbersome of these two terms might come into complete disuse in daily life and the shorter take its place, without the least change in social or marital conditions.

The causes which determine the formation, choice, and similarities of terms of relation are primarily linguistic. Whenever it is desired to regard terms of relationship as due to sociological causes and as indicative of social conditions, the burden of proof must be entirely with the propounder of such views.

Even the circumstances that the father's brother is frequently called father is not necessarily due to or connected with the custom of the Levirate; nor can group marriage be inferred from the circumstance that there is frequently no other term for mother's sister than mother. A woman and her sister are more alike than a woman and her brother, but the difference is conceptual, in other words linguistic, as well as sociological. It is true that a woman's sister can take her place in innumerable functions and relations in which a brother cannot; and yet a woman and her sister, being of the same sex, agree in one more category of relationship than the same woman and her brother, and are therefore more similar in relationship and more naturally denoted by the same term. There are so many cases where the expression of relationship cannot have been determined by sociological factors and must be purely psychological, as in the instances just discussed, that it is fair to require that the preference be given to the psychological cause, or that this be admitted as of at least equal probability, even in cases where either explanation is theoretically possible and supporting evidence is absent.

On the whole it is inherently very unlikely in any particular case that the use of identical terms for similar relationships can ever be connected with such special customs as the Levirate or group marriage. It is a much more conservative view to hold that such forms of linguistic expression and such conditions are both the outcome of the unalterable fact that certain relationships are more similar to one another than others. On the one hand this fact has led to certain sociological institutions; on the other hand, to psychological recognitions and their expression in language. To connect the institutions and the terms causally can rarely be anything but hazardous. It has been an unfortunate characteristic of the anthropology of recent years to seek in a great measure specific causes for specific events, connection between which can be established only through evidence that is subjectively selected. On wider knowledge and freedom from motive it is becoming increasingly apparent that causal explanations of detached anthropological phenomena can be but rarely found in other detached phenomena, and that it is even difficult to specify the most general tendencies that actuate the forms taken by culture, as the immediate causes of particular phenomena.

The following conclusions may be drawn:—

1.   The generally accepted distinction between descriptive and classificatory systems of terms of relationship cannot be supported.
2.   Systems of terms of relationship can be properly compared through an examination of the categories of relationship which they involve and of the degree to which they give expression to these categories.
3.   The fundamental difference between systems of terms of relationship of Europeans and of American Indians is that the former express a smaller number of categories of relationship than the latter and express them more completely.
4.   Terms of relationship reflect psychology, not sociology. They are determined primarily by language and can be utilized for sociological inferences only with extreme caution.

RIVERS ON THE PSYCHOLOGY
AND SOCIOLOGY OF KINSHIP

W. H. R. Rivers

The classificatory system may be the result neither of promiscuity nor of polyandry, and yet have been determined, both in its general character and in its details, by forms of social organisation.

Since the time of Morgan and McLennan few have attempted to deal with the question in any comprehensive manner. The problem has inevitably been involved in the controversy which has raged between advocates of the original promiscuity or the primitive monogamy of mankind, but most of the former have been ready to accept Morgan's views blindly, while the latter have been content to try and explain away the importance of conclusions derived from the classificatory system without attempting any real study of the evidence. On the side of Morgan there has been one exception in the person of Professor J. Kohler (*Zur Urgeschichte der Ehe*, 1897.) who has recognised the lines on which the problem must be studied, while on the other side there has been, so far as I am aware, only one writer who has recognised that the evidence from the nature of the classificatory system of relationship cannot be ignored or belittled, but must be faced and some explanation alternative to that of Morgan provided.

This attempt was made four years ago by Professor Kroeber (1909), of the University of California. The line he takes is absolutely to reject the view common to both Morgan and McLennan that the nature of the classificatory system has been determined by social conditions. He explicitly rejects the view that the mode of using terms of relationship depends on social causes, and puts forward as the alternative that they are conditioned by causes purely linguistic and psychological.

It is not quite easy to understand what is meant by the linguistic causation of terms of relationship. In the summary at the end of his paper Kroeber concludes that "they (terms of relationship) are determined primarily by language." Terms of relationship, however, are elements of language, so that Kroeber's proposition is that elements of language are determined primarily by language. In so far as this proposition has any meaning, it must be that, in the process of seeking the origin of linguistic phenomena, it is our business to ignore any but linguistic facts. It would follow that the student of the subject should seek the antecedents of linguistic phenomena in other linguistic phenomena, and put on one side as not germane to his task all reference to the objects and relations which the words denote and connote.

Professor Kroeber's alternative position is that terms of relationship reflect psychology, not sociology, or, in other words, that the way in which terms of relationship are used depends on chain of causation in which psychological processes are the direct antecedents of this use. I will try to make his meaning clear by means of an instance which he himself gives. He says that at the present time there is a tendency among ourselves to speak of the brother-in-law as a brother; in other words, we tend to class the brother-in-law and the brother together in the nomenclature of our own system of relationship. He supposes that we do this because there is a psychological similarity between the two relationships which leads us to class them together in our customary nomenclature. I shall return both to this and other of his examples later.

We have now seen that the opponents of Morgan have taken up two main positions which it is possible to attack: one, that the classificatory

From W. H. R. Rivers, *Kinship and Social Organization*, Monographs on Social Anthropology, No. 34 (1968), pp. 43–44. Reprinted by permission of Athlone Press. Originally published 1914.

system is nothing more than a body of terms of address; the other, that it and other modes of denoting relationship are determined by psychological and not by sociological causes.

SELECTED READINGS

A. Commentaries and Critiques

Harris, Marvin
1968 *The rise of anthropological theory: A history of theories of culture.* New York: Crowell, pp. 319–337.
Kardiner, Abram and Edward Preble
1961 *They studied man.* New York: World, ch. VIII.
Lowie, Robert H.
1937 *The history of ethnological theory.* New York: Holt, Rinehart, & Winston.
Tax, Sol
1937c From Lafitau to Radcliffe-Brown. In F. Eggan (ed.), *Social anthropology of the North American tribes.* Chicago: University of Chicago Press.

B. Original Works

Kroeber, Alfred L.
1909 Classificatory systems of relationships. *Journal of the Royal Anthropologial Institute,* 39:77–84. Reprinted in Paul Bohannan and John Middleton (eds.), *Kinship and social organization.* New York: The Natural History Press, 1968b, pp. 19–28.
————1917a California kinship systems. *University of California Publications in Archeology, Anthropology and Ethnology,* 12:9:340–396.
————1917b Zuni kin and clan. *American Museum of Natural History Anthropological Papers,* 19:39–204.
————1917c The matrilineate again. *American Anthropologist,* 19:571–579.
Rivers, William H. R.
1900 A genealogical method of collecting social and vital statistics. *Journal of the Royal Anthropological Institute,* 30:74–82.
————1906 *The Todas.* London: Macmillan Co.
————1907 On the origin of the classificatory systems of relationships. In *Anthropological essays presented to E. B. Tylor.* London: Oxford University Press.
————1910 The genealogical method of anthropological enquiry. *Sociological Review,* 3:1–11. (Also see Bobbs-Merrill reprint #A–190), pp. 1–11.
————1914a *Kinship and social organization.* London: Constable. London: Athlone Press and New York: Humanities Press, 1968.
————1914b *The History of Melanesian society.* 2 vols. Cambridge: Cambridge University Press.
————1914c Kin, kinship. In *Hastings encyclopedia of religion and ethics.* N.Y.: Scribner's, 1914. vol. 7. pp 700–707.
————1915a Marriage, introductory and primitive. *Ibid.* 8:423–432.
————1915b Mother-right. *Ibid.* 8:851–859.
————1924 *Social organization.* London: Kegan Paul, Trench, Trubner & Co. Ltd.

V

AMERICAN CAUTION AND PROGRESS: 1915–1935

After the Kroeber-Rivers controversy subsided, North American cultural anthropologists showed relatively little interest in the topics of kinship and social structure. Instead, they concentrated on matters of diffusion, culture area, and, later, culture and personality. These are the topics that the "ethnologists" thought were important and fundamental. It can be said, therefore, that most contributions to kinship and social structure theory during this period (1915–1935) were rather trivial. Also during this period, American linguistics made great strides and led the world in this area. The effect of this work on anthropology, however, could not be discerned until several decades had passed.

Robert H. Lowie was by far the most important contributor to kinship and social structure studies for these two decades. As a good student of Boas, Lowie was not, at first, interested in kinship and social organization. His reading of Rivers' works, however, stimulated him in this direction. Lowie became interested through the rather minor dispute over whether kinship terminology systems reflected special types of marriage or whether they were reflections of exogamous groups in societies. On this debate Lowie first took the latter view ("Social Organization," 1914) but gradually modified his stand to include more of the former, even though it was derived from Morgan. Most of the Americans following Lowie inclined to the "special marriage" idea, for example, the work of Sapir (1916a), Hallowell (1930), Aginsky (1935a and b), Strong (1929), etc.

The question of whether kinship terms reflected sociological institutions at all—or whether, as Kroeber claimed, they obeyed the laws of linguistics and diffusion (Lowie 1915, 1916, and later), was another dispute that Lowie debated, both with himself and with others. Lowie compromised but tended to accept the sociological view. In addition, he cast aspersions on all "psychological" explanations of the kind put forward by Frazer and Freud. It was his view that assumptions about the universal nature of the human psyche could not possibly explain the differences found in human social systems.

His *Primitive Society* (1920) was a landmark of synthesis and clear writing. It made little theoretical advance in kinship studies, however, and clung to compromise explanations and, in some cases, no explanations of any kind were provided. Perhaps it was a greater contribution in that it brought to the attention of anthropologists the *non*-kin-based structures of primitive societies, such as rank, caste, class, associations, clubs, and so on. However the majority of anthropologists did not then—and have not since —taken the hint. It is only in the very recent past that this began to change.

Intensive fieldwork was going on all through this period and masses of kinship data and data concerning kinship terminology were accumulated. Attempts at classification of kinship systems were made by Kroeber (1917a) and Gifford (*California Kinship Terminologies*, 1922) for California data on the basis of nonsociological criteria suggested by Kroeber (1909) and followed by a few others. Spier (*The Distribution of Kinship Systems in North America,* 1925) produced an empirically-based classification for all North America, based mainly upon the terminology systems for cousins and siblings and for the generations above and below ego, as partially suggested by Morgan (1870). Although Spier was concerned with the distribution of his types, these types did, in fact, have an implicit sociological rationale that could be traced back to Morgan. Lowie ("A Note on Relationship Terminologies," 1928) and Kirschoff (1932) independently presented another classification based on distinctions in the terminological categories for close relatives in the generation above ego. This classification had a logical and, hence, universal basis, but it made fewer and less useful distinctions than did Spier's (1925).

Lesser (1928, 1929, 1930) generally followed Lowie in making compromises but went further in trying to join historical and functional explanations. His works were forgotten or demolished by the adherents of both approaches—so much for compromise.

In general few of the actual contributions of this period made fundamental advances, though fundamental issues, such as the nature of ethnological explanations were raised. The problem of former and present cross-cousin marriage among the Northern Algonkians captured the interests of some (Hallowell 1930, Strong 1929). This controversy came to be a test of the ideas of "survivals" (Morgan, Tylor) and the ideas that marriage practices are reflected in kinship terminologies (Rivers, Lowie). The conflict has not been successfully resolved (Graburn, "Naskapi Family and Kinship," 1971).

The end of this period of stale-mate came about when (1) Radcliffe-Brown came to Chicago in 1931 and attracted followers and students, including Tax, Eggan, Opler, Lloyd Warner, and others, who were of different persuasions that the home-grown (Boas) group, and (2) when it was felt that culture area and diffusionist theory were beginning to be played out. It was found that these series did not really work outside of North America (cf. Herskovits'—1924, 1930—attempts to construct culture areas for Africa).

EXOGAMY AND THE CLASSIFICATORY SYSTEMS OF RELATIONSHIP

Robert H. Lowie

Some connection between exogamy and primitive relationship terminologies has been recognized for a long time. Morgan noted that among the Iroquois all clan members were brothers and sisters as if children of the same mother. And though in his theoretical treatment of the subject he does not derive the classificatory system as a whole from the exogamous principle, he does attribute the change from the older Malayan to the later and more common Turanian form of the system to Punaluan marriage as a predecessor of

Reproduced by permission of the American Anthropological Association from *American Anthropologist,* Vol. 17, 1915, pp. 223–239.

the institution of exogamy and to exogamy itself (1877, Chapters 1–3). Tylor, to my knowledge, was the first to view exogamy and the classificatory system as but "two sides of one institution" (1889: 245–269, 261 ff). More recently both Frazer (1910: 4:114) and Rivers (1907:70 *et seq.*) discovered the origin of the classificatory system in "a social structure which has the exogamous social group as its essential unit," both conceiving this group as an exogamous moiety, which indeed had already figured prominently in Tylor's essay.

It will be best to put this theory in somewhat more concrete form. Among the Iroquois, Morgan noted that a single term was applied to the maternal grandmother and her sisters; to the mother and her sisters; to the father and his brothers; and so forth. On the other hand, distinct terms were applied to the father's and to the mother's brother, to the father's and to the mother's sister. All these facts are readily formulated by deriving the classification from the exogamous groups extant among the Iroquois: /those relatives distinguished in our own nomenclature and not distinguished in that of the Iroquois are members of the same exogamous division, while those not distinguished by us and separated by the Iroquois are necessarily members of different divisions/ From this point of view the objection otherwise plausibly urged against denying the name "classificatory" to our own system since it, also, ranges certain relatives in *classes*, becomes impossible. It is no longer a question, whether our terms "uncle," "aunt," or "cousin" are "classificatory" in a purely etymological sense of the term; nor whether the classificatory principle is quantitatively more important in certain primitive systems than in our own. The point at issue is the *basis* of the classification, and having regard to this there obviously exists a real difference between a system that classifies, say, cousins from both the father's and the mother's side under a common term and a system that rigorously divides relatives of the paternal and the maternal line on the ground of their different clan or gentile affiliations. Thus, the Tylor-Rivers theory, on the one hand, briefly summarizes and makes intelligible certain modes of classification operative in many primitive systems that otherwise might seem purely capricious; and, moreover, it furnishes at last a logical basis for separating our civilized system from that of the primitive peoples concerned.

I am profoundly impressed with the influence of the exogamous principle on primitive kinship nomenclature, but I feel strongly that the principle has not yet been formulated with adequate precision and due regard to coordinate principles of a different type. It seems to me that most writers on the subject suffer from the familiar disease of conceptual realism: the concept "classificatory system" is for them a sort of Platonic idea in the essence of which particular systems of this type somehow participate.

Even Dr Rivers cannot be freed from this charge. In practice he does not treat classificatory systems as fully determined by the clan or gentile factor, but smuggles in additional elements that go hand in hand with exogamy in moulding relationship nomenclature. Most important among these is the principle, so strongly emphasized by Cunow, that members of the same generation are classed together and apart from other generations. Dr Rivers regards this as so general a feature of "classificatory" systems that departures from the rule at once elicit from him special hypotheses. Again, in a concrete illustration of his theory, he has it that in tribes possessing a classificatory system a person will apply a single term to all the members of his father's clan *of the same generation as his father*. I am certainly in favor of considering clan, generation, and other causes as jointly operative in the development of kinship nomenclature, but if this method is accepted an attempt must be made to indicate the interaction of these several principles. The fact is that the mode of interaction for the two factors that are here taken into account *varies*. In some cases, Dr Rivers's statement, that members of the same clan (or gens) *and* generation are united, holds. But in other cases, for example among the Tewa, Crow, Hidatsa, and Tlingit, the exogamous principle predominates and overrides the generation category. Here, then, is an empirical problem, to be settled for every people and only obscured by the characterization of classificatory systems generally as "clan" systems; to wit, the problem how the exogamous group is coordinated with other principles of classification.

The fact that Dr Rivers has not attempted to evaluate the several factors that together determine primitive relationship terminology has led him into the curious position of underestimating in practice the very factor that occupies the dominant position in his theory. Again and again he invokes special social usages to account for "relatively small variations of the classificatory system" that are at once explained by the prepotency of the exogamous principle. For example, he cites the East Indian term *bahu*, which is applied to son's wife, the wife, and the mother; and in explanation of this classification he assumes a one-time form of polyandry in which a man and his son had a wife in common. This assumption is *de trop* because with a dual organization and paternal descent, I and my son belong to my father's moiety, while my mother, my wife, and my son's wife must belong to the complementary moiety; hence, *bahu* may simply connote females of that exogamous group. Again, Dr Rivers cites the Pawnee use of one term for the wife and the wife of the mother's brother, explaining this by a special form of marriage. But, given a dual organization with maternal descent, I and my mother's brother are members of the same moiety, while my wife and his wife are fellow-members of the complementary moiety. Finally, the confusion of generations in the Banks Islands requires no special hypothesis. With maternal descent, my father's sister's son is classed with my father because, as among the Tewa of Hano, he is my father's clansman. My mother's brother's children are classed with my children because my mother's brother, being my clansman, is my brother; and because two brothers regard each other's children as their own. Thus, in the first confusion of generations the clan principle alone has been operative; in the second case, the clan principle has established a relationship from which a really nonexistent distinction of generation is the logical derivative.

Thus, on the one hand, the exogamous theory does not suffice to explain the classificatory systems in their totality; on the other hand, it eliminates certain auxiliary hypotheses considered necessary by the most eminent of its advocates. Obviously, there is something wrong with the formulation of the theory.

The solution of the difficulty lies implicity in the original and invaluable portion of Professor Kroeber's (1909) essay on the subject the very part ignored or misunderstood by his critics— where he lists the categories in which the North American Indians have ranged relatives, and by the quantitative importance of each of which a given system may be defined. Among these categories is that of distinguishing lineal and collateral relatives,—the father from the father's

brother, the mother from the mother's sister, the brother from the cousin. When we turn to Morgan's earliest description of what he afterwards took for the starting-point of his definition of the classificatory type of system (*League of the Iroquois*, 1851, Book I, Chapter 4), we find that what impressed him above all was the abeyance of the rule that collateral shall be distinguished from lineal relatives. This, then, forms the core of Morgan's concept, however obscured by adherent features that are logically quite unrelated. And from this point of view the Tylor-Rivers theory assumes a different aspect. Exogamy cannot explain why generations are so generally distinguished; it cannot explain the frequent differences between elder and younger *Geschwister*, or the frequent distinction between vocative and non-vocative forms; it cannot explain a hundred and one features of classificatory systems so-called. But it does explain why lineal and collateral lines of kinship are merged in the particular way characteristic of the Iroquois, Ojibwa, and many other primitive systems conforming to Morgan's Turanian type. Thus purged, the theory must now be subjected to empirical verification.

It might appear at first sight that such an empirical verification has already been given by Dr Rivers with regard to Oceania, though this, of course, would not render it unnecessary to collect corroborative evidence from other regions. However, Dr Rivers has in reality made a different point. In Oceania he is not dealing with classificatory and non-classificatory systems, but merely with the two forms of the classificatory system,—the Hawaiian and the Turanian. In both forms lineal and collateral relationship are merged, but in the Hawaiian nomenclature the terms are even more inclusive, no distinction being drawn between relatives of the maternal and paternal side. Setting out with his theory and these two forms of the classificatory system before him, Dr Rivers undertakes to show how the Hawaiian form could have developed from the Turanian form which alone follows logically from the exogamous principle. He finds that where the Hawaiian form is most clearly developed, traces of exogamy are lacking, while the highest development of exogamy is accompanied by a Turanian form of kinship system. An indefinate number of intermediate social organizations are accompanied, we are told, by intermediate kinship terminologies. The general interpretation of the phenomena offered is that a progressive change has occurred from the Turanian to the Hawaiian form, going hand in hand with the substitution of non-exogamous marriage regulations for regulation by exogamous divisions.

This is obviously not testing the theory that the classificatory system is a function of exogamy, but merely interpreting by a special historical hypothesis the occurrence of an aberrant type of classificatory system, on the supposition that the theory is already established. Granting that the hypothesis correctly represents the course of development in Oceania, we cannot assume that exogamy everywhere represents an older condition, and indeed in North America the evidence points in the opposite direction ("Social Organization," 1914, pp. 68–97). Without assuming the priority of either the exogamous or the loose social organization, we can test the Tylor-Rivers theory by grouping together exogamous tribes, on the one hand, and non-exogamous tribes, on the other hand, and comparing the corresponding kinship terminologies. North America, where the geographical distribution of types of organization is fairly well determined, offers a favorable field for such an inquiry.

In the first place, there can be little doubt that the custom of identifying in nomenclature lineal and collateral relatives is very largely coextensive with the exogamous practice. It is found in at least three of the four main exogamous areas of the continent,—east of the Mississippi, among the southern Siouan and northwestern Plains tribes, and on the Northwest coast. For the Southwest satisfactory data seem to be lacking except for the Tewa, where conditions are markedly anomalous. Both among the patrilineally organized Tewa of New Mexico and the matrilineal Tewa of Hano, Arizona, there are distinct terms for father's brother and father, although the term for "father" is "applied loosely to father, elder brother, father's brother, or other relatives older than self" in New Mexico, and at Hano to all father's clansmen, including of course his own

brothers. For the present purpose it is important to note that at Hano it is the distinct term for "father's brother" that seems to be the older mode of designation, now rendered obsolescent by the term for "father." Similarly, in both branches of the Tewa, the mother's sister is carefully distinguished from the mother; in Hano, we are told emphatically, a mother's sister is never addressed as mother; and conversely we find that a woman does not address her sister's children like her own children but by a reciprocal term with diminutive suffix. In New Mexico there is a further invasion of the exogamous principle inasmuch as no distinction is drawn between paternal and maternal uncles and aunts respectively.

For the Tewa, then, the hypothetical correlation does not hold.

Exogamy thus furnishes a sufficient explanation of the invasion of the generation principle as encountered in Melanesia, and various North American tribes. The chief value of the theory that kinship classification has followed exogamous groupings lies, however, in another direction. It explains the remarkable resemblance between the terminologies of widely separated and quite distinct peoples without recourse to hypothetical historical connections. If we abandon Morgan's theory that the development of the family has been unilinear, with the main stages impressing their stamp on kinship nomenclature, how can we account for the far-reaching similarity between, say, the system of the Seneca of North America and that of the South Indian Tamil? So widespread a custom as exogamy is admirably fitted to explain the distribution of the lineal-collateral category, and it seems eminently worth while to extend the verification of the Tylor-Rivers theory both extensively and intensively. Such a study will be far from exhausting the subject of kinship nomenclature. The merging of lineal and collateral relationships constitutes but one of a number of categories, the geographical distribution of each of which must be definitely ascertained. Moreover, we are sadly in need of the intensive investigation of particular systems, giving all the connotations of every term, and indicating by comparison with closely related systems how and why kinship nomenclature changes. A comparative study of all the Siouan, or all the Athapascan, or all the Southwestern systems would be of greatest value in this respect. However, the connection between exogamy and the "classificatory" system often hinted at but never systematically examined be-fore Dr Rivers's investigations in Oceania, con-stitutes even by itself a problem of great signifi-cance and its partial solution cannot help but to react on a study of other phases of the whole question of kinship terminology.

HISTORICAL AND SOCIOLOGICAL INTERPRETATIONS OF KINSHIP TERMINOLOGIES

Robert H. Lowie

Students of kinship terminology have been interested almost exclusively in the *sociological* inferences that may be derived from systems of relationship. They have generally failed to note that Morgan himself drew not merely sociological, but also startling *historical* conclusions from the observed phenomena. Indeed, in this regard Morgan may fairly be said to out-Graebner Graebner. He not only rejects the hypothesis that similari-ties in relationship nomenclature can be explained by independent development, but also summarily dismisses the suggestion of diffusion by borrow-ing: nothing will do but racial affiliation.

> In other words the Turanian and Ganowanian families drew their common system of consanguinity and affinity from the same parent nation or stock from whom both were derived, etc. . . . When the discoverers of the New World bestowed upon its inhabitants the name of *Indians*, under the impression that they had reached the Indies, they little suspected that children of the same original family, although upon a different continent, stood before them. By a singular coincidence error was truth. (*Systems of Consanguinity and Affinity*, p. 508.)

This extravagant view was quite correctly criticized by Lubbock when he pointed out that the Two-Mountain Iroquois can hardly be recog-nized as more closely akin to remote Oceanian tribes than to their fellow-Iroquois. But while this criticism (with an indefinite number of similar instances that lie at hand) eliminates the use of kinship terminologies for ascertaining *racial* affinity, it does not dispose of them as evidence of *cultural* connection. Indeed, Morgan himself repeatedly cites resemblances that be-come intelligible only from this point of view; yet with that characteristic lack of the logical sense that detracts so largely from his otherwise superb pioneer achievements he fails to see the bearing of his data. Professor Kroeber—the only writer since Morgan who has departed funda-mentally from the sociological point of view—assumes an historical position when he points out that differences in terminology are regional; but so far as I can see, he does not stress the obvious conclusion that the similarities within a given region are due to historical connection (1909, p. 81).

In the following pages I will cite a number of striking similarites that are explicable as the result of historical connection and will discuss the relation of these facts to a sociological in-terpretation.

While the differentiation of elder and younger brothers and sisters is of very common occur-rence, a tripartite classification of *Geschwister* is not found, so far as I know, except among the Eskimo. The Alaskan Eskimo, according to notes

From *Holmes Anniversary Volume* (Washington, D.C.: J. W. Bryan Press, 1916), pp. 293–300.

supplied by Dr. E. W. Hawkes, have distinct terms for elder brother, younger brother, and youngest brother. Corresponding to this, we find among the Chukchee three distinct terms for eldest brother, middle brother, and youngest brother; and a similar nomenclature among the Koryak. The peculiarly restricted distribution of the phenomenon is such as to at once suggest diffusion. Here, however, an alternative explanation may be given. Though diffusion be the ultimate cause, the immediate antecedent of the similarity may be similar social conditions. In other words, it is certain social peculiarites relating to the status of eldest and youngest brothers that may have been borrowed and the kinship terms may have developed independently from these borrowed usages.

A like perplexity confronts us when we consider the systems found east of the Mississippi and some of the adjoining Plains territory to the west. It is true that a characteristic trait of these systems—the merging of collateral and lineal kin—occurs in a continuous, though vast, area so that its distribution would, according to accepted criteria, be explained by dissemination from a single source. However, it is also true that this area is practically coextensive with the Eastern area of clan exogamy. The hypothesis is, therefore, *a priori* tenable that clan exogamy was the feature diffused, from which a corresponding kinship nomenclature developed independently in a number of cases. We must eliminate such possibilities if we are to establish the historical significance of kinship terms themselves.

Among the numerous tribes in the eastern and central United States which designate collateral kin by the terms used for lineal relatives there are nevertheless certain far-reaching differences connected with the tendency to recognize or to ignore differences of generation. Mr Leslie Spier's as yet unpublished researches in this field indicate that this tendency appears primarily in the designation of cross-cousins. This phenomenon had not escaped the attention of Morgan. As he points out, the Seneca, Ojibwa, and Dakota designate a mother's brother's and a father's sister's child as "cousin"; the Southern Siouans (and Winnebago) call the mother's brother's son

"uncle" and the father's sister's son "nephew"; the Crow and Hidatsa class the former with the son and the latter with the father: and at least part of the Crow-Hidatsa scheme occurs among the Choctaw and related tribes.

I have elsewhere shown that the striking difference between the Southern Siouans and their northern congeners, the Crow and Hidatsa, is a function of the difference in rules of descent. Owing to the very close linguistic affiliation of the Crow and Hidatsa, most ethnologists will agree that their kinship systems (which coincide in many points besides those cited) were neither borrowed from each other in recent times nor arose independently, but are survivals from the system of the parent tribe, which pristine system, then, expressed the maternal (clan) organization. For like reasons, a corresponding conclusion will be deemed permissible for the Omaha and their immediate relatives, whose pristine system, as already noted by Kohler and Cunow, reflected their paternal (gentile) organization.

But as the example of the matrilineal Seneca and the patrilineal Ojibwa indicates, the rule of descent *need* not be reflected in the kinship nomenclature; for here we have tribes of different rule of descent with the same mode of designating cross-cousins, who are *not* placed in a generation above or below that of the speaker. I will not now attack the more general problem why certain tribes emphasize rules of descent while others do not. I prefer to render the problem more specific, and therefore more amenable to solution by confining attention to a single linguistic stock and to a single branch of that stock, among whose members there is a cultural bond as well. Of the Central Algonquians, the Miami, Sauk and Fox, Kickapoo, Menomini, and Shawnee agree among themselves and differ from the Ojibwa in classing the mother's brother's son and the father's sister's son with the uncle and nephew, respectively; the corresponding female cousins with the mother and daughter, respectively. But this is precisely like the system of the Winnebago and Southern Siouans, as Morgan himself expressly states! Why do the Algonquian terminologies cited resemble those of a group of Siouan tribes rather than the Ojibwa nomenclature?

In order to appreciate the significance of the actual facts, we must plot them on some such map as that of Mooney in his paper on The Cheyenne Indians (1907). We then find that the system in question is spread over an absolutely continuous area, covering the territory of the Menomini, Winnebago, Iowa, Omaha, Ponca, Oto, Kansas, Osage, Illinois, Sauk and Fox, Miami, and Shawnee. But the Ojibwa also form part of a fairly continuous area,—that including besides their own habitat that of the Cree, Dakota, Wyandot, and Iroquois, all of whom designate cross-cousins as cousins. Since within both areas members of distinct linguistic families share the same kinship features, the similarities, unless explicable by similar social conditions, can be explained only by diffusion.

The similarities cannot be explained by similar social conditions. The Ojibwa do not possess either the clan or the moiety system of the Iroquois, yet they have a similar nomenclature. They do possess the gentile organization of the Central Algonquian, yet that similarity was not an adequate cause for the production or maintenance of a system similar to that of the Central Algonquians. No sociological condition can be conceived that might account for the empirical distribution of traits. On the other hand that distribution corresponds so closely to the criterion ordinarily demanded for a proof of diffusion that diffusion, and diffusion only, must be accepted as the explanatory principle.

For the present discussion the distribution of systems with a clear development of reciprocal terms is important. To choose a common example, grandparent and grandchild are designated in these systems by a common term, or at least by a common root to which a diminutive affix is attached to distinguish the junior relative. So far as I know, systems in which reciprocal terms figure at all conspicuously are completely lacking in the Eastern Woodland, Southeastern, and Plains areas. On the other hand, they have been recorded among the Lillooet, Squawmish, Okinagan, Spokane, and Nez Percé; the Wishram, Takelma, Uintah Ute and Kaibab Paiute; the San Carlos Apache; the Navaho; the Zuñi; the Tewa, Acoma and Cochiti; the Papago; the Yo-

kuts; the Kern River and Mono; the Paviotso, Moapa and Shivwits Paiute, Wind River and Lemhi Shoshone; and Kootenay. Having regard to our very meager information on some of the tribes concerned, every one must again be impressed with the fact that the trait discussed is spread over a large, practically continuous area, among more than half a dozen distinct linguistic families, while outside that area it is lacking.

This phenomenon of distribution cannot be explained sociologically. The tribes cited vary fundamentally in social organization and usage. Nothing could be more distinct in this regard than the clan division of the Pueblo tribes and the loose organization of the Plateau Shoshoneans. Moreover, no social usage that could conceivably unite grandparent and grandchild has ever been reported in North America, no trace of anything like the Australian class system being known.

A more minute examination supports the theory of diffusion. Sapir has shown that "in this matter of relationship terms two such closely related dialects as Ute and Southern Paiute differ on a point on which they respectively agree with neighboring Shoshonean and with a non-Shoshonean language (Tewa). Here, as often, a cultural dividing line runs clear across a homogeneous linguistic group." *American Anthropologist*, 1913, pp. 132–138.) Similarly, Mr. Gifford informs me that the Kern River people share with the Southern Paiute the use of diminutive suffixes for the junior relative designated by a reciprocal term. These tribes, though belonging to distinct branches of the Shoshonean family, are geographically contiguous. Why they should agree in a feature not common to the entire family is not at all clear unless we assume that the similarity is a contact phenomenon. Here again a sociological interpretation is barred at the outset: what social usage or institution *could* lead to the employment of a diminutive suffix.

I can refer only briefly to certain other points. The occurrence of the distinction between vocative and non-vocative forms is one of the phenomena that should be investigated and plotted on a map. It is markedly developed among the Siouan tribes, but has also been noted by Uhlenbeck for the Blackfoot, by Morgan for the Nez Percé and

Yakima, by Sapir for the Wishram. Before adopting any interpretation we must determine more definitely the distribution of this trait.

Another very interesting feature is the differentiation of maternal and paternal grandparents. This is so completely lacking in the immense area east of the Rocky mountains that Morgan has not even distinct tables for these relationships and notes their discrimination with some surprise for the Spokane. Yet in the Far West of the United States it is exceedingly common. Boas notes it for the Kalispelm and Okinagan, it occurs probably among the majority of Plateau Shoshoneans, among the Takelma and Wishram, and according to Professor Kroeber is widespread in California. According to Harrington and Kroeber, it exists also among the Tewa and Zuni; weakly developed, it occurs among the Navaho. It is a striking fact that in the North America areas in which clans, gentes, and moieties occur (including the Tlingit and Haida) and where accordingly a discrimination between maternal and paternal grandparents might a priori be expected, such a distinction exists only in the Southwest, while the discrimination occurs precisely in the region without definite social organization. We are clearly dealing with an historical problem.

Still another peculiarity may be mentioned here because its occurrence seems restricted to the same general area—the change of terms after the death of a near or connecting relative. This has been found by Professor Kroeber among the Yokuts and by Mr. Gifford among the neighboring Kern River and Kawaiisu Shoshoneans of California; Boas recorded it for several Salish tribes, the Chinook, and the Kootenay. Again one cannot think of a social custom prevalent among these tribes capable of producing the terminological feature and lacking among tribes without it.

Finally, I may refer to the absence of separate terms for elder and younger brothers and sisters. The failure to distinguish these differences within one's own generation marks the Pawnee system, and occurs in that of the Kiowa. The fact that so glaring an anomaly from the point of view of the ordinary North American system should occur in the same portion of the Plains area is hardly without significance; and, once more, we are tempted to ask what social usage can be lacking here that unites the rest of the North American tribes.

The foregoing remarks seem to me to establish the principle that features of kinship terminology are distributed like other ethnographical phenomena and must be approached in the same spirit. Like specific customs, beliefs, or implements, particular features of kinship nomenclature are sign-posts of cultural relationship. This being so, it becomes obvious that in order to get the full benefit of relationship systems for historical purposes it does not suffice to record the fundamental elements of a terminology. On the contrary, as in other cases apparently trifling features are the most important because when they are found to occur in distinct tribes a specific historical connection is indicated. It is likewise clear that after such a general orientation as I have given above, far more detailed and in some measure quantitative studies along lines suggested by Professor Kroeber must set in. It is not the same thing whether reciprocity is expressed only for the paternal grandfather and the son's son; nor whether classificatory terms (in an etymological sense) exist like our own "cousin" and "uncle" or whether the classification includes father's brothers with the father, as in many primitive systems. A much finer statistical treatment is likely to reveal the accentuation of traits in a particular center of distribution and their gradual diminution as we pass toward the periphery of the area in question. If, as appears rather likely from certain indications, the entire western slope of the United States should then be found to differ markedly from the rest of the continent in point of kinship terminology, that result would be of considerable historical significance, over and above the value of particular historical inferences.

It remains to say a word on the relation of the historical to the sociological point of view. In a paper already cited I have expressed my belief in the validity of sociological interpretation, and since I still adhere to this conviction I feel it incumbent to harmonize it with the apparently contradictory argument of the preceding pages.

As stated above, I am in favor of dealing with

kinship terms in the same way as with other ethnographic features. In the interpretation of cultural resemblances the criterion for historical connection generally applied by American investigators is occurrence in a continuous area or among tribes of known historical relations, while in other instances they assume independent development. This procedure does not solve all perplexities but seems the only one that can yield any assistance at all, and it is applicable in exactly the same way to the problems at hand. When I find a reciprocal system among the Yokuts and Kern River Indians, I explain the similarity by diffusion; when I find a reciprocal system among the Australian Arunta and the Kern River Indians, I do not. In this latter case the question naturally arises *how* the similarity could arise independently. If the Californians possessed a class system like that of the Arunta, I should not hesitate to ascribe the similarity to this institution; since neither they nor any other American tribes have anything of the sort, I confess that I have no explanation to offer. But we are not always so unfortunate. The fact that the Tlingit and Crow class the father's sister's daughter with the father's sister *is* intelligible from the common possession of a maternal exogamous grouping by these tribes. Here as among the Choctaw, certain Pueblo and some Melanesian tribes the clan factor has proved stronger as a classificatory device than the generation factor. Obviously clan exogamy does not furnish a complete explanation, since it does not produce the same effect among the Iroquois, to cite but one illustration. Whether we can adduce an additional sociological determinant, remains to be seen. At all events, we may say that the trait in question is a function of matrilineal descent *plus* certain unknown factors tending to an accentuation of the rule of descent. So, wherever we can connect empirical resemblances between unrelated tribes with actual social customs from which those resemblances naturally flow, we have an adequate explanation of the phenomenon of similarity and do not require recourse to borrowing or cultural relationship.

As everywhere, so here there will be room for doubt and subjective interpretation. For example, who would state categorically that the clan system of the Muskhogeans did or did not give rise to the merging of collateral and lineal kin independently of the development of this feature among the other tribes of the Eastern clan area? Here we find both similar conditions adequate to the production of the terminological trait *and* contiguity of territory. I can conceive the diffusion of a clan organization *with* a correlated terminology at a relatively early period over the entire Eastern area; but I can also conceive an independent development of the terminology from a mere diffusion of the clan concept (not to consider other logical possibilities). If the Tlingit and Haida developed a "classificatory" system independently, so could the Choctaw or the Iroquois. In such instances I think it best to admit frankly either that we cannot make up our minds or that our theoretical preferences rest on more or less subjective grounds. In this regard the study of kinship nomenclature does not differ in the least from like investigations of other cultural elements. And I hope the foregoing remarks have illustrated the axiom, sometimes ignored by ethnologists, that every ethnological problem is primarily a problem of distribution.

TERMS OF RELATIONSHIP
AND THE LEVIRATE

E. Sapir

Revived interest has been manifested of late in the relation which exists between systems of consanguinity and affinity on the one hand, and specific types or features of social organization on the other. It is to Rivers that we chiefly owe this revival of interest and it is he who, by discussion and example based chiefly on Melanesian material, has conclusively shown that many groupings of kinship terms are best understood as expressive of particular types of marriage. True, many of Rivers' inferences seem far-fetched and there is no necessity of following him in detail, but his main argument is certainly sound.[1]

[1] Lowie has tried to show that Rivers' line of argument is in many cases too exclusive in character, that he has explained by a specific form of marriage what would equally well result from a more general feature, that of group exogamy. It seems to me, however, that Lowie's own arguments are in part invalidated by his failure to show why only certain relationships covered by the same exogamic rule are included under a single term. In not at the same time defining the reasons for specific delimitation he may prove too much. Personally I believe that the factors governing kinship nomenclature are very complex and only in part capable of explanation on purely sociological grounds. In any event, I do not seriously believe that thoroughly satisfactory results can be secured without linguistic analysis of kinship terms. Moreover, for the proper historical perspective we must have some feeling for the lack of strict accord between linguistic and cultural change. This means that an existing nomenclature may be retained, at least for a time, in the face of sociological developments requiring its modification. Direct sociological interpretation of descriptive data may be as unhistorical as any other mode of direct interpretation of descriptive cultural facts. However, the purpose of this brief paper is not a polemic or broadly methodological one. It aims merely to call attention to a specific type of marriage as determining part of the kinship nomenclature. Some of the facts instanced in the text are instructive because, without other evidence, one might have inferred from them the actual or former existence of group exogamy. This inference, fortunately, we know to be impossible for the Yana and Chinook.

A widespread marriage custom among American Indians, and other peoples as well, is that of the levirate, in other words the custom by which a man has the privilege or, more often, duty of marrying the widow of his deceased brother and of bringing up the offspring of their union in his own household. Correlative to this is the custom by which a man has the privilege or duty of marrying the as yet unmarried sister of his deceased wife. For convenience we shall consider these two customs as different forms of the levirate. How can the levirate form of marriage find expression in kinship nomenclature? Obviously in two distinct ways. We may look upon the levirate as an accomplished fact, in which case it remains to define step-relationship in terms of the nepotic relationship, i.e., step-father as uncle, step-mother as aunt, step-child as nephew or niece. A reflection of the levirate in nomenclature naturally demands that identification of the step-father and step-mother with the paternal uncle and maternal aunt respectively in such tribes as possess distinct terms for paternal and maternal uncle, and paternal and maternal aunt; correlatively, in those tribes that distinguish between brother's and sister's children we must look for an identification of the step-child with the man's brother's child and the woman's sister's child. Or, secondly, we may look upon the levirate as a potential fact, in which case it remains to define certain nepotic and ensuing relationships in terms of filial (and fraternal) relationship, i.e., paternal uncle as father, maternal aunt as mother, man's brother's child as son and daughter, children of father's brother and mother's sister as brothers and sisters (as distinguished from "real" cousins, i.e., cross-cousins). We may also expect to find a

Reproduced by permission of the American Anthropological Association from *American Anthropologist*, Vol. 18, 1916, pp. 327–337.

man's sister-in-law and a woman's brother-in-law referred to as wife and husband respectively. I propose to show that such peculiarities of kinship nomenclature actually follow, as consequences of the levirate, among the Upper Chinook [2] and the Yahi or Southern Yana.[3]

The identification of step-relationship with the nepotic relationship is complete among the Upper Chinook. The nepotic relationships recognized by these Indians are as follows:—

> *i-mut* "paternal uncle" (vocative *amut*).
> *i-ɫEm* "maternal uncle" (vocative *aɫEm*).
> *a-ɫak* "paternal aunt" (vocative *aɫak*).
> *a-gutx* "maternal aunt" (vocative *agutx* or *aqxôda*).
> ⎡ *i-wulx* "man's brother's son; woman's sister's son" (vocative *qxēwulx*).
> ⎣ *a-wulx* "man's brother's daughter; woman's sister's daughter" (vocative *qxēwulx*).
> ⎡ *i-ɫatxan* "man's sister's son" (vocative *qxētatxEn*).
> ⎣ *a-ɫatxan* "man's sister's daughter" (vocative *qxēɫatxEn*).
> ⎡ *i-tkiu* "woman's brother's son."
> ⎣ *a-tkiu* "woman's brother's daughter."

The step-relationships which are identical with certain of these terms are:—

> *i-mut* "step-father."
> *a-gutx* "step-mother."
> ⎡ *i-wulx* "(man's or woman's) step-son."
> ⎣ *a-wulx* "(man's or woman's) step-daughter."

These facts speak for themselves. Their dependence on the levirate is too obvious to call for extended discussion. I need only add that the levirate itself is known to have been in force among most or all of the tribes of Washington and Oregon. We may infer with some degree of plausibility, for the Upper Chinook, that it was the custom of the levirate, more specifically the fact that both

[2] In Southern Washington. Data taken from as yet unpublished material secured at Yakima reserve in 1905. For orthography of Wishram terms see my "Wishram Texts," *Publications of the American Ethnological Society*, Vol. 2, 1909.

[3] Data taken from material recently (summer of 1915) obtained from Ishi, the last known survivor of the tribe.

the man's brother's child and the woman's sister's child were alike potentially the step-children, that was responsible for the grouping of these two relationships under a single term in contrast to the distinctive terms for the man's sister's child and the woman's brother's child.

Fully as instructive are the Yahi data. They are all the more significant in that the informant made it perfectly clear that he himself looked upon the facts that we are about to consider as simply another way of saying that it was customary for the widow to marry her former husband's brother and for the widower to marry his former wife's sister. The Yahi terms for parents and children, in so far as they are necessary for our argument, are:—

> *galsi* "father (vocative *galsinā*, *galsī*).
> *ganna* "mother" (vocative *gannā*).
> *'i‘sip!a* "son" (literally "little man") or *i'sip!ai'amauyāhi* (literally "person who is little man").
> *mari'mip!a* "daughter" (literally "little woman") or *mari'mip!ai'amauyāhi* (literally "person who is little woman").
> The terms involving the nepotic relationship are:—
> *galsi* "paternal uncle" (vocative *galsinā*, *galsī*).
> *u‘dji' yauna* "maternal uncle (vocative *u‘dji'yaunā*, *u‘dji'yau*).
> *mucdi* "paternal aunt" (vocative *mucdī*).
> *ganna* "maternal aunt" (vocative *gannā*).
> *'i‘sip!a* "man's brother's son; woman's sister's son" (vocative *'i‘sip!anā*, *'i‘sip!ā*).
> *mari'mip!a* "man's brother's daughter; woman's sister's daughter" (vocative *mari'mip!anā*, *mari'mip!ā*).
> *u‘dji'yauna* "man's sister's son" (vocative *u‘dji'yauna*); "man's sister's daughter" (vocative *u‘dji'yau*).
> *mucdi* "woman's brother's son, daughter" (vocative *mucdī*).

These lists show that the paternal uncle, as a potential father, is termed father; and the maternal aunt, as a potential mother, mother. As a necessary correlate of this we find that the man's brother's son and daughter, and the woman's sister's son and daughter, as potential children, are termed son and daughter. On the other hand, the maternal uncle and the paternal aunt are designated by distinctive terms, the correlative nephew or niece being in each case designated by the same term. In other words, the kinship terms involved in the nepotic relation fall into two very distinct groups: such as, through the custom of the levirate, have become identified with the filial relation and recognize the difference of generation, and such as enter into reciprocal pairs in which the difference of generation is not recognized. The latter type of kinship term also includes the terms for grandparents and grandchildren.

There is, furthermore, a specific term applied to the man's brother's son or daughter, *wa'dāt 'imauna* (plural *yēidat'imauna*). The analysis of this term, however, would seem again to show dependence on the levirate. *Wa'-*, to which *yēi-* corresponds as plural, is a verb stem meaning "to sit" but apparently also, when followed by an incorporated noun stem, conveying the idea of "to have, consider as"; *dāt'i* is a term for "child," regardless of sex; *-mauna* is a participial. The term would therefore seem to mean "had, considered as own child," i.e., potential son or daughter according to the levirate. The Northern Yana term for the man's brother's son is the cognate *wadāt'imauna*, for the man's brother's daughter *wadāt'imaumari'mi*, which is the same term compounded with the word for woman, *mari'mi*. A division into two kin groups of necessity prevails also in the cousin relationship. Cross-cousins, i.e., cousins related through parents of opposite sex, are designated by special terms (*'ô'yanmauna* and *'a'yansiya;* their exact definition does not concern us here), while cousins related through parents of like sex are brothers and sisters. In other words, if my paternal uncle and maternal aunt are my potential father and mother, their children must be my potential brothers and sisters.

The levirate is further reflected in the Yahi kinship system in the terms for the wife's sister and the husband's brother, which, as applying to potential wife and husband, are identical with the terms for these:—

> *'i'si* "husband" (literally "man, male"); also "husband's brother."
> *mari'mi* "wife" (literally "woman"); also "wife's sister."

Whether these terms also apply to the woman's sister's husband and the man's brother's wife respectively I do not know, as I have no data on this point, but it seems quite likely from the general analogies of the Yahi system that this is the case. This would be further confirmed by the fact that in Northern Yana a single term (*u'naiyāna*) is used for the wife's sister, the man's brother's wife, the husband's brother, and the woman's sister's husband; this term would thus seem to be about equivalent to "potential spouse." On the other hand, the wife's brother, the man's sister's husband, the husband's sister, and the woman's brother's wife are each designated, in both Northern Yana and Yahi, by a distinctive term; these terms differ only phonetically in the two dialects.

The influence of the levirate on Yahi kinship nomenclature may be still further pursued in certain other terms of affinity. The paternal uncle's wife and the maternal aunt's husband are not typical potential mother and father respectively, but the former, as the potential father's wife, may become a step-mother (or better perhaps co-mother); while the latter, on the death of one's brotherless father, may take the widow to wife and thus become a step-father. However, the terms "mother" and "father" are not respectively used for the paternal uncle's wife and the maternal aunt's husband. The special terms in use for these relationships are:—

> *p'êmo'o* "paternal uncle's wife" (vocative *p'êmo'onā, p'êmo'ô*).
> *'āp'dju'wīyauna* "maternal aunt's husband" (vocative *'āp'dji'wīyaunā*).

The significance of the term *p'êmo'o* for our problem will become apparent in a moment. While the *'āp'dju'wīyauna* himself is not named so as to refer to the levirate, it is highly significant as indicative of this custom that he was said by Ishi to address his wife's children as his own children thus implying a potential fatherhood in himself. Equally significant is the term applied by a woman to her husband's brother's child, *dāt'ip!a* (vocative *dāt'ip!ā*), for this is simply the diminutive of *dāt'i* "child." In other words, as the potential step-mother (or co-mother, for we are dealing with a polygamous society), she addresses her husband's brother's children as her children.

We may now take up the Yahi terms for the step-relationship. They are:—

wa'nimāsi "step-father; man's step-child"
   (vocative *wa'nimāsinā, wa'nimāsī*).
p'êmo'o "step-mother" (vocative *p'êmo'onā, p'êmo'ó*).
dāt'ip!a "woman's step-child" (vocative *dāt'ip!ā*).

The last term, in spite of its literal meaning ("little child"), is used by a woman even for a grown-up step-child. The most striking point about this step-nomenclature is the identity of the step-mother-step-child relation with that of the paternal uncle's wife to the husband's brother's child, a clear indication of one form of levirate marriage. The term *wa'nimāsi,* which is used reciprocally, finds no parallel, so far as my data go, in the Yahi kinship system, but comparison with Northern Yana demonstrates that it too is symptomatic of the levirate—and in a manner, indeed, directly comparable to the Upper Chinook usage. Its Northern Yana cognate is *un'īma* (vocative *un'īmanā*), which means "paternal uncle." This correspondence is of course indicative of the direct and most typical form of levirate, the marriage by a man of his brother's widow. It further implies the former use in Yahi of *wa'nimāsi* for the paternal uncle, its displacement, under the influence of the levirate, by the term for "father," and its survival in a specialized sense ("step-father").

This leads us to a point of considerable interest, the geographical distribution of the kinship terms implying the levirate. For some reason which I am at present unable to give, the identification of the paternal uncle with the father and of the maternal aunt with the mother is peculiar to Yahi, while the Northern and Central Yana have distinct terms for each of the four types of uncle and aunt. . . . we conclude that the Yahi peculiarities of terminology are secondary and that the influence upon it of the levirate was not on the wane, but on the increase. It would be highly interesting to have the Northern Maidu kinship system available for comparison in order to deter-mine whether this emphasis on the levirate is due to a southern influence, but unfortunately such material has not been made accessible.

The influence of the levirate on kinship terminology is doubtless traceable in other systems, and perhaps much of what has been explained with reference to other causes is ascribable to it. I should certainly not be disposed to hold, for instance, that the merging of lineal and collateral lines of descent necessarily points to the custom of group exogamy. The levirate may no doubt not infrequently be examined as an equally or more plausible determining influence.[4] Various features of a kinship system may be interpreted as symptomatic of the levirate, but care must always be taken to see whether in any specific case other explanations may not be more appropriate. One such symptomatic feature is the classification of cousins related through parents of like sex as brothers and sisters. The classification of all cousins as brothers and sisters, as among the Nootka, is naturally of no significance in connection with the levirate. A typical instance of the former mode of cousin classification I find among the Takelma, a tribe of southern Oregon. Among these Indians the term for "younger brother" (*wā"-xa*) was also applied to the father's younger brother's son and to the mother's younger sister's son; the term for "older brother" (*op-xa*) also to the father's older brother's son and to the mother's older sister's son; the term for "younger sister" (*t'awā"-xa*) also to the father's younger brother's daughter and to the mother's younger sister's daughter; and the term for "older sister" (*t'op-xa*) also to the father's older brother's daughter and to the mother's older sister's daughter. The cross-cousins, on the other hand, are classed partly with the paternal uncle and maternal aunt and partly under a distinctive kinship term. It may well be significant in connection with these facts that the levirate was obligatory among the Takelma.

---

[4] To avoid misconception, I wish expressly to state that I do not consider the explanation here given of certain features of kinship terminology to hold generally, but only in the two groups of cases specifically dealt with. Other possible applications of my line of argument must be examined on their merits.

The identification in nomenclature of the wife's sister or man's brother's wife with the wife, and of the husband's brother or woman's sister's husband with the husband, is also good presumptive evidence of the presence of the levirate. Thus, for the Tlingit, Swanton expressly states: "A woman's sister's husband was called husband; and a wife's sister, wife, because in case of the wife's death, the widower had a right to marry her sister" (J. R. Swanton, "Tlingit," 1918–1919, p. 196). That this "right" was really a duty and that both forms of levirate marriage are customary among the Tlingit is indicated by the following quotation from a recent work on the tribe:—

> The levirate custom regulates many marriages; that is, when a brother dies some one of his surviving brothers must take his widow to wife . . . On the other hand, if the wife dies, then a sister of the deceased, or a close relative, must be given to the surviving husband for a wife. (Livingston F. Jones, *A Study of the Thlingets of Alaska,* 1914, p. 129).

How much a matter of course the levirate is with the Tlingit may be gathered from further remarks of the author:—

> In levirate marriages no presents are passed from the man's people to the people of the woman he takes to wife, for this is only making good his loss. The surviving husband has the right even to select a married sister of his deceased wife. If this is done, she must leave her husband and become the widower's wife. Or the widow has the right to select even a married brother of her deceased husband. And if this is done, the husband must leave his wife and children and become the widow's husband. [Presumably not in earlier days, when polygamy was practised. E.S.] The writer is acquainted with more cases than one of this kind. (*Ibid.*, pp. 129, 130.)

In several Shoshonean languages there are similar examples of nomenclature. Many other examples could doubtless be found in America of this type of nomenclature. Among the Shoshonean tribes of the Plateau, aside from the Hopi, there can be no talk of group exogamy. The levirate is ready to hand as a plausible explanation.

Terms denoting step-relationship are also peculiarly apt to be symptomatic of the levirate, as we have seen. I believe that this brief study has served to accentuate the special importance in a study of the relation between kinship and social organization of considering the nomenclature of step-relationship.

SELECTED READINGS

A. Commentaries and Critiques

Eggan, Fred
1961 Introduction to *Primitive society* by R. H. Lowie. New York: Harper Torchbook, pp. vii–xii.
Harris, Marvin
1968 *The rise of anthropological theory: A history of theories of culture.* New York: Crowell, pp. 343–372.
Kroeber, Alfred L.
1920 Review of Lowie's *Primitive society* in *American Anthropologist,* 22:377–381.
Lowie, Robert
1937 *The history of ethnological theory.* New York: Holt, Rinehart & Winston, ch. XIV.
Tax, Sol
1937c From Lafitau to Radcliffe-Brown. In F. Eggan (ed.), *Social anthropology of the North American tribes.* Chicago: University of Chicago Press, pp. 474–477.

B. Original Works

Aginsky, Bernard W.
1935b The mechanics of kinship. *American Anthropologist,* 37:450–457.
Gifford, Edward W.
1916 Miwok moieties. *University of California Publications in Archeology, Anthropology and Ethnology,* 12:4:139–94.
——— 1922 California kinship terminologies. *University of California Publications in Archeology, Anthropology and Ethnology,* 18:155–219.
Hallowell, Alfred I.
1930 Was cross-cousin marriage formerly practiced by the North-Central Algonqian? *Proceedings of International Congress [1928] of Americanists,* 22:97–145.

Kirshhoff, Paul
1932 Verwandshaftsbezeichnungen und Ver-
wahdtenheirat. *Zeitschrift für Ethnologie*,
64:41–72.

Lesser, Alexander
1930 Some aspects of Siouan kinship. *Proceedings of International Congress [1928] of
Americanists*, 23:563–571.
———— 1929 Kinship origins in the light of some
distributions. *American Anthropologist*,
31:710–730.

Lowie, Robert H.
1914 Social organization. *American Journal of
Sociology*, 20:68–97.
———— 1915 Exogamy and the classificatory systems of relationship. *American Anthropologist*, 17:223–239.
———— 1916 Historical and sociological interpretations of kinship terminology. In *Holmes
anniversary volume*. Washington, D.C.: J. W.
Bryan, pp. 293–300.
———— 1917c Methods and principles [a review of
three works of Rivers published during the
years 1914–1915]. *American Anthropologist*,
19:269–272.
———— 1920 *Primitive society*. New York: H.
Liveright. (2nd edit. 1947). New York: Harper
Torchbook, 1961.
———— 1928 A note on relationship terminologies.
American Anthropologist, 30:263–268.
———— 1934a Some moot problems in social organization. *American Anthropologist*, 36:321–
330.
———— 1934b Omaha and Crow kinship terminologies. *Proceedings of International Congress
[1930] of Americanists*, 24:102–108.
———— 1948 *Social organization*. New York: Holt,
Rinehart & Winston.
———— 1959 *Robert H. Lowie, ethnologist*. Berkeley: University of California Press.

Sapir, Edward
1916a Terms of relationship and the levirate.
American Anthropologist, 18:327–337.

Spier, Leslie
1925 The distribution of kinship systems in
North America. *University of Washington
Publications in Anthropology*, 1:2:69–88.

Strong, William D.
1929 Cross-cousin marriage and the culture of
the Northeast Algonkian. *American Anthropologist*, 31:277–288.

VI

STRUCTURE AND FUNCTION: RADCLIFFE-BROWN AND MALINOWSKI

Both Radcliffe-Brown and Malinowski entered British anthropology around 1910 and both came under the influences of such men as Rivers, Haddon, Seligman, and Westermarck. Both owed a very great debt to the ahistorical sociological functionalism of Durkheim. As a result they both rejected the evolutionary and diffusionist methods and explanations of their mentors. They continued to reject "conjectural history" and the worst excesses of social evolutionary imaginations throughout their lives.

Under the influence of Westermarck, Malinowski became particularly interested in the presence, functions, and roles of the nuclear family, working first with library data from Australia (*The Family Among the Australian Aborigines*, 1913) and later with his own Trobriand materials. Early in his career, he was greatly influenced by Freud but, after examining his own data, he rejected the theory of the Oedipus complex because (1) Freud (1918) and Jones (1925) had given it an excessively evolutionary interpretation, and (2) he found it only relevant in patrilineal/patriarchal situations. He therefore invented the "matrilineal complex" as a counterpart and gave us the very valuable concepts of (a) the "split role" of the "father" (i.e., the separability of the roles of father into authoritarian *pater* and mother's sexual partner), and (b) the universal principle of legitimacy irrespective of consanguinity and descent (1927).

In working through his social and economic data, he gave importance to the rather vague concept of reciprocity as a basis of all social re-

lationships following the work of Thurnwald (*Die Gemeinde der Bánaro*, 1921) and Mauss (1925). He also wrote—and very persuasively—on the ambition and willfulness of the individual in primitive societies, combatting the notions of the "custom-bound" savage (1926). He continued work on the analysis of the functions of social sanctions, which he conceived of as customary, institutionalized, and essential to the maintenance of the norms of an integrated cooperating society.

Radcliffe-Brown started by trying to follow Rivers' ideas on historical reconstruction, but his own field experiences (1913, 1922), combined with Durkheim's influence, led him to give up such causal explanations. He then turned to synchronic functionalist explanations of social phenomena ("The Methods of Ethnology and Social Anthropology," 1923). While accepting Malinowski's (1913) ideas on the universality and importance of the nuclear family, he concentrated his own studies on the larger functions and groups in kinship and social structure. He rejected Rivers' ideas on the causal nature of social institutions and the idea of "survivals" and showed that in Australia (*The Social Organization of Australian Tribes*, 1930–1931) and many other areas, the kinship terms, kinship systems, and the total social world were bound up in an integrated whole, each part of which had the function of maintaining that whole. The "whole" was the social structure, or culture ("On Social Structure," 1940a) which had an adaptive function with respect to the total environment.

In Radcliffe-Brown's view, kinship systems

were generated from patterns found in the nuclear family so that affect and behavior were extended to more distant kinsmen ("The Mother's Brother in South Africa," 1924) according to certain sociological principles. He saw the function of the resulting classificatory kinship systems as the means by which a wide range of kinsmen were ordered into a few manageable categories. The units of the social system for Radcliffe-Brown were "positions" (statuses) within a structured arrangement and the task of social anthropology was the comparative study of structures. Little attention, therefore, was given to organization, activities, and roles. In that structures tend to be adaptive equilibria, Radcliffe-Brown's studies were essentially static.

Malinowski, however, viewed the units of comparison (of culture-structure) as *institutions* (*Argonauts of the Western Pacific*, 1922): organized groups with charters and goals, performing culture-maintaining functions that satisfied certain basic human (i.e., universal) biosociological needs (1944) for the individual and his society. Malinowski's theories, then, tended to overlook—and could not "explain"—diversity. On the other hand, however, they were better able to explain individual actions and motivations through his application of behaviorist psychology to sociological functionalism.

Both men had a revolutionary effect on anthropology all over the world. Their students, and many seem to have been shared, became the leaders of social and cultural anthropology in the 1930s, 1940s, and 1950s, but few of them were so revolutionary or so stubborn as their teachers.

By 1930 Malinowski had stated all of his ideas on the subject of kinship systems. He continually emphasized the paramount importance of the nuclear family and downgraded the importance of clans and other, larger, social groupings which he considered to be more the creations of anthropologists than the mainstays of primitive societies. In many places, he mentioned his "forthcoming book on kinship," but it never appeared, and it was left to Radcliffe-Brown to make the major contributions to that field.

Radcliffe-Brown (1923, 1924) often averred that the methods and goals of scientific anthropology, following the "biological analogy" were (1) classification and (2) systematic comparative analyses. In his book *African Systems of Kinship and Marriage* (1950), Radcliffe-Brown made a rather timid attempt at classification of kinship systems according to the nature of their descent systems:

I. Lineal Systems. A. Unilineal 1) Patrilineal
                                      2) Matrilineal
                      B. Bilineal or Double Descent
II. Cognatic Systems, i.e., Bilateral, without lineal descent groups.

This system was rather obvious for its time but, nonetheless, fundamental. It should be noted that this is a classification of kinship *systems*, and not of terminologies as were those of Spier (1925), Lowie (1928), and so on.

In addition to their important contributions to the study of structure and function in primitive societies, both Malinowski and Radcliffe-Brown trained and inspired a large number of brilliant students on all continents of the world. These students, many of whose works appear in the following chapters led the world of social anthropology for decades and made advances that place them among the most renowned senior anthropologists of the present time.

THE METHODS OF ETHNOLOGY
AND SOCIAL ANTHROPOLOGY

A. R. Radcliffe-Brown

In this address I cannot, I think, do better than deal with a subject which has for some years occupied, and is still occupying, the minds of ethnologists and anthropologists all over the world, namely that of the proper aims and methods to be followed in the study of the customs and institutions of uncivilized peoples. The subject is very obviously one of fundamental importance, for a science is hardly likely to make satisfactory progress, or to obtain general recognition, until there is some agreement as to the aims which it should pursue and the methods by which it should seek to attain those aims. But in spite of the many books and papers which have been devoted to the question of method in the past ten or fifteen years, agreement has not yet been reached. The subject is still open for discussion, is still, indeed, a burning one, and we cannot do better, I think than open our proceedings by considering it.

The names ethnology and social or cultural anthropology have been applied without any constant discrimination to the study of culture or civilization, which, according to the definition of Tylor, is "that complex whole which includes knowledge, belief, art, morals, law, custom, and any other capabilities and habits acquired by man as a member of society." Such being the subject matter of the study the question of method which arises is how we are to study the facts of culture, what methods of explanation we are to apply to them, and what results of theoretical interest or practical value we are to expect from our study.

Tylor himself, whose right to the title of the father of the science I think no one will dispute, pointed out that there are two different methods by which facts of culture may be explained (*Researches into the Early History of Mankind*,

Reprinted by permission of the South African Association for the Advancement of Science from the *South African Journal of Science*, Vol. XX (October 1923), pp. 124–147.

1865, p. 5.) and I believe that the confusion that has arisen in the sciences is in some large part due to the failure to keep these two methods carefully separated.

Let us first see what these two methods of explanation are. There is first what I propose to call the historical method, which explains a given institution or complex of institutions by tracing the stages of its development, and finding wherever possible the particular cause or occasion of each change that has taken place. If, for instance, we are interested in representative government in England, we may study its history, noting the changes that have taken place from the earliest times, and thus tracing the development down to the present. Wherever we have adequate historical data we may study the facts of culture in this way.

The important thing to note about explanations of this type is that they do not give us general laws such as are sought by the inductive sciences. A particular element or condition of culture is explained as having had its origin in some other, and this in turn is traced back to a third, and so on as far back as we can go. In other words, the method proceeds by demonstrating actual temporal relations between particular institutions or events or states of civilization.

Now with regard to the institutions of uncivilized peoples we have almost no historical data. If, for instance, we are interested in the customs of the native tribes of Central Australia, it is obvious at once that we can never obtain any direct information as to the history of these tribes. In such instances, therefore, the only possible way to apply the historical method of explanation is by making, on the basis of whatever evidence of an indirect kind we can find, a hypothetical reconstruction of the past history of these tribes.

A great deal of what is generally called

ethnology has consisted of such theoretical or conjectural history. Let me illustrate the method by reference to a specific example. Off the east coast of this continent there lies a large island— Madagascar. A first examination of the people of the island shows that they are in some ways related, as we should expect, to the peoples of Africa. You may find, particularly on the western side, many individuals of distinctly negro, i.e., African type, in respect, I mean, of their physical characters. And quite a number of the elements of Madagascar culture seem to be African also. But a closer examination shows that there are elements both of race and culture that are not African, and a study of these enables us to demonstrate without question that some of them have been derived from south-eastern Asia. A consideration of the racial and cultural features of Madagascar as they exist at the present time enables us to say with practical certainty that, at a period of time not many centuries ago, there was an immigration into the island of people from Asia who were related in language, in culture, and at least to some extent in race, to the present inhabitants of the Malay Archipelago. We can even fix dates, rather vague, it is true, between which this migration took place. It must have been earlier than our first historical accounts of Madagascar, and it must have been later than the introduction of ironworking into the region from which the immigrants came.

A more detailed study of the racial and cultural features of Madagascar would enable us to reconstruct a good deal more of the history of the island. We see that there are at least two elements that have been combined in the culture of the island, two culture-strata as they are sometimes, not very appropriately, called, and a thorough systematic examination of the culture in comparison with the cultures of S.E. Asia and of Africa would permit us to analyse the existing complex of culture traits, so that we could say of many of them whether they were brought by the immigrants or whether they belonged to the earlier population of the island. And in this way we should be able to reconstruct some of the characters of the culture that existed in the island before the invasion.

In this way we explain the culture of Mada-

gascar by tracing out the historical process of which it is the final result, and in default of any historical records we do this by means of a hypothetical reconstruction of the history based on as complete a study as possible of the racial characters, the language and the culture of the island at the present time, supplemented, if possible, by the information given by archaeology. In our final reconstruction some things will be quite certain, others can be established with a greater or less degree of probability, and in some matters we may never be able to get beyond mere guessing.

You will see from this example that we are able to apply the method of historical explanation even where we have no historical records. From written documents we can only learn the history of civilization in its most advanced stages during the last few centuries, a mere fragment of the whole life of mankind on earth. Archaeologists, turning over the soil, and laying bare the buildings or dwelling sites, and restoring to us the implements, and occasionally the bones, of races and peoples of long ago, enable us to fill in some of the details of the vast prehistoric period. The ethnological analysis of culture, which I have illustrated by the example of Madagascar, supplements the knowledge derived from history and archaeology.

This historical study of culture gives us only a knowledge of events and of their order of succession. There is another kind of study which I propose to speak of as "inductive," because in its aims and methods it is essentially similar to the natural or inductive sciences. The postulate of the inductive method is that all phenomena are subject to natural law, and that consequently it is possible, by the application of certain logical methods, to discover and prove certain general laws, i.e., certain general statements or formulae, of greater or less degree of generality, each of which applies to a certain range of facts or events. The essence of induction is generalisation; a particular fact is explained by being shown to be an example of a general rule. The fall of the apple from the tree and the motions of the planets round the sun are shown to be different examples of the law of gravitation.

Inductive science has conquered one realm of nature after another: first the movements of the stars and planets and the physical phenomena of the world around us; then the chemical reactions of the substances of which our universe is composed; later came the biological sciences which aim at discovering the general laws that govern the reactions of living matter; and in the last century the same inductive methods have been applied to the operations of the human mind. It has remained for our own time to apply these methods to the phenomena of culture or civilization, to law, morals, art, language, and social institutions of every kind.

There are then, these two quite different methods of dealing with the facts of culture, and, since they are different, both in the results they seek, and in the logical methods by which they strive to attain those results, it is advisable to regard them as separate, though doubtless connected, studies, and to give them different names. Now the names ethnology and social anthropology seem to be very suitable for this purpose, and I propose to devote them to it. There is already noticeable, I think, a distinct tendency to differentiate the use of the two terms in very much this

way, but it has never, so far as I am aware been carried out systematically. I would propose then, to confine the use of the term ethnology to the study of culture by the method of historical reconstruction described above, and to use the term social anthropology as the name of the study that seeks to formulate the general laws that underlie the phenomena of culture.[1] In making this suggestion I am doing nothing more, I think, than make explicit a distinction that is already implicit in a great deal of the current usage of the terms.

I think that the clear recognition of the existence of two quite different methods of dealing with the facts of culture will help us to understand the controversies on method that have been occupying the attention of students in recent years.

[1] It may be asked why I do not use the word "sociology" instead of the decidedly more cumbersome "social anthropology." Usage must count for something, and a good deal of what is commonly called sociology in English-speaking countries is a somewhat formless study of whose votaries Steinmetz says "on désire des vérités larges, éternelles, valables pour toute l'humanité, comme prix de quelques heures de spéculation somnolente."

ON RULES OF DESCENT AND INTERKIN BEHAVIOR

A. R. Radcliffe-Brown

Amongst primitive peoples in many parts of the world a good deal of importance is attached to the relationship of mother's brother and sister's son. In some instances, the sister's son has certain special rights over the property of his mother's brother. At one time it was usual to regard these customs as being connected with matriarchal institutions, and it was held that their presence in a patrilineal people could be regarded as evidence that the people had at some

Reprinted by permission of the South African Association for the Advancement of Science from A. R. Radcliffe-Brown, "The Mother's Brother in South Africa," *South African Journal of Science*, Vol. XXI (1924), pp. 542–555.

time in the past been matrilineal. This view is still held by a few anthropologists and has been adopted by Mr. Junod in his book on the BaThonga people of Portuguese East Africa. Referring to the customs relating to the behaviour of the mother's brother and the sister's son to one another, he says: 'Now, having enquired with special care into this most curious feature of the Thonga system, I come to the conclusion that the only possible explanation is that, in former and very remote times, our tribe has passed through the matriarchal stage.' (Junod, *The Life of a South African Tribe*, 1913, Vol. I, p. 253).

It is with this theory that I wish to deal in this paper; but I do not propose to repeat or add to the objections that have been raised against it by various critics in recent years. Purely negative criticism does not advance a science. The only satisfactory way of getting rid of an unsatisfactory hypothesis is to find a better one. I propose, therefore, to put before you an alternative hypothesis, but in showing that it does give a possible explanation of the facts, I shall at least have refuted the view of Mr. Junod that the explanation he accepts is the 'only possible' one.

For many African tribes we have almost no information about customs of this kind. Not that the customs do not exist, or are not important to the natives themselves, but because the systematic and scientific study of the natives of this country has as yet hardly begun. I shall, therefore, have to refer chiefly to the customs of the BaThonga as recorded by Mr. Junod. These are to be found in the first volume of the work quoted above (pp. 225 *et seq.*, and pp. 253 *et seq.*). Some of the more important of them may be summarised as follows:

1. The uterine nephew all through his career is the object of special care on the part of his uncle.
2. When the nephew is sick the mother's brother sacrifices on his behalf.
3. The nephew is permitted to take many liberties with his mother's brother; for example, he may go to his uncle's home and eat up the food that has been prepared for the latter's meal.
4. The nephew claims some of the property of his mother's brother when the latter dies, and may sometimes claim one of the widows.
5. When the mother's brother offers a sacrifice to his ancestors the sister's son steals and consumes the portion of meat or beer offered to the gods.

It must not be supposed that these customs are peculiar to BaThonga. There is evidence that similar customs may be found amongst other peoples in various parts of the world. In South Africa itself customs of this kind have been found by Mrs. Hoernle amongst the Nama Hottentots. The sister's son may behave with great freedom towards his mother's brother, and may take any particularly fine beast from his herd of cattle, or any particularly fine object that he may possess. On the contrary, the mother's brother may take from his nephew's herd any beast that is deformed or decrepit, and may take any old and worn-out object he may possess.

What is particularly interesting to me is that in the part of Polynesia that I know best, that is, in the Friendly Islands (Tonga) and in Fiji, we find customs that show a very close resemblance to those of the BaThonga. There, also, the sister's son is permitted to take many liberties with his mother's brother, and to take any of his uncle's possessions that he may desire. And there also we find the custom that, when the uncle makes a sacrifice, the sister's son takes away the portion offered to the gods, and may eat it. I shall, therefore, make occasional references to the Tongan customs in the course of this paper.

These three peoples, the BaThonga, the Nama, and the Tongans, have patrilineal or patriarchal institutions; that is, the children belong to the social group of the father, not to that of the mother; and property is inherited in the male line, passing normally from a father to his son. The view that I am opposing is that the customs relating to the mother's brother can only be explained by supposing that, at some past time, these peoples had matrilineal institutions, such as are found today amongst other primitive peoples, with whom the children belong to the social group of the mother, and property is inherited in the female line, passing from a man to his brother and to his sister's sons.

It is a mistake to suppose that we can understand the institutions of society by studying them in isolation without regard to other institutions with which they coexist and which they may be correlated, and I wish to call attention to a correlation that seems to exist between customs relating to the mother's brother and customs relating to the father's sister. So far as present information goes, where we find the mother's brother important we also find that the father's sister is equally important, though in a different way. The custom of allowing the sister's son to take liberties with his mother's brother seems to be generally accompanied with an obligation of particular respect and obedience to the father's sister. Mr. Junod says little about the father's sister amongst the BaThonga. Speaking of a man's behaviour to this relative (his *rarana*) he says simply: 'He shows her great respect. However, she is not in any way a mother (*mamana*)' (*op. cit.*, p. 223). About the Nama Hottentots we have better information, and there the father's sister is the object of the greatest respect on the part of her brother's child. In Tonga this custom is very clearly defined. A man's father's sister is the one relative above all others whom he must respect and obey. If she selects a wife for him he must marry her without even venturing to demur or to voice any objection; and so throughout his life. His father's sister is sacred to him; her word is his law; and one of the greatest offences of which he could be guilty would be to show himself lacking in respect to her.

Now this correlation (which is not confined, of course, to the three instances I have mentioned, but seems, as I have said, to be general) must be taken into account in any explanation of the customs relating to the mother's brother, for the correlated customs are, if I am right, not independent institutions, but part of one system; and no explanation of one part of the system is satisfactory unless it fits in with an analysis of the system as a whole.

In most primitive societies the social relations of individuals are very largely regulated on the basis of kinship. This is brought about by the formation of fixed and more or less definite patterns of behaviour for each of the recognised kinds of relationship. There is a special pattern of behaviour, for example, for a son towards his father, and another for a younger brother towards his elder brother. The particular patterns vary from one society to another; but there are certain fundamental principles or tendencies which appear in all societies, or in all those of a certain type. It is these general tendencies that it is the special task of social anthropology to discover and explain.

Once we start tracing out relationship to any considerable distance the number of different kinds of relatives that it is logically possible to distinguish is very large. This difficulty is avoided in primitive society by a system of classification, by which relatives of what might logically be held to be of different kinds are classified into a limited number of kinds. The principle of classification that is most commonly adopted in primitive society may be stated as that of the equivalence of brothers. In other words if I stand in a particular relation to one man I regard myself as standing in the same general kind of relation to his brother; and similarly with a woman and her sister. In this way the father's brother comes to be regarded as a sort of father, and his sons are, therefore, relatives of the same kind as brothers. Similarly, the mother's sister is regarded as another mother, and her children are therefore brothers and sisters. The system is the one to be found amongst the Bantu tribes of South Africa, and amongst the Nama Hottentots, and also in the Friendly Islands. By means of this principle primitive societies are able to arrive at definite patterns of behaviour towards uncles and aunts and cousins of certain kinds. A man's behaviour towards his father's brother must be of the same general kind as his behaviour towards his own father and he must behave towards his mother's sister according to the same pattern as towards his mother. The children of his father's brother or of the mother's sister must be treated in very much the same way as brothers and sisters.

This principle, however, does not give us immediately any pattern for either the mother's brother or the father's sister. It would be possible, of course, to treat the former as being like a father and the latter as similar to a mother, and this course does seem to have been adopted in a few societies. A tendency in this direction is found in some parts of Africa and in some parts of Polynesia. But it is characteristic of societies in which the classificatory system of kinship is either not fully developed or has been partly effaced.

Where the classificatory system of kinship reaches a high degree of development or elaboration another tendency makes its appearance: the tendency to develop patterns for the mother's brother and the father's sister by regarding the former as a sort of male mother and the latter as a sort of female father. This tendency sometimes makes its appearance in language. Thus, in South Africa the common term for the mother's brother is *malume* or *unalume*, which is a compound formed from the stem for mother—*ma*—

and a suffix meaning 'male.' Amongst the BaThonga the father's sister is called *rarana,* a term which Mr. Junod explains as meaning 'female father.' In some South African languages there is no special term for the father's sister; thus in Xosa, she is denoted by a descriptive term *udade bo bawo,* literally 'father's sister.' In Zulu she may be referred to by a similar descriptive term or she may be spoken of simply as *ubaba,* 'father,' just like the father's brothers. In the Friendly Islands the mother's brother may be denoted by a special term *tuasina,* or he may be called *fa'e tangata,* literally 'male mother.' This similarity between South Africa and Polynesia cannot, I think, be regarded as accidental; yet there is no possible connection between the Polynesian languages and the Bantu languages, and I find it very difficult to conceive that the two regions have adopted the custom of calling the mother's brother by a term meaning 'male mother' either from one another or from a common source.

Now let us see if we can deduce what ought to be the patterns of behaviour towards the mother's brother and the father's sister in a patrilineal society on the basis of the principle or tendency which I have suggested is present. To do this we must first know the patterns for the father and the mother respectively, and I think that it will, perhaps, be more reassuring if I go for the definition of these to Mr. Junod's work, as his observations will certainly not have been influenced by the hypothesis that I am trying to prove. The relationship of father, he says, 'implies respect and even fear. The father, though he does not take much trouble with his children, is, however, their instructor, the one who scolds and punishes. So do also the father's brothers' (*op. cit.,* p. 222). Of a man's own mother he says: 'She is his true *mamana,* and this relation is very deep and tender, combining respect with love. Love, however, generally exceeds respect' (*op. cit.,* p. 224). Of the mother's relation to her children we read that 'She is generally weak with them and is often accused by the father of spoiling them.'

There is some danger in condensed formulae, but I think we shall not be far wrong in saying that in a strongly patriarchal society, such as we find in South Africa, the father is the one who must be respected and obeyed, and the mother is the one from whom may be expected tenderness and indulgence. I could show you, if it were necessary, that the same thing is true of the family life of the Friendly Islanders.

If, now, we apply the principle that I have suggested is at work in these peoples it will follow that the father's sister is one who must be obeyed and treated with respect, while from the mother's brother indulgence and care may be looked for. But the matter is complicated by another factor. If we consider the relation of a nephew to his uncle and aunt, the question of sex comes in. In primitive societies there is a marked difference in the behaviour of a man towards other men and that towards women. Risking once more a formula, we may say that any considerable degree of familiarity is generally only permitted in such a society as the BaThonga between persons of the same sex. A man must treat his female relatives with greater respect than his male relatives. Consequently the nephew must treat his father's sister with even greater respect than he does his own father. (In just the same way, owing to the principle of respect for age or seniority, a man must treat his father's elder brother with more respect than his own father.) Inversely, a man may treat his mother's brother, who is of his own sex, with a degree of familiarity that would not be possible with any woman, even his own mother. The influence of sex on the behaviour of kindred is best seen in the relations of brother and sister. In the Friendly Islands and amongst the Nama a man must pay great respect to his sister, particularly his eldest sister, and may never indulge in any familiarities with her. The same thing is true, I believe, of the South African Bantu. In many primitive societies the father's sister and the elder sisters are the objects of the same general kind of behaviour, and in some of these the two kinds of relatives are classified together and denoted by the same name.

We have deduced from our assumed principle a certain pattern of behaviour for the father's sister and for the mother's brother. Now these patterns are exactly what we find amongst the BaThonga, amongst the Hottentots, and in the

Friendly Islands. The father's sister is above all relatives the one to be respected and obeyed. The mother's brother is the one relative above all from whom we may expect indulgence, with whom we may be familiar and take liberties. Here, then, is an alternative 'possible explanation' of the customs relating to the mother's brother, and it has this advantage over Mr. Junod's theory that it also explains the correlated customs relating to the father's sister. This brings us, however, not to the end but to the beginning of our enquiry. It is easy enough to invent hypotheses. The important and difficult work begins when we set out to verify them. It will be impossible for me, in the short time available, to make any attempt to verify the hypothesis I have put before you. All I can do is to point out certain lines of study which will, I believe, provide that verification.

The first and most obvious thing to do is to study in detail the behaviour of the sister's son and the mother's brother to one another in matriarchal societies. Unfortunately, there is practically no information on this subject relating to Africa, and very little for any other part of the world. Moreover, there are certain false ideas connected with this distinction of societies into matriarchal and patriarchal that it is necessary to remove before we attempt to go further.

In all societies, primitive or advanced, kinship is necessarily bilateral. The individual is related to certain persons through his father and to others through his mother, and the kinship system of the society lays down what shall be the character of his dealings with his paternal relatives and his maternal relatives respectively. But society tends to divide into segments (local groups, lineages, clans, etc.), and when the hereditary principle is accepted, as it most frequently is, as the means of determining the membership of a segment, then it is necessary to choose between maternal or paternal descent. When a society is divided into groups with a rule that the children belong to the group of the father we have patrilineal descent, while if the children always belong to the group of the mother the descent is matrilineal.

There is, unfortunately, a great deal of looseness in the use of the terms matriarchal and patriarchal, and for that reason many anthropologists refuse to use them. If we are to use them at all, we must first **give** exact definitions. A society may be called patriarchal when descent is patrilineal (i.e. the children belong to the group of the father), marriage is patrilocal (i.e. the wife removes to the local group of the husband), inheritance (of property) and succession (to rank) are in the male line, and the family is patripotestal (i.e. the authority over the members of the family is in the hands of the father or his relatives). On the other hand, a society can be called matriarchal when descent, inheritance and succession are in the female line, marriage is matrilocal (the husband removing to the home of his wife), and when the authority over the children is wielded by the mother's relatives.

If this definition of these opposing terms is accepted, it is at once obvious that a great number of primitive societies are neither matriarchal or patriarchal, though some may incline more to the one side, and others more to the other. Thus, if we examine the tribes of Eastern Australia, which are sometimes spoken of as matriarchal, we find that marriage is patrilocal, so that membership of the local group is inherited in the male line, the authority over the children is chiefly in the hands of the father and his brothers, property (what there is of it) is mostly inherited in the male line, while, as rank is not recognised, there is no question of succession. The only matrilineal institution is the descent of the totemic group, which is through the mother, so that these tribes, so far from being matriarchal, incline rather to the patriarchal side. Kinship amongst them is throughly bilateral, but for most purposes kinship through the father is of more importance than kinship through the mother. There is some evidence, for example, that the obligation to avenge a death falls upon the relatives in the male line rather than those in the female line.

We find an interesting instance of this bilateralism, if it may be so called, in South Africa, in the OvaHerero tribe. The facts are not quite certain, but it would seem that this tribe is subdivided into two sets of segments crossing one another. For one segment (the *omaanda*) descent is matrilineal, while for the other (*otuzo*) it is patrilineal. A child belongs to the *eanda* of its mother and inherits cattle from its mother's brothers, but it belongs to the *oruzo* of its father and inherits his ancestral spirits. Authority over the children would seem to be in the hands of the father and his brothers and sisters.

It is now clear, I hope, that the distinction between matriarchal and patriarchal societies is not an absolute but a relative one. Even in the most strongly patriarchal society some social importance is attached to kinship through the mother; and similarly in the most strongly matriarchal society the father and his kindred are always of some importance in the life of the individual.

. . .

Of one tribe of [the matrilineal peoples of South Central Africa] we have a fairly full description in the work of Smith and Dale (The *Ila-speaking People of Northern Rhodesia*, 1920). Unfortunately, on the very points with which I am now dealing the information is scanty and certainly very incomplete. There are, however, two points I wish to bring out. The first concerns the behaviour of the mother's brother to his sister's son. We are told that 'the mother's brother is a personage of vast importance; having the power even of life and death over his nephews and nieces, which no other relations, not even the parents, have; he is to be held in honour even above the father. This is *avunculi potestas*, which among the BaIla is greater than *patria potestas*. In speaking of the mother's brother, it is customary to use an honorific title given to people who are respected very highly' (*op. cit.*, Vol. I, p. 230). This kind of relation between the mother's brother and the sister's son is obviously what we might expect in a strongly matriarchal society. But how then, on Mr. Junod's theory, can we explain the change which must have taken place from this sort of relation to that which now exists among the BaThonga?

This brings me to another point which it will not be possible to discuss in detail but which has an important bearing on the argument. We have been considering the relation of the sister's son to his mother's brother; but if we are to reach a really final explanation, we must study also the behaviour of a man to his other relatives on the mother's side, and to his mother's group as a whole. Now in the Friendly Islands the peculiar relation between a sister's son and a mother's brother exists also between a daughter's son and his mother's father. The daughter's son must be honoured by his grandfather. He is 'a chief' to him. He may take his grandfather's property, and he may take away the offering that his grandfather makes to the gods at a kava ceremony. The mother's father and the mother's brother are the objects of very similar behaviour patterns, of which the outstanding feature is the indulgence on the one side and the liberty permitted on the other. Now there is evidence of the same thing amongst the BaThonga, but again we lack the full information that we need. Mr. Junod writes that a grandfather 'is more lenient to his grandson by his daughter than his grandson by his son' (*op. cit.*, p. 227). In this connection the custom of calling the mother's brother *kokwana* (grandfather) is significant.

Now here is something that it seems impossible to explain on Mr. Junod's theory. In a strongly matriarchal society the mother's father does not belong to the same group as his grandchild and is not a person from whom property can be inherited or who can exercise authority. Any explanation of the liberties permitted towards the mother's brother cannot be satisfactory unless it also explains the similar liberties towards the mother's father which are found in Polynesia, and apparently to some extent in South Africa. This Mr. Junod's theory clearly does not do, and cannot do.

But on the hypothesis that I have put forward the matter is fairly simple. In primitive society there is a strongly marked tendency to merge the individual in the group to which he or she belongs. The result of this in relation to kinship is a tendency to extend to all the members of a group a certain type of behaviour which has its origin in a relationship to one particular member of the group. Thus the tendency in the BaThonga tribe would seem to be to extend to all the members of the mother's group (family or lineage) a certain pattern of behaviour which is derived from the special pattern that appears in the behaviour of a son towards his mother. Since it is from his mother that he expects care and indulgence he looks for the same sort of treatment from the people of his mother's group, i.e. from all his maternal kin. On the other hand it is to his paternal kin that he owes obedience and respect. The patterns that thus arise in relation to the father and the mother are generalised and extended to the kindred on the one side and on the other. If I had time I think I could show you quite conclusively that this is really the principle that governs the relations between an individual and his mother's kindred in the patriarchal tribes of South Africa. I must leave the demonstration, however, to another occasion. I can do no more now than illustrate my statement.

The custom, often miscalled bride-purchase and generally known in South Africa as *lobola* is, as Mr. Junod has well shown, a payment made in compensation to a girl's family for her loss when she is taken away in marriage. Now, since in the patriarchal tribes of South Africa a woman belongs to her father's people, the compensation has to be paid to them. But you will find that in many of the tribes a certain portion of the 'marriage payment' is handed over to the mother's brother of the girl for whom it is paid. Thus, amongst the BaPedi, out of the *lenyalo* cattle one head (called *hloho*) is handed to the mother's brother of the girl. Amongst the BaSotho a portion of the cattle received for a girl on her marriage may sometimes be taken by her mother's brother, this being known as *ditsoa*. Now the natives state that the *ditsoa* cattle received by the mother's brother are really held by him on behalf of his sister's children. If one of his sister's sons or daughters is ill he may be required to offer a sacrifice to his ancestral spirits, and he then takes a beast from the *ditsoa* herd. Also, when the sister's son wishes to obtain a wife, he may go to his mother's brother to help him to find the necessary cattle and his uncle may give him some of the *ditsoa* cattle received at the marriage of his sister, or may even give him cattle from his own herd, trusting to being repaid from the *ditsoa* cattle to be received in the future from the marriage of a niece. I believe that the Native Appeal Court has decided that the payment of *ditsoa* to the mother's brother is a voluntary

matter and cannot be regarded as a legal obligation, and with that judgment I am in agreement. I quote this custom because it illustrates the sort of interest that the mother's brother is expected to take in his sister's son, in helping him and looking after his welfare. It brings us back to the question as to why the mother's brother may be asked to offer sacrifices when his nephew is sick.

In south-east Africa ancestor worship is patrilineal, i.e., a man worships and takes part in sacrifices to the spirits of his deceased relatives in the male line. Mr. Junod's statements about the BaThonga are not entirely clear. In one place he says that each family has two sets of gods, those on the father's side and those on the mother's; they are equal in dignity and both can be invoked (*op. cit.*, II, p. 349, and I., p. 256, note). But in another place it is stated that if an offering has to be made to the gods of the mother's family this must be through the maternal relatives, the *malume* (*op. cit.*, II, p. 367). Other passages confirm this and show us that ancestral spirits can only be directly approached in any ritual by their descendants in the male line.

. . .

This brings us to the final extension of the principle that I have suggested as the basis of the customs relating to the mother's brother. The pattern of behaviour towards the mother, which is developed in the family by reason of the nature of the family group and its social life, is extended with suitable modifications to the mother's sister and to the mother's brother, then to the group of maternal kindred as a whole, and finally to the maternal gods, the ancestors of the mother's group. In the same way the pattern of behaviour towards the father is extended to the father's brothers and sisters, and to the whole of the father's group (or rather to all the older members of it, the principle of age making important modifications necessary), and finally to the paternal gods.

The father and his relatives must be obeyed and respected (even worshipped, in the original sense of the word), and so therefore also must be the paternal ancestors. The father punishes his children, and so may the ancestors on the father's side. On the other hand, the mother is tender and indulgent to her child, and her relatives are expected to be the same, and so also the maternal spirits.

A very important principle, which I have tried to demonstrate elsewhere (*The Andaman Islanders*, 1922, Chapter V), is that the social values current in a primitive society are maintained by being expressed in ceremonial or ritual customs. The set of values that we here meet with in the relations of an individual to his kindred on the two sides must, therefore, also have their proper ritual expression. The subject is too vast to deal with at all adequately here, but I wish to discuss one point. Amongst the BaThonga, and also in Western Polynesia (Fiji and Tonga), the sister's son (or in Tonga also the daughter's son) intervenes in the sacrificial ritual. Mr. Junod describes a ceremony of crushing down the hut of a dead man in which the *batukulu* (sister's children) play an important part. They kill and distribute the sacrificial victims and when the officiating priest makes his prayer to the spirit of the dead man it is the sister's sons who, after a time, interrupt or 'cut' the prayer and bring it to an end. They then, among the BaThonga clans, seize the portions of the sacrifice that have been dedicated to the spirit of the dead man and run away with them, 'stealing' them (*op. cit.*, I, p. 162).

I would suggest that the meaning of this is that it gives a ritual expression to the special relation that exists between the sister's son and the mother's brother. When the uncle is alive the nephews have the right to go to his village and take his food. Now that he is dead they come and do this again, as part of the funeral ritual, and as it were for the last time, i.e. they come and steal portions of meat and beer that are put aside as the portion of the deceased man.

The same sort of explanation will be found to hold, I think, of the part played in sacrificial and other ritual by the sister's son both amongst the Bantu of South Africa and also in Tonga and Fiji. As a man fears his father so he fears and reverences his paternal ancestors, but he has no fear of his mother's brother, and so may act irreverently to his maternal ancestors; he is, indeed, required by custom so to act on certain occasions, thus giving ritual expression to the special social relations between a man and his maternal relatives in accordance with the general function of ritual, as I understand it.

It will, perhaps, be of help if I give you a final brief statement of the hypothesis I am advancing, with the assumptions involved in it and some of its important implications.

1.   The characteristic of most of these societies that we call primitive is that the conduct of individuals to one another is very largely regulated on the basis of kinship, this being brought about by the formation of fixed patterns of behaviour for each recognised kind of kinship relation.
2.   This is sometimes associated with a segmentary organisation of society, i.e. a condition in which the whole society is divided into a number of segments (lineages, clans).
3.   While kinship is always and necessarily bilateral, or cognatic, the segmentary organisation requires the adoption of the unilineal principle, and a choice has to be made between patrilineal and matrilineal institutions.
4.   In patrilineal societies of a certain type, the special pattern of behaviour between a sister's son and the mother's brother is derived from the pattern of behaviour between the child and the mother, which is itself the product of the social life within the family in the narrow sense.
5.   This same kind of behaviour tends to be extended to all the maternal relatives, i.e. to the whole family or group to which the mother's brother belongs.[1]

[1] This extension from the mother's brother to the other maternal relatives is shown in the BaThonga tribe in the kinship terminology. The term *malume*, primarily applied to the mother's brother, is extended to the sons of those men, who are also *malume*. If my mother's brothers are dead it is their sons who will have to sacrifice on my behalf to my maternal ancestors. In the northern part of the tribe the term *malume* has gone out of use, and the mother's father, the mother's brother, and the sons of the mother's brother are all called *kokwana* (grandfather). However absurd it may seem to us to call a mother's brother's son, who may be actually younger than the speaker, by a word meaning 'grandfather,' the argument of this paper will enable us to see some meaning in it. The person who must sacrifice on my behalf to my maternal ancestors is first my mother's father, then, if he is dead, my mother's brother, and after the decease of the latter, his son, who may be younger than I am. There is a similarity of function for these three relationships, a single general pattern of behaviour for me towards them all and this is again similar in general to that for grandfathers. The nomenclature is, therefore, appropriate.

6. In societies with patrilineal ancestor worship (such as the BaThonga and the Friendly Islanders) the same type of behaviour may also be extended to the gods of the mother's family.

7. The special kind of behaviour to the maternal relatives (living and dead) or to the maternal group and its gods and sacra, is expressed in definite ritual customs, the function of ritual here, as elsewhere, being to fix and make permanent certain types of behaviour, with the obligations and sentiments involved therein.

In conclusion, may I point out that I have selected the subject of my contribution to this meeting because it is one not only of theoretical but also of practical interest. For instance, there is the question as to whether the Native Appeal Court was really right in its judgment that the payment of the *ditsoa* cattle to the mother's brother of a bride is not a legal but only a moral obligation. So far as I have been able to form an opinion, I should say that the judgment was right.

KINSHIP

B. Malinowski

I.—MUST KINSHIP BE DEHUMANIZED BY MOCK-ALGEBRA?

Much ink has flowed on the problem of blood—"blood" symbolizing in most human languages, and that not only European, the ties of kinship, that is the ties derived from procreation. "Blood" almost became discoloured out of all recognition in the process. Yet blood will rebel against any tampering, and flow its own way and keep its own colour. By which florid metaphor I simply mean that the extravagantly conjectural and bitterly controversial theorizing which we have had on primitive kinship has completely obscured the subject, and all but blinded the observers of actual primitive life. Professor Radcliffe-Brown is all too correct when he says "that theories of the form of conjectural history, whether 'evolutionary' or 'diffusionist' exert a very pernicious influence on the work of the field ethnologist," and he gives a very significant example of the fact-blindness to which this leads (*Man*, 1929a, No. 35).

And these conjectural theories on kinship have

Reprinted by permission of the Royal Anthropological Institute of Great Britain and Ireland from *Man*, Vol. 30:2 (1930), pp. 19–29.

simply flooded anthropological literature from the times of Bachofen, Morgan and McLennan, to the recent revival in kinship enthusiasm, headed by Rivers and his school, A. R. Radcliffe-Brown, the late A. Bernard Deacon, T. T. Barnard, Mrs. Hoernle, Mrs. B. Z. Seligman, not to mention myself, or the Californian kinship-trinity, Kroeber, Lowie, and Gifford—one and all influenced by the work of Rivers. With all this, the problem has remained enshrined in an esoteric atmosphere. The handful of us, the *enragés* or initiates of kinship, are prepared to wade through the sort of kinship algebra and geometry which has gradually developed; memorize long lists of native words, follow up complicated diagrams and formulae, sweat through dry documents, endure long deductive arguments, as well as the piling of hypothesis upon hypothesis.

The average anthropologist, however, somewhat mystified and perhaps a little hostile, has remained outside the narrow ring of devotees. He has his doubts whether the effort needed to master the bastard algebra of kinship is really worth while. He feels, that, after all, kinship is a matter of flesh and blood, the result of sexual passion and maternal affection, of long intimate daily life, and of a host of personal intimate interests. Can all this really be reduced to formulae, symbols, perhaps equations? Is it sound, hopefully to anticipate

> that the time will come when we shall employ symbols for the different relationships . . . and many parts of the description of the social systems of savage tribes will resemble a work on mathematics in which the results will be expressed by symbols, in some cases even in the form of equations? (W. H. R. Rivers, *Melanesian Society,* 1914b, Vol. I, p. 10.)

A very pertinent question might be asked as to whether we should really get nearer the family life, the affections and tender cares, or again the dark and mysterious forces which the psychoanalyst banishes into the Unconscious but which often break out with dramatic violence—whether we could come nearer to this, the real core of kinship, by the mere use of mock-algebra. There is no doubt that whatever value the diagrams and equations might have must always be derived from the sociological and psychological study of the intimate facts of kinship, on which algebra should be based. The average common-sense anthropologist or observer of savages feels that this personal approach to kinship is sadly lacking. There is a vast gulf between the pseudo-mathematical treatment of the too-learned anthropologist and the real facts of savage life. Nor is this merely the feeling of the non-specialist. I must frankly confess that there is not a single account of kinship in which I do not find myself puzzled by some of this spuriously scientific and stilted mathematization of kinship facts and disappointed by the absence of those intimate data of family life, full-blooded descriptions of tribal and ceremonial activities, thorough enumerations of the economic and legal characteristics of the family, kindred and clan, which alone make kinship a real fact to the reader.[1]

And when, after all the floods of ink on kinship, the average anthropologist finds that an authority like Professor Westermarck maintains that most work on classificatory terminologies "has been a source of error rather than knowledge"; when he finds that A. R. Radcliffe-Brown, B. Malinowski and Brenda Z. Seligman cannot agree as to what they mean when they use the terms kinship, descent, unilateral and bilateral; when he discovers that no sooner has Mrs. Seligman restated the fundamental concept of classificatory terminologies than she is challenged in letters to *Man;* then he really feels justified in mistrusting all this terribly elaborate pseudo-mathematical apparatus and in discounting most of the labour which must have been spent on it.

I believe that kinship is really the most difficult subject of social anthropology; I believe that it has been approached in a fundamentally wrong way; and I believe that at present an impasse has been reached. I am convinced, however, that there is a way out of this impasse, and that some of the recent work, notably that of A. R. Radcliffe-Brown, of Brenda Z. Seligman and of the Californian trinity, has placed the problem on the correct foundation. This has been done by a full recognition of the importance of the family and by the application of what is now usually called the functional method of anthropology—a method which consists above all in the analysis of primitive institutions as they work at present, rather than in the reconstruction of a hypothetical past.[2]

All this recent work is bound to lead us to the correct solution of the many more or less superficial puzzles, as well as of the real and profound problems of kinship. This work is still somewhat diffused and chaotic, however, and there is the need of a comprehensive contribution which will

---

[1] In a book on kinship which I am preparing I shall substantiate this indictment in detail. All our data on kinship are insufficient linguistically and inadequate sociologically.

[2] I would like to mention Edward Westermarck and Ernest Grosse as the forerunners in matters of kinship of the modern movement. Perhaps the first monographic description of the family, from an area where its very existence has been most contested, is my *Family among the Australian Aborigines* (1913). In the same year there appeared an excellent article on "Family," in Hastings' *Encyclopedia of Religion and Ethics,* written by E. N. Fallaize. More recently Kroeber; in his *Zuni Kin and Clan,* and Lowie in his field work on the Crow Indians and in his book on *Primitive Society,* have very strongly emphasized the functional point of view in reference to kinship.

organize and systematically integrate the results of the functional work, and correct a few mistakes still prevalent. In my forthcoming book on kinship I am making an attempt at such a systematic treatment. Here I propose to indicate in a preliminary fashion some of its results.

II.—THE FUNCTIONAL PROBLEM OF KINSHIP

It is unnecessary, perhaps, in addressing the readers of *Man*, to labour the point of kinship remaining still in an impasse. The several interesting articles in the present periodical, as well as in the *Journal*, show how profoundly even the few most devoted and most spiritually related specialists disagree with one another. As a member of the inner ring, I may say that whenever I meet Mrs. Seligman or Dr. Lowie or discuss matters with Radcliffe-Brown or Kroeber, I become at once aware that my partner does not understand anything in the matter and I end usually with the feeling that this also applies to myself. This refers also to all our writings on kinship, and is fully reciprocal.

The impasse is really due to the inheritance of false problems from anthropological tradition. We are still enmeshed in the question as to whether kinship in its origins was collective or individual, based on the family or the clan. This problem looms very large in the writings of the late W. H. R. Rivers, of whom most of us in the present generation are pupils by direct teaching or from the reading of his works. Another false problem is that of the origins and significance of classificatory systems of nomenclature. This problem, or any problem starting from the classificatory nature of kinship terminologies, must be spurious, because the plain fact is that classificatory terminologies do not exist and never could have existed.[3] This sounds like a paradox but is a mere truism which I propose to develop later in another article. Connected with the classificatory obsession, there was the rage for the explanation of queer terms by anomalous marriages, which

led to one or two half-truths but also to half a dozen capital errors and misconceptions. The conception of mother-right and father-right as successive stages or self-contained entities, recently so well and convincingly stigmatized by Radcliffe-Brown (*Man*, 1929a, 35), has been embodied in yet another monument of brilliantly speculative erroneousness in Briffault's work on *The Mothers*.

The real trouble in all this is that we have been hunting for origins of kinship before we had properly understood the nature of kinship. We inquired whether mother-right preceded father-right or vice versa, without allowing the facts to convince us, as they must, that mother-right and father-right are always indissolubly bound up with each other. Because we have profoundly misunderstood the linguistic nature of kinship terms, we are able to make the monstrous mistake of regarding them as "survivals," as petrified remains of a previous social state. It is almost ludicrous with what naïvité Morgan assumes throughout his writings that the terminologies of kinship invariably lag one whole "stage of development"—neither more nor less—behind the sociological status in which they are found; and yet that they mirror the past sociological status perfectly. The mere logical circle of the argument is appalling. But even worse is the complete misconception of the nature of kinship terminologies which, in fact, are the most active and the most effective expressions of human relationship, expressions which start early in childhood, which accompany human intercourse throughout life, which embody all the most personal, passionate, and intimate sentiments of a man or woman.

The modern or functional anthropologist proposes, therefore, to understand what kinship really means to the native; he wishes to grasp how terminologies of kinship are used and what they express; he wishes to see clearly the relations between the family, the clan and the tribe. But the more he studies all these elements of the problem and their inter-relation, the more clearly he realizes that we have to do here not with a number of isolated entities but with the parts of an organically connected whole. In the first place,

[3] For the most recent, brief, clear and most erroneous statements concerning the nature of classificatory terminologies, see the letter in *Man* by Mr. J. D. Unwin (1929, No. 124).

the family and the clan, for instance, which have hitherto been regarded as domestic institutions at various stages of development, appear invariably together. That is, while the family exists in many societies alone, the clan never replaces it, but is found as an additional institution. Again, though certain tribes use kinship terms in a wider sense, they also use them in the narrower sense, denoting the actual members of the family. Or, again, there is no such thing as pure mother-right or father-right, only a legal over-emphasis on one side of kinship, accompanied very often by a strong emotional, at times even customary, reaction against this over-emphasis. And, in all communities, whatever the legal system might be, both lines are *de facto* counted and influence the legal, economic, religious and emotional life of the individual. It is, therefore, nothing short of nonsensical to perform this sort of illegitimate preliminary surgery, to cut the organically connected elements asunder, and "explain" them by placing the fragments on a diagram of imaginary development. The real problem is to find out how they are related to each other, and how they *function,* that is, what part they play respectively within the society, what social needs they satisfy, and what influence they exert.

To put it clearly, though crudely, I should say that the family is always the domestic institution *par excellence.* It dominates the early life of the individual; it controls domestic co-operation; it is the stage of earliest parental cares and education. The clan, on the other hand, is never a domestic institution. Bonds of clanship develop much later in life, and, though they develop out of the primary kinship of the family, this development is submitted to the one-sided distortion of matrilinial or patrilineal legal emphasis, and it functions in an entirely different sphere of interests: legal, economic, above all ceremonial. Once the functional distinction is made between the two modes of grouping, the family and the clan, most of the spurious problems and fictitious explanations dissolve into the speculative mist out of which they were born.

I shall have, however, to qualify and make much more detailed the above contention. Here I only wish to point out that kinship presents really several facets corresponding to the various phases or stages of its development within the life history of the individual. For kinship is the phenomenon which begins earliest in life and which lasts longest, even as the word *mother* is usually the first word formed and often the last word uttered. Kinship, as it appears in the social horizon of a developed adult tribesman is the result of a long process of extensions and transformations. It starts early in life with the physiological events of procreation; yet even these are profoundly modified in human society by cultural influences. The original ties of kinship, which I believe firmly are invariably individual, later on develop, multiply and become largely communal. So that, at the end, the individual finds himself the centre of a complex system of multiple ties; a member of several groups: the family, always; the extended household, in many communities; the local group, almost invariably; the clan, very often; and the tribe, without any exception. I am convinced that if the study of kinship ties had been carried out in the field along the life history of the individual, if terminologies, legal systems, tribal and household arrangements had been studied in process of development and not merely as fixed products—that we would have been completely free of the whole nightmare of spurious problems and fantastic conjectures. It is almost an irony in the history of anthropology that the most ardent evolutionists as well as the most embittered prophets of the historical method have completely missed development and history of kinship in the one case in which this development and history can be studied empirically.[4]

III.—THE INITIAL SITUATION OF KINSHIP

Whenever we become convinced that a phenomenon must be studied in its development, our attention naturally must become focussed on its origins, and let us remember that here we are dealing, not with a fanciful, reconstructed evolution, but with observable development of kinship

[4] My friend Mr. T. J. A. Yates suggests the adjective "biographical" as the simplest description of the method of approach to kinship through its study along the life-history of the individual.

in human life and that *origins* here mean simply the whole set of initial conditions which determine the attitudes of the actors in the kinship drama.

These actors are obviously three in number at the beginning—the two parents and their offspring. And, at first sight, it might appear that the drama itself is of no real interest; for is it not merely the physiological process of conception, gestation and child-birth? In reality, however, the process is never a merely physiological one in human societies. However primitive the community, the facts of conception, pregnancy and the childbirth are not left to Nature alone, but they are reinterpreted by cultural tradition: in every community we have a theory as to the nature and causes of conception; we have a system of customary observances, religious, magical or legal, which define the behaviour of the mother, at times also of the father; we have, specifically, a number of taboos observed during pregnancy by both parents.

Thus, even the biological foundation of kinship becomes invariably a cultural and not merely a natural fact. This unquestionably correct principle has become at the hands of some modern anthropologists the starting point for a new reinterpretation of Morgan's hypothesis of a primitive communal marriage. Rivers, the most conspicuous modern supporter of Morgan's theories, is fully aware that group-marriage implies group-parenthood. Yet group-parenthood, above all group-motherhood, seems to be an almost unthinkable hypothesis. As such it has been in fact ridiculed by Andrew Lang, E. Westermarck and N. W. Thomas. Rivers, however, following in this the brilliant suggestions of Durkheim, Dargun, and Kohler, argues that, since cultural influences can modify maternity in every other respect, it can transform it even from an individual motherhood into a sort of sociological group-motherhood. This writer, and a number of his followers, notably Mr. Briffault, would lead us to believe that what I like to call the *initial situation* of kinship is not individual but communal.

I have adduced these very recent hypotheses about the initial situation of kinship in order to show that its study, far from being an obvious and superfluous statement of a physiological fact, raises a number of sociological questions, even of controversial points. With all this, the study of real empirical facts seems to show that the communal interpretation of the initial situation is definitely erroneous. I can but anticipate here the full presentation of my argument, and say that while I recognize that kinship, even in its origins, is a cultural rather than a biological fact, this culturally defined kinship is, I maintain, invariably individual. All the primitive theories of procreation, though they are a mixture of animistic beliefs and crude empirical observations, invariably define parenthood as an individual bond. The taboos of pregnancy, the rites observed at certain stages of gestation, customs of the couvade type, ceremonial seclusion of mother and child, all these individualize the relationship between the actual parents and their offspring.

While most of these facts refer to the individual tie between mother and child, a number of them, such as the couvade, the taboos kept by the pregnant woman's husband, his economic contributions toward pregnancy ceremonies, culturally define paternity, and at the same time individualize this relationship. There is one fact, however, of paramount importance as regards paternity, a generalization so cogent, so universally valid, that it has, to my knowledge, been almost completely overlooked, as it so often happens to the "obvious." This generalization I have called, in some of my previous writings, the Principle of Legitimacy.[5] This principle declares that, in all human societies, a father is regarded by law, custom and morals as an indispensable element of the procreative group. The woman has to be married before she is allowed legitimately to conceive, or else a subsequent marriage or an act of adoption gives the child full tribal or civil status. Otherwise the child of the unmarried mother is definitely stigmatized by an inferior and anomalous position in society. This is as true of the polyandrous Todas (where the child

[5] *Cf.* article on the "Psychology of Sex in Primitive Societies," *Psyche*, Oct., 1923.

has, in fact, to be sociologically assigned to one father among the several husbands); of the matrilineal Melanesians, of primitive peoples in Australia, North America, and in Africa, as of monogamous and Christian Europe. The principle of legitimacy works at times in indirect ways, but on the whole the law which demands marriage as the preliminary to family seems to be universal.

I believe that a correct inductive survey of all the evidence at our disposal would lead us to the answer that the initial situation of kinship is a compound of biological and cultural elements, or rather that it consists of the facts of individual procreation culturally reinterpreted; that every human being starts his sociological career within the small family group, and that whatever kinship might become later on in life, it is always individual kinship at first. At the same time this general statement gives us only the broad outlines of the initial situation; this becomes from the outset deeply modified by such elments as maternal or paternal counting of kinship, matrilocal or patrilocal residence, the relative position of husband and wife in a community, length of lactation, types of seclusion and taboos. The study of the initial situation, far from being trite and insignificant, is a rich field of sociological investigation, and a field on which the anthropologist and the modern psychologist meet in common interest.

IV.—THE PROCESS OF EXTENSION IN KINSHIP

With the conclusion that individual parenthood, defined by cultural as well as biological forces, forms invariably the initial situation of kinship, the foundations of a correct theory have been laid. But the task is not yet complete. What I have named the initial situation is important in its influence on later life. Parenthood interests the sociologists not only in itself, whether as an exhibition of human tenderness or as an example of the cultural transformation of instinct, but rather in that it is the starting point of most other sociological relationships and the prototype of the characteristic social attitudes of a community. It is, therefore, the processes of the extension of kinship from its extremely simple beginnings in

plain parenthood, to its manifold ramifications and complexities in adult membership of tribe, clan and local group, which, in my opinion, forms the real subject-matter of the study of kinship. It is in the study of these processes that the true relationship between clan and family, between classificatory systems and individual attitudes, between the sociological and the biological elements of kinship, can be discovered.

Most of the mistakes were due to the following false argument: all kinship is biological; the cohesion of a clan is based on kinship; ergo, clanship has a direct biological basis. This conclusion has led to such capital howlers as that "the clan marries the clan and begets the clan" that "the clan, like the family, is a reproductive group"; and that "a domestic group, other than the family" is the environment of primitive childhood. The perpetrators of these and similar are no lesser anthropologists than Fison, Spencer and Gillen, Briffault, and Rivers.

All this nonsense could never have obsessed some of the clearest minds in anthropology, had the study of the initial situation been made the starting point, and the study of subsequent processes of extension the main theme, of social anthropology. For the "origins of the clan system" are not to be found in some nebulous past by imaginary speculations. They happen nowadays under our very eyes. Any reasonably intelligent and unprejudiced anthropologist who works within a tribe with clan organization can see them taking place.

I have, myself, witnessed the "origins of the clan" in Melanesia, and I think that even from this one experience I am able to draw a universally valid conclusion, or at least a generalization which ought to be universally tested. Especially since all the fragmentary evidence from other areas fits perfectly well into the scheme based on Melanesian facts.

The process by which clanship and other forms of communal kinship develop out of the initial situation is in reality not easy to grasp or define. The main difficulty consists in the fact that it is a lengthy and interrupted process; that its threads are many, and that the pattern can only be discovered after an integration of detailed and intimate observations over a lengthy period of time. And so far, it has been the custom of competent sociologists to pay only flying visits to savage tribes, for which practice the euphemism of "survey work" has been invented. While the long-residence amateur was unable to see the wood for the trees.

But there is one definite source of difficulty. This is the fact that in the biographical development of kinship we have a two-fold extension of family ties, the other a process in which the family is over-ridden, in which kinship is submitted to a process of one-sided distortion, and in which the group or communal character of human relations, is definitely emphasized at the expense of the individual character.

I shall proceed to amplify this statement, but I want to mention here that this duality of kinship growth has given rise to most of the misconceptions, above all to the quarrel as to whether primitive kinship is communal or individual, whether it is essentially bilateral or unilateral.

Kinship in primitive communities has invariably the individual aspect, it has in most cases also the communal one. Each aspect is the result of a different process, it is formed by different educational mechanisms, and it has its own function to fulfil. The real scientific attitude is, not to quarrel as to which of the two actually existing phases of kinship has a moral right or a logical justification for its existence but to study their relation to each other.

V.—THE CONSOLIDATION AND THE ONE-SIDED DISTORTION OF KINSHIP

Let me first outline briefly the process of consolidation of the family. For it must be remembered that, clan or no clan, the individual's own family remains a stable unit throughout his lifetime. The parents, in most societies, not only educate and materially equip the child, but they also watch over his adolescence, control his marriage, become the tender and solicitous grandparents of his children and in their old age often rely on his help. Thus the early bonds of kinship which start in the initial situation, persist throughout life. But they undergo along process which, on

the one hand, as we have said, is one of consolidation, and on the other one of partial undermining and dissolution.

The consolidation in its early phases starts with the physiological dependence of the infant upon its parents, which shades into the early training of impulses, and that again passes into education. With education there are associated already certain wider sociological implications of parenthood. The child has to be educated in certain arts and crafts, and this implies that he will inherit the occupations, the tools, the lands or hunting-grounds of his father or his mother's brother. Education again, embraces the training in tribal traditions, but tribal traditions refer to social organization, to the rôle which the child will play in society, and this the child usually takes over from his father or his mother's brother.

Thus, already, at the phase of education, kinship may either simply and directly confirm the father's rôle in the family, or, in matrilineal societies, it may partly disrupt the family by introducing an outsider as the man in power.

At the same time the dependence of the child upon the household varies to a considerable extent in different societies. He or she may either remain as an inmate in the parents' house, sleeping, eating and spending most of his time there; or else the child moves somewhere else, becomes influenced by other people, and forms new bonds. In communities where there are ceremonies of initiation the sociological function of such customs consists often in divorcing the child from the family, above all from maternal influences, and in making him aware of his unilateral bonds of clanship, especially with his male clansmen. This is obviously an influence of a disruptive rather than a consolidating character so far as the family is concerned.

When it comes to adolescence and sexual life, there is an enormous variety of configurations but usually sexuality removes the boy or girl from the family and through the rules of exogamy makes him or her aware of their participation in the clan. At marriage, on the other hand, the own father and mother, at times some other near relative, always individual, come into prominence. The founding of a new household means to a large extent a final detachment from the parent one. But the parents, whether of the husband or the wife, reaffirm the relationship by the already mentioned fact of grandparenthood. Finally, in old age, new duties define the relationship between an adult man and his decrepit father or mother. Thus, throughout all the varieties which we find scattered over the globe, in main outline we find that the individual relation of offspring to parents, develops, receives several shocks and diminutions, becomes reaffirmed again, but always remains one of the dominant sentiments in human life, manifesting itself in moral rules, in legal obligations, in religious ritual. For, last not least, at death, parent or offspring alike have to fulfil some of the principal mortuary duties and, in ancestor-cults—which, in a more or less pronounced form are to be found everywhere—the spirits of the departed are always dependent on their lineal descendants. The consolidation of family ties, and of the concept of family and household, manifests itself in the extensions of the early kinship attitudes to members of other households. Thus in most primitive communities, whatever be their way of counting descent, the households of the mother's sister and of the father's brother play a considerable part and in many ways become substitute homes for the child.

I have stressed, so far, the elements of consolidation, let me now muster those of disruption. The actual weaning, the removal from the family, especially from the mother's control, outside influences such as that of the mother's brother, at times of the father's sister or brother, initiation and the formation of a new household— all these influences run counter to the original ties and militate against the persistence of parental bonds and influences. At the same time most of these disruptive influences are not really negations of kinship. They are rather one-sided distortions of the original parental relationship. Thus, the mother's brother, in a matrilineal society, becomes the nucleus of the matrilineal clan. The training in tribal law, especially and dramatically given at initiation, while it removes the boy from the exclusive tutelage of the family, imbues him with ideas of clan identity and solidarity.

Clan identity becomes especially prominent in certain phases of tribal life. During big tribal gatherings, whether for economic enterprise or war, or enjoyment, the bonds of clanship become prominent, the family almost disappears. Especially is this the case in large religious or magical ceremonies such as those reported from Central Australia, Papua, Melanesia and the various districts of North America. On such occasions there takes place a recrystalization of the sociological structure within the community, which brings vividly to the minds of young and old the reality of the clan system.

VI.—THE CLAN AND THE FAMILY

We can see, therefore, that the clan develops as a derived sociological form of grouping by empirical processes which can be followed along the life history of the individual, which always take place later in life—full clanship taking hold of an individual only at maturity—and which embrace a type of interests very different from those obtaining within the family.

As I have tried to show elsewhere there is something almost absurd in the tendency of anthropologists to treat the family and the clan as equivalent units which can replace one another in the evolution of mankind.[6] The relation between parents and child—that is, family relations—are based on procreation, on the early physiological cares given by the parents to the child and on the innate emotional attitudes which unite offspring and parents. These elements are never found in clanship. This institution, on the other hand, is based on factors which are quite alien to the family: on the identity of a totemic nature; on mythological fictions of a unilateral common descent from an ancestor or an ancestress; and a number of religious or magical duties and observances. It may be safely laid down that the family, based on marriage, is the only domestic institution of mankind, that is, the only institution the function of which is the procreation, the early cares and the elementary training of the offspring. Kinship thus always rests on the family

[6] See B. Malinowski, article on "Kinship," in *Ency. Brit.*, 14th Edn., 1929b, esp. xxiii.

and begins within the family. The clan is essentially a non-reproductive, non-sexual and non-parental group, and it is never the primary source and basis of kinship. But the clan always grows out of the family, forming round one of the two parents by the exclusive legal emphasis on the one side of kinship, at times backed by a one-sided reproductive theory. The functions of the clan are mostly legal and ceremonial, at times also magical and economic.

Family and clan differ thus profoundly in origins, in the functions which they fulfil, and in the nature of the bonds which unite their members. They differ also in structure. The family always embraces the two principles essential to procreation—motherhood and fatherhood. The clan is based on the partial negation of one of these principles. But the difference goes farther. The family is self-contained as regards its functions. The clan, by the very nature of its formation, is a dependent and correlated unit. The body of actually recognized relatives in the widest, that is classificatory, sense never consists of clansmen alone. It embraces the own clansmen—that is, kinsmen on the relevant side,—the clansmen of the irrelevant parent, the clanspeople of the consort, and members of the other clans which take part in the communal game of exchange of services, so characteristic of the tribes organized on the basis of the clan. It is the tribe, as the body of conjoined and mutually related clans, which at the classificatory level corresponds to the family. The sociological equivalence of family and clan, which has played so much havoc with social anthropology, is a misapprehension due to the omission of functional analysis and of the biographical method in the study of kinship problems.

VII.—CONCLUSIONS AND ANTICIPATIONS

I have started with a protest against the subordination of the flesh and blood side of kinship to the formal, pseudo-mathematical treatment to which it has been so often subjected. I have justified my criticism in a positive manner by showing that there are fundamental problems of kinship which demand a great deal of first-hand sociological observation and of theoretical analy-

sis: problems which must be solved even before we start kinship algebra. The *initial situation*, the *principle of legitimacy*, the *two correlated processes of extension*, the *multiplicity of kinship groupings*—this is an extensive field for full-blooded sociological research in the field and in the study. Through the biographical approach and the functional analysis which I have advocated, most of these problems become transferred to the realm of empirical research from that of hypothetical reconstruction.

There remain a number of questions, however, on which I was hardly able to touch, above all the notorious puzzle of classificatory terminologies. I have left this latter question on purpose: words grow out of life, and kinship words are nothing else but counters or labels for social relations. Even as, sociologically, kinship is a compound and complex network of ties, so every native nomenclature consists of several layers or systems of kinship designations. One system is used only to the parents and members of the household. Another stratum of kinship appellations is extended to the next nearest circle of relatives, the mother's sister and brother, the father's brother and sister, their offspring and the grandparents. Yet another type of kinship words applies to the wider relatives of the immediate neighbourhood. Finally there are kinship words used in a truly classificatory sense, based partly but never completely on the distinctions of clanship. The sounds used in these different senses are the same, but the uses, that is the meanings, are distinct. Each use, moreover, the individual, the extended, the local and the classificatory, are differentiated by phonetic distinctions, however slight, by fixed circumlocutions, and by contextual indices. It is only through the extraordinary incompetence of the linguistic treatment in kinship terminologies that the compound character of primitive terminologies has, so far, been completely overlooked. "Classificatory terminologies" really do not exist, as I have said already. But I shall have to return to this question once more.

After that, it will be possible for me to criticize directly the logical game of kinship algebra from Morgan and Kohler to Rivers and Mrs. B. Z. Seligman; and to show within which limits this game is legitimate and where it becomes spurious. There remain one or two questions: the definition of kinship and descent, on which I have been recently criticized by A. R. Radcliffe-Brown in the present periodical; the nature of kinship extensions, where I have to deal with the strictures of my friend E. E. Evans-Pritchard (also in *Man*); the nature of the functional treatment of kinship, where I have drawn some kindly, but I think irrelevant criticism from Lord Raglan in the last number of *Man*.

SELECTED READINGS

A. Commentaries and Critiques

Eggan, Fred and William Lloyd Warner
1956 A. R. Radcliffe-Brown. (Obituary). *American Anthropologist*, 58:544–547.

Evans-Pritchard, Edward E.
1951a *Social anthropology*. London: Cohen & West, chs. III, IV, V.

Firth, Raymond W. (ed.)
1957a *Man and culture*. (The work of Malinowski). London: Routledge & Kegan Paul. New York: Harper Torchbook, 1964.

Fortes, Meyer
1957 Malinowski and the study of kinship. In R. Firth (ed.) *Man and culture, ibid.*, pp. 157–188.

Gluckman, Max
1949 Malinowski's sociological theories. In *Rhodes-Livingston paper no. 16*. London: Oxford University Press. (One essay of this book was first published in *Africa*, 1947, 27:103–121.)

Harris, Marvin
1968 *The rise of anthropological theory: a history of theories of culture*. New York: Crowell, pp. 514–538, 547–562.

Kardiner, Abram and Edward Preble
1961 *They studied man*. New York: World, pp. 140–162.

Leach, Edmund R.
1957a The epistemological background to Malinowski's empiricism. R. Firth (ed.), *Man and culture*. London: Routledge & Kegan Paul, 1957, pp. 119–138.

Lowie, Robert H.
1937 *The history of ethnological theory*. New York: Holt, Rinehart & Winston, chs. XII, XIII.

Murdock, George P.
1943 B. Malinowski. (Obituary). *American Anthropologist*, 45:441–451.

Parsons, Talcott
1957 Malinowski and the theory of social systems. In R. Firth (ed.), *Man and culture*. London: Routledge & Kegan Paul, 1957a, pp. 53–70.

Tax, Sol
1937c From Lafitau to Radcliffe-Brown. In F. Eggan (ed.), *Social anthropology of North American tribes*. Chicago: University of Chicago Press, pp. 478–481.

White, Leslie
1966 The social organization of ethnological theory. In *Rice University studies*, 52:4. Houston: Rice University Press. (Pp. 28–51 deal with Radcliffe-Brown's school.)

B. Original Works

Evans-Pritchard, Edward
1929 The study of kinship in primitive societies. *Man*, 29:190–195.
——— 1932 The nature of kinship extensions. *Man*, 32:12–15.

Hocart, Arthur M.
1937 Kinship systems. *Anthropos*, 32:545–551. Reprinted in *The life-giving myth*. London: Methuen, 1952.

Jones, E.
1925 Mother-right and the sexual ignorance of savages. *International Journal of Psychoanalysis*, 6:2:109–130.

Lowie, Robert H.
1933 Queries. *American Anthropologist*, 35:288–296.

Malinowski, Bronislaw
1913 *The family among the Australian aborigines*. London: University of London Press. New York: Schocken, 1963.
——— 1926 *Crime and custom in savage society*. New York: Harcourt Brace Jovanovich.
——— 1927a *Sex and repression in savage society*. New York: Harcourt Brace Jovanovich.
——— 1929a *The sexual life of savages in Northwest Melanesia*. London: George Routledge, and Sons. New York: H. Liveright.
——— 1930 Kinship. *Man*, 30:19–29.
——— 1944 *A scientific theory of culture (and other essays)*. Chapel Hill: University of North Carolina Press.

————1945 *The dynamics of culture change.* Later edited by P. Kaberry. New Haven: Yale University Press.

Radcliffe-Brown, Alfred R.

1913 Three tribes of western Australia. *Journal of the Royal Anthropological Institute,* 43:143–194.

———— 1914 Review of Malinowski's *The family among the Australian aborigines. Man,* 14:16.

———— 1922 *The Andaman islanders.* Cambridge: Cambridge University Press.

———— 1923 The methods of ethnology and social anthropology, *South African Journal of Science,* XX:124–147. Reprinted in M. N. Srinivas (ed.), *Method in Social Anthropology.* Chicago: University of Chicago Press, 1958, pp. 3–38.

———— 1924 The mother's brother in South Africa. *South African Journal of Science,* XXI: 542–555. Reprinted in Radcliffe-Brown, 1952, pp. 15–31.

———— 1930–1931 The social organization of Australian tribes. *Oceania,* 1, 34–63, 206–256, 426–456.

———— 1935a On the concept of function in social science. *American Anthropologist,* 37:394–402. Reprinted in Radcliffe-Brown, 1952c, pp. 178–187.

———— 1935b Patrilineal and matrilineal succession. *Iowa Law Review,* 20:2:286–306. Reprinted in Radcliffe-Brown, 1952c, pp. 32–48.

———— 1935c Kinship terminologies in California. *Amerian Anthropologist,* 37:530–535.

———— 1940a On social structure. *Journal of the Royal Anthropological Institute,* 70:1–12. Reprinted in Radcliffe-Brown, 1952c, pp. 188–204.

———— 1940b Preface. In M. Fortes and E. Evans-Pritchard (eds.), *African political systems.* London: Oxford University Press, pp. xi–xxiii.

———— 1941 The study of kinship systems. *Journal of the Royal Anthropological Institute,* 70:1–18. Reprinted in Radcliffe-Brown, 1952c, pp. 49–89.

———— 1944 *A natural science of society.* New York: Free Press, 1948.

———— 1950 Introduction. In Radcliffe-Brown and C. D. Forde (eds.), *African systems of kinship and marriage.* London: Oxford University Press, pp. 1–85.

———— 1952c *Structure and function in primitive society.* London: Cohen and West. (This volume also contains Radcliffe-Brown, 1924, 1933a, 1933b, 1935a, 1935b, 1940a, 1941, as well as a valuable introduction.)

Srinivas, Mysore N. (ed.)

1958 *Method in social anthropology.* Chicago: University of Chicago Press. (Contains Radcliffe-Brown, 1923, and other valuable essays.)

VII

THE STUDY OF CHANGING KINSHIP SYSTEMS

The study of change in kinship and social structure has paralleled the history of the total study of these systems and has reflected the major anthropological approaches to the study of change. The two basic philosophies, which stand at the opposite ends of a continuum, are those that (1) see change as an ever-present and major feature of the history of human social organization, and (2) those that take a static state or equilibrium as "normal" and view change as the exception or merely the transition between two stable forms. While the difference lies largely in the length of the historical perspective taken, the ramifications are much wider.

The first approach has been exemplified by the "evolutionists" from Morgan (1870), Marx (1857–1858), Engels (1884), through White (1949) and, to some extent, Steward (1955) to Sahlins (1958, 1960), Fried (1960), Service (1960, 1962), and some of the contemporary Soviet anthropologists. These authorities have concentrated on the larger picture of the whole of social organization and on all of—or large segments and regions of—the world's societies. One of their basic axioms is that societies are nowhere perfectly functional and that the internal adaptations that each society makes generate the evolution of new social forms. The American evolutionists have tended to stress the specific *ecological* adaptations characteristic of various types of societies (particularly Steward), and, more recently, have pointed out the role of adaptation leading to increased population densities. These densities have led, in turn, to new and more complex social forms, such as class and caste stratification, in Polynesia, for example. (See Harris, 1968, Chapters 5–8, 22, 23.)

Boasian thought was not particularly concerned with processes of change, except as exemplified in specific area histories (e.g., Swanton, 1905; Lowie 1915) but tended to diffusionary explanations, as in its work on culture areas. Hallowell, however, used recorded history to trace and explain the changes in Abenaki kinship (1926–28) in his refutation of Morgan. This constituted a forerunner to anthropologists' increasing concern with acculturated and, therefore, changed societies.

The study of social change also came to be extrapolated from the static functionalist ideas of Radcliffe-Brown and Malinowski, though the former paid little attention to change and the latter (*The Dynamics of Culture Change*, 1945) used an approach based in his ideas of "institutions" (see Chapter VI). This was unsuccessful because it assumed a biopsychological basis of society and neglected the role of individuals (Gluckman, 1947).

It is easy to see that the successful combination of history and sociology depended on throwing out *conjectural* history and replacing it with *recorded* history, which is what Hallowell attempted to do. The functionalist approach was successfully combined with the historical through the works of the students of Radcliffe-Brown and Malinowski, and particularly through the work of Eggan (1937b) and, later, his students (Spoehr 1947; Bruner 1955). Other functionalist analyses followed, in particular Fortes' (1949b) essay on the concept of Time and Social Structure, and Gough's (1952) historical analysis of Nayar kinship.

Detailed case studies of changing kinship systems have shown that:

1. The changes tend to be gradual, from one system to another, through a series of divergencies and consistencies.
2. Complete changes from one type of system to another can only be made where there is a model for the new system within the nuclear family, by intermarriage and the consequent bicultural socialization.
3. Diffusion of kinship systems between adjacent peoples is rare and slow except in conditions described in (2), above, or where there is mass adoption. To put it another way, terminology systems are rarely taken over and relearned in adulthood.
4. *Systemic* changes, as opposed to flexible "giving," only tend to occur over long periods under continued pressure from *external* conditions, especially economic changes. The latter tend to change living arrangements and other aspects of socioeconomic organization which, in turn, effect basic changes in the structural rules.

E. R. Leach's important study of the changing *Political Systems* [of the Kachin] *of Highland Burma* (1946) dealt with an unusual case wherein the society carried within it two opposed models of social structure and had been in a state of dynamic equilibrium between the two for over 2,000 years. This functionalist analysis accounted for the change on ecological-political terms, but the case falls short of total systemic change (cf. Gellner, 1958).

More recently intensive studies have been made concerning the kinship systems of complex societies (see Chapter XVI). Such studies should become increasingly important as increasing numbers of the world's people are affected by urbanization and industrialization. Although impressionistic comparisons tend to show a trend toward nuclear family units and neolocality under such circumstances, it has also been demonstrated that the underlying cultural themes of kinship relationships are very persistent (e.g., Hammel, 1969a) and that family ties may remain extremely important though the superficial content of the relationships may change drastically.

The traditional holistic societies that anthropologists used to study are becoming increasingly rare in the modern pluralistic world. The scale of societies is becoming larger and the importance of kinship as the underlying structure for political, economic, and legal institutions is diminishing. Corporate kin groups are giving way to single-purpose institutions and less well-bounded networks and personal dyadic relationships are taking their place (see Chapter XVI: Dávila, 1971; Mangin, 1963).

HISTORICAL CHANGES IN THE CHOCTAW KINSHIP SYSTEM

Fred Eggan

I

The Southeast furnishes an interesting field for studies in social organization. Here is to be found a bewildering array of unilateral institutions, territorial groupings, and social classes which cross-cut one another in various ways. Most historical and comparative studies have concerned themselves with the more formal groupings, largely ignoring the underlying kinship systems.

The importance of kinship systems, particularly in relation to other aspects of social organi-

Reproduced by permission of the author and the American Anthropological Association from *American Anthropologist*, Vol. 39, 1937, pp. 34–52.

zation, is beginning to be apparent. The present paper, while presenting an instance of historical change in the field of kinship which has important theoretical implications, also attempts to furnish the basis for a preliminary classification of Southeastern kinship systems.

One of the important problems in social organization is an adequate classification of kinship systems according to types. Such a classification seems essential for either historical or comparative studies of social organization. Dr. Leslie Spier has worked out a preliminary classification of kinship systems for North America into eight types, largely on the basis of the terminology used for cross cousins. In regard to two of these types he finds the terminology indicative of a more comprehensive classification of relatives:

> Cross cousin terminology also offers a clue for the discrimination of the Omaha and Crow types. The first class together the mother's brother and his descendants through males: their daughters are always called mothers. The paternal cross cousins are then conceptual equivalents. Similarly systems of the Crow type class the father's sister with her female descendants through females and their sons with the father. Again, equivalent forms are used for the maternal cross cousins. That is, both systems ignore differences of generation in one or the other type of unilateral descent. (Spier, "The Distribution of Kinship Systems in North America," 1925, Vol. 1, No. 2, p. 72.)

If we look at the distribution of the Crow and Omaha types we find it to be somewhat irregular, though within rather widely scattered areas the distribution tends to be continuous. Furthermore, if we examine various Crow and Omaha kinship systems we find a series of variations on each pattern, so that often there is some difficulty in deciding whether a given kinship system is a Crow type or something else.

II

A preliminary survey of Southeastern social organization indicated such a situation in regard to the various kinship systems studied. While Spier has classified the Choctaw, Chickasaw, Creek, Cherokee, Timucua, and (less probably)

Yuchi as belonging to the Crow type, an inspection of the source materials led to some preliminary doubts as to the correctness of this classification.

The formal social organization of the Southeastern tribes seems to have been based on the matrilineal clan, but otherwise few generalizations may be made at present. The Choctaw, for example, had matrilineal exogamous moieties divided into non-totemic clans, a territorial division into three or four groups of "towns," and four social classes. The Chickasaw, close linguistic relatives of the Choctaw, had matrilineal totemic clans with a dual-division which was not exogamous, along with various local groupings. The Creek, just to the east, in addition to the "Upper" and "Lower" tribal divisions, had numerous matrilineal totemic clans grouped into phratries and moieties, with a further dual-division into "red" and "white" towns, associated with "war" and "peace," respectively. The Cherokee (W. H. Gilbert, Jr., *Eastern Cherokee Social Organization*, 1934) had a simpler organization: matrilineal totemic clans which were exogamous, and possibly grouped into seven phratries. The Yuchi had matrilineal totemic clans which were exogamous and which varied in rank; these were cut across by a patrilineal division of the men into "chiefs" and "warriors," associated with "peace" and "war," respectively. This dual patrilineal organization tended toward endogamy in that a "chief" preferred his daughter to marry other "chiefs." The Natchez apparently combined a matrilineal clan system with a system of social classes, the whole regulated by definite rules of marriage. In addition the Natchez had a dual organization of "red warriors" and "white warriors." The Chitimacha seem to have had totemic clans and endogamous classes which approached true castes.

The kinship systems of the Southeastern tribes are all "classificatory" in that the father's brother is classed with the father, and the mother's sister with the mother, as far as terminology is concerned. In the following chart (fig. 1) we have outlined the kinship structures of the Southeastern tribes for which there is adequate data, in terms of the pattern of descent from the father's sister. The Crow type (A) is well known. Both

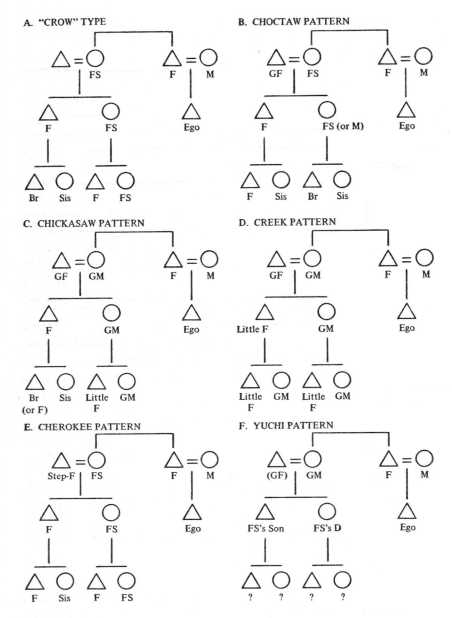

Figure 1. Kinship Structures in the Southeast. △ is male and ○ is female; Ego is male in each case. The equal sign indicates marriage. English equivalents are used for the native terms: F, M, GF, GM, FS, Br, Sis, etc., standing for father, mother, grandfather, grandmother, father's sister, brother, and sister, respectively. For sources see the text.

Spier and Lowie agree that its essential characteristic is the classification of the father's sister's female descendants through females with the father's sister, and their sons with the father, thus giving a definite descent pattern. Lowie considers this classification an "overriding of the generation principle in favor of the clan or lineage principle."[1]

[1] R. H. Lowie, *The Omaha and Crow Kinship Terminologies* (Proceedings, Twenty-fourth International Congress of Americanists, Hamburg, 1930), p. 103. While Lowie specifically refers to the Omaha type, the same

If we now examine the kinship structures of the Southeastern tribes with special reference to the pattern of descent from the father's sister, we find some interesting variations. In the Choctaw kinship system (B), for example, the pattern seems to be "turned around." Here the father's sister's son and *his* descendants through *males* are classed as "fathers," whereas the children of the father's sister's daughter (who is classed with the father's sister) become "brothers" and "sisters." Morgan is quite explicit on this point:

> My father's sister's son is my father, *Ah'-kĭ*, whether *Ego* be a male or female; his son is my father again; the son of the latter is also my father; and this relationship theoretically continues downward in the male line indefinitely. The analogue of this is to be found in the infinite series of uncles among the Missouri nations, applied to the lineal male descendants of my mother's brother.[2]

This is clearly something quite different from the typical Crow pattern of descent.

There are some interesting variations in the other tribes. The Chickasaw pattern of descent (C) as given by Morgan is identical with that of the Crow type, except for the minor variation of "little father" for the father's sister's daughter's son. Swanton, however, gives "father" as an alternative to "brother" for the father's sister's son's son. The Creek kinship structure (D) fur-

nishes another pattern of descent. Here the descendants of the father's sister, in *both* the male and female lines, are classed as "father" or "grandmother" rather than "brother" and "sister," as in the normal Crow pattern. The Cherokee kinship structure (E) gives a pattern of descent from the father's sister much like that of the Chickasaw, except that the father's sister's son's son is regularly classed with the father, as are his male descendants through males. Information concerning the Yuchi kinship system (F) is difficult to interpret. We have no early accounts, but Speck indicates that the father's sister was classed with the grandmother, while her children were called by descriptive terms. Recent information indicates an Omaha pattern of descent, the mother's brother's children being classed as "mother's brother" and "little mother," with the father's sister's children, reciprocally, being "nephew" and "niece," male speaking, or "little son" and "little daughter," female speaking. Information concerning the kinship systems of the Natchez and other tribes is too fragmentary to be of much value. The Natchez, according to Swanton, classified the father's sister with the grandmother. While no information is available concerning the terminology employed for descendants, other features of the system, e.g., the classification of the brother's children as "children," male speaking, and "grandchildren," female speaking, and the sister's children as "nephew" and "niece," male speaking, and "children," female speaking, closely resemble those found in the tribes mentioned above.

III

On the basis of this preliminary survey it is possible to formulate some of the problems involved. One of the important problems is: do these patterns of descent represent new fundamental types of kinship systems or are they simply variations from a Crow type? If they are fundamental types they are unique; the writer is not aware of other kinship systems with these patterns of descent. If we examine the variants we find it possible to arrange them in a series between the Crow and Choctaw types: the Chickasaw have practically a pure Crow type, the Chero-

---

principle obviously holds for the Crow. This seems to be a basic principle for the classification of kinship systems. If this be so the Omaha and Crow types might be considered sub-types of a more fundamental "Crow-Omaha" type. The extent to which this principle operates can be best illustrated by constructing "lineage diagrams."

[2] Morgan, L. H., *Systems of Consanguinity and Affinity of the Human Family* (Smithsonian Contributions to Knowledge, Vol. 17, 1870), p. 191. The last sentence is probably responsible for much of the confusion which exists in regard to the Choctaw kinship system. Structurally this pattern of descent is not *analogous* in the way that the Crow and Omaha are. J. Kohler (*Zur Urgeschichte der Ehe*, Zeitschrift für vergleichende Rechtswissenschaft, Vol. 12, 1897, pp. 187–353) almost forty years ago considered the Choctaw system as analogous to the Omaha (tribal) system, and attempted to explain both on the basis of certain types of secondary marriages, types which had to be assumed for the Choctaw.

kee vary slightly, the Creek are intermediate, while the Choctaw have an almost completely reversed line of descent. All of these tribes had a similar culture, resided in the same area, were removed to Indian Territory under similar conditions, and were subjected to similar influences while there. This suggests that the variations found may represent historical changes. A further problem may be set up: if these are variants from a Crow type, do they represent a series brought about by the action of some common acculturation process, or are they merely "random," the separate results of unrelated circumstances?

These wider problems grew out of an interest in the Choctaw kinship system. On the basis of a preliminary study the writer had come to a tentative conclusion: the Choctaw system probably represented a pure Crow type which had altered under the stress of missionary and governmental activities. To *prove* this it would be necessary to find the older kinship system in operation in some relatively uninfluenced region, or to find an earlier account of the kinship system. Morgan thought highly of his Choctaw schedules. The Reverends Byington and Edwards collaborated on one, Copeland furnished the other; these missionaries had long resided among the Choctaw and knew their language and customs. Furthermore the two independent schedules checked remarkably well. Hence they must be accepted as basic data—as representing the Choctaw kinship system as it was in 1860.

In 1933, on the advice of Dr. John R. Swanton, the writer visited the old Choctaw country in an attempt to find some traces of the assumed older kinship system among the Bogue Chito and other groups which had remained in Mississippi following the general removal of the Choctaw to Indian Territory in the 1830's. This quest was completely unsuccessful, though a considerable body of contemporary material was gathered. The results, where they had any bearing, merely confirmed those presented by Morgan and Swanton.

Later in the summer, while studying Cheyenne and Arapaho social organization, the writer found in the "Chronicles of Oklahoma" the text of a speech which John Edwards made to the students of the University of California about 1880, outlining the *earlier* social organization of the Choctaw. This is the same Edwards who collaborated with Byington in furnishing the basic schedule for Morgan; when the Civil War broke out in the next year he was forced to leave and went to reside in California. In this speech (edited by Dr. J. R. Swanton) we find the following statements concerning the older Choctaw kinship system:

> A third important principle was that kinship was not lost by remoteness. This involved a very peculiar system of nomenclature. For instance, with them, my father's brothers are all my fathers, and my mother's sisters are all my mothers, and their children are my brothers and sisters; but my mother's brother is my uncle, and his sons and daughters are mine; and my father's sister is my aunt, her son is my father, her daughter is my aunt, and *her* daughter is my aunt, and *her* daughter is my aunt, and so on, so far as it is possible to go. This is what they call *aunts* in a row. The farthest removed of one's kindred by consanguinity are aunt, uncle, nephew, and niece. The line of relationship, after turning aside thus far, returns into the direct line, and becomes that of father to son, or grandfather to grandson. To us it seems a very complicated system.[3]

Here is a clear, unequivocal, documentary proof that the Choctaw formerly had a Crow type of kinship system.

There is good evidence, then, of a definite change in the Choctaw kinship system from the time of removal in the 1830's to the time when Morgan collected the schedules in 1860. Can the influences affecting the Choctaw from the time of removal to the Civil War be historically controlled? Fortunately this question may be answered in the affirmative; Grant Foreman and Miss Debo have both assembled and surveyed the available documentary evidence for precisely this period, 1830–1860.

[3] John Edwards, *The Choctaw Indians in the Middle of the Nineteenth Century* (Chronicles of Oklahoma, Vol. 10, Oklahoma City, 1932, pp. 392–425), pp. 400–401. The italics are Edwards. This is a precise and excellent statement of the Choctaw kinship structure, and one which is consistent with what we know of other aspects of early Choctaw social organization.

The Choctaw were subjected to longer and more intensive acculturational influences than were the Chickasaw, Creek, or Cherokee. Missions were established among them as early as 1819. They were the first tribe from the Southeast to be removed to Indian Territory; they set up a new system of government on the model of our territorial governments; they early established a school system and encouraged education. Their leaders were more friendly to attempts to alter the old ways of life in favor of white ways.

There are many statements in Foreman indicating the efforts—and success—of missionaries, teachers, and government agents in changing the mode of life of the Choctaw. The fact that women worked in the fields and that a father (in accordance with the matrilineal system of inheritance) failed to provide for his own children, particularly worried the missionaries. There were introduced new regulations in regard to land which emphasized the position of the man as head of the family; by others leaders no longer represented the clan but the male membership of the district, being elected by adult male voters. Marriage was regulated by law, and widows were entitled to a dower and children to inherit their father's estate.

For our purposes these statements indicate a change from a *matrilineal* emphasis to a *patrilineal* emphasis; though the missionaries and others concerned were not aware of the significance of the changes they were bringing about. The effect on the social organization of the Choctaw was to break down the clan structure and emphasize the territorial tie. In the later periods the clan structure became largely a memory, many individuals not knowing their own clans. Specifically, this change seems to have affected the kinship structure by "turning around" the pattern of descent from the father's sister, making "fathers" descend in the male line, rather than "father's sisters" in the female line, as Edwards indicates for the old Choctaw system.

This conclusion, if it is of any value, should also "explain" the changes which have taken place in the kinship systems of the other tribes in the Southeast who were subjected to similar influences. Foreman presents evidence to indicate that the Chickasaw in particular were backward. They were a smaller tribe, less sedentary, and more warlike. Their removal to Indian Territory took place later than that of the Choctaw and under less favorable circumstances. They were settled on the western portion of the Choctaw reservation, where they led a restless and unsettled existence, continually harassed by the unpacified Plains tribes. Attempts to merge them with the Choctaw were resented by both tribes, and delayed their advancement. Missionaries and schools were much later in influencing them; in 1847 there were no preachers or schools in their territory, schools not getting started until after 1850. Hence the Chickasaw retained their aboriginal customs to a greater degree, and for a longer time, than did the Choctaw. The Creek, on the other hand, made more rapid "progress" than the Chickasaw. The first few years, after the removal of the majority of the Creek in 1836, were taken up with a continuation of the quarrel between the Upper and Lower Creek. They were suspicious and resentful of the efforts of missionaries to change their customs; in fact they expelled them from the Creek Nation in 1836 with the injunction, "Go teach your white men!" The missionaries returned in 1842, however, and their influence gradually increased. After a measure of tribal unity was restored, some interest was taken in schools, there being a few schools by 1841. The Lower Creek settlements advanced faster than those of the Upper Creek, abandoning compact town settlements and communal cultivation at an earlier date. By 1844 chiefs were beginning to be elected, but in general they were prejudiced against the whites because they felt their authority to be lessened. By 1850–1860 many changes were in progress: new laws were replacing old customs, property was being inherited according to legal provisions, schools were well established, men were doing the agricultural work, and missions were expanding.

On the basis of Foreman's material it is possible to arrange the Choctaw, Chickasaw, and Creek in a rough series, in so far as the *general degree of acculturation* is concerned. The Choctaw were subjected to the greatest influence, the Chickasaw the least, while the Creek were intermediate.

The Chickasaw had a Crow type in Morgan's time; the Choctaw earlier. There is good reason to believe the Creek formerly had a Crow type of kinship structure also. An early writer makes the following statement:

> All the men of the father's clan or family are called their father, the women are generally called their grandmother, all the men of the mother's family older than themselves are their uncles, being their mother's brothers. All of their own age and under are called brothers, and all the old women of their mother's clan are called grandmother or aunt. (Swanton, *Social Organization . . . of the Creek Confederacy*, p. 87, quoting from the Stiggins ms., no date.)

Swanton agrees to this but says:

> In spite of the emphasis which Stiggins places on clans in determining the application of terms of relationship, an examination of the usages assigned to them shows that all the terms not individual cut across, or at least may cut across, the lines of the exogamous groups. (Swanton, *op. cit.*)

The writer would like to suggest, in view of the above analysis, that both Stiggins and Swanton were right; that the Creek have changed the applications of terms to the descendants of the father's sister. Their early institutions and behavior patterns, so far as we know them, seem to be consistent with such an assumption.

If we may tentatively assume that the Creek system represents a variant from a Crow type, we thus have a series of variations which corresponds with the series worked out with reference to the general degree of acculturation. If this be so we have an "explanation" for certain discrepancies which exist in the source materials. In regard to the Choctaw, for example, Reverend Copeland's schedule gives "mother" as the term for the father's sister's daughter. If the Choctaw system were in a process of change, the term "mother" might be considered more suitable than "father's sister," since the children of the father's sister's daughter were called "brother"

and "sister" in both schedules. This variation apparently was not popular for long, but the earlier process of shortening the line of aunts continued: thus Swanton found that the term for father's sister "sometimes extends to the father's sister's daughter." (Swanton, *Source Material for . . . the Choctaw Indians*, p. 87.) The Chicasaw materials furnishes us with an illustration of the first steps in this change. In Morgan's time the father's sister's son's son was classed as a "brother," but Swanton later reports both "brother" and "father" being used for this particular relative. The Creeks apparently have reached a relatively stable state in which the matrilineal and patrilineal emphases are more or less balanced.

The Cherokee furnish an additional group against which our conclusions may be tested. They belong to a different linguistic stock and have a different early history. On the other hand they were removed to Indian Territory and subjected to much the same acculturational influences that affected the other tribes, though if we may judge by Foreman's account, these influences were less intensive than for either the Choctaw or Creek. During the first period after removal there was considerable trouble between the "Western" Cherokee, who had voluntarily migrated to Arkansas early in the 19th century and then had moved to Indian Territory in 1828, and the "Eastern" Cherokee, who were subjected to a forcible removal ten years later. Again white influence gradually brought about a change in the sentiments relating to females, a new division of labor, new laws and government, but these did not become well developed until after 1850. A national school system was established in 1841 and gradually grew as the leaders perceived the advantages of education.

A small group of Cherokee refused to be removed to Indian Territory and remained in the hills of North Carolina, where they still reside on the Eastern Cherokee Reservation. This group, numbering at present less than 2,000 persons, has been studied recently by Dr W. H. Gilbert, Jr. He found them relatively uninfluenced in many respects, particularly in regard to social organization. He was fortunate enough to find the old kinship system in operation; his account of the terminological structure and the accompanying social behavior or relatives gives us our first relatively complete picture of the kinship system of a Southeastern tribe.

This system, as far as the pattern of descent is concerned, represents a pure Crow type. Relatives are recognized in four clans: one's own matrilineal clan, one's father's clan, one's mother's father's clan, and one's father's father's clan. In each of these, relatives are classified on a "lineage" principle. In the father's matrilineal lineage (and clan), for example, all men are "fathers," their wives "mothers" or "stepmothers," their children "brothers" and "sisters;" all women of the father's generation and below are "father's sisters," those above being "grandmothers" or "father's sisters," all husbands of these women are "grandfathers," all children are "father's sisters" and "fathers."

We have, then, existing among the Cherokee, the situation which the writer had hoped to find among the Choctaw. The evidence suggests that the Cherokee formerly had a Crow type of kinship structure, but that influences affecting the portion of the tribe in Oklahoma have modified the descent system in the same direction as in the other Southeastern tribes considered, so that the father's sister's male descendants through males are classed as "father."

These acculturational influences are of course not completely lacking in North Carolina, but seem to have been much less intensive. Gilbert mentions the loss of political power of clan heads, the gradual decline in family control, particularly in regard to marriage. Also:

> The mother's brother is no longer a power in the family and the transmission of family names for the last three generations through the father's line has tended to shift the emphasis in lineality to the paternal ancestry. (Gilbert, *op. cit.*, p. 278.)

This shift in emphasis from the matrilineal to the patrilineal line among the Cherokee still residing in North Carolina should result eventually in similar changes in the pattern of descent, assuming other factors remain the same. Our hypothesis may therefore be verified, or modified, by future investigations of these groups.

The Yuchi furnish a separate and more complicated problem; they are considered partly to illustrate the value of our historical analysis, and partly to extend our survey of Southeastern tribes. Speck studied the Yuchi in Oklahoma in 1904–5; they then resided in three scattered settlements in the northwestern corner of the Creek Nation. The Yuchi had belonged to the Creek Confederation in the later period and were removed to Indian Territory with the Creek. In Speck's time they seldom mixed with the Creek, but were friendly with the Shawnee and Sauk and Fox.

We have outlined the kinship structure above, as far as it relates to the pattern of descent (fig. 1, F). In describing the kinship system Speck notes that

> The family, in our sense of the word, as a group is of very little political importance in the tribe. The father has a certain individual social standing according to his clan and according to his society. The woman on the other hand carries the identity of the children, who may be said to belong to her. The bonds of closest kinship, however, being chiefly reckoned through the mother, it would appear that the closest degrees of consanguinity are counted in the clan. (F. G. Speck, *Ethnology of the Yuchi Indians*, 1909, pp. 68–9.)

It seems probable that by Speck's time (1904–5) the kinship system had already been considerably modified. The use of descriptive terms for the father's sister's children is unique in this area, and suggests a breakdown from some earlier pattern. The classification of the father's sister as a "grandmother" is suggestive of a Crow type of system, especially when coupled with a matrilineal clan system.

This is mere conjecture, based on probabilities. We will never know precisely what the earlier system was unless new historical evidence is discovered. On the other hand we have evidence of important changes since Speck's visit. Dr Wagner has recently completed a linguistic study of the Yuchi and was kind enough to furnish me with a list of the current kinship terms. These, interestingly enough, seem to represent an Omaha type of structure. The father's sister is now called "little mother," her children are "nephew" and "niece," male speaking, or "little son" and "little daughter," female speaking. The children of the mother's brother are, reciprocally, "mother's brother" and "little mother." That the shift of the term for father's sister is recent is further indicated by the fact that the father's sister's husband is still called "grandfather."

In connection with this shift there are several factors which must be considered. Within the aboriginal Yuchi system there was a patrilineal emphasis through the "War" and "Peace" societies, which were confined to males and definitely patrilineal in membership. Secondly, the same factors influencing the Creeks since their removal in 1836 have necessarily affected the Yuchi, though probably in a varying degree. Finally we have evidence of close contact with the Shawnee and the Sauk and Fox in recent years, both of whom have an Omaha type of kinship system. The Yuchi, then, possibly have gone through the whole sequence of changes from a Crow to an Omaha type of descent, though we have definite evidence for the last series of changes only.

IV

The immediate conclusions which may be drawn from this survey of historical changes in Southeastern kinship structures can be briefly summarized. (1) The evidence indicates that a Crow type of kinship structure was widespread over the Southeast. The Choctaw, Chickasaw, Creek, and Cherokee all seem to have had such a system in historic times; the evidence for the Yuchi is inconclusive but favorable. Even the Natchez may have had a Crow type of kinship structure. (2) These kinship structures, originally Crow in type, were progressively modified by being subjected to varying degrees of the same acculturational process. For the Choctaw, Chickasaw, and Creek there seems to be a precise correlation between the degree of general acculturation and the degree of modification of the pattern of descent. The evidence available for the Cherokee and Yuchi confirms this correlation.

These conclusions have a firm foundation in documentary and other evidence. Further, they have a definite value; they make possible the reconciliation of inconsistencies between accounts for different periods, and thus afford a foundation for preliminary classifications and comparative studies, whether historical or generalizing.[4]

These conclusions also raise a whole series of problems which have implications for both acculturational studies and studies in kinship theory, though many of these problems require the analysis of much more material than is here presented. Since Hallowell (1928), in a study of recent changes in the kinship terminology of the Abenaki, came to conclusions concerning certain of these problems which differ to some extent from those which the above material suggests, it seems to examine some of these problems briefly.

The solid distribution of the Crow type in the Southeast is important. Lowie (1930: 102) has pointed out that this is a characteristic feature of the two main regions in North America where the Omaha type occurs, and suggests that "there is only one conceivable explanation of the distributional data—historical connection within each of the two areas." In the Southwest we also find a solid block of Crow types in the western Pueblos, though the other occurrences of the Crow type in North America are rather isolated. In general the Crow and Omaha types occupy geographically separate areas; only in California and the Southeast do we find the two occurring side by side. For the Yuchi we know the change to the Omaha type to be relatively recent. While Lowie utilizes historical connection to explain the distribution within an area he finds no indication of any borrowing between areas. Furthermore, borrowing as a *complete* explanation of the distribution within an area breaks down in the case of California where one of the Pomo subdivisions, as well as the Wappo, have a Crow type system in the midst of Omaha types. The case of the Yuchi has some bearing on this problem. Superficially we might consider that the Yuchi have borrowed the Sauk and Fox kinship system through con-

---

[4] Unfortunately, they also indicate that Morgan's schedules cannot always be accepted as representing the aboriginal kinship systems unaffected by white contact.

tact. But obviously a *pattern* of grouping relatives is not borrowed, particularly when the actual terms are not taken over, and the languages are not even mutually intelligible. I have attempted above to indicate some of the factors which have influenced this change among the Yuchi; borrowing is only one. If the situation were reversed in California, i.e., if there were one or two Omaha types among a large number of Crow types, we might suspect an acculturational factor such as we find in the Southeast.

In this study we have not been concerned primarily with kinship terminology, but rather the patterns and principles which may be abstracted from native usage. In the systems of the tribes considered there have been few lexical changes; terms have changed primarily in regard to their applications. Thus we find different patterns for grouping relatives at different periods. Kinship terminology and the kinship pattern may vary independently: the terms may change without affecting the pattern, as when a simple substitution occurs, or the pattern may change without affecting the terminology, or both may change. From this standpoint the traditional dispute over whether linguistic factors or social factors are involved in the kinship system has little point. One or the other may be dominant in different situations. Hallowell, for example, found new terms replacing old ones among the Abenaki, as well as shifts in application; in the Southeastern tribes considered, the latter change seems more important.

From the standpoint of acculturation we have here an instance of culture change which is reflected to a certain extent by specific changes in the kinship pattern. While the acculturational process has not been adequately analyzed, its effects on the social organization seem to have been in the direction of emphasizing "patrilineal" tendencies at the expense of "matrilineal." The precise way in which the social factors affected the kinship pattern is an important problem. Even in this preliminary study a "causal" relationship of some sort is indicated, direct or indirect. It does not seem likely that these social factors have operated directly on the kinship patterns, which as we have indicated is an abstraction. Other aspects of the social organization have changed concurrently. Among the Choctaw, for example, the moiety and clan organizations gradually broke down under the impact of acculturational influences. The close correlation of the Crow type with matrilineal clans has been pointed out by Lowie; in his earlier papers he attempted to explain kinship terminology as far as possible in terms of the clan. While it is possible that the acculturational process operated through the clan organization, the nature of the changes taking place in the Choctaw system does not make this hypothesis very likely. The clan organization apparently gradually disintegrated; the kinship system, on the other hand, developed a new type of organization which did not directly reflect the clan system.

One important effect of the acculturational process was to modify the attitudes and behavior patterns which existed between various relatives. The patrilineal emphasis brought definite changes in the roles of males and females in the family and in the local group. The relation of a father to his children, in particular, was changed, largely at the expense of the relations between the child and the mother, and the child and the mother's brother. Specifically the relation of father and child was strengthened; the father gradually took over control of his children, became responsible for their education and training and for their behavior and marriage. Property came to be largely owned by the father and inherited by his children. Such changes must have influenced attitudes toward relatives, as well as weakening matrilineal descent. It is this change in behavior patterns and attitudes which seems to be the medium through which the kinship patterns were modified. This is consonant with recent studies of kinship systems where a close correlation has been observed between the terminological structure and the social behavior of relatives. The changes in behavior patterns and attitudes seem to operate through affecting the choice of alternate principles of classifying relatives.

Hallowell, studying the historical changes in the Abenaki terminology, came to the conclusion that there was no precise correlation between the kinship nomenclature and social institutions.

The major lexical changes, as well as the readjustments in the usage of terms (pattern changes), were found to be most satisfactorily explained as "contact phenomena," resulting from the influence exerted upon Abenaki speakers by those of related Indian languages and Europeans. (A. I. Hallowell, *Recent Changes in the Kinship Terminology of the St. Francis Abenaki*, 1928, p. 145.)

But Hallowell had no data indicating possible changes in social behavior except those inferable from the family hunting territory complex and the levirate. He particularly agrees with Speck that the kinship terminology is in agreement with the social structure in earlier times, but fails to see how the specific changes in relationship terms can be directly connected with the gradual disintegration of the family hunting band.

These conclusions do not necessarily conflict with those reached in the present study. Hallowell was forced to infer the nature of the changes resulting from the contact phenomena: "local differences and custom must have been remoulded to some extent under these new conditions," (*ibid.*, p. 143). In the Southeast there is more evidence for these changes. On the basis of our analysis it seems likely that acculturational factors affect the kinship system through influencing social behavior and attitudes, rather than directly affecting the terminology.

Changes in social organization presumably may go on at different rates among different tribes. The rapidity of the changes reported for the Southeast is significant in indicating the sensitiveness of the kinship system to certain social influences, and raises some doubts as to "survivals" in kinship structures. A more important problem is concerned with the nature of the changes which have been described for the Southeastern tribes. Here a *similar* change seems to have taken place in most of the tribes considered. These changes vary in extent but may be arranged in a series (from a Crow type to a Choctaw type, and perhaps even to an Omaha type), and this series is correlated with the degree of acculturation. This suggests that we may have here a *general* type of change. If so we might expect other Crow systems, under similar acculturational influences, to undergo a similar series of changes.

The fundamental problem of the explanation of the kinship system in terms of correlated social institutions is too complex to be considered in any detail in this paper. In a future paper on the Southeast the writer proposes to bring together the relevant material and indicate its bearing on this problem. Lowie attempts to bolster the lack of preciseness in the correlations of matrilineal and patrilineal organizations with the Crow and Omaha systems by reference to special forms of marriage, though he points out that these are in many instances logical rather than empirical explanations. More fruitful, in my opinion, is Lowie's insistence that "the more specific matrimonial arrangements are themselves a function of the rule of descent." (Lowie, *op. cit.*, p. 108.) It should be possible to go even further and consider them both as functions of some factor or principle which they have in common. Incidentally, the levirate as a causal factor in kinship systems receives a setback in Hallowell's study. He finds, for example, an increase in the number of equations which might reflect the influence of the levirate during the period that the levirate is declining as an institution.

Finally we might point out that in the present study, at least, it seems possible to unite "functional" and "historical" points of view without doing too much violence to either. In studies of acculturation both would seem essential: we need to know something of the interrelations of social institutions before we can deal adequately with cultural change. Without the concept of a *kinship system* for example, the changes recorded in terminology for the Southeastern tribes have very little meaning. On the other hand, without the historical analysis the kinship structure of the Southeast remains blurred. This analysis must be based on documentary evidence, however, since at present we have no satisfactory technique for reconstructing such changes as have been outlined. In terms of an ultimate interest in systematic general "laws" we have here an instance supporting the general hypothesis that "any marked functional inconsistency in a social system tends to induce change." (A. R. Radcliffe-

Brown, *Kinship Terminologies in California* 1935c, pp. 533–34.) The kinship systems of the Southeastern tribes seem to have partially re-covered their internal consistency by means of a series of similar changes.

TWO PROCESSES OF CHANGE IN MANDAN-HIDATSA KINSHIP TERMINOLOGY

Edward M. Bruner

INTRODUCTION

We already have some understanding of the progressive stages in the breakdown of a Crow type kinship system under conditions of social change (Spoehr 1947; Eggan 1950), but we lack sufficient information on the actual processes and interactions involved in the shift from one basic kinship type to another. This paper deals with processes of kinship change in one village of Mandan-Hidatsa Indians living on the Fort Berthold Reservation in North Dakota.

HISTORICAL BACKGROUND

The Mandan and Hidatsa are both small Siouan-speaking tribes with a long history of residence in the Missouri River Valley. Although the Mandan and Hidatsa had different origins, spoke mutually unintelligible languages, and lived in separate villages, they have been in intimate and peaceful association for over two hundred years, with constant cultural borrowings and intermarriage. For the problem to be dealt with here, we may consider the two tribes as one.

Both groups were part of the Prairie earth lodge complex, which included the Chiwere and Dhegiha Sioux and the Caddoan tribes and covered the area encompassed by the Arkansas and Missouri River valleys. A dual subsistence economy of agriculture and hunting was adjusted to an abundant ecological setting in the fertile creek and river bottom lands. Each tribe was com-posed of a number of independent villages integrated by social and ceremonial ties. The characteristic dwelling was the earth lodge, occupied by matrilocal extended families. The social structure of the Mandan-Hidatsa included a clan and Moiety system, matrilineal lineages, an elaborate set of societies, and a Crow type kinship system.

In the early nineteenth century, the two tribes were severely reduced in population by a series of small-pox epidemics. By 1862, the remnants of the Mandan-Hidatsa had consolidated with the Arikara in one village for mutual defense against hostile nomads. With the Indian Bureau allotment program in the last decade of the nineteenth century, the people of the village were scattered into a number of separate and smaller communities on the Fort Berthold Reservation. A group of Mandan and Hidatsa families established themselves in one of these communities located on an isolated segment of the reservation between the Missouri and the Little Missouri rivers. The village is called Lone Hill by the Indian people. In 1951, Lone Hill had a total Indian population of 267 individuals forming 48 nuclear families.

THE PROBLEM

In the summer of 1951 and continuing in 1952–3, I studied social and cultural change in Lone Hill village. Starting with an investigation of kinship using the genealogical method I obtained kinship schedules essentially similar to those reported by Morgan (1871: 291–382), Lowie (1917b), and Bowers (1950, ms.) as characterizing the traditional Crow lineage system. It became apparent that for some mem-

Reproduced by permission of the author and the American Anthropological Association from *American Anthropologist*, Vol. 57, 1955, pp. 840–849.

bers of Lone Hill, both old and young, the terminological system had not changed. While the majority of the schedules gathered in the village represented the Crow lineage system, this was not so in every case. A number of schedules were obtained with English terms and were directly comparable to the American type of system. Thus, within one community I obtained two kinds of kinship patterns, the first aboriginal Indian and the second modern near-white.

This extreme variation is not too surprising if one considers previous work on kinship change in other American Indian tribes which have had a comparable Crow lineage system. Spoehr (1947), comparing related tribes within the Southeastern area, found direct evidence of a complete series from a pure Crow type to a variant of an American generational system with intermediate forms showing a regular pattern of change. The Schmitts (n.d.), within one community of Wichita, found variations in kinship terminology which fitted into the latter part of Spoehr's more complete series. The direction of the Wichita data tends to validate Spoehr's conclusions—when a Crow system changes under modern acculturative influence, there is an increasing patrilineal emphasis, a shift from a lineal to a generational pattern in classification, and a diminishing importance of kinship in regulating social life.

The point to be stressed here is that the terminological systems gathered among the Indian people of Lone Hill village were either pure Crow or white generation types—both extremes without the intermediate variations. While a generational type kinship system is found among the Mandan-Hidatsa and in the cases reported upon by Spoehr and the Schmitts, the absence of intermediate variations on Lone Hill suggests a significant difference in the kind of acculturation taking place. This difference may be clarified by a description of the types of terminological systems found in Lone Hill, followed by an analysis of the mechanisms of kinship change.

THE KINSHIP PATTERNS

Of the two terminological kinship patterns found in Lone Hill, the pure Crow type remains the operating functional system for the majority of the people of the village. Figure 1 is a diagram of the system in the Hidatsa language with English equivalents. The orthography follows Bowers (ms.). Although Lone Hill is composed of members of the Hidatsa and the Mandan tribes, the Hidatsa language has become standard in the village while the Mandan language is rapidly becoming extinct. This may have been due to the small percentage of Mandan-speaking people in Lone Hill when the community was formed. The Crow terminology is used in the Indian language in daily face-to-face contact among most of the people in the village. The meanings and applications of the terms have not changed. Bowers (1950: 1) notes that "the kinship system has been affected little by recent events." Figure 1 is based upon observations of usage throughout the village and was checked by formal schedules obtained from 14 individuals: 8 males ages 34 to 70, and 6 females ages 23 to 60.

In certain situations the people of Lone Hill make a direct linguistic translation of the Crow terminology from the Indian language into the English language. Classificatory fathers are called uncle, classificatory mothers and fathers' sisters are called aunt, while niece, nephew, and cousin terms are applied indiscriminately and usually incorrectly from the white point of view. There are no uncle, cousin, niece, or nephew terms in the Indian language. Figure 2 is offered as an illustration—note particularly the descendants from the father's sister. As the diagram shows, the generation principle does not apply. This use of English is not a variation of the Crow system but is rather the same system with an alternate language. The English kinship terms do not form a reciprocal system and do not conform to expected white usage, for example, an individual whom you address as uncle may call you cousin or brother rather than nephew. It is an egocentric system and is used only when an individual in Lone Hill finds himself in a situation in which he is forced to speak English. All but two of the 137 adults of the village are bilingual, as they speak English in addition to the Indian language. English is most often learned in government schools as a second language and is used by

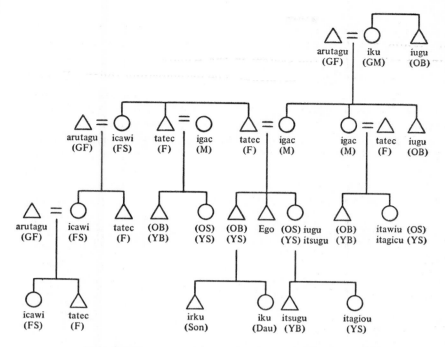

(Note—For a female ego, sister's children are son and daughter.)

Figure 1.

the Indian people to deal with the outside world: in contact with Indian Bureau employees, local white merchants, or when members of alien tribes visit or marry into the village.

The second major kinship pattern in Lone Hill consists of cases in which English terms are used in the white generation pattern, as indicated in Figure 3. My observations indicate that the generational system was used only by seven acculturated families. Many of the individuals in

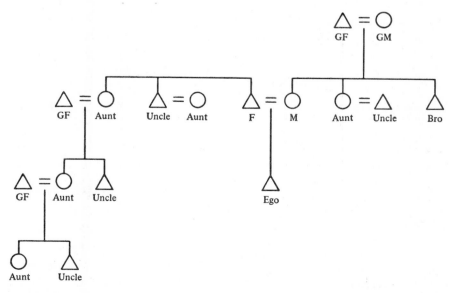

Figure 2.

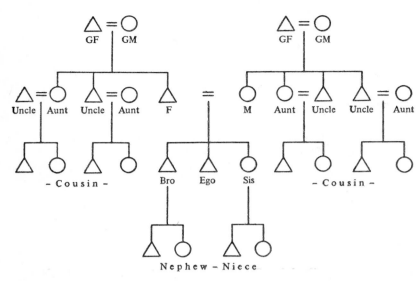

Figure 3.

these families have spent most of their lives away from the village in off-reservation schools. The system was checked in formal interviews with six people, all between the ages of 20 and 30. In one instance a father's brother was called a cousin rather than an uncle because, as my informant said, "He is too young to be my uncle." The situations in which the generational system is employed tend to be relatively restricted and occur when acculturated individuals relate to one another, their close relatives, and whites in or outside the village.

An additional kinship complication arises in those homes in which a member of an alien tribe —usually Crow, Sioux, Blackfoot or Arikara— marries a Mandan-Hidatsa resident of the village. No schedule can be given as there is no general pattern, but one case will be briefly described as an illustration.

As shown in Figure 4, John Bear Leg is the child of a mixed Hidatsa-Arika marriage. The family lives in Lone Hill and speaks only English at home as Mrs. Bear Leg, an Arikara woman, does not understand Hidatsa. While discussing kinship, John referred to his father's sister's daughter, Mary White Duck, by the term "sister" and told me, "That's the white way." This is incorrect, of course, as in the American way Mary would be a cousin to John, while in the Hidatsa

way, she would be an *icawi* or father's sister. I became excited here, as I thought I had found a case of ironing out generation differences which would represent an internal shift in kinship type. Further inquiry revealed that John's Arikara mother had told him to regard Mary as a sister. Mrs. Bear Leg wants her son to take all of his relationships in the Arikara way, and she attempts to teach him Arikara kinship. I checked with Mary, who informed me, "I know it's not right, but he calls me sister so I call him brother." The use of sibling terms for cross-cousins is one stage in Spoehr's series in the breakdown of a pure Crow system. But in this case it is a borrowed change introduced by an Arikara and not one that arose from the situation in lone Hill.

John's total kinship pattern indicates that he follows Hidatsa usage with most of his father's relatives and Arikara usage with all of his mother's relatives, who reside in another village at Fort Berthold. As his mother seems to be the dominant member of the family in these matters, John also refers to some of his father's relatives according to the Arikara way. I pointed out this apparent confusion to John, who replied, "I still don't know about these relationships yet, except what they say to me. The old folks each tell me their way. I'm catching on slow but sure." The net result of this situation is that while John

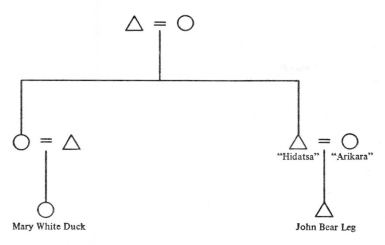

Figure 4. Two Processes

knows how to interact with each specific relative he does not have a consistent total kinship system. John, now 24 years old, understands neither the Hidatsa, Arikara, nor the white kinship pattern. His case illustrates the confusion found among the children of mixed marriages in which the parents have not established a clear-cut identification with any one social system.

To summarize thus far, the two kinship patterns found in Lone Hill are: (1) the traditional Crow terminological system, which remains the basic type for the village and has not changed, at least since 1862 when Morgan first gathered Mandan and Hidatsa kinship terms; and (2) a white generational system employed primarily by acculturated families. There is also a separate set of English terms used in the Crow pattern for the benefit of outsiders and an inconsistent terminological pattern in some Indian homes in which a member of an alien tribe has come to Lone Hill through marriage.

TWO PROCESSES

These data, considered in conjunction with the findings of Spoehr and of the Schmitts, indicate that there are two distinct processes involved in kinship change. The first process consists of the slow modification of a kinship system as evidenced by an orderly and progressive shift in type. This process is best illustrated by Spoehr's complete series in the transition from a pure Crow to an American generation type. Although the shift de-scribed by Spoehr was an indirect result of ac-culturative factors, the slow modification of a social structure may be due to internal forces that are not necessarily associated with culture contact (Eggan 1941; Gough 1952). The second process is a more radical change evidenced by an abrupt jump from one type of kinship system to another. In the second case, reported upon in this paper, the Indian and the white systems exist simultaneously without intermediate variations in kinship patterns.

Both processes of change, slow modification and sudden transformation, occur together in Lone Hill—and they also take place together among the Southeastern tribes. Spoehr emphasized the progressive stages in the breakdown of a Crow lineage system but he also recognized the more rapid type of kinship change (1947: 198). The Mandan-Hidatsa seem to differ from the Southeastern tribes in terms of the relative importance of each process.

The first process of slow modification has not affected the Crow kinship terminology and associated behavior in Lone Hill, but it has changed other aspects of social life in the village. There are many changes in content. A man recently modified the strict mother-in-law respect relation, not by the aboriginal practice of giving his mother-in-law a scalp, but by presenting her with an imitation war bonnet purchased from a mail order house. Innumerable other examples could be cited in which known changes in cultural content have not precipitated changes in the established social structure (cf. Gough 1952:85). An extreme illustration of this is provided by the previously mentioned case of English kinship terminology being used in the Crow kinship pattern. There are, however, many structural changes: the destruction of the native ceremonial life has descreased the religious importance of the father's lineage, the moieties are almost inoperative, the clans have diminished in importance, there is a general laxity among the youth in meeting certain kinship obligations, village organization has shifted from a close-knit unit to one of widely separated households, the matrilocal extended family is no longer a residence unit, and the lineage has ceased to be a corporate group. The only change in the Crow terminology is that vocative terms are rarely used except on public and community-wide occasions. The important point is that the gradual modification of the social structure has not proceeded far enough in Lone Hill to cause an internal shift in kinship type.

The significance of the second process of radical change in Lone Hill may be seen in broader perspective by examining the kind of acculturation now taking place among the Mandan-Hidatsa (Bruner 1953). In every acculturated family that uses the American generational system there has been an Indian-white intermarriage within three ascending generations. Individuals in these families make an abrupt and almost total conversion to white ways, while the rest of the people in the village continue to live by more traditional Indian standards. In the families in which there has been a mixed marriage, the entire white system comes across in the socialization process. Among the Southeastern tribes the shifts in kinship terminology were the result of adaptive responses to changing conditions (Spoehr 1947: 225). The presence of the white generational system in Lone Hill is due to neither cultural "borrowing," adult learning, nor rearrangements in the social structure precipitated by new conditions. Individuals in Lone Hill learn the American kinship system in the English language within the intimate domestic family situation. Although no single factor is ever sufficient to explain a highly complex acculturation situation, it would seem that these differences in the mechanisms of change may account for the differences in kinship patterns found among the Southeastern tribes and the Mandan-Hidatsa. (In a future paper, I shall document and describe the process of individual conversion to white ways in greater detail.)

The converted Indian embraces a new way of life and comes to internalize a set of goals and values which are incongruent with the Crow lineage system. The kinship ties and obligations of the Crow system incorporate and reaffirm the older societal values. Kinship provides the means for mutual aid and cooperation in the village as well as a mechanism of social control for ridiculing and cajoling the nonconformist. While the Mandan-Hidatsa social system, with its wide range, embodies the primary societal values of sharing, generosity, group cooperation, and village unity, the converted Indian shifts to the more individualistic American values of accumulating goods and wealth as ends in themselves. Any member of Lone Hill who interacts with others in terms of the Crow kinship system and who meets the obligations of that system will remain an "Indian."

The majority of the Indians who have converted to white ways tend to leave the village to seek their fortunes elsewhere (cf. Spicer 1940; Tax 1941). For this reason, there were few cases of American type kinship systems found in Lone Hill—most such people had already left their village. If all the individuals who adopted a new kinship system as part of a more inclusive conversion experience were to remain in Lone Hill, they might well produce radical changes in the existing social structure of the community. Their departure is a major factor making for the retention of traditional Indian ways. However, some of the converted Indians do continue to live in Lone Hill and do become sources of change in the Crow kinship system.

Individuals in Lone Hill who do not fulfil their kinship obligations destroy the solidarity of the group and the unity of the system. The converted Indian will avoid any kinship tie which involves his sharing material wealth or giving of his time or possessions. One man has developed devious means to accomplish this. He deposits all his money in a bank so that when people ask him for a loan he can honestly reply that he does not have any money around. He avoids any situation in which he might be called upon to make donations, and, as such, he never attends the social "give-away" dances. This man has consciously narrowed the range of his relationships but he has done so selectively. He will not address another by a kinship term if there is any possibility that he may have to help that person. On the other hand, he does not avoid his joking relatives, for through structured joking he can make critical remarks about Indian ways which would not be permitted in any other context.

SITUATIONAL DETERMINANTS

As converted Indians who use the generational system do interact with their many relatives in the village who use the traditional lineage system, some mechanism of adjustment is necessary. Two relatives who follow different kinship systems may have different conceptions of the proper way of relating to one another. The adjustment is usually made through one of the persons' adopting the other's system for that *particular* relationship. Every acculturated individual in the village who ordinarily uses the generational system will use the Indian lineage system with *some* of his relatives. The converse also occurs, as unacculturated Indians sometimes use the American generational system. Individuals thus adjust to the alternate kinship systems, which tends to minimize the changes in the systems themselves.

Individual adjustment to alternate ways of structuring relationships is neither alien nor unique to the Mandan-Hidatsa (Firth, 1930). Overlapping kinship ties tend to be characteristic of small societies with widely extended kinship systems. In addition to consanguineal and affinal-relations, the Mandan-Hidatsa extended kinship to the clan, linked clan, moiety, ceremonial system, and the supernatural world. As a result, almost every individual in the village was related to everyone else in more than one way. The closest relationship, as defined by the Mandan-Hidatsa, was usually taken in any given case, but factors

unique to the individuals involved were also important (Bowers ms.) Today people often discuss these dual ways of being related and they tend to regard the white way of reckoning kinship as one more way of being related, comparable to the alternate ways within the Indian system.

The following examples will illustrate how the adjustment takes place.

A young girl teased an acculturated woman, after which the woman said to her, "You're supposed to be my *icawi* [father's sister] and you are not supposed to tease me, but that's O.K., we can take it the white way."

In referring to an acculturated girl, an older woman remarked, "She don't talk Indian. She is supposed to call me mother but she calls me auntie. I would be glad to hear it if she called me mother but she won't use it any more. She's my daughter but she won't understand so I call her niece. All of that family acts like white kids."

.   .   .

Schneider (1953a: 228) has suggested "that one important function of the use of kinship terms as forms of address is in imposing on the situation a kind of sanction which enforces conformity with the social definition of the relationship." In some situations the people of Lone Hill consciously manipulate kinship terms to serve their personal ends. Interaction between the acculturated and unacculturated is not unstructured or losely defined, but it does have an element of ambiguity as there are two relatively clear-cut alternate systems. A few individuals take advantage of this in rather subtle ways.

At a political meeting, a converted Indian, who ordinarily uses the generational system, addressed a prominent member of the opposing faction as "father." He used the Crow system in this situation knowing full well that his political rival would not be so indiscreet as to criticize his "son" in public.

An unacculturated woman of the village came into the house of a wealthy converted Indian and addressed him as "older brother." She sat down and indicated that she had some important business in town but had no means of transportation. The converted Indian, as he was preparing to drive her to town, whispered to me, "The only time she ever calls me 'brother' is when she wants something."

CONCLUSION

In earlier times both the Mandan-Hidatsa and the Southeastern tribes had a pure Crow type lineage system. After acculturative influence an American generational type kinship system is found among the two groups. In the Southeast the orderly and progressive shift in kinship type was characterized as a process of slow modification of the existing system due to adaptive responses to changing conditions. In Lone Hill, the lack of intermediate variations in kinship patterns suggests a rapid process of change caused by early socialization in those families in which there has been white intermarriage.

The comparison of static types and categories at different times will yield only partial information on the processes of change and persistence. If we are satisfied simply with answers to the question of *what* change has taken place, it may be sufficient to study the beginning and the end of a cultural sequence. But only through examination of an ongoing sequence and of the actual contexts in which a choice of alternatives is made can we say *how* the change has happened and thereby gain insight into the process itself. And the deepest understanding of social change may best be achieved by direct study of the actual mechanisms and processes involved.

ECONOMIC CHANGE, SOCIAL MOBILITY, AND KINSHIP IN SERBIA

E. A. Hammel

This paper is an interim report on a research project concerned with the interrelationships between economic development, social mobility, and changes in kinship and friendship networks in the city of Belgrade. However, I would like to place the report in a wider theoretical and historical framework.

With respect to theory, studies of changing kinship exhibit some nagging deficiencies. They do not always distinguish the cultural from the social aspects of kinship systems; that is, they do not always distinguish ideology and attitudes from behavior. Further, they often fail to distinguish different structural levels in a given kinship system, so that the analyst is hard put to identify the structural locus of change. In a recent and very cogent paper on change in the Croatian kinship system, Professor Lorraine Barić (1967) remedies the latter problem by

Reprinted from the *Southwestern Journal of Anthropology* (1969), Vol. 25, pp. 188–197, by permission of the author and the Editors of the *Journal*.

separating out an infrastructure of general, bilateral kinship ties that form a network supporting a superstructure of corporate groups based on more selective kinship linkages. All societies have the former, infrastructural level; some also have the latter. I would suggest only one improvement in Professor Barić's scheme—that dichotomization is not sufficient, and that there are or can be several levels in the structure. In fact, one might visualize kinship systems as a potentially limitless network of relationships on which were drawn a series of cultural boundaries (including the outer limit) that specified the extent to which a particular kind and degree of corporacy and solidarity would apply. These boundaries connecting points of similar corporacy and solidarity for particular social purposes—which, Heaven forbid, we could even call isocorps—could be arranged on the presumed *tabula rasa* of available relationships in a variety of ways. They could be largely concentric, as they tend to be in a bilateral, "degree-counting" system like the ancient

Anglo-Saxon one. They could be warped along mono-sexual lines but still lie along a gradient of intensity of corporacy, as they do in segmentary unilineal systems. They could all be very close to one another near the center of the network, with only a few rather unimportant lines of ritual corporacy beyond them, as they are in a society like our own, in which most kinship functions are concentrated in the conjugal family. My point here is that one way to study changing kinship is to study the way the various demarcating lines of corporacy, solidarity, and mutual involvement *move* across the network of available ties. This is only a little different from Professor Barić's concept of infrastructure and superstructure, but it does allow one to make somewhat finer distinctions, if need be. In our own European society, for example, the last few centuries have seen progressive collapse of some lines of corporacy toward the center of the network and the outward disappearance of some others beyond the realm of kinship, as the *size* of the functioning kin group has decreased toward the conjugal family, and as some *functions* of kin groups (such as political action, part of the socialization process, or elements of authority over spouses and children) have moved beyond the kinship zone of social relations.

Before trying to describe the changes in the kinship system of the inhabitants of Belgrade, and their antecedents, I should first describe something of the other changes that have affected their society. Long before the Slavs entered the Balkans in the sixth century A.D., and in their early years in the Balkans they probably subsisted by herding and crude agriculture. After the Serbian empire fell to the Turks in the 14th century, herding became the almost exclusive occupation of *those* Slavs who were pushed back into the inhospitable karst-lands of the Dinaric Alps, where they remained bottled up in rather a tribal state until the middle of the 18th century. As the Turks began to withdraw from the Balkans, these herding groups flowed back down from their meager pastures into the more hospitable valleys they had abandoned four centuries earlier. For about 100 years, there was an extraordinary series of migrations pioneering the deserted lower slopes and bottom lands, clearing the oak forests, and shifting to a system of mixed farming on dispersed homesteads. About the turn of the century (1800), maize was introduced; the population increased in consequence, and also because Slavs from the still occupied areas of Macedonia and southern Serbia began to flee northward to escape Turkish pressure. The population of Serbia tripled between 1840 and 1900. There were great losses of population in the Balkan wars of 1912–1913 and in the Great War of 1914–1918, but little extensive destruction of property. Destruction in the Second War was incredible, and the involvement of the Jugoslav population was very direct. By 1943 the Partizans alone numbered 300,000 men under arms and tied up 30 to 36 enemy divisions and Chetnik forces. Jugoslav losses in the war included about a million civilian deaths plus over 300,000 military, or about 10% of the prewar population and the majority of some male age cohorts. Losses to mining and industry were 50%, to communications 100%, to livestock 60%.

During and on top of all this there was a vicious civil war, ending in domination by the Communist Party and a concerted effort to transform a traditional agrarian society into an industrial one, with both carrot and stick. The revitalization movement of 1942–1968 has been characterized not only by massive changes in culture content, but also by a marked and fluctuating alteration of goals and norms. Jugoslav socialism in its early administrative period was a Stalinist dictatorship with a command economy and a national front *qua* front. Its character as a mobilization regime has steadily diminished, Lenin has been largely replaced by early Marx, and the democratic and decentralist fervor of one wing of the Party finds no match even in last summer's Czechoslovakia. The economic and demographic as well as the ideological changes have been massive. The proportion of the Jugoslav population living in cities of over 20,000 persons has doubled since 1921. The percentage of persons engaged in agriculture has fallen from 80% to 69%. The share of the national income from agriculture has fallen from a half to a fifth. A quarter of the population moved to cities from the countryside in the decade following the war. A quarter of the peasant households have at least one member working off the land, and 16% of the labor force lives on the farm but works in industry or other nonagricultural pursuits.

If a country can go through all of this, from nomadic pastoralism to mixed farming to industrialization, through massive population losses and displacements, and through repeated transformations of ideology—and if there are no discernible effects on the kinship system, then functionalism is dead. Careful examination reveals a fluttering pulse.

There are two questions I would like to explore here. One is, what has happened to the people in Serbia as opposed to the population of Serbia in the most recent changes? The second is, what has happened to the kinship system under the changing conditions of the last several centuries?

. . .

Analysis . . . demonstrates that the occupational and prestige unity of sibling groups is broken up by economic development. During periods of economic expansion, respondents moved ahead of their siblings; as intensity of the expansion lessened, and in periods of retraction, siblings retained their similarity *inter se* and also with respect to their fathers. Similarly, the overall occupational dispersion within sets composed of fathers, fathers' brothers, and mothers' brothers (living largely in a period of economic stagnation) is less than that within corresponding sets of brothers and cousins (living largely in a period of economic expansion). My point is simply that in a scenario of mobility as extreme as that of modern Jugoslavia, the massive changes of history have had more to do with the lives of individuals than our Horatio Algerish impressions or Protestant-ethic disposition would lead us to believe. Personal factors *are* important, but are secondary within lines drawn on a greater stage.

Now let us examine some of the changes in the kinship system. Before entering the Balkans, the Slavs had a kinship system that was probably patrilineal, with strong and extensive agnatic corporacy, and with some terminological features

of Omaha systems. In the refuge areas of Montenegro and parts of Herzegovina, during the Turkish occupation of the rest of the Balkans, the kinship system was one of segmentary patrilineages, stretching from joint households (minimal lineages) at the bottom to maximal lineages as much as 14 generations deep, several of which were combined into each of the various tribes. The lines of corporacy were drawn along agnatic dimensions, modified by coresidence of wives and occasional adoption of individuals or groups at lower levels, and by contractual ties at the tribal level. Individual nuclear families within the joint families had maximal corporacy, including ownership of cattle and common consumption. Closely related nuclear families, constituting the joint family, were coresident. The maximal lineage was the largest group with a common name and icon and with joint responsibility in blood feuds. The tribe was not restricted to agnates and was seemingly the largest unit within which common territory was acknowledged, which might occasionally be solidary in war, and within which there was an institutionalized means for settling feuds.

As the former refugees moved down the slopes to repossess their lands from the Turk, changing demographic and political conditions seem to have effected changes in the kinship system. The more complex and settled tasks of mixed farming demanded a more specific division of labor, and the superior subsistence base permitted larger aggregations within the same household. The solution reached was the classic Serbian *zadruga,* an agnatic core which might include second degree patrilateral cousins and from ten to 100 members, operating as a joint-family corporation. The difference between this joint family and the previous Montenegrin one is that the Serbian joint family was corporate not only in residence but also in production and consumption. There may also have been some relaxation of agnatic bias and increase in frequency of other-kin and non-kin inclusion in the joint family. The lines of economic corporacy had *expanded* to include all of the joint household under new demographic and ecological conditions.

As the households grew in size, and as the

Serbs moved into areas still under nominal Turkish control, and particularly as the nomadic basis of life faded, so also the agnatically biased superstructure of the political system began to lessen in importance. The maximal lineages that covered so much territory in Montenegro now formed just a hamlet or section of a scattered village (although at least as many people might be included in the hamlet as in the former maximal lineage), and the contractually based tribal organization was replaced by the contractually based village. Feuding disappeared as lineages became attenuated, and most of the larger political functions of the maximal lineage passed to the emerging Serbian monarchy and its bureaucracy. The lines of political corporacy had passed *out* of the kinship system.

In the twentieth century, particularly between the wars, the increasing scarcity of good land, monetization of the economy, some inheritance by women, and the acceptance of modern ideas made the maintenance of large extended households difficult. By the time of the first World War, few households in Serbia numbered over 25 persons, most were less than 10, and few included relatives of wider span than married brothers and their young children. Political functions passed even more into the hands of the State, socialization was assumed in part by emerging village schools, and the economic self-sufficiency of the households was diminished by increasing reliance on money, credit, and manufactured goods. Nevertheless, the *ideology* of kinship remained agnatic, males retained their public roles as managers of property, and the zadruga differed more in its reduced size and decreased fission span than it did in its cultural style.

As late as the 1960's, many upland farm families in Serbia retained much the same style of household organization that they had had between the wars. Sons more frequently left the farm for good, and many families had some members working off the land, but the old correlation between economically substantial peasant households and extended family organization, and between poverty and nuclear family organization, persisted. While lines of major political functions remained outside the system, corporacy

in residence and economy collapsed slowly into the nuclear or three-generation household.

My concern here, however, is more with those persons who have felt the brunt of the economic and political changes since World War II, those who have moved to the cities. Urban families are almost exclusively nuclear, but often more because of the housing shortage and cramped apartment quarters; some families contain aged parents, and relatives will take apartments or build squatters' houses near one another if they can. The new urban population retains strong ties to the village. Even families resident in Belgrade for a half-century still visit relatives remaining in the country, and many wealthier families have summer homes in a village, sometimes in their native village. With modern transportation and increasing literacy, maintenance of contact with village kinsmen is less a problem than it was in the days of the old migrations. As recently as 1965, over half the men in a sample of 350 rural-born Serbian industrial workers spent their annual vacation in the village of their birth.

Kin are still important to one another. Villagers come to the city to make major purchases or take care of legal business; they stay with city relatives and seek their advice. Urbanites return periodically to the village to buy in the cheaper market, show off their finery, attend religious feasts, or go to cattle fairs. About a fifth of the sample of Belgrade workers said that a kinsman had helped them to find a job; in a mobile urban environment in which kin are seldom in a position to help with finding jobs, that is a significant level of involvement. In rating their degree of obligation to help relatives and friends, informants expressed greater obligation to close relatives, less to distant ones, and least of all to friends. In most Western industrial countries, friends rank before distant relatives.

Agnatic and viricentric biases continue in the system. In assessing their liking for cousins, informants of both sexes consistently preferred their male cousins to female ones, the children of uncles to the children of aunts, and patrilateral cousins to matrilateral ones. In fact, they even tended to report that they *had* more cousins in direct proportion to the agnatic character of the relationship. In naming the relative who had the greatest influence on them, the one they liked the most, the one they regarded as the most capable and successful, and the one they liked the least, informants indicated a *stronger*, more charged relationship with male relatives than with female; the only exception was that children liked their mothers better than their fathers.

In public and private behavior, sex-roles are still relatively traditional. Women seldom have positions of authority in industry, and when they do, the positions are minor and involve few subordinates. In council meetings, men listen politely to their female colleagues, and then vote as they see their own interests. There are, of course, exceptions, but they are just that. With their spouses, men make a great public show of being in command—it is still, "Wife, serve the guests." Husbands seldom assist their wives publicly in household chores, although they will do very heavy jobs, such as carrying coal, and men with working wives will help by going to market. Some statistics will illustrate: In over 60% of households, the wife alone did the marketing, with 23% sharing equally between husband and wife. In 68% of households, major purchases were decided jointly by husband and wife. In over 70%, husbands left all minor purchases totally to their wives. In over 90%, wives did all the housecleaning. In over 60%, supervision of children's schooling was a joint affair. In 60% of households, husbands did all the heavy chores, and in another 20% husband and wife shared them. This pattern does not differ much from that found in the villages, except that there husbands and wives will share much more of the heavy, agricultural work. In Montenegro even today, mountain men often do all the market-going, because they do not feel that their wives should appear in public places. In serving guests at the traditional feast of the household saint, a peasant still roasts the meat himself, carves it, and often serves it to his guests, while his wife takes care of other foods. In the city, men sometimes prepare the roast for a ceremonial dinner, although in an apartment oven.

It is of course impossible to maintain that there has been no change in the kinship system. There has been change in the size of groups: households have decreased from the nineteenth century zadruga norm to the one-child families of the Belgrade middle class. Agnatic groups have decreased from the extended politically active lineages of Montenegro to a shadowy information network in the cities. There has been change in the degree to which only agnates are admitted to critical economic activities; the emphasis is now much more bilateral. There has been a shift in the lines of corporacy, with a collapse of many functions into the nuclear family and the abandonment of others, such as political activity and some aspects of social control, to the State. Nevertheless, the ideology of kinship in much the same as it always was. Linkages of kinsmen are still *phrased* largely in agnatic terms. Preferences for and affective and instrumental ratings of kin stress men and agnatic linkages. Important assets (other than affect) are still controlled largely by men, and men take precedence in ritual activities. It is a far cry from protohistoric cattle herders with an Omaha kinship terminology to a Belgrade bureaucrat roasting a suckling pig in his two-room apartment on the anniversary of the Revolution, but there is an underlying consistency in cultural attitudes, for all the changes in lines of corporacy and solidary behavior. The maps in peoples' heads really are the last thing to go.

SELECTED READINGS

A. Commentaries and Critiques

Gellner, Ernest
    1958 Time and theory in social anthropology. *Mind; a quarterly review of psychology and philosophy,* 67:182–202.

Gluckman, Max
    1949 Malinowski's sociological theories. In *Rhodes-Livingston papers no. 16.* London: Oxford University Press.

Harris, Marvin
    1968 *The Rise of Anthropological theory: A History of Theories of Culture.* New York: Crowell, pp. 539–540, 634–687.

Schapera, Isaac
    1950 Kinship and marriage among the Tswana. In A. R. Radcliffe-Brown and C. D. Forde (eds.) *African systems of kinship and marriage.* London: Oxford University Press.

B. Original Works

Bruner, Edward M.
1955 Two processes of change in Mandan-Hidatsa kinship terminology. *American Anthropologist*, 57:840–850.

Eggan, Fred
1937b Historical changes in the Choctaw kinship system. *American Anthropologist*, 39: 34–52.
——— 1966 *The American Indian: Perspectives in the Study of Social Change.* Chicago: Aldine.

Fortes, Meyer
1949b Time and social structure. In M. Fortes (ed.), *Social Structure: Essays presented to Radcliffe-Brown.* Oxford: Clarendon Press, pp. 54–84.

Freed, Stanley A.
1960 *Changing Washo kinship,* Anthropological Records, 14:6.

Fried, Morton H.
1960 On the evolution of social stratification and the state. In S. Diamond (ed.), *Culture in history: Essays presented to Paul Radin.* New York: Columbia University Press, 1960, pp. 713–731.

Gearing, Frederick O.
1958 The structural poses of 18th-century Cherokee villages. *American Anthropologist*, 60:1148–1157.

Goode, William J.
1966 Industrialization and family change. In B. F. Hozelitz and W. E. Moore (eds.), *Industrialization and Society.* The Hague: UNESCO.

Gough, E. Kathleen
1952 Changing kinship usages in the setting of political and economic change among the Nayars of Malabar. *Journal of the Royal Anthropological Institute,* 82:71–88.

Hallowell, Alfred I.
1928 Recent changes in the kinship terminology of the St. Francis Abenaki. In *Proceedings of International Congress [1926] of Americanists.* Vol. II, pp. 97–145.

Hammel, Eugene A.
1969a Economic change, social mobility and kinship in Serbia. *Southwestern Journal of Anthropology,* 25:188–197.

Herskovits, Melville J.
1948 *Man and his works,* Part VI. New York: Knopf.

Kroeber, Alfred L.
1933 Process in the Chinese kinship system. *American Anthropologist,* 35:151–157.

Leach, Edmund R.
1954b *Political systems of Highland Burma.* Cambridge: Harvard University Press.

Linton, Ralph, Melville J. Herskovits and Robert Redfield
1935 Memorandum on the study of acculturation. In *Man,* 35:162, 145–148. Also in *American Anthropologist,* 38:149–52; *Africa,* 9:114–18.

Malinowski, Bronislaw
1945 *The dynamics of culture change.* Edited by P. Kaberry. New Haven: Yale University Press.

Moore, Wilbert E.
1964 *Social Change.* Englewood Cliffs, N.J.: Prentice-Hall.

Murdock, George P.
1949 *Social structure.* New York: Macmillan, ch. 8, appendix A.

Murphy, Robert F.
1956 Matrilocality and patrilocality in Mundurucú society. *American Anthropologist,* 58:414–433.
——— 1960 *Headhunter's heritage.* Berkeley: University of California Press.

Nett, B. R.
1952 Historical changes in the Osage kinship system. *Southwestern Journal of Anthropology,* 8:164–181.

Sahlins, Marshall D.
1958 *Social stratification in Polynesia.* Seattle: University of Washington Press.

Sahlins, Marshall D. and Elman R. Service (eds.)
1960 *Evolution and culture: Essays presented to Leslie White.* Ann Arbor: University of Michigan Press.

Service, Elman R.
1960 Kinship terminology and evolution. *American Anthropologist,* 62:747–763.
——— 1962 *Primitive social organization: An evolutionary perspective.* New York: Random House.

Spöehr, Alexander
1947 Changing kinship systems. Field Museum of Natural History Anthropological Series, 33:4:153–235.

Steward, Julian H.
1955 *Theory of culture change: The methodology of multilinear evolution.* Urbana, Ill.: University of Illinois Press.

VIII

STRUCTURE AND FUNCTION: FURTHER DEVELOPMENTS

In the two decades that followed Malinowski's and Radcliffe-Brown's rise to preeminence in the anthropological world, the outstanding development was the stimulation and output of their students. Adopting the intensive field work methods that Malinowski had started with his Trobriand work, these younger anthropologists spent considerable lengths of time "in the field." However, their method actually contrasted with the also considerable amounts of field work that the American anthropologists of the same period generally undertook. The Americans tended to spend shorter lengths of time in each field situation (e.g., summer vacations and, if more data was needed, they would return for similarly short periods). The British, on the other hand, tended to remain in a particular society for a longer time and were thus, often, removed from their "normal" lives. Furthermore, once a project was completed, many of them never returned to the particular field area again.

The result of these extended periods of field work were generally written up as more than ethnographic descriptive monographs. They were analytical-descriptive essays—often focusing on one major set of institutions—but usually purporting to present a relatively complete idea of the functional interrelationships of all parts of the society. The first such work was published by Fortune (*The Sorcerers of Dobu*, 1932a) and this was followed by Firth (*We, the Tikopia*, 1936), Lloyd Warner (*A Black Civilization*, 1937), and many others. Many of the American contributions were presented in more condensed form. An example is Eggan's *Social Anthropology of the North American Tribes* (1937c) that contained the analytic and field work results of many of Radcliffe-Brown's Chicago students. These summaries had to concentrate on a more "skeletal" description of the major features of kinship and social organization. This idea of a series of "condensed monographs" dealing with a particular set of institutions was later followed by Fortes and Evans-Pritchard (1940) and Radcliffe-Brown and Daryl Forde (1950).

Apart from the more general structural-functional analyses of particular societies which, though much needed, tended to be more descriptive than theoretical, anthropologists continued to examine subjects of more general concern. The nature of the relationships between kinship nomanclatures and social systems was reexamined in the light of better data and Radcliffe-Brown was shown to be basically correct in his assertions, though often incorrect in his detailed conjectures concerning the mechanisms for classification (cf. Opler, 1937b; Firth, 1936). It appears that the type of society studied seriously affected the degree and the nature of the correlation between terminology systems and categories of relatives.

One topic that came to the fore during this period was the examination of "special" social relationships, such as joking and avoidance relationships. These, because of their "curiosity value" had long been noted by anthropologists (cf. Tylor, 1889; Lowie, 1920) and some of the methods used in the attempts to explain them had been derived from the now popular theories of Freud concerning sexual ambivalence. Eggan

("The Cheyenne and Arapaho Kinship Systems," 1937a) tackled the subject in a more general framework, and showed how these relationships were functional mechanisms for solving structural problems that had led to ambivalence. His suggestions were much like those of Tax (1937a) concerning the functional nature of "kinship accomodation" in general.

Radcliffe-Brown himself took an interest in the subject (1940c, 1949) and also thought that joking relationships were mechanisms for the resolution of hostility (disjunction) and alliance (conjunction). He then proceeded to a more general level, opposing the emphasis on the ties of *alliance* over those of *contract* (corporateness). He demonstrated that the former concerned divergent interests and rights and that the latter emphasized convergent or similar interests. Of these two major types of social relationships, he stated that the former is often associated with marital links and the latter with descent. However, he suggested, joking relationships are only one of four possible types of alliance relationship, along with economic exchange, blood brotherhood, and intermarriage. Thus Radcliffe-Brown touched upon a general theory of exchange and dualism that was also developed by Mauss (1925) and, later, by Lévi-Strauss (1949).

GENERAL OBSERVATIONS UPON THE CLASSIFICATORY SYSTEM

Raymond Firth

Analysis of . . . Tikopian data . . . has shown that certain conclusions can be drawn which are of general interest to the theory of primitive kinship. The more important of them may be reformulated in conjunction as follows: In a native community where the classificatory system of relationship is in force, and kinship is counted with almost equal strength through both the male and the female lines, it is clear that the more limited in numbers the population the more likelihood there is of the existence of a previous tie of kinship between people who marry. In the matter of this prior relationship it is immaterial whether the social organization is based upon exogamous clan groups or not. Marriage, then, involves a change of status not only for the husband and wife, but also for their relatives who have to make a readjustment of their kinship bonds to meet the altered situation.

This change is not automatic, a simple reclassification *in toto*. It takes place on the basis of individual circumstances and even personal selection, the most significant relationship, that one which has the greatest social weight, being adopted from among the several possible or inferential relationships. Such a process is seen in its extreme form in what may be termed the "parting" or "splitting" of relationships, as in those cases quoted above where a husband holds the status of father-in-law, and his wife that of sister, to the same man, or where a father and his own son enter the same kinship grade, one being the son-in-law, the other the nephew of a third person. There is no attempt to combine or fuse the status or the terminology of kinship. The mode of such selection shows, incidentally, the existence of a very strong *individual element* in the classificatory system. The terms as used in ordinary life by the native connote for him not abstract undifferentiated groups of kinsfolk, but definite concrete persons each linked to him by personal individual bonds.

This process of individuation, of selection and exclusion in adjustment, is necessary for the preservation of this particular type of kinship structure. It is, in fact, the compensatory principle which the classificatory system bears within itself for the purpose of its own functioning.

Reprinted by permission of the Royal Anthropological Institute of Great Britain and Ireland from the *Journal of the Royal Anthropological Institute*, Vol. 60 (1930), pp. 266–268.

Under this form of social organization, where the classificatory system of relationship is in association with the bilateral recognition of kinship, and consequently marriage with a relative is the rule, the major proportion of such unions takes place between persons of the same kinship grade, as between those termed "brother" and "sister," that is, between cousins. Natural birth sequence, however, operating it may be over several generations, tends to cause a variation of kinship grade between persons of essentially the same age. Hence, a proportion of marriages tend to occur between people of different kinship grades, as between classificatory uncle and niece, nephew and aunt, father and daughter. To this extent such marriages are anomalous. It may be noted that they have not been deduced from any "correspondences" in kinship terminology, but have actually been observed and recorded from native life. These marriages, however, are truly normal in character, their essential feature being that the union is contracted between people of approximately the same age, the same *tupuraya*, "growth-stage," as the natives say. Really anomalous marriages between people of widely different ages are rare and contracted for some special reason—as desire for children, or physical disability of one partner.

In general, then, the natural tendency of man to seek a mate in a woman of equivalent age, that is, soon after both have attained maturity, renders it inevitable that where such differences of kinship grade occur with no great disparity of age, marriage in many cases will eventuate, and the discrepancies in the kinship grading disappear. Age and status are thus once more reduced to a level of equality. Nature herself tends to correct in the sphere of marriage the balance of the social mechanism which was originally displaced by her own operations in the field of birth.

It seems to me probable that a careful study of the social organization of further Polynesian peoples, and perhaps of other culture types as well, will yield similar results to those obtained in the case of Tikopia.

To have given an adequate account of this subject of Tikopian kinship would have meant the inclusion of a vast mass of data showing the manner in which the system operates against the background of economic and religious affairs. Such ample treatment is impossible here. Its absence is to be regretted in that examination of it might, perhaps, have brought home to the reader what the observer cannot help but perceive as he is actual studying the native culture in all its bearings, namely, the essential practical utility of the classificatory system of counting relationship in its own cultural surroundings. Unlike the rigid travesty of it which it sometimes put forward by theorists for comment and criticism, it reveals itself as a convenient, flexible and commonsense piece of the social mechanism.

MARRIAGE VS. DESCENT IN MATRILINEAL DOBU

Reo Fortune

OUTLINE OF SOCIAL ORGANIZATION

The ideal village of Dobu is a circle of huts facing inward to a central, often elevated mound, which is the village graveyard.

In point of fact there are usually gaps in the

From the book *The Sorcerers of Dobu* by R. F. Fortune. Copyright, 1932, by E. P. Dutton & Co., Inc. Renewal, ©, 1960 by Reo Franklin Fortune. Dutton Paperback Edition. Reprinted by permission of the publishers and the author. Pp. 1–10.

circle of huts as at a, b, c, and d. These gaps represent old house sites of extinct family lines. A path, f, goes around the village behind the backs of the houses. This is for the use of passers by, who are not allowed to enter the village unless they are closely related to its members, or unless they have legitimate business of moment to transact.

In the centre of the village a clear space lies open with only scattered brilliant leaved croton

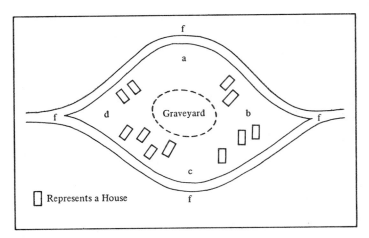

Figure 1. Village plan

shrubs upon it. Here below the sod within their stone set circular enclosure lie the mothers, and mothers' brothers, the grandmothers on the distaff side and their brothers, and so, for many a generation back, the ancestors of the villagers on the distaff side. From the dead who lie in the central space individual ownership vested in soil and palm has come to the living. On the paternal side the ancestors of the village owners lie utterly dispersed in the villages of many stranger clans, the villages of their respective mothers and female ancestors.

In the following discussion I shall use the term villager in the restricted meaning of owner of village land and village trees. This use excludes those who have married into the village and who claim residence only through their spouses.

Each villager, male, or female, owns a house site and a house. A woman inherits her house site from her mother, or from her mother's sister. The husband in every marriage must come from another village than that of his wife. His house site is in one village, his wife's house site is in another. A man's son cannot inherit the house site of his father in his father's village. After his father's death he must scrupulously avoid so much as entering his father's village. His father bequeaths his house site to his own sister's son. His own son inherits house site and village status from his mother's brother in his mother's village.

For the purpose of diagrammatic representa-

tion we may represent the village as one of its constituent units only.

We may represent the Dobuan situation, graphically as below [in Fig. II].

The oval enclosing lines mark off villages A, B, and C. For brother and sister own house sites in the same village, and children inherit house sites in their mother's village, not possibly in their father's. Hence a man, his sister and his sister's children are the owners or potential owners of all village house site land.

Where a man's house land is inherited there is he buried in the central place adjoining the outer ring of house land. Thus no father is ever buried in the place of his children. A, B, and C represent a legal unit which keeps village land and the disposal of the corpses of its members strictly within itself.

The unit I have ringed about, of a man, his sister, and his sister's children, is called in Dobuan the *susu*. It extends down the generations so that it may include a man, his sister, his sister's children, and his sister's daughter's children, but not his sister's son's children, and so on. The children of any male member of the *susu* go out of it. In the above diagram I have represented each *susu* as a separate village in order to represent marriage out of the village. In reality, each village is a small number of *susu*, from four or five to ten or twelve, all claiming a common female ancestress and unbroken descent from her through females only. In practice only some of

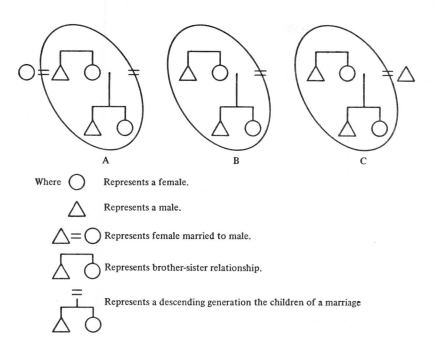

Where ◯ Represents a female.

△ Represents a male.

△=◯ Represents female married to male.

△⌐◯ Represents brother-sister relationship.

△=◯ (descending) Represents a descending generation the children of a marriage

Figure 2.

the number of *susu* can demonstrate this claim of common ancestry in their short known genealogies. But the claim is probably well founded, although not fully substantiated except by mythological validation in a mythical common ancestress.

All virtue in this system comes from descent through the mother. Every woman claims by right the inheritance of her brother for her male children. Hence this grouping is called *susu*, the term for mother's milk. A husband beating his wife falls out with her mother's brother, or with her brother whose inheritance she claims for her children. Her children are independent of her husband for legal endowment—they *must* by law be independent, and differently endowed. She is greatly independent of her husband, and only bound if he cares to indulge, as often happens, in suicidal self pity, and does not succeed in killing himself. Nevertheless, the suicidal resort is taken in a minority of cases; divorce is possible in the majority. It has become popular now for offended men to embark for work in the white man's centres, rather than to attempt suicide, the more so since the old point of suicide, forcing one's kin to avenge on one's cruel wife's kindred, is difficult

now owing to the white man's laws against murder being fairly well enforced. Nevertheless, despite the new fashion, the old way still persists side by side with the new.

If we come upon the village in its everyday aspect, when all is quiet, all its marriages going smoothly, it gives little apparent evidence of the strength of the *susu*. The *susu* does not live in a house. A man lives with his wife and children, and the interior of their house is strictly forbidden to anyone else, except at night to a lover of the daughter of the house. The man's sister or the woman's brother, or any other visitor, cannot ascend into the house but must rest under its elevated floor on the sheltered ground beneath, or, in the case of two men who are friends meeting, they may sit together on the elevated platform in front of the house, a small roof-sheltered "verandah".

The *susu* has no common house for its exclusive use. Its only exclusive communal resting place is the graveyard, the centre ring with its red croton plants upon it; each hut of the many that surround the communal place of the *susu* shelters a biological family, the marital grouping as I shall term it throughout this account.

Normally the house interior is as rigidly restricted to man, wife, and their children, as the graveyard that the house fronts is rigidly restricted to the corpses of brothers, sisters, and sisters' children, it being understood that the house is restricted to the one unit, the biological family only, whereas the graveyard is common to all the *susu* of the village. But in case of serious illness the patient is always removed on a litter to his or her own village, village of the mother, if residence at the time of sickness is otherwise. Then, and then only, entrance to the house is possible to the matrilineal kin of the patient despite the presence of the patient's spouse in the house. If serious illness turns to death the dead's spouse is immediately prohibited from the house and the village of death. Within the house the near matrilineal kin mourn their dead. The alignment of kin within the house is, for the first and only time, the same as the alignment of kin within the graveyard. The house has ceased to be a house in its normal function. It is deserted for a season then destroyed.

Each marital grouping possesses two house sites, each site with a house built upon it. The woman has her house in her village, the man has his house in his village. The couple with their children live alternately in the woman's house in the village of the woman's matrilineal kin, and in the man's house in the village of the man's matrilineal kin. The change in residence usually takes place each gardening year, so that the one spouse spends alternate years in the other's place and alternate years in own place; but some couples move more frequently to and fro. It is thus required that every person spend at least every alternate year, he with his sister and mother, she with her brother and mother (and, of course, mother's brothers and sisters). Since every family grouping moves in this fashion, it follows that when a man is in his village his wife is there also, if his mother is in her village his father or his stepfather is also there, and if his sister is in her village his sister's husband is also there. His mother's brother may also be at home. Then his mother's brother's wife will be there. He and his sister, his mother with her sisters and brothers are all owners of the village land where they are

resident, owners of the houses built upon it, and owners of the palms growing about the village.

They are the *susu*. His wife, his father, his sister's husband, his mother's brother's wife, on the other hand, own land, houses, and palms in their own different villages. They are representatives of the various *susu* of other places, and they are in the place of their affinal relatives temporarily for the year.

Now, although these incoming visitors, who are not local owners, have each a retiring place in the village exclusively to themselves with their respective husbands or wives—the interior of the house—they spend a great part of the day and the early evening outside their houses in sight and in frequent communication with the local owners and the wives and husbands of others of the local owners. Certain rules and observances govern this communication.

The incomers are called Those-resulting-from-marriage, or strangers, as a collective class by the collective class which is called Owners of the Village. Owners of the village use personal names between themselves freely to persons of their own or a younger generation. To their elders they prefer to use relationship terms, though the personal name is not forbidden. But Those-resulting-from-marriage cannot use the personal name of any one of the owners down to the smallest child, except in the case of a father to his own child. They must use a term of relationship. Owners of an ascendant generation can and do use their names freely, however. Moreover, one of Those-resulting-from-marriage cannot use the personal name of any other person in the same class. Again, a relationship term must be used. Those-resulting-from-marriage, while they are yet newly married, must approach an owner's family sitting beneath the owner's house by a roundabout way, circling in unobtrusively and bending apologetically while they do so—their own spouse being the only owner excepted. By the time one or two children are born this behaviour is usually discarded towards the own mother-in-law's *susu*. But it remains even later towards other *susu* in the village (at least when an unusual mode of behaviour is set up, as when I might ask a man to come and introduce me to some of the more distant village relatives of his own mother-in-law's *susu*).

"Those-resulting-from-marriage" are not supposed to be themselves kinsmen. It happens sometimes that they are. But this develops from linked parallel marriages between the same two places which are strongly disapproved. "Those-resulting-from-marriage" are supposed to be on entirely formal terms with each other when they are resident in the owner's village, avoiding each other's personal names. It is not fitting that they should be kinsmen and of the one village; and economic arrangements, as we shall see later, discriminate against such linked marriages. Moreover, in case two villages are linked by several marriages, as they are becoming nowadays in places where the population has receded seriously, a suicidal ending to one marriage might rend the others into two opposing groups bound to revenge and defence against revenge respectively. In the state of uneasy marriage found in Dobu it is fitting that one village should hesitate to involve itself over deeply with another, but prefer to spread its marriages widely. This is actually stated as the ideal.

"Those-resulting-from-marriage," if they are men, are always abnormally uneasy about their wives' fidelity. Now when a woman is in her own village, she has her kin next door and only too ready to eject her husband if he dares to lift a hand against her, or use foul language to her. She has no great dependence on her husband for care for her children, since a woman can nearly always get a new husband for future help, and her brother ultimately provides for them in any case. Consequently she behaves very much as she likes in secret. Suspicion and close watching are not relaxed by her jealous resultant-from-marriage. Sooner or later anger between man and wife flares up in public. Then the woman's kin tell the man to get out. He has no sympathy from the others-resultant-from-marriage. They are for the most part no kin of his, and they are not a united body as the collective class formed of the several *susu* Owners of the Village are. The result is that the unfortunate resultant-from-marriage gets out precipitately, usually being designated in uncomplimentary obscene terms by irate owners as he

goes. Dobuan folklore is full of husbands pathetically packing up their goods and going home to their mothers and sisters after a child has informed them that their wife has been consorting secretly with a male member of a distantly related *susu* of her own village. All men of the village call all women of the village of their own generation sister, but some are not close parallel cousins in reality, their relationship being of a degree that cannot be determined from known genealogy. Marriage within the village is strongly discountenanced, but casual sex affairs between distant "brothers" and "sisters" of other *susu* of the village occur often. The husband either gets out without insulting or striking his wife as in the folk-lore, or else both insults and strikes her and then gets out before he is injured, but under danger of injury, as I saw happen in real life. Conversely, when a woman is in her husband's place she is jealous of him and watches for signs of his intrigues with village "sisters" of his. I do not know how much actual village "incest" of this order there is, but I do know that suspicion of it is frequently flaring up into as much trouble as if the suspicion were perfectly founded. The offended husband always believes his suspicion is true, the owners invariably repudiate it, and no conciliatory mechanism exists, apart from the husband sometimes pocketing his pride later, sometimes not, and sometimes resorting to a suicidal attempt on his life. In reality, as in the legends, children are enlisted as informers. Jealousy normally runs so high in Dobu that a man watches his wife closely, carefully timing her absences when she goes to the bush for natural functions. And when it is time for women's work in the gardens here and there one sees a man with nothing to do but stand sentinel all day and play with the children if any want to play with him. It will be apparent that the strength of the marital grouping is not improved by the solidarity of the *susu*, which is maintained by the rule of alternate residence. Incest prohibition is not too difficult to enforce within the small family. But when the children are grown adults, many with dead parents, belonging to different family lines that have only mythological validation of common ancestry, all thrust closely together by local residence and taught to regard their village mates as brothers and sisters, and people of other villages as dangerous sorcerers and witches, enemies all, then it is not unnatural that the strain of considering a woman of a friendly group as a sister sometimes breaks down. One's wife, after all, is a member of a group that may only modify its underlying hostility at best. Parents-in-law are frequently divined by the diviner as the sorcer or witch that is making one ill. In the lower social forms the bee's division into three classes of queen, worker, and drone is a type that works with no strain. But sister-brother solidarity with an artificial extension of the sister-brother relationship does not work with the husband-wife solidarity very well under Dobuan conditions. One solidarity tends to gain predominance. Then friction tends to occur between the two groupings. This friction is expressed in sorcery and witchcraft terms as well as in terms of jealousy, quarrel, attempted suicide, and village "incest."

The following diagram [Fig. III] of marital grouping and *susu* respectively may be useful for a summary of the argument as far as it has gone:—

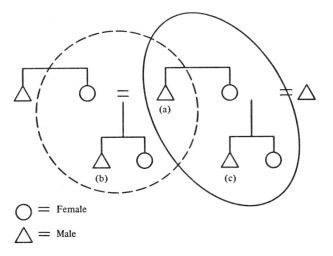

◯ = Female

△ = Male

Figure 3.

The circle enclosed group is the marital grouping, the oval enclosed group is the *susu*. It is evident that the man (a) is a member of both groupings. He has a loyalty to each group. The gain of one group from him will be at the expense of the other.

The *susu*, with the brother-sister solidarity at its base, has as its gains:—

(1) The inheritance and exclusive possession of a's corpse.

(2) The inheritance and exclusive possession of a's village land and palms.

(3) The right to exclude a's children from entering a's *susu*'s village after he is dead.

(4) The right to enforce a to live in his sister's village every alternate year in despite of marriage ties, and reciprocally he is forced in aternate years to live in his wife's brother's village.

The marital grouping has as its losses the inheritance of a's corpse, the inheritance of a's village land and palms, the right to enter a's village after a is dead (for widows as well as widow's children are excluded), and the right to live in one place in a settled manner, such as would probably be more in accord with marital congeniality. Related culture's, neighbors to Dobu, have fixed patrilocal marriage with *susu* right otherwise similar to Dobu. I studied one such culture fairly intensively. Divorce is not one-fifth as frequent as in Dobu. Moreover, "those-resulting-from-marriage" are all women come into their husband's place more or less permanently. The Dobuan custom makes "those-resulting-from-marriage" half man, half women, of non-permanent residence, and non-permanent even in changing residence, because the chances of divorce are high. The oldest Dobuan in my main genealogy had had eight successive marriages, one of the youngest men in the genealogy had had four, one other youth, three, and this is fairly typical of an overwhelming majority of Dobuans. It is so in every separate sea-divided district that is Dobuan in culture. The result is that each Dobuan village shelters a heterogenous collection of men of different village allegiance who distrust one another thoroughly. Suspicion of sorcery and poisoning tactics *within* the village runs very high at times. In the patrilocal marriage of neighboring cultures all the men of the village are "brothers," owners of the village in every sense. All resultants-from-marriage are women and suspicion of foul tactics *within* the village is not found.

There can be no doubt that the rule of alternate residence, while it enjoins and expresses a solidarity between the owners, disrupts the relations between the owners and their separate spouses, "Those-resulting-from-marriage." We can quite fairly assign this custom as a gain to *susu* right and a loss to marital grouping right. Conversely a brother-sister tabu, if it were inaugurated and carried far enough, would prevent the alternate residence rule, or, at least, tend to prevent the extended "incest" that follows with alternate residence as it exists in Dobu. Such a brother-sister tabu would be a gain for the marital grouping over the *susu*. It would tend to put (a) with his wife and her children more, and less with his sister and her children (see Fig. III). It will be clear from the Dobuan situation how a brother-sister *tabu* would strengthen the family by marriage. There is no hint of any such *tabu*, however, in Dobu, except that young unmarried men do not sleep in the same house with their young unmarried sisters. The young man is turned out of the parental house, the daughter of the house remains in it. The youths go and sleep with the daughters of other houses, and the brothers of other girls of other villages come to sleep with their sisters. It is not a brother-sister *tabu*, for a youth with no sister is excluded from his parents' house, but an active arrangement whereby the young men seek out the sisters of other young men who live afield. The full estimation of the disruptive possibilities in the Dobuan rule of alternate residence can only be reached after a discussion of Dobuan sorcery. That I cannot do within the limits of this chapter. Meanwhile, pending later substantiation, it must be provisionally accepted from the results that the rule is a gain of *susu* right, a loss for the marital grouping.

RESPECT AND JOKING RELATIONSHIPS AMONG THE CHEYENNE AND ARAPAHO

Fred Eggan

The social usages involving restrictions on behavior or privileged familiarity are well developed among the Cheyenne and Arapaho, practically every relative being involved in one category or the other. Thus a man must respect his parents, sisters, and children-in-law's parents, and must "avoid" his parents-in-law, particularly his mother-in-law. On the other hand, he may joke "mildly" with his father's sisters, mother's brother's, grandfathers, and brothers, and must joke "roughly" with his brothers-in-law and sisters-in-law. A woman has parallel respect and joking relationships, except for her parents-in-law where avoidance is not involved.

Lowie has furnished a foundation for further studies of these social usages by reviewing the available data in the light of various theories. He finds ample evidence for a correlation "between social and sexual taboos, and between social license and the possibility of sex relations," but is aware that "this by no means explains all the phenomena," (1920: 104). He is skeptical of any all-inclusive theory and sets down as a principle of method:

> The regulations in any particular locality should rather be viewed in conjunction with the whole culture, . . . whatever interpretations appear from such an inquiry may then be compared with corresponding results from other regions (*ibid*: 101–2).

From Fred Eggan (ed.), *Social Anthropology of the North American Tribes* (Chicago: University of Chicago Press, 1937), pp. 75–81. Copyright 1937 by the University of Chicago. Copyright 1955 by the University of Chicago Press. Reprinted by permission of the author and the University of Chicago Press.

The social usages centering around avoidance and joking have attracted a good deal of theoretical attention, particularly in terms of sex. In the following analysis a more inclusive formulation of these social usages will be attempted, based on a study of the social situations in which they occur and utilizing the descriptive principles outlined above. This will furnish a preliminary interpretation, which can then be compared with others, and eventually may result in a general formulation with regard to joking and respect.

Respect and joking relationships seem to represent mutually exclusive forms of social behavior which stand at opposite poles of conduct.[1] Each of these relationships may vary in intensity. Thus avoidance seems to represent an intensification of the respect relationship, while "rough joking" seems to be an extreme form of the "mild joking" relationship. We may state our problem as follows: Is there any correlation between the categories of joking and respect relationships and the social situations which exist in Cheyenne and Arapaho life, which will throw light on the classification of relatives in one or the other of these categories?

Among the Cheyenne and Arapaho (as elsewhere) respect relationships seem the more fundamental and involve the members of the elementary family as well as parents-in-law. The parents are responsible for transmitting the social heritage; this transmission involves authority on the part of the parents and obedience and respect on the part of the children.[2] The marked social differentiation on the basis of sex is another factor; the brother must respect his sister at the same time that he looks out for her welfare, and vice versa. The relation of a man to his parents-in-law is more complex. By the general

rule of matrilocal residence he must reside in his parents-in-law's camp and must help support them economically, though to begin with he may feel an intruder. The mother-daughter relationship is a respect relationship; this respect is intensified in the case of the son-in-law by the difference in sex. There is a further factor in the rivalry of the mother-daughter and husband-wife relationships; in order that the affairs of the camp may run smoothly, the son-in-law and the mother-in-law avoid each other completely, though manifesting the highest respect for each other. It is significant, in this connection, that the restrictions may be removed when a satisfactory adjustment has been reached by a public exchange of gifts. The relation of a son-in-law and father-in-law is not so restricted. The factor of sex differentiation is absent, and there is the necessity for economic co-operation between father-in-law and his son-in-law; while there is a reserve felt, there is no avoidance.

A daughter-in-law, on the other hand, has a different relation to her parents-in-law. Normally she is not in close contact with them, unless they should happen to belong to the same band. A daughter-in-law must respect her husband's father because he is of the opposite sex and in the generation above, but there is no avoidance. The mother-in-law, on the other hand, is of the same sex and has an active interest in her sons's and daughter-in-law's children; the daughter-in-law may speak freely with her mother-in-law and may argue with her and even tease her mildly—a privilege which is reciprocal. Two sets of parents-in-law are of the same generation, usually, and are related only through the marriage of their children.

All these relationships, centering largely about the domestic household, involve the possibility of social conflict, and in the case of the son-in-law the conflict of interests is inevitable. In certain of these relationships, also, there is a social necessity for avoiding or minimizing conflict if the household organization is to function properly. In these cases the conflict situation seems to be solved largely by suppressing the possibility of conflict.

Joking relationships among the Cheyenne and

[1] Tax has suggested, on the basis of Fox material, that psychologically respect may take two forms: (1) a "teacher-student" relationship in which social distance is emphasized and (2) a "shame" relationship between blood-relatives of different sex. Joking represents a release from an emotionally uncertain situation, in part, and involves the psychology of laughter.

[2] (The father is primarily responsible for the training of his son and hence usually exacts more obedience from the son than he does from a daughter; the mother, vice versa.)

Arapaho obtain between more distant relatives in general. Mild joking relationships occur between consanguineal relatives, for the most part, and are not obligatory. Between brothers there is a feeling of equality and an absence of any particular restraint, which results in an attitude of familiarity and which allows mild teasing and joking.[3] Grandparents are in a somewhat similar position, except for the difference in age which introduces an attitude of respect to some extent, but they have no specific duties in regard to the transmission of the social heritage. The father's sister and the mother's brother are in the parental generation, and hence represent authority, but are not directly concerned with the training of their nephews and nieces. On the other hand, their affection for each other manifests itself in their behavior toward each other's children, a father's sister being particularly close to her niece and a mother's brother to his nephew. These relationships involve some conflict in attitudes but no particular conflict in interests. A conflict situation which develops seems to be adjusted by establishing a mild joking relationship which regulates its expression in a socially desirable manner.

These joking relationships take a more extreme form among siblings-in-law, where they become obligatory and involve horseplay, practical jokes, satire, and sexual play. The relationship of siblings-in-law is not affected by differences of generation but is by differences of sex. A man must work in close co-operation with his wife's brother, yet since a husband has control over his wife and a brother over his sister, conflict is almost inevitable. A woman is in a parallel position in regard to her husband's sister; they are supposed to help each other and never show any jealousy in public, but there is a similar rivalry and conflict of interests. A man's relations to his wife's sisters and a woman's relations to her husband's brothers represent apparent exceptions to the general restriction in behavior between members of the opposite sex. But the husband-wife relationship is the one socially recognized exception to the general rule; since sisters are socially equivalent, the wife's sister seems to be brought into the range of the husband-wife relationship and may actually become a second wife, of course. But here, also, there is the possibility of conflict between the husband-wife relationship and the sister-sister relationship. The relationship of a woman to her husband's brother is parallel; she may marry him if her husband dies, but there is a similar possibility of conflict of interests. The behavior of siblings-in-law of the opposite sex centers around obscene jests and sexual play, in addition to ordinary joking.

The relations of siblings-in-law thus involve fundamental conflicts which are inevitable in view of the household organization and the social relations of siblings and spouses. These conflicts must be regulated in some way if the social order is to operate smoothly; respect as a device for suppressing these conflicts is not possible, since there are no generational differences involved and the factor of sex difference is socially nullified, but obligatory joking seems to serve quite well. Essentially it seems to be a device for organizing hostility in socially desirable ways; such relationships not only make an adjustment to an ambivalent situation but create a definite bond between the relatives as well.

Thus respect and joking relationships seem to be a part of a single system of social behavior. We may summarize this brief survey of these relationships among the Cheyenne and Arapaho as follows:

1. *Respect relationship*—where there is some possibility of conflict and the social necessity for avoiding it.
2. *Mild joking relationship*—where there is some possibility of conflict but no particular social necessity for avoiding it.
3. *Avoidance relationship*—where the conflict situation is inevitable, where there is the social necessity of avoiding it, and where generation differences are present.
4. *Obligatory joking relationship*—where the conflict situation is inevitable, where there is the social necessity of avoiding it, but where no differences of generation are involved.

Some insight into the nature of respect and joking relationships may be gained from this

---

[3] There is some slight conflict involved between their "social equivalence" and the actual differences in age which give some authority to the older brother.

survey. They seem to correlated with conflict situations and to represent alternate ways of adjusting social conflicts. Respect seems to be the more fundamental relationship, based as it is on the necessity for transmitting the social heritage and on the differentiation of sex. Where respect is not involved, the relationship tends to be one of equality and familiarity, other things being equal. Conflicts are inevitable in any social system, and each social group must regulate them, either by suppressing them or by organizing them in socially desirable ways. The kinship system deals with the conflicts which arise in the elementary family largely by establishing a relationship of authority and obedience among its members, and also by limiting the possibility of conflict in the sexual sphere. With the enlargement of the elementary family through the marriage of the children (or otherwise) new conflict situations arise for which there has been little preparation on the part of the adult individuals concerned. These new relationships are more complex in that they usually involve indirect relationships by way of a third relative and also involve ambivalent attitudes. New relatives are brought into a new social group in one sense and excluded in another, so that they are in an uncertain social position. Where marriage creates a separate household group, these conflicts, except those between husband and wife, may not cause too great disruption. But when larger households are created by marriage, these conflicts must be regulated if the household is to operate efficiently. In systems of the Cheyenne and Arapaho type the regulation seems to be by establishing a relationship of extreme respect or avoidance, on the one hand, or of obligatory joking, on the other. Which of these is chosen depends on several circumstances: the nature of the situation, the generation and sex differences involved, and the social necessity for a solution. Avoidance relationships usually involve generation and sex differences and a situation in which an immediate solution is essential, but since avoidance operates by eliminating social relations, it is not very satisfactory in terms of the social

structure. Where generation differences are not involved, obligatory joking relationships are likely to be utilized. The latter furnish a standardized way of behaving in socially uncertain situations as well as a release of emotional tensions. Also they establish bonds between such relatives which gradually bind them together. In regard to the relationships between relatives in different households the same factors seem to be involved, but the conflict situations are normally less numerous and less important, and their regulation is less rigid. The importance of the household structure is evident in these various relationships.

The widespread distribution of respect and joking relationships among the Plains tribes indicates that they are important in this area, but except for Lowie's pioneer account of these relationships among the Crow (1912a) there is little comparative material available in the literature. The papers in the present volume will remedy this deficiency to some extent, and the data presented on these relationships among the Kiowa-Apache, the Fox, Cherokee, and Southern Athabaskan groups may be utilized to test and modify the tentative correlations here advanced on the basis of the Cheyenne and Arapaho materials. An adequate classification of these various tribes is essential before comparative studies can take place, however, since the conflict situations vary according to the social structure of the group. There is nothing directly comparable in the Cheyenne and Arapaho system, for example, to the Crow joking relationships between children whose fathers belong to the same clan, since neither tribe emphasizes the lineage principle or has a clan organization. They are comparable in more general terms, however, since this Crow relationship is an example of an indirect relationship through the men of the father's clan who are considered as a unit. When comparative studies between the Plains types have been carried out, the results can be compared with those of other regions, and a more general formulation of respect and joking relationships may then be possible.

ON JOKING RELATIONSHIPS

A. R. Radcliffe-Brown

The publication of Mr. F. J. Pedler's note (1940: 170) on what are called 'joking relationships,' following on two other papers on the same subject by Professor Henri Labouret (1929) and Mademoiselle Denise Paulme (1939), suggests that some general theoretical discussion of the nature of these relationships may be of interest to readers of *Africa*.

What is meant by the term 'joking relationship' is a relation between two persons in which one is by custom permitted, and in some instances required, to tease or make fun of the other, who in turn is required to take no offence. It is important to distinguish two main varieties. In one the relation is symmetrical; each of the two persons teases or makes fun of the other. In the other variety the relation is asymmetrical; A jokes at the expense of B and B accepts the teasing good humouredly but without retaliating; or A teases B as much as he pleases and B in turn teases A only a little. There are many varieties in the form of this relationship in different societies. In some instances the joking or teasing is only verbal, in others it includes horseplay; in some the joking includes elements of obscenity, in others not.

The theory that is here put forward, therefore, is that both the joking relationship which constitutes an alliance between clans or tribes, and that between relatives by marriage, are modes of organising a definite and stable system of social behaviour in which conjunctive and disjunctive components, as I have called them, are maintained and combined.

To provide the full evidence for this theory by following out its implications and examining in detail its application to different instances would take a book rather than a short article. But some confirmation can perhaps be offered by a consideration of the way in which respect and disrespect appear in various kinship relationships, even though nothing more can be attempted than a very brief indication of a few significant points.

In studying a kinship system it is possible to distinguish the different relatives by reference to the kind and degree of respect that is paid to them (c.f. Eggan 1937c). Although kinship systems vary very much in their details there are certain principles which are found to be very widespread. One of them is that by which a person is required to show a marked respect to relatives belonging to the generation immediately preceding his own. In a majority of societies the father is a relative to whom marked respect must be shown. This is so even in many so-called matrilineal societies, i.e. those which are organized into matrilineal clans or lineages. One can very frequently observe a tendency to extend this attitude of respect to all relatives of the first ascending generation and, further, to persons who are not relatives. Thus in those tribes of East Africa that are organised into age-sets a man is required to show special respect to all men of his father's age-set and to their wives.

The social function of this is obvious. The social tradition is handed down from one generation to the next. For the tradition to be maintained it must have authority behind it. The authority is therefore normally recognised as possessed by members of the preceding generation and it is they who exercise discipline. As a result of this the relation between persons of the two generations usually contains an element of inequality, the parents and those of their generation being in a position of superiority over the children who are subordinate to them. The unequal relation between a father and his son is maintained by requiring the latter to show respect to the former. The relation is asymmetrical.

When we turn to the relation of an individual to his grandparents and their brothers and sisters we find that in the majority of human societies

Reprinted by permission of the International African Institute from *Africa*, Vol. XIII:3 (1940), pp. 195–210.

relatives of the second ascending generation are treated with very much less respect than those of the first ascending generation, and instead of a marked inequality there is a tendency to approximate to a friendly equality.

Considerations of space forbid any full discussion of this feature of social structure, which is one of very great importance. There are many instances in which the grandparents and their grandchildren are grouped together in the social structure in opposition to their children and parents. An important clue to the understanding of the subject is the fact that in the flow of social life through time, in which men are born, become mature and die, the grandchildren replace their grandparents.

In many societies there is an actual joking relationship, usually of a relatively mild kind, between relatives of alternate generations. Grandchildren make fun of their grandparents and of those who are called grandfather and grandmother by the classificatory system of terminology, and these reply in kind.

Grandparents and grandchildren are united by kinship; they are separated by age and by the social difference that results from the fact that as the grandchildren are in the process of entering into full participation in the social life of the community the grandparents are gradually retiring from it. Important duties towards his relatives in his own and even more in his parents' generation impose upon an individual many restraints; but with those of the second ascending generation, his grandparents and collateral relatives, there can be, and usually is, established a relationship of simple friendliness relatively free from restraint. In this instance also, it is suggested, the joking relationship is a method of ordering a relation which combines social conjunction and disjunction.

This thesis could, I believe, be strongly supported if not demonstrated by considering the details of these relationships. There is space for only one illustrative point. A very common form of joke in this connection is for the grandchild to pretend that he wishes to marry the grandfather's wife, or that he intends to do so when his grandfather dies, or to treat her as already being his wife. Alternatively the grandfather may pretend that the wife of the grandchild is, or might be, his wife. The point of the joke is the pretence at ignoring the difference of age between the grandparent and grandchild.

In various parts of the world there are societies in which a sister's son teases and otherwise behaves disrespectfully towards his mother's brother. In these instances the joking relationship seems generally to be asymmetrical. For example the nephew may take his uncle's property but not vice versa; or, as amongst the Nama Hottentots, the nephew may take a fine beast from his uncle's herd and the uncle in return takes a wretched beast from that of the nephew.

The kind of social structure in which this custom of privileged disrespect to the mother's brother occurs in its most marked forms, for example the Thonga of South-East Africa, Fiji and Tonga in the Pacific, and the Central Siouan tribes of North America, is characterised by emphasis on patrilineal lineage and a marked distinction between relatives through the father and relatives through the mother.

In a former publication (1924), I offered an interpretation of this custom of privileged familiarity towards the mother's brother. Briefly it is as follows. For the continuance of a social system children require to be cared for and to be trained. Their care demands affectionate and unselfish devotion; their training requires that they shall be subjected to discipline. In the societies with which we are concerned there is something of a division of function between the parents and other relatives on the two sides. The control and discipline are exercised chiefly by the father and his brothers and generally also by his sisters; these are relatives who must be respected and obeyed. It is the mother who is primarily responsible for the affectionate care; the mother and her brothers and sisters are therefore relatives who can be looked to for assistance and indulgence. The mother's brother is called 'male mother' in Tonga and in some South African tribes.

I believe that this interpretation of the special position of the mother's brother in these societies has been confirmed by further field work since I wrote the article referred to. But I was quite aware at the time it was written that the discussion and interpretation needed to be supplemented so as to bring them into line with a general theory of the social functions of respect and disrespect.

The joking relationship with the mother's brother seems to fit well with the general theory of such relationships here outlined. A person's most important duties and rights attach him to his paternal relatives, living and dead. It is to his patrilineal lineage or clan that he belongs. For the members of his mother's lineage he is an outsider, though one in whom they have a very special and tender interest. Thus here again there is a relation in which there is both attachment, or conjunction, and separation, or disjunction, between the two persons concerned.

But let us remember that in this instance the relation is asymmetrical. The nephew is disrespectful and the uncle accepts the disrespect. There is inequality and the nephew is the superior. This is recognised by the natives themselves. Thus in Tonga it is said that the sister's son is a 'chief' (eiki) to his mother's brother, and Junod (1913) quotes a Thonga native as saying 'The uterine nephew is a chief! He takes any liberty he likes with his maternal uncle.' Thus the joking relationship with the uncle does not merely annul the usual relation between the two generations, it reverses it. But while the superiority of the father and the father's sister is exhibited in the repect that is shown to them, the nephew's superiority to his mother's brother takes the opposite form of permitted disrespect.

It has been mentioned that there is a widespread tendency to feel that a man should show respect towards, and treat as social superiors, his relatives in the generation preceding his own, and the custom of joking with, and at the expense of, the maternal uncle clearly conflicts with this tendency. This conflict between principles of behaviour helps us to understand what seems at first sight a very extraordinary feature of the kinship terminology of the Thonga tribe and the VaNdau tribe in South-East Africa. Amongst the Thonga, although there is a term malume (-male mother) for the mother's brother, this relative is also, and

perhaps more frequently, referred to as grandfather (kokwana) and he refers to his sister's son as his grandchild (ntukulu). In the VaNdau tribe the mother's brother and also the mother's brother's son are called 'grandfather' (tetekulu, literally 'great father') and their wives are called 'grandmother' (mbiya), while the sister's son and the father's sister's son are called 'grandchild' (muzukulu).

This apparently fantastic way of classifying relatives can be interpreted as a sort of legal fiction whereby the male relatives of the mother's lineage are grouped together as all standing towards an individual in the same general relation. Since this relation is one of privileged familiarity on the one side, and solicitude and indulgence on the other, it is conceived as being basically the one appropriate for a grandchild and a grandfather. This is indeed in the majority of human societies the relationship in which this pattern of behaviour most frequently occurs. By this legal fiction the mother's brother ceases to belong to the first ascending generation, of which it is felt that the members ought to be respected.

It may be worth while to justify this interpretation by considering another of the legal fictions of the VaNdau terminology. In all these southeastern Bantu tribes both the father's sister and the sister, particularly the elder sister, are persons who must be treated with great respect. They are also both of them members of a man's own patrilineal lineage. Amongst the VaNdau the father's sister is called 'female father' (tetadji) and so also is the sister. Thus by the fiction of terminological classification the sister is placed in the father's generation, the one that appropriately includes persons to whom one must exhibit marked respect.

In the southeastern Bantu tribes there is assimilation of two kinds of joking relatives, the grandfather and the mother's brother. It may help our understanding of this to consider an example in which the grandfather and the brother-in-law are similarly grouped together. The Cherokee Indians of North America, probably numbering at one time about 20,000, were divided into seven matrilineal clans. A man could not marry a woman of his own clan or of his father's clan. Common membership of the same clan connects him with his brothers and his mother's brothers. Towards his father and all his relatives in his father's clan of his own or his father's generation he is required by custom to show a marked respect. He applies the kinship term for 'father' not only to his father's brothers but also to the sons of his father's sisters. Here is another example of the same kind of fiction as described above; the relatives of his own generation whom he is required to respect and who belong to his father's matrilineal lineage are spoken of as though they belonged to the generation of his parents. The body of his immediate kindred is included in these two clans, that of his mother and his father. To the other clans of the tribe he is in a sense an outsider. But with two of them he is connected, namely the clans of his two grandfathers, his father's father and his mother's father. He speaks of all the members of these two clans, of whatever age, as 'grandfathers' and 'grandmothers'. He stands in a joking relationship with all of them. When a man marries he must respect his wife's parents but jokes with her brothers and sisters.

The interesting and critical feature is that it is regarded as particularly appropriate that a man should marry a woman whom he calls 'grandmother,' i.e. a member of his father's father's clan or his mother's father's clan. If this happens his wife's brothers and sisters, whom he continues to tease, are amongst those whom he has previously teased as his 'grandfathers' and 'grandmothers.' This is analogous to the widely spread organisation in which a man has a joking relationship with the children of his mother's brother and is expected to marry one of the daughters.

It ought perhaps to be mentioned that the Cherokee also have a one-sided joking relationship in which a man teases his father's sister's husband. The same custom is found in Mota of the Bank Islands. In both instances we have a society organised on a matrilineal basis in which the mother's brother is respected, the father's sister's son is called 'father' (so that the father's sister's husband is the father of a 'father'), and there is a special term for the father's sister's husband. Further observation of the societies in which this custom occurs is required before we can be sure of its interpretation. I do not remember that it has been reported from any part of Africa.

What has been attempted in this paper is to define in the most general and abstract terms the kind of structural situation in which we may expect to find well-marked joking relationships. We have been dealing with societies in which the basic social structure is provided by kinship. By reason of his birth or adoption into a certain position in the social structure the individual is connected with a large number of other persons. With some of them he finds himself in a definite and specific jural relation, i.e. one which can be defined in terms of rights and duties. Who these persons will be and what will be the rights and duties depended on the form taken by the social structure. As an example of such a specific jural relation we may take that which normally exists between a father and son, or an elder brother and a younger brother. Relations of the same general type may be extended over a considerable range to all the members of a lineage or a clan or an age-set. Besides these specific jural relations which are defined not only negatively but also positively, i.e. in terms of things that must be done as well as things that must not, there are general jural relations which are expressed almost entirely in terms of prohibitions and which extend throughout the whole political society. It is forbidden to kill or wound other persons or to take or destroy their property. Besides these two classes of social relations there is another, including many very diverse varieties, which can perhaps be called relations of alliance or consociation. For example, there is a form of alliance of very great importance in many societies, in which two persons or two groups are connected by an exchange of gifts or services (see Mauss 1925:30–186; 1954). Another example is provided by the institution of blood-brotherhood which is so widespread in Africa.

The argument of this paper has been intended to show that the joking relationship is one special form of alliance in this sense. An alliance by exchange of goods and services may be associated with a joking relationship, as in the instance recorded by Professor Labouret. Or it may be comoined with the custom of avoidance. Thus in the Andaman Islands the parents of a man and the parents of his wife avoid all contact with each other and do not speak; at the same time it is the custom that they should frequently exchange through the medium of the younger married couple. But the exchange of gifts may also exist without either joking or avoidance, as in Samoa, in the exchange of gifts between the family of a man and the family of the woman he marries or the very similar exchange between a chief and his 'talking chief.'

So also in an alliance by blood-brotherhood there may be a joking relationship as amongst the Zande; and in the somewhat similar alliance formed by exchange of names there may also be mutual teasing. But in alliances of this kind there may be a relation of extreme respect and even of avoidance. Thus in the Yaralde and neighbouring tribes of South Australia two boys belonging to communities distant from one another, and therefore more or less hostile, are brought into an alliance by the exchange of their respective umbilical cords. The relationship thus established is a sacred one; the two boys may never speak to one another. But when they grow up they enter upon a regular exchange of gifts, which provides the machinery for a sort of commerce between the two groups to which they belong.

Thus the four modes of alliance or consociation, (1) through intermarriage, (2) by exchange of goods or services, (3) by blood-brotherhood or exchanges of names or sacra, and (4) by the joking relationship, may exist separately or combined in several different ways. The comparative study of these combinations presents a number of interesting but complex problems. The facts recorded from West Africa by Professor Labouret and Mademoiselle Paulme affords us valuable material. But a good deal more intensive field research is needed before these problems of social structure can be satisfactorily dealt with.

What I have called relations by alliance need to be compared with true contractual relations. The latter are specific jural relations entered into by two persons or two groups, in which either party has definite positive obligations towards the other, and failure to carry out the obligations is subject to a legal sanction. In an alliance by blood-brotherhood there are general obligations of mutual aid, and the sanction for the carrying out of these, as shown by Dr. Evans-Pritchard, is of a kind that can be called magical or ritual. In the alliance by exchange of gifts failure to fulfil the obligation to make an equivalent return for a gift received breaks the alliance and substitutes a state of hostility and may also cause a loss of prestige for the defaulting party. Professor Mauss has argued that in this kind of alliance also there is a magical sanction, but it is very doubtful if such is always present, and even when it is it may often be of secondary importance.

The joking relationship is in some ways the exact opposite of a contractual relation. Instead of specific duties to be fulfilled there is privileged disrespect and freedom or even licence, and the only obligation is not to take offence at the disrespect so long as it is kept within certain bounds defined by custom, and not to go beyond those bounds. Any default in the relationship is like a breach of the rules of etiquette; the person concerned is regarded as not knowing how to behave himself.

In a true contractual relationship the two parties are conjoined by a definite common interest in reference to which each of them accepts specific obligations. It makes no difference that in other matters their interests may be divergent. In the joking relationship and in some avoidance relationships, such as that between a man and his wife's mother, one basic determinant is that the social structure separates them in such a way as to make many of their interests divergent, so that conflict or hostility might result. The alliance by extreme respect, by partial or complete avoidance, prevents such conflict but keeps the parties conjoined. The alliance by joking does the same thing in a different way.

All that has been, or could be, attempted in this paper is to show the place of the joking relationship in a general comparative study of social structure. What I have called, provisionally, relations of consociation or alliance are distinguished from the relations set up by common membership of a political society which are defined in terms of general obligations, of etiquette, or morals, or of law. They are distinguished also from true contractual relations, defined by some specific obligation for each contracting party, into which the individual enters of his own volition. They are further to be distinguished from the relations set up by common membership of a domestic group, a lineage or a clan, each of which has to be defined in terms of a whole set of socially recognised rights and duties. Relations of consociation can only exist between individuals or groups which are in some way socially separated.

This paper deals only with formalised or standardised joking relations. Teasing or making fun of other persons is of course a common mode of behaviour in any human society. It tends to occur in certain kinds of social situations. Thus I have observed in certain classes in English-speaking countries the occurrence of horse-play between young men and women as preliminary to courtship, very similar to the way in which a Cherokee Indian jokes with his 'grandmothers.' Certainly these unformalised modes of behaviour need to be studied by the sociologist. For the purpose of this paper it is sufficient to note that teasing is always a compound of friendliness and antagonism.

The scientific explanation of the institution in the particular form in which it occurs in a given society can only be reached by an intensive study which enables us to see it as a particular example of a widespread phenomenon of a definite class. This means that the whole social structure has to be thoroughly examined in order that the particular form and incidence of joking relationships can be understood as part of a consistent system. If it be asked why that society has the structure that it does have, the only possible answer would lie in its history. When the history is unrecorded, as it is for the native societies of Africa, we can only indulge in conjecture, and conjecture gives us neither scientific nor historical knowledge.

SELECTED READINGS

A. Commentaries and Critiques

Berliner, Joseph S.
1962 The feet of the natives are large. *Current Anthropology*, 3:1:47–77.

Evans-Pritchard, Edward E.
1951a *Social anthropology*. London: Cohen & West, chs. IV, V.

Harris, Marvin
1968 *The rise of anthropological theory: A history of theories of culture*. New York: Crowell, pp. 541–545.

Homans, George C.
1965 Anxiety and ritual: The theories of Malinowski and Radcliffe-Brown. In W. Lessa and E. Vogt (eds.), *Reader in comparative religion*. (2nd edit.) New York: Harper & Row, pp. 123–138.

Lowie, Robert H.
1936 Introduction to *A black civilization* by W. L. Warner. New York: Harper & Row, 1937, pp. xiii–xvi.

Malinowski, Bronislaw
1932b Introduction to *The sorcerers of Dobu* by R. F. Fortune. New York: Dutton. Dutton Paperback edition, 1963, pp. xv–xxxii.
—— 1936 Preface to *We, the Tikopia* by R. Firth. New York: G. Allen & Unwin. Boston: Beacon, 1963, pp. vii–xi (abridged edit.).

B. Original Works

Eggan, Fred
1937a The Cheyenne and Arapaho kinship system. In F. Eggan (ed.), *Social anthropology of the North American tribes*. Chicago: University of Chicago Press, pp. 35–98.
—— 1937c (ed.) *Social anthropology of the North American tribes*. (1st edit.). Chicago: University of Chicago Press. (2nd edit., 1955).

Firth, Raymond W.
1930 General observations upon the classificatory system of relationships. *Journal of the Royal Anthropological Institute*, 60:266–267.
—— 1936 *We, the Tikopia*. New York: G. Allen & Unwin. Boston: Beacon, 1963.
—— 1959 *Social change in the Tikopia*. London: G. Allen & Unwin.

Fortune, Reo F.
1932a *The Sorcerers of Dobu*. New York: Dutton. Dutton Paperback edition, 1963.

Opler, Morris E.
1937a An outline of Chiracahua Apache social organization. In F. Eggan (ed.), *Social anthropology of the North American tribes*. Chicago: University of Chicago Press, 1937, pp. 173–242.
—— 1937b Apache data concerning the rela-

tions of kinship terminology to social classification. *American Anthropologist,* 39:201–212.

Radcliffe-Brown, Alfred R.
1940c On joking relationships. *Africa,* 13:195–210. Also in A. R. Radcliffe-Brown, *Structure and function in primitive society.* London: Cohen and West, 1952c, pp. 190 ff.

———— 1949 A further note on joking relationships. *Africa,* 19:133–140. A. R. Radcliffe-Brown, *Structure and function in primitive society.* London: Cohen and West, 1952c, pp. 105 ff.

Tax, Sol
1937a Some problems of social organization. In F. Eggan (ed.), *Social anthropology of the North American tribes.* Chicago: University of Chicago Press, pp. 3–34.

———— 1937b The social organization of the Fox Indians. *Ibid.,* 243–284.

Warner, William Lloyd
1937 *A black civilization.* New York: Harper & Row. Harper Torchbook edition, 1964.

IX

STRUCTURE AND FUNCTION: REVIEWS AND THE COMPARATIVE METHOD

The 1940s witnessed the publication of a number of monographs that were based upon field work done in Africa during the 1930s. Most of the authors were students of Malinowski but their structural-functional approaches tended to follow the methods of Radcliffe-Brown. Outstanding were the works of Evans-Pritchard on the Nuer (1940a, 1951b), Nadel on the Nupe (1943), and Fortes on the Tallensi (1945, 1949a). Other structural-functional analyses of very high quality appeared in the anthologies *African Political Systems* (1940) and *African Systems of Kinship and Marriage* (1950).

Each of the authors tended to emphasize certain approaches and particular aspects of their societies, in fact the nature of the societies studied may well have influenced the analysts' approaches. The Nuer with their transhumant annual cycle, expansionist territorial groups, and strongly agnatic kinship ideology led Evans-Pritchard to examine the relationships between social structure and time and between social structure and ecology. The Nupe, a culturally complex political state with a long history, led Nadel to take a more historical approach, to concentrate on the economic and political systems, and to examine the relationship between "culture" and "society." The Tallensi, with a strongly agnatic structure involving ancestor worship and territorial-based kin groups, led Fortes to use a classically Durkheimian approach, concentrating on the segmentary solidarity of the descent groups and an examination of the relationship between descent and other forms of affiliation.

Eggan continued the presentation of his struc-

tural-historical analyses in his publications on the Hopi (1949) and the Western Pueblo groups (1950). He too examined the relationship between social relations, social usages, social structure, and culture. Though the synchronic aspects of his analyses stemmed from Radcliffe-Brown, Eggan continued to operate within his own type of comparative framework—that of closely related cultures within one "type" or area (c.f. Eggan, 1954—see Chapter IX).

At the end of the 1940s, this era had been effectively closed. During the following decade, a number of position and review papers were written concerning the methods and results of the structural-functional approach. Some analytical concepts were clarified or redefined, and Fortes pointed out (1953c) the contributions of British anthropologists—like himself—who had studied unilineal descent systems in great detail using a comparative approach. He claimed that though the efforts of British anthropologists seemed narrow by comparison with those of the Americans, the concentration and depth of analysis had led to fruitful understandings and generalizations on particular topics such as descent systems.

The various methods of comparative sociological analyses were also reexamined at this time. These methods had been espoused by older writers such as Comte, Morgan, Tylor, Durkheim, and Rivers and had been stressed and redefined by Radcliffe-Brown and, to an extent, Boas. Murdock (1947; *Social Structure,* 1949) used sophisticated statistical methods to test old and new anthropological generalizations against a vast body of data gathered from more than 250 of the world's societies. Though impressive, some criticisms were levelled at the quality and representativeness of his data (See Ackerknecht, 1954; Leach, 1950; Schapera, 1953; Spoehr, 1950).

Radcliffe-Brown continued to urge world-wide comparisons and classifications (1951). Eggan suggested, in 1954, that narrower but better controlled comparisons could be more fruitful considering the extreme complexity of anthropological data. His many works bore out the success of his methods. Evans-Pritchard (1951a), emphasizing the inability of any one man to know more than a very few societies, opted for penetrating insights or very limited comparisons. He later (*The Comparative Method in Social Anthropology*, 1963), became doubtful that any kind of comparison could be useful as a method of producing universal generalizations or predictions. Tending to the historical view, he emphasized the extreme complexity and relative arbitrariness of all human behavior.

STATISTICAL COMPARISONS OF KINSHIP SYSTEMS

George Peter Murdock

A person's consanguineal relatives are either lineal or collateral. Lineal relatives are those who lie in a direct line of descent, such as grandparents, parents, children, and grandchildren. Collateral relatives are those lying outside the direct line of descent, e.g., uncles, aunts, cousins, nephews, and nieces. Collateral relatives of an equivalent degree of relationship may be related to Ego either through a male connecting relative or through a female relative. They are, in short, "bifurcated" by the sex of the intervening relative. Some kinship systems distinguish in terminology between two kinsmen if one is related to Ego through a woman and the other through a man, whereas others make no such distinctions. The combinations of these alternatives yield four possible types of kinship terminology, to which Lowie (1928) has given the convenient names of "bifurcate collateral," "bifurcate merging," "lineal," and "generation."

Recognition of both collaterality and bifurcation produces bifurcate collateral terminology, in which collateral relatives like uncle and aunt are distinguished not only from lineal relatives like father and mother but also from one another on the basis of the sex of the connecting relatives. The father, the father's brother, and the mother's brother, for example, would be called by three distinct terms. Similar differentiation would also prevail for the following trios, Mo, MoSi, FaSi; So, BrSo, SiSo; Da, BrDa, SiDa. By extension, terminological distinctions would be made between Si, FaBrDa, and FaSiDa, and between Si, MoSiDa, and MoBrDa. The recognition of bifurcation but not of collaterality produces bifurcate merging terminology, in which FaSi, MoBr, SiSo, and SiDa are called by distinct terms, whereas MoSi is terminologically equated with Mo, FaBr with Fa, BrSo with So, and BrDa with Da. The recognition of collaterality but not of bifurcation results in lineal terminology, as in our own kinship system, paternal and maternal uncles being called by the same terms, which differ from those for father and mother, while nephews and nieces are similarly classed together and differentiated from sons and daughters. Finally, the nonrecognition of both collaterality and bifurcation produces generation terminology, in which the terms for father, mother, son, and daughter are extended respectively to all uncles, aunts, nephews and nieces, and even to remoter relatives of the same generation.

All four types of kinship terminology occur widespread over the earth, and specialists have

Reproduced by permission of the American Anthropological Association from "Bifurcate Merging: A Test of Five Theories," *American Anthropologist*, Vol. 49, 1947, pp. 56–63.

sought to account for them in different ways. Bifurcate merging has been particularly productive of speculation. Five distinct hypotheses have been advanced to account for this phenomenon, each propounded by an anthropologist of outstanding reputation, to wit: W. H. R. Rivers, R. H. Lowie, A. L. Kroeber, E. Sapir, and A. R. Radcliffe-Brown. In the past it has often proved difficult, if not impossible, to make a definite decision as between alternative scientific theories in anthropology, especially when none seems obviously to contravene the distributional evidence. As a consequence, each author clings to the hypothesis for which he feels a personal preference, and anthropological science makes no advance. It so happens, however, that the present writer is able to subject the five theories on bifurcate merging to a quantitative test on the basis of a current study. The results, presented below, indicate that the several theories have markedly different claims to reliability.

The test consists of a statistical analysis of the data on social organization and kinship from 221 societies, distributed as follows: 62 from Africa, 28 from Eurasia, 66 from North America, 50 from Oceania, and 15 from South America. The tribes are listed, with a tabulation of the pertinent data, at the end of this paper. They were selected, as nearly as possible, to give equal representation to all continents, culture areas, and sub-areas, but the lack of adequate sources prevented perfect sampling, especially in South America and Eurasia. A few peoples with complex cultures are included, e.g., the Chinese, Manchus, Syrian Christians, and Yankees. Unfortunately the test is confined to male-speaking terms for female relatives, since only these were gathered for the study.

The earliest theory is that of Rivers (1914a: 72–3) who attributed bifurcate merging to the influence of moieties. Moieties include in the same social group a lineal kinsman and his sibling of the same sex, and segregate in different groups collateral relatives related to Ego through connecting relatives of different sex. This social classification and differentiation, it is alleged, should tend to produce a corresponding effect on kinship terminology, and thus result in the phenomenon of bifurcate merging. An analysis of

the kinship terms for Mo, MoSi, and FaSi, and for Da, BrDa, and SiDa from our 221 societies according to the presence or absence of moieties yields the following [Table 1] results:

Table 1.

TYPE OF KINSHIP TERMINOLOGY	Mo-MoSi-FaSi		Da-BrDa-SiDa	
	Moieties Present	Moieties Absent	Moieties Present	Moieties Absent
Bifurcate merging	24	59	25	79
Bifurcate collateral	8	63	7	41
Lineal	3	29	1	18
Generation	1	21	2	19

These figures show a definite tendency for bifurcate merging to be associated with moieties, for other types of kinship terminology to be associated with the absence of moieties. This tendency can be expressed statistically by coefficients of association, which are calculated as +.59 and +.41 for aunt and niece terms respectively.

An additional test of this hypothesis can be made with terms for cousins. Bifurcate merging would equate parallel cousins with siblings and distinguish cross cousins by special terms. The data are analyzed below [Table 2] for two series: Si, MoSiDa, and MoBrDa; Si, FaBrDa, and FaSiDa:

Table 2.

TYPE OF KINSHIP TERMINOLOGY	Si-MoSiDa-MoBrDa		Si-FaBrDa-FaSiDa	
	Moieties Present	Moieties Absent	Moieties Present	Moieties Absent
Bifurcate merging	28	72	29	81
Bifurcate collateral	2	23	5	16
Lineal	2	53	2	52
Generation	4	21	2	21

The coefficients of association for this series are +.65 and +.56 for maternal and paternal cousins respectively.

The theory advanced by Rivers emerges from this statistical test with positive, uniformly high, and unquestionably reliable coefficients of an average value of +.55. It must be accepted as valid. It should be noted, however, that this hypothesis explains the occurrence of bifurcate merging only in tribes possessing moieties, of which there are only 38 in our sample of 221, and that this type of kinship terminology is commoner than any other even among the tribes which lack moieties. The problem remains of accounting for bifurcate merging where there are no moieties. Rivers, of course, assumes that the occurrence of bifurcate merging in the absence of moieties is due to the former existence of moieties in societies that now lack them. This assumption, however, is not supported by such historical evidence as we have, and it is rebutted by strong theoretical considerations which cannot be presented here. We are forced to the conclusion, therefore, that the hypothesis of Rivers explains bifurcate merging in only a minority of societies, and that the high coefficients noted above are merely a consequence of its validity in a considerable number of special cases.

Recognizing the inadequacy of the moiety theory as a general explanation of bifurcate merging, Lowie (1915, 1917a) has sought to supplement it by invoking the influence of exogamy, irrespective of whether the rule of out-marriage applies to moieties or to sibs, lineages, or other social groups in which kinsmen are uni-linearly aggregated. An analysis of the kinship terminology for the same groups of relatives in accordance with this hypothesis yields the following [Table 3] results:

	(Si-MoSiDa-MoBrDa)		(Si-FaBrDa-FaSiDa)	
Bifurcate merging	85	12	95	13
Bifurcate collateral	21	4	16	4
Lineal	16	15	9	15
Generation	17	36	15	37

These figures demonstrate a strong tendency for bifurcate merging to be associated with exogamy and to be lacking in the absence of exogamy. This tendency is statistically expressed by coefficients of association of +.41, +.50, +.73, and +.82 in regard to the terms for aunts, nieces, maternal cousins, and paternal cousins respectively.

From this test one must conclude that Lowie's hypothesis is superior to that of Rivers. In the first place, the coefficients are more strongly positive and even more reliable, averaging nearly +.62 as against +.55 for the moiety theory. In the second place, the hypothesis is applicable to all societies and not merely to a minority. Lowie's theory, therefore must be conceded to represent a definite scientific advance.

Kroeber (1917b: 86–7), like Lowie, accepts the influence of unilinear groupings of kinsmen, but whereas Lowie emphasizes exogamy as the crucial factor, Kroeber believes that unilinear descent itself may suffice to produce bifurcate merging. Our data enable us to discriminate between the two hypotheses. While the great majority of peoples are either unilinear and exogamous at the same time, or else neither, two small groups of tribes provide critical examples, lending support to either hypothesis but not to both. The first is the group which possesses unilinear but non-exogamous sibs or lineages, like the Fox, Tikopia, and Tswana. The second consists of tribes like the Yaghan and Yurok which follow a rule of local exogamy, and by virtue of customary patrilocal residence align in one place a group of patrilineally related men without, however, defining them as constituting a lineage or sib. Kroeber would expect bifurcate merging terminology in the first group of tribes and not in the

Table 3.

TYPE OF KINSHIP TERMINOLOGY	Mo-MoSi-FaSi		Da-BrDa-SiDa	
	Exogamy Present	Exogamy Absent	Exogamy Present	Exogamy Absent
Bifurcate merging	65	17	80	22
Bifurcate collateral	45	27	30	19
Lineal	8	13	7	12
Generation	24	8	9	7

second; Lowie, in the second but not in the first. An analysis of the kinship terminology in accordance with Kroeber's hypothesis yields the following [Table 4] results:

Table 4.

TYPE OF KINSHIP TERMINOLOGY	Mo-MoSi-FaSi		Da-BrDa-SiDa	
	Unilinear Groups	No Unilinear Groups	Unilinear Groups	No Unilinear Groups
Bifurcate merging	73	10	88	15
Bifurcate collateral	49	23	31	19
Lineal	7	14	7	14
Generation	25	7	10	6
	(Si-MoSiDa-MoBrDa)		(Si-FaBrDa-(FaSiDa)	
Bifurcate merging	91	9	100	10
Bifurcate collateral	24	1	19	1
Lineal	17	13	11	13
Generation	18	36	18	35

These figures offer very strong support to Kroeber's theory. The tendency for bifurcate merging to be associated with unilinear kin groups is expressed statistically by coefficients of +.60, +.65, +.79, and +.82 in respect to the terms for aunts, nieces, maternal cousins, and paternal cousins respectively.

The differential effect of the two groups of critical tribes is notably to increase the already strongly positive coefficients from an average of approximately +.62 to an average of nearly +.72. This clearly demonstrates that Kroeber's hypothesis, insofar as it differs from Lowie's is appreciably more satisfactory. It is even preferable to a combination of the two theories, for when tribes that are both unilinear and exogamous are compared with all others the coefficients, while higher than for Lowie's theory, do not attain the level of Kroeber's.

An alternative or supplementary hypothesis has been advanced by Sapir (1916a) and accepted by a number of other anthropologists. According to Sapir, rules of preferential mating, especially the levirate and sororate, may produce an effect similar to that of unilinear kin-groups. The levirate, by bringing the father's brother into the family through marriage with the widowed mother, either actually or potentially, might result in equating him terminologically with the father, while the mother's brother, whom incest taboos would exclude from such a secondary marriage, would be terminologically differentiated. In consequence, the father's brother's children should be equated with siblings and the brother's children with own children, whereas the father's sister's children and the sister's children would be unaffected thereby and thus presumably called by different kinship terms. The sororate, similarly, might operate to equate the mother's sister with the mother and to distinguish the father's sister from both, and indirectly to class MoSiDa with Si and to differentiate MoBrDa from both. Sororal polygyny should have the same effect as the sororate, and fraternal polyandry as the levirate. These various rules of secondary marriage could be expected to have an influence on kinship terminology only when they are customary and preferential, and hence repetitive, and not when they are merely permissive and occur occasionally. Hence in the following tables these usages are classed as absent unless they are definitely stated in the sources to be preferential. The data are analyzed below [Table 5] for the levirate, the sororate, and sororal polygyny in that order:

Table 5.

TYPE OF KINSHIP TERMINOLOGY	Da-BrDa-SiDa		Si-FaBrDa-FaSiDa	
	Levirate Present	Levirate Absent	Levirate Present	Levirate Absent
Bifurcate merging	57	24	60	19
Bifurcate collateral	28	8	11	4
Lineal	8	4	8	9
Generation	5	9	32	13

	Mo-MoSi-FaSi		Si-MoSiDa-MoBrDa	
	Sororate Present	Sororate Absent	Sororate Present	Sororate Absent
Bifurcate merging	29	16	38	16
Bifurcate collateral	31	14	7	7
Lineal	9	4	8	9
Generation	9	11	24	13
	Mo-MoSi-FaSi		Si-MoSiDa-MoBrDa	
	No		No	
	Sororal Polygyny	Sororal Polygyny	Sororal Polygyny	Sororal Polygyny
Bifurcate merging	22	35	22	42
Bifurcate collateral	19	26	1	7
Lineal	3	9	4	17
Generation	4	19	18	21

The coefficients of association are as follows: +.10 for the levirate and bifurcate merging in the case of nieces, +.23 in the case of paternal cousins, +.04 for the sororate in the case of aunts, +.28 in the case of maternal cousins, +.13 for sororal polygyny in the case of aunts, and +.01 in the case of maternal cousins. If the sororate and sororal polygyny are combined, the coefficient for aunts is +.20 or −.05, and that for maternal cousins is +.37 or +.11, the larger figure in each instance being obtained by not counting absences when attested for only the sororate or sororal polygyny, the occurrence of the other being unreported.

The above coefficients range in magnitude from +.37 to −.05, averaging +.14. Even the highest is lower than the lowest coefficient obtained in testing the previous three theories, and the majority are so close to .00, indicating complete absence of any tendency toward association, as to be statistically unreliable, i.e. due possibly to pure chance. One reason why the coefficients have on the average a positive value, however slight, is that some societies with unilinear kin-groups,

notably the Australian tribes with sub-sections, so greatly limit the number of marriageable persons that levirate and sororate usages become practically inevitable. As a general explanation of bifurcate merging, therefore, Sapir's theory must be adjudged unacceptable. It may still, however, retain a modest value as a supplementary theory to account for the occurrence of bifurcate merging in societies which lack unilinear kin-groups, since in these societies sororate and levirate usages tend to be slightly associated with bifurcate merging, the coefficients of association are +.15 for aunts, +.23 for nieces, +.47 for maternal cousins, and +.22 for paternal cousins.

Radcliffe-Brown (1930–1: 429) accepts Sapir's alleged correlation between the levirate and bifurcate merging but refuses to regard the one as the cause and the other as the effect. On the contrary, he asserts, both are derived from a single more basic sociological principle, namely, "the social equivalence of brothers." If this principle is supposed to be universally operative, then we should expect bifurcate merging also to be universal, and since we find in fact that it is out-numbered by other types of kinship terminology the principle is thereby demonstrated to be invalid. If, on the other hand, the principle is supposed to be operative in some societies and inoperative in others, it should produce both levirate and bifurcate merging in the former and both should be lacking in the latter. In other words, the same effects would be expected as are anticipated by Sapir's theory. Since, as has already been demonstrated, these effects do not appear except to a very moderate and statistically unreliable degree, the hypothesis of Radcliffe-Brown must be rejected on the same grounds as that of Sapir.

We are now in a position to summarize the results of our statistical test of the five hypotheses of bifurcate merging. Those advanced by Sapir and Radcliffe-Brown must be rejected as unproven and presumably invalid. The moiety theory of Rivers and the exogamy theory of Lowie both receive strong statistical support and must be regarded as valid within limits. Both take into account at least some of the significant factors. The hypothesis advanced by Kroeber, which attributes bifurcate merging to the presence of unilinear kin-groups, receives appreciably more substantial statistical confirmation than any other. In addition it subsumes the essential factors dealt with by Rivers and Lowie. It is further supported by theoretical considerations which the present author intends to discuss at length in a future publication. In fine, Kroeber's theory survives the acid test of science and must be accepted as valid, at least until some new theory is found to better accord with the facts.[1]

[1] A recheck of the data subsequent of the writing of the article, adding new tribes and making minor corrections, yields similar results but shows less difference in favor of Kroeber's over Lowie's hypothesis.

SOCIAL STRUCTURE AND SOCIAL ORGANIZATION

Raymond Firth

In studying a field of social relations, whether we are using the notions of society, of culture, or of community, we can distinguish their structure, their function, and their organization. These are separable but related aspects. All are necessary for the full consideration of social process. Briefly, by the structural aspect of social relations we mean the principles on which their form depends; by the functional aspect we mean the way in which they serve given ends; by the organizational aspect we mean the directional activity which maintains their form and serves their ends. Each of the critical words here is heavy with implications for our study. So we had better examine each concept in turn.

To the layman the term social structure may sound simple enough. In fact anthropologists and other social scientists—for example, Herbert Spencer—used it for many years without feeling the need to define it. They simply took it as meaning generally the form or morphology of society, and took for granted that everyone would know broadly what the idea meant. They were concerned with substantial propositions rather than formal propositions. When, forty years ago, a pair of economic historians set out to examine the results of the eighteenth-century enclosure of the common fields, they said, "Our business is

From Raymond Firth, *Elements of Social Organization*, Chapter I. (London: C. A. Watts, 1951), pp. 28–36. Reprinted by permission.

with the changes that the enclosures caused in the social structure of England . . ." (J. L. Hammond and Barbara Hammond, *The Village Labourer*, 1911). They assumed that every reader would accept this to mean changes in the form of English society, especially rural society. Their analysis accordingly dealt with such themes as changes in the system of social classes in the village, the conversion of the peasant to a labourer, modifications in his rights to assistance, in his relations to the courts, the magistrates, the parish authorities. When later two other social analysts made what they termed "A Survey of the Social Structure of England and Wales" (A. M. Carr-Saunders and D. Caradog Jones, 1927), using a great deal of statistical material, they also did not give any specific definition of what they meant by social structure. It was merely stated that the aim of the book was to treat contemporary social data from the morphological point of view; to construct a picture of social conditions as a whole; to present a coherent picture of some of the more important aspects of social life in this country so far as they can be illustrated by statistics. It was assumed that what was wanted was classification and assessment of magnitude of social units of the more important types, and demonstration of the relations between them. The analysis began with population units, and went on to examine units of marital association, housing, urbanization, distribution of industrial facilities, of occupations, of national income, of social services; special attention was also given to such important matters as the breadth of the educational ladder.

As against this rather broad use of the term social structure, many social anthropologists and some sociologists have in recent years spent much time in trying to get a more precise idea of its meaning. Their differences of view suggest that any science must have a budget of terms of general application, not too closely defined, and that "structure" may be one of these. On the other hand, they have drawn attention to significant elements in the social process, and in the process of social study itself.

The idea of the structure of society, if it is to be in conformity with the general concept of structure, must fulfil certain conditions. It must be concerned with the ordered relations of parts to a whole, and with the arrangement in which the elements of the social life are linked together. These relations must be regarded as built up one upon another—they are series of varying orders of complexity. They must be of more than purely momentary significance—some factor of constancy or continuity must be involved in them. Current anthropological use of the notion of social structure conforms to this. But there is room for difference of opinion as to what kinds of social relations shall be of main account in describing a social structure, and how much continuity they ought to have before they are included. Some anthropologists have argued that a social structure is the network of all person-to-person relations in a society. But such a definition is too wide. It makes no distinction between the ephemeral and the more enduring elements in social activity, and makes it almost impossible to distinguish the idea of the structure of a society from that of the totality of the society itself. At the opposite extreme is the idea of social structure as comprising only relations between major groups in the society—those with a high degree of persistence. This includes groups such as clans, which persist for many generations, but excludes those such as the simple family, which dissolves from one generation to another. This definition

is too narrow. A different idea of social structure stresses not so much the actual relations between persons or groups as the expected relations, or even the ideal relations. According to these views, what really gives a society its form, and allows its members to carry on their activities, is their expectations, or even their idealized beliefs, of what will be done, or ought to be done, by other members. There is no doubt that for any society to work effectively, and to have what may be called a coherent structure, its members must have some idea of what to expect. Without some pattern of expectations and a scheme of ideas about what they think other people ought to do, they would not be able to order their lives. But to see a social structure in sets of deals and expectations alone is too aloof. The pattern of realizations, the general characteristics of concrete social relations, must also form a part of the structural concept. Moreover, to think of social structure as being comprised only of the ideal patterns of behaviour suggests the covert view that these ideal patterns are the ones of primary importance in the social life, and that actual behaviour of individuals is simply a reflection of standards which are socially set. It is equally important, I think, to stress the way in which the social standards, the ideal patterns, the sets of expectations, tend to be changed, recognizably or imperceptibly, by the acts of individuals in response to other influences, including technological developments.

If we bear in mind that the only way in which we can learn of a person's ideals and expectations is from some aspect of his behaviour—either from what he says or from what he does—the distinction between the norms of action and the norms of expectation to some extent disappears. The concept of social structure is an analytical tool, designed to serve us in understanding how men behave in their social life. The essence of this concept is those social relations which seem to be of critical importance for the behaviour of members of the society, so that if such relations were not in operation, the society could not be said to exist in that form. When the economic historian describes the social structure of eighteenth-century rural England he is concerned, for instance, with relations of different classes of people to the common land and to one another. These were fundamental to the society of the time. As the commonfield system changed to one of private enclosure, consequential changes affected the various classes. The small farmer and the cottager, for example, emigrated to an industrial town or became day labourers. The relations of the new type of labourer with his employer and with local authorities, how that he was deprived of land and many other rights to minor income, were very different from before. The social structure of the country had radically altered—though the ideals of many people were still much as before, and even some of their earlier expectations lingered on.

In the types of society ordinarily studied by anthropologists, the social structure may include critical or basic relationships arising similarly from a class system based on relations with the soil. Other aspects of the social structure arise through membership of other kinds of persistent groups, such as clans, castes, age-sets, or secret societies. Other basic relations again are due to position in a kinship system, status in regard to a political superior, or distribution of ritual knowledge. In many African or Oceanic societies an important structural element is the special relation between a mother's brother and a sister's child. The senior has obligations to protect the junior, to make him or her gifts, to help in sickness or misfortune. So important is the relationship that where a person has no true mother's brother he is provided socially with a "stand-in." This will be a son of the dead mother's brother, or some more distant kinsman who will act as representative of the mother's brother, take on the kinship term, and behave appropriately. Such a relation, then, is one of the cardinal elements of the social structure. If, through external influence on the society, the role of the mother's brother becomes less marked, and the duties cease to be performed, then the structure of the society has altered. Different social structures are contrasted in terms of the differences in such critical or basic relations. For example, among some Malays, in the matrilineal communities of Negri Sembilan, the mother's brother has the role just described. But among other Malays elsewhere in the Malay peninsula this relative has no special importance. On the other hand, in accordance with Muslim law, all Malays attach great importance to what is termed a *wali*. This is the guardian of a young woman for certain legal purposes, including marriage. The *wali* represents her in the marriage contract, and must give his consent to the union. Usually it is the girl's father who is the guardian. But if he be dead, then the grandfather, brother, or other nearest kinsman of the girl, according to rules laid down in the Muslim books of the law, takes his place. In some circumstances the duties and powers of guardians go so far as to allow a guardian in the ascending male line the titular right to dispose of a maiden's hand without her consent. The *wali* relation is therefore a major element in the structure of a Muslim society. In comparing different Malay and Muslim social structures as such, then, the difference between the role of the mother's brother and that of the *wali* is a useful structural feature.

This discussion of the notion of social structure has taken us some way towards understanding the kinds of questions with which some anthropologists are concerned in trying to grasp the bases of human social relations. It also helps to clarify two other concepts, social function and social organization, which are as important as that of social structure.

Every social action can be thought of as having one or more social functions. Social function can be defined as the relation between a social action and the system of which the action is a part, or, alternatively, as the result of the social action in terms of the means-ends scheme of all those affected by it.[1] By Malinowski the idea of function was extended into a major scheme of analysis of social and cultural material. The basic emphasis in this scheme has influenced modern

[1] See A. R. Radcliffe-Brown, "On the Concept of Function in Social Science," *American Anthropologist*, 1935, vol. 37, pp. 394–402; B. Malinowski, *A Scientific Theory of Culture*, Chapel Hill, 1944, p. 53. Illuminating treatment of the general theme is given by Talcott Parsons, *Essays in Sociological Theory: Pure and Applied*, Glencoe, Illinois, 1949, passim. (A)

social anthropology considerably. It stresses the relation of any social or cultural item to other social or cultural items. No social action, no element of culture, can be adequately studied or defined in isolation. Their meaning is given by their function, the part they play in an interacting system. In studying the grosser units, the more abstract sets of behaviour patterns known as institutions—such as marriage system, a family type, a type of ceremonial exchange, a system of magic—the scheme distinguishes various associated components. The charter is the set of traditionally established values and principles which the people concerned regard as the basis of the institution—it may even be embodied in a mythical tale. The norms are the rules which govern the conduct of the people; and these must be distinguished from their activities, which may diverge from the norms according as their own individual interests pull them. The institution is carried on by means of a material apparatus, the nature of which is to be understood only by consideration of the uses to which it is put, and by a personnel, arranged in the appropriate social groups. Finally, there is the function or set of functions to which the institution as a whole corresponds. By function in this sense Malinowski meant the satisfaction of needs, including those developed by man as a member of a specific society as well as the more directly biologically based needs.

This imputation of needs to human social behaviour raises some difficult questions. Needs can be fairly easily recognized in the sense of those proximate ends giving immediate direction to an activity and normally envisaged by the participants themselves. The proximate ends of a feast, for instance, clearly include the aim of consuming food, and this in itself involves certain social and economic consequences. But it is less easy to identify and separate ultimate ends —those which give basic significance to the activity as part of the total pattern of the social life. The ultimate end of a feast is not the satisfaction of hunger, which could be done much more simply. Is it a form of sociability, the pleasure in assembly and excitation through company? Or is it in the exchange system of

which a single feast is only one item? Or is it in the status-display and personal enhancement for which the feast gives opportunity? Or is it a form of mystic compulsion, by which periodic assembly is necessary to the integration of the social body? The more abstract the conception of needs, the greater is what may be called the personal refraction of the student—the conditioning of the social image by his own views of purpose in social life. At a certain point in the analysis, indeed, it becomes difficult to do more than infer the human needs from the behaviour that is being studied—men act socially in such and such ways, therefore we judge from this consistent behaviour that some social need is met. For reasons such as these, many modern social anthropologists, while drawing much from Malinowski, have found it preferable to approach the classification of types of social action through study of the structural aspects of behaviour. Elements which can be isolated by reference to their form, their continuity of relation, are more easily classed.

But any attempt at describing the structure of a society must embody some assumptions about what is most relevant in social relations. These assumptions, implicitly or openly, must use some concepts of a functional kind, by reference to the results or effects of social action. This also includes some attention to the aims or directional quality of the actions. Take the exogamy associated with a lineage structure. The exogamous rule requiring that a lineage member shall not marry anyone who is a member of the same lineage is said to be one of the defining characteristics of that structural unit: it helps to mark off lineage members as a body. But for this statement to be true it is assumed necessarily that prohibition of marriage has some effect upon actual marital attitudes; that this effect is considerable; and that there are also positive effects on non-marital behavior. The translation of "forbidden to marry" into "reinforcement of lineage ties" may be justified, but only after consideration of effects. From this point of view one may use a term of A. N. Whitehead's, and say that the function of a social action or relation is the "concern" which the action or relation has for all other elements in the social system in which it appears. Even minimally, their orientations are affected by its presence. As it tends to exhibit variation, so also do they tend to vary within the total sphere of social activity.

The study of social structure needs, then, to be carried farther, to examine how the forms of basic social relations are capable of variation. It is necessary to study social adaptation as well as social continuity. A structural analysis alone cannot interpret social change. A social taxonomy could become as arid as classification of species in some branches of biology. Analysis of the organizational aspect of social action is the necessary complement to analysis of the structural aspect. It helps to give a more dynamic treatment.

Social organization has usually been taken as a synonym for social structure. In my view it is time to distinguish between them. The more one thinks of the structure of a society in abstract terms, as a group of relations or of ideal patterns, the more necessary it is to think separately of social organization in terms of concrete activity. Generally, the idea of organization is that of people getting things done by planned action. This is a social process, the arrangement of action in sequences in conformity with selected social ends. These ends must have some elements of common significance for the set of persons concerned in the action. The significance need not be identical, or even similar, for all the persons; it may be opposed as between some of them. The process of social organization may consist in part in the resolution of such opposition by action which allows one or other element to come to final expression. Social organization implies some degree of unification, a putting together of diverse elements into common relation. To do this, advantage may be taken of existing structural principles, or variant procedures may be adopted. This involves the exercise of choice, the making of decisions. As such, this rests on personal evaluations, which are the translation of general ends or values of group range into terms which are significant for the individual. In the sense that all organization involves allocation of resources, it implies within the scheme of value judgments a concept of efficiency. This infers a notion of the relative contributions which means of different amount and quality can make to given ends. The sphere of allocation of resources is one in which economic studies are pre-eminent. (See Chapter IV.) But of necessity economics has been restricted primarily to the field of exchange relations, especially those which are measurable in monetary terms. In the social field beyond this the processes resulting from the possibilities of choice and the exercise of decision are also of major importance.

THE STRUCTURE OF UNILINEAL DESCENT GROUPS

Meyer Fortes

The most important feature of unilineal descent groups in Africa brought into focus by recent field research is their corporate organization. When we speak of these groups as corporate units we do so in the sense given to the term "corporation" long ago by Maine in his classical

Reproduced by permission of the author and the American Anthropological Association from *American Anthropologist*, Vol. 55, 1953, pp. 25–39.

analysis of testamentary succession in early law (Maine, 1861). We are reminded also of Max Weber's sociological analysis of the corporate group as a general type of social formation (Weber, 1947), for in many important particulars these African descent groups conform to Weber's definition. British anthropologists now regularly use the term *lineage* for these descent groups. This helps both to stress the significance of descent in their structure and to distinguish them from wider often dispersed divisions of society ordered to the notion of common—but not demonstrable and often mythological—ancestry for which we find it useful to reserve the label *clan*.

The guiding ideas in the analysis of African lineage organization have come mainly from Radcliffe-Brown's formulation of the structural principles found in all kinship systems (cf. Radcliffe-Brown, 1950). I am sure I am not alone in regarding these as among the most important generalizations as yet reached in the study of social structure. Lineage organization shows very clearly how these principles work together in mutual dependence, so that varying weight of one or the other in relation to variations in the wider context of social structure gives rise to variant arrangements on the basis of the same broad ground-plan.

A lineage is a corporate group from the outside, that is in relation to other defined groups and associations. It might be described as a single legal personality—"one person" as the Ashanti put it (Fortes, 1950). Thus the way a lineage system works depends on the kind of legal institutions found in the society; and this, we know, is a function of its political organization. Much fruitful work has resulted from following up this line of thought. As far as Africa is concerned there is increasing evidence to suggest that lineage organization is most developed in what Evans-Pritchard and I (1940), taking a hint from Durkheim, called segmentary societies. This has been found to hole for the Tiv of Nigeria (P. J. Bohannan, 1951), for Guisii (Mayer, 1949) and other East and South African peoples, and for the Cyrenaican Beduin (Peters, 1951), in addition to the peoples discussed in *African Political Systems*. In societies of this type the lineage is not only a corporate unit in the legal or jural sense but is also the primary political association. Thus the individual has no legal or political status except as a member of a lineage; or to put it another way, all legal and political relations in the society take place in the context of the lineage system.

But lineage grouping is not restricted to seg-mentary societies. It is the basis of local organization and of political institutions also in societies like the Ashanti (Fortes, 1950; Busia, 1951) and the Yoruba (Forde, 1951b) which have national government centered in kingship, administrative machinery and courts of law. But the primary emphasis, in these societies, is on the legal aspects of the lineage. The political structure of these societies was always unstable and this was due in considerable degree to internal rivalries arising out of the divisions between lineages; that is perhaps why they remained federal in constitution. In Ashanti, for instance, this is epitomized by the fact that citizenship is, in the first place, local not national, is determined by lineage membership by birth and is mediated through the lineage organization. The more centralized the political system the greater the tendency seems to be for the corporate strength of descent groups to be reduced or for such corporate groups to be nonexistent. Legal and political status are conferred by allegiance to the State not by descent, though rank and property may still be vested in descent lines. The Nupe (Nadel, 1943), and Zulu (Gluckman in Fortes and Evans-Pritchard, 1940), and Hausa (Dry, 1950), and other state organizations exemplify this in different ways. There is, in these societies, a clearer structural differentiation between the field of domestic relations based on kinship and descent and the field of political relations, than in segmentary societies.

However, where the lineage is found as a corporate group all the members of a lineage are to outsiders jurally equal and represent the lineage when they exercise legal and political rights and duties in relation to society at large. This is what underlies so-called collective responsibility in blood vengeance and self-help as among the Nuer (Evans-Pritchard, 1940a and b) and the Beduin (Peters, 1951).

Maine's aphorism that corporations never die draws attention to an important characteristic of the lineage, its continuity, or rather its presumed perpetuity in time. Where the lineage concept is highly developed, the lineage is thought to exist as a perpetual corporation as long as any of its members survive. This means, of course, not merely perpetual physical existence ensured by the replacement of departed members. It means perpetual structural existence, in a stable and homogeneous society; that is, the perpetual exercise of defined rights, duties, office and social tasks vested in the lineage as a corporate unit. The point is obvious but needs recalling as it throws light on a widespread custom. We often find, in Africa and elsewhere, that a person or descent group is attached to a patrilineal lineage through a female member of the lineage. Then if there is a danger that rights and offices vested in the lineage may lapse through the extinction of the true line of descent, the attached line may be some jural fiction permitted to assume them. Or again, rather than let property go to another lineage by default of proper succession within the owning lineage, a slave may be allowed to succeed. In short, the aim is to preserve the existing scheme of social relations as far as possible. As I shall mention presently, this idea is developed most explicit among some Central African peoples.

But what marks a lineage out and maintains its identity in the face of the continuous replacement by death and birth of its members is the fact that it emerges most precisely in a complementary relationship with or in opposition to like units. This was first precisely shown for the Nuer by Evans-Pritchard, and I was able to confirm the analysis among the Tallensi (Fortes, 1949a). It is characteristic of all segmentary societies in Africa so far described, almost by definition. A recent and most interesting case is that of the Tiv in Northern Nigeria, (P. J. Bohannon, 1951). This people were, until the arrival of the British, extending their territory rapidly by moving forward *en masse* as their land became exhausted. Among them the maximal lineages are identified by their relative *positions* in the total deployment of all the lineages and they maintain these positions by pushing against one another as they all move slowly forward.

The presumed perpetuity of the lineage is what lineage genealogies conceptualize. If there is one thing all recent investigations are agreed upon it is that lineage genealogies are not historically accurate. But they can be understood if they are seen to be the conceptualization of the existing lineage structure viewed as continuing through time and therefore projected backward as pseudo-history. The most striking proof of this comes from Cyrenaica. The Beduin there have tribal genealogies going back no more than the fourteen generations or thereabouts which we so commonly find among African Negro peoples; but as Peters points out, historical records show that they have lived in Cyrenaica apparently in much the same way as now for a much longer time than the four to five hundred years implied in their genealogies. Dr. P. J. and Dr. L. Bohannan have actually observed the Tiv at public moots rearranging their lineage genealogies to bring them into line with changes in the existing pattern of legal and political relations within and between lineages. A genealogy is, in fact, what Malinowski called a legal charter and not an historical record.

A society made up of corporate lineages is in danger of splitting into rival lineage factions. How is this counteracted in the interests of wider political unity? One way is to extend the lineage framework to the widest range within which sanctions exist for preventing conflicts and disputes from ending in feud or warfare. The political unit is thought of then as the most inclusive, or maximal, lineage to which a person can belong, and it may be conceptualized as embracing the whole tribal unit. This happens among the Gusii (Mayer, 1949) as well as among the Nuer, the Tiv and the Beduin; but with the last three the tribe is not the widest field within which sanctions against feud and war prevail. A major lineage segment of the tribe is the *de facto* political unit by this definition.

Another way, widespread in West Africa but often associated with the previously mentioned structural arrangement, is for the common in terest of the political community to be asserted periodically, as against the private interests of the component lineages, through religious institutions and sanctions. I found this to be the case among the Tallensi (Fortes, 1940) and the same principle applies to the Yakö (Forde 1950 (c)) and the Ibo (Forde and Jones, 1950). I believe it will be shown to hold for many peoples of the

Western Sudan among whom ancestor worship and the veneration of the earth are the basis of religious custom. The politically integrative functions of ritual institutions have been described for many parts of the world. What recent African ethnology adds is detailed descriptive data from which further insight into symbolism used and into the reasons why political authority tends to be invested with ritual meaning and expression can be gained. A notable instance is Dr. Kuper's (1947) account of the Swazi kingship.

As the Swazi data indicate, ritual institutions are also used to support political authority and to affirm the highest common interests in African societies with more complex political structures than those of segmentary societies. This has long been known, ever since the Divine Kingship of the Shilluk (cf. Evans-Pritchard, 1948) brought inspiration to Sir James Frazer. But these ritual institutions do not free the individual to have friendly and co-operative relations with other individuals irrespective of allegiance to corporate groups. If such relations were impossible in a society it could hardly avoid splitting into antagonistic fractions in spite of public ritual sanctions, or else it would be in a chronic state of factional conflict under the surface. It is not surprising therefore to find that great value is attached to widely spreading bonds of personal kinship, as among the Tallensi (Fortes, 1949a). The recent field studies I have quoted all confirm the tremendous importance of the web of kinship as a counterweight to the tendency of unilineal descent grouping to harden social barriers. Or to put it slightly differently, it seems that where the unilineal descent group is rigorously structured within the total social system there we are likely to find kinship used to define and sanction a personal field of social relations for each individual. I will come back to this point in a moment. A further point to which I will refer again is this. We are learning from considerations such as those I have just mentioned, to think of social structure in terms of levels of organization in the manner first explicitly followed in the presentation of field data by Warner (1937). We can investigate the total social structure of a given community at the level of local organization, at that of kinship, at the level of corporate group structure and government, and at that of ritual institutions. We see these levels are related to different collective interests, which are perhaps connected in some sort of hierarchy. And one of the problems of analysis and exposition is to perceive and state the fact that all levels of structure are simultaneously involved in every social relationship and activity. This restatement of what is commonly meant by the concept of integration has the advantage of suggesting how the different modes of social relationship distinguished in any society are interlocked with one another. It helps to make clear also how certain basic principles of social organization can be generalized throughout the whole structure of a primitive society, as for instance the segmentary principle among the Nuer and the Tallensi.

This way of thinking about the problem of social integration has been useful in recent studies of African political organization. Study of the unilineal descent group as a part of a total social system means in fact studying its functions in the widest framework of social structure, that of the political organization. A common and perhaps general feature of political organization in Africa is that it is built up in a series of layers, so to speak, so arranged that the principle of checks and balances is necessarily mobilized in political activities. The idea is used in a variety of ways but what it comes to in general is that the members of the society are distributed in different, nonidentical schemes of allegiance and mutual dependence in relation to administrative, juridical and ritual institutions. It would take too long to enumerate all the peoples for whom we now have sufficient data to show this in detail. But the Lozi of Northern Rhodesia (Gluckman, 1951) are of such particular theoretical interest in this connection that a word must be said about them. The corporate descent group is not found among them. Instead their political organization is based on what Maine called the corporation sole. This is a title carrying political office backed by ritual sanctions and symbols to which subjects, lands, jurisdiction, and representative status, belong. But every adult is bound to a number of titles for different legal and social purposes in such a way that what is one allegiance group with respect to one title is split up with reference to other titles. Thus the only all-inclusive allegiance is that of all the nation to the kinship, which is identified with the State and the country as a whole. A social structure of such a kind, knit together moreover by a widely ramifying network of bilateral kinship ties between persons, is well fortified against internal disruption. It should be added that the notion of the "corporation sole" is found among many Central African peoples. It appears, in fact, to be a jural institution of the same generality in any of these societies as corporate groups are in others, since it is significant at all levels of social structure. A good example is the Bemba (cf. Richards, 1936, 1940) among whom it is seen in the custom of "positional inheritance" of status, rank, political office and ritual duty, as I will explain later.

What is the main methodological contribution of these studies? In my view it is the approach from the angle of political organization to what are traditionally thought of as kinship groups and institutions that has been specially fruitful. By regarding lineages and statuses from the point of view of the total social system and not from that of an hypothetical EGO we realize that consanguinity and affinity, real or putative, are not sufficient in themselves to bring about these structural arrangements. We see that descent is fundamentally a jural concept, as Radcliffe-Brown argued in one of his most important papers (1935b); we see its significance, as the connecting link between the external, that is political and legal, aspect of what we have called unilineal descent groups, and the internal or domestic aspect. It is in the latter context that kinship carries maximum weight, first, as the source of title to membership of the groups or to specific jural status, with all that this means in rights over and towards persons and property, and second as the basis of the social relations among the persons who are identified with one another in the corporate group. In theory, membership of a corporate legal or political group need not stem from kinship, as Weber has made clear. In primitive society, however, if it is not based on kinship it seems generally to presume some formal procedure of incorporation

with ritual initiation. So-called secret societies in West Africa seem to be corporate organizations of this nature. Why descent rather than locality or some other principle forms the basis of these corporate groups is a question that needs more study. It will be remembered that Radcliffe-Brown (1935b) related succession rules to the need for unequivocal discrimination of rights *in rem* and *in personam*. Perhaps it is most closely connected with the fact that rights over the reproductive powers of women are easily regulated by a descent group system. But I believe that something deeper than this is involved; for in a homogeneous society there is nothing which could so precisely and incontrovertibly fix one's place in society as parentage.

Looking at it from without, we ignore the internal structure of the unilineal group. But African lineages are not monolithic units; and knowledge of their internal differentiation has been much advanced by the researches I have mentioned. The dynamic character of lineage structure can be seen most easily in the balance that is reached between its external relations and its internal structure. Ideally, in most lineage-based societies, the lineage tends to be thought of as a perpetual unit, expanding like a balloon but never growing new parts. In fact, of course, as Forde (1938) and Evans-Pritchard (1940a and b) have so clearly shown fission and accretion are processes inherent in lineage structure. However, it is a common experience to find an informant who refuses to admit that his lineage or even his branch of a greater lineage did not at one time exist. Myth and legend, believed, naturally, to be true history, are quickly cited to prove the contrary. But investigation shows that the stretch of time, or rather of duration, with which perpetuity is equated varies according to the count of generations needed to conceptualize the internal structure of the lineage and link it on to an absolute, usually mythological origin for the whole system in a first founder.

This is connected with the fact that an African lineage is never, according to our present knowledge, internally undifferentiated. It is always segmented and is in process of continuous further segmentation at any given time. Among some of the peoples I have mentioned (e.g. the Tallensi and probably the Ibo) the internal segmentation of a lineage is quite rigorous and the process of further segmentation has an almost mechanical precision. The general rule is that every segment is, in form, a replica of every other segment and of the whole lineage. But the segments are, as a rule, hierarchically organized by fixed steps of greater and greater inclusiveness, each step being defined by genealogical reference. It is perhaps hardly necessary to mention again that when we talk of lineage structure we are really concerned, from a particular analytical angle, with the organization of jural, economic, and ritual activities. The point here is that lineage segmentation corresponds to gradation in the institutional norms and activities in which the total lineage organization is actualized. So we find that the greater the time depth that is attributed to the lineage system as a whole, the more elaborate is its internal segmentation. As I have already mentioned, lineage systems in Africa, when most elaborate, seem to have a maximal time depth of around fourteen putative generations. More common though is a count of five or six generations of named ancestors between living adults and a quasi-mythological founder. We can as yet only guess at the conditions that lie behind these limits of genealogical depth in lineage structure. The facts themselves are nevertheless of great comparative interest. As I have previously remarked, these genealogies obviously do not represent a true record of all the ancestors of a group. To explain this by the limitations and fallibility of oral tradition is merely to evade the problem. In structural terms the answer seems to lie in the spread or span (Fortes, 1945) of internal segmentation of the lineage, and this apparently has inherent limits. As I interpret the evidence we have, these limits are set by the condition of stability in the social structure which it is one of the chief functions of lineage systems to maintain. The segmentary spread found in a given lineage system is that which makes for maximum stability; and in a stable social system it is kept at a particular spread by continual internal adjustments which are conceptualized by clipping, patching and telescoping genealogies to fit. Just what the optimum spread of lineage segmentation in a particular society tends to be depends presumably on extra-lineage factors of political and economic organization of the kind referred to by Forde (1947).

It is when we consider the lineage from within that kinship becomes decisive. For lineage segmentation follows a model laid down in the parental family. It is indeed generally thought of as the perpetuation, through the rule of the jural unity of the descent line and of the sibling group (cf. Radcliffe-Brown, 1950), of the social relations that constitute the parental family. So we find a lineage segment conceptualized as a sibling group in symmetrical relationship with segments of a like order. It will be a parental sibling group where descent is patrilineal and a maternal one where it is matrilineal. Progressive orders of inclusiveness are formulated as succession of generations; and the actual process of segmentation is seen as the equivalent of the division between siblings in the parental family. With this goes the use of kinship terminology and the application of kinship norms in the regulation of intra-lineage affairs.

As a corporate group, a lineage exhibits a structure of authority, and it is obvious from what I have said why this is aligned with the generation ladder. We find, as a general rule, that not only the lineage but also every segment of it has a head, by succession or election, who manages its affairs with the advice of his co-members. He may not have legal sanctions by means of which to enforce his authority in internal affairs; but he holds his position by consent of all his fellow members, and he is backed by moral sanctions commonly couched in religious concepts. He is the trustee for the whole group of the property and other productive resources vested in it. He has a decisive jural role also in the disposal of rights over the fertility of the women in the group. He is likely to be the representative of the whole group in political and legal relations with other groups, with political authorities, and in communal ritual. The effect may be to make him put the interests of his lineage above those of the community if there is conflict with the latter. This is quite clearly recognized by some peoples.

Among the Ashanti for instance, every chiefship is vested in a matrilineal lineage. But once a chief has been installed his constitutional position is defined as holding an office that belongs to the whole community not to any one lineage. The man is, ideally, so merged in the office that he virtually ceases to be a member of his lineage, which always has an independent head for its corporate affairs (cf. Busia, 1951).

Thus lineage segmentation as a process in time links the lineage with the parental family; for it is through the family that the lineage (and therefore the society) is replenished by successive generations; and it is on the basis of the ties and cleavages between husband wife, between polygynous wives, between siblings, and between generations that growth and segmentation take place in the lineage. Study of this process has added much to our understanding of well known aspects of family and kinship structure.

I suppose that we all take it for granted that filiation—as contrasted with descent—is universally bilateral. But we have also been taught, perhaps most graphically by Malinowski, that this does not imply equality of social weighting for the two sides of kin connection. Correctly stated, the rule should read that filiation is always complementary, unless the husband in a matrilineal society (like the Nayar) or the wife in a patrilineal society, as perhaps in ancient Rome, is given no parental status or is legally served from his or her kin. The latter is the usual situation of a slave spouse in Africa.

Complementary filiation appears to be the principal mechanism by which segmentation in the lineage is brought about. This is very clear in patrilineal descent groups, and has been found to hold for societies as far apart as the Tallensi in West Africa and the Gusii in East Africa. What is a single lineage in relation to a male founder is divided into segments of a lower order by reference to their respective female founders on the model of the division of a polygynous family into separate matricentral "houses." In matrilineal lineage systems, however, the position is different. Segmentation does not follow the lines of different parental origin, for obvious reasons; it follows the lines of differentiation between sisters. There is a connection between this and the weakness in law and in sentiment of the marriage tie in matrilineal societies, though it is usual for political and legal power to be vested in men as Kroeber (1938) and others have remarked. More study of this problem is needed.

Since the bilateral family is the focal element in the web of kinship, complementary filiation provides the essential link between a sibling group and the kin of the parent who does not determine descent. So a sibling group is not merely differentiated within a lineage but is further distinguished by reference to its kin ties outside the corporate unit. This structural device allows of degrees of individuation depending upon the extent to which filiation on the non-corporate side is elaborated. The Tiv, for example, recognize five degrees of matrilateral filiation by which a sibling group is linked with lineages other than its own. These and other ties of a similar nature arising out of marriage exchanges result in a complex scheme of individuation for distinguishing both sibling groups and persons within a single lineage (L. Bohannan, 1951). This, of course, is not unique and has long been recognized, as everyone familiar with Australian kinship systems knows. Its more general significance can be brought out however by an example. A Tiv may claim to be living with a particular group of relatives for purely personal reasons of convenience or affection. Investigation shows that he has in fact made a choice of where to live within a strictly limited range of nonlineage kin. What purports to be a voluntary act freely motivated in fact presupposes a structural scheme of individuation. This is one of the instances which show how it is possible and feasible to move from the structural frame of reference to another, here that of the social psychologist, without confusing data and aims.

Most far-reaching in its effects on lineage structure is the use of the rule of complementary filiation to build double unilineal systems and some striking instances of this are found in Africa. One of the most developed systems of this type is that of the Yakö; and Forde's excellent analysis of how this works (Forde, 1950 b and c) shows that it is much more than a device for classifying kin. It is a principle of social organization that enters into all social relations and is expressed in all important institutions. There is the division of property, for instance, into the kind that is tied to the patrilineal lineage and the kind that passes to matrilineal kin. The division is between fixed and, in theory, perpetual productive resources, in this case farm land, with which goes residence rights, on the one hand, and on the other, movable and consumable property like livestock and cash. There is a similar polarity in religious cult and in the political office and authority linked with cult, the legally somewhat weaker matrilineal line being ritually somewhat stronger than the patrilineal line. This balance between ritual and secular control is extended to the fertility of women. An analogous double descent system has been described for some Nuba Hill tribes by Nadel (1950) and its occurrence among the Herero is now classical in ethnology. The arrangement works the other way round, too, in Africa, as among the Ashanti, though in their case the balance is far more heavily weighted on the side of the matrilineal lineage than on that of the jurally inferior and noncorporate paternal line.

These and other instances lead to the generalization that complementary filiation is not merely a constant element in the pattern of family relationships but comes into action at all levels of social structure in African societies. It appears that there is a tendency for interests, rights and loyalties to be divided on broadly complementary lines, into those that have the sanction of law or other public institutions for the enforcement of good conduct, and those that rely on religion, morality, conscience and sentiment for due observance. Where corporate descent groups exist the former seem to be generally tied to the descent group, the latter to the complementary line of filiation.

If we ask where this principle of social structure springs from we must look to the tensions inherent in the structure of the parental family. These tensions are the result of the direction given to individual lives by the total social structure but they also provide the models for the working of that structure. We now have plenty of evidence to show how the tensions that seem normally to arise between spouses, between successive generations and between siblings find expression in custom and belief. In a homogeneous society they are apt to be generalized over wide areas of the social structure. They then evoke controls like the Nyakyusa separation of successive generations of males in age villages that are built into the total social structure by the device of handing over political power to each successive generation as it reaches maturity, (Wilson, 1951 a and b). Or this problem may be dealt with on the level of ritual and moral symbolism by separating parent and first born child of the same sex by taboos that eliminate open rivalry, as among the Tallensi, the Nuer, the Hausa and other peoples.

Thus by viewing the descent group as a continuing process through time we see how it binds the parental family, its growing point, but a series of steps into the widest framework of social structure. This enables us to visualize a social system as an integrated unity at a given time and over a stretch of time in relation to the process of social reproduction and in a more rigorous way than does a global concept of culture.

I do want to make clear, though, that we do not think of a lineage as being just a collection of people held together by the accident of birth. A descent group is an arrangement of persons that serves the attainment of legitimate social and personal ends. These include the gaining of a livelihood, the setting up of a family and the preservation of health and well-being as among the most important. I have several times remarked on the connection generally found between lineage structure and the ownership of the most valued productive property of the society, whether it be land or cattle or even the monopoly of a craft like blacksmithing. It is of great interest, for instance, to find Dr. Richards attributing the absence of a lineage organization among the Bemba to their lack of heritable right in land or livestock (Richards, 1950). A similar connection is found between lineage organization and the control over reproductive resources and relations as is evident from the common occurrence of exogamy as a criterion of lineage differentiation. And since citizenship is derived from lineage membership and legal status depends upon it, political and religious office of necessity vests in lineages. We must expect to find and we do find that the most important religious and magical concepts and institutions of a lineage based society are tied into the lineage structure serving both as the necessary symbolical representation of the social system and as its regulating values. This is a complicated subject about which more needs to be known. Cults of gods and of ancestors, beliefs of a totemic nature, and purely magical customs and practices, some or all are associated with lineage organization among the peoples previously quoted. What appears to happen is that every significant structural differentiation has its specific ritual symbolism, so that one can, as it were, read off from the scheme of ritual differentiation the pattern of structural differentiation and the configuration of norms of conduct that goes with it. There is, to put it simply, a segmentation of ritual allegiance corresponding to the segmentation of genealogical grouping. Locality, filiation, descent, individuation, are thus symbolized.

Reference to locality reminds us of Kroeber's careful argument of 1938 in favor of the priority of the local relationships of residence over those of descent in determining the line that is legally superior. A lineage cannot easily act as a corporate group if its members can never get together for the conduct of their affairs. It is not surprising therefore to find that lineage in African societies is generally locally anchored, but it is not necessarily territorially compact or exclusive. A compact nucleus may be enough to act as the local center for a group that is widely dispersed. I think it would be agreed that lineage and locality are independently variable and how they interact depends on other factors in the social structure. As I interpret the evidence, local ties are of secondary significance, *pace* Kroeber, for local ties do not appear to give rise to structural bonds in and of themselves. There must be common political or kinship or economic or ritual interests for structural bonds to emerge. Again spatial dispersion does not immediately put an end to lineage ties or to the ramifying kin

ties found in cognatic systems like that of the Lozi. For legal status, property, office and cult act centripetally to hold dispersed lineages together and to bind scattered kindred. This is important in the dynamic pattern of lineage organization for it contains within itself the springs of disintegration, at the corporate level in the rule of segmentation, at the individual level in the rule of complementary filiation.

As I have suggested before, it seems that corporate descent groups can exist only in more or less homogeneous societies. Just what we mean by a homogeneous society is still rather vague though we all use the term lavishly. The working definition I make use of is that a homogeneous society is ideally one in which any person in the sense given to this term by Radcliffe-Brown in his recent (1950) essay, can be substituted for any other person of the same category without bringing about changes in the social structure. This implies that any two persons of the same category have the same body of customary usages and beliefs. I relate this tentative definition to the rule of sibling equivalence, so that I would say that, considered with respect to their achievable life histories, in a homogeneous society all men are brothers and all women sisters.

Societies based on unilineal descent groups are not the best in which to see what the notion of social substitutability means. For that it is better to consider societies in which descent still takes primacy over all other criteria of association and classification of persons in the regulation of social life but does not serve as the constitutive principle of corporate group organization. Central Africa provides some admirable instances (cf. Richards, 1950; Colson and Gluckman, 1951). Among the Bemba, the Tonga, the Lozi and many of their neighbors, as I have already remarked, the social structure must be thought of as a system of interconnected politico-legal statuses symbolized and sanctioned by ritual and not as a collection of people organized in self-perpetuating descent units. The stability of the society over time is preserved by perpetuating the status system. Thus when a person dies his status is kept alive by being taken up by an heir; and this heir is selected on the basis of descent rules. At any given time an individual may be the holder of a cluster of statuses; but these may be distributed among several persons on his death in a manner analogous to the widespread African custom by which a man's inherited estate goes to his lineage heir and his self-acquired property to his personal heir. Ideally, therefore, the network of statuses remains stable and perpetual though their holders come and go. Ritual symbols define and sanction the key positions in the system. What it represents, in fact, is the generalization throughout a whole society of the notion of the corporation sole as tied to descent but not to a corporate group. Descent and filiation have the function of selecting individuals for social positions and roles—in other words, for the exercise of particular rights and obligations—just as in cross cousin marriage they serve to select ego's spouse.

The concept of the "person" as an assemblage of statuses has been the starting point for some interesting enquiries. A generalization of long standing is that a married person always has two mutually antagonistic kinship statuses, that of spouse and parent in one family context and that of child and sibling in another, (cf. Warner, 1937). This is very conspicuous in an exogamous lineage system; and the tensions resulting from this condition, connected as they are with the rule of complementary filiation, have wide consequences. A common rule of social structure reflected in avoidance customs is that these two statuses must not be confounded. Furthermore, each status can be regarded as a compound of separable rights and obligations. Thus a problem that has to be solved in every matrilineal society is how to reconcile the rights over a woman's procreative powers (rights *in genetricem* as Laura Bohannan has called them in her paper of 1949) which remain vested in her brother or lineage, with those over her domestic and sexual services (rights *in uxorem*, cf. Laura Bohannan, *loc. cit.*) which pass to her husband. Among the Yao of Nyassaland, as Dr. Clyde Mitchell has shown (1950), this problem underlies the process of lineage segmentation. Brothers struggle against one another (or sisters' sons against mothers' brothers) for the control of their sisters' procreative powers and this leads to fission

in the minimal lineage. It is of great significance that such a split is commonly precipitated by accusations of witchcraft against the brother from whose control the sisters are withdrawn. By contrast, where rights over a woman's childbearing powers are held by her husband's patrilineal lineage the conflicts related to this critical interest occur between the wives of a lineage segment; and among the Zulu and Xhosa speaking tribes of South Africa these lead to witchcraft accusations between co-wives (cf. Hunter, 1936). As Laura Bohannan's paper shows, many widespread customs and institutions connected with marriage and parenthood, such as the levirate and the sororate, wife-taking by women, exchange marriage as practiced by the Tiv, and ghost marriage was found among the Nuer (Evans-Pritchard, 1951b) have structural significance not hitherto appreciated if they are regarded from the point of view I have indicated.

But one thing must be emphasized. This method of analysis does not explain why in one society certain kinds of interpersonal conflict are socially projected in witchcraft beliefs whereas in another they may be projected in terms of a belief in punitive spirits. It makes clear why a funeral ceremony is necessary and why it is organized in a particular way in the interest of maintaining a stable and coherent social system. It does not explain why the ritual performed in the funeral ceremonies of one people uses materials, ideas and dramatizations of a different kind from those used by another people. In short, it brings us nearer than we were thirty years ago to understanding the machinery by which norms are made effective, not only in a particular primitive society but in a type of primitive society. It does not explain how the norms come to be what they in fact are in a particular society.

In this connection, however, it is worth drawing attention to certain norms that have long been recognized to have a critical value in social organization. Marriage regulations, incest prohibitions and laws of homicide and warfare are the most important. Analysis of lineage structure has revealed an aspect of these norms which is of great theoretical interest. It is now fairly evident that these are not absolute rules of conduct which men are apt to break through an outburst of unruly instinct or rebellious self-assertion, as has commonly been thought. They are *relatively* obligatory in accordance with the structural relations of the parties. The Beduin of Cyrenaica regard homicide within the minimal agnatic lineage, even under extreme provocation, as a grave sin, whereas slaying a member of a different tribal segment is an admirable deed of valor. The Tallensi consider sex relations with a near sister of the same lineage as incest but tacitly ignore the act if the parties are very distant lineage kin. Among the Tiv, the Nuer, the Gusii and other tribes the lineage range within which the rule of exogamy holds is variable and can be changed by a ceremony that makes formally prohibited marriages legitimate and so brings marriage prohibitions into line with changes in the segmentary structure of the lineage. In this way previously exogamous units are split into intermarrying units. In all the societies mentioned, and others as well, an act of self-help that leads to negotiations if the parties belong to closely related lineages might lead to war if they are members of independent—though not necessarily geographically far apart—lineages. Such observations are indications of the flexibility of primitive social structures. They give a clue to the way in which internal adjustments are made from time to time in those structures, either in response to changing pressures from without or from the momentum of their own development. They suggest how such societies can remain stable in the long run without being rigid. But this verges on speculation.

The contributions to African ethnography mentioned in this paper are only a small and arbitrary selection from a truly vast amount of new work that is now going on in several countries. My aim has been to suggest how this work links up with a theoretical approach that is much in evidence among British social anthropologists. It is perhaps needless to add that this approach is also being actively applied by American, French, Belgian and Dutch anthropologists concerned with the problems of social organization. What I wish to convey by the example of current studies of unilineal descent group structure is that we have, in my belief, got to a point where a number of connected generalizations of wide validity can be made about this type of social group. This is an advance I associate with the structural frame of reference. I wish to suggest that this frame of reference gives us procedures of investigation and analysis by which a social system can be apprehended as a unity made of parts and processes that are linked to one another by a limited number of principles of wide validity in homogeneous and relatively stable societies. It has enabled us to set up hypotheses about the nature of these principles that have the merit of being related directly to the ethnographic material now so abundantly at hand and of being susceptible of testing by further field observation. It cannot be denied, I think, that we have here a number of positive contributions of real importance to social science.

★ SOCIAL ANTHROPOLOGY AND THE
METHOD OF CONTROLLED COMPARISON

Fred Eggan

I

The contemporary student of anthropology is in a difficult position in attempting to achieve a

Reprinted by permission of the author and the American Anthropological Association from the *American Anthropologist*, Vol. 56 (1954), pp. 743–760.

sound orientation in our rapidly changing and developing discipline. Nowhere is this more true than in the general field of cultural anthropology, where there is an apparent schism between those who call themselves ethnologists and the newer group of social anthropologists. Ethnology, which has had its major development in the United States, has been concerned primarily with culture history and culture process; social anthropology, on the other hand, is primarily a product of British anthropology and has emphasized social structure and function as its major concepts. These differences in emphasis and interest have led to considerable misunderstanding on both sides. As one who has had a foot in both camps for some two decades I may perhaps be permitted some observations on this situation, along with some suggestions as to a common meeting-ground.

Since World War II rapid changes have taken place in all branches of anthropology. Genetics and the experimental method, plus a host of new fossil finds from Africa, are revolutionizing physical anthropology; archeology, with the aid of radiocarbon dating and other new techniques, is beginning to achieve a world-wide chronology and is turning to cultural anthropology for further insight into cultural development; linguistics, with structural methods well established, is returning anew to historical problems and re-examining the relations of language and culture. But ethnology, one of whose tasks it is to synthesize and interpret the conclusions reached by its sister disciplines, is lagging behind.

It is not clear how long anthropology can remain partly a biological science, partly a humanity, and partly a social science. As we shift from the descriptive, data-gathering phases of anthropology to analysis, interpretation and theory, it is inevitable that realignments will come about. My predecessors in the presidency during the postwar period have sketched some of these new developments and realignments as they have seen them [Benedict (1948), Hallowell (1950), Beals (1951), Howells (1952), and Bennett (1953)]. It is highly probable that the forces for fusion will prevail over the tendencies to fission in the near future, so far as the United States is concerned; in England the forces are more nearly balanced, and the outcome is more uncertain. In the long run we may or may not follow the patterns set by other disciplines.

Turning to the field of cultural anthropology,

one of the important developments of the last few years has been the series of articles and books defining, denouncing, or defending "social anthropology." Murdock, in the most outspoken attack, notes that: "For a decade or more, anthropologists in other countries have privately expressed an increasingly ambivalent attitude toward recent trends in British anthropology—a curious blend of respect and dissatisfaction" (1951: 465). His analysis of the strengths and weaknesses of British social anthropology, as revealed in current productions, and his diagnosis of the social anthropologists as primarily "sociologists" have led to replies and counterreplies.

At the International Symposium on Anthropology sponsored by the Wenner-Gren Foundation a special session was devoted to "Cultural/Social Anthropology," in which various scholars presented the usages current in their respective countries. Tax's (Tax and others 1953: 225) summary of the consensus is to the effect that we ought to "use the words 'cultural' and 'social' anthropology interchangeably and forget about the question of terminology"; but Kroeber in his "Concluding Review" (1953: 357–76) returns to the problem of society and culture and finds distinctions. If these distinctions were merely a question of factional dispute or of alternate terms for similar activities, we could agree, with Lowie (1953: 527–28), on some neutral term such as "ethnography"—or allow time to make the decision in terms of relative popularity.

But the distinctions being made are not merely a matter of British and American rivalry or of terminology, and it is essential that we realize that there is a problem and that it is an important one. After accepting contemporary British social anthropologists as "true ethnographers" interested in the realities of culture, Lowie (1953: 531) goes on to unequivocally reject Fortes' contention that "social structure is not an aspect of culture but the entire culture of a given people handled in a special frame of theory" (Fortes 1953c: 21). However, many British social anthropologists would go even further than Fortes! In general they make a clear distinction between the concepts of *society* and *culture* and think of social anthropology as concerned primarily with the former. Murdock's (1951: 471) startling conclusion that the Britishers are sociologists was anticipated by Radcliffe-Brown (1931) and recently reaffirmed by Evans-Pritchard: "I must emphasize that, theoretically at any rate, social anthropology is the study of all human societies . . . Social anthropology can therefore be regarded as a branch of sociological studies, that branch which chiefly devotes itself to primitive societies" (1951a: 10–11). In contrast, the current Americanist opinion subsumes social structure as one aspect of culture, following Tylor (Lowie 1953: 531), or separates the two but gives primacy to the concept of culture.

Before we read our British brethren out of the anthropological party, however, it might be wise to see whether we may not have taken too narrow a view of cultural anthropology. Lowie, who, along with many American anthropologists, takes his cultural text from Tylor, defines the aim of ethnography as "the *complete* description of all cultural phenomena everywhere and at all periods" (1953: 528, italics Lowie's). It may be both possible and useful to view the "capabilities and habits acquired by man *as a member of society*" under the heading of social structure, despite the fact that Lowie finds it inconceivable. We might wait for the remainder of Fortes' materials on the Tallensi before rendering a verdict. And if we look more closely at Tylor's famous definition it seems clear that anthropology should be concerned with *both* society and culture, as they are interrelated and reflected in human behavior. We need a complete description and interpretation of both social and cultural phenomena, not to mention those concerned with the individual, if we are going to think in global terms. I would agree with Hallowell that society, culture, and personality may "be conceptually differentiated for specialized types of analysis and study. On the other hand, it is being more clearly recognized than heretofore that society, culture and personality cannot be postulated as completely independent variables" (1953: 600). We can wait until we know more about each of these concepts before we rank them as superior and inferior.

More important, we cannot afford to ignore the contributions of the British social anthropologists to both theory and description. In the last thirty years they have been developing a new approach to the study of man in society, which is currently producing significant results. It is no accident that many of the best monographs of the postwar period have come out of the small group of British social anthropologists. Reviewing *African Systems of Kinship and Marriage* Murdock states (1951: 465) that "the ethnographic contributions to the volume reveal without exception a very high level of professional competence in field research and in the analysis of social structural data, equalled only by the work of the very best men in other countries." What some of these contributions are has been recently pointed out by Firth (1951 a and b), Evans-Pritchard (1951a) and Fortes (1953 a and c), among others. While Fortes recognizes that they lack the wide and adventurous sweep of American anthropology, "the loss in diversity is amply balanced by the gains we have derived from concentration on a limited set of problems" (1953c: 17). Most American anthropologists are inclined to attribute the relative excellence of these contributions to good field techniques or perhaps to superior literary abilities, considering the British theoretical approach as rather barren and lifeless. But this seems to me to be a mistake. The structural point of view makes possible a superior organization and interpretation of the cultural data, and good monographs may well be related to this point of view. If we are to meet this competition (particularly in view of Firth's [1951a] account of their new directions), we need to do more than label our British colleagues as "comparative sociologists" or invoke the magical figures of Tylor and Franz Boas.

If I may venture a prescription based on my own experience, we need to adopt the structural-functional approach of British social anthropology and integrate it with our traditional American interest in culture process and history. For the weaknesses of British social anthropology are in precisely those aspects where we are strong, and if we can develop a way of relating the two approaches we can perhaps save ethnology from the destiny to which Kroeber has assigned it— "to a premature fate or a senescent death as one may see it" (1953: 366). I feel encouraged in this attempt because I have a genuine interest in both culture and social structure and because Murdock believes I have succeeded in "fusing functional analysis with an interest in history and an awareness of process in a highly productive creative synthesis" (1951: 469).

In contrast to most of my contemporaries I arrived at this synthesis without too many conflicts. My early anthropological education was in the Boas tradition as interpreted by Cole, Sapir and Spier—with additions from Redfield. But before the mold had hardened too far I came under the influence also of Radcliffe-Brown. The early thirties was a period of intense excitement among graduate students at Chicago, enhanced by debates between Linton and Radcliffe-Brown and heated arguments about functionalism. Redfield's (1937) account gives something of the flavor of this period, as well as a brief characterization of Radcliffe-Brown's contributions to anthropology. And Linton's *Study of Man* (1936) shows definite evidence of the impact of the structural and functional points of view on his thinking: culture and society are clearly differentiated, though they are mutually dependent, and concepts such as social system, status and role, integration and function are intermixed with the more usual cultural categories. But *The Study of Man,* while widely admired, was little imitated by Linton's colleagues —though it has had important effects on social science as a whole and on some of his students.

Once we were in the field, however, some of us discovered that the alternatives about which we had been arguing were in reality complementary. We found that the structural approach gave a new dimension to the flat perspectives of American ethnography and allowed us to ask new kinds of questions. Functionalism gave us meaningful answers to some questions and enabled us again to see cultures as wholes. But we also maintained an interest in cultural regions and a concern for culture process and cultural development. The resulting data were utilized for a variety of purposes. Some students prepared "descriptive integrations" which approximated to that complex reality which is history. Others were attracted to the formulation of general propositions as to so-

ciety or culture. I, myself, began by working in limited areas on problems of kinship and social structure, utilizing comparison as a major technique and attempting to see changes over time. When Radcliffe-Brown went to Oxford in 1937 we put together some of these studies under the ambitious title, *Social Anthropology of North American Tribes.*

The distinction between society and culture, far from complicating the procedures of analysis and comparison, has actually facilitated them. Generalization requires repeatable units which can be identified, and social structures, which tend to have a limited number of forms, readily lend themselves to classification and comparison. Cultural data, on the other hand, tend to fall into patterns of varying types which are most easily traced through time and space. Social structures and cultural patterns may vary independently of one another, but both have their locus in the behaviour of individuals in social groups. Depending on our problems one or the other may be central in our analysis, and we may utilize one or another of the basic methods of investigation— history or science. I would agree with Kroeber (1935: 569) that these latter need differentiation, "precisely because we shall presumably penetrate further in the end by two approaches than by one," but I see no reason why we should not use the two approaches together when possible.

The crucial problem with regard to generalization, whether broad or limited, is the method of comparison which is used. In the United States, for reasons which I will mention later on, the comparative method has long been in disrepute and was supplanted by what Boas called the "historical method." In England, on the other hand, the comparative method has had a more continuous utilization. Nadel (1951: 222–55) discusses the techniques and limitations of the comparative method and the nature of the results which may be obtained from its application. As Radcliffe-Brown has stated:

> It is only by the use of the comparative method that we can arrive at general explanations. The alternative is to confine ourselves to particularistic explanations similar to those of the historian. The two kinds of explanation are both legiti-

mate and do not conflict; but both are needed for the understanding of societies and their institutions (1952b: 113–14).

The particular adaptation of the comparative method to social anthropology which Radcliffe-Brown has made is well-illustrated in the Huxley Memorial Lecture for 1951, where he begins with exogamous moiety divisions in Australia and shows that the Australian phenomena are instances of certain widespread general tendencies in human societies. For him the task of social anthropology is to "formulate and validate statements about the conditions of existence of social systems . . . and the regularities that are observable in social change," (1951: 22). This systematic comparison of a world-wide variety of instances, while an ultimate objective of social anthropology, is rather difficult to carry out in terms of our present limited knowledge of social systems. We can make some general observations about institutions such as the family; and the war between the sexes in aboriginal Australia has some interesting parallels with the world of Thurber. But I am not sure, to give one example, that the "Yin-Yang philosophy of ancient China is the systematic elaboration of the principle that can be used to define the social structure of moieties in Australian tribes" (1951b: 21), though Radcliffe-Brown's analysis and wide experience give it a certain plausibility.

My own preference is for the utilization of the comparative method on a smaller scale and with as much control over the frame of comparison as it is possible to secure. It has seemed natural to utilize regions of relatively homogeneous culture or to work within social or cultural types, and to further control the ecology and the historical factors so far as it is possible to do so. Radcliffe-Brown has done this with great skill in *The Social Organization of Australian Tribes* (1930–1). After comparing the Australian moiety structures and finding their common denominators, I would prefer to make a comparison with the results of a similar study of moiety structures and associated practices of the Indians of Southern California, who approximate rather closely the Australian sociocultural situation. The results of this comparison could then be matched against

comparable studies of Northwest Coast and other similar moiety systems, and the similarities and differences systematically examined by the method of concomitant variation. I think we would end up, perhaps, with Radcliffe-Brown's relationship of "opposition," or the unity of opposites, but we would have much more, as well, in the form of a clearer understanding of each type or subtype and of the nature of the mechanisms by which they are maintained or changed. While I share Radcliffe-Brown's vision of an ultimate science of society, I think that we first have to cultivate more intensively what Merton (1949: 5) has called the middle range of theory. I suggest the method of controlled comparison as a convenient instrument for its exploration, utilizing covariation and correlation, and avoiding too great a degree of abstraction.

Before examining the ramifications and possible results of such exploration it may be useful to glance at selected aspects of the history of anthropology to see how certain of the present differences between American and British anthropologists have come about. We are somewhere in the middle of one of Kroeber's "configurations of culture growth" and it is important to see which patterns are still viable and which are close to exhaustion.

II

The early developments in American cultural anthropology have been delineated by Lowie (1937) and parallel in many respects those which were occurring in England. In addition to Morgan, Bandelier, Cusing, J. O. Dorsey, Alice Fletcher, and others were among the pioneers whose work is today largely forgotten in the United States. For with the advent of Franz Boas a major break was made with the past, resulting not so much from his program for cultural anthropology as in its selective implementation. Boas in "The Limitations of the Comparative Method" (1896) outlined a program which included two major tasks. The first task involved detailed studies of individual tribes in their cultural and regional context as a means to the reconstruction of the histories of tribal cultures and regions. A second task concerned the comparisons of these tribal histories, with the ultimate objective of formulating general laws of cultural growth, which were psychological in character (1940: 278–79). This second task, which Boas though of as the more important of the two, was never to be fully implemented by his students.

Boas formulated this program in connection with a destructive criticism of the comparative method as then practiced in England and America. After stating as a principle of method that uniformity of process was essential for comparability, he goes on to say:

> If anthropology desires to establish the laws governing the growth of culture it must not confine itself to comparing the results of growth alone, but whenever such is feasible, it must compare the processes of growth, and these can be discovered by means of studies of the cultures of small geographical areas (1940: 280).

He then compares this "historical method" with the "comparative method," which he states has been remarkably barren of results, and predicts that it will not become fruitful until we make our comparisons "on the broader and sounder basis which I ventured to outline." The requirement that only those phenomena can be compared which are derived psychologically or historically from common causes, valuable as it may have been at that time, has had the effect of predisposing most of Boas' students against the comparative method—except in linguistics where genetic relationships could be assumed—and hence against any generalizations which require comparison. And the processes which Boas sought in a study of art and mythology on the Northwest Coast proved more difficult to isolate than was anticipated. Kroeber notes that though Boas was "able to show a multiplicity of processes in culture, he was not able—it was impossible in his day and perhaps is still—to formulate these into a systematic theory" (1953: 368).

In the "Formative Period" of American ethnology, from 1900 to 1915, these were minor considerations. There were the vanishing Indian cultures to study, and it was natural for the students of Boas to concentrate on the first portion of his program. They wrote theses, for the most part, on specific problems, or to test various theories which had been advanced to explain art, or myth, or ritual, generally with negative results. This clearing of the intellectual air was essential, but it also led to excesses, as in Goldenweiser's famous study of totemism (1910). It also resulted in the ignoring of earlier anthropologists and even contemporaries. Alice Fletcher's *The Hako: A Pawnee Ceremony* (1904) excellently describes and interprets a ritual but was never used as a mode.

The major attention of the early Boas students was devoted to the tasks of ordering their growing data on the American Indian in tribal and regional context. During this and the following periods many important monographs and studies were published, which formed a solid base for future work. The climax of this fact-gathering revolution was reached with the culture-area concept as crystallized by Wissler (1914, 1922), and in the studies by Boas on the art, mythology, and social organization of the Northwest Coast.

The period which followed, from 1915 to 1930, was a "Florescent Period" in American ethnology. The culture area provided a framework for the analysis and interpretation of the cultural data in terms of history and process. Sapir opened the period with his famous *Time Perspective* (1916b), which began: "Cultural anthropology is more and more rapidly getting to realize itself as a strictly historical science. Its data cannot be understood, either in themselves or in their relation to one another, except as the endpoints of specific sequences of events reaching back into the remote past." Wissler, Lowie, Kroeber, Spier, Benedict, and many others provided a notable series of regional studies utilizing distributional analyses of cultural traits for chronological inferences—and for the study of cultural process. Wissler developed the "law of diffusion" and then turned his attention to the dynamic factors underlying the culture area itself. In *The Relation of Nature to Man in Aboriginal America* (1926) he thought that he had found them in the relationship of the culture center to the underlying ecology. The great museums dominated this period, and American anthropology shared in the general prosperity and optimism which followed the First World War.

One result of these distributional studies was that chronology tended to become an end in itself, and some ethnologists became so preoccupied with seeking time sequences that they did not pay much attention to culture as such. The analysis of culture into traits or elements and their subsequent treatment often violated principles of historical method by robbing them of their context. The normal procedure of historians of basing their analysis of chronology was here reversed—the chronology resulted from the analytic study. The generalizations as to process which were formulated were used as short-cuts to further historical research.

Another important result of these studies was the conception of culture which gradually developed. Culture came to be viewed as a mere aggregation of traits brought together by the accidents of diffusion. Here is Benedict's conclusion to her doctoral dissertation:

> It is, so far as we can see, an ultimate fact of human nature that man builds up his culture out of disparate elements, combining and recombining them; and until we have abandoned the superstition that the result is an organism functionally interrelated, we shall be unable to see our cultural life objectively, or to control its manifestations (1923: 84–85).

The revolt against this mechanical and atomistic conception of culture came both from within and from without. Dixon (1928) criticized both Wissler's procedures and his conceptions of the processes of culture growth, as well as his formulation of the dynamics of the culture area. Spier (1929: 222) renounced historical reconstruction as misleading and unnecessary for understanding the nature of the processes of culture growth, advocating in its place a consideration of the actual conditions under which cultural growth takes place. Benedict was soon engaged in the study of cultural patterns and configurations, and her *Patterns of Culture* (1934) represents a complete reversal of her earlier position—here superstition has become reality.

During this period there was little interest in social structure as such, even though Kroeber, Lowie, and Parsons all studied Pueblo life at first hand. The shadows of Morgan, McLennan, Spencer, and Maine still loomed over them, and sociological interpretations were generally rejected in favor of psychological or linguistic ones. Lowie, however, began to develop a moderate functional position and sociological orientation with regard to social organization, perhaps best exemplified in his article on "Relationship Terms" (1929).

The "Expansionist Period" which followed, 1930–1940, was a time of troubles and of transition for American ethnology. The old gods were no longer omniscient—and there was an invasion of foreign gods from overseas. The depression brought the great museums to their knees and temporarily ended their activities in ethnological research; the center of gravity shifted more and more to the universities, as the social sciences grappled with the new social problems. This was a period of considerable expansion for cultural anthropology, much of it in terms of joint departments with sociology. Archeology also experienced a remarkable expansion during the decade, partly as a by-product of its ability to utilize large quantities of WPA labor. The chronological framework that resulted, based on stratigraphy and other techniques, further emphasized the inadequacy of the reconstructions made from distributional analyses alone.

In the meantime *Argonauts* and *The Andaman Islanders* had been published but had made relatively little impression on American scholars. Malinowski's field methods were admired, and his functional conception of culture struck some responsive chords; as for Radcliffe-Brown, his "ethnological appendix" was utilized but his interpretations of Andamanese customs and beliefs were largely ignored. Soon afterwards, however, Malinowski began developing social anthropology in England on the basis of the functional method and new techniques of field research. Brief visits by Malinowski to the United States, including a summer session at the University of California, plus the work of his early students in Oceania and Africa, led to considerable increase in his influence, but during the 1930's he was largely preoccupied with developing a program of research for Africa.

In 1931 Radcliffe-Brown, who had been first in South Africa and then in Australia, brought to this country "a method for the study of society, well defined and different enough from what prevailed here to require American anthropologists to reconsider the whole matter of method, to scrutinize their objectives, and to attend to new problems and new ways of looking at problems. He stirred us up and accelerated intellectual variation among us" (Redfield 1937: vii).

As a result of these and other forces American ethnologists began to shift their interests in a variety of directions. Kroeber re-examined the relationship between cultural and natural areas in a more productive way and formulated the concept of culture climax to replace Wissler's culture center. He also explored the problem of culture elements more thoroughly, in the course of which he organized the Culture Element Survey; at the other end of the cultural spectrum he wrote *Configurations of Culture Growth* (1944). Herskovits, who had earlier applied the culture-area concept to Africa, developed a dynamic approach to the study of culture (1950) which has had important results. Redfield, in the meantime, was beginning the series of studies which resulted in *The Folk Culture of Yucatan* (1941)—a new and important approach to the study of social and cultural change.

During this period, also, Steward was beginning his ecological studies of Great Basin tribes, Warner was applying social anthropological concepts and methods to the study of modern American communities, and Sapir was shifting his interests in the direction of psychiatry. Linton, with his perception of new and important trends, had put them together with the old, but his interests also shifted in the direction of personality and culture. Acculturation became a respectable subject with Redfield, Linton, and Herskovits' "Memorandum on the Study of Acculturation" (1936), and applied anthropology secured a foothold in the Indian Service and in a few other government agencies.

These developments, which gave variety and color to American ethnology, also tended to leave a vacuum in the center of the field. We will never know for sure what might have developed out of this interesting decade if World War II had not come along.

The "Contemporary Period"—the decade since the war—is difficult to characterize. In part there has been a continuation of prewar trends, in part a carry-over of wartime interests, and in part an interest in new problems resulting from the war and its aftermath. There is a growing interest in complex cultures or civilizations, such as China, Japan, India, and Africa, both at the village level and at the level of national culture and national character, and new methods and techniques are in process for their study and comparison.

One postwar development of particular interest in connection with this paper has been the gradual but definite acceptance in many quarters in this country of social anthropology as a separable but related discipline. Of even greater potential significance, perhaps, is the growing alliance between social psychology, sociology, and social anthropology as the core groups of the so-called "behavioral sciences," a relationship also reflected in the Institute of Human Relations at Yale and in the Department of Social Relations at Harvard, as well as elsewhere.

Perhaps most important of all the postwar developments for the future of anthropology has been the very great increase in the interchange of both students and faculty between English and American institutions, including field stations in Africa. The Fulbright program, the Area Research Fellowships of the Social Science Research Council, the International Symposium on Anthropology of the Wenner-Gren Foundation, and the activities of the Carnegie, Rockefeller, and Ford Foundations have all contributed to this increased exchange. I am convinced that such face-to-face contacts in seminar and field represent the most effective way for amalgamation of techniques and ideas to take place. The testimony of students back from London or Africa is to the general effect that our training is superior in ethnography and in problems of culture history, but is inferior in social anthropology: kinship, social structure, political organization, law, and so on. There are exceptions, of course, but we would like the exceptions to be the rule.

III

For the details of the complementary developments in England we are indebted to Evans-Pritchard's account in *Social Anthropology* (1951a) and to Fortes' inaugural lecture entitled *Social Anthropology at Cambridge Since 1900* (1953b). There are differences in emphasis between the Oxford and Cambridge versions, but in general the developments are clear.

In England cultural anthropology got off to a fine start through the efforts of Tylor, Maine, McLennan and other pioneers of the 1860's and 1870's, but their attempts to construct universal stages of development ultimately fell afoul of the facts. The nineteenth-century anthropologists in England were "armchair" anthropologists; it wasn't until Haddon, a zoologist by training, organized the famous Torres Straits expedition of 1898–1900 and converted an assorted group of psychologists and other scientists into ethnologists that field work began. But from this group came the leaders of early twentieth-century British anthropology: Haddon, Rivers, and Seligman. According to Evans-Pritchard, "This expedition marked a turning point in the history of social anthropology in Great Britain. From this time two important and interconnected developments began to take place: anthropology became more and more a whole-time professional study, and some field experience came to be regarded as an essential part of the training of its students" (1951a: 73).

During the next decade a gradual separation of ethnology and social anthropology took place, culminating, according to Radcliffe-Brown (1952a: 276), in an agreement to use "ethnography" for descriptive accounts of nonliterate peoples, "ethnology" for historical reconstructions, and "social anthropology" for the comparative study of the institutions of primitive societies. The institutional division of labor also took a different organization which has led to different views as to how anthropology should be constituted.

Sir James Frazer dominated social anthropology in the early decades of this century, and the conceptions of evolution and progress held sway long after they had given way in American anthropology. But Fortes notes that, while anthropologists had a magnificent field of inquiry, the subject had no intrinsic unity: "At the stage of development it had reached in 1920, anthropology, both in this country and elsewhere, was a bundle-subject, its data gathered, so to speak, from the same forest but otherwise heterogeneous and tied together only by the evolutionary theory" (1953b: 14).

Ethnology flourished for a period under Haddon, Rivers, and Seligman, but with the advent of Malinowski and Radcliffe-Brown "social anthropology has emerged as the basic discipline concerned with custom and social organization in the simpler societies" (Fortes 1953b: 16). From their predecessors the latter received their tradition of field research and the principle of the intensive study of limited areas—a principle that Malinowski carried to its logical conclusion.

Beginning in 1924 Malinowski began to train a small but brilliant group of social anthropologists from all parts of the Commonwealth in the field techniques and functional theory that he had developed from his Trobriand experience, but his approach proved inadequate for the complex problems encountered in Africa. This deficiency was remedied in part by the advent of Radcliffe-Brown, who returned to the newly organized Institute of Social Anthropology at Oxford in 1937 and proceeded to give British Social anthropology its major current directions. Evans-Pritchard discusses this period with the authority of a participant and I refer you to his *Social Anthropology* for the details—and for a summary of what a social anthropologist does.

The postwar developments in England have been largely a continuation of prewar developments together with a considerable expansion stimulated by government support of both social anthropological research and applied research.

Unlike the situation in the United States there is no large established group of sociologists in England, and social anthropology has in part filled the gap. Major theoretical differences as to the nature of social anthropology as a science or as a humanity are developing, but these differences are subordinate to a large area of agreement as to basic problems, methods, and points of view. Just as the American ethnologists of the 1920's had a common language and a common set of problems, so do the British social anthropologists today.

One important key to the understanding of British social anthropology resides in their conception of social structure. The contributions in this field with regard to Africa have been summarized by Fortes in "The Structure of Unilineal Descent Groups" (1953c). Here he points out that the guiding ideas in the analysis of African lineage organization have come mainly from Radcliffe-Brown's formulation of the structural principles found in all kinship systems, and goes on to state that he is not alone "in regarding them as among the most important generalizations as yet reached in the study of social structure" (p. 25). For Fortes the social structure is the foundation of the whole social life of any continuing society.

Not only have the British social anthropologists produced an outstanding series of monographs in recent years but they have organized their training programs in the universities and institutes to insure that the flow will continue. In the early stages of training there is a more concentrated program in social anthropology in the major British universities, though the knowledge demanded of other fields is less, and linguistics is generally conspicuous by its absence. Only the top students are given grants for field research. As Evans-Pritchard (1951a: 76–77) sketches the ideal situation, the student usually spends at least two years in his first field study, including learning to speak the language of the group under observation. Another five years is allotted to publishing the results, or longer if he has teaching duties. A study of a second society is desirable, to avoid the dangers of thinking in terms of a single society, but this can usually be carried out in a shorter period.

Granted that this is the ideal procedure, it still offers a standard against which to compare our American practices. My impression is that our very best graduate students are approximating this standard, but our Ph.D. programs in general require considerably less in terms of field research and specific preparation. We tend to think of the doctorate as an earlier stage in the development of a scholar and not a capstone to an established career.

This proposed program, however, has important implications for social anthropology itself. If each anthropologist follows the Malinowskian tradition of specializing in one, or two or three societies and spends his lifetime in writing about them, what happens to comparative studies? Evans-Pritchard recognizes this problem: "It is a matter of plain experience that it [the comparative study] is a formidable task which cannot be undertaken by a man who is under the obligation to publish the results of the two or three field studies he has made, since this will take him the rest of his life to complete if he has heavy teaching and administrative duties as well" (1951a: 89).

In place of the comparative method he proposes the "experimental method," in which preliminary conclusions are formulated and then tested by the same or other social anthropologists on other societies, thus gradually developing broader and more adequate hypotheses. The old comparative method, he says, has been largely abandoned because it seldom gave answers to the questions asked (1951a: 90).

This concentration on intensive studies of one or two selected societies has its own limitations. The hypotheses advanced on such a basis can often be modified in terms of studies easily available for comparison. Thus Schneider (1953b: 582–84) points out that some of Evans-Pritchard's generalizations about the Nuer could well have been tested against the Zulu data. The degree to which comparison may sharpen hypotheses is well illustrated by Nadel's study of "Witchcraft in Four African Societies" (1952).

There is a further reason for this lack of interest in comparative studies on the part of Evans-Pritchard in that he thinks of social anthropology as "belonging to the humanities rather than to the natural sciences" (1951a: 60) and conceives of his task as essentially a historical one of "descriptive integration." His colleagues are currently disagreeing with him (Forde 1950a; Fortes 1953b).

Schapera (1953) has recently reviewed a number of studies utilizing some variation of the comparative method and finds most of them deficient in one respect or another. The comparative approach he advocates involves making an intensive study of a given region and carefully comparing the forms taken among the people of the area by the particular social phenomena which are under scrutiny, so as to classify them into types. These types can then be compared with those of neighboring regions. "Social anthropology would benefit considerably, and have more right to claim that its methods are adequate, if in the near future far more attention were devoted to intensive regional comparisons" (p. 360).

One difficulty in the way of any systematic and intensive comparison of African data is being remedied by the Ethnographic Survey under the direction of Daryll Forde. The absence of any interest in linguistics is a major criticism of a group who advocate learning a language to carry out researches in social structure but who ignore the structure in the languages which they learn. Lévi-Strauss (1951) has pointed out some of the problems in these two fields, and it is difficult to see why they are neglected.

Ultimately the British anthropologists will discover that time perspective is also important and will encourage archeology and historical research. The potentialities of Greenberg's recent genetic classification of African languages, and the subgrouping of Bantu languages through shared correspondences and lexico-statistical techniques, are just beginning to be appreciated. And for those who demand documents there are the Arab records and historical collections such as the Portuguese records for Delagoa Bay. That the same tribes speaking the same languages are still in this region after four hundred years suggests that there is considerable historical material which needs to be utilized. For our best insights into the nature of society and culture come from seeing social structures and culture patterns over time. Here is where we can distinguish the accidental from the general, evaluate more clearly the factors and forces operating in a given situation, and describe the processes involved in general terms. Not to take advantage of the possibilities of studying social and cultural change under such relatively controlled conditions is to do only half the job that needs to be done.

IV

These brief and inadequate surveys indicate that cultural anthropology has had quite a different development in the United States and England and suggest some of the reasons for these differences. They also suggest that the differences may be growing less. In the United States ethology began with a rejection of Morgan and his interest in the development of social systems, and an acceptance of Tylor and his conception of culture. Tylor's views by-and-large still prevail, though since the 1920's there have been many alternative definitions of culture as anthropologists attempted to get a more *rounded* view of their subject. In England, as Kroeber and Kluckhohn (1952) have pointed out, there has been more resistance to the term "culture;" on the other hand, Morgan is hailed as an important forerunner, particularly for his researches on kinship. Prophets are seldom honored in their own country.

Both Kroeber (1953) and Redfield (1953) have recently reviewed the role of anthropology in relation to the social sciences and to the humanities and have emphasized the virtues of a varied attack on the problems that face us all. With Redfield, I believe we should continue to encourage variety among anthropologists. But I am here particularly concerned with cultural anthropology, and I am disturbed by Kroeber's attitude toward ethnology: "Now how about ethnology?" he writes in his Concluding Review of *Anthropology Today*, "I am about ready to abandon this baby to the wolves." He goes on to detail some of the reasons why ethnology appears to be vanishing: the decrease in primitives, the failure to make classifications and comparisons, and the tendencies to leap directly into large-scale speculations (1953: 366–67). His solution is to merge ethnology with culture history and, when that is soundly established, to extricate the processes at work and "generalize the story of culture into its causal factors." This is a return to the original Boas program.

My own suggested solution is an alternate one. While there are few "primitives" in our own backyard, there are the new frontiers of Africa, India, Southeast Asia, Indonesia, and Melanesia to exploit. Here is still a complete range in terms of cultural complexity and degree of culture contact. Africa alone is a much more challenging "laboratory" in many respects than is the American Indian. And for those who like their cultures untouched there is interior New Guinea.

The failure to make adequate classifications and comparisons can in part be remedied by borrowing the methods and techniques of the social anthropologists or by going in the directions pioneered by Murdock (1949). Social structure gives us a preliminary basis for classification in the middle range while universals are sought for. Steward's "sociocultural types" are another step in the directions we want to go.

The tendency to leap directly into large-scale speculations is growing less and will be further controlled as we gradually build a foundation of well-supported hypotheses. Speculations are like mutations in some respects—most of them are worthless but every now and then one advances our development tremendously. We need to keep them for this reason, if no other.

If we can salvage cultural anthropology in the United States, I do not worry too much about the "anthropological bundle" falling apart in the near future. As a result of the closer co-operation among the subdisciplines of anthropology in this country new bridges are continually being built between them, and joint problems, and even new subfields, are constantly being generated. So long as our interaction remains more intensive than our relations with other disciplines, anthropology will hold together.

One thing we can do is to return to the basic problems American ethnologists were tackling in the 1920's and 1930's, with new methods and points of view and a greater range of concepts. I have elsewhere (1952: 35–45) discussed the potential contributions that such a combined approach could achieve, and for the Western Pueblos I have tried to give a specific example (1950). But in terms of present possibilities, not one single region in North America has had adequate treatment. Nor are the possibilities of field research in North America exhausted. The Cheyenne, for example, are still performing the Sun Dance pretty much as it was in Dorsey's day. But despite all the studies of the Sun Dance we still do not have an adequate account giving us the meaning and significance of the rituals for the participants and for the tribe. One such account would enable us to revalue the whole literature of the Sun Dance.

The Plains area is now ripe for a new integration which should be more satisfying then the older ones. In addition to Wissler's and Kroeber's formulations, we now have an outline of cultural development firmly anchored in stratigraphy and radiocarbon dates, and a considerable amount of documentary history as well as a series of monographs on special topics. By centering our attention on social structure, we can see the interrelations of subsistence and ecology, on the one hand, and political and ritual activities, on the other. For those interested in process we can ask: Why did tribal groups coming in to the Plains from surrounding regions, with radically different social structures, tend to develop a similar type. The answer is not simply diffusion (Eggan 1937a). Once this new formulation of the Plains is made, new problems will arise which will require a more complex apparatus to solve.

Another type of comparative study which has great potentialities is represented by the investigation of the Southern Athabascan-speaking peoples in the Plains and Southwest. Here the same or similar groups have differentiated in terms of ecology, contacts, and internal development. Preliminary studies by Kluckhohn, Opler, Hoijer, Goodwin, and others suggest the possibilities of a detailed comparative attack on the problems of cultural development in this relatively controlled situation. Bellah's (1952) recent study of Southern Athabascan kinship systems, utilizing Parsons' structural-functional categories, shows some of the possibilities in this region.

In the Southwest I have attempted to work within a single structural type in a highly integrated subcultural area and to utilize the archeological and historical records, which are here reasonably complete to delimit and interpret the variations which are found (1950). Clyde Kluckhohn looks at the Southwest from a broader standpoint and with a different but related problem:

> One of the main rewards of intensive study of a culture area such as the Southwest is that such study eventually frees investigators to raise genuinely scientific questions—problems of process. Once the influence of various cultures upon others in the same area and the effects of a common environment (and its variant forms) have been reasonably well ascertained, one can then operate to a first approximation under an "all other things being equal" hypothesis and intensively examine the question: Why are these cultures and these modal personality types still different—in spite of similar environmental stimuli and pressures and access over long periods of time to the influence of generalized area culture or cultures? We are ready now, I believe, for such studies—but no one is yet attempting them seriously (1954:693).

The Ramah Project, directed by Kluckhohn, has been planned so as to furnish a continuous record of a series of Navaho from childhood to maturity and of the changes in their culture as well. This project is in its second decade, and a variety of participants have produced an impressive group of papers. So far Kluckhohn's major monograph has concerned *Navaho Witchcraft* (1944), which he has interpreted in both psychological and structural terms and which breaks much new ground. A newer project in the same region involves the comparison of the value systems of five groups: Navaho, Zuni, Mormon,

Spanish-American, and Texan, but the results are not yet available.

Comparative studies can also be done on a very small scale. The few thousand Hopi are divided into nearly a dozen villages, each of which differs in independence, degree of acculturation, and specific sociocultural patterns. And on First Mesa the Hano or Hopi Tewa, who came from the Rio Grande around A.D. 1700, still maintain their linguistic and cultural independence despite biological assimilation and minority status—and apparently differ significantly in personality traits as well. Dozier's (1951) preliminary account of this interesting situation suggests how valuable this comparison may eventually be.

How much can be learned about the processes of social and cultural change by comparative field research in a controlled situation is illustrated by Alex Spoehr's researches in the Southeast. Here some preliminary investigations by the writer (1937b) had led to tentative conclusions as to the nature of changes in kinship systems of the Creek, Choctaw, Chickasaw, and other tribes of the region after they were removed to reservations in Oklahoma. Spoehr (1947) not only demonstrated these changes in detail but has analyzed the historical factors responsible and isolated the resulting processes.

Here Redfield's (1941) comparative study of four Yucatecan communities in terms of progressive changes in their organization, individualization, and secularization as one moves from their tribal hinterland through village and town to the city of Merida should also be mentioned. The significance of its contributions to comparative method has been largely overlooked in the controversies over the nature of the "folk society" and the usefulness of ideal types.

We can also begin to study particular social types wherever they occur. Murdock's *Social Structure* (1949) demonstrates that similar social structures and kinship systems are frequently found in various parts of the world. We can compare matrilineal social systems, or Omaha kinship systems, in different regions of the world without restricting ourselves to the specific requirements originally laid down by Boas. Thus Audrey Richards' (1950) comparison of matrilineal organizations in Central Africa will gain in significance when set against the Northwest Coast data. When variant forms of matrilineal or patrilineal social systems are compared from the standpoint of structure and function, we will have a clearer idea of the essential features of such systems and the reasons for special variants. The results for matrilineal systems promise to give quite a different picture than Lowie originally drew of the "Matrilineal Complex" (1919), and they will help us to see more clearly the structural significance of cultural patterns such as avunculocal residence and cross-cousin marriage.

These and other studies will enable us ultimately to present a comprehensive account of the various types of social structure to be found in the regions of the world and to see the nature of their correlates and the factors involved in social and cultural change. It is clear that new methods and techniques will need to be developed for the evaluation of change over time; quantitative data will be essential to establish rates of change which may even be expressed in statistical terms.

I have suggested that there may be some virtues in combining the sound anthropological concepts of structure and function with the ethnological concepts of process and history. If we can do this in a satisfactory manner we can save the "ethnological baby" from the fate to which Kroeber has consigned it—what we call the infant when it has matured is a relatively minor matter. In suggesting some of the ways in which comparative studies can be made more useful I have avoided questions of definition and ultimate objectives. This is only one of the many ways in which our science can advance, and we have the personnel and range of interests to cultivate them all.

After this paper was substantially completed the volume of papers in honor of Wilson D. Wallis entitled *Method and Perspective in Anthropology* (Spencer 1954) became available. Much of what Herskovits says with regard to "Some Problems of Method in Ethnography" is relevant to points made above, particularly his emphasis on the historical approach and the comparative study of documented change (1954: 19) as well as on the

importance of repeated analyses of the same phenomena. And Ackerknecht's scholarly survey of "The Comparative Method in Anthropology" emphasizes the importance of the comparative method for cultural anthropology: "One of the great advantages of the comparative method will be that in a field where the controlled experiment is impossible it provides at least some kind of control." He sees signs of a renaissance: "In whatever form the comparative method may reappear, it will express the growing desire and need in cultural anthropology to find regularities and common denominators behind the apparent diversity and uniqueness of cultural phenomena" (p. 125).

Kroeber, in commenting on the papers in this volume, subscribes "whole-heartedly to Ackerknecht's position. My one criticism is that he doesn't go far enough. He sees the comparative method as something that must and will be revived. I would say that it has never gone out; it has only changed its tactic" (1954: 273). He goes on to point out that all science ultimately seeks knowledge of process, but that this must be preceded by "description of the properties of the form and substance of the phenomena, their ordering or classification upon analysis of their structure, and the tracing of their changes or events" (pp. 273–274). These are the essential points that I have tried to make with reference to cultural anthropology.

On both sides of the Atlantic there is an increasing willingness to listen to one another and a growing conviction that the varied approaches are complementary rather than competitive. We can agree, I think, with Radcliffe-Brown: "It will be only in an integrated and organized study in which historical studies and sociological studies are combined that we shall be able to reach a real understanding of the development of human society, and this we do not yet have" (1951b: 22). It seems to me that it is high time we made a start—and indeed it is well under way.

In time we may be able to simplify and further order our conceptual schemes in terms of direct observations on human behavior. Sapir, in perhaps a moment of insight, once defined culture as "a systematic series of illusions enjoyed by people." But culture, like the "ether" of the nineteenth-century physicists, plays an essential role today and will do so for a considerable time to come. The distant future is more difficult to predict—I think it was Whitehead who remarked that the last thing to be discovered in any science is what the science is really about!

THE FAILURE OF THE COMPARATIVE METHOD

E. E. Evans-Pritchard

This brings me to concluding observations. I suppose that no one would dispute that there is no other method in social anthropology than observation, classification and comparison in one form or another. This can be taken as axiomatic. There is nothing fundamentally different in method from its use by Montesquieu and what Radcliffe-Brown and others have recently said about it. But it is over two hundred years since *L'Esprit des lois* was written, and we may well ask once more what has been achieved by use of the comparative method, in whatever form, over this long period of time. Certainly little which could be acclaimed as laws commensurable with those which in the natural sciences have been reached in the two centuries. We are no nearer the *mathématique sociale* contemplated by Condorcet and those laws of succession and coexistence Comte believed would be revealed by the *méthode historique* (the comparative method). The method has not yielded the hoped-for results.

What are the reasons? Method in all sciences is the same; it is in the techniques that they vary, different kinds of phenomena requiring different treatment. Why then have the social sciences lagged behind? It has sometimes been said that we will be able to establish the laws of social life when we know more and better attested facts, but the contrary appears to be the case. It was

From the Hobhouse Memorial Trust Lecture No. 33 published by the Athlone Press on behalf of the London School of Economics and reprinted with their permission. Reprinted from *The Comparative Method in Social Anthropology* (1963), pp. 24–28.

easy for anthropologists to speculate about primitive institutions when little was known about them. It is not so easy now, when negative instances, vouched for by competent professional research, crop up everywhere to dispute any general theory. Here we can learn something from historiography. As Collingwood pointed out (1946: 127), the positivist historians used to take the line that when sufficient facts had been collected the laws of history would emerge, but in their happy engagement in collecting mountains of new facts they finally forgot about the laws.

The complexity of the phenomena is another reason advanced to account for the slow progress of social anthropology. Comte, who, for all his verbosity, had a clear understanding of scientific method, has told us that in the hierarchy of the sciences, each can be established only when the one below it has firm foundations, and so, since sociology, the queen of the sciences, heads the hierarchy it has been the last to come into being, having had to await the development of psychology or what he called cerebral physiology. The reason for this succession of the sciences, with mathematics at one end and sociology at the other, is that the phenomena studied become more and more complex the higher up the scale we go, so that those studied by sociology are the most complex of all; and furthermore, we must recognize that the greater the complexity the smaller the generality in each science of respective concepts. Now, it is true that the simplest institutions of the most primitive peoples can be bafflingly complex, the factors at play being so many and so varied that it would be difficult to isolate correlations between independent variables, assuming, that is, that there are any; but that does not sufficiently explain why social anthropology, in spite of the volume of research in the past few decades, has not reached more than very low-level generalizations. It can also be said, and has been, that while the natural sciences can experiment, we cannot. But it may also be said not only that some natural sciences are not able to experiment, or only to a limited degree, but also that, if we cannot make much use of laboratory conditions, both the vast range of societies open to observation and the history of institutions experiment for us, even though not subject to control; and further that there is a large element of experimentation in our field research. Doubtless other reasons could be adduced: e.g. that the comparative method has been employed for too ambitious ends, and that what have been compared have too often been customs, 'things,' rather than quantitative relations between qualities or properties—a charge which would require a separate lecture to sustain adequately.

But these difficulties and defects, taken singly or together, do not convincingly explain how it is that so little of what was aimed at has been attained. Would it therefore be temerarious (I may as well be hung for a sheep as a lamb) to ask ourselves if we should not question the basic assumption which has so long been taken for granted, that there are any sociological laws of the kind sought; whether social facts, besides being remarkably complex, are not so totally different from those studied by the inorganic and organic sciences that neither the comparative method nor any other is likely to lead to the formulation of generalizations comparable to the laws of those sciences. We have to deal with values, sentiments, purposes, will, reason, choice, as well as with historical circumstances. It is true that some social processes may take place without conscious direction or even awareness, e.g., languages (this may be why the scientific study of language, both with regard to history and structure, is more exact than that of other social activities), but the same cannot be said of, shall

we say, the organization of an army and its strategy and tactics. It is also doubtless to a large extent true, as Adam Ferguson has remarked, that though men always have a choice they cannot know to what their choice may ultimately lead. Everyone knows that in human affairs it is impossible to predict with any exactitude what will happen. Tomorrow's discoveries and decisions which will play their part in shaping future development are unknown today and at best can only vaguely be foreseen. That there are limiting principles in social organization no one would deny, but within those limits there is nothing inevitable about human institutions. Men have continuous choice in the direction of their affairs, and if a decision is found to be disadvantageous it is not beyond their wit to make a second to correct the first. To deny this is not only to ignore the rôle of values and sentiments but also to deny that of reason in the social life. 'The fault, dear Brutus, is not in our stars.' In investigating the nature of social institutions we have moved from the realm of natural law to the realm of positive law, to make the old Greek distinction between natural and moral philosophy as phrased by Montesquieu, who states it in a celebrated passage (1750: 4): 'Man, as a physical being, is, like other bodies, governed by invariable laws. As an intelligent being, he incessantly transgresses the laws established by God, and changes those which he himself has established.'

I have no intention of stating in this Lecture what I think should be the aims of social anthropology or how the subject could, or ought to, develop, or what it may one day become, but rather what appears to me have been its aims and development over two centuries to the present day.

I do not believe that, whatever the final outcome may be, a life spent in the study of primitive ways of life and thought—next year I shall have spent forty years at the task—is not well spent, that the portrayal of these ways is not in itself of supreme value for an understanding of human beings; I have no regrets. Perhaps I should regard myself first as an ethnographer and secondly as a social anthropologist, because I believe that a proper understanding of the ethnographic facts must come before any really scientific analysis.

If, therefore, I cannot share the optimism of my teacher and friend Professor Ginsberg, on whom the mantle of Hobhouse fell, when he thinks it possible that in the next hundred years or so progress in the social sciences may equal that in the biological sciences and even in the physical sciences, my scepticism does not mean that I think we should cease to look for such regularities as can be established by various forms of the comparative method. It would be a great convenience were we to succeed in finding them. If we do not, we shall at least in the search have achieved a deeper understanding of human society.

SELECTED READINGS

A. Commentaries and Critiques

Ackerknecht, Erwin H.
1954 On the comparative method in anthropology. In R. F. Spencer (ed.), *Method and Perspective in anthropology*. Minneapolis: University of Minnesota Press, pp. 117–125.

Berliner, Joseph S.
1962 The feet of the natives are large: An essay on anthropology by an economist. *Current Anthropology*, 3:1 (Feb.), pp. 47–77.

Eggan, Fred
1955 Social anthropology: Methods and results. In F. Eggan (ed.), *Social anthropology of the North American tribes*. (2nd edit.). Chicago: University of Chicago Press, pp. 485–551.

Evans-Pritchard, Edward Evan
1951a *Social Anthropology*. London: Cohen and West, chs. III, IV, V.

Fortes, Meyer
1953b *Social Anthropology at Cambridge since 1900*. Cambridge: Cambridge University Press.

Harris, Marvin
1968 *The rise of anthropological theory: A history of theories of culture*. New York: Thomas Y. Crowell, pp. 605–633.

Herskovits, Melville J.
1944 Review of Evans-Pritchard (1940). *American Anthropologist*, 46:396–400.

Kobben, A. J.
1952 New ways of presenting an old idea: The statistical method in social anthropology. *Journal of the Royal Anthropological Institute*, 82:89.

Leach, Edmund R.
1950b Review of Murdock (1949). *Man*, 50:169.

Sahlins, Marshall D.
1961 The segmentary lineage: An organization of predatory expansion. *American Anthropologist*, 63:322–345.

Schapera, Isaac
1953 Some comments on the comparative method in social anthropology. *American Anthropologist*, 55:353–362.

Singer, M. B.
1953 Summary of comments and discussion [of Schapera (1953)]. *American Anthropologist*, 55:362–366.

Spoehr, Alexander
1950 Observations on the study of kinship. *American Anthropologist*, 52:1–15.

B. Original Works

Bohannan, Laura and Paul
1953 The Tiv of central Nigeria. In *Ethnographic survey of Africa: Western Africa*. Part VIII. London: International African Institute.

Bohannan, Paul
1954 The migration and expansion of the Tiv. *Africa*, 24:2–16.

Eggan, Fred
1949 The Hopi and the lineage principle. In M. Fortes (ed.) *Social structure: Essays presented to Radcliffe-Brown*. 1949. Oxford: Clarendon, pp. 121–144.
————1950 *The social organization of the western Pueblos*. Chicago: University of Chicago Press.
————1954 Social anthropology and the method of controlled comparison. *American Anthropologist*, 56:743–763.

Evans-Pritchard, Edward Evan
1937 *Witchcraft, oracles and magic among the Azande*. London: Oxford University Press.
————1940a *The Nuer*. London: Oxford University Press.
————1951b *Kinship and marriage among the Nuer*. London: Oxford University Press.
————1963 *The comparative method in social anthropology*. London: Athlone.

Firth, Raymond W.
1951b *Elements of social organization*. London. Watts. Boston: Beacon paperback, 1963.

Fortes, Meyer
1940 The political systems of the Tallensi of the Northern Territories of the Gold Coast. In M. Fortes and E. E. Evans-Pritchard (eds.),

African political systems. London: Oxford University Press, for the International African Institute.

————1945 *The dynamics of clanship among the Tallensi.* London: Oxford University Press for the International African Institute.

————1949a *The web of kinship among the Tallensi.* London: Oxford University Press for the International African Institute.

————1949b Time and social structure. In M. Fortes (ed.), *Social Structure.* London: Oxford University Press for the International African Institute.

———— 1953b *Social anthropology at Cambridge since 1900.* Cambridge: Cambridge University Press.

———— 1953c The structure of unilineal descent groups. *American Anthropologist* 55:17–41.

————1969 *Kinship and the social order: The legacy of Lewis Henry Morgan.* Chicago: Aldine.

Fortes, Meyer and E. E. Evans-Pritchard (eds.)
1940 *African political systems.* London: Oxford University Press for the International African Institute. Reprinted in 1955.

Gluckman, Max
1950 Kinship and marriage among the Lozi of northern Rhodesia and the Zulu of Natal. In A. R. Radcliffe-Brown and C. D. Forde (eds.), *African systems of kinship and marriage.* London: Oxford University Press for the International African Institute.

Kroeber, Alfred L.
1938 Basic and secondary patterns of social structure. *Journal of the Royal Anthropological Institute,* 68:299–310.

Murdock, George P.
1947b Bifurcate merging: A test of five theories. *American Anthropologist,* 49:56–63.

————1949 *Social structure.* New York: Macmillan.

Nadel, Seigfried F.
1940 The Kede: A riverian state in northern Nigeria. In M. Fortes and E. E. Evans-Pritchard (eds.), *African political systems.* London: Oxford University Press for the International African Institute, pp. 165–196.

————1943 *Black Byzantium.* London: Oxford University Press.

————1950 Dual descent in the Nuba Hills. In C. D. Forde and A. R. Radcliffe-Brown (eds.), *African systems of kinship and marriage.* London: Oxford University Press for the International African Institute, pp. 333–359.

Radcliffe-Brown, Alfred R.
1951b The comparative method in social anthropology. *Journal of the Royal Anthropological Institute,* 81:15–22.

Radcliffe-Brown, Alfred R., and C. D. Forde (eds.)
1950 *African systems of kinship and marriage.* London: Oxford University Press for the International African Institute.

Schapera, Isaac
1950 Kinship and marriage among the Tswana. In *ibid.* Pp. 140–165.

Warner, William L.
1937 *A Black civilization.* New York: Harper & Row.

X

NONUNILINEAL KINSHIP

Nonunilineal kinship systems had long been included in the schemes of earlier anthropologists such as McLennan, Morgan, and so on. However they always concentrated on the bilateral nature of kinship and the nuclear family itself rather than on nonunilineal kinship groups at a higher level than the domestic group.

Westermarck (1891) and Malinowski (1913, 1930) were vitally interested in the nonunilineal nuclear family but not in kinship structure in general. The vast majority of British functional anthropologists spent their efforts on the analyses of unilineal systems mainly in Africa (Fortes 1953c).

After World War II, there was a great rise in interest in nonunilineal kinship structures. This can be attributed to the following: (1) Murdock (1949) showed that both data and theory on such systems were inadequate and (2) the United States Navy's occupation of the Pacific following World War II, brought in its train a host of anthropologists, a majority of whom worked with such systems.

Both Murdock and Radcliffe-Brown pointed out the relative scarcity of nonunilineal systems both in the world and in the ethnographies. Their apparent scarcity, they explained, was due to (1) the need for avoiding confusion of rights *in rem* and *in personam* (Radcliffe-Brown "Patrilineal and Matrilineal Succession," 1935b) and, relatedly, (2) the inability of bilateral groupings to be corporate and continuous over time. The latter statement also applied to that enigmatic group, the *kindred*.

The first field reports and consequent analyses of nonunilineal descent structures that appeared in the 1950s showed that some societies had been able to solve the problems of kindred noncorporateness and kindred noncontinuity, e.g. Pehrson ("Bilateral Kin Groupings as a Structural Type," 1954) on the Lapp. Thus, for a time, it was thought that the kindred could be a landholding (corporate) group through various social mechanisms. The other main thrust of such studies was concerned with the nature of kinship structures resulting from ambilineal descent, in which each person has a choice of affiliation. Such choices were classified as optative, producing ambilineages or ramages, or obligatory in turn, producing non-overlapping groups also called ramages, but better called (utro-)septs, by, e.g., Freeman (*Iban Agriculture*, 1955; "The Family System of the Iban of Borneo," 1958).

The emphasis during the 1950s, then, was on accumulating more data and also producing new classifications of what had previously been subsumed under the grab bag name of "cognative" (e.g., Radcliffe-Brown, 1935b, 1950). The trouble was that no two classifications were alike and that many analysts used different criteria when they assigned structures to the classes within their schemes. One of the pioneers in the study of these kinds of social structures was Firth whose original field work among the Maori (1929) and the Tikopia (1936) forced him to consider the nature of nonunilineal descent systems. When theoretical consideration of the subject became important, in the 1950s, Firth ("A

Note on Descent Groups in Polynesia," 1957b) helped to clarify the difference between those nonunilineal descent groups in which affiliation is optative and those in which it is compulsory. At the end of the decade, Davenport ("Nonunilinear Descent and Descent Groups," 1959) attempted to classify all the forms of nonunilineal descent that had been discussed in the literature to date.

In the 1960s a number of reexaminations of the previous analytical and classificatory schemes took place (Scheffler 1964). For one thing, it was realized that a true bilateral kindred could neither be corporate nor a continuing group, much as Murdock (1949) and Radcliffe-Brown had asserted. The concept of kindred could only embrace relatives bilaterally and, therefore, only unmarried members of a sibling group could share exactly the same kindred. However, the existence of a number of kindred-based groups that had corporateness and continuity had been witnessed. Whereas the true kindred might be only a "temporary action group," the stem-kindred (Arensburg and Kimball, *Family and Community in Ireland,* 1940), the nodal kindred

(Goodenough, "Kindred and Hamlet in Lalakai," 1962), and the assymetrical kindred could all be structural entities comparable in function and permanence to lineages and clans. It was also realized that there could be unrestricted bilateral groups (Goodenough, *A Problem in Malayo-Polynesian Social Organization,* 1955) which, though never real, could be of social significance for diadic, although not group, purposes.

The classification of ambilineal descent structures did not need such revision. The criterion of overlapping versus exclusive had become obvious and by this time most anthropologists realized the implications of such systems. By the 1960s, it was felt that the major need was for more field work among such types of societies to improve our understanding of how such groups are able to work within any situation. All types of nonunilineally-based societies have a degree of flexibility not approached by unilineal societies. Thus they may "change" without breaking the rules. On the other hand, such flexibility makes for great diversity of social forms which is probably the major reason why anthropologists had previously neglected these problems.

BILATERAL KIN GROUPINGS AS A STRUCTURAL TYPE: A PRELIMINARY STATEMENT

Robert N. Pehrson

A good deal of anthropological theory concerning social organization is derived from investigations of societies based upon unilateral descent groups. The lineage looms large in our picture of non-Western societies. It is frequently assumed that societies based upon the bilateral principle of descent are "amorphous," "unstructured," "loosely organized" or "infinitely complex." I wish to examine the local group organization and marriage residence patterns of one bilaterally

Reprinted by permission of the University of Manila from the *University of Manila Journal of East Asiatic Studies,* Vol. III (January 1954), pp. 199–202.

organized society in order to suggest that there is structure to this type of society but that the structure may be obscured by approaching it from a unilateral point of view.

My model of bilateral organization derives from research among the North Lapp reindeer nomads who migrate near Karesuando, Sweden; Enontekio, Finland, and Kautokeino, Norway. The fundamental bilateralism of Lapp society first becomes apparent in the reindeer nomads' inheritance rules and kinship nomenclature.

Among the Lapps, property is owned individually. Wealth is determined by the number of reindeer possessed and these are inherited and transmitted equally through the male and female lines. The reindeer are herded collectively by the migratory local group on pasturelands allocated according to customary rights of usage.

Neither is there any unilateral emphasis in the kinship terminology as shown by the complete bilaterality and symmetry of Lapp consanguineal kinship terms and by the rigid differentiation into generations. A third significant feature is the equivalence of siblings (in Ego's generation, the term of cousin is derived from the sibling term). This equivalence of siblings also occurs in the affinal terminology; Ego classes together his or her spouse's sister and female cousin and brother and male cousin and brother's wife and male cousin's wife.

These terminological features are parallel in local group organization which, among the Lapps, takes the form of migratory units or bands. Within the band, each generation has its own sphere of activities, rights and obligations. Band members of the same generational level are unified by the classification of cousins with siblings. The principle of equivalence of siblings also acts to increase the number of band members available for economic activities. In examining kinship behavioural patterns, I came to the conclusion that sibling solidarity is the fundamental kinship bond of Lapp society.

A cursory glance at Lapp band genealogies does not, at first, reveal any clear organizational pattern. The reason for this, I believe, is that a Lapp migratory unit is not a corporate body as such is generally conceived in Social Anthropology. That is, it lacks such corporate attributes of unilateral kin groupings as perpetuity through time, collective ownership of property and unified activity as a legal individual. Instead of thinking of the Lapp band as a corporate body, we must think of it as a series of alliances between sibling groups. Since these alliances have varying degrees of permanence, a Lapp may be a member of several bands during his life. Within the band, every person is related by blood or marriage to every other person either directly or through a third person. However, the Lapp band is not an "extended family" but, to repeat, an alliance between sibling groups, one of which is

dominant. The dominant sibling group also gives continuity to leadership since the leader is one of the dominant siblings and his successor is chosen from his sons or sons-in-law.

One of the problems involved in analyzing local group organization is the problem of marriage residence patterns. (I might add in passing that this is not the only problem involved in local group organization as some social anthropologists have assumed. It is also necessary to account for the presence of such unmarried adults as the hired herders found in many Lapp bands.) In analyzing marriage residence, I found no clear-cut matrilocal or patrilocal rules. I also found that the bands are not exclusively exogamic or endogamic. The concepts of complete exogamy or endogamy in relation to local groups may be useful in dealings with societies based on unilateral descent. However, where the local group is neither exclusively exogamic or endogamic (and this seems to be true of many bilateral societies in addition to the North Lapps), the problem becomes one of determining effective range of relationship covered by incest taboos. This is so because the Lapp band is not a corporate entity. By analyzing Lapp sociological concepts, it becomes apparent that the Lapp conceives of himself as a point in a network of kinship relations and not as a member of any corporate entity greater than the sibling group. In selecting a spouse, the Lapp must determine his position on his framework of kinship ties in relation to the position of his perspective mate rather than whether or not she belongs to his local group. Thus, if two people in the same band are not directly related or if they are not too closely related, then they marry. Ideally, incest taboos extend to third cousins but I found in analyzing genealogical connections between spouses that there is a certain amount of cousin marriage. Here there was a discrepancy between the statements of informants and a statistical analysis of the actual situation.

I noted the same discrepancy in statements as to change of residence upon marriage. The Lapps invariably state that at marriage, the woman should join her husband's band but an analysis of all marriages shows that about equally often, the man joins his wife's band and remains there. Occasionally, the spouse who moves brings his or her parents and parental siblings and families into the new band. Thus, it became apparent that the Lapps have no simple rules of residence, that the matrilocal and patrilocal characterizations do not apply to a society where parents change residence on the marriage of their children and that each case of residence change has to be investigated to determine the sociological factors at work.

Such an investigation reveals the following factors underlying marriage residence patterns (although not necessarily in the following order of importance):

1. *Relative wealth.* The spouse with less reindeer often moves to the band of the richer spouse. Rich Lapps frequently consider it desirable to marry off their children to poorer Lapps since, by so doing, they gain an addition to their labour force and do not lose their children's reindeer.

2. *Relative status of the spouses' parents or siblings.* Status is not determined exclusively by the individual's wealth. It may also derive from membership in the dominant sibling group of a particular band.

3. *Relative labour convenience.* A person who has several siblings may join his spouse's band if the latter lacks sufficient manpower to herd efficiently.

4. *Relative age considerations.* These are of two sorts. First, one must consider the age of the partners relative to their respective siblings. The eldest son tends to remain at home upon marriage if he is the son of a band leader or wealthy man. In poor families where the mother is widowed, the youngest son often remains at home upon marriage so that he may herd his family's reindeer while the elder siblings are employed as servants in other bands. If there is a great age difference, the younger spouse may join the band of the elder spouse since the latter has had more time to accumulate property.

Demographic factors are also important in determining residence after marriage. If a herding leader has only daughters, then most of the adult males in the band are liable to have come from other bands (as Mr. Ian R. Whitaker, University of Edinburgh, has shown).

Finally, ecological factors help to determine marriage residence. For example, the son of a rich man may decide to join his wife's band if his father and his own siblings have too many reindeer in relation to the available pastureland.

Now, throughout this consideration of factors determining residence, you may have noted that people may move in relation to their siblings instead of in relation to their parents. This may be correlated with the tendency for Lapps to marry at a relatively late age or when they have attained enough reindeer to set up their own household. By the time a Lapp is ready to marry, band and family leadership may reside in the person of a sibling or cousin rather than in a member of the parental generation. In other words, a Lapp's relation to his siblings may be as important as his relation to his parents in determining local group membership. Therefore, the terms "matrilocalism" and "patrilocalism" do not correctly characterize the whole situation. The terms "virilocal" and "uxorilocal" are more useful here. Virilocalism means that the married couple lives at the locality of the husband's kinsmen, uxorilocalism that the married couple lives at the locality of the wife's kinsmen. The uxorilocal-virilocal characterization emphasize relationships within one generation, a relationship which may be diagrammed as follows [*sic*]:

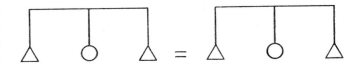

This relationship I believe to be crucial in bilateral society. The matrilocal and patrilocal characterizations emphasize the relationship over several generations, a relationship important in unilateral societies and diagrammed as follows:

Thus, when dealing with a bilaterally organized society which emphasizes sibling solidarity it seems apropos to use the terms "virilocal" and "uxorilocal" in place of the terms "matrilocal" and "patrilocal" with their implications of unilaterality.

Leonhard Adam, writing in *Man* (1948: 12), suggests that virilocal and uxorilocal are preferable to matrilocal and patrilocal which he considers etymologically incorrect and logically misleading. I also found the former terms more helpful in analyzing marriage residence patterns in a bilateral society. In using them to characterize all marriages, it became clear that Lappish marriage residence patterns are, in fact, bilocal, that there appears to be equal chances of uxorilocalism and virilocalism with the issue settled in each case by the various factors I have discussed before (as was suggested to me by Mr. Ralph Bulmer, Cambridge University).

The structural features of Lapp bilateral organization which emerge from these considerations of kinship, marriage and local group affiliation may be summarized as follows:

1. The society is horizontally separated into generations.

2. The sibling group is the fundamental structural unit of the society. The sibling group is the basic point of reference of Lapp social structure.

3. When the society must act as a unit, these sibling groups form alliances by bilaterally tracing relationship over a network of kinship ties. The temporary nature of these alliances gives flexibility to the structure.

I have not tried in this paper to trace all of the structural ramifications of bilateral organization. Rather, I have attempted to establish that bilateral organization has more structure than has been allowed and that this structure must be studied in its own terms.

A NOTE ON DESCENT GROUPS IN POLYNESIA

Raymond Firth

Now that the study of corporate descent groups is well advanced, and interest has been awakened in the existence and function of 'bilateral' systems, it seems appropriate to reexamine material from Polynesia. In such a study it is simplest to start by consideration of the criteria conventionally assigned to lineage structures. Lineage is essentially a unilineal descent group with some corporate functions, normally related by segmentary process to other descent groups of the same type, and with them usually covering the entire society. Empirically, lineages in the African field have been treated as exogamous. Descent groups in Polynesia for the most part offer a contrast to practically every one of these criteria. In Tikopia they are unilineal but in most other Polynesian societies they are not. They are formed by seg-

Reprinted by permission of the Royal Anthropological Institute of Great Britain and Ireland from *Man*, Vol. 57 (1957), pp. 4–7.

mentary process but the level of segmentation does not in itself necessarily have structural significance. In most Polynesian societies a person is a member of some descent group of some scale, but in at least one, Tonga, by no means every member of the society is a member of a 'lineage.' In no Polynesian society are the descent groups fully exogamous; even in Pukapuka, where the matrilineal sub-lineages are said to be exogamous, the lineages themselves are specifically stated not to be so.

Discovery of these facts is not particularly new. But the interest in the exploration of the varieties of unilineal systems has meant that for the most part the more general significance of the Polynesian units as descent-group variants has tended to be overlooked. To use them effectively at this stage, however, some reconsiderations is necessary.

Two pieces of evidence may be revived here.

In 1929 I drew attention to the curious structure of the Maori *hapu,* pointing out that it contravened the then generally accepted principle of unilineal transmission of membership of a descent group. I referred to this group as ambilateral in type (1929). I pointed out that such a group had two characteristics, that it was nonexogamous in distinction from the current view of the 'clan' (which term had often been used to describe *hapu*), and that it was not unilateral since both parents were eligible for purposes of descent-group affiliation. In the same year E. W. Gifford described for Tonga what he termed 'lineages,' an equivalent for the Tongan term *ha'a,* which previously had been described as 'tribe, class, family' (1929). Gifford cited what he called the splitting of major lineages into minor ones and likened the whole system of lineages to a tree with trunk, limbs, and twigs. He pointed out three interesting facts. One was how a minor segment (a 'limb') becomes huge and flourishing while a major segment (the 'trunk') ceases to flourish. This process was linked with chieftainship, since a succession of chiefs who could command authority was necessary as a nucleus for the lineage. 'Without such chiefs it appears to wilt and die and its membership gradually aligns itself with other rising lineages.' The second point was that not all members of Tongan societies in his day belonged to lineages. Some of the commoners seemed not to be aware of their lineage and even some modern descendants of former powerful chiefs were in this position. Thirdly, Gifford explained the mechanism of descent. He first described the lineages as 'patrilineal.' But he qualified this by saying that though tracing lineage through the mother was not considered 'appropriate,' it did sometimes occur, usually when it gave greater prestige or because the father was a foreigner. If a person were annoyed at something, he might shift his alliance from his father's to his mother's chief, which in effect would mean shifting his *ha'a.* Moreover, he pointed out that the process of realignment of allegiance from a dying to a flourishing lineage contravened the theoretical rule of patrilineal descent.

Later, I took up this main theme in regard to the flexibility of Polynesian descent (1936). In general, I noted how in Polynesia descent, i.e., membership in a named group, is usually not unilateral, but is conditioned to a large extent by residence. For the Maori I stated specifically that descent and the formal structure of the kinship grouping can be understood only by reference to residence and land holding. I suggested that the patriliny of Tikopia may be correlated with a 'patrilocal' form of marriage settlement, whereas the ambilaterality of the Maori and the mechanics of absorption from female into male side of the house of Samoa and Tonga are correlates of the tendency to 'uxorilocal' settlement at marriage. I also used the generic term 'ramage' to describe the various Polynesian descent groups, primarily because of their branching character.

From the synoptic viewpoint one may organize the Polynesian material in various ways. But one of the most important distinctions is that between descent-group systems which do not allow choice in affiliation as regards membership through male and female, and those which do. The former may be termed *definitive* descent-group systems, the latter *optative.* Taking as a criterion the rigidity of descent-group principle, one may single out two Polynesian societies of a *definitive* type. One is the single unilineal system of Tikopia with patriliny as its established theory. Patriliny is indeed operative in practice for all normal occasions. The other is the double unilineal system of Pukapuka in which a set of matrilineal units ('lineages') operates in conjunction with a set of patrilineal units. Varying from these are *optative* systems such as those of the Maori, Tonga or Samoa, in which the major emphasis is upon descent in the male line, but allowance is made, in circumstances so frequent in some societies as to be reckoned as normal, for entitlement to membership through a female. In such societies there are no purported matrilineal units. But closer analogy with Pukapuka is presented by Ontong Java, in which descent units with patrilineal predominance are combined with house-and-garden-owning units of matrilateral character with normal uxorilocal residence. A similar structure exists in Tokelau.

In considering Polynesian descent groups, there are three main concepts to be discussed. One is the concept of attachment to the group, the tracing of linkage with a particular descent group by the principle of *affiliation*. Another is the concept of the *constitution* of the group, the notion of what is meant when it is said that a person 'belongs' to a particular group, is a member of it. The third concept is that of the *formation* of the group, the process whereby new groups arise.

The principle of affiliation is of particular interest in Polynesia because of the relative lack of importance attached in most of the societies to the particular parent through whom it is traced. In theory as regards field of choice there are three possibilities:

(a)   Unilaterality by tracing affiliation consistently through *one* kind of parent only to the exclusion of the other.
(b)   Bilaterality by tracing affiliation through *both* kinds of parents equally and consistently.
(c)   Ambilaterality, in which, in any one generation, *both* kinds of parents are feasible for affiliation but some selectivity is possible, with difference of emphasis.

This opens up a range of variants. If affiliation is traced through both parents who are themselves members of different descent groups, then their child is a member of these two groups. Such a claim may in fact be made, as often occurs among the Maori. A person will say that he 'belongs' to both Group A and Group B, or that he is half Group A and half Group B. In practice, however, the claim to membership of one group tends to be emphasized at the expense of the claim to membership of the other, either permanently or varying according to context. When affiliation is traced through one parent only but it is immaterial which, the descent-group membership established may be unalterable. But an alternative, as already indicated, is that a person may switch from one group to another as circumstances dictate. Such reversible affiliation is probably more common than the unalterable or irreversible type. I should doubt if irreversible affiliation occurs in the ambilateral field in Polynesia (see Freeman 1955). Finally, since exogamy is not characteristic of Polynesian descent groups, there is always the possibility that both parents

may belong to the same descent group. The child thus has a double bond of affiliation. He does not need in such societies to emphasize one type of affiliation against the other, although for status purposes within the group he may stress the tie through father rather than through mother, or *vice versa*. (This gives a virtual though not theoretical bilaterality.)

One point about ambilateral affiliation is that a descent-group traced through the father in one generation may continue through the mother in the next generation and so on, using males and females as links without set order. The descent-group structure at any given moment looks like that of a lineage, as Leach has pointed out, though it lacks consistent unilineality.

In Polynesia, unilateral affiliation occurs in respect of the Tikopia *paito,* as also with the Pukapuka patrilateral *po* and *wakavae* and matrilateral *wua* and *keinanga*. Ambilaterality occurs among the Maori, the Tongans and the Samoans and also very generally in Polynesia.

As regards the constitution of descent groups, what are the implications of the choice found in ambilateral systems? A unilateral system of affiliation provides invariant group membership and presumably a less flexible group structure. An ambilateral system provides for variant group membership and presumably a more flexible group structure. This flexibility is seen, for example, in the Tongan situation where, taking advantage of the possibilities of choice, persons of relatively low status realign themselves with those of higher status and correspondingly give more impetus to the waxing and waning of lineage magnitudes. Again, the variant possibilities of group membership in the ambilateral scheme may tend to a more dispersed sense of responsibility. If not leading to divided allegiance, the possibilities of transferable allegiance in regard to one's descent group tend to modify the structural principle of the unity of the lineage group. What in unilineal descent systems must be provided by conflicting ties of neighborhood and political attachment, is given freer range within the very structure of the descent-group system itself in Polynesia. The ultimate outcome may not be so different, but the details of process are different. But the flexibility of Polynesian descent groups has its limitations. For the most part, while an individual may choose fairly freely the descent group in which he wishes membership, once his choice is made he tends to abide by it. Only rarely does he change. His ties with other groups remain dormant and in succeeding generations they tend to atrophy. With the Maori there is traditionally a tendency for claims to descent and land rights to 'grow cold' after a few generations if they are not revived by residence. Hence the variant structure provided in theory by ambilaterality is much less so in fact. The descent configuration is different from that of a unilineal lineage structure but the operational effects are very similar. (cf. Leach, 1950a)

From the point of view of an individual the mode of laterality in descent affiliation is of first importance: he is primarily concerned with the parent tie by which he is attached to the group. But from the point of view of analysis of a social structure the mode of lineality is equally important: group responsibility, claims and rights are concerned with the lines along which membership is transmitted from one generation to another.

Individuals are concerned with the principle of descent in their societies, in particular as regards status and rights—when they have to decide between competing claims or when they wish to establish a special relation to someone in a previous generation. But bearing in mind the

bilateral kin unit is of a corporate order, with specific functions in regard to land holding, status rights, etc. Here it is possible that completely bilateral groups may function for two or even three generations in descent from a common ancestor, both males and females consistently and invariably being reckoned in tracing membership. But unless birth and marriage are highly restricted or there is a high degree of endogamy, such bilinear continuity is unlikely. Unequal stress on the parental tie is necessitated by the ordinary conditions of living and handling resources. There may be a bias in favour of a tie with the male parent or through males generally and this patrilineal emphasis, though not exclusiveness, is characteristic of most Polynesian societies. Or again, the issue may be left to contiguity. Where the parents are from different villages residence tends to crystallize in one. It is clearly simpler to attach oneself to the group of the parent who is living in 'his own' village. Thus, a descent group behaving in most respects like a lineage tends to be formed.

I attach no great importance to terms as such. But considering the wide distribution of descent-group systems where there is some selectivity of parentage as a basis for membership, it would seem appropriate to have a set of terms to describe such systems. It would seem useful to include among such terms the following:

Ambilateral for the mode of attachment in which both parents are feasible as links in group membership.
Ambilineal for the maintenance of group continuity through the generations by using male or female links without set order.
Ramage for the kind of group constituted by using both/either parents as links in group membership.

need for economy in the handling of social resources, it is highly improbable that persons will be allowed to claim or establish membership in any wide series of descent groups through both parents and their ancestors. In other words, bilaterality is a feasible operational procedure; consistent, complete bilineality is not. It is for this reason that in speaking of 'bilateral kin group' it has seemed necessary to distinguish by name as well as in fact between two different types. One is the type illustrated by the Tikopia *kano a paito*, which is bilateral—but not bilineal —and is ego-oriented, having no persistence beyond the single generation. The other type of

In former publications I have used *ramage* to include the Tikopia unilineal descent group. This, I think, is better described functionally as a lineage, keeping the term ramage for those descent groups which are not unilineal. Ramage would then be defined as a corporate descent group of a non-unilinear (ambilineal) character, membership being obtained ambilaterally, i.e. through either parent according to circumstances. Such a group ethnographically is normally found to be non-exogamous.

Now consider the constitution of such a group. What is meant by saying that a person 'belongs' to a kin unit? One such concept is that of *recog-*

nition, in which the person himself and—of equal importance—other members of the society, ordinarily speak of him and regard him as properly associated with that group. (This is essentially a process of social classification.) Such recognition is commonly given by use of the group name. But the other concept into which recognition is almost at once translated is that of rights and obligations. The operation of status rights becomes one of the conditioning factors in the working of ambilineal descent. While most Polynesian societies, including those of the Maori and the Tongans, allow membership in a descent group through females, they attach greater importance for status purposes to descent through males. The Maori stress the prestige of chieftainship, boasting of unbroken descent through a line of firstborn sons; they also emphasize descent through males in the exercise of public privileges in oratory in general assemblies. Similar stresses in Tonga explain Gifford's opening statement that in Tonga patrilineal descent theoretically and largely in practice determines 'lineage' membership. As rank and status decrease, it becomes less important whether the individual's tie of membership is through male or female, and in the idiosyncratic case of Tonga the tie may be so reduced in importance that people of low status are ignorant even whether it exists. (This is as far as membership in the major named *ha'a* is concerned; they presumably belong to small unnamed descent groups.) From this point of view the Polynesian ramage is a unit of political significance, though it usually also involves ritual and other social rights, obligations and services outside the political field.

One question in regard to rights and obligations concerns the lack of exogamy. It may be argued that the difference between exogamous and non-exogamous lineage structures is not very important because with the latter there is always some degree of incest ban on unions between close kin, and the distinction is, therefore, only a matter of degree. But where a person's mother's and father's descent groups are identical there is a constriction upon the social circulation of goods and services which do not go out to another group and therefore do not serve to enlarge and maintain social ties. The whole system of pattern reciprocities may be affected. The Tikopia, for example, recognize this overtly. Moreover, the absence of exogamy means that when an intra-group marriage has occurred, the offspring will have a more limited set of kin in typical roles. When a marriage has been exogamous between Groups A and B, members of Group A provide the father's kin, those of Group B the mother's kin. When social support of any scale is needed and normally the parents' groups are mobilized, the child of a non-exogamous marriage has a more restricted field of support.

The importance of rights to group membership being associated with locality is now fairly clearly understood, and in respect of ambilineal groups has recently been reexamined and clarified by Goodenough. But a distinction can be drawn between theoretical and operational membership of such a group. In a unilineal group system, a person living in one place may be regarded for local purposes, especially the exercise of land rights, as a member of a kin group, the rest of whose members live elsewhere (this is the situation in Tikopia). Residence is irrelevant as a determinant of descent-group membership, but residence is, of course, very important for operational purposes. People who have plenty of land tend to cultivate themselves those parts of 'their' lands which are nearer to their homes. In a completely bilineal group ('unrestricted bilateral' in Goodenough's term) the same is possible. But in an ambilateral group, a ramage, theoretical and operational limitations of land rights tend to coincide. Residence by itself does not give title to descent-group membership, but land rights established by descent-group membership tend to remain operational only through residence. Conditions here vary. In some communities several generations must pass before absentee land rights can be extinguished. Among the Maori, for instance, a change in residence traditionally implied a diminishing validity for a land claim. But it should be noted that in some Polynesian communities, e.g. Rarotonga and Maori, the institution of a new political and legal system has facilitated some change. New markets for products have given a more pronounced economic value to land. Peaceful conditions have allowed people to move about more easily and maintain multiple residence. Record of title has given a legal validity to what otherwise might have been disputable. The result has been to allow the operation of dispersed land rights to an extent apparently much greater than in traditional times. In this respect the land operations of ambilateral groups have tended to resemble those of lineages, though as yet there does not seem to be any sign that in the Maori system, for example, rights through women are tending to become more restricted than rights through men.

A few words about processes of group formation.

Anthropologists speak with confidence about the process of lineage segmentation, yet it must be remembered that most of the evidence is inferential rather than observed. It rests largely upon the interpretation of genealogical and other social data. Actual observation of changes that have taken place over a period of time during which documentary or other evidence about such segmentation was available has been scanty. One line of enquiry in the Polynesian field would be to take the classic material of, say, Elsdon Best on Tuhoe *hapu*, now nearly half a century old, and trace the changes in segmentation and rearrangement since Best's work. I discussed briefly 'progressive segmentation' among the Maori, but it would be interesting to ascertain how far segmentation of Maori ramages is, in fact, progressive.

One may distinguish here four concepts. One is the *segmentation model*, the anthropologist's description of what he understands to have taken place as a type of process. Then there is the *segmentation charter*, the local type of what the people themselves, or sections of them, regard as the 'historical' order of events. Then there is *operational segmentation*, the way the descent group splits for various social ends, recombining where necessary for other ends. Finally, there is what may be termed *definitive segmentation*, the irreversible process leading to the formation of new groups which do not then recombine. This process, progressive in character and sometimes described as 'polysegmentation,' may also be described as *gemmation*, referring to the way in which budlike growths become detached and develop into new individuals. This term might perhaps be most aptly used for those cases of segmentation in which connexions with the parent descent group are lost, so that what have been sometimes called 'truncated lineages' occur. This is a process which historically would seem to have taken place in many of the smaller Polynesian communities with the growth of population.

Segmentation is not a process which is difficult to understand. What is sometimes difficult is to relate the segmentation model of the anthropologist to the operational segmentation of the society—the way in which the actual descent groups order their personnel for social purposes. Here it may be suggested that segmentation in any social structure is not an automatic process but is related to the available resources. The relation cannot be simple but it would appear that increasing pressure of population upon land is likely to lead to a speeding-up on the segmentation process for operational purposes, though not necessarily in terms of the structural frame.

NONUNILINEAR DESCENT AND DESCENT GROUPS

William Davenport

For many years interest in social structure has been directed towards unilinear systems, while

Reproduced by permission of the author and the American Anthropological Association from *American Anthropologist*, Vol. 61, 1959, pp. 557–569.

bilateral structures have been allowed to remain an unstudied residual category for everything that is not unilinear. Some writers (e.g. Fortes 1953c: 33) have stressed the universality of certain bilateral features, while others (e.g. Radcliffe-Brown 1935b: 302) have considered the absence of a unilinear principle of some kind to be unusual or rare. Even the more cursory glance at the now voluminous literature on societies with bilateral structures reveals the great variation among them and suggests the need, not only for a better understanding of what these variations are, but also of what structural principles are being varied.

Murdock (1949: 56–58), Pehrson (1954), and Spoehr (1950: 3) have stressed the need for studies of bilateral social structure, and in his study of the Konkama Lapps, Pehrson (1957) set forth and defined the concept of "bilateralism." Also aware of the inadequacies in the current bilateral concept, Freeman (1957: 55) has offered the term "utrolateral filiation" to describe some features of Iban social structure. Others have run into special problems in describing and classifying societies where the ordinary bilateral unilinear distinctions are either inappropriate or inadequate. Most notable of these have been Boas (1920) with the Kwakiutl, Firth (1929: 98) with the Maori, Gifford (1929: 29–33) with the Tongans, McIlwraith (1948: I: 117–162) with the Bella Coola, Gluckman (1951: 71–76) with the Lozi, and Goodenough (1955: 73–75) with the Gilbertese.

The plan of this paper is first to survey a number of selected examples of what Goodenough (1955: 72) has called nonunilinear descent groups, and then to compare these with the well-known unilinear types and with variations in the so-called kindred type of structure. In comparing these systems, however, one does not get far before it also becomes clear that a new look at the concept of descent itself, as well as the related concepts of inheritance and succession, might be rewarding. The purpose of this paper is not just to set up a series of types or to study bilaterality as a special type, but to offer at least tentatively three structural features which seem to operate in all systems, and which in their various combinations produce the rich variety of kin groups we find described.

Let us look briefly at the concept of descent. This has been variously defined, depending upon the interests of the investigator and the unit of analysis with which he starts. The most common

American usage seems to begin with the existence of a kin group; descent is then defined as the manner in which persons affiliate with this group by birth (see Murdock 1949: 15). A similar procedure is to start with society as the unit and to define descent as a means of grouping or of dividing the society into segments of kin (see Lowie 1948: 7–9, 57–59). Another approach is to regard descent as a way of ascribing jural rights by means of kinship relationships (Radcliffe-Brown 1935b). These several usages do not really differ essentially from each other, and each has certain advantages when it comes to describing or comparing systems. It should be pointed out that, whatever else a kin group may be, its membership is characterized by some commonality of status with respect to other groups of kin, and that descent is as much a way of limiting a social unit and excluding some persons as it is of including others. As a minimal definition, therefore, let us consider descent as a way in which statuses are ascribed and/or withheld on the basis of kin relationships. Statuses can be defined either by their associated behavioral roles or in legal or quasi-legal terms.

A rule of descent will be considered unilinear when ascription through a specified kin relationship approaches a frequency of 100 percent and when the norms of the society do not under normal conditions provide alternatives. Emphasis is placed on normal conditions, for few if any societies are so rigid as not to provide alternatives for special situations (e.g., adoption, *ambil anak*). The matrilineal and patrilineal subtypes are well known, but it is well to keep in mind that these are not the only unilinear variations that have been described.

Nonunilinear descent, then, is ascription or exclusion through specified kin relationships, but where societal norms provide more than one possibility or where no single alternative rule approaches a frequency of 100 percent. However, nonunilinearity is not to be confused with double descent, where different statuses are ascribed by different unilinear rules (e.g., Ranon, Arunta; see Lowie 1949: 58–59, 260; Murdock 1949: 50–52).

A major step toward better understanding of bilateral social structure was taken by Goodenough (1955: 71–72) when he differentiated between two types of groups on Onotoa in the Gilberts and at the same time untangled the terminological confusion in the use of the term "kindred." Following American usage and a precedent which seems to have been established by Phillpotts (1913: 5) in her study of Teutonic kin groupings, Goodenough retained the term kindred for the kind of nonperpetuating kin grouping we have in the United States, namely, a set of kinsmen who are related through males and females within a specified degree of collaterality to a particular common relative. Different from the kindred is a group in which the members trace their relationship lineally through either or both sexes to a common known or unknown ancestor; Goodenough aptly called this the "nonunilinear descent group."

These nonunilinear descent groups resemble unilinear ones in several ways. For instance, the members believe they are descended from a common ancestor, though frequently they cannot state the precise genealogical connections; the groups are commonly named and have identifying emblems; land and other productive property are to be found under their collective control; and often myth, ritual, and religious beliefs are closely associated with them. Marriage may also be regulated by group membership, but more often than not exogamy does not prevail. To be sure, the Mangaian kopu is exogamous, with maximal extension to both mother's and father's groups, but on the other hand, the Kwakiutl numaym is actually agamous, even though marriages are preferentially exogamous. The Bella Coola minmint is also agamous, but with endogamic marriages preferred.

The fact that these descent groups are not all exogamous divests them of a feature that has often been used to characterize the clan and sib (see Lowie 1948: 9; Murdock 1949: 47), but it must be remembered that there are many instances of agamous or even preferentially endogamous unilinear kin groups The Tikopian kainanga (Firth 1936) and the Arab lineages are but two well-known instances. Admittedly, an endogamous kin group is quite different from an exogamous one, and the consequences of this difference become especially significant in the

case of nonunilinear kin groups. Nevertheless, we should bear in mind that all or nearly all societies prescribe both exogamy and endogamy in accordance with various principles, including such diverse ones as age, race, social class, religion, and kinship.

Nonunilinear descent groups resemble unilinear ones in still other structural characteristics. One finds restricted segments of larger groups that seem to correspond to the lineage divisions of unilinear descent groups. For example, prior to 1746 the Highland Scottish clan, an endogamous nonunilinear descent group and not a unilinear clan, was frequently segmented into smaller lineage-like divisions called septs on the basis of descent from particular clan members (Adam 1952). The exogamous 'aiga sa of Samoa has similar segments based on the same principle, and in both these cases the smaller divisions organize and control activities that the larger descent group does not. One also finds nonunilinear descent groups compounded into phratries or moieties for special purposes. The New Zealand Maori iwi is made up of constituent hapu on the basis of legendary associations, while the Mangaian kopu are similarly linked into "right" and "left" moiety-like divisions.

Finally, nonunilinear descent groups, in combination with rules of post-marital residence, occur in localized and in dispersed or purely consanguineal forms. This is of course the distinction which Murdock (1949: 65–78) has made between sib and clan for unilinear kin groups. It is pertinent to note here that it seems to be the localized forms of nonunilinear descent groups that are the more frequently described, since the kinds of activities, rights and obligations most often regulated by them are those requiring residence and participation with other members of the group. Rules of post-marital residence, too, like those of inheritance and succession, can be thought of as systems of ascription that pertain to particular statuses or activities.

Let us now look at some of the varieties of nonunilinear descent itself. In Mangaia, affiliation with the exogamous kopu occurs through either the father or the mother, but the choice is not left to the individual. Children are assigned alternately to the father's then the mother's kopu, according to prearrangement between representatives of the two groups. In Nukuoro a similar system prevails. The descent groups, called *te-haka-sa-aluna,* do not regulate marriage, but in case of intergroup marriages the children are assigned first to one parent's group then to the other, beginning with the father's.

With the Iban of the Baleh region of Sarawak, affiliation with the independent, corporate, exogamous three-generation apartment group called *bilek,* is with that of either the husband or wife, depending upon with which the married couple chooses to reside. This means that rights in land, ritual obligations, and other activities which come under bilek control, as well as membership in the corporate longhouse village, are subject to some degree of choice at marriage. A couple which affiliates with one thereby relinquishes its potential claim on the other, so that there is no overlapping membership. Their children can belong only to the bilek with which their parents have affiliated, and like them, when they marry they must decide with which bilek (and longhouse group) they will live and affiliate (Freeman 1957).

On Onotoa one of the descent groups which controls land, feuding, and other economic activities, but does not regulate marriage in any way, is called the *kainga.* As in the case of the Iban bilek, affiliation is with either spouse's group, and only the one which is chosen by them becomes a possible choice for their children (Goodenough 1955). In both societies, economic factors exert some influence on the married couple's choice.

Among the Kwakiutl (southern branch) the descent groups are called numaym, and affiliation with one is dependent upon possession of a summer potlatch name that traditionally belongs to the group. Residence with and use of numaym lands are also contingent upon possession of the name. A man acquires his name from his father, from a close agnate such as a brother or a father's brother, or from his mother's father. Only one instance is recorded where a man actually took a potlatch name from, and participated with, his wife's father's group instead of holding it and passing it on to his son. Marriage is not completely regulated by numaym affiliation, but exogamy is preferred. In Boas' time, individuals could be simultaneously affiliated with more than one numaym through the possession of several names.

The Bella Coola have a similar descent system, with groups called minmint. As with the Kwakiutl, affiliation depends upon having an ancestral name belonging to a group. A man may receive names from a number of his paternal and maternal relatives, and may thus possess more than one. However, having a name obliges him to validate it by potlatch, and it is difficult to fulfill this obligation for more than one name. Some men do so and thus belong to more than one minmint, but most return unvalidated names to their respective groups and thereby relinquish their claims of affiliation. Here again a choice of descent is made among alternatives, and relative social and economic advantages seem to influence the choice. Since marriage is preferentially within the minmint, endogamy tends to reduce the number of different groups among which a man can exercise his choice of affiliation.

With the Lozi of Barotseland, each person is affiliated with a "descent name" group called *mishiku.* Each of these has an ancestral village site located on a small mound that rises above the flood level of the Zambezi River. Participation with one of these groups involves living in its ancestral village, and one may choose any of the villages where his or his spouse's parents or grandparents have lived. Since the mishiku does not regulate marriage in any way, intra-mishiku marriages frequently reduce the number of possible choices to less than the maximum. Since land is very limited on these mounds, a married couple's choice is partly influenced by the availability of space for a house.

The Samoan *'aiga sa* is a descent group controlling garden land, house sites, and certain ceremonials. It is exogamous, since the incest taboo is extended to all known relatives. Associated with each 'aiga sa is one or more titles, from the senior of which the group takes its name. Title holders are selected from among the eligible males participating with the group. Affiliation with a descent group is through either father or mother, and a married couple may affiliate with the groups of either spouse. A person is mainly associated with one group— that with which he lives—but he may participate to some extent in several. Living with and using lands belonging to a particular 'aiga sa, as well as the right to speak at meetings of the group, are dependent upon the consent of its members, and this may be denied if there is doubt about a person's genealogical relationship to the group or if he has failed to fulfill his obligations to it. Here, too, indefinitely extended relationships through consanguinity become limited by the obligations of participation. Even though there is considerable overlapping membership, the number of potential affiliations is appreciably reduced by both remissness in obligations and failure to remember genealogical connections.

This kind of nonunilinear descent is also exemplified by the Maori *hapu*. A person usually affiliates with either of his parents' or his spouse's parents' hapu, but it is also possible to obtain membership in the hapu of a grandparent and even a great-grandparent, provided the genealogical connection is recognized by the hapu in question. Such recognition depends upon the extent to which the claimant has participated in or maintained reciprocal ties with the group. If he has allowed these ties to "grow cold" they lapse, and it is difficult to maintain them with a large number of hapu. Here again potential affiliations are reduced by obligations to participate.

Nonunilinear affiliation is of course not limited to sedentary societies like those just cited. Among the Könkämä Lapps, band membership is determined through either spouse's kin relationships to the pair of male siblings who form the nucleus of the band and by whose name the band is called (Pehrson 1957). A comparable situation probably occurs in nonunilocal bands elsewhere, including those with hunting economies, but we frequently lack sufficient data to determine what the rules of affiliation are.

Several distinct trends are to be noted in the above examples. One is toward an either/or sort of affiliation, whereby an individual is assigned to, or chooses among, limited alternatives and relinquishes all other potential affiliations for himself and his children. Like classic unilinear descent, this is best understood as establishing one right of membership, albeit through the exercise of choice rather than automatic ascription, and at the same time giving up all other such rights, i.e. establishing a no-right, in other groups. Contrasted with this is the overlapping kind of membership where a person may continue to participate, even though partially, in more than one group. Residence and social participation with a group frequently serve as either contingent or final factors in fixing present affiliation and that of descendants. Nonunilinear affiliation also differs as to whether choice for a married couple includes alternatives through one or both spouses. Possible modes of affiliation may also be narrowed by group agamy and endogamy. Variable as they are, these examples demonstrate the need for classifying such kin groups in a manner that makes them coordinate in most structural respects with unilinear descent groups.

The "descent group" serves equally well for both unilinear and nonunilinear types, and in accordance with current usage, when they are unilinear they are called sibs or lineages, depending on internal segmentation and genealogical depth. For nonunilinear descent groups the term "sept" is proposed. Though employed by others in various senses, this term is used by Boas (1920: 114–115) for the Kwakiutl numaym in an attempt to distinguish it from unilinear kin groups elsewhere on the Northwest Coast. The term "clan" (Murdock 1949: 47–50, 65–78) may be used for the localized core of sib and sept plus their inmarrying spouses and other dependents.

The fact that septs are comparable to sibs can be demonstrated by some areal distributions and the evolutionary trends to be inferred from them. The sept can be considered one of the distinguishing traits of social organization of Polynesia, for they are found in Tonga, Samoa, the Societies, the Cook Islands, New Zealand, the

Marquesas, Easter Island, and Hawaii. In all these cultures very similar activities are found to be organized by this system. Among the so-called outliers of Polynesia, however, we find certain of these same activities organized by unilinear descent. Tikopia (Firth 1936) organizes some of them by patrilineal descent, Kapingamarangi (Emory 1956) regulates certain of them in part through matrilineal descent, while Ontong Java (Hogbin 1934) organizes by both, i.e. by double descent. Pukapuka (Beaglehole 1938), though not strictly an outlier, resembles Ontong Java, and in addition organizes a third set of activities by nonunilinear descent.

A similar areal variation was noted many years ago by Boas on the Northwest Coast of North America, but unlike Polynesia, it cannot be assumed that this differentiation occurred within one genetic group, speaking closely related languages of a single linguistic stock.

Let us now turn to the other major form of bilateral organization, the kindred. Here the means of ascribing and restricting statuses differs radically from that which we have termed the sept. Each person has his own kindred, the personnel and boundaries of which coincide only with those of his siblings, and siblings are members of as many different kindreds as there are kin types in their own (see Murdock 1949: 56–58). In making this distinction between kin groups which are identical for siblings only and descent groups whose personnel is the same for all members, Phillpotts (1913: 268, 275) used for the former the terms "shifting kindred" and "fluctuating kindred," while more recently Leach (1950a: 61–62) has suggested "personal kindred." These terms merit serious consideration in this area where terminological confusion has been the rule and not the exception. The term personal kindred will be adopted here, since it most clearly describes the most salient feature of this kind of organization.

One of the most complete descriptions of personal kindreds comes from the Ifugao. Here the kin group, or "family" as Barton has called it, consists of all the descendants of an individual's eight pairs of great-grandparents. It may include as many as two thousand persons, many more than in most of the septs already described. In discussing legal relationships, Barton clearly shows that the only kin types with the same "family" composition are siblings. The extent of one's involvement in legal disputes is a positive function of one's genealogical closeness to the litigants. In reference to property, a rich man who owns much land has a definite obligation which decreases as a function of collateral distance. The Kalinga have a similar organization, although some form of sept may also be present in connection with the endogamous tribal districts.

Leach (1950a) presents some interesting comparative data on personal kindreds, as defined by marriage regulations, among several peoples of Sarawak. The Semambu Murut prefer marriage with kin who are more distant than fourth cousins, or just within this range, i.e., with third cousins, by paying a fine for incest, but marriage with first cousins is absolutely prohibited. The Iban, however, prescribe marriage with second to fifth cousins and prohibit marriage with both first cousins and kin beyond fifth cousins.

The generalized version of Eskimo culture presented by Hoebel (1954: 67–99) reveals a personal kindred range for extension of the incest taboo, obligatory action in blood revenge, and other kin-organized statuses which extends only to lineals and siblings. With the contemporary Nunamiut Eskimo of Alaska, Pospisil (1957) reports that the incest taboo is extended only to primary relatives, all other kin being eligible as spouses. Strict obligations to attend life-crisis rites and to extend special hospitality are extended to a wider range of kinsmen, including lineals to great-grandparents and great-grandchildren, first collaterals to siblings' great-grandchildren, second collaterals to children of first cousins, third collaterals to second cousins, and fourth collaterals to siblings of great-grandparents, but never beyond these limits. All relatives outside this scope, even though their relationship is known, are sociologically non-kin.

Clearly, the most variable feature of the personal kindred is its collateral limits. In the same society, moreover, different statuses may be ascribed by different degrees of collateral extension. This can occur in two ways, by a sharp break in status ascriptions across collateral lines (e.g., Iban marriage regulations and the wider extension of obligations in Nunamiut kindreds) or by a gradual transition as collateral distance increases (e.g., Ifugao land distribution and litigations).

The distinction between personal kindreds and descent groups seems clear enough if one recalls their differences in point of reference (an individual or siblingship as contrasted with an ancestor or ancestors), clarity of group boundaries (overlapping and diffuse as contrasted with distinct and discrete), and the presence of some variable degree of collateral limitation in the former and no collateral limitation in the latter. But Leach (1950) gives an example where these differences begin to fade. The Iban longhouse village is composed of a number of apartment groups, all of which are related by consanguineal or affinal ties. Consanguinity is reckoned to include fifth cousins and, at least theoretically, each member of the longhouse community should have a different set of persons in his personal kindred which is calculated to this limit. But consanguine relationships are not accurately calculated to the sixth degree of collaterality, so every member of the longhouse community acts as if he had the same personal kindred. Even though the norms of organization here are not those of a sept, behaviorally and structurally the result is the same.

Collateral limitation may be important, but in a different way, in unilinear descent groups as well. The Garia of New Guinea (Lawrence 1955), for example, have land-owning patrilineages with considerable genealogical depth. Land may be lent to nonmembers through an affinal link, but after four generations of continuous holding in the same lineage, the jurisdiction over this loaned land passes from the lineage to which it originally belonged to the lineage of the borrowers. These changes are tied in with supporting beliefs about the destiny of the souls of deceased agnatic ancestors.

Commenting on the continuity and corporate function of personal kindreds, Goodenough (1955: 71) states that, because there is no continuity of membership from one generation to the next, kindreds cannot function as land-owning bodies (see also Murdock 1949: 61.) This argument follows only if one assumes that ownership of land is an all-or-none kind of relationship. But Hoebel (1954: 54–63) and others have clearly demonstrated that ownership, whether by groups or by individuals, can consist of a number of different kinds of rights and limitations which cannot be collected under a single term with any degree of precision. A personal kindred can become a land-owning and land-holding group with continuity, just like a descent group, if the title to the land is vested in a single individual with the limitation that it must be distributed and redistributed among his personal kindred and cannot be alienated without their consent. A member of this kindred who does not hold the title has the right to claim some land for his use and the power to approve or disapprove its transfer or alienation from the group. If there is a patterned rule of succession to the title, regardless of what form this might be, the system has continuity through time. There will be a genealogical line of title holders, at the end of which is the incumbent's personal kindred. In each generation some genealogically related persons are born outside the collateral range of the kindred and are thereby excluded from it, while those born within this range continue to exercise their rights toward the title holder.

Such a system differs very little from that which occurs in many unilinear systems where land and other valued goods associated with the kin group are held by a title holder or head of that group for distribution and redistribution to members. The nonunilinear version outlined above is not just a hypothetical case, but is exactly what occurs with the Ifugao and Kalinga. In both these societies, primogenitural inheritance keeps lands intact, but each society has a different way of amalgamating lands inherited in other ways. We find related systems in European societies as well. Among the small farmers of County Clare in Ireland (Arensberg and Kimball 1940:61–157), for example, an agnatic line of title holders constitutes the genealogical line of land holders toward whom a small personal kindred have definite obligations, even though they may not be resident on the land. As a consequence of the permanence of the farmstead and the continuity provided by the line of successive title holders, the kin unit itself has a kind of perpetuity. The term suggested for this kind of organization is "stem kindred."

The features that might clearly differentiate the stem kindred from the sept become blurred in some instances, and the Tongan haa provides an excellent example. Each haa is composed of a set of kin who claim consanguine ties through males or females from a common ancestor. It is localized in an unambiguously bounded district, and each haa is headed by a noble in whose title is vested the power to distribute and withhold all lands within his district. The title holders of all haa are related to each other through an official genealogy of the Polynesian sort that goes back to the mythological past. Since each member of a haa claims to be related to its title holder, although he may not know what the precise relationship is, he can trace his relationship through the latter's genealogy to all title holders of other haa and through them to all members of those haa. This system functions not only in relationship to land, but also determines some everyday kinds of behavior as well. When, for example a person meets someone from a different haa to whom he cannot trace a direct relationship, their reciprocal behavior is determined by the genealogical relationship of their respective title holders.

Similar stem relationships within septs can be found in other Polynesian societies. Some emphasize an agnatic line of succession; others, like Hawaii, exhibit no sex preference but stress primogeniture alone, while in Samoa the title holders are selected from among the male members of the 'aiga sa so the genealogical relationship between them is obscure. This same kind of stem structure gives both the Iban longhouse community and its constituent bilek a special kind of continuity by way of a line of special status holders which connect the founders with the present-day inhabitants (Freeman 1955: 7–9).

While some of the examples given above were selected to reveal a number of kin group types—sib, sept, personal kindred, and stem kindred—some were also chosen to show how these types are not qualitatively distinct, but merge into one another in graduated series. The summary to follow is largey a recapitulation of the features, already discussed, which seem to unite them all. It must be kept in mind that although the unit of analysis is the kin group, the ultimate frame of reference is the society, and that different activities and statuses in the same society are frequently organized by different combinations of features, so that kin groups of several types may occur. Moreover rarely is an activity or status organized by kin relationships alone, but by kinship in combination with other criteria such as sex, age, maturity, race, religion, and ability. Each of the three features presented below will be defined qualitatively as traits, although they might be ordered into variables.

The first feature is descent, of which the unilinear and nonunilinear subtypes and their measures have already been discussed. The limiting case of nonunilinear descent results in the personal kindred type of kin group, in which any and all means of reckoning relationship are utilized. This is what Parsons (1943: 26) has called "multilineal" in reference to the United States personal kindred, and what Fortes (1953c: 33) has termed "filiation" in order to contrast it with unilinear descent. However, the term "bilateral descent" seems adequately to describe the symmetrical and nonlinear aspects of this kind of ascription, and since it has been used in this way for many years, there seems no reason to adopt a new term. Where descent is nonunilinear and choice is exercised among a limited number of alternatives, as with the septs described above, then the term "multi linear" would be appropriate and will distinguish this form from both unilinear and bilateral forms.

The second feature, which will be called "jural exclusiveness," refers to whether a status is ascribed by only one of the alternative rules of descent at a time, or is simultaneously ascribable to the same individual by more than one. Put into terms of group affiliation, it refers to whether an individual is permitted to affiliate with only one of the alternative kin groups, relinquishing his claims to all others, or may affiliate with more than one. In the examples above, affiliation in the Mangaian kopu, the Nukuoro te-haka-sa-aluna, and the Lozi mishiku is "exclusive," since there is no overlapping membership. With the Kwakiutl numaym, the Bella Coola minmint, and the Samoan 'aiga sa descent is also multilinear, but individuals are permitted to belong to and participate with more than one group, making affiliation "nonexclusive." Personal kindreds are always nonexclusive, sibs and lineages are always exclusive, while septs may be either. Exclusiveness is specified by Freeman's (1955: 7–9) term "utrolateral" (Latin uter-, either of two) which he applies to the Iban bilek, where an individual may have and transmit membership in either his father's or his mother's birth group, but not both. Unfortunately, this term is not quite applicable to instances like the Lozi, where there may be more than two alternative choices. Nonexclusiveness is implied by Firth's (1929: 98–100) term "ambilateral," which he applied to the Maori hapu, but it is not certain that this is exactly what he intended it to mean.

Important details of these two features are often missing from ethnographies reporting them. The potential kinds and number of choices permitted in multilinear descent systems are also frequently omitted, as are discussions of the means by which some of these choices of affiliation in parent's generation are eliminated as possible choices in the children's. Likewise, it is not always clear whether septs are jurally exclusive or nonexclusive, or whether individuals may change affiliation from one group to another during the course of their lives.

The third feature concerns the ascription of statuses collaterally along a type of descent. In sib and sept organization, statuses are ascribed to every eligible person without diminution or limitation, and they are indefinitely extensible to future generations. Since no collateral restrictions apply, this may be called "unrestricted collateral extension." The incest taboo in exogamous descent groups is usually extended in this

way, and the same principle may be found in assigning rights to land, ritual obligations, and other activities.

Personal kindreds differ from septs and sibs in this respect by always imposing some degree of collateral limitation on the extension of statuses. In the examples given above, this "collateral restriction," as it will be called, varied from one degree (Nunamiut Eskimo extension of incest) to six degrees (Semambu Murut extension of incest), as measured by the number of ascending generations from Ego to the relative who connects the most removed collateral line. For the sake of clarity, the measure of collateral restriction in personal kindreds should include both the number of ascending generations to the branching of the most distant collateral line as well as the number of descending generations down this and each included line to their limits.

If they were to be expressed in terms of collateral extension, individual ownership of property, occupancy of offices, and possession of titles, together with their associated rules of inheritance and succession, would be instances of maximal collateral restriction. That is, there is no extension of the status along any consanguineal relationship until the occupant of the status is removed; yet ascription, like descent, is by kin relationships.

As noted above, different statuses may be ascribed by different degrees of collateral extension and restriction of bilateral descent (e.g., Iban and Semambu Murut). This is similar in several ways to the internal differentiation of unilinear descent groups. Tiv lineages provide an interesting comparison. As the Bohannans (1953) describe them, each patrilineage has several spans of different degrees of inclusiveness. Each of these spans regulates specific activities which the less inclusive spans do not. These spans, however, are reckoned by agnatic descent from particular ancestors who stand in ascending genealogical relationship to each other, not by a fixed number of ascending generations from an Ego as they are in personal kindreds.

The structural significance of this similarity is that a kind of segmentary organization can be associated with bilateral as well as with unilinear descent where it is very frequently to be found. It was also noted above that septs may have segmentary divisions (e.g., Highland Scottish clan and Samoan 'aiga sa). It is interesting to note again the different means by which this internal differentiation occurs in descent groups and personal kindreds, and the way it underscores the different structural characteristics of the two kinds of organization. Descent groups, having a fixed point of origin in some real or hypothetical ancestor, segment by reckoning descent from particular members of the group. Personal kindreds, having no ancestral point of origin, are reckoned bilaterally from an Ego, and since bilateral descent does not exclude consanguines in any way, some degree of collateral restriction must be established in order to form a limited set of kin. Internal differentiation, then, can only take place by a recognition of different degrees of collateral relationship from Ego as the principle of division. When kindreds have the kind of continuity they possess in stem kindreds, we might expect them to differentiate internally on somewhat the same basis that lineages do.

Comparing unilinear and multilinear descent from the point of view of kin group continuity, some differences are worth noting. As Fortes (1953c: 27) points out, when a unilinear kin group is faced with extinction, some "fiction" of descent will be resorted to in order to provide a member through whom the group can maintain its continuity (see also Murdock 1949: 45). Many societies even formalize and name these emergency fictions. With multilinear descent, and particularly those systems permitting a high degree of choice affiliation, these emergency measures are built in, so to speak. What Fortes (1953c: 33–45) has termed "complementary filiation" in unilinear systems—the link between a sibling group and the kin of the parent who does not determine descent—is raised to equal or near-equal importance for affiliation.

When descent is considered from the point of view of a means by which the use of valued resources (e.g., land and spouses) are allocated to members of the society, still other differences between unilinear and multilinear types become apparent. In relatively inflexible unilinear systems, unforeseen events may produce what the society considers to be an inequitable distribution of these resources in relation to the size of the groups. Frequently, there are means by which the surplus of one group is used by and ultimately passes under control of other groups. In effect, a reallocation takes place. The Garia, mentioned above, are an example of this; the transfer for use takes place through complementary filiation, and after four generations of use, title and control of the resources pass to the using lineage. With multilinear descent this kind of readjustment may go on constantly through the exercise of choice in affiliation. When an imbalance occurs, it is corrected by the influence this exerts on affiliation. Instead of reallocating resources to different groups, as above, individuals may be redistributed among the groups.

The important aspects of any multilinear descent system are the patterns of affiliation and the social and ecological factors which influence them. In some, like the Mangaian kopu and the Nukuoro te-haka-sa-aluna, the guiding principle seems to be the equal claims of the groups of both parents over the children. In others, like the Lozi mishiku and the Onotoa kainga, membership seems largely influenced by the availability of resources controlled by the group, while affiliation in both Kwakiutl and Bella Coola septs seems best understood in terms of motivation provided by the social status system. The number of societies for which these multilinear groups have been well described are still too few to permit anything but the most superficial kind of comparison, but even if they prove to be rare phenomena, the fact that multilinear descent can and does exist sheds light on some of the structural characteristics of unilinear groups.

Concerning bilateral descent and the resulting personal and stem kindreds, only the obvious is clear—this type of structure occurs where collective and corporate control is absent or minimal. Even though a partial case has been made here for studying these seemingly changing and ephemeral kin groups from the point of view of continuity, i.e., as stem kindreds, this may in fact prove to be misleading and unproductive.

But it is obvious that we need more detailed analyses of kindred systems and particularly the manner in which different degrees of collateral extension and restriction are used as principles of organization; the ways in which important individuals and the bilateral kin who group around them may constitute the significant kin groups; the function of kindreds as networks which bind other groups together; and as reservoirs of kin from which household groups are increased and sustained.

In framing hypotheses about the evolution of the different kinds of ascription through kinship, the first and third features listed above are of greatest relevance. The first question that arises is, what conditions favor the descent group as opposed to the personal kindred? That is, under what circumstances are bilateral and nonbilateral (unilinear and multilinear) descent most likely to occur? Given this answer, the next questions are, what circumstances favor no degrees of freedom in ascription (unilinear), some degrees of freedom (multilinear), and complete freedom with varying degrees of collateral restriction (bilateral). Intuitively, the answers seem to lie in the idea that control and regulation are greatest over those items which have the highest value. Thus, when something has high value or is scarce, its scarcity is insured by greater control and fewer degrees of freedom in allocating it, and vice versa. Whether or not this is correct could be determined by testing a number of derived hypotheses dealing with such matters as the limitation of resources, population density, social class, and bride price.

SELECTED READINGS

A. Commentaries and Critiques

Hubbell, Linda J.
1966 *Non-unilineal kinship studies.* (Unpublished manuscript, University of California, Berkeley.)

B. Original Works

Barton, Roy F.
1919 Ifugao law. *University of California Publications in Archeology, Anthropology and Ethnology,* XV:1–127.

Bohannan, Paul
1957 An alternate residence classification. *American Anthropologist* 59:126–31.

Coult, Allan D.
1964 Role allocation, position structuring, and ambilineal descent. *American Anthropologist,* 66:29–40.

Davenport, William
1959 Nonunilinear descent and descent groups. *American Anthropologist,* 61:557–72.

Eggan, Fred
1937c (ed.) *Social anthropology of the North American tribes.* Chicago: University of Chicago Press.

Firth, Raymond W.
1957b A note on descent groups in Polynesia. *Man,* 57:4–8.
——— 1963 Bilateral descent groups, an operational viewpoint. In I. Schapera (ed.), Studies in kinship and marriage. *Royal Anthropological Institute Paper,* No. 16, pp. 22–37.

Forde, C. Daryll
1950b Double descent among the Yako. In A. R. Radcliffe-Brown and C. D. Forde (eds.), *African systems of kinship and marriage.* London: Oxford University Press for the International African Institute.

Freeman, J. D.
1955 Iban agriculture. *Colonial Research Studies,* No. 18. London: Colonial Office.
——— 1958 The family system of the Iban of Borneo. In J. Goody (ed.), 1958. The developmental cycle in domestic groups. *Cambridge Papers in Social Anthropology,* No. 1. Cambridge: Cambridge University Press, pp. 15–52.
——— 1961 On the concept of the kindred. *Journal of the Royal Anthropological Institute,* 91:192–220.

Gluckman, Max
1950 Kinship and marriage among the Lozi of Northern Rhodesia and the Zulu of Natal. In A. R. Radcliffe-Brown and C. D. Forde (eds.), *African systems of kinship and marriage.* London: Oxford University Press for the International African Institute, pp. 166–206.

Goodenough, Ward H.
1951 Property, kin and community: The social organization on Truk. *Yale University Publications in Anthropology,* No. 46.
——— 1955 A problem in Malayo-Polynesian social organization. *American Anthropologist,* 57:71–83.

1956b Residence Rules. *Southwestern Journal of Anthropology* 12:22–37.

——— 1962 Kindred and hamlet in Lalakai. *Ethnology,* 1:5–12.

Graburn, Nelson H. H.
1964 Taqagmiut Eskimo kinship terminology. Northern Coordination and Research Centre—64–1. Ottawa: Dept. of Northern Affairs and Natural Resources, ch. XI.

Lambert, Bernd
1966 Ambilineal descent groups in the north Gilbert Islands. *American Anthropologist,* 68:641–664.

Leach, Edmund R.
1950a Social science research in Sarawak. *Colonial Research Studies,* No. 1. London: Colonial Office.

Lowie, Robert H.
1920 *Primitive society.* New York: Liveright. (2nd edit., 1947).

Mitchell, William E.
1963 Theoretical problems in the concept of kindred. *American Anthropologist,* 65:343–354.

Murdock, George P.
1949 *Social structure.* New York: Macmillan.

——— 1951 Forward In W. Goodenough, *Property, kin and community on Truk.* Yale University Publications in Anthropology, No. 46, pp. 5–8.

——— 1959 Evolution of social organization. In *Evolution and anthropology.* Washington, D.C.: Anthropological Society of Washington.

——— 1960 Cognatic forms of social organization. In G. Murdock (ed.), *Social structure of Southeast Asia.* Chicago: Quadrangle, pp. 1–14.

Nadel, Siegfried F.
1950 Dual descent in the Nuba Hills. In A. R. Radcliffe-Brown and C. D. Forde (eds.), *African systems of kinship and marriage.* London: Oxford University Press for the International African Institute, pp. 333–359.

Pehrson, Robert N.
1954 Bilateral kin groupings as a structural type. *Journal of East Asiatic studies,* 3:199–202.

——— 1957 The bilateral network of social relations in Könkämä Lapp district. *Indiana University Publications, Slavic and East European Series,* 5.

Radcliffe-Brown, Alfred R.
1935b Patrilineal and matrilineal succession. *Iowa Law Review,* 20:2. Reprinted in *Structure and function in primitive society.* London: Cohen and West, 1952, pps. 32–48.

——— 1950 Introduction to A. R. Radcliffe-Brown and C. D. Forde (eds.), *African systems of kinship and marriage.* London: Oxford University Press, pp. 1–85.

Sahlins, Marshall D.
1962 *Moahla: Culture and nature on a Fijian island.* Ann Arbor: University of Michigan Press.

Scheffler, Harold
1964 Descent concepts and descent groups: The Maori case. *Journal of the Polynesian Society,* 73:126–133.

Yalman, Nur
1962 The structure of the Sinhalese kindred: A re-examination of the Dravidian terminology. *American Anthropologist,* 64:548–575.

XI

✱ ALLIANCE AND DESCENT

The development of alliance theory—as opposed to descent theory (Dumont, "Descent, Filiation and Affinity," 1961)—has been inextricably involved with a number of more or less fundamental arguments in recent social anthropology: the nature of society and culture, the nature of social structure and analytical models, the origin of incest, marriage rules, marriage stability, descent, affinity, affiliation, and so on. The selections in this chapter, therefore, can only begin to deal with the main theoretical arguments. The entire subject was reviewed at greater length and with greater sophistication by Schneider ("Some Muddles in the Models," 1965a).

Alliance theory is an examination of the nature of social integration in the Durkheimian sense. Descent theory, with its emphasis on the analysis of unilineal descent groups (Fortes, "The Structure of Unilineal Descent Groups," 1953c), tends to view society as a set of separate but equal units bounded by the extent of their internal relationships and unified into a society by mechanical-segmentary solidarity. Such theories stemmed in part from the large amount of field work that writers of descent theory had done in Africa and Australia.

Alliance theory similarly recognizes the separateness and equality of social groups, but it concentrates on the nature of the bonds between these groups. Since all exogamous groups, from the nuclear family to the moiety, are *functionally dependent* on other wife-giving and wife-taking groups, the bonds that integrate them into the larger society are those of organic solidarity, and those bonds are expressed in the *exchange of women*. All social bonds of mutual interdependence, according to Mauss (1925) and, later, to Lévi-Strauss (1949), are bonds of reciprocity. Lévi-Strauss went on to say that the incest taboo and exogamous prohibitions must have been the foundations of culture because (1) they are part natural and part cultural and (2) they are the rules by which the nuclear family or any other biological group comes to be integrated into the larger society through the reciprocal exchange of women.

In Lévi-Strauss' view, there are two basic kinds of marital exchanges: (1) general exchange, between the family group and any other group, and (2) restrictive exchange, involving the positive rule to marry within a certain kin class. Within the second type of exchange, with which he was concerned, marriages between a mother's brother's daughter and father's sister's son are possible—the former is a matrilateral cross-cousin marriage and the latter is a patrilateral cross-cousin marriage. As Fortune (1933) has shown, the former type generates a "direct current" and the latter type an "alternating current" of women. Lévi-Strauss thought that the reason so few of the latter type took place, was because such a marriage produced a lowe_ level of integration in that women were exchanged between groups only in every other generation; he claimed that the rule of descent in a particular society had no influence on the direction of cross-cousin marriage.

Leach ("The Structural Implications of Matrilateral Cross-Cousin Marriage," 1951) claimed that (a) mother's brother's daughter marriage systems often are not closed, that is, reciprocity is not completed solely in the exchange of women, (b) that balances in the system are restored by intangibles such as rights and prestige or power, and (c) that women may or may not be the "highest good" whose exchange produces the reciprocity and the best kind of integration. He was able to show, by the detailed examination of selected systems, that cultural items other than women could assume, in some societies, the highest value in exchanges between groups of men. Homans and Schneider (*Marriage, Authority, and Final Causes*, 1955) using a different theoretical approach, stated that the assymetry of marriage rules is dependent on the particular rule of descent in the society or, more importantly, the rules concerning potestality (i.e., whether the real power over children lies with the father or the mother's brother). They claimed that mother's brother's daughter marriage is common because it is compatible with patrilineality. Father's sister's daughter rules are, conversely, compatible with matrilineality. By a theory of the extension of sentiments (cf. Radcliffe-Brown, 1924), they explained why a mother's brother or, in the converse case, a father's sister, were likely to give their daughters to a male Ego: because they are the parents of the female cross-cousins on the nonpotestal side of the family.

Needham (*The Formal Analysis of Prescriptive Patrilateral Cross-Cousin Marriage*, 1958b; 1962) attacked Homans and Schneider on many grounds (see Lounsbury, 1962; Dumont, 1968). He claimed that (1) they misunderstood Lévi-Strauss, (2) Lévi-Strauss was concerned with prescriptive rules, not preferential ones, (3) that prescriptive father's sister's daughter marriage rules could not and did not exist, and (4) that Homans and Schneider's survey of the ethnographic literature was inadequate. He tried to reaffirm Lévi-Strauss' original theory in his own way. Recently, in the Preface to Needham's (1969a) translation of the French original (1949), Lévi-Strauss stated that Needham misunderstood the use of the term "prescriptive" (1969a: xxx–xxxv). It was not, according to Lévi-Strauss, meant to be as absolutely differentiated from "preferential" as Needham had assumed. Needham replied (Lévi-Strauss 1969a: xix) that perhaps Lévi-Strauss had misinterpreted the original intent and meaning of his own argument.

With respect to wider issues, alliance theorists claimed that *social structure* is concerned with models that are statements of rules at a higher level than descent theory (Lévi-Strauss, *Social Structure*, 1953; 1964). These rules are not overt to the actors in the system, and the models are therefore analytical. Descent theorists' models have been only slightly abstracted from social relations and are at the level of "structures which continue over time," such as lineages and clans—ties that are observable to the "folk" themselves. The arguments, particularly those concerning the relationships between descent, affinity, and affiliation have continued (see Chapter XV), and alliance theory has been applied to nonkinship aspects of culture, (e.g., Lévi-Strauss 1966, 1969b).

THE NATURE OF SOCIAL RECIPROCITY

Marcel Mauss

PRESTATION, GIFT AND POTLATCH

This work is part of the wider research carried out by M. Davy and myself upon archaic

forms of contract, so we may start by summarizing what we have found so far. It appears that there has never existed, either in the past or in

Reprinted with permission from *The Gift* by Marcel Mauss, translated by Ian Cunnison, Introd. by E. E. Evans-Pritchard, 1954, Cohen & West, London. Pp. 3, 10–12.

modern primitive societies, anything like a 'natural' economy. By a strange chance the type of that economy was taken to be the one described by Captain Cook when he wrote on exchange and barter among the Polynesians. In our study here of these same Polynesians we shall see how far removed they are from a state of nature in these matters.

In the systems of the past we do not find simple exchange of goods, wealth and produce through markets established among individuals. For it is groups, and not individuals, which carry on exchange, make contracts, and are bound by obligations; the persons represented in the contracts are moral persons—clans, tribes, and families; the groups, or the chiefs as intermediaries for the groups, confront and oppose each other. Further, what they exchange is not exclusively goods and wealth, real and personal property, and things of economic value. They exchange rather courtesies, entertainments, ritual, military assistance, women, children, dances, and feasts; and fairs in which the market is but one element and the circulation of wealth but one part of a wide and enduring contract. Finally, although the prestations and counter-prestations take place under a voluntary guise they are in essence strictly obligatory, and their sanction is private or open warfare. We propose to call this the system of *total prestations*.

. . .

THE OBLIGATION TO GIVE AND THE OBLIGATION TO RECEIVE

To appreciate fully the institutions of total prestation and the potlatch we must seek to explain two complementary factors. Total prestation not only carries with it the obligation to repay gifts received, but it implies two others equally important: the obligation to give presents and the obligation to receive them. A complete theory of the three obligations would include a satisfactory fundamental explanation of this form of contract among Polynesian clans. For the moment we simply indicate the manner in which the subject might be treated.

It is easy to find a large number of facts on the obligation to receive. A clan, household, association or guest are constrained to demand hospitality, to receive presents, to barter or to make blood and marriage alliances. The Dayaks have even developed a whole set of customs based on the obligation to partake of any meal at which one is present or which one has seen in preparation.

The obligation to give is no less important. If we understood this, we should also know how men came to exchange things with each other. We merely point out a few facts. To refuse to give, or to fail to invite, is—like refusing to accept—the equivalent of a declaration of war; it is a refusal of friendship and intercourse. Again, one gives because one is forced to do so, because the recipient has a sort of proprietary right over everything which belongs to the donor. This right is expressed and conceived as a sort of spiritual bond. Thus in Australia the man who owes all the game he kills to his father- and mother-in-law may eat nothing in their presence for fear that their very breath should poison his food. We have seen above that the *taonga* sister's son has customs of this kind in Samoa, which are comparable with those of the sister's son (*vasu*) in Fiji.

In all these instances there is a series of rights and duties about consuming and repaying existing side by side with rights and duties about giving and receiving. The pattern of symmetrical and reciprocal rights is not difficult to understand if we realize that it is first and foremost a pattern of spiritual bonds between things which are to some extent parts of persons, and persons and groups that behave in some measure as if they were things.

All these institutions reveal the same kind of social and psychological pattern. Food, women, children, possessions, charms, land, labour, services, religious offices, rank-everything is stuff to be given away and repaid. In perpetual interchange of what we may call spiritual matter, comprising men and things, these elements pass and repass between clans and individuals, ranks, sexes and generations.

SOCIAL STRUCTURE

Claude Lévi-Strauss

The investigations we may enter into, in treating this subject, must not be considered as historical truths, but only as mere conditional and hypothetical reasonings, rather calculated to explain the nature of things, than to ascertain their actual origin; just like the hypotheses which our physicists daily form respecting the formation of the world.

J. J. Rousseau, On the Origin of Inequality

The term "social structure" refers to a group of problems the scope of which appears so wide and the definition so imprecise that it is hardly possible for a paper strictly limited in size to meet them fully. This is reflected in the program of this symposium, in which problems closely related to social structure have been allotted to several papers, such as those on "Style," "Universal Categories of Culture," and "Structural Linguistics." These should be read in connection with the present paper.

On the other hand, studies in social structure have to do with the formal aspects of social phenomena; they are therefore difficult to define, and still more difficult to discuss, without overlapping other fields pertaining to the exact and natural sciences, where problems are similarly set in formal terms or, rather, where the formal expression of different problems admits of the same kind of treatment. As a matter of fact, the main interest of social-structure studies seems to be that they give the anthropologist hope that, thanks to the formalization of his problems, he may borrow methods and types of solutions from disciplines which have gone far ahead of his own in that direction.

Such being the case, it is obvious that the term

Excerpted from Chapter XV, "Social Structure" of *Structural Anthropology* by Claude Lévi-Strauss, translated by Claire Jacobson and Brooke Grundfest Schoepf, © 1963 by Basic Books, Inc., Publishers, New York. Pp. 277–289, 314–315. Also published by Penguin Books, Ltd., London. Reprinted by permission.

"social structure" needs first to be defined and that some explanation should be given of the difference which helps to distinguish studies in social structure from the unlimited field of descriptions, analyses and theories dealing with social relations at large, which merge with the whole scope of social anthropology. This is all the more necessary, since some of those who have contributed toward setting apart social structure as a special field of anthropological studies conceived the former in many different manners and even sometimes, so it seems, came to nurture grave doubts as to the validity of their enterprise. For instance, Kroeber writes in the second edition of his *Anthropology:*

"Structure" appears to be just a yielding to a word that has a perfectly good meaning but suddenly becomes fashionably attractive for a decade or so—like "streamlining"—and during its vogue tends to be applied indiscriminately because of the pleasurable connotations of its sound. Of course a typical personality can be viewed as having a structure. But so can a physiology, any organism, all societies and all cultures, crystals, machines—in fact everything that is not wholly amorphous has a structure. So what "structure" adds to the meaning of our phrase seems to be nothing, except to provoke a degree of pleasant puzzlement. (1948: 325).

Although this passage concerns more particularly the notion of "basic personality structure," it has devastating implications as regards the generalized use of the notion of structure in anthropology.

Another reason makes a definition of social structure compulsory: From the structuralist point of view which one has to adopt if only to give the problem its meaning, it would be hopeless to try to reach a valid definition of social structure on an inductive basis, by abstracting common elements from the uses and definitions current among all the scholars who claim to have made "social structure" the object of their studies. If these concepts have a meaning at all, they mean, first that the notion of structure has a structure. This we shall try to outline from the beginning as a precaution against letting ourselves be submerged by a tedious inventory of books and papers dealing with social relations, the mere listing of which would more than exhaust the limited space at our disposal. At a further stage we will have to see how far and in what directions the term "social structure," as used by the different authors, departs from our definition. This will be done in the section devoted to kinship, since the notion of structure has found its chief application in that field and since anthropologists have generally chosen to express their theoretical views also in that connection.

DEFINITION AND PROBLEMS OF METHOD

Passing now to the task of defining "social structure," there is a point which should be cleared up immediately. The term "social structure" has nothing to do with empirical reality but with models which are built up after it. This should help one to clarify the difference between two concepts which are so close to each other that they have often been confused, namely, those of *social structure* and of *social relations*. It will be enough to state at this time that social relations consist of the raw materials out of which the models making up the social structure are built, while social structure can, by no means, be reduced to the ensemble of the social relations to be described in a given society (c.f. Leach 1945). Therefore, social structure cannot claim a field of its own among others in the social studies. It is rather a method to be applied to any kind of social studies, similar to the structural analysis current in other disciplines.

The question then becomes that of ascertaining what kind of model deserves the name "structure." This is not an anthropological question, but one which belongs to the methodology of science in general. Keeping this in mind, we can say that a structure consists of a model meeting with several requirements.

First, the structure exhibits the characteristics of a system. It is made up of several elements, none of which can undergo a change without effecting changes in all the other elements.

Second, for any given model there should be a possibility of ordering a series of transformations resulting in a group of models of the same type.

Third, the above properties make it possible to predict how the model will react if one or more of its elements are submitted to certain modifications.

Finally, the model should be constituted so as to make immediately intelligible all the observed facts.

These being the requirements for any model with structural value, several consequences follow. These, however, do not pertain to the definition of structure, but have to do with the chief properties exhibited and problems raised by structural analysis when contemplated in the social and other fields.

Observation and experimentation

Great care should be taken to distinguish between the observational and the experimental levels. To observe facts and elaborate methodological devices which permit the construction of models out of these facts is not at all the same thing as to experiment on the models. By "experimenting on models," we mean the set of procedures aiming at ascertaining how a given model will react when subjected to change and at comparing models of the same or different types. This distinction is all the more necessary, since many discussions on social structure revolve around the apparent contradiction between the concreteness and individuality of ethnological data and the abstract and formal character generally exhibited by structural studies. This contradiction disappears as one comes to realize that these features belong to two entirely different levels, or rather to two stages of the same process. On the observational level, the main—one could almost say the only—rule is that all the facts should be carefully observed and described, without allowing any theoretical preconception to decide whether some are more important that others. This rule implies, in turn, that facts should be studied in relation to themselves (by what kind of concrete process did they come into being?) and in relation to the whole (always aiming to relate each modification which can be observed in a sector to the global situation in which it first appeared).

This rule together with its corollaries has been explicitly formulated by K. Goldstein (1939) in relation to psychophysiological studies, and it may be considered valid for any kind of structural analysis. Its immediate consequence is that, far from being contradictory, there is a direct relationship between the detail and concreteness of ethnographical description and the validity and generality of the model which is constructed after it. For, though many models may be used as convenient devices to describe and explain the phenomena, it is obvious that the best model will always be that which is *true*, that is, the simplest possible model which, while being derived exclusively from the facts under consideration, also makes it possible to account for all of them. Therefore, the first task is to ascertain what those facts are.

Consciousness and unconsciousness

A second distinction has to do with the conscious character of the models. In the history of structural thought, Boas (1908) may be credited with having introduced this distinction. He made clear that a category of facts can more easily yield to structural analysis when the social group in which it is manifested has not elaborated a conscious model to interpret or justify it. Some readers may be surprised to find Boas' name quoted in connection with structural theory, since he has often been described as one of the main

obstacles in its path. But this writer has tried to demonstrate that Boas' shortcomings in matters of structural studies did not lie in his failure to understand their importance and significance, which he did, as a matter of fact, in the most prophetic way. They rather resulted from the fact that he imposed on structural studies conditions of validity, some of which will remain forever part of their methodology, while others are so exacting and impossible to meet that they would have withered scientific development in any field.

A structural model may be conscious or unconscious without this difference affecting its nature. It can only be said that when the structure of a certain type of phenomena does not lie at a great depth, it is more likely that some kind of model, standing as a screen to hide it, will exist in the collective consciousness. For conscious models, which are usually known as "norms," are by definition very poor ones, since they are not intended to explain the phenomena but to perpetuate them. Therefore, structural analysis is confronted with a strange paradox well known to the linguist, that is: the more obvious structural organization is, the more difficult it becomes to reach it because of the inaccurate conscious models lying across the path which leads to it.

From the point of view of the degree of consciousness, the anthropologist is confronted with two kinds of situations. He may have to construct a model from phenomena the systematic character of which has evoked no awareness on the part of the culture; this is the kind of simpler situation referred to by Boas as providing the easiest ground for anthropological research. Or else the anthropologist will be dealing on the one hand with raw phenomena and on the other with the models already constructed by the culture to interpret the former. Though it is likely that, for the reasons stated above, these models will prove unsatisfactory, it is by no means necessary that this should always be the case. As a matter of fact, many "primitive" cultures have built models of their marriage regulations which are much more to the point than models built by profession anthropologists. Thus one cannot dispense with studying a culture's "home-made" models for two reasons. First, these models might prove to be accurate or, at least, to provide some insight into the structure of the phenomena; after all, each culture has its own theoreticians whose contributions deserve the same attention as that which the anthropologist gives to colleagues. And, second, even if the models are biased or erroneous, the very bias and type of error are a part of the facts under study and probably rank among the most significant ones. But even when taking into consideration these culturally produced models, the anthropologist does not forget—as he has sometimes been accused of doing (see Firth 1951b: 28–31)—that the cultural norms are not of themselves structures. Rather, they furnish an important contribution to an understanding of the structures, either as factual documents or as theoretical contributions similar to those of the anthropologist himself.

This point has been given great attention by the French sociological school. Durkheim and Mauss, for instance, have always taken care to substitute, as a starting point for the survey of native categories of thought, the conscious representations prevailing among the natives themselves for those stemming from the anthropologist's own culture. This was undoubtedly an important step, which, nevertheless, fell short of its goal because these authors were not sufficiently aware that native conscious representations, important as they are, may be just as remote from the unconscious reality as any other.

Structure and measure

It is often believed that one of the main interests of the notion of structure is to permit the introduction of measurement in social anthropology. This view has been favored by the frequent appearance of mathematical or semi-mathematical aids in books or articles dealing with social structure. It is true that in some cases structural analysis has made it possible to attach numerical values to invariants. This was, for instance, the result of Kroeber's study of women's dress fashions, a landmark in structural research (Richardson and Kroeber, 1940) as well as of a few other studies which will be discussed below.

However, one should keep in mind that there is no necessary connection between measure and structure. Structural studies are, in the social sciences, the indirect outcome of modern developments in mathematics which have given increasing importance to the qualitative point of view in contradistinction to the quantitative point of view of traditional mathematics. It has become possible, therefore, in fields such as mathematical logic, set theory, group theory, and topology, to develop a rigorous approach to problems which do not admit of a metrical solution. The outstanding achievements in this connection—which offer themselves as springboards not yet utilized by social scientists—are to be found in J. von Neumann and O. Morgenstern, *Theory of Games and Economic Behavior;* N. Wiener, *Cybernetics;* and C. Shannon and W. Weaver, *The Mathematical Theory of Communication.*

Mechanical models and statistical models

A last distinction refers to the relation between the scale of the model and that of the phenomena. According to the nature of these phenomena, it becomes possible or impossible to build a model, the elements of which are on the same scale as the phenomena themselves. A model the elements of which are on the same scale as the phenomena will be called a "mechanical model;" when the elements of the model are on a different scale, we shall be dealing with a "statistical model." The laws of marriage provide the best illustration of this difference. In primitive societies these laws can be expressed in models calling for actual grouping of the individuals according to kin or clan; these are mechanical models. No such distribution exists in our own society, where types of marriage are determined by the size of the primary and secondary groups to which prospective mates belong, social fluidity, amount of information, and the like. A satisfactory (though yet untried) attempt to formulate the invariants of our marriage system would therefore have to determine average values—thresholds; it would be a statistical model. There may be intermediate forms between these two. Such is the case in societies which (as even our own) have a mechanical model to determine prohibited marriages and rely on a statistical model for those which are permissible. It should also be kept in mind that the same phenomena may admit of different models, some mechanical and some statistical, according to the way in which they are grouped together and with other phenomena. A society which recommends cross-cousin marriage but where this ideal marriage type occurs only with limited frequency needs, in order that the system may be properly explained, both a mechanical and a statistical model, as was well understood by Forde (1941) and Elwin (1947).

It should also be kept in mind that what makes social-structure studies valuable is that structures are models, the formal properties of which can be compared independently of their elements. The structuralist's task is thus to recognize and isolate levels of reality which have strategic value from his point of view, namely, which admit of representation as models, whatever their type. It often happens that the same data may be considered from different perspectives embodying equally strategic values, though the resulting models will be in some cases mechanical and in others statistical. This situation is well known in the exact and natural sciences; for instance, the theory of a small number of physical bodies belongs to classical mechanics, but if the number of bodies becomes greater, then one should rely on the laws of thermodynamics, that is, use a statistical model instead of a mechanical one, though the nature of the data remains the same in both cases.

The same situation prevails in the human and the social sciences. If one takes a phenomenon such as suicide, for instance, it can be studied on two different levels. First, it is possible by studying individual situations to establish what may be called mechanical models of suicide, taking into account in each case the personality of the victim, his or her life history, the characteristics of the primary and secondary groups in which he or she developed, and the like; or else one can build models of a statistical nature, by recording suicide frequency over a certain period of time in one or more societies and in different types of primary and secondary groups, etc.

These would be levels at which the structural study of suicide carries a strategic value, that is, where it becomes possible to build models which may be compared (1) for different types of suicides, (2) for different societies, and (3) for different types of social phenomena. Scientific progress consists not only in discovering new invariants belonging to those levels but also in discovering new levels where the study of the same phenomena offers the same strategic value. Such a result was achieved, for instance, by psychoanalysis, which discovered and means to set up models in a new field, that of the psychological life of the patient considered as a whole.

The foregoing should help to make clear the dual (and at first sight almost contradictory) nature of structural studies. On the one hand, they aim at isolating strategic levels, and this can be achieved only by "carving out" a certain constellation of phenomena. From that point of view, each type of structural study appears autonomous, entirely independent of all the others and even of different methodological approaches to the same field. On the other hand, the essential value of these studies is to construct models the formal properties of which can be compared with, and explained by, the same properties as in models corresponding to other strategic levels. Thus it may be said that their ultimate end is to override traditional boundaries between different disciplines and to promote a true interdisciplinary approach.

An example may be given. A great deal of discussion has taken place lately about the difference between history and anthropology, and Kroeber and others have made clear that the time dimension is of minor significance in this connection. From what has been stated above, one can see exactly where the difference lies, not only between these two disciplines but also between them and others. Ethnography and history differ from social anthropology and sociology, inasmuch as the former two aim at gathering data, while the latter two deal with models constructed from these data. Similarly, ethnography and social anthropology correspond to two different stages in the same research, the ultimate result of which is to construct mechanical models, while history (together with its so-called "auxiliary" disciplines) and sociology end ultimately in statistical models. The relations between these four disciplines may thus be reduced to two oppositions, one between empirical observation and model building, which characterizes the initial stage of research, and the other between the statistical and the mechanical nature of models, which constitutes the products of research. By arbitrarily assigning the sign + to the first term of each opposition and the sign − to the second, we obtain the following [Table 1] chart:

Table 1.

	HISTORY	SOCIOLOGY	ETHNOG-RAPHY	SOCIAL ANTHRO-POLOGY
Empirical observation/model building	+	−	+	−
Mechanical models/statistical models	−	−	+	+

This is the reason why the social sciences, though they all have to do with the time dimension, nevertheless deal with two different categories of time. Anthropology uses a "mechanical" time, reversible and non-cumulative. For instance, the model of, let us say, a patrilineal kinship system does not in itself show whether or not the system has always remained patrilineal, or has been preceded by a matrilineal form, or by any number of shifts from patrilineal to matrilineal and vice versa. On the contrary, historical time is "statistical;" it always appears as an oriented and non-reversible process. An evolution which would take contemporary Italian society back to that of the Roman Republic is as impossible to conceive of as is the reversibility of the processes belonging to the second law of thermodynamics.

This discussion helps to clarify Firth's distinction (*op. cit.*: 40) between social structure, which he conceives as outside the time dimension, and social organization, where time re-enters.

Also in this connection, the debate which has been going on for the past few years between followers of the Boasian anti-evolutionist tradition and of Professor Leslie White (1949) may become better understood. The Boasian school has been mainly concerned with models of a mechanical type, and from this point of view the concept of evolution has no operational value. On the other hand, it is certainly legitimate to speak of evolution in a historical and sociological sense, but the elements to be organized into an evolutionary process cannot be borrowed from the level of a cultural typology which consists of mechanical models. They should be sought at a sufficiently deep level to insure that these elements will remain unaffected by different cultural contexts (as, let us say, genes are identical elements combined into different patterns corresponding to the different racial [statistical] models) and can accordingly permit the drawing of long statistical runs. Boas and his followers are therefore right in rejecting the concept of evolution, since it is not relevant on the level of the mechanical models which they employ exclusively. As for Leslie White, he is mistaken in his attempts to reintroduce the concept of evolution, since he persists in utilizing models of the same type as those of his opponents. The evolutionists would find it easier to regain their position if they consented to substitute statistical for mechanical models, that is, models whose elements are independent of their combinations and which remain identical through a sufficiently long period of time.

The distinction between mechanical and statistical models has also become fundamental in another respect; it makes it possible to clarify the role of the comparative method in structural studies. This method was greatly emphasized by both Radcliffe-Brown and Lowie. The former writes:

> Theoretical sociology is commonly regarded as an inductive science, induction being the logical method of inference by which we arrive at general propositions from the consideration of particular instances. Although Professor Evans-Pritchard . . . seems to imply in some of his statements that the logical method of in-

duction, using comparison, classification and generalization, is not applicable to the phenomena of human social life . . . I hold that social anthropology must depend on systematic comparative studies of many societies. (1952)

Writing about religion, he states:

> The experimental method of social religion . . . means that we must study in the light of our hypothesis a sufficient number of diverse particular religions or religious cults in relation to the particular societies in which they are found. This is a task not for one person but for a number. (1945: 1)

Similarly, Lowie, after pointing out that "the literature of anthropology is full of alleged correlations which lack empirical support," (*op. cit:* 48) insists on the need for a "broad inductive basis" for generalization (*ibid:* 68). It is interesting to note that by this claim for inductive support these authors dissent not only from Durkheim—"When a law has been proved by a well performed experiment, this law is valid universally," (1912: 543)—but also from Goldstein, who, as already mentioned, has lucidly expressed what may be called "the rules of structuralist method" in a way general enough to make them valid outside the more limited field in which they were first applied by their author. Goldstein remarks that the need to make a thorough study of each case implies that the amount of cases to be studied should be small; and he proceeds by raising the question whether or not the risk exists that the cases under consideration may be special ones, allowing no general conclusions about the others. His answer is as follows:

> This objection completely misunderstands the real situation . . . an accumulation of facts even numerous is of no help if these facts were imperfectly established; it does not lead to the knowledge of things as they really happen . . . We must choose only those cases which permit of formulating final judgments. And then, what is true for one case will also be true for any other. (*op. cit.:* 25)

Probably very few anthropologists would be ready to support these bold statements. However, no structuralist study may be undertaken without a clear awareness of Goldstein's dilemma: either to study many cases in a superficial and in the end ineffective way; or to limit oneself to a thorough study of a small number of cases, thus proving that in the last analysis one well done experiment is sufficient to make a demonstration.

Now the reason for so many anthropologists' faithfulness to the comparative method may be sought in some sort of confusion between the procedures used to establish mechanical and statistical models. While Durkheim and Goldstein's position undoubtedly holds true for the former, it is obvious that no statistical model can be achieved without statistics, that is, without gathering a large amount of data. But in this case the method is no more comparative than in the other, since the data to be collected will be acceptable only insofar as they are all of the same kind. We remain, therefore, confronted with only one alternative, namely, to make a thorough study of one case. The real difference lies in the selection of the "case," which will be patterned so as to include elements which are either on the same scale as the model to be constructed or on a different scale.

Having thus clarified these basic questions revolving around the nature of studies in social structure, it becomes possible to make an inventory of the main fields of inquiry and to discuss some of the results achieved so far.

. . .

A few words may be added as a conclusion. This chapter was started by working out the notion of "model," and the same notion has reappeared at its end. Social anthropology, in its incipient stage, could only seek, as model for its first models, among those of the simplest kinds provided by more advanced sciences, and it was natural enough to seek them in the field of classical mechanics. However, in doing so, anthropology has been working under some sort of illusion, since, as Von Neumann puts it, "an almost exact theory of a gas, containing about 10^{25} freely moving particles, is incomparably easier than that of the solar system, made up of 9 major bodies." (*op. cit.:* 14) But when it tries to construct its models, anthropology finds itself in a situation which is neither the one nor the other: The objects with which we deal—social roles and human beings—are considerably more numerous than those dealt with in Newtonian mechanics, and at the same time, far less numerous than would be required to allow a satisfactory use of the laws of statistics and probability. Thus we find ourselves in an intermediate zone: to complicated for one treatment and not complicated enough for the other.

The tremendous change brought about by the theory of communication consists precisely in the discovery of methods to deal with objects—signs—which can be subjected to a rigorous study despite the fact that they are altogether much more numerous than those of classical mechanics and much less than those of thermodynamics. Language consists of morphemes, a few thousand in number; significant regularities in phoneme frequencies can be obtained by limited counts. The threshold for the use of statistical laws becomes lower, and that for operating with mechanical models higher, than was the case when operating on other grounds. And, at the same time, the size-order of the phenomena has become significantly closer to that of anthropological data.

Therefore, the present conditions of social-structure studies can be summarized as follows: Phenomena are found to be of the same kind as those which, in strategics and communication theory, were made the subject of a rigorous approach. Anthropological facts are on a scale which is sufficiently close to that of these other phenomena as not to preclude their similar treatment. Surprisingly enough, it is at the very moment when anthropology finds itself closer than ever to the long-awaited goal of becoming a true science that the ground seems to fail where it was expected to be the firmest: The facts themselves are lacking, either not numerous enough or not collected under conditions insuring their comparability.

Though it is not our fault, we have been behaving like amateur botanists, haphazardly picking up heterogeneous specimens, which were further distorted and mutilated by preservation in our herbarium. And we are, all of a sudden, confronted with the need of ordering complete series, ascertaining original shades, and measuring minute parts which have either shrunk or been lost. When we come to realize not only what should be done but also what we should be in a position to do, and when we make at the same time an inventory of our material, we cannot help feeling in a disheartened mood. It looks almost as if cosmic physics were asked to work with Babylonian observations. The celestial bodies are still there, but unfortunately the native cultures from which we used to gather our data are rapidly disappearing and that which they are being replaced by can only furnish data of a very different type. To adjust our techniques of observation to a theoretical framework which is far more advanced is a paradoxical situation, quite opposite to that which has prevailed in the history of sciences. Nevertheless, such is the challenge to modern anthropology.

AN ALTERNATIVE THEORY

Edmund R. Leach

INTRODUCTION

At first glance the theme of this essay might seem excessively narrow and pedantic; in fact, as I hope to show, it is very appropriate to the terms of the Curl Bequest competition. Firstly it is a topic that lies at the very heart of anthro-

Reprinted by permission of the Royal Anthropological Institute of Great Britain and Ireland from *The Structural Implications of Matrilateral Cross-Cousin Marriage*,

Journal of the Royal Anthropological Institute, Vol. 81 (1951), pp. 24–29, 51–53.

pological kinship theory. Secondly it is a branch of kinship theory to which a number of significant, and perhaps very important, contributions have been made during the past ten years. Thirdly it is a field to which I myself, from my own experience, can make a new and original contribution.

The essay is arranged in four sections.

Part 1—serves to establish certain basic definitions, assumptions and theoretical objectives.

Part 2—reviews the literature of the theme under discussion. [omitted]

Part 3—provides material from my own field work, and examines the relevance of this new material for the analysis of two other well documented societies which have not previously been considered from quite this point of view. [omitted]

Part 4—summarises the conclusions that may be drawn from this review of theory and ethnographic fact, and specifies a series of propositions, which not only accord with the facts as now known, but which are in a form which permits of further empirical testing in the field.

PART 1. BASIC ASSUMPTIONS AND SPECIAL CONCEPTS

Local descent groups

There are two kinds of marriage. The first results from the whims of two persons acting as private individuals; the second is a systematically organized affair which forms part of a series of contractual obligations between two social groups. When I mention an institutionalized or 'type' form of marriage, it is to this latter kind of arrangement that I refer.

In my view the social groups which 'arrange' such a marriage between themselves are, in almost all societies, of essentially the same kind. The core of such a group is composed of the adult *males* of a kin group all resident in one place. By this I do not mean to argue that women have no part to play in the arrangement of a marriage or that remotely situated kinsfolk are wholly ignored; I merely mean that the corporate group of persons who have the most decisive say in bringing about an arranged marriage is always a group of co-resident males representing,

as a rule, three genealogical generations, namely: the old men or grandfathers, the normal adults or fathers, and the young adults or sons.

In practice, membership of such groups is defined by descent as well as residence. In this essay I am concerned only with systems of unilateral (and double unilateral) descent so that I can formulate the above proposition as follows:

In a unilaterally defined descent system where a clan, or large scale lineage, ceases, for one reason or another, to be a localised group, then, in general, it ceases to be a corporate unit for the purposes of arranging a marriage. The corporate group which does arrange a marriage is, in such circumstances, always a group of males who, besides being members of the same lineage or clan, share a common place of residence.

In this essay I shall refer to corporate groups of this kind as *local descent groups*, or more simply, wherever the context in unambiguous, simply as 'groups.'

Logically speaking *local descent groups* thus defined can come about only in a limited number of ways. The following would appear to be the most likely possibilities:

(a)   with patrilineal descent and patrilocal residence.

(b)   with matrilineal descent and 'avuncolocal' (Murdock 1949: 17) residence (i.e., residence in the community of the mother's brother), succession to male authority being from mother's brother to sister's son.[1]

(c)   with matrilineal descent and 'matrilocal' residence (i.e., residence in the community of the wife) coupled with matrilateral cross cousin marriage (father's sister's son-mother's brother's daughter); succession to male authority being from father-in-law to son-in-law.

Diagram Lines: local lines and descent lines

Figs. 1, 2a and 2b illustrate Diagrammatically the notion of *local descent groups* as resulting from each of the above situations. In this essay I shall refer to such diagrammatic local descent

---

[1] The normal Trobriand rule; Malinowski (1932a, pp. 10, 83). A man moves to his mother's brother's village when adolescent and then brings his wife to join him in that village.

groups as local lines. This in these figures the lines A.1-A.2-A.3; B.1-B.2-B.3; C.1-C.2-C.3 each represent *local lines*. The kinship relation between any two individuals in such a diagram is always intended to be classificatory rather than

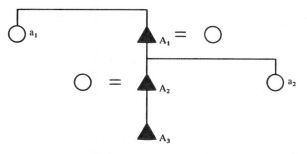

Figure 1.   The line A.1–A.2–A.3 indicates a patrilineal local descent group resulting from patrilocal residence

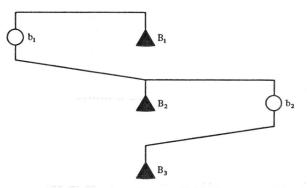

Figure 2a.   The line B.1–B.2–B.3 indicates a matrilineal local descent group resulting from avunculocal residence

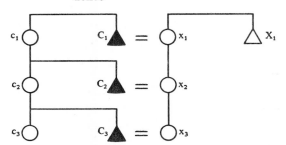

Figure 2b.   The line C.1–C.2–C.3 indicates a matrilineal local descent group resulting from matrilocal residence and matrilateral cross cousin marriage
In this system C_2 succeeds C_1 because he is husband of x_2 and potential husband of x_1. Only with matrilateral cross cousin marriage are C_1 and C_2 of the same descent group

actual; thus A.2 is classificatory son of A.1: B.2 is classificatory sister's son to B.1.

This notion of a *local line* is to be distinguished from the parallel concept of a *descent line* ('line of descent') which has frequently been used by Radcliffe-Brown and his pupils. Descent lines have nothing whatever to do with local grouping, they are merely a diagrammatic device for displaying the categories of the kinship system in relation to a central individual called Ego. The number of basic descent lines in such a diagram depends merely upon how many different kinds of relative are recognised in the grandfather's generation. It has nothing to do with the number of local descent groups existing in the society. (see Radcliffe-Brown 1951b: 43).

Failure to distinguish between the notion of *local line* (indicating a *local descent group*) and *descent line* (indicating a set of kinship categories) has been the source of much confusion.

One particularly important difference between these two types of diagram is this: A *descent line* commonly comprises at least five generations, e.g., grandfather, father, Ego, son, grandson and each of these individuals is given equal weight. A *local line* on the other hand seldom contains more than three generations at any one time. (A man may have classificatory grandfathers and classificatory grandchildren alive at the same moment, but it is not likely that they will both be members of Ego's own local group.) As a child, Ego is a member of a system comprising the local descent groups of himself and his wife, and the local descent groups into which his children are married. These two systems of kinship association overlap but do not normally both exist in their totality at one and the same time. Ego's father and grandfather and their contemporaries are mostly dead before Ego's grandchildren are born. A diagram designed to show *descent lines* instead of local lines tends to obscure this very important fact.

Type marriages

Readers of this essay will be familiar with the notion of type marriages which has been developed by Radcliffe-Brown to describe the various forms of institutionalised marriage regulation found among Australian tribes (Radcliffe-Brown, 1930, *passim;* 1951a, pp. 41–42). Type marriages form a very convenient shorthand notation and in this essay I shall employ the following series:

1. *Kariera type*—'symmetrical cross cousin marriage.' This system approves the simultaneous exchange of women between two local descent groups. In the ideal type a man marries the mother's brother's daughter who is sister to his own sister's husband.

I am not concerned with the other Australian symmetrical type marriages but it may be noted that the Aranda type, and the Kumbaingeri type, both approve marriage with the sister of a man's own sister's husband. They differ from the Kariera type only in excluding from marriage certain categories of women who would be admissible as 'mother's brother's daughter/father's sister's daughter' in the Kariera system of kinship.

2. *Trobriand type*—'asymmetrical cross cousin marriage (patrilateral).' This system precludes the reciprocal marriage of a man with the sister of his own sister's husband, but it amounts nevertheless to a systematic exchange of women between two local descent groups. The exchange is completed only after a time lag of one generation. In the ideal type a man marries the father's sister's daughter; he is forbidden to marry the mother's brother's daughter.

This kind of marriage regulation occurs in patrilineal as well as matrilineal societies. I shall use the description *Trobriand type marriage* in both cases.

3. *Kachin type*—'asymmetrical cross cousin marriage (matrilateral).' This system precludes altogether the exchange of women between two local descent groups. If group B gives a woman to group A, the service is never reciprocated in kind, though it may of course be reciprocated in other ways—e.g., by marriage payments. In the ideal type a man marries the mother's brother's daughter; he is forbidden to marry the father's sister's daughter.

My Kachin type includes the Australian Karadjeri type and thus includes the much discussed Murngin system. It should be noted however that, in general, Kachin type systems lack those features of the Karadjeri type which make the latter characteristically Australian—e.g., the formal division of the local descent group into sections composed of alternating generations (Radcliffe-Brown, 1951a, pp. 43, 55.)

Assumptions and objectives

For the purposes of this essay I assume that the three varieties of cross cousin marriage defined above, the Kariera type, the Trobriand type and the Kachin type, can usefully, for purposes of comparison, be treated as institutional isolates. I am interested in the implications of such institutionalised behaviour for the societies in which such rules occur.

The total literature on the subject of cross cousin marriage is very large; the major part of it has been recently reviewed by Lévi Strauss (1949). In this essay I am primarily concerned only with that part of this material which deals with Kachin type marriage; I shall concern myself with Kariera and Trobriand type marriages only so far as is necessary to provide contrasts and comparisons.

The particular aspect of Kachin type marriage which interests me is this. Where such a system of institutionalised marriage rules exists in association with local descent groups, then a group B which provides wives for group A is not compensated in kind. There are then three possibilities:

(1) That the principle of reciprocity does not apply at all and that group B obtains no compensation;

(2) that reciprocity is achieved by group A giving group B some form of economic or political compensation—e.g., marriage payments, work service, political fealty;

(3) that three or more groups A, B, C, make mutual arrangements to 'marry in a circle'—C giving wives to B, who give wives to A, who give wives to C again. In this case the wives that C gives to B are, in a sense, compensation for the wives that B gives to A.

The implications of these alternative possibilities form the subject matter of this essay.

But let me be quite clear about what I mean by *implication*. I am not concerned with the origins of institutional rules. It seems to me probable that such marriage rules as we are discussing may have originated in quite different ways in different societies. I am also not greatly interested in what Malinowski might have called the overt function of such behaviour. I have no doubt that in different societies one and the same rule will serve different immediate ends; comparison in terms of such ends can therefore only lead to purely negative results. What I am interested in however is the 'function' of such rules in a mathematical sense. For example: Given a rule such as that which defines Kachin type marriage, and given various other common elements between society A and society B, can we infer, by logical arguments, that some other unknown characteristic 'x' must also be common to our two societies? And if we think we can do this, how far do empirical facts justify such a claim?

Diagrams

In my discussion of the literature in the later sections of this essay it will become apparent that serious misunderstandings have constantly arisen from a tendency to confuse structural diagrams with ethnographic reality. (Cf. Radcliffe-Brown [1951a, *passim*] for criticism of Lawrence and Murdock on this score). In my own argument I shall constantly refer to diagrams such as those of Figs. 3 and 4. It is important that the reader should clearly understand just how these diagrams relate to reality.

In a system of unilineal descent, either patrilineal or matrilineal, Kachin type marriage has the effect of grouping Ego's relatives into at least three mutually exclusive categories, namely:

A. Groups containing 'father's sister's daughters'.
B. Groups containing 'sisters'.
C. Groups containing 'mother's brother's daughters'.
   Ego (male) is permitted to marry only into groups C.
   Ego (female) is permitted to marry only into groups A.

With Trobriand type marriage, on the other hand, a group which contains a father's sister's daughter in one generation will contain a mother's brother's daughter in the next. (E.g., in Fig. 4 c_2^1 is father's sister's daughter to B_2^1 but c_3^1 is mother's brother's daughter to B_3^1). There is thus no category of local descent groups which are 'non-marriageable' for Ego (male) although outside his own clan.

This distinction between Kachin type and Trobriand type is made clear in Figs. 3 and 4. In Fig. 3 the three lines, A, B, C, can be taken to represent three patrilineal local descent groups intermarrying according to Kachin type marriage. In Fig. 4 the three lines, A^1, B^1, C^1, can be taken to represent three matrilineal local descent groups intermarrying according to Trobriand type marriage. In the first case the relationship of group B to group A and of group B to group C is quite distinct. B receives wives from C and

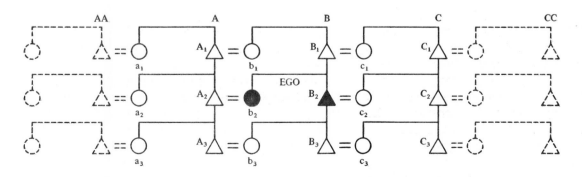

Figure 3.   Kachin type marriage system (patrilineal). Lines A, B, and C alone can be thought of as local lines. If the whole scheme be considered including lines AA and CC then the vertical lines are descent lines (see text).

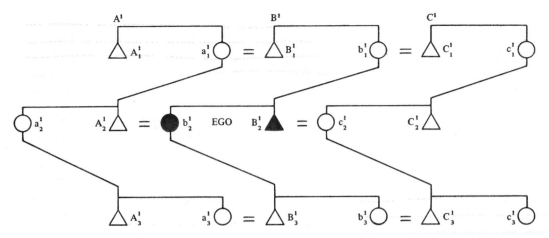

Figure 4. Trobriand type marriage system (matrilineal). Lines A^1, B^1, C^1 can be thought of as local lines.

gives wives to A. In the second case the general type of relationship between B^1 and A^1 is the same as that which exists between B^1 and C^1, but merely shifted one generation. This argument first appears clearly stated in Fortune (1933).

In Kachin type systems the division of Ego's relatives into three mutually exclusive categories is a minimum; there may be further categories of a like kind. In theory for example it might seem, as in Fig. 3, that there must always be a further group AA related to A in the same way as A is related to B, and that there must always be a group CC related to C in the same way as C is related to B.

If we are merely seeking to display the categories of the kinship system by a diagram of *descent lines*, it is very probable that these extra lines AA and CC will be necessary. In the actual Kachin system this is the case (Leach, 1945), and also in the Australian Yir-Yoront system (Sharp, 1934). The much discussed Murngin system requires in all no less than 7 lines (Warner, 1930–31), so that the diagram contains further lines AAA and CCC to the left and right respectively.

But this wide extension of the descent line diagram does not necessarily imply that an equal number of *local descent groups* are associated with Ego's own group. If Fig. 3 denotes *local lines* (local descent groups) instead of *descent lines* then there is no reason why AA should not coincide o at any rate overlap with B. This is the

crux of Murdock's and Lévi-Strauss's misunderstanding of the Murngin system which has been criticised by Radcliffe-Brown (1951a).

If we are concerned with *descent lines* it is always true that the most satisfactory diagram model which will represent the whole of a Kachin type marriage system will consist of some uneven number of lines, Ego's own line being centrally placed. In contrast, any system of marriage regulations, which approves the marriage of a man with his sister's husband's sister (e.g., Kariera, Aranda, Ambryn types) can be most easily represented by a diagram model containing an even number of lines, Ego's own position being immaterial. This fact also has led to much confusion.

In Fig. 3 the central part, lines A, B, C, can be taken as a diagram of *local lines;* but the full scheme, including lines AA and CC, can only be a diagram of *descent lines*—it merely shows the categories into which Ego's relatives necessarily fall. It says nothing at all about the totality of Ego's society. That total society may contain any number of local descent groups; Fig. 3 only specifies three of them, namely, A, B, and C; the remainder might potentially fit in anywhere. For instance, suppose there is a local descent group X to which B is either unrelated, or only remotely related; then if Ego (male) marries a woman of X, X will thereafter be rated as category C— 'wife giving'; but if Ego (female) marries a man of X, X will thereafter be rated as category A—'wife taking.'

The majority of writers who have discussed Kachin type marriage systems have failed to understand this. Instead they have been led to assume that a diagram such as Fig. 3 can serve to represent not merely the whole kinship system, but the whole of Ego's society. Once this assumption is made certain erroneous inferences appear to follow immediately. In the first place if lines AA and CC denote local descent groups, then AA has no husbands and CC has no wives; it must then follow that CC take wives from AA. The system then becomes circular. Furthermore the five lines AA, A, B, C, CC, now cease to denote merely categories of Ego's relatives, they become actual segments of the total society, and can be thought of as 'marriage classes,' or perhaps as five strictly exogamous phratries which by some mystical process always manage to remain of exactly equal size and sex composition.

Radcliffe-Brown (1951a, *passim*) has rightly criticised Murdock's analysis of the Murngin system on this score; I shall likewise criticise the work of Hodson, Mrs. Seligman, Granet, Lévi-Strauss and others. But I would like to make it clear that the problem at issue is not simply one of understanding the ethnographic facts. In a number of societies which possess Kachin type marriage systems the native informants themselves habitually explain the intricacies of their kinship system by saying that the society consists of 3 or 5 or 7 clans which 'marry in a circle,' and it requires the collection of genealogies to prove that this description is a fiction. Furthermore, cases can be found where three or more local descent groups do in fact, as well as in theory, 'marry in a circle' on a continuous and more or less exclusive basis. The correspondences as well as the contradictions between ideal and model and empirical fact therefore call for comment and analysis. . . .

PART 4. CONCLUSION

What then can be inferred from the theoretical discussions of the first half of this essay and the three brief structural analyses given in the second?

1. A review of the literature has shown that if we ignore various quite hypothetical historical reconstructions the most popular 'explanation' of Kachin type marriage is to see it as the hallmark of an imaginary type of structural system in which 'marriage classes' marry in a circle. Radcliffe-Brown has shown that this analysis is invalid for the Murngin; I have shown it to be equally invalid for the Kachins.

2. Two major errors are involved in the 'marriage class' argument. The first is to suppose that the groups which are paired as 'wife giving' and 'wife receiving' by the marriage rule are major segments of the society. In fact, in all cases closely examined, they are local descent groups domiciled in the same or closely neighbouring communities. The second error is to suppose that the marriage system in itself constitutes a closed system. In fact, as we have seen, Kachin type marriage is only understandable if it is thought of as one of many possible types of continuing relationship between paired local descent groups.

3. Despite the stimulating quality of Lévi-Strauss's argument, his main proposition is back to front. He argues that the fundamental characteristic of Kachin type marriage is that it is egalitarian—women must be exchanged for goods, on a sort of fixed price equilibrium basis. He perceives that in fact differences of price and differences of status will result, but regards this as the breakdown of the system, and hence as a mechanism in the general process of social evolution. My own argument is almost the reverse of this. As far as the marriage system is concerned, the status relations between group A and group B must be taken as given factors in the situation; a marriage is only one of many possible ways of 'expressing' those relations.

4. When two local descent groups A and B are in relation the 'things' which can be exchanged to express this relationship can be roughly categorised as follows:

I. *Tangibles*
   (a) 'women' and 'men'
   (b) labour of men or women
   (c) consumer goods and money
   (d) capital goods
   (e) ritual objects of no intrinsic value

II. *Intangibles*
  (f) 'rights' of a territorial and political nature
  (g) relative 'status' or 'prestige'

The last item cannot be defined except in terms of the cultural situation; it is simply 'that kind of reputation which gains a man the admiration of his fellows,' it may be derived from murder in one society, philanthropy in a second, saintliness in a third.

In every relationship between individuals and between groups, items in the above list are exchanged. It is in the nature of most such 'exchanges' that, as regards the tangible items *a, b, c, d, e* there is always an imbalance on one side or the other. The exchange account is balanced by the intangible items *f* and *g*.

If this argument be admitted then the role of women in the total exchange system cannot be discovered from first principles.

It is the error of Hodson, Murdock and the other 'marriage class' enthusiasts to suppose that in a marriage exchange the equivalent of a woman is always another woman. Lévi-Strauss argues that the equivalent of a woman may also be in goods and labour and symbolic objects; but he perceives much less clearly that intangible factors such as rights and reputation can play a part in this exchange without damage to the system. The fact that the Chinese who practise Kachin type marriage pay on balance a dowry and not a brideprice, while their neighbours the Kachins pay a brideprice and not a dowry is a crucial fact of which Lévi-Strauss's theory takes no account.

What can be said on the positive side? I suggest the following minimal propositions which are capable of empirical testing in the field.

1. With Kachin type marriage the relationship between wife giving and wife receiving groups is asymmetrical; hence differentiation of status one way or the other is more likely than not. Such differentiation can be avoided if a small number of neighbouring local descent groups marry in a circle, or if there is a system of balancing rights and obligations—as with the Murngin; but any such system of balances will be unstable.

2. If the status between wife givers and wife receives is unequal one cannot predict from first principles which of the two groups will be the senior. It seems probable however that in any one cultural situation the position will be consistent. One would not expect that all wife givers are ranked high in one village, and all wife receivers ranked high in the next.

3. The status relations between wife givers and wife receivers must conform to the status relations implicit in other (non-kinship) institutions: e.g., where wife givers are socially superior to wife receivers, one can predict that the political and territorial rights of wife givers will be superior to those of wife receivers, etc.—and *vice versa*. In other words, where Kachin type marriage occurs, it is part of the *political* structure.

4. It seems probable that a costly brideprice *in terms of consumer goods and labour* implies that wife givers rank higher than wife receivers. Conversely a dowry *expressed in consumer goods* implies that wife givers rank lower than wife receivers. A substantial brideprice consisting of objects of symbolic and ritual value only probably goes with high rank and equality of status. The absence of either work payment, brideprice or dowry suggests a breakup of the Kachin type marriage institution.

5. It is a notable characteristic of all the societies considered—Murngin, Kachin, Batak, Lovedu—that the usual characteristics of a tribal organisation are lacking. The network of kinship relations embraces a great number of local groups and ties them into a kind of loosely knit political system; but throughout the population so linked there is no strong sense of social solidarity and in some cases there are even wide differences of language and culture between different parts of the one system.

It seems probable that this is a characteristic that may normally be expected to be associated with Kachin type marriage systems, since the asymmetrical relationship between wife givers and wife receivers tends always to push the ramifications of the system to wider and wider limits. The whole structure, in fact, does bear close resemblance to the feudal organisation of medieval Europe, which in the same way drew a number of culturally divergent communities into a single political system, though admittedly the integration of that system was, at best, extremely weak.

I certainly do not hold, as Lévi-Strauss seems to do, that the origin of feudal structures is to be found in the breakdown of Kachin type marriage systems; but it does appear to be the case that Kachin type marriage systems correlate very well with political structures of a somewhat feudal type.

This series of hypothetical correlations with Kachin type marriage appear to fit all the cases examined in this essay and also, so far as the ethnography permits one to judge, those other Kachin type societies such as the Gilyak, the Lakher and the Old Kuki which have been commented upon by Lévi-Strauss; moreover they do so without straining the facts to fit a world embracing theory of social evolution—which can hardly be said of some of Lévi-Strauss's arguments.

In the more general field I suggest that the concept of local descent group developed at the beginning of this essay may have important analytical implications in many cases where the pure descent concept lineage lacks precision. Moreover the arguments which have here been propounded regarding the relevance of status concepts to the analysis of brideprice and dowry have relevance also outside the immediate context of Kachin type marriage.

Finally there emerges from this discussion an important principle of method. If anthropologists are to arrive at any valid principles of social organisation, the general method must be comparative. But the original comparative method, exemplified in its most overwhelming form by the work of Frazer, rested on the comparison of cultural traits. Under the impact of functionalism, which insisted upon the analysis of whole cultural systems, this type of comparative method fell into disrepute simply because it appeared to be an impossibility—the body of data that would be involved in an adequate comparison was altogether too vast.

Since 1930, however, Radcliffe-Brown and his followers have had some success in applying a different kind of comparison, namely, that of whole political systems. In a comparative method of this latter kind cultural features are to a large extent ignored, and the 'things' which are compared are really simplified models of the societies under discussion, as observed from a particular point of view. In practice 'the particular point of view' has been that of kinship, and despite the very great value of works such as *Social Organisation of Australian Tribes, Social Anthropology of North American Tribes, African Political Systems* and other kindred studies the generalisations that emerge are liable to be distorted on this account.

My own argument, in which to a great extent I follow Lévi-Strauss, is that the comparison of models rather than of 'whole cultures' is a necessary and valid method—indeed I would go much further in such abstraction than has usually been the case with the followers of Radcliffe-Brown But at the same time I would insist that the comparison must always take into account the whole range of institutional dimensions with which the anthropologist normally has to deal and must start from a concrete reality—a local group of people—rather than from an abstract reality—such as the concept of lineage or the notion of kinship system.

The content of this essay should make it clear why I hold this view. It also provides an excellent illustration of how very misleading comparisons based on the analysis of the kinship dimension alone are liable to be.

MARRIAGE ALLIANCE

Louis Dumont

All societies prohibit marriage with certain relatives, but some societies complement this prohibition by prescribing, or preferring, marriage with other relatives. In this way two kinds of cousins are sometimes distinguished, marriage being prohibited between those who are children of siblings of the same sex ("parallel cousins"), while it is prescribed between children of siblings of opposite sex ("cross-cousins"). This disposition is generally accompanied by exogamy. This article attempts to sum up recent developments in the theory of cross-cousin marriage.

DESCENT AND ALLIANCE

The expression "marriage alliance," in which "alliance" refers to the repetition of intermarriage between larger or smaller groups, denotes what amounts to a special theory of kinship, a theory developed to deal with those types of kinship systems that embody positive marriage rules, though it also affords certain general theoretical insights regarding kinship. Two points may be noted at the outset: (1) The combination of the positive marriage rule with exogamy, or at the very least with a prohibition against marriage between parallel cousins, is essential to the type of system under description here; a preference for marriage with the father's brother's daughter, as found among some Islamic peoples, is a quite different phenomenon. (2) The approach here presented is essentially common to several writers, though an element of personal interpretation is inevitable.

In the initial stages of kinship studies, the reconstruction of fanciful marriage rules (or mating arrangements) as having supposedly existed in the past was widely used in order to explain seemingly strange ways of classifying relatives

"Marriage Alliance" by Louis Dumont. Reprinted with permission of the Publisher from the *International Encyclopedia of the Social Sciences*, David L. Sills, Editor. Volume 10, pp. 19 to 23. Copyright © 1968 by Crowell Collier and Macmillan, Inc.

(kinship terminologies). This practice has brought discredit, in the eyes of some, to the study of both marriage rules and terminologies. In 1871 Lewis Henry Morgan made two assumptions: (1) terminology reflects behavior, and hence, (2) if a terminology cannot be understood from present behavior, it must be because the behavior it reflects belongs to the past.

Quite apart from the difficulty of reconstructing past behavior, anthropological thought in this matter is still ethnocentric. The underlying assumption is that all peoples entertain the same *ideas* about kinship; their classifying of relatives in different ways is, therefore, due to differences in *behavior*. Fully excusable in Morgan, such an assumption is less so today.

W. H. R. Rivers recognized the link between an actual marriage rule (symmetrical cross-cousin marriage) and a certain type of terminology (often called "bifurcate merging"). For Rivers, the marriage rule was the cause, the terminology the effect, and he saw his task as explaining the marriage rule itself. Once again, terminology reflects behavior, and again historical speculation is called in, this time to discover the "origin" of one item, which is in fact essentially a normative trait. In our time the different features of a kinship system are, in practice, often considered in isolation or are hierarchized according to what is assumed to be their degree of reality or determinativeness. This tendency, if not found in such crudity as in the past, still exerts considerable pressure even on the best minds, and that it constitutes a major obstacle to the understanding of certain kinship systems can be shown by the example of Australian kinship, a classical subject for kinship theory. In Australian section systems, descent is overstressed; the reasons that may elsewhere justify this emphasis are here misplaced, for it prejudices the consideration of other elements in the system.

In writing about Australian kinship systems, authors vie with each other in stressing that in symmetrical cross-cousin marriage arrangements, double descent is always present or implied. This is unobjectionable in itself, but in the literature it is accompanied by a bias which makes itself obvious by repetition, whether it be in B. Z. Seligman's attempt to reduce the "type of marriage" to "forms of descent" (1928, p. 534), however strange the latter forms may appear, or in Radcliffe-Brown's overemphasis upon descent, or in Murdock's outbidding of Radcliffe-Brown in this respect. Radcliffe-Brown was not content with finding an underlying matrilineal exogamy in his classic Australian patrilineal systems and with seeing in what is now called "double descent" a widespread principle of Australian kinship. He claimed that his second kind of exogamous group actually "existed," whereas he had only inferred it (1931, pp. 39, 439); the point is insisted upon by Goody (1961, pp. 6ff.). It is perplexing later on to find Murdock opposing Radcliffe-Brown, while praising the same discovery in others; but the crux of the matter is that in Murdock's opinion Radcliffe-Brown had not gone far enough in stressing descent and descent groups, for Radcliffe-Brown had maintained, at another level, the primacy of individual relationships and marriage rules over the arrangement of groups (Murdock 1949, pp. 51 ff.).

Actually, the hypothesis of underlying matrilineal exogamy among the Kariera and Aranda accounts for the allocation of alternate generations to different groups. Among them, the patrilineal group is conceived not as a unity over a continuous series of generations but as a duality made up of two alternate generation-sections, called by different names and following different marriage rules (the grandson falling back, so to speak, into the grandfather's section). This is the simple, concrete sociological fact, widespread in Australia. If we take this for granted, together with intermarriage between the named sections, we can in each case draw a simple diagram of the whole tribe. In Figure 1 the sign [=] denotes intermarriage in both directions, the letters A, B, etc. represent patrilineal groups, and the numbers 1 and 2 are used for the two alternating generation-sections in each patrilineal group. The system of Ambrym (Balap) is easily represented in the same fashion (Deacon 1927). All three systems represent variations on the same theme, the number of patrilineal groups being respectively two, four, and three, the number of sections four, eight, and six. Each of the three systems may be conceptualized as forming a single whole through a regular chain of intermarriage and patrilineal descent. The differences in the arrangement follow necessarily from the numbers of groups (for details, see Dumont 1966). I do not pretend that a second unilineal principle cannot be said to underlie these systems, but only that the above is a simpler view of them. Let us now turn to the general theory that, like the above analysis, recognizes inter-

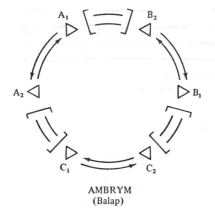

KARIERA

ARANDA
(North)

AMBRYM
(Balap)

Figure 1.

marriage as a basic element in those systems which possess a preferential or prescriptive marriage rule.

LEVI-STRAUSS

We must neglect the scholars who had previously advanced the distinction and description of the types of cross-cousin marriage (e.g. Fortune 1933; Wouden 1935) and start with the general theory of Lévi-Strauss. His monumental book *Les structures élémentaires de la parenté* (1949) goes far beyond our limits. Josselin de Jong (1952) has provided an able summary of the book, while Leach (1961) and Needham (1960) have sympathetically, but sharply, criticized its detail. Our concern here is only with its leading ideas.

From the present point of view, the work is first of all a comparative study of positive marriage rules, informed by a general theory of kinship. Preferential marriage rules and marriage prohibitions are accounted for within an integrated body of theory. The prohibition of incest is recognized as universal; it is seen as a basic condition of social life. A man cannot take in marriage the women who are his immediate kin; on the contrary, he has to abandon them as wives to others and to receive from others his wife or wives. Lévi-Strauss considers this situation as a universal principle which lies beyond sociological explanation—and which implies an opposition between consanguinity and affinity as the cornerstone of kinship systems. He views marriage as predominantly a process of exchange (between one man and other men or between one domestic group and others), and he sees in positive marriage rules devices through which this exchange is directly regulated, giving rise to what he has called "elementary" structures.

Let us note that a kinship system is viewed here, starting from its basis in the incest prohibition, as an entirety resting on an opposition and not as a mere collection of features in which one feature might, for a priori reasons, be considered to determine the others. Abstractly, a kinship system is taken as combining a number of features (descent, inheritance, residence, affinity), and an effort is made to characterize the whole by the relations that prevail between the different features. Thus, a system is called harmonic if all transmission between generations takes place in one and the same line, dysharmonic if some features are transmitted patrilineally, others matrilineally. The rule of cross-cousin marriage, where it exists, correlates with this. Theoretically three types may be distinguished: bilateral, matrilateral, and patrilateral. In bilateral cross-cousin marriage, the spouse is at the same time mother's brother's child and father's sister's child. Two intermarrying groups exchange women as wives and thus constitute a self-sufficient unit. Lévi-Strauss has called this form "closed" or "restricted" exchange (*échange restreint*) and correlated it with dysharmonic transmission. In opposition to this type, he has stressed the quite different properties and implications of matrilateral cross-cousin marriage. This type had been less clearly recognized by previous writers, though he does not consider the Dutch literature on Indonesia in which the type had been characterized (e.g. Fischer 1935; 1936; Wouden 1935). In this type, a man marries his mother's brother's daughter; a given line B takes wives from line A and gives wives to line C, generation after generation. Intermarriage is thus asymmetrical, and if the society is conceived as a number of discrete groups giving and receiving women in marriage, the simplest system is that of a circle: at the end of the series, Z receives from Y and gives to A (called the "circulating connubium" by the Dutch scholars). This is what Lévi-Strauss calls "generalized exchange." In opposition to the closed type, it requires at least three groups and may accommodate any number of groups. This type correlates with harmonic transmission, which may be either matrilineal or patrilineal. Here the identity of the intermarrying group emerges from the network of relationships, for one group is not closely dependent on any other single group, nor are two successive generations distinguished. Relatives belonging to different generations within the same group of affines are terminologically equated. Since intermarriage is directionally oriented—a group does not receive wives from the group to which it gives its daughters—there is a probability of difference of status between wife-givers and wife-takers. For a discussion of the further consequences, see Leach (1961, chapter 3; cf. Fischer 1935).

The third type, the patrilateral, is only cursorily treated in Lévi-Strauss's treatise; it appears there as a kind of abortive crossbreed between the first two types and is omitted here because it is somewhat controversial (Needham 1958b; Lane 1962).

Some of the objections that have been leveled at Lévi-Strauss's theory can be briefly mentioned. One, forestalled by Lévi-Strauss, is that he argues exclusively about viripotestal societies; another is that his idea of marriage is naive, although this is beside the point, since he was actually concerned solely with the forms and implications of intergroup marriage. A more radical criticism can be directed at the fundamental character and explanatory value of "exchange" in Lévi-Strauss's scheme (discussed in Wolfram 1956). To view the prohibition of incest as the basis for the opposition between consanguinity and affinity appears tautological to those who think of consanguinity itself as fundamental and self-explanatory or appears insufficient to those who would like a psychological explanation. Viewing marriage as an exchange may be questioned on two accounts. First, it introduces an arbitrary analogy between women and chattels, women being supposed, for instance, to be universally the most prized of "valuables." Second, "exchange" here tends to be given so wide and indeterminate a meaning as to be practically devoid of content. While this is true of "indirect exchange" and even more so of "reciprocity," the notion of exchange is certainly useful within limits. In still another critique of Lévi-Strauss, Homans and Schneider (1955) argue, in the last analysis, that to look at kinship systems as wholes having explanatory value in relation to their parts is to resort to "final causes." This critique has itself been carefully refuted by Needham (1962).

DEVELOPMENTS

Since 1949 the Lévi-Straussian theory has been tested and has undergone partial modifications

and developments. To mention only the major themes, we have first the clear-cut distinction, advocated by Needham, between prescription and preference in marriage rules. He claims that prescription alone has "structural entailments" in the total social system, and that Lévi-Strauss has dealt only with prescription or at any rate should have done so (Needham 1962). "Prescription" is here defined more as the characteristic of a system than as simply a marriage rule: it involves the combination of a rule prescribing some relatives and prohibiting others, a corresponding terminological distinction, and a sufficient degree of observation of the rule in practice (Needham 1958a, p. 75; 1958b, p. 212). The advisability of the distinction has been challenged by R. B. Lane (1962, p. 497). At first sight the distinction seems justified, and there is no objection to isolating a clear-cut type of "prescriptive alliance." That there is a danger of underestimating the importance of other types is apparent from the exacting criteria by which the author excludes the recognition of forms of patrilateral intermarriage as "prescriptive" in his sense (Needham 1958b). These latter forms, like preferential marriage in general, do have "structural entailments" of a kind, as we shall see. Moreover, the two forms are not easily distinguishable; the distinction, so presented, is more one of levels than of systems (for a recent clarification of this question, see Maybury-Lewis 1965).

The main development has probably been a refinement of the concept of alliance and the substitution of a more structural for a more empirical notion. At the start the theory, although anchored in the notion of complementarity, was in large part concerned with the exchange or circulation of women between the major exogamous components of the society. To begin with, three authors have asserted that the units which may be said to exchange women are, in concrete cases, smaller than the exogamous units. In 1951 Leach sternly insisted—with empirical, if somewhat dogmatic, good sense—that the agents arranging marriages are as a rule the males of the local descent groups, as distinct from the wider exogamous units and from the "descent lines" used in terminological diagrams and often unwittingly reified by the analyst into actual groups (see Leach 1961, p. 56; cf. Needham 1958a). Quite logically, Leach went on to criticize the assumption that a matrilateral marriage rule should necessarily result in the groups intermarrying "in a circle," an idea which Needham, on the other hand, tried to refine (1958a; 1962). A criticism from Berting and Philipsen may also be noted: to be meaningful, they suggest, the "marriage cycles" must be limited in number, and the people themselves must be aware of them (Needham 1961, p. 98). While such "alliance cycles" (Needham) do meaningfully exist in some cases, their existence does not exhaust the function or meaning of marriage alliance. On this all our authors agree, for Lévi-Strauss (1962, p. 333) himself recently recognized—if my interpretation is correct—that "conscious rules" have emerged from recent research as more important than their results in terms of "exchange." Leach had pointed out that, in the absence of cycles, the basic relationship is "one of the many possible types of continuing relationship between paired local descent groups" (1961, p. 101). Elsewhere, while marriage alliance does not result in a system of exchange at the level of the group as a whole, it is an integral part of the system of categories and roles as conceived by the people studied (Dumont 1957, pp. 22, 34).

Needham has gone furthest in submitting Lévi-Straussian structuralism to criticism from the inside and in referring the "mediating" concepts of exchange and reciprocity back to that of (distinctive) opposition (1960, p. 103). The more fundamental "integration" is not that of groups but rather that of the categories as it occurs within the social mind: the marriage rule is part and parcel of this system of ideas. Like everything else, social relationships are defined by classification. Studying the "symbolic order" of the Purum and others, Needham (1958a) found that asymmetrical intermarriage, although it could not function with less than three intermarrying or "alliance groups," can be dualistically conceptualized (wife-givers and wife-takers) in accordance with an over-all dualist

scheme. Here are found "structural entailments" different from the group arrangements on which attention had first focused. The expression "marriage alliance" thus covers both the general phenomenon of mental integration and the particular phenomenon of group integration.

In its restricted field this truly structural theory alone transcends the bias inherent in our own culture. Such expressions as "cross-cousin marriage" are technically useful but basically misleading. Real understanding is reached when the marriage rule understood as marriage alliance is seen as giving affinity the diachronic dimension that we tend to associate only with descent and/or consanguinity. By this means we are able to transcend the limitations of thinking based upon our own society and make comparisons in terms of the basic concepts involved (consanguinity and affinity).

Much remains to be done. Certainly the implications of marriage alliance for status, economy, and political organization (i.e. the physiology of the system) should be worked out (Leach 1961, chapter 3). But even regarding the morphology, our analyses are as yet imperfectly structural; we still take too much for granted in the study of terminologies. Before attempting ambitious (re)constructions, the basis in comparative data must be strengthened and extended, and we must obtain a clearer view of the limits of the logical integration of features, or conversely, of the plasticity and tolerance of systems, which can in some cases go so far as to deny in effect the ideological primacy postulated above in principle.

SELECTED READINGS

A. Commentaries and Critiques

Eggan, Fred
1956 Review of Homans and Schneider (1955). *American Sociological Review*, 21:402–403.

Fox, Robin
1967 Exogamy and direct exchange. In *Kinship and Marriage*. R. Fox (ed.), London: Penguin, pp. 175–207.

Hart, Charles M.
1950 Review of Lévi-Strauss (1949). *American Anthropologist*, 53:392.

Josselin de Jong, Jan P. de
1952 *Lévi-Strauss's theory on kinship and marriage.* Leiden: Museum voor volkekunde, Nedelelingen 10. E. J. Brill, publisher.

Lévi-Strauss, Claude
1955b *Tristes tropiques.* Paris: Librairie Plon.

Lounsbury, Floyd G.
1962 Review of Needham (1962) *American Anthropologist,* 64:1302–1311.

Lowie, Robert H.
1956 Review of Homans and Schneider (1955). *American Anthropologist,* 58:1144.

Nicholas, Ralph W.
1964 Review of Needham (1962). *Man,* 64:71.

Richards, Audrey I.
1952 Review of Lévi-Strauss (1949). *Man,* 52:12–13.

Scheffler, Harold W.
1970 The elementary structures of kinship by Claude Lévi-Strauss: A review article. *American Anthropologist,* 72:251–268.

Schneider, David M.
1965a Some muddles in the models: Or, how the system really works. In M. Banton (ed.), The relevance of models for social anthropology. *Association of Social Anthropologists of the Commonwealth. Monographs,* No. 1. London: Tavistock, pp. 25–85.

B. Original Works

Dumont, Louis
1957 *Hierarchy and marriage alliance in South Indian kinship.* London: Royal Anthropological Institute.
——— 1961 Descent, filiation and affinity. *Man,* 61:11.
——— 1968 Marriage alliance. In *International encyclopedia of social sciences.* New York: Macmillan, and Free Press.

Fortes, Meyer
1959 Descent, filiation and affinity. *Man,* 59:309, 331.

Fortune, Reo F.
1933 A note on some forms of kinship structure. *Oceania,* 4:1–9.

Goody, Jack R.
1959 The mother's brother and sister's son in West Africa. *Journal of the Royal Anthropological Institute,* 89:61–87.
——— 1961 The classification of double descent systems. *Current Anthropology,* 2 (February), pp. 3–25.

Homans, George C., and David M. Schneider
1955 *Marriage, authority and final causes: A study of unilateral cross-cousin marriage.* New York: Free Press.

Leach, Edmund R.
1951 The structural implications of matrilateral cross-cousin marriage. *Journal of the Royal Anthropological Institute,* 81:23–55. Reprinted in E. R. Leach, *Rethinking anthropology.* London: Athlone, pp. 54–104.
——— 1962 *Rethinking anthropology.* London: Athlone.

Lévi-Strauss, Claude
1943 The social use of kinship terms among Brazilian Indians. *American Anthropologist,* 45:398–409.
——— 1949 *Les structures élémentaires de la parenté.* Paris: Presses Universitaires de France.
——— 1951 Language and the analysis of social laws. *American Anthropologist,* 53:155–163.
——— 1953 Social structure. In A. L. Kroeber et al. (eds.), *Anthropology today.* Chicago: University of Chicago Press, pp. 524–553.
——— 1955a The structural study of myth. *Journal of American Folklore,* 68:428–444.
——— 1963a *Totemism.* Translated by R. Needham. Boston: Beacon.
——— 1963b *Structural anthropology.* New York: Basic Books.
——— 1969a The elementary structures of kinship (*Les structures élémentaires de la parenté*). R. Needham (ed.). Translated by J. H. Bell and I. R. von Sturmer. Boston: Beacon.

Mauss, Marcel
1925 *The gift.* Translated by I. Cunnison. London: Cohen and West, 1954.

Needham, Rodney
1958a A structural analysis of Purum society. *American Anthropologist,* 60:75–101.
——— 1958b The formal analysis of prescriptive patrilateral cross-cousin marriage. *Southwestern Journal of Anthropology,* 14:199–219.
——— 1962 *Structure and sentiment: A test in social anthropology.* Chicago: University of Chicago Press.

Schneider, David M.
1961 The distinctive features of matrilineal descent groups. In D. M. Schneider and E. K.

Gough (eds.), *Matrilineal kinship*. Berkeley: University of California Press.

——— 1965a Some muddles in the models: Or, how the system really works. In M. Banton (ed.), The relevance of models for social anthropology. *Association of Social Anthropologists of the Commonwealth Monographs*, No. 1. London: Tavistock.

Yalman, Nur
1962 The structure of the Sinhalese kindred: A re-examination of the Dravidian terminology. *American Anthropologist*, 64: 548–575.

XII

THE MEANING OF KIN TERMS: FORMAL AND COMPONENTIAL ANALYSES

Formal and componential are adjectives that describe two approaches to the analysis of kinship terminology systems as well as other domains of language. They are by no means mutually exclusive. Formal analysis refers, first, to those methods of model building that satisfy the canons (1) of accuracy (they can predict), and (2) of parsimony (they are the most efficient, neat models that can be built from the data). Formal analyses have been used to build models that generally have no claim to psychological reality. Componential analyses, in addition to satisfying the above criteria, construct models that are paradigms within linguistic domains such that (a) all the terms considered have something in common in their meaning and (b) the boxes in the paradigm are divided by area or "distinctive features" that have been derived from the data. It has often, though not always, been claimed that componential analyses approach psychological reality, that is, represent the "folk models" that the people have in their own heads.

Kroeber's 1909 paper attempted a formal analysis by using criteria derived from an *internal* anlysis of terminology systems—the very patterns that made the system what it was. Kroeber's criteria (principles) were geneological in nature and, he assumed, universally applicable. He also claimed that they were psychologically real. In a reaction to the many sociological analyses of kinship systems that appeared in the three decades following Kroeber's paper, Davis and Warner (1937) produced another "structural analysis" that, again, was based on geneology and assumed to be universally, although not necessarily psychologically real. Leach ("Jinghpaw Kinship Terminology," 1945), in his analysis of the Kachin system, was concerned with the relationship between norms and models and showed that a terminology system is a guide to *ideal* norms with sociological reference. He analyzed the Jinghpaw system in terms of a social structural model that was not primarily geneological. Therefore his criteria of distinctive meaning were sociological. He did not assume that his model was universal and said little about psychological reality.

Goodenough (*Property, Kin and Community,* 1951; 1956b) and Lounsbury ("A Semantic Analysis of Pawnee Kinship Usage," 1956) developed a more rigorous type of analysis for kinship terminology systems, drawing upon the methods of semantic linguistics. In these two initial componential analyses, the "reference languages" were geneological, as were their criteria. The particular cultural data determined these distinctive features and, therefore, the features were not universal. Goodenough, at least, claims psychological reality for his paradigms and criteria. Further analyses, in the same vein, followed. Wallace and Atkins ("The Meaning of Kinship Terms" 1960), in a major review, pointed out some of the problems of this approach, particularly those concerning (a) their inability to deal with alternate or multiple terms, and (b) the problem of psychological (cognitive) versus structural (predictive) reality. However the search for a method to prove the psychological reality of the analysis has continued (Romney and D'Andrade, "Cognitive Aspects of English Kin Terms," 1964). Other criticisms of these claims to psychological reality have been made by Burling ("Cognition and Componential Analysis," 1964) and Berreman ("Anemic and Emetic Analysis in Social Anthropology," 1966) and, in the recent past, anthropologists have shied away from such attempts.

Lounsbury (1956, 1964 a and b) has led the way in performing structural analyses that only claim analytical reality, that is, correctness and parsimony, as exhibited by most of the authors in Hammel (ed.) 1965. Leach ("Concerning Trobriand Clans and the Kinship Category Tabu," 1958) presented a sociological (semi-componential) analysis of Malinowski's Trobriand data, demonstrating the relative irrele-

vance of geneology. This analysis was attacked by Lounsbury ("Another View of Trobriand Kinship Catagories," 1965), who claimed that a formal geneologically based analysis was, in fact, closer to psychological reality! Graburn (*Taqagmiut Eskimo Kinship Terminology*, 1964) performed geneologically and sociologically based componential analyses on the same body of data from the Eskimos, demonstrating the superiority of the latter on the grounds of both correctness and parsimony as well as the method's far greater relevance to psychological reality. Many of the "ethnoscientists," using componential and taxonomic methods for the analysis of linguistic domains, have clung to the possibilities of reconstructing psychologically real folk models: though the arguments continue, their efforts may yet succeed and satisfy the canons of formal analysis too.

KINSHIP, MARRIAGE RULES AND RESIDENTIAL MODELS

Edmund R. Leach

I. THEORY

Kinship systems have a perennial fascination. From Morgan's day to the present, a long succession of authors have produced their diagrams and algebraic explanations. Indeed the explanations are so many and varied that it is possible to suspect that this particular type of jigsaw puzzle fits together in several different ways.

In an important paper Professor Radcliffe-Brown (1941) has recently discussed two such ways, which he labels respectively "conjectural history" and "structural analysis" (p. 1). Whether the argument which follows can rightly

Reprinted by permission of the Royal Anthropological Institute of Great Britain and Ireland from "Jinghpaw Kinship Terminology: An Experiment in Ethnographic Algebra," *Journal of the Royal Anthropological Institute,* Vol. 75 (1945), pp. 59–66, 70–71.

be held to fall into either category I find it hard to determine. Granted that the objective of the social anthropologist is the elucidation of general laws concerning the nature of human society, the particular study of kinship systems may prove deceptively attractive. Kinship terminology and its diagrammatic arrangement provide, ready-made, a delightful series of mathematical abstractions and it is all too easy to develop their analysis into a 'system' having little relation to sociological facts. In another recent paper Radcliffe-Brown (1940a) has remarked that

if in an Australian tribe I observe in a number of instances the behaviour towards one another of persons who stand in the relation of mother's brother and sister's son, it is in order that I may be able to record as precisely as possible the general or normal form of this relationship, abstracted from the variations of particular instances, though taking into account those variations (p. 4).

I would suggest, however, that the existence of any "general or normal form" cannot be taken for granted, but must be demonstrated. In this quotation, the "persons who stand in the relation of mother's brother and sister's son" might be taken to mean either persons standing in that blood relationship, biologically defined, or persons categorised by a particular pair of native kinship terms. Identification of these two meanings may lead to confusion. To me it seems that many of the artificial dogmas that have arisen during the development of kinship theory have their source in too great a readiness to translate native terminology into what is arbitrarily deemed to be the primary English equivalent. The focal point of apparent norms may thereby be displaced. For example, in the system I shall describe, the mother's brother and the wife's father fall into the same term category, *tsa*, which includes also other relatives. There may be a norm of behaviour which characterises a man's attitude towards his *tsa*, but it is not legitimate to assume that this characteristic attitude is especially typical either of the respect for a mother's brother or of that for a wife's father.

In my own field work, I have found the determination of sociological norms extremely difficult, and at no level of analysis would such a norm coincide with the cultural ideal put forward by a good informant, well versed in native law and custom. The field worker has three distinct 'levels' of behaviour pattern to consider. The first is the actual behaviour pattern of individuals. The average of all such individual behaviour patterns constitutes the second, which may fairly be described as 'the norm.' But there is a third pattern, the native's own description of himself and his society, which constitutes 'the ideal.' (cf. Malinowski [1932a], p. 120: also Gordon Brown and Barnett [1942], p. 30. The latter speak of "ideal," "anticipated" and "actual" behaviour.) Because the field worker's time is short and he must rely upon a limited number of informants, he is always tempted to identify

the second of these patterns with the third. Clearly the norm is strongly influenced by the ideal, but I question whether the two are ever precisely coincident. In the study of kinship this is an important distinction, because any structural analysis of a kinship system is necessarily a discussion of ideal behaviour, not of normal behaviour.

In the account which follows, the "explanation" of Jinghpaw kinship terminology rests on a rule of preferred marriage. The reader should remember throughout that the preference is for marriage between *gu* and *nam* (and not, let us say, for marriage between a 'father's sister's son,' and a 'mother's brother's daughter'). This marriage rule is an item of ideal behaviour with mythological sanction, but it cannot be regarded as a statistical norm of behaviour, nor even as an element of conjectural history. I see no reason to suppose that in the past the norm was any closer to the ideal than I have found it to be today. In short, while I claim to demonstrate that the rule in question has a functional significance in the society as it now exists, I am not concerned with any teleological argument as to whether the marriage rule is causal to the form of society, or vice versa.

I seek to show that Jinghpaw kinship terminology, which is superficially extremely complex, would appear simple and consistent to a man living in an ideal society, organised according to certain very simple rules. These rules constitute the ideal pattern of Jinghpaw society, to which the actual society is now, and probably always has been, a somewhat remote approximation.

I will first demonstrate that in a hypothetical society organised in accordance with seven structural principles, the terminology actually used by the Jinghpaw Kachins is the simplest possible. Consider a hypothetical society organised as follows:

Hypothesis 1—Descent is patrilineal.
Hypothesis 2—Marriage is patrilocal (that is, a man always continues to live in the house of his father, while a woman, on marriage, leaves her own home and goes to that of her husband).
Hypothesis 3—Each patrilineal-patrilocal group is exogamous.

Hypothesis 4—Polygyny is permissible; polyandry is not.

Hypothesis 5—All women marry immediately upon reaching puberty; therefore the patrilineal-patrilocal group at no time contains *adult* females who have been born into that group.

Hypothesis 6—A man must always marry a woman from the original patrilineal-patrilocal group of his own mother; and that woman must not be older than himself.

Hypothesis 7—A woman can never be given in marriage to a man from the original patrilineal-patrilocal group of her own mother; she will always be given in marriage to a man of the patrilocal group into which her father's sister has already married.

Hypothesis 5 is an exaggeration introduced for purposes of simplified demonstration. Hypotheses 6 and 7 are logically identical; they are given separately here because, while a modified permissive form of Hyp. 6 is common to many actual societies, it is the negative (incest) aspect of Hyp. 7 which is most heavily stressed in the Jinghpaw reality. If 'may' were substituted for 'must' in Hyp. 6, we could find a wide range of societies which approximate to the pattern of Hyp. 1–6, but the ban on marriage to the father's sister's daughter, stressed in Hyp. 7, is relatively rare. The principle involved has been described by some writers as "asymmetrical descent," and is found, here and there, in all parts of the world. But clearly no actual society could conform rigidly to the ideal pattern here laid down.

Granted these hypothetical conditions, our problem is to devise a system of kinship terminology which, *in the simplest manner possible,* will be logically consistent with the given conditions. It is necessary first to specify the rules of classification which I intend to apply and then to try to justify the claim that these rules are the simplest possible in the circumstances.

Rule 1.—Two distinct terms will never be used where one can serve. A speaker will only differentiate terminologically between two individuals if failure to do so would imply a situation either contrary to the listed hypotheses or contrary to the universal law of incest (the ban on sexual relations between parent and child, and between brother and sister).

The primacy and universality of the biological human family has repeatedly been stressed by both anthropologists and psychologists. It is in any case generally conceded that relationships within the biological family are, of all relationships, by far the most significant psychologically, the most highly charged with emotion. From this fact we derive

Rule 2.—In any patrilineal kinship system, the only sentiments which may be claimed as universal are those associated with the elementary human family, namely: father-child, mother-child, brother-brother, brother-sister, sister-sister. Where terms exist to identify such relationships, they may legitimately be presumed to represent sentiments at least broadly analogous to those covered by the English terms. (In no other case can it be assumed that any term has a primary meaning which can be exactly translated into an English equivalent).

Sociologically speaking, the sex of a small child is usually irrelevant to its elders, and there is nothing in our hypotheses to suggest the contrary. From this fact derives Rule 3:

Rule 3.—An elder addressing a child will make no distinction as to sex, unless the implications of the listed hypotheses demand it.

A corollary of Rules 1 and 3 is Rule 4:

Rule 4.—Except where it is contrary to hypothesis, an adult woman will address any child by the same term as does her husband.

In Rule 1, I have assumed that a child distinguishes between the members of its own biological family on a basis of (a) sex, and (b) age status. To the adult, the essential difference between the father and the elder brother rests on the biological connection, but this the child cannot comprehend. To the child, the difference is rather one of behaviour, of appearance, of authority. The classifications natural to a child in considering its elders derive from a sentimental enlargement of this axiomatic principle (cf. Radcliffe-Brown's "unity of the sibling group" 1941: 7). The limits of extension of the basic sentiments are defined by our hypotheses, especially Hyp. 2, 3, 6, and 7. Hence:

Rule 5.—For the child, terms applicable to members of the speaker's own biological family (see Rule 2) will be extended to other persons living within the same patrilocal group, the extension being made on the basis of sex and age; such terms will not be extended to persons living outside the speaker's own patrilocal group.

Rule 6.—A term applied to a member of any patrilocal group other than the speaker's own will apply also to all other persons of the same group, of similar sex and age status.

It must be emphasized that these last two rules are meant here to apply only to the special conditions of our hypothetical society. In practice they apply to a wide range of societies organised on an exogamous, patrilineal lineage basis (cf. Lowie 1929).

Two other special differentiations derive from Hyp. 7:

Rule 7.—Among members of the opposite sex in patrilocal groups other than the speaker's own, the child must distinguish between persons with whom marriage will be permitted and those with whom it will be forbidden.

Rule 8.—For a male child, the potential wife's father, and for a female child, the potential husband are males of potential authority status. The *child* must distinguish such classes of persons from all others.

With the exception of members of the speaker's own biological family, the precise blood relationship between any two individuals is, generally speaking, irrelevant. In the hypothetical society under consideration relationship is defined by:

(a)   The patrilineal-patrilocal group into which the individual is born.
(b)   The patrilocal group in which the individual resides.
(c)   The permissibility of sex relations.
(d)   In the case of males, the age-group status of the individual in the line of patrilineal descent.

Let us now consider five distinct patrilineal-patrilocal groups, designated AA, A, B, C, and CC, respectively, which conform to the required conditions. Men of AA always take their wives from A; men of A take their wives from B; men of B take their wives from C; men of C take their wives from CC. At any given instant the community resident in B will consist of:

(i)   Adult males who were born into B.
(ii)   The wives of B males, who by birth are adult females of C.
(iii)   The children of B males and C females, of either sex.

There will be no adult females of B group birth still resident in B; by Hyp. 5, all such are now married and resident in A.

Let us construct a terminology adequate for the use of a child born into B. In place of symbols we will use the monosyllables of the Jinghpaw terminology.

First, from Rule 2, we need terms with the primary biological meaning: mother (*nu*), father (*wa*), brother (*hpu*), sister (*na*). By Rule 5, these terms can be extended to other persons resident in B, as follows:

Definition 1: *wa*. The real father, and all other males of the father's age group resident within the speaker's own group, are addressed as *wa*.
Definition 2: *nu*. The real mother, and all other women of the mother's age group resident within the speaker's own group, are addressed as *nu*.
Definition 3: *hpu*. All males of the speaker's own age group belonging to the speaker's own group by birth, are addressed as *hpu*.
Definition 4: *na*. All females of the speaker's own age group belonging to the speaker's own group by birth, are addressed as *na*.

Though of the same age group, *hpu* and *na* are necessarily older than the child speaker, since we presume that the latter, when first learning to talk, is the younger of any pair of persons in reciprocal speech relationship.

A theoretical point which may be stressed is that a kinship term in isolation has no significance; it is the relationship expressed by a pair of reciprocal terms which has structural importance and which can be interpreted in terms of behaviour (cf. Radcliffe-Brown 1941:11. This view has, however, been disputed by Kroeber and others.) Any particular term (T) may have a variety of different reciprocals (R, R′, R″, etc.), and the relationship denoted by T-R has not necessarily much in common with the relationship T-R′. Nevertheless, in view of the rules set out above, we are here concerned with only two forms of reciprocal, namely, relationships of the form T-R, where the sex of T and R are both defined, and relationships of the form T-R′, where the sex of T is defined but that of R′ is not.

Reverting to our hypothesis, we require reciprocals for the four terms already defined. Applying Rules 3 and 4, we see that two reciprocals are sufficient.

Definition 5: *sha*. *Wa* and *nu* address the speaker as *sha*, irrespective of sex.

Definition 6: *nau*. *Hpu* and *na* address the speaker as *nau*, irrespective of sex.

The term *nau*, thus defined, might almost be translated as 'youngster.' The child itself will in due course use the same term to address infants of its own patrilocal group, younger than itself.

Within the child's own patrilocal group there still remain the members of age groups senior to *wa* and *nu* (Def. 1, 2). Without considering factors of behaviour, it may be seen from purely algebraic arguments that in the given conditions the extension of any of the terms already defined to members of the second ascending generation would be inappropriate. Since the sex of *sha* is indeterminate (Def. 5) and the sex of the children of *sha* will be indeterminate (Rule 3), we logically require a term of relationship T-R′, which covers four reciprocal biological relationships: father's father-son's son, father's father-son's daughter, mother's father-daughter's son, mother's father-daughter's daughter. Of these, however, mother's father, daughter's daughter, and daughter's son are not members of the speaker's own patrilocal group, hence (according to Rule 5) none of the terms so far defined can be extended to cover these categories. Since a child distinguishes the sex of its elders, father's father must be distinct from father's mother. Hence three new terms are required:

Definition 7: *ji*. Males whom the father addresses as *wa*, or *ji*, are addressed as *ji*.

Definition 8: *woi*. Females whom the father addresses as *nu*, or *woi*, are addressed as *woi*.

Definition 9: *shu*. *Ji* and *woi* address the speaker as *shu* irrespective of sex.

As long as the child remains at home, it needs no further extension of its kinship terminology; but as soon as the mother's parents are visited, a further group of relatives require classification. It follows from the argument of the last paragraph that the father's father and the mother's father must be covered by the same term. Hence, by Rule 6, it follows that *ji* and *woi* can be extended to all members of age groups senior to the mother, resident in the patrilocal group of the mother's father.

Definition 7—*Extension: ji*. All males whom the mother addresses as *wa*, or *ji*, are addressed as *ji*.

Definition 8—*Extension: woi*. All females whom the mother addresses as *nu*, or *woi*, are addressed as *woi*.

For simplicity, we will refer to the patrilocal group of mother's father as 'the mother's group,' and to the speaker's own patrilocal group as 'the speaker's group.'

The males of the mother's age group in the mother's group are important to a child of either sex. For the male child, these are in the class of potential wife's father (Hyp, 6, Rule 8). For the female child, they are in the class of males with whom sex relations are forbidden (Hyp. 7, Rule 7). According to Rule 5, the term *wa* cannot be extended to any males of the mother's group; similarly none of the other terms so far defined is appropriate. A new term is therefore needed:

Definition 10: *tsa*. Males of the mother's group who belong to the mother's own age group are addressed as *tsa*.

Among the females of the mother's group, the male child must distinguish between those who are marriageable and those who are unmarriageable. A woman may be unmarriageable because she is married already, or because she stands in a prohibited degree of relationship to the speaker. Hence:

Definition 11: *ni*. A male addresses the wives of the males of the mother's group, other than *woi*, as *ni*.

Definition 12: *rat*. A male child addresses the female children of the mother's group who are older than himself as *rat*.

Definition 13: *nam*. A male addresses the women younger than himself who belong by birth to his mother's group as *nam*.

Since, by Hyp. 5, *rat* on reaching puberty become the wives of *hpu*, they are for the most part resident members of the speaker's own group.

The speaker (male) stands in a non-marriageable relationship to *ni* and *rat*, but in a marriageable relationship to *nam* (female). If the speaker is by birth a member of B, then *nam* and *rat* were both born into C and *ni* into CC. If our B group child is female, this threefold classification is unnecessary. After marriage, the B group female child will reside in A, and will be remote from C and CC relatives. Hence:

Definition 14: *ning*. A female addresses all the female individuals whom her brother would address as *ni*, *rat*, or *nam*, as *ning*.

Initially, therefore, a female child does not use the terms *ni*, *rat* and *nam* at all. Later she will use *rat* towards males younger than herself (see Def. 12, Ext.), and *nam* towards members of the junior generation who are *nam* to her husband; but a female will never use the term *ni*.

The adult extension of the term *nam* follows from Rules 3 and 4:

Definition 13—*Extension* A: *nam*. An adult male addresses as *nam* the *hpu* and *nau* of all females of age group junior to himself whom he addresses as *nam* in accordance with Def. 13, above.

Definition 13—*Extension* B: *nam*. An adult female addresses as *nam* all those, of either sex, who would be addresses as *nam* by her husband, with the exception of females who are already *nau* to herself in accordance with Def. 6, above.

In the mother's group, there remain only the males of the speaker's own age group. For the female child these are covered by Hyp. 7 and Rule 7 (see Def. 10, above):

Definition 10—*Extension*: *tsa*. A female addresses all males (other than *ji*) in the mother's group as *tsa*.

This category will include even the males of age group junior to the speaker whom a male would

address as *nam* in accordance with Def. 13, Ext. A (above).

A male child first encounters the males of his own age in his mother's group as playmates. Their social attitude towards him is very similar to that of his *hpu-nau*, but the extension of the latter terms is excluded by Rule 5. The emphasis is strongly on equality of status, and the authority content of the term *tsa* (Def. 10, Rule 8) is inappropriate. A new term is therefore needed:

Definition 15: *hkau*. A male addresses all males in the mother's group, of the speaker's own age group, as *hkau*.

Reciprocals for the terms covered by Definitions 10–15 are now required. The equality of status emphasized by *hkau* is reciprocal:

Definition 15—*Extension*: *hkau*. A male addresses as *hkau* all males who would address the speaker as *hkau*.

Applying Rules 3 and 4, only one reciprocal is required for the terms *ni* and *tsa*:

Definition 16: *hkri*. Persons addresses as *ni* or *tsa* address the speaker of either sex as *hkri*.

The term *rat* expresses a non-marriageable relationship between persons of the same age group. This condition is mutual:

Definition 12—*Extension*: *rat*. Persons addresses as *rat* address the speaker as *rat*.

The term *nam* (Def. 13) expresses primarily a marriageable relationship which is mutual. The term cannot, however, be made into its own reciprocal, since the sex of *nam* is indeterminate (Def. 13, Ext.) and its reciprocal use would lead to implications contrary to Hyp. 6 and 7. Moreover the male reciprocal of *nam* (female) is the class of potential husbands (Rule 8). Hence two reciprocals are required for the term *nam*, differentiating as to sex:

Definition 17: *gu*. Males who address persons of either sex as *nam* are themselves addressed as *gu*.

Definition 18: *moi*. Females who address persons of either sex as *nam* are themselves addressed as *moi*.

It may reasonably be objected that this is a highly artificial way of reaching the relationship with the father's sister, who is included in the class *moi*. Circumlocution seems, however, unavoidable, despite the fact that, according to Radcliffe-Brown (1949), the unity of the sibling group may be so firm that the father's sister can be regarded as "a sort of female father" (p. 7). It must be remembered that the father's sister is here not a resident member of the child's own group; although biologically a close relative, sociologically she is somewhat remote. The basic unity here is the local group which, for the individual, is stratified into age groups or generations: this implies the unity of the sibling group (in Radcliffe-Brown's sense) in the case of children, but not in the case of adults. Kroeber and others have argued that place of residence may be a more fundamental social grouping than lineage descent, a contention borne out by this example (Kroeber: 1938:308 and *passim*). Later we shall see that the term *moi* is extended in practice to cover wives of *gu* who are not blood relatives of the real father at all, which lends support to the rather artificial interpretation given here.

The term *ning* (Def. 14) covers primarily a wide group of unimportant relatives of the same sex. This unimportance is mutual:

Definition 14—Extension: ning. Females addressed as *ning* address the speaker as *ning*.

The eighteen terms thus defined (Def. 1–18) suffice to identify the kinship status of any two individuals within the hypothetical system composed of groups A, B, and C, since all needs are met by considering the relationship of the individual to members of his own and of his mother's group. We have studied, above, the relationship of a B group child to its own (B) group and to its mother's group (C). The B group child's relationship to members of its father's sister's husband's group (A) is analogous to the reciprocal relationship between a C group individual and the original B group child. The table of Reciprocal Terms (Table I) recapitulates the foregoing definitions.

While the use of these terms, in accordance with the definitions given, defines the relationship of any B group individual to all persons belonging to A and C groups, certain more re-

Table I.   Reciprocal Terms

SENIOR		JUNIOR	
MALE	FEMALE	MALE	FEMALE
Wa	*Nu*	*Sha*	*Sha*
Ji	*Woi*	*Shu*	*Shu*
Hpu	*Na*	*Nau*	*Nau*
Tsa	*Ni*	*Hkri*	*Hkri*
	Rat	*Rat*	
Gu	*Moi*	*Nam*	*Nam*
	Ning		*Ning*
Hkau		*Hkau*	

NOTE—In the *ni-hkri* relationship, the *hkri* is always male (Def. 14). In the *tsa-hkri* relationship, the *hkri* is male or female (Def. 10), and if female, unmarriageable (Hyp. 7).

NOTE: The terms in the two right-hand columns are the reciprocals of those in the two left-hand columns and vice versa.

mote individuals, belonging to groups AA and CC, are also relevant to the social context. We have already noted that *ni* is by birth a CC individual, in relation to a B speaker; it follows that the males of CC (i.e., the *hpu-nau* of *ni*) are also socially significant relatives. The child's approach to members of both C and CC groups is through its mother. From Def. 10, Ext., it follows that the mother of a B child addresses all males of CC either as *ji* or as *tsa*. If we compare these two terms as to affective tone, we see that the *ji-shu* relationship implies, *inter alia*, remoteness of relationship; in contrast, the *tsa-hkri* has the specialised affect of constraint. Where *hkri* is female, it implies a sexual taboo; where *hkri* is male, it implies, among other attitudes, that of a son-in-law. It follows that *ji*, rather than *tsa*, is the appropriate term to extend to a category of affinal relatives chiefly characterised by remoteness of relationship:

Definition 7—Secondary Extension: ji. All males whom the speaker's mother would address either as *ji* or as *tsa* are addresses as *ji* by a speaker of either sex.

Reciprocally it follows that all persons of AA group, of either sex and any age, are *shu* to a male speaker of B. Thus, in logic, a whole clan is comprised under a single relationship term, and if we insist upon translating terms, it would be formally correct to say that a Jinghpaw addresses his son's wife's brother's wife's brother as 'grandfather.' But translation of terms invites complicated explanations. I feel they are unnecessary. Diagrammatic analysis, on the other hand, by imputing equal weight to all parts of the diagram, tends to exaggerate the practical complexity. In our hypothetical system, for instance, the clan which is treated as a unity is also remote. Only one or two of these AA or CC relatives are ever likely to have dealings with a B group individual. In such circumstances, the undifferentiated classification of a whole clan grouping need not imply ambiguity. The principle of unification is, in fact, clearly the locality of residence, rather than lineage descent.

Table II reproduces our whole system in diagrammatic form. In each Local Group column, the terms on the left designate females, the terms on the right, males. The males have married, or will marry, the females in the column immediately to their right; they are the brothers (hpu-nau) of the females in the column immediately to their left; they are the sons (sha) of the males in the age-group level immediately above them; and they are the fathers (wa) of both the males and the females in the age-group level immediately below, in the same column. The central B group male is shown as 'EGO,' his sister as 'ego' (representing the 'speaker' in the text above). In respect of each individual represented in the diagram, the term of address used by 'EGO' is shown in capital letters, and the corresponding term used by 'ego' is shown in lower case letters immediately below, thus:

RAT
ning

The terms DAMA, HPU-NAU, MAYU, shown at the head of columns A, B, and C, are the Jinghpaw terms for these clan groupings, as used by both 'EGO' and 'ego' (see Section II). *Madu wa* and *Madu jan* signify 'husband' and 'wife,' respectively.

In practice, the terms denoting affinal relationship are used in the same sense, whether or

Table II. Diagram Illustrating Jinghpaw Relationship System

LOCAL GROUP	AA (SHU)		A DAMA		B HPU-NAU		C MAYU		CC (JI)	
	FEMALE	MALE	FEMALE	MALE	FEMALE	MALE	FEMALE	MALE	FEMALE	MALE
Age groups senior to parents'			HKRI ning	GU gu	MOI moi	JI ji	WOI woi	JI ji	WOI woi	JI ji
Parents' age group	SHU ning	SHU hkri	HKRI ning	GU gu	MOI moi	WA wa	NU nu	TSA tsa	NI ning	JI ji
Older than speaker	SHU ning	SHU hkri	HKRI ning	HKAU gu	NA na	HPU hpu	RAT ning	HKAU tsa	NI ning	JI ji
Speaker's own age group			(madu wa)		ego	EGO	(MADU JAN)			
Younger than speaker	SHU ning	SHU hkri	HKRI ning	HKAU rat	NAU nau	NAU nau	NAM ning	HKAU tsa	NI ning	JI ji
Son's age group	SHU ning	SHU hkri	HKRI sha	HKRI sha	SHA nam	SHA nam	NAM ning	NAM tsa	NI ning	JI ji
Age groups junior to son's	SHU shu	SHU shu	SHU shu	SHU shu	SHU nam	SHU nam	NAM ning	NAM tsa		

not all the marriages envisaged by the ideal system have actually taken place. Thus EGO's wife's father may not stand in any blood relationship to EGO's mother, but EGO's wife's father is nevertheless called *tsa*, EGO's wife's father's sister *nu*, EGO's wife's father's sister's husband *wa*, and so on. It is this type of adoptive relationship which makes the system appear unduly complicated when first encountered in the field.

In reading the diagram it should be understood that siblings of the same sex are always denoted by the same term, and that the children of siblings of the same sex are treated as siblings (Rule 5 and 6); thus the mother's sister is called *nu*, the mother's sister's husband *wa*, and the mother's sister's son (older than the speaker) *hpu*.

II. PRACTICE

The system of relationship terms described in Section I is the terminology actually employed by the Jinghpaw Kachins of North Burma. It has been described several times before; but these earlier studies merely give lists, necessarily incomplete, of alternative translations of the different terms. In the field, these dictionary translations merely serve to make the practical application of the terminology seem more confusing than ever.

The various Jinghpaw dialects, including Gauri, Hkahku, Duleng, and Tsasen, appear to have systems structurally identical. Concerning Zi (Atsi), I am doubtful. The other Maru dialects, including Lashi, Nung, and Daru, although associated with a form of society very similar to that of the Jinghpaw, have systems which cannot be translated word for word into Jinghpaw, with identical extensions of meaning. I have therefore avoided the use of the rather vague term 'Kachin' in the title of this paper.

The correspondence between the Jinghpaw reality and the hypothetical 'ideal' situation described in Section I is somewhat remote. The actual society is patrilineal; marriage is usually, but not always, patrilocal; the patrilineal lineage remains strictly exogamous for a few generations only; Hyp. 4 is valid; Hyp. 5 is an exaggeration

(most girls are married before they are 20, an elderly spinster is a great rarity); there is a marked preference for a man to marry into his *mayu*, but not necessarily into his mother's group (this distinction is explained below); the ban upon marriage between *hkri* and *tsa* is rigidly enforced only with respect to near relatives.

The normal Jinghpaw village (*gahtawng*) consists essentially of a single patrilineal-patrilocal group, even though the presence of ex-slaves and various affinal relatives may obscure the superficial picture. Larger settlements (*mareng*) consist of a number of such distinct *gahtawng*, grouped together on a kinship basis: that is to say, the component *gahtawng* are either distinct lineages of the same clan, or else lineages of different clans linked in *mayu-dama* affiliation. In the ritual organisation of the *mareng* as a whole, the differentiation into component groups of *mayu ni*, *dami ni*, and *hpu-nau ni* is fundamental. Any marriage between *hkri* and *tsa*, within the *mareng* is inconsistent with such a structure. This fundamental structure is heavily obscured near Government Stations and Mission Centres, and also in certain areas, especially in the Bhamo District, where for administrative reasons the authorities have either forcibly altered the lay-out of house sites or else exerted strong official pressure to bring about the amalgamation of unrelated and even hostile *gahtawng*.

In Section I, terms such as 'clan' and 'lineage' were avoided as far as possible, and I have given no indication of the size of the idealised patrilineal patrilocal group. In the real society, there is no specific point at which the collateral group, comprising all the agnates of a common male ancestor, cease to regard themselves as forming an exogamous group. Lineage fission is, however, a normal feature of the society.

An important feature of Jinghpaw custom is that succession follows the rule of ultimogeniture. In the semi-historical past, this rule was clearly linked with a tradition of expansion whereby, before the death of a chief (or head of a lineage), his elder sons broke away from the parent locality to found new settlements of their own. On the other hand there were various pressures, political and economic, which made drastic expansion of this kind very difficult. The net result was (and is) a clan distribution pattern in which the patrilocal group, at any one time, consists of a few households only, while the clan unit comprises a number of such patrilocal groups, distributed over a wide area and intermingled with the patrilocal groups of other clans. In general the clan-lineage grouping is somewhat more stable than the local grouping. In practice, therefore, the patrilineal-patrilocal groups referred to in Section I (i.e., persons who regard one another as *hpu-nau*) are not all to be found in one place; a man may be in *hpu-nau* relationship with the inhabitants of numerous different settlements.

. . .

III. DISCUSSION

The inverted presentation of the first two sections of this paper was chosen in order to make it easy to see that the practice of the Jinghpaw is a modification of the formal simplicity of a theoretical scheme. Had the practice been described first, it would have been difficult to demonstrate that it had any formal shape at all. In the field, the actual use of Jinghpaw kinship terminology impressed me as highly complex, yet it must be, I argued, *from the users' point of view*, the simplest possible logical system consistent with the rules of the society. The classifications of our own kinship terminology appear to us "logical," the classifications of such a system as the Jinghpaw appear at first sight fantastic; yet they are simple to the Jinghpaw. The problem was, therefore, to find the ideal frame of reference, in terms of which the vagaries of Jinghpaw usage could appear logical and simple.

I found that the use of individual terms was, as it were, secondary; the basic ideology was the grouping of relatives, or rather of the households of relatives, into the three categories *hpu-nau, mayu, dama*. In practice, as we have seen these groupings are not necessarily permanent, but they "ought" to be; any Jinghpaw will tell the inquirer that, despite the contrary evidence provided by his own genealogy. What then is the significance of this 'ought,' the assertion that "in the old days" the *mayu-dama* relationship

was permanent? I suggest that it is simply the logical framework against which the Jinghpaw themselves conceptualise their own kinship system. Granted the uniqueness and permanence of the *mayu-dama* relationship, the whole kinship terminology falls into place as a consistent whole, in the manner demonstrated in Section I; without that assumption the classifications are chaotic. For the Jinghpaw, the idealisation that the *mayu-dama* relationship is permanent and unique implies in effect my original seven hypotheses; and I suggest that the Jinghpaw child does in fact learn to classify its relatives on the basis of this simplification, and that in consequence of its mental classifications are closely similar to my 'definitions.' I repeat once more, however, that this does not imply that the reality ever coincided with the idealisation.

The result of 'simplification,' as expressed in diagram form in Table II, may still appear somewhat complicated, but the practical situation is not. A Jinghpaw classes all his relatives by locality as *hpu-nau, mayu* and *dama*, with the *ji ni* and *shu ni* as remote and little mentioned appendages of the last two categories. Indeed the term *ji ni* is most frequently used as an expression for the ancestors in the speaker's own lineage; if the phrase refers instead to the *mayu ni* of the *mayu ni*, the context makes this obvious. Thus if a man announces his intention to visit his *ji ni*, one can presume that he is not contemplating a visit to Hades! To arrive at the specific relationship within the major grouping involves no special feat of memory.

Turning to general theory, it is of interest to reflect that the system I have described might have been approached from several different viewpoints, with differing results. Historical reconstruction could find evidence of a five-clan structure and submerged matriliny in a patrilineal state; linguistic analysis would place the form of the term-diagram in a particular category, such as Lowie's 'bifurcate merging' type; structural analysis would arrive at structural principles similar, in part at least, to my structural rules. I hold, however, that the type of structural analysis favoured by Radcliffe-Brown postulates a formal rigidity which is not found in practice, so that it is always necessary to consider carefully in what sense these formal simplifications are a reflection of actual behaviour. In my treatment, I have stressed the distinction between the ideal and the normal pattern of behaviour. I suggest that the kinship terminology bears a specific relationship to an idealised form of the social order, but that there is no such obvious relationship between the kinship terminology and the social order as manifested in actual behaviour.

The system of kinship terminology displays the categories into which the speaker divides the individuals with whom he has social contact; in that sense there is a functional relationship between the use of a term and the behaviour adopted towards a particular individual. But this is a tenuous relationship. In the Jinghpaw system, the mother's brother and the wife's father fall into the same category. Undoubtedly in certain contexts these two individuals fulfil somewhat similar ritual roles, but that is as far as the identity goes, and that link is not sufficient in itself to explain the kinship classification. This classification is, on the other hand, immediately understandable in terms of the idealisation that the *mayu-dama* relationship should be both permanent and unique.

I must confess that I started this paper simply in a spirit of curiosity, to discover whether it was possible to deduce from 'first principles' a system which in the field had caused me many hours of exasperation. I am not suggesting that the result has yielded anything very original with regard to basic principles of structure, but I find it interesting that, after I had made the initial assumptions that differentiation would be on the basis of age and sex, and that simplicity should always prevail (that is, that the number of differentiated kinship categories should always be minimal), it proved possible to start with a highly simplified pattern of a society, and then deduce the categories of kinship terminology actually employed in the same society. In the process, a number of structural principles which have previously been enunciated by Radcliffe-Brown, Lowie, Kroeber and others have come to the surface. This probably means no more than

that these principles are implied in the simplified pattern provided by the initial hypotheses. There is, however, one point which I would like to stress. I assume with Radcliffe-Brown that when individuals are comprised within a single kinship "class," there is a principle of unification underlying that classification which can be discerned from an analysis of the social system. But I would contrast two types of unification. On the one hand, individuals are classed together because, individually and as a group, they stand in a significant and important relationship to the speaker; but on the other hand they may be classed together precisely because they are unimportant and remote. In the Jinghpaw system *rat* is a class resulting from the first type of unification; *ning* a class resulting from the second. The same term may even comprise different groups of individuals and express different principles of unification at different stages of life. To a woman speaker, the term *tsa* signifies sexual constraint during her youth and is limited to age-group seniors of the *mayu* group with whom she has much social contact. In later life it comprises *all* males of the *mayu* group, including those younger than herself, this being a group with whom she now has little social contact.

Despite the abstraction, my treatment, while omitting the documentary detail of a normal intensive study, follows what Malinowski has called the 'biographical approach,' that is, the development of kinship terminology as it is used from childhood to old age. This treatment brings out clearly two points which have been frequently stressed before: first, that the extensions of a classificatory kinship system are merely elaborations and modifications of simple childhood sentiments developed in the normal context of home life; and secondly, that although a classificatory system includes, in theory, an unlimited number of individuals, the practical number of persons involved is quite small, and in no case so large as to lead to ambiguity.

Finally there is the question of the functioning of kinship terminology in conditions of social change. I have pointed out that if marriages between closely related *hkri* and *tsa* came to be generally recognised as correct, then the structural shape of the community, by which I mean the relationship of the kinship pattern to the local group pattern, would be radically altered. I have also mentioned that such marriages already occur, even if they are not yet regarded as orthodox. It follows, therefore, that ultimately there must come a stage where the divergence between practice and ideal is so great that there is a basic inconsistency; this must result in a terminological regrouping and a reconstruction of the ideal pattern. Such a prospect suggests a useful basis for attempting a compartive analysis of other societies in the Assam-Burma area, in which the same asymmetrical marriage rules are theoretically maintained, while other structural features differ.

The material which I have presented is based on my own field work, carried out at intervals between 1939 and 1943. An extensive literature on the Kachin already exists, a full bibliography being given by Leach (1947). Only the main contributions to the immediate subject matter of this paper are included among the References below. I may mention that the secondary extension of the *ji-shu* relationship has not previously been recorded explicitly, although it is implied by Hanson (1913), who gives *shu* as including 'sister's children's (*hkri ni a*) husbands and children.' This lack of previous observation may be accounted for by the fact that the brothers of *ni* are in any case remote relatives, while in many practical instances the use of *ji* to denote collaterals is avoided by the substitution of a closer relationship.

I am grateful to Mr. J. L. Leyden, of the Burma Frontier Service, for clarifying a number of doubtful and obscure points regarding Northern Kachin usage.

A NEW METHOD OF ANALYSING KINSHIP SYSTEMS: COMPONENTIAL ANALYSIS

Ward H. Goodenough

THE FUTUK

Anyone who can be referred to by a kinship term may be called *tefej* (my relative). As noted, however, not all relatives are considered among one's close kin. The group which forms what the Trukese calls his close kin consists of his primary and secondary relatives, the members of his own and his father's lineage, and the *jëfëkyr* of both. The natives call this group a *futuk* (flesh), considering its members to be of "one flesh with oneself." Their use of the concept of "one flesh" is similar to our own concept of consanguinity.

It will be noted that patrilineally as well as matrilineally related persons are included in the *futuk*. As broken down further it consists of:

From Ward H. Goodenough, "Property, Kin and Community on Truk," *Yale University Publications in Anthropology*, no. 46 (1951), pp. 102–110. Reprinted by permission.

1. All four grandparents.
2. Both parents.
3. The siblings of both parents (including all members of their respective lineages).
4. Siblings (including all members of one's lineage).
5. The children of all the siblings of both parents (including the *jëfëkyr* of their respective lineages).
6. Children.
7. The children of all siblings (including the *jëfëkyr* of one's lineage).
8. All grandchildren.

It is apparent that the *futuk* represents a modification of the bilateral kindred as defined by Rivers (1926:16), just as the Trukese kinship system is a modification of an earlier Hawaiian type. The development of matrilineal corporations and of the *jëfëkyr* concept has modified the basis for extending membership in the *futuk* beyond primary and secondary relatives and has unquestionably transferred to the lineage functions which at one time were associated with the earlier kindred.

The *futuk* corresponds to what we mean by the "family," "relatives," or "kin-folk" in the wider sense, as when we speak of family gatherings in connection with such events as Christmas, Thanksgiving, weddings, and funerals. It is the members of the *futuk* who assemble at births, marriages, and deaths on Truk. If there are members of his *futuk* living on other islands, a native can always look to them for food and shelter while away from home. In his own community he can turn to such kinsmen for a meal if there is no food in his own house. Sex relations with persons in one's *futuk* are considered incestuous.

A native may also have active kin relations with persons who are not strictly members of his *futuk*. Such persons are his *määräär*, who may be defined as affinal relatives and consanguineal relatives who are remoter than those in the *futuk*, but with whom an active relationship is maintained. One's *määräär* may include persons who are not covered by any kinship terms, but who wish to consider themselves related to one another by virtue of some affinal or remote consanguineal tie. The members of one's *futuk* are automatically counted among one's active relatives, but the *määräär* relationship is one which must be activated by mutual consent, though based on the potentialities of a remote kinship connection. As with the *futuk*, one can count on a meal from one's *määräär* when need arises. Visiting at the homes of others within a community tends also to be largely confined to *määräär*. A record of the people who stopped off at one native house on Romonum for visiting and gossiping was kept for a period of several weeks. Virtually everyone who stopped by was at least a *määräär* or ramage mate, if not a closer relative, of one of the adult occupants of the house.

A native may loosely refer to any kinsman by blood or marriage as a *määräär*, provided he is not of the same lineage, and even may use the term collectively to cover all active relatives, including those in the *futuk*. The Trukese regularly refer to a kinsman as a *määräär* when they wish to avoid expressing more precisely the nature of the relationship.

SOME METHODOLOGICAL CONSIDERATIONS

In our discussion of kinship so far, we have presented a set of terms as comprising a "system" and have followed this with other terms which we called "special" in the sense that they did not fit into the system. By what criteria have we decided to treat some terms as belonging and others as not belonging to a terminological system? Little validity can be claimed for the foregoing description without an answer to this question. In order to see its implications more clearly, we can restate it as follows: By what methods can we derive social categories from native terminology; how can the structural relationships of such categories to each other be determined; and what must be the manner of their relationship in order to classify them as members of a system of categories? Our problem starts in linguistics and ends in ethnography with semantics bridging the two, for we start with linguistic forms and, by defining their symbolic values, arrive at the categories of kin which they denote. In the discussion to follow, our methods of analysis in the present instance will be outlined step by step.

In order to isolate the verbal behavior patterns which would be relevant to kinship analysis, it was first ascertained that there is a group of persons any of whom can be referred to as *tefej* (my kinsman). Our genealogical census of Romonum revealed that nearly all people who can be referred to by this term have the common characteristic of being connected genealogically to an ego or to an ego's spouse. It is this fact which led to a definition of *tefej* as meaning "my kinsman." In order to isolate other kinship terms, it was necessary to find verbal behavior patterns which in their role as symbols denote persons who are included among those denoted by *tefej*, but who have more characteristics in common.

Employing the genealogical method, we obtained a series of symbolic behavior patterns which satisfy these criteria, e.g., the terms *jinej*, *jääj mwään*, *nëwyn neji* (child of my child), and *ʒōmwomw* (your father). Morphological analysis of these verbal behavior patterns—and there are a great many of them—indicated that whether or not the persons denoted are kinsmen depends on the presence of a limited number of morphemes, some one of which has to be a part of the behaviour pattern. These morphemes consist of the following base forms: *sam-*, *jin-*, *mwään-*, *feefin-*, *mwëgej-*, *newjëës-*, and *pwyny-*. Some of these have corresponding forms appearing as independent words, uncompounded with other morphemes. They are *mwään*, *feefin*, *saam* (*sam-*), and *jiin* (*jin-*). The remaining morphemes seem to occur only when compounded with other morphemes or with repetition of their own base form in complex words, e.g., *pwii-j* or *pwii-pwi* (*pwi-*).

The independent words *mwään* and *feefin* do not signify kinship at all. The characteristics of persons which they denote are such that they signify "man" and "woman" respectively. Nor do *saam* and *jiin* signify relationship with respect to some ego. The persons which they denote have characteristics in common such that these words signify "father" and "mother" in the sense of "he is a father" and "she is a mother" or "everyone who is a father (or mother)." Thus, they signify social attributes which people may or may not have rather than kinship with respect to a specific ego.

This raises an important distinction that must be made between types of social categories. There are categories to which a person may belong regardless of the category membership of others. For example, an old man is an "old man" regardless of anyone else's age, and he has a social role as such. Similarly a man who has children may have a role in his community as one who is a father. On the other hand, there are categories to which a person may belong only as they are polar to specified categories of others. In this context, one can be an "older man" only in relation to those who are younger than oneself. A man can be a "father" only in relation to persons who are "children" to him. In deriving the categories into which the members of a society are classified it is necessary to distinguish between these two types. The first may be called *absolute*

categories and the second *relative categories*. With this distinction in mind, analysis revealed that there are only two Trukese terms denoting absolute categories of kin: *saam* and *jiin*. Beyond them it is not possible to construct a system of kinship nomenclature based on terms of this semantic type.

We turned our attention, therefore, to the forms denoting relative categories of kin, those categories which exist only with reference to a specified ego or egos. This immediately raised the problem of how such reference is expressed in the Trukese language, and what the possible categories of reference are.

Reference or possession may be expressed for the following categories of persons or egos: first person singular, second person singular, third person singular, first person plural inclusive (we including you), first person plural exclusive (we excluding you), second person plural, and third person plural. Any of the morphemes which may signify kinship can occur compounded with a suffixed form denoting any one of the above categories of ego-reference. There is also a suffix expressing reference or possession for an unspecified category of egos. Any compound with this form must be followed by a specifying word or phrase. All resulting compounds, unless further modified, denote relative categories of kin and may be said to belong to a semantic class of verbal behavior patterns on the basis of this common characteristic.

Having thus derived a series of verbal behavior patterns which regularly denote persons who are genealogically connected with an ego or ego's spouse, our next problem was to define the boundaries of each category of kin. Since relative categories of kin are denoted only by behavior patterns which include referential or possessive forms as one of their components, it was necessary to hold the ego constant, that is we have to ascertain all the persons who can be denoted by each term as given consistently in the first person singular or some other referential form. Having derived a set of persons who can be denoted by each kinship term in the first person singular, we proceeded to do the same thing for each term in the second person singular, and so on for all the referential categories. We then compared the set of persons denoted by a term in the first persons with sets denoted by it in the other referential categories, and found them all to be congruent. For example, the persons who can be "your father" in relation to "you" have the same characteristics as those who can be "my father" in relation to "me." In our description of the kinship system, therefore, it was necessary to present only the first person singular forms, for the same picture would have obtained had the terms been presented in any other possessive form.

The next step in our analysis was to see how each category of persons denoted by a term is related to the other categories as denoted by the other terms. This involved comparing them with respect to the characteristics by which membership in each category is defined. We shall refer to the characteristic which defines what a term denotes as what the term *signifies* or as the *significatum* of the term (from Morris 1946:17). Our problem, then was to derive the significatum of each kinship term and to compare these significata with one another to see how they are related, if, of course, they are related at all beyond the fact that all persons denoted have the common characteristic of being genealogically connected to an ego or ego's spouse.

In order to derive significatum of a term we compared all the persons who were denoted by it on the occasion of all of its utterances as we had experienced them. The characteristics which these persons had in common, but which they shared with no one who could not be denoted by the term, were considered to be the criteria for membership in the category of persons which they constituted, and hence to comprise the significatum of the kinship term. Thus, for example, the significatum of *semej* (my father) consists of the following characteristics or attributes: (1) kin to ego (as contrasted with non-kin), (2) higher generation than that of ego (as contrasted with same or lower generations), and (3) male (as contrasted with female). According to our data, anyone with this combination of characteristics, and no one else, may be called *semej*.

The method used in comparing significata can be illustrated by analysis of the English words "go," "went," and "gone." While there is no constant phonemic segment among them, they can all be classed as parts of the same verb because of the fact that when any utterance in which they occur is varied only with respect to tense, the others must be substituted for it. In other words, the differences in their significata are a simple function of a variable of tense. This can be expressed symbolically as follows:

Let A equal the characteristic of motion away from an ego.
Let B equal the variable characteristic of tense with B_1 (present), B_2 (imperfect), and B_3 (perfect).
Thus: "go" has the significatum AB_1
  "went" has the significatum AB_2
  "gone" has the significatum AB_3

The significata of these words are mutually contrasting and at the same time complement each other with respect to the variable of tense.

For our purposes we must complicate this example further by examining the relation of "come," "came," "come" to "go," "went," "gone."

Let A equal the characteristic of motion.
Let B equal the variable characteristic of direction, with B_1 (towards ego) and B_2 (away from ego).
Let C equal the variable characteristic of tense, with C_1 (present), C_2 (imperfect), and C_3 (perfect).
Thus: "come" has the significatum AB_1C_1; AB_1C_3
  "came" has the significatum AB_1C_2
  "go" has the significatum AB_2C_1
  "went" has the significatum AB_2C_2
  "gone" has the significatum AB_2C_3

All of the above forms have the common characteristic of motion in their significata. The differences between their significata are simultaneously functions of two variable characteristics, those of direction in relation to an ego and of tense. Because the differences between the significata of "go," "went," and "gone" in the first paradigm are functions of only one variable, they are forms which belong together in what may be called a *simple semantic system*. Because the differences between the significata of all the forms in the second paradigm are functions of more than one variable, we shall consider them members of what may be called a *complex semantic system*.

We can say that a series of symbolic behavior patterns belong to the same semantic system if (1) their significata include one characteristic in common, (2) the differences between their significata are functions of one (simple system) or more (complex system) variable characteristics, and (3) the differences between their significata are mutually contrasting and complement each other.

With this in mind we are now in a position to examine the significata of Trukese kinship terms. Taking them all collectively, their significata involve, in addition to the common characteristic kinship, characteristics which are expressions of seven different variable. In accordance with the procedure outlined above we may list them as follows:

Let A equal the characteristic of being someone who is *tefej* (my kinsman) to an ego.

Let B equal the variable characteristic of generation in relation to that of ego, with B_1 (higher generation), B_2 (same generation), and B_3 (lower generation), generation here to be taken in the Trukese sense.

Let C equal the variable characteristic of the sex of ego's kinsman, with C_1 (male) and C_2 (female).

Let D equal the variable characteristic of the sex of ego's kinsman in relation to the sex of ego, with D_1 (same sex) and D_2 (opposite sex).

Let E equal the variable characteristic of the age of ego's kinsman in relation to ego's age, with E_1 (older) and E_2 (younger).

Let F equal the variable characteristic of the lineage of the kinsman in relation to ego's lineage, with F_1 (ego's lineage) and F_2 (ego's father's lineage).

Let G equal the variable characteristic of affinal as opposed to consanguineal connection, with G_1 (no affinal connections), G_2 (one affinal connection), and G_3 (two affinal connections).

Let H equal the variable characteristic of lineality versus collaterality, with H_1 (lineal relative) and H_2 (collateral relative).

Comparison of the kinship terms in relation to these characteristics of their significata reveals that they fall into three distinct semantic systems, as illustrated in Table 1.

Table 1.   Semantic Systems of Kinship

	KINSHIP TERM	SIGNIFICATUM
System 1	semej	AB_1C_1
	jinej	AB_1C_2
	pwiij	$AB_2D_1G_1$; $AB_2D_1G_3$
	jëësej	$AB_2D_1G_2$
	mwääni; mwëgëjej	$AB_2D_2G_1C_1$
	feefinej	$AB_2D_2G_1C_2$
	pwynywej	$AB_2D_2G_2$
	neji	AB_3
System 2	jääj mwään	$AF_1D_1E_1$
	mwääninyki	$AF_1D_1E_2$
	jinejisemej	AF_2C_2
System 3	semenapej	$AB_1H_1C_1$
	jinenapej	$AB_1H_1C_2$

NOTE: There is no term for the complementary possibility of $AB_2D_2G_3$ in System 1, other than the descriptive phrase *pwynywen jëësej*. There are no terms for the remaining complementary possibilities implied by the significata of the three terms in System 2 and the two terms in System 3, both systems being fragmentary.

It will be noted that none of these systems contains terms for all the complementary categories which are made possible by the significata actually represented. In this respect they are all what may be called incomplete semantic systems. The first system is nearly complete with only one unrealized possibility, while the other two are fragmentary.

Each system is composed of kinship terms whose significata meet the requirements of our definition of a semantic system. The first system, for example, consists of terms whose significata have characteristic A common to all of them. The differences between the significata are functions primarily of the variable characteristic of generation (B) and secondarily of other variables which subdivide the major categories of generation into complementary subcategories. All of the significata are mutually contrasting and complement one another with respect to their variable characteristics.

The significata of the kinship terms composing the second and third systems are not mutually contrasting with those of the first system, nor do they complement them, despite the fact that they share the common characteristic A. For example, at least one person denoted by *jinenapej* may also be denoted by *jinej*. People who may be denoted by *jääj mwään* are partially included among those who may be denoted by *semej* and *pwiij*.

This constitutes the method whereby we derived the criteria by which kinsmen are differentiated as presented in our description of the Trukese kinship system. It explains why the kinship system was described with respect to the terms found in the first semantic system given in Table 5, whereas the others were treated as "special" terms which could not be fitted into it. All of the kinship categories denoted by terms belonging to one semantic system are considered as constituting a single system of social categories. It is in this sense that we have used the expression "kinship system."

In the writer's opinion, the method of analysis just presented has important implications for comparative studies of kinship. It reveals what are the primary variables out of which a given kinship system is constructed and what are the secondary variables. Systems can therefore be compared on the basis of the particular variables selected by different societies as the primary ones on which to base differentiation of kin. For example, the primary variable differentiating the significata of contemporary American kinship terms is that of lineality versus collaterality, with three categories which are expressions of this variable: (1) those who are lineal ancestors or descendants, including siblings; (2) those who are the siblings of lineal ancestors or reciprocally the lineal descendants of siblings; and (3) those who are the lineal descendants of the siblings of lineal ancestors. Within the first two categories we also distinguish by sex and generation of kinsman, but within the third category we make no distinctions at all, referring to everyone as "my cousin" unless the requirements of the situation demand such further description as "second cousin, once removed." This, of course, contrasts markedly with the Trukese system (system 1), where the primary variable is that of generation. Classification of kinship systems for comparative study has so far been based mainly on differences in the way in which relatives in the first ascending or in ego's generation are distinguished. Our method of analysis makes possible the systematic comparison of total kinship systems, taking completely into account the larger range of differentiating criteria which were first isolated by Kroeber (1909).

In conclusion, we may summarize our procedures for the empirical derivation of the Trukese kinship system as follows:

1. Isolating the symbolic, verbal behavior patterns whose significata included blood or affinal kinship as one of their constituent characteristics.
2. Determining just who could and who could not be denoted by each of these verbal behavior patterns.
3. Deriving the significata of these behavior patterns as defined by the characteristics common to all persons who could be denoted by each of them.
4. Comparing the significata of each of these behavior patterns in order to determine which of them could be included in the same semantic system.

These procedures provide a method for the precise derivation of social categories and systems of social categories. Analysis of the significata of kinship terms in effect establishes the criteria for determining an individual's social category within the framework of a category system. By a social category is meant that aspect of social organization whereby persons are differentiated from each other and classified in accordance with attributes which they may or may not possess. In the present instance the relevant attributes are non-behavioral. There was no need to analyze any interaction patterns between ego and his kinsman in order to derive the Trukese categories of kin. They are quite different, therefore, from what will be referred to as statuses in the next chapter. A status may be defined as a pole of interaction, something which can be isolated only with reference to the combination of behavior patterns which are exclusively and consistently associated with it. In this definition we follow Linton (1936: 113), who defines a status as "simply a collection of rights and duties." We shall define a role, as he does, as "the dynamic aspect of a status." There will be occasion to reexamine this definition of status and role in discussing the implications of our methods for the empirical derivation of status positions in the next chapter.

THE NATURE OF FORMAL ANALYSIS

Floyd G. Lounsbury

Let us distinguish at the outset between a "formal account" of a kinship terminological system, and such other kinds of accounts as anthropologists may be interested in—e.g., a functional account, a historical account, or any other kind of causal account.

We may consider that a "formal account" of a collection of empirical data has been given when there have been specified (1) a set of primitive elements, and (2) a set of rules for operating on these, such that by the application of the latter to the former, the elements of a "model" are generated; which model in turn comes satisfactorily close to being a facsimile or exact replica of the empirical data whose interrelatedness and systemic nature we are trying to understand. A formal account is thus an apparatus for predicting back the data at hand, thereby making them "understandable," i.e., showing them to be the lawful and expectable consequences of an underlying principle that may be presumed to be at work at their source.

A formal account should be distinguished both by its sufficiency and by its parsimony. Its "sufficiency" consists in its ability to account *in toto* for what is at hand in the empirical data, with no elements of this collection wrongly predicted or left unpredicted in the model, and with none of the predictions of the model remaining empirically unverifiable (assuming adequate documenta-

tion or documentability of the source). That is to say, the model should not underpredict, overpredict, or wrongly predict. To the extent that it achieves this goal, it satisfies the requirement of sufficiency. Theories, formal or otherwise, purporting to account for the application of terms of relationship in Crow- and Omaha-type systems, including the ones proposed in this paper, can and should be judged against this criterion of sufficiency.

The "parsimony" of a formal account consists in its specifying only the absolute minimum of assumptions that are necessary to account for the data of the empirical collection, or to generate an exact replica thereof. The theories just mentioned may be judged against this criterion also. One that purports to be "formal" is expected to be so judged.

Now it is a fact, deriving from this very parsimony, that formal accounts are likely to be peculiarly unsatisfying to many anthropologists. Thus, for example, a simple rule that tells one the exact minimum he needs to know in order to predict accurately who gets called what in such and such a system of kinship terminology, *and nothing else*, is quite likely to be rejected because it fails to tell him other (and doubtless more important) things that he wants to know about the society, its culture, its legal structure, its patterns of social interaction, value orientations, etc. In fact, it may well reinforce in him the common prejudice that kinship terminologies are of no importance to the study of social structure—"so why bother with the kinship algebra?"

This, I hope to convince the reader, would be a

From " A Formal Account of Crow- and Omaha-type Kinship Terminologies" in *Explorations in Cultural Anthropology*, Ward Goodenough (ed.). Copyright 1964 by McGraw-Hill Book Company. Used with permission of McGraw-Hill Book Co. Pp. 351-352.

premature and unfortunate conclusion. It is the parsimony of formal accounts—the fact that they do not tell one more than the barest necessary minimum—that is precisely the characteristic that can give them their value in terms of cross-cultural generality; and it is the habit of over-explanation, so common in attempts at functional description, that robs the latter of their generality. I suggest, then, that it is only the parsimonious "formal" account that can point to the common and essential features of the various causal matrices out of which any given type of kinship terminology crystalizes.

This is not meant to disparage functional accounts. Quite to the contrary, it is a hope and a legitimate expectation that a formal analysis will be of help—as a kind of direction indicator—in getting functional analyses profitably oriented. All of us, surely, formalist and functionalist alike, have this as an objective. It is something of a commonplace in linguistics that the functional account of a system requires, or is at least facilitated by, a prior formal account; and that the functional account is but a part of the formal account of some larger system within which the first is embedded.

THE STRUCTURAL ANALYSIS OF KINSHIP SEMANTICS *

Floyd G. Lounsbury

The set of KIN-TYPE designations—such as *father, father's brother, mother's brother, father's sister's son*, etc.—specifying the genealogical positions of one's known kin in relation to himself, can be regarded as constituting a semantic field. Linguistic usage, in any given community, groups these kin types into a smaller number of labeled KIN CLASSES, such as "father," "uncle," "cousin," etc. The set of linguistic forms employed to designate such kin classes in a speech community constitutes its KINSHIP VOCABULARY. Any one of the forms is a KIN TERM. The classificatory structure imposed on this semantic field by conventional usage of kinship vocabulary varies greatly from society to society. We shall consider one single instance of such usage—that

of the Seneca Indians, an Iroquois tribe of western New York State, as documented by Lewis Henry Morgan in the middle of the nineteenth century.

A kinship vocabulary can be regarded as constituting a paradigm. It can be subjected to a kind of analysis similar to that given other paradigmatic sets in a language. The Seneca data will be analysed in this manner. The application of the method yields results which are not common knowledge and which run counter to a classic but erroneous anthropological view concerning the nature of the "Iroquois type" of kinship system. Our interest in this paper, however, is not in correcting an anthropological error, but in illustrating a method of semantic analysis.

PRELIMINARY NOTIONS

Paradigm

We shall regard as a paradigm any set of linguistic forms wherein: (a) the meaning of every form has a feature in common with the meanings of all other forms of the set, and (b) the meaning of every form differs from that of every other form of the set by one or more additional features. The common feature will be said to be the

* Earlier versions of this paper, or of parts of it, were presented at the Fifth International Congress of Anthropological and Ethnological Sciences in Philadelphia, September 5, 1956 (under the title, "The Componential Structure of the Iroquois-type Kinship System"); at the Tenth Conference on Iroquois Research, Redhouse, N.Y., October 13, 1956; and at the Yale Linguistic Club, November 11, 1957.

From H. G. Hunt (ed.), *Proceedings of the 9th International Congress of Linguistics* (The Hague: Mouton & Co., 1964), pp. 1073–1092. Reprinted by permission of the author and the publisher.

ROOT MEANING of the paradigm. It defines the semantic field which the forms of the paradigm partition. The variable features define the SEMANTIC DIMENSIONS of the paradigm.

Dimension; feature

A dimension of a paradigm is a set of mutually exclusive (i.e., non-cooccurent) features which share some or all of the same privileges of combination ("bundling") with features not of this dimension.—A feature is an ultimate term of characterization in a set of descriptive terms appropriate for the analysis of a particular given paradigm. A dimension is thus an "opposition," and the features of a dimension are the terms of the opposition. Reduction to dichotomous oppositions is always possible, but is normally carried out only when a resulting increase in clarity and simplicity warrants it.

Meaning

In §1 above, where we have written "meaning," one may read "meaning and/or distribution" without departing from the sense intended. The term is meant to be interpreted broadly, covering both (a) objects and conditions of reference, and (b) restrictions and special privileges of context. In the instance of the kinship paradigm given below, however, we have only to deal with reference.

Componential definitions

A term belonging to a paradigm can be defined componentially in terms of its coordinates in the paradigm. The definition represents a bundle of features: one from each of several, or of all, of the dimensions of the paradigm. This bundle of features states the necessary and sufficient conditions which an object must satisfy if it is to be a DENOTATUM of the term so defined. Terms having single denotata are the exception; multiple denotation is more generally the case. The class of all possible denotata of a term constitutes its DESIGNATUM. The defining features of this class—i.e. the necessary & sufficient conditions for membership in it—are its SIGNIFICATUM. The componential definition of a term is the expression of its significatum.

Conjunctive definitions

A componential definition represents a Boolean class product, and is thus a "unitary" or "conjunctive" definition. It is assumed that the meaning of any term belonging to a properly defined paradigm—one whose semantic field is itself unitary—will be susceptible to such a definition. This is perhaps a stronger item of faith than we have a right to hold at this moment; but it furnishes the motivation for the analysis of kinship systems at least. We proceed from extensional definitions (definitions by listing of denotata) to intensional definitions (definitions by specification of distinctive features). We feel that we have failed if we cannot achieve conjunctive definitions for every terminological class in the system. Were we to compromise on this point and admit disjunctive definitions (class sums, alternative criteria for membership) as on a par with conjunctive definitions (class products, uniform criteria for membership), there would be no motivation for analysis in the first place, for definitions of kin classes by the summing of discrete members—as in the table of Seneca data given below—are disjunctive definitions par excellence.

SENECA KINSHIP DATA

Following is a list of the Iroquois kinship terms, given in the language of the Seneca. Each term designates a class of one's kinsmen. The reference of each term is defined by naming all of the more closely related types of kinsmen, as well as a small sample of the more distant ones, to which the term is applied. We restrict our discussion here to consanguineal types.

Abbreviations

Primary kin types are abbreviated as follows: F = *father*; M = *mother*; B = *brother*; S = *sister*; s = *son*; d = *daughter*.[1] Higher-order kin types are abbreviated with compound symbols, e.g.: Bd = *brother's daughter*; FSs = *father's sister's son*; MMBsd = *mother's mother's brother's son's daughter*; etc. Since we shall deal here

---

[1] As a mnemonic device one can remember that lower case means lower generation.

only with the consanguineal system, we shall not need to employ the additional symbols H (= *husband*) and W (= *wife*) which are necessary in the writing of affinal and step types.

Sex of propositus

All kin types listed after any given kinship term are assumed to be possible referents of that term in relation to a propositus *of either sex*, except when otherwise indicated. Such indication is either written out (unabbreviated), as in the list of data at the close of this section, or is indicated by the prefixed signs ♂ and ♀, as in some of the later discussion. Thus, ♂ s = *a man's son;* ♀ s = *a woman's son;* ♂ Ss = *a man's sister's son;* etc.

Translation labels

English labels are also given for the Seneca terms. In each case the label is the word which we would use in English, in our kinship usage, to refer to the pivotal member or members of the class—that one which is (or those which are) the most closely related to the propositus. It

should be borne in mind that these English labels are *not* proper English translations, for they do not cover the same areas of denotation. English translations can be achieved only by descriptive circumlocution after the classificatory features defining the Iroquois kin classes have been discovered. The purpose of the English labels is merely to save the reader the task of learning an Iroquois vocabulary, and also to identify the pivotal member or members, i.e., the focus or foci, of each class. Translation labels will always appear in double quotation marks (e.g., "my father") to mark them as Iroquois concepts and to distinguish them from the normal English meanings of the same words.

ANALYSIS

The root of the paradigm

An individual related to a propositus in any of the ways specified by the various kin-type designations given under the kin terms of the above list is also *akyatēnōhk*, "my kinsman," and can be referred to as such. This general term subsumes all of the special terms of the kinship

hakso:t, "my grandfather"	FF, MF; FFB, FMB, MFB, MMB, FFFBs, etc.; *also* FFF, MMF, etc.
akso:t, "my grandmother"	FM, MM; FFS, FMS, MFS, MMS; FFFBd, etc.; *also* FFM, MMM, etc.
ha?nih, "my father"	F; FB; FMSs, FFBs, FMBs, FFSs; FFFBss, etc.
no?yēh, "my mother"	M; MS; MMSd, MFBd, MMBd, MFSd, MMMSdd, etc.
hakhno?sēh, "my uncle"	MB; MMSs, MFBs, MMBs, MFSs; MMMSds, etc.
ake:hak, "my aunt"	FS; FMSd, FFBd, FMBd, FFSd; FFFBsd, etc.
hahtsi?, "my elder brother"	B; MSs, FBs; MMSds, FFBss, MFBds, FMSss, MMBds, FFSss, MFSds, FMBss; MMMSdds, etc., *when older than Ego.*
he?kē:?, "my younger brother"	Same, *when younger than Ego.*
ahtsi?, "my elder sister"	S; MSd, FBd; MMSdd, FFBsd, MFBdd, FMSsd, MMBdd, FFSsd, MFSdd, FMBsd; MMMSddd, etc., *when older than Ego.*
khe?kē:?, "my younger sister"	Same, *when younger than Ego.*
akyä:?se:?, "my cousin"	MBs, FSs; MMSss, FFBds, MFBss, FMSds, MMBss, FFSds, MFSss, FMBds; MMMSdss, etc.; *and* MBd, FSd; MMSsd, FFBdd, MFBsd, FMSdd, MMBsd, FFSdd, MFSsd, FMBdd; MMMSdsd, etc.
he:awak, "my son"	s; Bs; MSss, FBss, MBss, FSss; MMSdss, etc., *of a man; but:* s; Ss; MSds, FBds, MBds, FSds; MMSdds, etc., *of a woman.*
khe:awak, "my daughter"	d; Bd; MSsd, FBsd, MBsd, FSsd; MMSdsd, etc., *of a man; but:* d; Sd; MSdd, FBdd, MBdd, FSdd; MMSddd, etc., *of a woman.*
heyē:wō:tē?, "my nephew"	Ss; MSds, FBds, MBds, FSds; MMSdds, etc., *of a man.*
hehsō?neh, "my nephew"	Bs; MSss, FBss, MBss, FSss; MMSdss, etc., *of a woman.*
kheyē:wō:tē?, "my niece"	Sd; MSdd, FBdd, MBdd, FSdd; MMSddd, etc., *of a man.*
khehsō?neh, "my niece"	Bd; MSsd, FBsd, MBsd, FSsd; MMSdsd, etc., *of a woman.*
heya:te?, "my grandson"	ss, ds; Bss, Bds, Sss, Sds; FBsss, etc.; *also* sss, dds, etc.
kheya:te?, "my granddaughter"	sd, dd; Bsd, Bdd, Ssd, Sdd; FBssd, etc.; *also* ssd, ddd, etc. (The data are from Morgan 1871)

vocabulary, each of which in turn subsumes all of the kin types listed after it. It thus defines the common feature of meaning required of a set of forms if they are to be regarded as constituting a paradigm. It represents, therefore, the root of the paradigm. This feature will be written as K (for *kinsman*) in the kin-class definitions below.

The dimension of generation

Inspection of the data shows that one of the dimensions of the system is obviously GENERATION. This presents a set of five features, which represent obligatory categories in the system. These are: *second-or-higher ascending generation; first ascending generation; the generation of the propositus; first descending generation;* and *second-or-lower descending generation.* In the kin-class definitions below, these will be written as G^2, G^1, G^0, G^{-1}, G^{-2}, respectively.

The categories of generation in Seneca, unlike those in our own system of kinship terminology, are overriding categories. Seneca kin-classes do not cross generation lines, whereas some of ours do (e.g., our classes cousin, uncle, aunt, etc.). Seneca kin classes, on the other hand, cross degrees of collaterality, whereas none of our English classes transgress the boundaries of the three DEGREES OF COLLATERALITY obligatorily distinguished in our system, viz.: the *zero degree* (i.e., lineal kin); *first degree* (brother, sister, uncle, aunt, nephew, niece); and *second-or-higher degree* (cousin).

The dimension of sex

Another obvious dimension of the system is that of SEX. Its features are *male* and *female.* In the kin-class definitions below, these will be written as ♂ and ♀ respectively.

The features from the dimensions of generation and sex are sufficient to distinguish and define four of the kin classes of the list:

hakso:t, "grandfather"	♂·G^2·K.
akso:t, "grandmother"	♀·G^2·K.
heya:te?, "grandson"	♂·G^{-2}·K.
kheya:te?, "granddaughter"	♀·G^{-2}·K.

Note that, unlike the analogous terms in English, these four Seneca terms include known collateral kin of all degrees, as well as lineal kin. The componential definitions given here recognize this fact, inasmuch as they do not incorporate any features drawn from a dimension of collaterality distinctions, as definitions for our English terms must.

The classification in the first ascending generation

Four kin classes are distinguished in the first ascending generation: *ha?nih* ("father"), *no?yēh* ("mother"), *hakhno?sēh* ("uncle"), and *ake:hak* ("aunt"). Assuming that we may be dealing with two dimensions of dichotomizing features, we may try pairing the terms.

Given any four terms, there are three possible ways of pairing them. In the present case, we might first pair "father" with "uncle" and oppose these to the remaining pair consisting of "mother" and "aunt." Inspection of the data will show that, if we do this, the opposition is in the dimension of sex. (It should be noted that we *must* inspect the data to determine this; we cannot simply assume it as natural, or infer it from the translation labels. Anthropological literature furnishes many examples of systems that have both females and males in the "mother" class, and both males and females in the "father" class.)

Inspection of the data also suggests another plausible pairing: that of "father" with "aunt," as opposed to "mother" and "uncle." In this case the dimension can be characterized as SIDE, and the opposed features which constitute it as *patrilateral* and *matrilateral*. These we may write as π and μ, resp. As can be seen from the table, the types of kinsmen who are called by the "father" term, *ha?nih*, in Seneca are male first-ascending-generation kinsmen related to the propositus on his father's side (patrilateral), while those called "uncle," *hakhno?sēh*, are all on his mother's side (matrilateral). Similarly, all of those who are "aunt," *ake:hak*, are female kin of that generation on the father's side, while those that are "mother," *no?yēh*, are on the mother's side. These features from the dimension of side, together with those from the dimension of sex, suffice to differentiate the kin classes of the first ascending generation. The definitions are as follows:

ha?nih, "father"	♂·π·G¹·K.
ake:hak, "aunt"	♀·π·G¹·K.
hakhno?sēh, "uncle"	♂·μ·G¹·K.
no?yēh, "mother"	♀·μ·G¹·K.

There is however a third possible way of pairing these terms, which, because it may appeal to us as a more or less reasonable and natural kind of pairing, at least should not be overlooked. This is to pair "father" with "mother," and to oppose them to the pair consisting of "uncle" and "aunt." Study of the data, with the aim of discovering a feature shared by all of the members of both the "father" and the "mother" classes, and some other opposed feature common to the members of the "uncle" and "aunt" classes, shows that, from the standpoint of the data, this is a less obvious manner of pairing and will require a more contrived set of features. It is possible, nonetheless, to define such features. And this fact suffices to show that this is indeed a natural pairing; for arbitrary and unnatural pairings never allow the discovery of common features.

Accordingly we may define a feature, $L^=$, which will be said to inhere in any kin type in which *the sex of the designated kin is the* SAME *as that of the first link;* and an opposed feature, $L^{\neq}$, which will be said to inhere in any kin type in which *the sex of the designated kin is* OPPOSITE *to that of the first link.* Now, the second of these features is common to all of the members of both the "uncle" and the "aunt" classes, while the first is common to all of the members of both the "father" and "mother" classes. Thus, in the types MB, MMSs, MFBs, MMBs, MFSs, etc. ("uncles"), and in the types FS, FMSd, FFBd, FMBd, FFSd, etc. ("aunts"), it is true that the sex of the designated kinsman or kinswoman (given by the last term in any kin-type abbreviation) is in every case opposite to that of the first link to the propositus (given by the first term in the abbreviation). *The sexes of intervening links, when present, are irrelevant to the reckoning.*[2]

[2] The italicization, for emphasis, is to call this point to the attention of anthropologists. The "classic but erroneous anthropological view concerning the nature of the 'Iroquois type' of kinship systems," to which reference was made at the beginning of this paper, is that this kind of system classifies kin by membership in unilineal descent groups. Thus, given exogamous matrilineal moieties (as the Seneca are said to have had), all of one's "fathers" should be found in one's father's moiety, and all of one's "maternal uncles" should be found in one's own moiety, A glance at the data shows that this theory of the Iroquois system gives about fifty percent right predictions and nearly fifty percent wrong predictions. Of the "maternal uncles"; for example, MB, MMSs, and MFBs would indeed be found in one's own exogamous matrilineal moiety, but MMBs and MFSs would be in the opposite moiety. Similarly one has classificatory "fathers" in *both* moieties, his own as well as his father's.—Another version of the theory, thought to be applicable where matrilineal clans (sibs) exist but moieties do not, or where kinship is reckoned to clan limits but not to moiety limits, is that the "father" term refers to men of one's father's clan in his generation or age grade, and that the "maternal uncle" term refers to men of one's own clan in the generation or age grade of one's mother's brother. The facts, however, correspond as little to the predictions of this clan theory of Iroquois kinship as they do to those of the moiety theory; for one may have "fathers" in any clan, and one may also have "maternal uncles" in any clan. The predictions of these theories are as far off for the other kinclasses of the system as they are for these.—These facts are true not only of the Iroquois Indians themselves, but also of every "Iroquois-type" system included in Morgan's tables in *Systems of Consanguinity and Affinity*. While I was becoming acquainted with this for the first time in 1954–55 by reading these tables, my colleague Leopold Pospisil was finding out the same thing for the Kapauku Papuans while engaged in field work in the highlands of the (then) Netherlands New Guinea. (Cf. L. Pospisil, "The Kapauku Papuans and their Kinship Organization," *Oceania* 30 Sidney, 1960, 188–205.) My astonishment at discovering the real principle operative in the reckoning of bifurcation in an Iroquois-type kinship system was matched by his. It was contrary to all of the expectations to which we had been led by the anthropological theoretical writings on the subject. It is surprising that the essential data pertinent to a subject about which so much has been written should have been in print and available to all for nearly a century without anyone's having taken account of the classification of any but the closest collateral kin-types. The classic theory predicts correctly only to the immediate (closest) uncles and aunts [FB, MB, FS, MS] and first cousins. Beyond this its predictions are half right and half wrong. Morgan himself, already under the influence of a clan theory of kinship (of his own making), is partly responsible for this error. Statements in Chapter IV, Book I, of his *League of the Ho-de-no-sau-nee or Iroquois* (New York, 1851) can be derived from a metaphoric use of "sibling" terms and from the ignoring of all but the closest kin-types included in his own tables of data that he published in *Systems*.

There *do* exist systems which classify kin-types in the way that the Iroquois type was imagined to. These are

Similarly, in the types F, FB, FMSs, FFBs, FMBs, FFSs, etc. ("fathers"), and in the types M, MS, MMSd, MFBd, MMBd, MFSd, etc. ("mothers"), the sex of the designated kinsman or kinswoman is in every case the same as that of the first link. [Note: F and M are the limiting cases, where "designated kin" (last term) and "first link" (first term) coincide. In the case of coincidence, the condition of equality of sex can of course be said to be satisfied.]

With three possible pairings of the four G^3 kinship terms, we are now in possession of one more dimension than is necessary for uniquely characterizing them. The features from any two of these dimensions might be chosen as defining features, and those of the third dimension regarded as "redundant." ("Redundant" in a logical sense, not merely in an empirical sense, since the features of any one of the dimensions can be defined in terms of those of the other two.) It may be objected that in the case of the third pair of features we are attempting to impose on the Seneca system a pairing which is natural and reasonable from our point of view, as members of our society, but which, because of its contrived nature, may be inappropriate to the Seneca system. We can leave the judgment on that point until later. For the time being, we recognize that there are three possible alternative definitions for each of the first-ascending-generation kin classes:

ha?nih, "father"	♂·L⁼·G¹·K,	or	♂·π·G¹·K,	or	π·L⁼·G¹·K.
no?yẽh, "mother"	♀·L⁼·G¹·K,	or	♀·μ·G¹·K,	or	μ·L⁼·G¹·K.
hakhno?sẽh, "uncle"	♂·L≠·G¹·K,	or	♂·μ·G¹·K,	or	μ·L≠·G¹·K.
ake:hak, "aunt"	♀·L≠·G¹·K,	or	♀·π·G¹·K,	or	π·L≠·G¹·K.

the "Dravidian" type of systems. Interestingly, they are *not* generally founded on clan or moiety reckoning, but on a mode of reckoning of bifurcation that, unlike the Iroquois, takes account of the sexes of all intervening links. The Dravidian and Iroquois types are rarely distinguished in anthropological literature, all passing under the label 'Iroquois type.' Actually, they are systems premised on very different principles of reckoning, and deriving from social structures that are fundamentally unlike.

[3] I.e., the children of his brother and of *all* of his male cousins, regardless of whether the latter be classificatory "brothers" to him (e.g., MSs, FBs) or "cousins" to him (e.g., MBs, FSs).

The classification in the first descending generation

Six kin terms are given in the list for kin types of the first descending generation, but only four of them are available to any given propositus.

First let us consider the four terms for the kin of a male. As before, we seek all possible ways of pairing the terms. We may begin with the sex pairing, of "son" (*he:awak*) with "nephew" (*heyẽ:wõ:tẽ?*), as opposed to "daughter" (*khe:-awak*) and "niece" (*kheyẽ:wõ:tẽ*).

A second possible pairing is that of "son" with "daughter," these being opposed to "nephew" and "niece." This pairing, as can be seen from the list, opposes a class consisting of the children of a male propositus and of all of his male generation-mates, to a second class consisting of the children of his female generation-mates.[4] The features of this opposition we may symbolize with the letters φ and σ (suggested by the partially—though not completely—descriptive terms "fratrifilial" or "sororifilial").

There should be a third manner of pairing these four kin terms. This can only be to set "son" with "niece," and to oppose these to "daughter" and "nephew." While this might not appeal to us (or to the Iroquois either) as a natural pairing, it is nonetheless possible to define a feature which would unite the "son" and the "niece" classes (viz., sameness of sex of designated kin and last link), and an opposing feature which would unite the "daughter" and "nephew" classes (viz., oppositeness of sex of designated kin and last link). We might symbolize these features as P$^=$ and P$^≠$, respectively (suggested by: *kinsman's* PARENT *of* SAME *sex as kinsman*, and *kinsman's* PARENT *of* OPPOSITE *sex to kinsman*).

[4] I.e., the children of his sister and of *all* of his female cousins, regardless of whether the latter be classificatory "sisters" to him (e.g., MSd, FBd) or "cousins" to him (e.g., MBd, FSd).

Thus, one may write three alternative definitions of each of the four G^{-1} kin classes for a *male propositus:*

he:awak, "son"	♂·φ·G^{-1}·K,	*or*	♂·P⁼·G^{-1}·K,	*or*	φ·P⁼·G^{-1}·K.
khe-awak, "daughter"	♀·φ·G^{-1}·K,	*or*	♀·P⁺·G^{-1}·K,	*or*	φ·P⁺·G^{-1}·K.
heyē:wō:tē, "nephew"	♂·σ·G^{-1}·K,	*or*	♂·P⁺·G^{-1}·K,	*or*	σ·P⁺·G^{-1}·K.
kheyē:wō:tē?, "niece"	♀·σ·G^{-1}·K,	*or*	♀·P⁼·G^{-1}·K,	*or*	σ·P⁼·G^{-1}·K.

If we consider not the classification of kin in relation to a *female propositus,* we find we can write the following definitions:

he:awak, "son"	♂·σ·G^{-1}·K,	*or*	♂·P⁺·G^{-1}·K,	*or*	σ·P⁺·G^{-1}·K.
khe:awak, "daughter"	♀·σ·G^{-1}·K,	*or*	♀·P⁼·G^{-1}·K,	*or*	σ·P⁼·G^{-1}·K.
hehsō?neh, "nephew"	♂·φ·G^{-1}·K,	*or*	♂·P⁼·G^{-1}·K,	*or*	φ·P⁼·G^{-1}·K.
khehsō?neh, "niece"	♀·φ·G^{-1}·K,	*or*	♀·P⁺·G^{-1}·K,	*or*	φ·P⁺·G^{-1}·K.

It will be seen that none of these definitions are invariant to the sex of the propositus. In fact, the definitions of "nephew" (*hehsō?neh*) of a female are identical to those of "son" (*he:-awak*) of a male, while those of "son" (*he:awak*) of a female are identical to those of "nephew" (*heyē:wō:tē?*) of a male. Preferable, surely, would be definitions invariant to the sex of the propositus—at least where the same linguistic forms are involved (*he:awak, khe:awak*).

These can be obtained by employing a pair of features which are the reciprocals of those used to obtain the pairing of "mother" with "father," and "uncle" with "aunt" in G^1, as follows. Let us define a feature L⁼, which will be said to inhere in any kin type in which *the sex of the last link is the* SAME *as that of the propositus;* and an opposed feature, L⁺, which will be said to inhere in any kin type in which *the sex of the last link is* OPPOSITE *to that of the propositus.* The first of these features is common to all the members of both the "son" (*he:awak*) and the "daughter" (*khe:awak*) classes, regardless of whether this be in relation to a male or to a female. Inspection of the data will verify that this is so. E.g., ♂ Bs, ♀ Ss, ♂ MBss, ♀ MBds, etc. [Note: s (i.e., ♂ s and ♀ s) and d (i.e., ♂ d and ♀ d) are the limiting cases, where last link (second-last term) coincides with the propositus. In such a case it can of course be said that their sexes are the same.]

We may redefine the G^{-1} terms as follows:

he:awak, "son"	♂·L⁻·G^{-1}·K.
khe:awak, "daughter"	♀·L⁻·G^{-1}·K.
heyē:wō:tē? / hehsō?neh, "nephew"	♂·L⁺·G^{-1}·K.
kheyē:wō:tē? / khehsō?neh, "niece"	♀·L⁺·G^{-1}·K.

Now, instead of having *he:awak* a being a pair of homonymous words, it is just one word with one signification; and similarly with the *khe:-awak.* And we get a bonus out of it besides; the two "nephew" terms end up being synonyms of a sort, differing only by an additional component specifying the sex of the propositus; and similarly the two "niece" terms. [This is a useful bonus, especially in a related language such as Tuscarora, which lacks the extra synonym and has but one term (Tusc. *kheyēhwa?nē?*) undifferentiated for either sex of propositus or sex of kin, for the meaning L⁺·G^{-1}·K.]

The classification in the 'zero' generation

Five kin terms are employed in $G°$. Four of them, the "sibling" terms *hahtsi?, he?kē:?, ahtsi?, khe?kē:?,* form a readily analysable set based on the differentiations of RELATIVE AGE and SEX. The fifth term, *akyä:?se:?,* "cousin," has a range of denotation comparable in magnitude to that of the four "sibling" terms conjointly. Within this range, no distinctions are made either for sex or for relative age.

We wish now to find out the dimension of

difference that opposes the combined "sibling" class (the sum of the four special "sibling" classes) to the "cousin" class. Study of the data reveals one, and only one, possibility. Let us accordingly define a feature, $A^=$, which will be said to inhere in any kin type in which *the sex of the last link is the* SAME *as that of the first link;* and an opposed feature, $A^{\neq}$, which will be said to inhere in any kin type in which *the sex of the last link is* OPPOSITE *to that of the first link.* The second of these features is common to all of the members of the "cousin" class (e.g., MBs, FSs, FFSds, FMSds, etc.), while the first is common to all of the members of the four "sibling" classes (e.g., MSs, FBs, FFSss, FMSss, etc.). [Note: B and S are the limiting cases, where the last link and the first link coincide—a fact that is not obvious simply from the writings B and S but that can be readily seen when it is remembered that B is Fs and/or Ms, and that S is Fd and/or Md. (There are empirical reasons why B and S are admitted as "primary" kin types in kinship reckoning, and why the ambiguity inherent in them can be tolerated.)]

Now we may write the definitions for the G° terms. (A^+ and A^- are for the features of RELATIVE AGE.)

hahtsi?, "elder brother"	$A^+ \cdot \male \cdot A^- \cdot G^\circ \cdot K.$
he?kē:?, "younger brother"	$A^- \cdot \male \cdot A^- \cdot G^\circ \cdot K.$
ahtsi?, "elder sister"	$A^+ \cdot \female \cdot A^- \cdot G^\circ \cdot K.$
khe?kē:?, "younger sister"	$A^- \cdot \female \cdot A^- \cdot G^\circ \cdot K.$
akyä:?se:?, "cousin"	$A^{\neq} \cdot G^\circ \cdot K.$

The dimension of bifurcation

Reviewing the definitions given in preceding paragraphs for kin classes in G^1, G^{-1}, and G°, it is seen (*a*) that the features $L^=$ and $L^{\neq}$ occur only in the context G^1; (*b*) that the features $L_=$ and $L_{\neq}$ occur only in the context G^{-1}, and (*c*) that the features $A^=$ and $A^{\neq}$ occur only in the context G°. They are thus in complementary distribution. This may suggest that they may be but conditioned variants of one basic pair of features; and that they may, if the similarity condition can be met, be grouped into a single pair of units in the metalanguage which we use to spell out the semantic content of the Seneca kin terms. They may thus be reduced to one opposition of wider

applicability in the system, instead of three oppositions of more limited applicability.

The condition of similarity can indeed be met (all three contrasts involve comparisons in the generation just above the lowest represented by propositus and/or kin), and we may take $L^=$, $L_=$, and $A^=$, as defined previously, to be conditioned variants of one basic feature. Similarly, $L^{\neq}$, $L_{\neq}$, and $A^{\neq}$ can be taken as conditioned variants of the opposed feature. These features we can call by the traditional names of *parallel* and *cross*, respectively, although the real meanings of these terms in their application to Iroquois-type kinship systems have been rather poorly understood in the past. And the dimension which these features constitute can similarly be called by the traditional name of BIFURCATION. The symbols $\|$ and $\times$ will be used to represent the features in the writing of definitions.

The structure of the field

The definitions of the kin classes in the middle three generations may now be rewritten; and the entire paradigm may be presented, so as to show the structure of its semantic field, in a four-dimensional diagram, a four-column matrix, or a four-margin outline.

The field dealt with up to this point has been that of the consanguineal kin-types. The step-kin and in-law types, and the terms that classify them, can be dealt with in a similar fashion. Step and in-law categories are obligatorily distinguished from the consanguineal ones, as well as from each other, and their classification is peculiar to the Iroquois system.

Also not dealt with yet are the many forms designating the superclasses which are obtained by neutralizing the oppositions of sex, relative age, and generation "direction"—i.e., *ascending* vs *descending*. These neutralizations are accomplished by grammatical devices provided in the Iroquoian inflectional and derivational systems. The existence of these does not invalidate the claim to "obligatoriness" that was made for the distinctions drawn in the sections above, for the neutralizing forms are cover-terms that are appropriate only to rather particular contexts, having a status in usage (though not in grammar) somewhat comparable to our cover-terms "parent," "child," "parent-and-child," "sibling," and such artificial ones like "grandkin"—as anthropologists occasionally employ.

These various aspects of the Iroquois kinship system cannot be treated here. To do so would expand this article to a length inappropriate to the present occasion. One matter of some general interest deserves comment however. It will be noted that, of the four dimensions employed in the analysis of the consanguineal system, three of them—sex, bifurcation, and relative age—were dimensions representing a *dichotomous opposition* of just two features; but one of them—generation—was a dimension whose variable could assume five values. Two questions may be raised. One of these is whether the five-valued dimension is reduceable in fact to a larger number of dimensions of dichotomous oppositions. The other is whether, in dichotomous oppositions, one member of the opposition can be said to be the marked member (a positive feature), and the other the unmarked member (the absence, or negation, of the positive).

In regard to the first question it may be remarked that, since kinship terms come in reciprocal sets, it is always possible to analyse out the polarity between the reciprocals as a separate dimension of opposition. Thus, in place of the five-valued dimension of GENERATION (G^2, G^1, G^0, G^{-1}, G^{-2}), we may have a three-valued dimension of GENERATION DISTANCE (consisting of the absolute values G^2, G^1, G^0) and a dimension of POLARITY (*senior* vs. *junior*) or GENERATION DIRECTION (*plus* vs. *minus*). This is especially appropriate in Iroquoian where, for example, a set such as that consisting of the two "parent" terms, together with their reciprocal "child" terms, is covered by a single cover-term that neutralizes the generation direction (or polarity), as well as the sex, of the basic terms. Thus:

$$\{[ha\mathord{?}nih + no\mathord{?}y\bar{e}h] + [he{:}awak + khe{:}awak]\}$$
$$= \{akyatathawak\},$$

i.e., $\{[(\text{♂}\cdot\|\cdot G^1\cdot K) + (\text{♀}\cdot\|\cdot G^1\cdot K)] + [(\text{♂}\cdot\|\cdot G^{-1}\cdot K)$
$+ (\text{♀}\cdot\|\cdot G^{-1}\cdot K)]\} = \{\|\cdot G^{\pm 1}\cdot K\};$

and similarly with the other reciprocal sets of the system.

This new dimension can be equated with that already set up for RELATIVE AGE, for the polarity relation between the "parent" and "child" terms is similar to that beween the "elder sibling" and "younger sibling" terms. Thus also:

$$\{[hahtsi\mathord{?} + ahtsi\mathord{?}] + [he\mathord{?}k\bar{e}{:}\mathord{?} + khe\mathord{?}k\bar{e}{:}\mathord{?}]\}$$
$$= \{akyatate\mathord{?}k\bar{e}{:}\mathord{?}\},$$

i.e., $\{[(\text{♂}\cdot\|\cdot A^+\cdot G^0\cdot K) + (\text{♀}\cdot\|\cdot A^+\cdot G^0\cdot K)]$
$+ [(\text{♂}\cdot\|\cdot A^-\cdot G^0\cdot K) + (\text{♀}\cdot\|\cdot A^-\cdot G^0\cdot K)]\} = \{\|\cdot G^0\cdot K\}.$

Thus the analytic simplification of the dimension of generation can be accomplished at no cost to economy in the total number of dimensions.

As for the possibility of reducing the remaining three-valued dimension of GENERATION DISTANCE still further, I know of no *good* natural basis for doing this; though it can, of course, always be done by fiat. One might cut it in either of two places: between G^2 and all else, or between G^0 and all else. More-or less plausible arguments might be adduced for either of these, but it can be done only at the expense of adding a dimension to the system. This *is* an 'expense,' for it would take two dimensions of dichotomous opposition to account for only three values.

As for the second of the questions posed above, viz. whether a distinction can be made between a 'marked' and an 'unmarked' member of every opposition, it may be stated that there are good reasons—primarily semantic-structural, but with strong linguistic as well as social correlates—for regarding the *first* term of each of the following oppositions as the *marked* member:

POLARITY: *senior*, vs. *junior*
SEX: *male*, vs. *female*
BIFURCATION: *cross*, vs. *parallel*.

The fourth dimension of the system, GENERATION DISTANCE, remains a three-valued one unless reduced by fiat. Just as I have not yet found any good basis, linguistic or social, for dividing this into two taxonomic dichotomics, so I am also without any basis for determining which features might best be regarded as marked and which as unmarked if this were done.

To justify the above choices of "marked" members (*senior, male, cross*) would require an extended treatment of the transitive pronominal prefix system, the gender system, and the stem-derivational system of Iroquois grammar, together with a "Whorfian" exegesis of the same, and an additional discussion of the typology of so-called 'Iroquois-type' kinship systems. It must suffice here to say that in each case the marked member is a "special" one in some sense, that is opposed to a "general" or "common" one. In positions or contexts of contrast, the unmarked member is specific. In positions or contexts of no contrast, it is general.[5] Thus, the "common gender" of Iroquois is the feminine (not the masculine as in English); the general root for the parent-child relation is -hawak; and the extension of bifurcation into G⁰ (making the system "Iroquois type" as opposed to "Cheyenne type") in fact rests rather lightly on the Iroquois.

INTRODUCTION TO THE DISCUSSION

This paper is presented as an example of the structural analysis of a lexical set which covers and partitions a semantic field. It was noted that this particular kind of lexical set can be regarded as constituting a paradigm, and that it can be subjected to a kind of analysis similar to that given other paradigmatic sets in a language. Certain common linguistic notions basic to this treatment were also defined, or briefly discussed, with special reference to their use in semantic analysis. These included the notions of semantic field, paradigm, root, dimension, feature, componential definition, the route from extensional to intensional definitions, the possibility of dichtomous dimensions of contrast, and the identification of the marked feature of an opposition. Also, something of the reason for the desideratum of conjunctive definitions was indicated.

[5] ". . . a marked category states the presence of a certain (whether positive or negative) property A; . . . the corresponding unmarked category states nothing about the presence of A, and is used chiefly, but not exclusively, to indicate the absence of A. On the level of general meaning the opposition . . . may be interpreted as 'statement of A' vs. 'no statement of A', whereas on the level of 'narrowed,' nuclear meanings, we encounter the opposition 'statement of A' vs. 'statement of non-A'."—Roman Jakobson, *Shifters, Verbal Categories, and the Russian Verb* (Harvard University: Russian Language Project, 1957), p. 5.

A rather frequent response of linguists to such kinship exercises, I have found, is that they are of limited interest so far as the general problems of semantic analysis are concerned because, it is said, kinship vocabularies and their meanings are something special in lexicology, permitting as they do, the specification and analysis of reference with a satisfactory degree of rigor; but it is felt that they are, for this very reason, unrepresentative of linguistic-semantic, or lexicological, problems in general. I would not care to make any exaggerated claims for the particular methods that are of utility in the analysis of systems of kinship terminology, though I do think that their potentialities are rather generally underestimated. In any case, I would like to comment on a few further points of general relevance that arise out of the exercise presented in the preprint paper.

The first of these is the question of whether there are other content fields represented in language that are susceptible to this kind of analysis. On this point I will only say that anthropologists have applied this or similar sorts of analysis to the vocabularies representing a number of lexical and cultural domains of special interest to them. Among them are color vocabularies, native ethnobotanical terminologies, vocabularies of disease taxonomy in primitive societies, those of primitive cosmologies, systems of religious concepts, etc. The work is still new, and much needs to be done yet in the development of the method. A review of this work and a bibliography of some relevant items are contained in a recent paper by Harold Conklin ("Lexicographical Treatment of Folk Taxonomies," in *Problems in Lexicography*, ed. by F. W. Householder and S. Saporta [=*Indiana Univ. Res. Center in Anthrop., Folkl., and Ling.*, Publ. 21], 1962a).

The second point has to do with the formal characteristics of the structure of semantic fields. There *is* something a bit special about the structure of kinship systems, viz., that their structure is in large part that of the "paradigm." While there are numerous sets of this sort in lexicon, this is by no means the general case. More typical, perhaps, is the "taxonomy." In the perfect paradigm, the features of any dimension combine with *all* of those of any other dimension. In the perfect taxonomy on the other hand, they never do; they combine with *only one* feature from any other dimension. In the perfect paradigm there is no hierarchical ordering of dimensions that is not arbitrary; all orders are possible. In the perfect taxonomy there is but one possible hierarchy. To illustrate the difference we may consider a set of eight elements constituting a field *F*. If these represent a paradigm, it takes but three dimensions of dichotomous opposition to fully characterize them (Fig. 1). If they represent a taxonomy, it takes seven (Fig. 2). Kinship

F							
a_1				a_2			
b_1		b_2		b_1		b_2	
c_1	c_2	c_1	c_2	c_1	c_2	c_1	c_2

Figure 1.

F							
a_1				a_2			
b_1		b_2		c_1		c_2	
d_1	d_2	e_1	e_2	f_1	f_2	g_1	g_2

Figure 2.

terminologies usually represent something intermediate between these, the imperfect or asymmetrical paradigm, which combines principles of both kinds. In the analysis of content fields other than kinship, one must be prepared to find both kinds of structures. Anthropological work on folk taxonomies reckons with both.

A third point has to do with the question of metaphor, the delimitation of a semantic field, and the possibility of conjunctive definitions. I should confess at once that I have not included *all* of the meanings of the Iroquois kinship terms in the tabulation of data given in the paper. Not

included, for example, are *the moon* in the list of denotata of the "grandmother" term, or *the thunderers* amongst the "grandfathers," or *the earth* as our "mother," or *the sun* as our "elder brother." Nor have I included the metaphoric uses of the "brother" and "cousin," "father" and "son," "elder brother" and "younger brother" terms, in ceremonial discourse, for divisions of the Longhouse and of the political confederacy of the Six Nations; or that of the "uncle" term for the Bigheads (certain masked dancers at Midwinter ceremonies) or, formerly, for prisoners at the stake. There is no difficulty here in identifying these as "marginal" or "transferred" meanings, to use Bloomfields' terms. (Cf. Prof. Jakobson's comments after Dr. Strang's paper on Tuesday.) Metaphoric extensions can be expected for any lexical item. In the structural analysis of a semantic field, however, they are excluded. We have not intended to deal with all of the meanings of the Iroquois kinship terms here, but only with those that fall within the field defined as *genealogical kin*. All of these have one common feature of meaning which is lacking from the metaphoric extensions. Determining the criteria for the delimitation of fields is the first important step in semantic analysis. Determining the bases for metaphoric extensions beyond the field is one of the last, and sometimes one of the most interesting. Normally it is not possible to subsume *all* of the meanings of a lexical item under one *conjunctive* definition. We expect that it should be possible to do this, however, for all of those meanings of an item *that lie within a properly defined field*.

A fourth point has to do with the way of entry into a problem of meaning. Bloomfield was of the opinion that "signals can be analyzed, but not the things signalled about," and that "this reinforces the principle that linguistic study must always start from the phonetic form and not from meaning" (*Language*, p. 162). The entry into phonology for Bloomfield was the same-or-different test applied to the meanings (*Language*, Chapter 5, esp. pp. 74–78). I have suggested elsewhere that the entry into *semantics* could be a same-or-different test *applied to forms*, and that this also offered a possible starting place

("A Semantic Analysis of the Pawnee Kinship Usage," *Lang.*, 32, 1956, 158–194, esp. pp. 190–192). C. M. Ebeling has an important and interesting discussion of this possibility, and of the symmetry, or parallelism, between the analytic constructs of semantics and those of phonology (*Linguistic Units*, The Hague, 1960, Chapter III). And a comment by Jakobson, that "meaning can and must be stated in terms of linguistic discriminations and identifications, just as, on the other hand, linguistic discriminations are always made with regard to their semantic value," is fundamental to this view ("Boas' View of Grammatical Meaning," *Memoir* 89, Amer. Anthrop. Assn., 1959, pp. 139–145, quote from p. 143). For purposes of the analysis of the Iroquois kinship semantics that was made in the paper submitted to the Congress, it was not really necessary for us to know anything about the Seneca forms other than whether any two responses of Morgan's informants were *the same* or *different*. Even Morgan, poor phonetician that he was, was able to tell that, and he has given us the necessary information. I have used spellings based on Chafe's analysis of Seneca phonology only because Morgan's clumsy and inaccurate ones offend me, not because more precise information about the forms is necessary. It suffices only know that they are different. They could as well be called alpha, beta, gamma, etc., or assigned random numbers.

A fifth and final point has to do with the analysis of multiple denotation *within a field*. It should be noted that dimensional analysis of a field, and componential definitions of the elements that constitute it, are as applicable to sets of forms having only single denotata as to sets of forms having multiple denotata. Only in the latter case—of which the Seneca kinship vocabulary has furnished an example—does one face the typical *"allo*-unit" problem. I want to point out that there are two ways of handling this, at least in kinship analysis. One is by the method of *total class definitions;* the other is by a method of *basic member definitions* and supplementary *rules of extension.* Much of linguistic method as we have known it in the recent past is based on the former method. The first attempts at com-

ponential analysis of kinship terminologies (Goodenough, 1951), as well as the present paper, take an analogous approach in the handling of multiple denotata. Differences of degree within the class of denotata of a term are of course recognized, but these are treated as "nondistinctive."

There is, as I have mentioned, another way of handling this. It is to regard one, or sometimes two, members of a terminological kinclass as the basic members and to fit the definition of the kinship term to these. The other members of the class are then treated as extensions ("metaphoric" in relation to the narrow field covered by the basic types and their definitions, but yet not "metaphoric" when considered in relation to the wide field which is the subject of analysis). These extensions are then accounted for by rules. The rules may be written either as expansion rules or as reduction rules. In the former case they derive distant members of the class from the basic member or members; in the latter they reduce the distant ones to the basic ones.

To illustrate this method let me take an example of a type of system somewhat more complicated than that of the Iroquois, for it will allow perhaps a more convincing demonstration of the potentialities of the method. There are kinship systems called "Crow" type (after the Crow Indians, whose system was one of the first of these to receive notice) which are found in many parts of the world. Actually, the Crow type is not one, but many. I shall speak of one particular subvariety which we might as well call the Choctaw subtype. I shall not give you another whole kinship system, but will mention only the classification of two particular kin-types (cousins to us), viz., *father's sister's son* [FSs] which goes by the "father" term in these systems, and *father's sister's daughter* [FSd] which goes by the "grandmother" term. These two can usually be taken as quick diagnostics of this particular variety of kinship system.

This system can be generated by a set of three rules, which I shall write here as reduction rules. These account not only for FSs and FSd, but for the whole system. They are:

(1) Skewing Rule: *Let any woman's brother,*

as linking relative, be regarded as equivalent to that woman's son, as linking relative.

♀B . . . → ♀s . . .

From this follows a corollary stating the consequent relationship of the reciprocals: *Any male linking relative's sister will then be equivalent to that male linking relative's mother.*

. . . ♂S → . . . ♂M

(2) Merging Rule: *Let any person's sibling of same sex, as linking relative, be equivalent to that person himself directly linked.*

♂B . . . → ♂ . . . ; ♀S . . . → ♀ . . .

From this follows the corollary pertaining to the reciprocals: *Any linking relative's sibling of same sex as himself (or herself) will then be equivalent to that relative himself (or herself) as an object of reference.*

. . . ♂B → . . . ♂; . . . ♀S → . . . ♀

(3) Half-sibling Rule: *Let any child of one of one's parents be regarded as one's sibling.*

Fs → B; Fd → S; Ms → B; Md → S

This rule contains its own reciprocal corollary.

Of these three rules, the third one is—so far as I know—universal in kinship systems; the second is widespread, applying to many systems besides the one now under consideration, but is by no means universal; while the first of these is the one of most restricted occurrence, being peculiar to this subvariety of so-called Crow" systems, but being found in quite a number of unrelated systems in many parts of the world nonetheless.

The rules constitute an unordered set. When we scan the rules for applicability in reducing a kin-type, if any is applicable, there is never more than one that is applicable at any particular step in the reduction. And if we write them as expansion rules rather than as reduction rules (which can be done by merely reversing the arrows), all possible orders of application of the rules must be exploited in generating a system. Since the rules cannot come into conflict, there is no basis for ordering.

We may apply them now to the kin-types

father's sister's son [FSs] and *father's sister's daughter* [FSd].

FSs → FMs	(by skewing rule corollary),
→ FB	(by half-sibling rule),
→ F	(by merging rule),
→ "father"	(by definition).
FSd → FMd	(by skewing rule corollary),
→ FS	(by half-sibling rule)
→ FM	(by skewing rule corollary),
→ "grandmother"	(by definition).

Now you can see by what logic one's father's sister's son may be called "father," and one's father's sister's daughter be called "grandmother." (Cf. Lounsbury, 1964a)

I have mentioned this alternative method not just to exhibit a bit of the variety in systems of kinship semantics, or the methodological resources of their devotees, but to raise also a more general point concerning the possible nature of relationships *between* the various denotata of a form. I am not prepared at this point to show that there are other semantic fields where a few generative rules may account for all instances of multiple denotation for all of the forms of an entire lexical set; but I think it might be suggested that the derivation of denotatum from denotatum, and the formulation of the principles involved, is a rather general problem in structural semantics.

DISCUSSION

Galton:

Where exactly does the contribution of structural linguistics to the treatment of kinship terminology lie, as against Delbrück's work (*Die indogerm. Verwandtschaftsnamen*, 1890) or my own ("The Indo-European Kinship Terminology," *Zeitschrift für Ethnologie*, Braunschweig, 1957) ? We are indeed dealing here with an interrelated structure, but the sole reason is to be sought in referential reality, in which the degrees of kinship form a closely knit and coherent pattern.

Just one example of a semantic shift, not due to any structural pressure within the terminological system, but purely to a relationship in the underlying reality. In some Slavic and other languages, the original term for "son-in-law" is also applied to the "brother-in-law," because the man who was son-in-law to the patriarch, the head of the clan, the grandfather, was also brother-in-law to the son of the patriarch who (the son) therefore transferred the term to denote his own relationship to the entrant into the clan. The semantic shift within the system of the kinship terminology goes back to an external factor, and it seems to me that the arguments Lounsbury adduces against my point of view are all extralinguistic.

Lounsbury:

Professor Galton has raised a crucial question, and one that I think many social anthropologists would also want to raise, viz., what does a "linguistic" or "structural-semantic" approach contribute to the treatment of kinship terms that is not adequately taken care of by a direct "social-structural" approach to their explanation? The answer that I would give to this question is that a prior formal analysis of the semantic structure will shift, and I believe simplify, the problem of relating the phenomena of linguistic usage to the social and cultural realities that lie behind them. It will do this by revealing a few underlying *principles of classification* whose effects are far-reaching. Both componential definitions and rules of extension describe such "principles of classification."

The usage of the "son-in-law" term in Slavic, that Professor Galton has referred to, finds a parallel in Latin. I believe that the extension of this term to include a man's sister's husband is an old trait of at least some of the branches of the Indo-European family, and that it is only one of many details that were the automatic consequences of one deep-lying structural principle. The example is an especially appropriate one in the context of the present discussion, because the principle involved is the precise mirror image of the "Choctaw" type of skewing rule that I have just mentioned and illustrated. If you reverse the

sex of every term in that rule and its corollary, you will have formulas that account not only for the inclusion of a man's sister's husband in the son-in-law class (L. *gener*), but also for the inclusion of a man's sister's children in the grandchild classes (L. *nepos* and *neptis*), the characterization of one's mother's brother by an essentially grandparental term (L. *avunculus*, diminutive of *avus*, the diminutive distinguishing collateral members from lineal members of the original class), etc. In this skewing rule, which generates one of the so-called "Omaha" types of kinship systems, a man's sister as linking relative is made equivalent to his daughter as linking relative, and by the corollary, a female linking relative's brother becomes equivalent to her father. A *raison d'être* for all this is not too difficult to discern in the structure of the early Roman gens, the filial position of women in relation to adult male members of their natal gens, their attainment of an adult status only in their husband's gens, etc. When these early conditions changed however, and the laws pertaining to them, then the nature of the skewing rule and the principles of kin classification also changed. The "Omaha" type of asymmetrical skewing of terminological generation gave way to a bilaterally symmetrical form of skewing such as persists in Italian and Roumanian to the present day. In French, Spanish, and Portuguese this in turn also gave way, and was replaced by principles that emphasize a pervasive contrast between lineal and collateral relatives. Analogs to these developments can be shown for Germanic as well. I am not prepared to say anything specific about the Slavic case, but I am told that there is some evidence that at least the early stage is similar to what I have posited for Latin and Germanic. With structural analysis, it becomes possible not only to trace the details of semantic change of particular words through time, but also to trace structural mutations, i.e. changes in underlying principles of classification that affect the whole system.

COGNITIVE ASPECTS OF ENGLISH KIN TERMS

A. Kimball Romney and Roy Goodwin D'Andrade

The study of kinship terminology has long been of central interest in anthropology. Formal methods of description developed by linguists, such as componential analysis, have been applied with success to kinship terminologies. It has been claimed that such descriptions, in addition to representing the data in an abstract, structural, and elegant manner, uncover and represent psychological reality for the native users of these systems. For example,

> Goodenough repeatedly states in his paper on Trukese terminology that the purpose of the componential analysis of kinship terms is to provide psychologically real definitions. . . .
>
> . . .
>
> Now this is a major theoretical commitment. It happens to be one we share: a part of anthropology's mission which is of particular concern to us is the development of formal theories and methods which will describe the relationship between cultural forms and processes, and their social-structure correlates, whose locus is a society, and psychological (cognitive) forms and processes, whose locus is the individual (Wallace and Atkins 1960: 75).

This claim is, we believe, an important hypothesis: This paper reports the results of an attempt to test this hypothesis with American-English kinship terminology. However, we are equally interested in the other side of the coin, that is, in those aspects of the individual's psychological or cognitive structure which are not represented in formal analyses.

We begin with the presentation of two alternative componential analyses of American-English kin terms. Then the results of a series of

Reproduced by permission of the author and the American Anthropological Association from *American Anthropologist*, Vol. 66, 1964, pp. 146–155.

psychological tests, designed to measure different aspects of the individual's cognitive structure concerning kin terms, are related to these componential models. An attempt is made to assess the validity of each of these models and the psychological implications of componential analyses in general.

COMPONENTIAL ANALYSES OF AMERI-CAN-ENGLISH KINSHIP TERMINOLOGY

Wallace and Atkins in a review of the methods of componential analysis, present a componential paradigm for American-English kin terms. The steps involved in this analysis are given as:

> The componential analysis of a kinship lexicon commonly consists of five steps: (1) the recording of a complete set (or a defined subset) of the terms of reference or address, using various boundary-setting criteria, such as a constant syntactic context, a type of pragmatic situation, or common inclusion within the extension of a cover term for "kinsmen;" (2) the definition of these terms in the traditional kin-type notation (i.e., as Fa, FaBr, DaHuBr); (3) the identification, in the principles of grouping of kin-types, of two or more conceptual dimensions each of whose values ("components") is signified (not connoted) by one or more of the terms; (4) the definition of each term, by means of a symbolic notation, as a specific combination, or set of combinations, of the components; (5) a statement of the semantic relationship among the terms and of the structural principles of this terminological system (Wallace and Atkins 1960: 60).

The recorded subset which Wallace and Atkins select is made up of consanguineal kin terms whose denotata in kin types are given as

Grandfather:	FaFa, MoFa
Grandmother:	FaMo, MoMo
Father:	Fa
Mother:	Mo
Brother:	Br
Sister:	Si
Son:	So
Daughter:	Da
Grandson:	SoSo, DaSo
Granddaughter:	SoDa, DaDa
Uncle:	FaBr, MoBr, FaFaBr, MoFaBr, etc.
Aunt:	FaSi, MoSi, FaFaSi, MoFaSi, etc.
Cousin:	FaBrSo, FaBrDa, MoBrSo, MoBrDa, FaSiSo, FaSiDa, MoSiSo, MoSiDa, FaFaBrSo, FaMoBrSo, MoFaSiDa, etc.
Nephew:	BrSo, SiSo, BrSoSo, SiSoSo, etc.
Niece:	BrDa, SiDa, BrDaDa, SiDaDa, etc.

Wallace and Atkins point out that the range of kin types is bound (for the sake of simplicity) at two generations above and below ego and that the last five terms have been used in their "extended sense," thus including cousin the sense of second cousin once removed, aunt in the sense of great aunt, and nephew in the sense of grand nephew, and so on. Stages 3, 4, and 5 are presented by them as follows:

Stage 3: we observe that all but one of these terms (cousin) specifies sex of relative; some specify generation; all specify whether the relative is lineally or nonlineally related to ego; and nonlineal terms specify whether or not all the ancestors of the relative are ancestors of ego, or all the ancestors of ego are ancestors of the relative, or neither. From these observations we hypothesize that three dimensions will be sufficient to define all the terms: sex of relative (A): male (a_1), female (a_2); generation (B): two generations above ego (b_1), one generation above ego (b_2), ego's own generation (b_3), one generation below ego (b_4), two generations below ego (b_5); lineality (C): lineal (c_1), co-lineal (c_2), ablineal (c_3). We use Goodenough's definition of the values on this dimension of lineality; lineals are persons who are ancestors or descendants of ego; co-lineals are non-lineals all of whose ancestors include, or are included in, all the ancestors of ego: ablineals are consanguineal relatives who are neither lineals nor co-lineals (Goodenough, private communication). Stage 4: we define the terms now by components, adopting the convention that where a term does not discriminate on a dimension, the letter for that dimension is given without subscript. The definitions are represented paradigmatically:

| | c_1 | | c_2 | | c_3 | |
	a_1	a_2	a_1	a_2	a_1	a_2
b_1	grandfather	grandmother	uncle	aunt		
b_2	father	mother				
b_3	[ego]		brother	sister	cousin	
b_4	son	daughter	nephew	niece		
b_5	grandson	granddaughter				

Figure 1. A componential paradigm of American English consanguineal core terms.

Note: Evidently each term has been so defined, with respect to the components selected, that no term overlaps or includes another; every component is discriminated by at least one term; and all terms can be displayed on the same paradigm. We do not wish to argue that this is the best representation; only that it is adequate to define the set of terms chosen (Wallace and Atkins 1960: 61–62).

A second method developed by Romney uses a different set of operations and yields slightly different results. This method begins with a basic set of symbols as follows:

m   represents male
f   represents female
a   represents person of either sex
=   represents marriage bond
0   represents sibling link (used only where individuals share both parents, i.e., "full" siblings)
+   represents parent link
—   represents child link
( )   represents an expansion
superscripts represent number of expansions
subscripts represent sex correspondences

These basic symbols are combined to represent kin types in the same way as standard abbreviations except that ego or sex of speaker is always explicitly indicated.

The notation and a subsequent analysis will be applied to the hypothetical English system reported by Wallace and Atkins (1960: 61). The terms defined by kin types written in the present notation are:

Grandfather	$a + m + m$
	$a + f + m$
Grandmother:	$a + m + f$
	$a + f + f$
Father:	$a + m$
Mother:	$a + f$
Brother:	$a \, 0 \, m$
Sister:	$a \, 0 \, f$
Son:	$a - m$
Daughter:	$a - f$
Grandson:	$a - m - m$
	$a - f - m$
Granddaughter:	$a - m - f$
	$a - f - f$
Uncle:	$a + m \, 0 \, m$
	$a + f \, 0 \, m$
	$a + m + m \, 0 \, m$
	$a + f + m \, 0 \, m$
	etc.,

(also the following not included by Wallace)
$a + m \, 0 \, f = m$
$a + f \, 0 \, f = m$
etc.

Aunt:
$a + m \, 0 \, f$
$a + f \, 0 \, f$
$a + m + m \, 0 \, f$
$a + f + m \, 0 \, f$
etc.,
(also the following not included by Wallace)
$a + m \, 0 \, m = f$
$a + f \, 0 \, m = f$
etc.

Nephew:
$a \, 0 \, m - m$
$a \, 0 \, f - m$
$a \, 0 \, m - m - m$
$a \, 0 \, f - m - m$
etc.,
(also the following not included by Wallace)
$f = m \, 0 \, m - m$
$m = f \, 0 \, m - m$
etc.

Niece:
$a \, 0 \, m - f$
$a \, 0 \, f - f$
$a \, 0 \, m - m - f$
$a \, 0 \, f - m - f$
etc.,
(also the following not included by Wallace)
$f = m \, 0 \, m - m$
$m = f \, 0 \, m - m$
etc.

Cousin:
$a + m \, 0 \, m - m$
$a + m \, 0 \, m - f$
$a + f \, 0 \, m - m$
$a + f \, 0 \, m - f$
$a + m \, 0 \, f - m$
$a + m \, 0 \, f - f$
$a + f \, 0 \, f - m$
$a + f \, 0 \, f - f$
$a + m + m \, 0 \, m - m$
$a + m + f \, 0 \, m - m$
$a + f + m \, 0 \, f - f$
etc.

The list of kin types following each kin term will be called the *range* of that term. An analysis of the terminological system begins with a listing of the *range* of each term as above. The next step is to reduce the *range* of each term to a single notational expression. (In the above example, Father, Mother, Brother, Sister, Son, and Daughter are already single expressions.)

The rules of the reduction of *ranges* to single expressions are outlined below.

Rule 1. *Rule of Minimum Difference Within Range.* Where two kin types within a range are identical except for a difference in sex markers in the same position, the two kin types may be written as one with an a in the contrasting position. Apply Rule 1 before all others.

The rule may be exemplified by the range of Grandfather where the range is indicated as:

$$a + m + m \text{ and}$$
$$a + f + m$$

The two kin types differ only in the sex markers of the medial position. Thus, the two kin types may be rewritten as: $a + a + m$. The rule of minimum difference will reduce all ranges in the above system to a single expression except for Uncle, Aunt, Nephew, Niece, and Cousin. For these, another rule is necessary.

Rule 2. *Rule of Sequence Difference Within Range.* Where two expressions are identical except for one additional "link" (i.e., a pair consisting of one sex and one relation marker), the "link" may be written in parentheses. The parentheses will indicate an optional expansion. This rule may be applied in sequence but must be labeled with a superscript indicating number of reductions made.

For example, assume the following range:

$$m + f \ 0 \ m$$
$$m + f \ 0 \ m - m$$
$$m + f \ 0 \ m - m - m$$

where it is desired to reduce these kin types to a single expression. Rule 2 provides the following convention:

$$m + f \ 0 \ (m -)^{0,1,2} m$$

where the parentheses indicate optional inclusion of the enclosed link, and the superscripts indicate number of applications of option.

The same rule holds for "affinal" links. Thus:

$$a + m \ 0 \ m$$
$$a + m \ 0 \ f = m$$
$$a + f \ 0 \ m$$
$$a + f \ 0 \ f = m$$

reduce to

$$a + a \ 0 \ (f =) \ m$$

The application of these two rules completely reduces the ranges of the English system to single expressions as follows:

Grandfather	$a + a + m$
Grandmother	$a + a + f$
Father	$a + m$
Mother	$a + f$
Brother	$a \ 0 \ m$
Sister	$a \ 0 \ f$
Son	$a - m$
Daughter	$a - f$
Grandson	$a - a - m$
Granddaughter	$a - a - f$
Uncle	$a + a(+a)^{0,1} \ 0 \ (f =)m$
Aunt	$a + a(+a)^{0,1} \ 0 \ (m =)f$
Nephew	$a(=a) \ 0 \ (a -)^{0,1}a - m$
Niece	$a(=a) \ 0 \ (a -)^{0,1}a - f$
Cousin	$a + a(+a)^{0,1,2} \ 0 \ (a -)^{0,1,2}a - a$

Before proceeding to the analysis of the structure of the above terms and expressions, two additional rules for the reduction of kin types within ranges to a single expression will be mentioned. These rules, though not necessary for the analysis of the English system, are useful for other systems.

Rule 3. *The Rule of Paired Sequence Difference Within Ranges.* This rule is used widely for the analysis of systems recognizing the parallel vs. cross distinction. It may be thought of as an extension of Rule 2. Where two expressions are identical except for "paired links," the "paired links" may be written in parentheses The parentheses will indicate an expansion, and superscripts will indicate number of expansions. In addition, the subscripts i and j will be used on the sex markers to indicate appropriate handling of sex when the expression is expanded.

Take for example the following hypothetical range:

$$a + m \, 0 \, m - a$$
$$a + f \, 0 \, f - a$$
$$a \, 0 \, a$$

Rule 3 provides the following single expression:

$$a(+ \, a_i)^x \, 0 \, (a_j -)^y a$$
where $x = y = 0, 1$
and $i = j$

The subscripts i and j may also be used for relative sex of speaker.

Rule 4. *The Rule of Reciprocals Within Ranges.* Where two expressions differ only by the fact that they are complete reciprocals of one another, either expression may be written between slashes and be taken to represent both. In the present notation, a reciprocal of any kin type is found by writing the expression in reverse order and changing all +'s to −'s and *vice versa*, without changing 0 and = links.

For example, if a range included the kin types $m + f \, 0 \, m$ and $m \, 0 \, f - m$, they could be reduced to the single expression, $/m + f \, 0 \, m/$. In practice, we have found it most convenient to put the ascending generations between slashes.

Perhaps at this point the rationale behind the development of this new notational system can be stated clearly. This notational system contains exactly the same information as the traditional systems. The difference is that in this notation, all information is represented explicitly. For example, if one wished to program a computer with the traditional notation to identify those kin terms which refer solely to male kin types, it would be necessary to give the machine special instructions that the symbols "Fa," "Br," "So," and "Hu" stand for males (as well as other things). Such additional instructions are not necessary for the notation given here.

Structural analysis of terms. We return to the task of completing a structural analysis of the expressions given above. A structural analysis may proceed on the basis of a set of rules in much the same way that within-range reductions were made. The essential difference is that the operations at this stage of analysis reveal structural principles rather than produce reduced expressions of ranges. The following rules are to be applied in ordered sequence as listed. They apply to the reduced expressions produced by procedures outlined above.

Sex of relative. If two expressions are identical except for the final sex marker, then *sex of relative* is a distinctive variable. Whenever a distinctive variable is discovered by any of the procedures in this section, it is noted for the appropriate terms. Then the expressions involved are combined and carried along in the analysis.

For example, the expressions of Grandfather and Grandmother above are $a + a + m$ and $a + a + f$, and they differ only by the final sex marker. Hence, *sex of relative* is a distinctive variable. It may be marked as R and takes the values R_1 male and R_2 female. We then mark Grandfather as R_1 and Grandmother as R_2. We now combine the expressions into $a + a + a$ (or more simply, $+ +$), which is caried along for further analysis.

Sex of speaker. If two expressions are identical except for the initial sex marker, then *sex of speaker* is a distinctive variable. It may be marked as S and takes the values S_1, male speaking, and S_2, female speaking. Where a variable is nowhere recognized in a system, it would not be marked anywhere. Thus S does not appear in the description of English.

Relative sex. If two expressions are identical except for the fact that in one, sex of speaker is the same as the relative and in the other, it is different, then *relative sex of speaker* is the distinctive variable. It may be marked as D and takes the values D_1, different, and D_2, the same.

Relative age. If two expressions are identical except for relative age, then *relative age* is a distinctive variable. It may be marked as A and takes the values A_1, relative older than ego, and A_2, relative younger than ego. (Sometimes relative age of intervening relatives is criterial.)

Reciprocity. If two expressions are identical except for being reciprocals, then *polarity* is a distinctive variable. It may be marked by P and takes the values P_1, senior or ascending generation, and P_2, junior or descending generation.

Sex of intervening relative. Where two expressions are identical except for intervening relative, then *cross vs. parallel* is a distinctive variable. It may be marked by C and takes the value C_1, cross, and C_2, parallel.

Further differences in expressions. Let us summarize the appearance of the analysis of English to this point. The application of the procedures in this section produce the following:

Table 1

TERM	EXTRACTED COMPONENTS	REMAINING EXPRESSION
Grandfather	R_1P_1	
Grandmother	R_2P_1	
Grandson	R_1P_2	/++/
Granddaughter	R_2P_2	
Father	R_1P_1	
Mother	R_2P_1	
Son	R_1P_2	/+/
Daughter	R_2P_2	
Uncle	R_1P_1	
Aunt	R_2P_1	
Nephew	R_1P_2	/+(+) 0 /
Niece	R_2P_2	
Cousin	R P	+(+) 0 (−) −
Brother	R_1P	
Sister	R_2P	0

In order to complete the analysis, it is necessary to have a small list of common distinctive variables that characterize systems. Examples of such variables include direct vs. collateral, generation, etc. Up to this point the steps in the analysis are explicit. The procedures have reduced 15 kin terms to five range-sets. We know of no way to specify a single best solution for the classification or arrangement of these five range-sets. Taste, previous knowledge of the system, emphasis on core kin types, and other factors affect the outcome. Three possible solutions are shown in Fig. 1:

Primary	Secondary	Tertiary
/+/	/++/	+(+) 0 (−) −
0	/+(+) 0/	

Figure 1. First analysis of American kinship system.

	Lineal	Co-lineal	Ablineal
±2	/++/	/+(+) 0/	+(+) 0 (−) −
±1	/+/		
0	ego	0	

Figure 2. Second analysis of American kinship system.

This solution stresses the distinction between relatives in the nuclear family and those outside the nuclear family. This is a simplification of Parson's picture of the American kinship system where "primary" relatives correspond to his "inner" circle (Parson 1943: 179).

The second solution (Fig. 2) corresponds to the distinction referred to by Wallace and Atkins above (1960:62).

The third solution (Fig. 3) is the one we prefer and the one that will be used in the remainder of the paper. It emphasizes the core or kernel kin type and hence treats "cousin" as a zero generation relative.

	Direct		Collateral		
	male	female	male	female	
+2	GrFa	GrMo	Un	Au	+
−2	GrSo	GrDa			
+1	Fa	Mo	Ne	Ni	−
−1	So	Da			
0	Br	Si	Co		0

Figure 3. Third analysis of American kinship system.

Note that the dotted lines in Fig. 3 represent the relations between terms obtained with simple operations on the notation scheme. Since the notation scheme represents the genealogical elements, it may be assumed that terms joined by dotted lines are somehow "closer" than terms separated by solid lines. (Although Wallace and Atkins use dotted lines between sex pairs, e.g., mother and father, they are not derived from steps in the analysis.) The dotted lines arise from the analytic procedures. Terms within solid lines (separated only by dotted lines) are defined as constituting a range-set.

COGNITIVE IMPLICATIONS AND INDIVIDUAL BEHAVIORAL MEASURES

There appear to be two separate issues with respect to the cognitive implications of the analyses presented above. The first issue deals with the problem of alternative componential structures, while the second issue involves the selection of behavioral measures that would be affected if a componential analysis were isomorphic with cognitive structure.

There are two possible solutions to the first issue; that is, either one analysis is more efficient than the other in providing a cognitively accurate representation, or individuals have more than one cognitive structure with which they may operate. If the individuals in a culture have alternative cognitive structures, it is possible that either different individuals have arrived at different cognitive structures or that the same individual operates with alternative structures.

It is our feeling that there will usually be several alternative analyses possible for any set of kin terms. If we are to talk about psychological or cognitive implications of an analysis, we must specify what these implications might be. Probably some analyses will be more useful for some purposes and less useful for others. Thus there may be no single best solution for a given system.

It should be pointed out that differences in Romney's and Wallace and Atkins' analyses are due to more than one factor. One difference is due to the definition of components, especially in the definition of collaterality. Another source of difference is that Romney uses an entirely different component (reciprocity) as a basic means of aligning range sets. These alternative results highlight the fact that componential analysis is not an automatic method of uncovering individual cognitive structures. Slight differences in the operations or the definition and number of components imply different pictures of psychological reality. We feel that the solution to this problem

lies in further behavioral measures of individual cognitive operations.

As Wallace and Atkins (1960: 78) say,

But the only way of achieving definite knowledge of psychological reality will be to study the semantics of individuals both before and after a formal, abstract, cultural-semantic analysis of the terms has been performed. Simple demands for verbal definition, the use of Rivers' genealogical method, and analysis of the system of kinship behaviors may not be sufficient here: additional procedures, by individual representative informants, of matching and sorting, answering hypothetical questions, and description of relationships in order to reveal methods of reckoning will probably all be required.

Following this suggestion, we have collected a variety of data on English kinship from large samples of high school students, utilizing a number of different techniques. The techniques that we have used include the following:

1. A listing of kin terms in free recall.
2. The semantic differential.
3. Direct judgments of similarity and difference with the triad method.

The general prediction we have made from componential analyses to cognitive measures is that the more components any two terms have in common, the greater will be the similarity, of response to these terms. This prediction is derived from the assumption that the components of a term constitute the meaning of that term for an individual; hence, the more components which are shared, the more similar the meaning. We use component at two levels of contrast: first, as a dimension, e.g., generation or sex; second, as a value on a dimension, e.g., zero generation or male sex. Context should make clear which level is being referred to.

At this point we have not differentiated between denotative or referential meaning and affective or connotative meaning (although we believe componential analysis would correspond most closely to denotative meaning). Nor have we attempted to prejudge which measures of similarity actually measure similarity in meaning. These issues will be discussed later in the paper as data are presented.

COGNITION AND COMPONENTIAL ANALYSIS: GOD'S TRUTH OR HOCUS-POCUS?

Robbins Burling

I

Many anthropologists have been attracted by procedures of formal semantics, such as componential analysis, and some have noted the possibility of alternative solutions (Goodenough 1956a: 211 ff; Wallace and Atkins 1960: 75 ff). To my knowledge, however, none have given consideration to the total number of alternative solutions that are logically possible, and to the implications of that number for the problem of indeterminacy, and to the implications of indeterminacy for semantic analysis. Componential analysis is applied to a set of terms which form a culturally relevant domain and proceeds by recognizing semantic distinctions (components) which apportion the terms of the set into contrasting sub-sets, such that every item is distinguished from every other item by at least one component. Subsets can be arrived at in many alternative ways, however, and in the following

II

My first objective will be to clarify the ways in which the items in a set may be distinguished from each other and divided among individual cells. The theoretical possibilities are most easily understood by considering very small sets of items. If we have a set of only one item, there is no problem of partitioning at all. Two items can presumably be distinguished in only one way, allowing only one possible division of a set of two terms. If there are three items in the set (call the items a, b, c) the possibilities become slightly more complex. For a first partition, one has three obvious choices: use a component which separates a from b and c; one which separates b from a and c; or one which separates c from a and b. As a matter of fact, any two of these components acting together will partition the set of three items completely, so that, to start with, there are three possible componential analyses of a set of

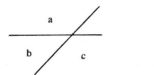

Figure 1.

discussion I will first consider the wider number of possible choices (II). Then I will consider the relation of the number of possibilities to the "cognitive" status of solutions, and conclude by stating what limited but real value I consider componential analyses to have (III).

Reproduced by permission of the author and the American Anthropological Association from *American Anthropologist*, Vol. 66, 1964, pp. 20–27.

three items (Figure 1). However, one further possibility must also be allowed for. After a first partition (which, let us say, separates a from b and c) it is possible to make a second partition which distinguishes b from c, but which is irrelevant for a. Such components have been regularly used in analyses which have actually been carried out. For instance, in giving a semantic analysis of the third person singular pronouns in English, one might first suggest an animate/inanimate distinc-

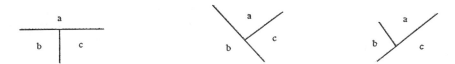

Figure 2.

tion to separate *it* on the one hand from *he* and *she* on the other. A second component, separating male from female can distinguish *he* from *she*, but sex is simply irrelevant for *it*. If we recognize this type of secondary partitioning, which makes use of a component that is significant for some but not all of the items in the set, three additional methods of discretely partitioning a set of three items become possible—for instance, a component distinguishing *a* from *b* and *c*, together with a second component separating *b* from *c* but irrelevant for *a*. This makes six possible analyses in all (Figure 2).

When we consider a set of four items, the possibilities increase considerably. In the hope of keeping the discussion as clear as possible, I will arbitrarily label the items *a*, *b*, *c*, and *d*, and I will call any partition which is significant over the entire set a "primary component." A component which is significant for less than the total number of items of the set I will call a "secondary component." A secondary component can only act after the particular sub-set to which it applies has been set off and distinguished either by one of the primary components or by a more inclusive secondary component. The initial partition of any set must always be made by a primary component. To label particular components I will use abbreviations of the following type: *ab/cd* means a component that divides the set of four items into two sub-sets, *ab* on the one hand and *cd* on the other. Secondary components can be labeled by such formulae as *bc/d* which would indicate a component which acts after *a* has been separated from the others and which is not itself applicable to *a* but which distinguishes *b* and *c* from *d*.

In a set of four items, seven different primary components can be recognized. These fall into two distinctive types, which I will call *Type I* and *Type II*, respectively.

Type I	a/bcd	b/acd	c/adb	d/abc
Type II	ab/cd	ac/bd	ad/bc	

These primary components can be combined in various ways to produce "discrete" but "non-redundant" solutions to the set. By a "discrete" solution I mean an analysis which apportions each item into a separate cell and which distinguishes between every pair of items by at least one component. By a "non-redundant" solution I mean an analysis in which no component can be eliminated without breaking down the distinction between at least one pair of items. Both discreteness and non-redundancy have implicitly been considered desirable in componential analysis. The discrete but non-redundant solutions, using the primary components only, are as follows:

A. Any three Type I components: 4 possible solutions.
B. Any two Type II components: 3 possible solutions.
C. Any one of the Type II components may be combined with any of four pairs of Type I components. The Type I components must be chosen to partition the sets already set up by the Type II components. For instance, ab/cd can be combined with any one of the following pairs of Type I components, but with no others:

> a/bcd and c/abd
> a/bcd and d/abc
> b/acd and c/abd
> b/acd and d/abc

Combining each of the three Type II components with the four appropriate Type I components gives: 12 possible solutions: $3 \times 2 \times 2$.

Taking A, B, and C together, we have, so far, 19 ways of apportioning the four items into discrete cells by using primary components only. If secondary components (which do not cut across the entire set) are used as well, the possibilities increase. We can recognize two types of secondary components, those which make a distinction among three items and those which distinguish only two. These can be added to the earlier types and called Types III and IV. There are, respectively, 12 and 6 Type III and Type IV components, as follows:

Type III	a/bc	b/ac	c/ab
	a/bd	b/ad	d/ab
	a/cd	c/ad	d/ac
	b/cd	c/bd	d/bc

Type IV	a/b	a/c	a/d	b/c	b/d	c/d

Several new possibilities now arise by which components of the several Types can be combined to obtain discrete but non-redundant solutions.

D. Any two Type I components acting together may be combined with any one of four Type III components: a/bcd and b/acd, for instance, may be combined with any of the four Type III components which distinguish c from d.

E.g. a/bcd, b/acd, c/ad
24 solutions: $(3 + 2 + 1) \times 4$

E. Any two Type I components acting together may be combined with one particular Type IV component:

E.g. a/bcd, b/acd, c/d
6 solutions: $(3 + 2 + 1) \times 1$

F. Any Type I component when acting with any Type II component may be combined with any one of four Type III components: a/bcd with ab/cd fails to distinguish only c and d. Any of the four Type III components which do distinguish cd from d will complete the job.

E.g. a/bcd, ab/cd, c/bd
48 solutions: $4 \times 3 \times 4$

G. Any Type I component acting together with any Type II component can then be combined with one particular Type IV component. I.e. once a choice of the Type I and Type II components has been made, one and only one of the Type IV components will complete the partitioning:

E.g. a/bcd, ab/cd, c/d
12 solutions: $4 \times 3 \times 1$

H. Any Type II component may be combined with the two Type IV components which redivide the sub-sets specified by the Type II components.

E.g. ab/cd with a/b with c/d
3 solutions: $3 \times 1 \times 1$

I. Any Type I component together with any one of three Type III components (one of the three which do not include the item designated by the letter to the left of the slash in the Type I component which was chosen) can then be combined with one particular Type IV component to complete the partitioning.

E.g. a/bcd with b/cd with c/d
12 solutions: $4 \times 3 \times 1$

In D through I, by combining primary and secondary components, we have added 105 possible analyses to the 19 which use primary components only for a total of 124 ways in which a set of four terms can be discretely but non-redundantly apportioned into cells by the application of components. Clearly with five or more items the possibilities would rapidly become astronomical.

One hundred and twenty-four possible analyses for four items may seem surprising, but they do not exhaust the complications. Others deserve at least brief mention: 1) *Homonomy*. Analysts of kinship terminology have occasionally found it expedient to provide two different formulae for a single term and suggest that it has (by such an analysis) two different meanings. 2) *Empty semantic spaces*. Authors of some semantic analyses have pointed out that when a number of components cross-cut each other in several ways, it may be found that there is no lexeme at all for some particular combination of components. 3) *Non-binary components*. There is no necessary reason why an analysis must be confined to binary distinctions, although some workers seem to have felt them to be esthetically more pleasing and my discussion has been limited to them. 4) *Parallel components*. There seems no reason to suppose that in real systems only a single distinction can separate the same sub-sets, though in the abstract formulation given here only one distinction is possible. 5) *Redundancy*. Finally, there seems no real reason to limit the available analyses to the non-redundant ones, except that by admitting redundant analyses, we open the way to vastly increased possibilities: ab/cd/ac/bd, and a/bcd form a discrete analysis of four items. It is redundant since the third component can be eliminated without destroying the discreteness of the solution. Redundant components have not traditionally been allowed in semantic analyses, though it is difficult to justify this limitation as a matter of principle. Homonomy, empty spaces, non-binary distinctions, parallel components, and redundant solutions all add considerable complexity to the possibilities for analysis of a set of terms. In principle, the number of possible analyses becomes infinite.

III

Readers may doubt whether this abstract and formalistic argument has any great relevance to the practical analysis of real systems. Later, I will try to suggest that it does, but since its relevance is entirely dependent upon one's objectives in conducting a semantic analysis, we must be clear about our objectives before considering its relevance.

Anthropologists who have advocated the use of componential analysis and similar formal methods as a way of studying the meaning of sets of terms seem to have had two contrasting objectives. Their first and more modest goal has been to specify the conditions under which each term would be used. The problem has been posed in the following way: What do we have to know in order to say that some object is to be called by a given term (cf. Goodenough 1956a: 195)? That is, analysts have searched for a set of rules which would unambiguously state the criteria by which it could be decided whether or not a particular

term could be applied to some object, and the test for the validity of the analysis has been the accuracy with which it predicts such naming. If it can be used to predict what term will be used for a particular object, then this is taken to justify the analysis.

The more ambitious objective of the method is to use it to lead us to an understanding of the criteria by which speakers of the language themselves decide what term to use for a particular item. This view was suggested in Goodenough's original paper (1956a: 196) when he said: "[the semantic analyst] aims to find the conceptual units out of which the meanings of linguistic utterances are built. . . ." and more forcefully by Wallace (1962: 352): "The problem is to define the taxonomic system itself—that is, to explicate the rules by which users of the terms group various social and genealogical characteristics into concepts." Frake (1962: 74) described one of his papers as containing ". . . some suggestions toward the formulation of an operationally-explicit methodology for discovering how people construe their world of experience from the way they talk about it."

These two objectives differ in an important way. Specifically, any of hundreds or thousands of logically alternative solutions might predict which term can be used, but the success of that prediction does not demonstrate that the speaker of the language uses the same scheme, or indicate whether or not all speakers use the same one.

It is a long and difficult leap from an analysis which is adequate in the sense of discriminating which term should be used to denote an object to that particular analysis which represents the way in which people construe their world. I will try to suggest briefly that the difficulty is not a purely hypothetical one by considering the attempts that have been made to analyze such sets as botanical and disease terminology. Conklin (1962a) and Frake (1961, 1962) have suggested that such terms can be arranged into a hierarchical taxonomy. In colloquial English, for instance, (not necessarily in the special English of taxonomic botany) we have a class of objects which we call plants, and within the class of plants we have a class of trees. Within the class of trees is a class of "needled trees" (which, in my part of the country where little account is taken of broad-leafed evergreens, seems nearly synonymous with "evergreen"). "Needled trees" include "pines" and "pines" in turn include "jackpines." At each taxonomic level are other coordinate terms: "Flowers" and "bushes" may be coordinate with "trees"; "palms" and "leafy trees" with "needled trees"; "spruce" and "hemlocks" with "pines"; and "white" and "Norway pines" with "jackpines" (Figure 3). Taxonomies existed for plants in all languages long before Linnaeus codified the idea and laid the basis for systematic biology.

A taxonomy of the sort suggested by this example constitutes a special form of componential analysis. After a primary component has been used to divide the entire set of terms, the next distinction is a secondary component which divides one of the sub-sets but which typically does not cross the first component into the other sub-set. Each component operates only within a single undifferentiated set which has been set off by earlier components but which is not yet divided itself. Intersecting components may be used for botanical terminology as well as for kinship, but they have less commonly been recognized.

It is my feeling that the analyses of terms into hierarchical taxonomies that have lately been discussed have rather glossed over the problems of indeterminacy. In fact, in my example I also glossed over some difficult problems of this sort. I am not at all certain, for instance, that "flower" and "bush" are really coordinate to "tree." Perhaps on the basis of size English speakers distinguish "trees" from "bushes," and "bushes" from "plants" (homonymous, but not synonymous with "plants" used as a general cover term for the entire set), and then on the basis of use, divide "plants" into "flowers," "vegetables," and "weeds." What about "cedars"? Are they "needled trees"? Not really, of course, but they are not "leafy trees" either. Should "balsam," "hemlock," and "spruce" be classed together as "short needled trees" (Christmas trees) as opposed to "pines"? Or should they all have equivalent taxonomic status? What is the essential "cognitive" difference between hemlock and spruce? Is it gross size, type of needle, form of bark, or what? I do not know how to answer these questions, but they are the types of questions which must be answered before any single semantic analysis can claim to represent the cognitive organization of the people, or even claim to be much more than an exercise of the analyst's imagination. The questions which I raise about English botanical terms represent precisely the sort of indeterminacy that arose in the abstract example which began this paper.

Analyses of terms in exotic languages may obscure the range of possible alternatives. For instance, Frake (1961) discusses some disease terms in Subanun, a language of Mindanao, and he makes appealing suggestions for their analysis; yet I cannot help wondering if he does not convey an unjustified certainty in the particular analysis he offers. Frake gives a diagram (1961:18) of the same form as my diagram of English plant terms (Figure 3), in which certain skin diseases are assigned to various taxonomic categories and sub-categories. Not know-

PLANTS						
ETC.	BUSHES	FLOWERS	TREES			
ETC.			LEAFY TREES	PALM TREES	NEEDLED TREES	
ETC.			ETC.	ETC.	SPRUCE	HEMLOCK	PINE

Figure 3.

ing the language, the reader can hardly question the data, and yet he may still wonder if this diagram is any less subject to question than my diagram of plant terms. This is particularly the case since Frake does not give a complete analysis of all disease terms, but limits himself to examples which illustrate the problems he is considering, and he implies that once having solved the problems one may easily provide the full analysis. In fact, in my judgment, the field of structural semantics has had a surfeit of programmatic articles, glowing with promise of a new ethnography (Conklin 1962a; Frake 1961, 1962; Wallace and Atkins 1960; Wallace 1962), and a dearth of substantive descriptions of whole systems or definable sub-systems.

Students who claim that componential analysis or comparable methods of semantic analysis can provide a means for "discovering how people construe their world" must explain how to eliminate the great majority of logical possibilities and narrow the choice to the one or few that are "psychologically real." I will not be convinced that there are not dozens or hundreds of possible analyses of Subanun disease terms until Frake presents us with the entire system fully analyzed and faces squarely the problem of how he chooses his particular analysis. In the meantime, I will doubt whether any single analysis tells us much about people's cognitive structure, even if it enables us to use terms as a native does.

The hope that we could somehow use our knowledge of language to gain understanding of the workings of the human mind has had a long history. Whorf's ideas have fallen into disrepute largely because the relationships which he claimed to see between patterns of language and patterns of thought could be checked only from the side of language. The language patterns were there to be sure, but how, except through intuition, could one tell whether the patterns corresponded to anything else? Structural semantics has the advantage over Whorf's more naive ideas in that it attempts to relate two observable types of data with one another—language use and events in the non-linguistic world. I cannot see that it has any advantage over Whorf's procedures in gaining an understanding of cognition.

This conclusion may sound harsh, but it does not imply that "structural semantics" is useless. There is a real problem of formulating rules which will predict the use of terms, or to put it another way, of specifying the relationship between terms, on the one hand, and events and situations in our extra-linguistic experience, on the other. In still other words, it is legitimate to try to specify precisely what terms "mean." The exercise of carrying out a formal analysis, moreover, is certainly useful in checking the completeness and adequacy of one's data, in exactly the same way that writing up a grammatical statement may make one aware of previously unimagined possibilities, whether or not these are attributed to the speaker. If nothing else, a precise statement of the objects to which terms are applied is certainly a help to someone wishing to learn the language or use behaviour which will be effective. I am convinced that componential analysis and other formal semantic methods can help us in this task. As we learn more about all aspects of language use and its relation to non-linguistic events and as we bring studies of various semantic domains into harmony with each other and take wider and wider account of all aspects of behaviour, we may be able to narrow down the alternatives. I expect, however, that a large degree of indeterminacy will always remain. I can be proven wrong by analyses which admit to no alternatives, but until such analyses are given, I will regard it as gratuitous to attribute our analyses to the speakers.

Linguists, in referring to attitudes toward grammatical analyses, have sometimes made a distinction between the "God's truth" view and the "hocus-pocus" view (Householder 1952). When a linguist makes his investigation and writes his grammar, is he discovering something about the language which is "out there" waiting to be described and recorded or is he simply formulating a set of rules which somehow work? Similarly, when an anthropologist undertakes a semantic analysis, is he discovering some "psychological reality" which speakers are presumed to have or is he simply working out a set of rules which somehow take account of the observed phenomena? The attitude taken in this paper is far over on the "hocus-pocus" side. It is always tempting to attribute something more important to one's work than a tinkering with a rough set of operational devices. It certainly sounds more exciting to say we are "discovering the cognitive system of the people" than to admit that we are just fiddling with a set of rules which allow us to use terms the way others do. Nevertheless, I think the latter is a realistic goal, while the former is not. I believe we should be content with the less exciting objective of showing how terms in language are applied to objects in the world, and stop pursuing the illusory goal of cognitive structures.

FURTHER COMMENTS ON COMPONENTIAL ANALYSIS

E. Hammel

Burling's recent article, "Cognition and Componential Analysis: God's Truth or Hocus-Pocus?" (1964), the comments by Hymes (1964) and Frake (1964) and Burling's rejoinder (1964) raise a number of important points about this aspect of anthropological investigation and throw some crucial issues into sharp focus. However, part of the discussion seems to me to ignore, perhaps even obscure, certain critical issues and to introduce at least one that is irrelevant.

Burling's initial point, the demonstration of the multiplicity of solutions, is an interesting logical exercise but important only as a springboard for his argument on the "reality" of a solution. The non-uniqueness of solutions is not a new phenomenon in anthropology, in linguistics, or in physics. What is needed here is not just a proof that multiple solutions are possible but that some non-unique solutions are redundant and unimportantly different, while others may contain in their differences major consequences for further analysis. As Hymes notes (1964: 116), Burling's demonstration is forced, because of the limitation of possibilities inherent in a native terminology by virtue of its own imposition of order on observed data. One might also suggest that the abstract demonstration was

empty, by considering the limiting case of a set defined by continuous variables infinitesimally divided; the number of analyses is then not only infinite "in principle" (Burling 1964: 24) but in fact. The remainder of Burling's argument and his rejoinder, however, strike a crucial problem —how real is a semantic analysis?

The problem of whether reality exists "out there" or in someone's head is at least as old as Plato and probably as old as people's heads. The issue has been debated by scientists and philosophers at every level from that of the reality of the basic sense datum to that of the reality of embracing theoretical constructs. I am not aware that complete agreement has ever been reached. However, agreement has been attained on the problem of how to decide between perceptions or constructs that are in the heads of different observers. The criteria for such a decision are replicability, internal consistency, correspondence with observation, and economy of statement. One may, of course, satisfy these criteria through different styles of research—by the sweat of one's brow and dogged induction or by insight and deductive confirmation. Nevertheless, the acceptability of one hypothesis over another rests on the grounds noted and, I venture to say, only on those grounds, although one might place greater weight on some criteria than on others. (One might even apply the last of them to Burling's demonstration and reject his Figure 1

Reproduced by permission of the author and the American Anthropological Association from *American Anthropologist*, Vol. 66, 1964, pp. 1167–1170.

because it contains empty sets and is thus un-economical, compared to his Figure 2; for Figure 2, the most economical solution, in the abstract, would seem to be B [1964: 22].)

At this level, as Frake suggests, the problem faced by the semantic analyst is no different from that of any scientist. It is one of deciding which hypothesis, of a redundant set of hypotheses, is most convenient or pleasing, or which hypothesis, or a non-redundant set of hypotheses, best describes the correspondence between at least two observed sets of data. The real problem for us lies in the identification of the sets. One of these has by custom always been linguistic. The other sets can be points on a genealogical grid, the results of sorting and selecting tests (Romney and D'Andrade 1964), other terminological sets, morphological or other linguistic sets, gestures, interaction patterns, expressions of affect and avoidance—in fact any other set of observable behavior which can be construed as having an observable referent and which is thus a kind of "pointing" even if not of "naming" in the restricted sense. (See also Hymes' discussion of this point [1964: 116–117].) The semantic analyses which have been most successful in a formal sense have employed at least one termi-nological set, since terms are usually (but not always) discrete objects specifiable by discon-tinuous variables, and a set of referential objects also specifiable by discontinuous variables—for example, most genealogical dimensions. It is this discontinuity which gives rise to the limitation of possibilities noted by Hymes (1964: 116).

Just as the structure or structures of the atom can only be apprehended through its behavior and its effects on sensors, so the structure of a cognitive system can only be approached through the observable behaviors of its possessors. Since, as noted, these behaviors can be of many differ-ent kinds, the analyst's first problem is to con-sider as many of them as he thinks necessary or convenient. His second problem is to determine their mutual correspondences, if these exist, *and* the differences between actors (Wallace 1961a). We may assume that these behaviors are not likely to be infinite in number or randomly differ-ent in kind, but any specification of some *one* behavioral set as more important for psycho-

logical understanding, or more real in any other sense, is a less tenable assumption. Having described the correspondences between native sets, the analyst may proceed to the construction of that set of his own which most closely cor-responds to the largest number of native sets or to their central tendency in sorting (again, see Frake 1964). At this point his only legitimate concern is with the isomorphism between his sorting and the native sorting. It is not necessary that the dimensions or principles of the anthro-pologist's model be expressed by informants in a direct fashion or even that their models, as given verbally or by other means, have some cor-respondence in their principles or dimensions with those of the analyst, unless the analyst's concern is the *translation* of the native model. If his concern is the accurate and economical de-scription of native behavior, or, further, of human behavior, selection of some particular native model and its translation may indeed be undesirable. It is not likely that the natives will have an *observable* general model for behavior; even if they do, it need not be as good a predictor of behavior as the anthropologist's. (I am not attempting to be humerous when I point out that we have Ph.D's in anthropology and the natives do not; for a particularly pungent example of the small power of native explanations, see Galbraith 1955. Who is to say *a priori* that a na-tive explanation is more "real" than the ana-lyst's?) (The functional value and *general* utility of ambiguity in native models should, however, be clear.)

Burling and Hymes make an important point when they agree that it would be futile to seek "what is inside people" only on linguistic grounds. But I would go further and side with Burling on the futility of the entire attempt, so phrased. That internal essence which is "inside people," in whatever form it may exist, is only knowable when it is outside them, and when it is outside them it takes a variety of forms which can, with effort and good fortune, only be sum-marized in externally valid and verifiable ways. Like Burling, I am an "outside" man, and, like Frake, I suspect that God's truth *is* hocus-pocus. From that position, however, I would suggest that the difference of opinion is irrelevant in a practical sense, since a good analysis by an "inside" man and a good analysis by an "outside" man are likely to be equivalent and only redundantly different, if not identical.

One further point should be raised, namely, whether "sitting at a desk with a set of terms uncertainly constituting a native set, and playing with analysis into dimensions uncertainly corresponding to native features" (Hymes 1964: 118–119) is a legitimate and useful activity. The full force of Hymes' criticism, to paraphrase his summary of Burling's remarks, applies to those who construct a model and claim that it is the natives' model; only an inside man, and an unsophisticated one at that, would make such a claim. Playing with dimensions is neither legitimate nor illegitimate; it either works or it does not, on the basis of the data at hand. It is further not a final solution (if these ever exist) but a hypothesis which may be tested as other data become available. If the directions of research change, it may even become irrelevant; note, for example, the change which occurred in the taxonomic model of biology when the purposes of that model shifted from convenient classification to the reflection of evolutionary genetic connections. This playing with dimensions is ideally only an initial step involving "sorting" and tentative "assignment of semantic features" (Hymes 1964: 117). It may, however, be final. While the best analyses can only be done in the field, we cannot always go to the field. The additional data may in fact be unrecoverable because the groups involved are extinct or vastly changed. In this, our position is no different from that of the philologist, the historian, the archaeologist, or the astronomer observing the birth of a star. Not only is armchair analysis inexpensive, but we also learn from it so that our field analyses may be more sophisticated in their manipulation of data. The bogey that kinship may be dehumanized by mock-algebra, which lurks under too many desks, should not deter us from the attempt. To be frightened by it is to retreat into a romanticist position which insists on the reality of internal essence but denies all rigorous attempts to know its manifestations. Some of the best technical work in semantic and structural analysis has mocked the bogey. I can think of no

more powerful justification for experimenting with dimensions than the highly abstract work of Lounsbury on Iroquois (1964a) and Crow-Omaha (1964b) and on even less recoverable bodies of data, Colonial Quechua and Latin, and the formalistic treatment of Australian section systems by Lawrence (1937). These are constructs of elegance and utility, even if they may eventually be proved "false" in terms of better hypotheses or of some additional sets of data. Truth is only correspondence, and the answer to one hypothesis is only another.

SELECTED READINGS

A.   Commentaries and Critiques

Berreman, Gerald
1966 Anemic and emetic analyses in social anthropology. *American Anthropologist,* 68: 346–354.

Burling, Robbins
1964 Cognition and componential analysis: God's truth or hocus pocus? *American Anthropologist,* 66: 20–28.

Graburn, Nelson H. H.
1964 Taqagmiut Eskimo kinship terminology. *Northern Coordination and Research Center-64-1.* Ottawa: Dept. of Northern Affairs and National Resources, ch. XI.

Hammel, Eugene A.
1965 Introduction. In E. A. Hammel (ed.), Formal semantic analysis. *American Anthropologist,* 67: 5 (Part 2): 1–8. Special Publication.

Harris, Marvin
1968 *The rise of anthropological theory: A history of theories of culture.* New York: Thomas Y. Crowell, pp. 568–603.

Kay, Paul
1966 Comment on Colby's Ethnographic semantics: A preliminary survey. *Current anthropology,* 7: 1: 20–23.

Wallace, Anthony F. C., and John Atkins
1960 The meaning of kinship terms. *American Anthropologist,* 62: 58–80.

B.   Original Works

Bloomfield, Leonard
1933 *Language.* New York: Holt, Rinehart and Winston.

Burling, Robbins
1965 Burmese kinship terminology. In E. A.

Hammel (ed.). Formal semantic analysis. *American Anthropologist*, 67:5 (Part 2):106–117. Special Publication.

D'Andrade, Roy
1965 Trait psychology and componential analysis. In Hammel (ed.), 1965, pp. 215–218.

Davis, Kingsley, and W. Lloyd Warner
1937 The structural analysis of kinship. *American Anthropologist*, 39:91–313.

Friedrich, Paul
1964 Semantic structure and social structure: An instance from Russian. In W. Goodenough (ed.), *Explorations in cultural anthropology*. N.Y.: McGraw-Hill, pp. 111–130.

Geoghegan, William
1970 Information processing systems in culture. In P. Kay (ed.), *Explorations in mathematical anthropology*. Cambridge: M.I.T. Press.

Goodenough, Ward H.
1951 Property, kin, and community: The social organization on Truk. *Yale University Publications in Anthropology*, No. 46.
——— 1956a Componential analysis and the study of meaning. *Language*, 32:195–216.
——— 1965 Yankee kinship terminology: A problem in componential analysis. In E. A. Hammel (ed.), Formal semantic analysis. *American Anthropologist*, 67:5 (Part 2): 259–287. Special Publication.

Graburn, Nelson H. H.
1964 Taqagmiut Eskimo kinship terminology. Northern Coordination and Research Centre-64–1. Ottawa: Dept. of Northern Affairs and National Resources.

Hammel, Eugene A.
1964 Further comments on componential analysis. *American Anthropologist*, 66: 1167–1171.
——— 1965 (ed.) Formal semantic analysis. *American Anthropologist*, 67:5 (Part 2). Special Publication.

Kroeber, Alfred L.
1909 Classificatory systems of relationship. *Journal of the Royal Anthropological Institute*, 39: 77–84.

Leach, Edmund R.
1945 Jinghpaw kinship terminology. *Journal of the Royal Anthropological Institute*, 75: 77–84. Reprinted in E. R. Leach, *Rethinking Anthropology*. London: Athlone.
——— 1958 Concerning Trobriand clans and the kinship category *Tabu*. In J. Goody (ed.), The developmental cycle in domestic groups. *Cam-*

bridge Papers in Social Anthropology, No. 1. Cambridge: Cambridge University Press, pp. 120–145.

Lounsbury, Floyd G.
1956 A semantic analysis of Pawnee kinship usage. *Language*, 32: 158–194.
——— 1964a A formal account of Crow- and Omaha-type kinship terminologies. In W. Goodenough (ed.), *Explorations in cultural anthropology*. N.Y.: McGraw-Hill, pp. 351–393.
——— 1964b The structural analysis of kinship semantics. In H. G. Hunt (ed.), *Proceedings of the 9th International Congress of Linguists*. The Hague: Mouton, pp. 1073–1092.
——— 1965 Another view of Trobriand kinship categories. In E. A. Hammel (ed.), Formal semantic analysis. *American Anthropologist*, 67: 5 (Part 2): 143–187. Special Publication.

Morris, Charles
1946 *Signs, language and behavior*. New York: Prentice-Hall.

Pospisil, Leopold
1964 Law and societal structure among the Nunamiut Eskimo. In W. Goodenough (ed.), *Explorations in cultural anthropology*. N.Y.: McGraw-Hill, pp. 395–432.

Romney, A. Kimball, and Roy D'Andrade
1964 Cognitive aspects of English kin terms. *American Anthropologist*, 66: 3 (Part 2): 146–170.

Sapir, Edward
1921 *Language*. New York: Harcourt Brace Jovanovich. Harvest Book, 1949.

Schneider, David M.
1965b American kin terms and terms for kinsmen. In E. A. Hammel (ed.), Formal semantic analysis. *American Anthropologist*, 67: 5 (Part 2): 288–308. Special Publication.

Schneider, David M., and George C. Homans
1955 Kinship terminology and the American kinship system. *American Anthropologist*, 57: 1194–1208.

Schneider, David M., and John M. Roberts
1956 *Zuni kin terms*. Notebook No. 3. Lincoln, Neb.: University of Nebraska Laboratory of Anthropology.

Wallace, Anthony F. C.
1965 The problem of psychological validity of componential analysis. In E. A. Hammel (ed.), Formal semantic analysis. *American Anthropologist*, 67: 5 (Part 2): 229–248. Special Publication.

The concept of role has long been present in lay ideas on the nature of society. Implicit in this concept is the notion that life is a drama and that individuals, throughout their lives, play parts in this drama, as Shakespeare explicitly expressed it. Similarly, the idea of status or "position" is also part of our folk notions about society. Here, however, the concept is comparative in that the "more" status one has, the "higher" is the position that one occupies in a hierarchically organized social system. The social scientific use of status shares the notion of position in a social network or pattern but, does not equate status with power or elevated prestige. Maine (1861) (see chapter III) was one of the first to use this notion of status and to distinguish between societies or social relations where one's position in the society (i.e., one's status) is determined at birth ("ascribed") and those in which one's position may depend upon one's actions during one's lifetime ("achieved"). The division of the world's societies into those two fundamentally different types was followed later by Tönnies and even Durkheim.

During the first three decades of this century, the notions of status and role were not thoroughly examined in social anthropology and were rarely used in precise ways. Nevertheless, these concepts were implicit in the discussions of anthropologists concerned with social relationships and social structure. For example, Radcliffe-Brown conceived of social structure (1952a: 191) as a set of actually existing social relationships of which the basic unit was the dyadic relationship, i.e., the relationship between any two people. Each individual in the dyad, in this structural framework, had a set of rights and duties with respect to the other person. Thus, social structure was seen as a network of social persons bound together by normatively specified rights and duties.

It was from this position that Linton, a student of Boas (*The Study of Man*, 1936), took off. Linton's major contribution was a clarification of the nature of status and role. He pointed out that if status were the position an individual occupied in the total social network, the individual would have to have a number of "statuses" with respect to every other individual with whom he shared a normative relationship in the pattern or network. With respect to each other individual, the person had certain rights and duties and, therefore, the person's total status was the sum of his total collection of rights and duties in that society. Linton further pointed out that rights and duties are only potentials and that role, therefore, is the "dynamic aspect of status," that is, the actions normatively performed by each social person towards other social persons, to whom he is related by certain rights and duties. Obviously, the total role is the collection of all social actions; and the role vis-à-vis one other person is the actions of that social person performed as part of the reciprocal interaction between the members of the social dyad.

American sociologists following Linton (1936) and Mead (1934), found the notion of role and, to a lesser extent, that of status—often called position—useful in their analyses of Western society. The concept expanded to include role, role expectations—the expectations of a social person vis-à-vis the other person in the relationship—role perception—how one sees one's role —and role performance—how, normatively, the person carried out his rights and duties: In fact, contemporary sociologists have developed a whole set of working propositions, called role theory. Role theory is one sociological method of examining the nature of the social system (see T. Parsons; Sarbin; Merton, 1957a, 1957b). Merton, one of the leading American sociologists, further refined the notion of role by introducing the idea of the role set, which is a refinement of Linton's (1936) ideas. Merton proposed that each social status (vis-à-vis another social person) is associated not with a single role but, rather, a whole array of roles, and that this set of roles is a basic feature of social structure

Nadel, a student of Malinowski, much influenced by the structural ideas of Radcliffe-Brown, tried to develop a whole logical theory of society in his book on *Social Structure* (1957), published posthumously. Examining critically the notions of social structure used by various different anthropologists, he attempted to build a new model of the nature of society using role, that is, expected ways of acting towards another social person, as the basic unit. Developing formal notions from this basis, he examined the nature of structure, pattern, and network and went on to differentiate among different kinds of roles in a society, particularly those that are necessary, and those that are incidental. Although the book was probably not as refined as it would have been had Nadel seen it through to publication himself, it has had a lasting influence on social theorists.

The Chicago school of sociologists, influence by Merton, Redfield, and Robert Park, further developed the notion of social life as a drama involving the idea that people may be seen as "actors" playing "roles." Goffman (*The Presentation of Self in Everyday Life,* 1959) has been a leader among these writers and the resulting branch of Sociology-Anthropology has come to be known as "interaction theory." Interaction theory concentrates upon the examination of social life in terms of "encounters" between social persons in particular situations. Abandoning the more static anthropological concepts of people playing normative, culturally defined roles, interaction theorists have shown how individuals modify their behavior in terms of their perceptions of situations, their self-perceptions, and their perceptions of how the other social person expects them to act. Thus, interaction theory resembles, in many ways, a detailed study of "face," the mechanisms by which a social person chooses what role to play in each situation. These detailed studies have been performed, mainly, in institutions of Western society, such as hospitals, mental institutions, small group encounters, power relationships, and so on. Berreman (*Behind Many Masks,* 1962) used this kind of approach to advantage in his analysis of a field situation in which he described the "faces" or roles put on by the anthropologist and by various informants in Himalayan India.

More recently, Goodenough, a student of Murdock, attempted to refine ("Rethinking Status and Role," 1964) the concepts of status and role in anthropology, illustrating his contentions from his well-known Truk material. Goodenough was able to show that dyadic roles are not entirely different from each other, but form a continuum; the differences are certain culturally diagnostic expected behaviors. Thus, kin roles, for example, can be scaled according to the presence or absence of these particular features. In order to do this, Goodenough differentiated between status as a bundle of rights and duties, and the social "positions," *social identities,* as he calls them, associated with each status and bundle. Consequently, as a general rule, he makes the useful distinction between "rights, duties, privileges, powers, liabilities, and immunities and *identity relationships.*" Each person has a number of social identities, vis-à-vis other people and a social identity is "an aspect of self that makes a difference in how one's rights and duties distribute to specific others." While agreement is not complete on how to use the concepts of status and role, and their various derivatives, in social anthropology, the variety of approaches now available gives us some powerful tools for our analysis of social systems and social behavior.

STATUS AND ROLE

Ralph Linton

In the preceding chapter we discussed the nature of society and pointed out that the functioning of societies depends upon the presence of patterns for reciprocal behavior between individuals or groups of individuals. The polar positions in such patterns of reciprocal behavior are technically known as *statuses*. The term *status*, like the term *culture*, has come to be used with a double significance. A *status*, in the abstract, is a position in a particular pattern. It is thus quite correct to speak of each individual as having many statuses, since each individual participates in the expression of a number of patterns. However, unless the term is qualified in some way, the *status* of any individual means the sum total of all the statuses which he occupies. It represents his position with relation to the total society. Thus the status of Mr. Jones as a member of his community derives from a combination of all the statuses which he holds as a citizen, as an attorney, as a Mason, as a Methodist, as Mrs. Jones' husband, and so on.

A status, as distinct from the individual who may occupy it, is simply a collection of rights and duties. Since these rights and duties can find expression only through the medium of individuals, it is extremely hard for us to maintain a distinction in our thinking between statuses and the people who hold them and exercise the rights and duties which constitute them. The relation between any individual and any status he holds is somewhat like that between the driver of an automobile and the driver's place in the machine. The driver's seat with its steering wheel, accelerator, and other controls is a constant with ever-present potentialities for action and control, while the driver may be any member of the family and may exercise these potentialities very well or very badly.

A *role* represents the dynamic aspect of a status. The individual is socially assigned to a status and occupies it with relation to other statuses. When he puts the rights and duties which constitute the status into effect, he is performing a role. Role and status are quite inseparable, and the distinction between them is of only academic interest. There are no roles without statuses **or** statuses without roles. Just as in the case of *status*, the term *role* is used with a double significance. Every individual has **a** series of roles deriving from the various patterns in which he participates and at the same time *a role*, general, which represents the sum total of these roles and determines what he does for his society and what he can expect from it.

Although all statuses and roles derive from social patterns and are integral parts of patterns, they have an independent function with relation to the individuals who occupy particular statuses and exercise their roles. To such individuals the combined status and role represent the minimum of attitudes and behavior which he must assume if he is to participate in the overt expression of the pattern. Status and role serve to reduce the ideal patterns for social life to individual terms. They become models for organizing the attitudes and behavior of the individual so that these will be congruous with those of the other individuals participating in the expression of the pattern. Thus if we are studying football teams in the abstract, the position of quarterback is meaningless except in relation to the other positions. From the point of view of the quarter-back himself it is a distinct and important entity. It determines where he shall take his place in the line-up and what he shall do in various plays. His assignment to this position at once limits and defines his activities and establishes a minimum of things which he must learn. Similarly, in a social pattern such as that for the employer-employee relationship the statuses of employer and employee define what each has to know and do to put the pattern into operation. The employer does not need to know the techniques involved in the employee's labor, and the employee does not need to know the techniques for marketing or accounting.

It is obvious that, as long as there is no interference from external sources, the more perfectly the members of any society are adjusted to their statuses and roles the more smoothly the society will function. In its attempts to bring about such adjustments every society finds itself caught on the horns of a dilemma. The individual's formation of habits and attitudes begins at birth, and, other things being equal, the earlier his training for a status can begin the more successful it is likely to be. At the same time, no two individuals are alike, and a status which will be congenial to one may be quite uncongenial to another. Also, there are in all social systems certain roles which require more than training for their successful performance. Perfect technique does not make a great violinist, nor a thorough book knowledge of tactics an efficient general. The utilization of the special gifts of individuals may be highly important to society, as in the case of the general, yet these gifts usually show themselves rather late, and to wait upon their manifestation for the assignment of statuses would be to forfeit the advantages to be derived from commencing training early.

Fortunately human beings are so mutable that almost any normal individual can be trained to the adequate performance of almost any role. Most of the business of living can be conducted on a basis of habit, with little need for intelligence and none for special gifts. Societies have met the dilemma by developing two types of statuses, the *ascribed* and the *achieved*. *Ascribed* statuses are those which are assigned to individuals without reference to their innate differences or abilities. They can be predicted and trained for from the moment of birth. The achieved statuses are, as a minimum, those requiring special qualities, although they are not necessarily limited to these. They are not assigned to individuals from birth but are left open to be filled through competition and individual effort. The majority of the statuses in all social

systems are of the ascribed type and those which take care of the ordinary day-to-day business of living are practically always of this type.

In all societies certain things are selected as reference points for the ascription of status. The things chosen for this purpose are always of such a nature that they are ascertainable at birth, making it possible to begin the training of the individual for his potential statuses and roles at once. The simplest and most universally used of these reference points is sex. Age is used with nearly equal frequency, since all individuals pass through the same cycle of growth, maturity, and decline, and the statuses whose occupation will be determined by age can be forecast and trained for with accuracy. Family relationships, the simplest and most obvious being that of the child to its mother, are also used in all societies as reference points for the establishment of a whole series of statuses. Lastly, there is the matter of birth into a particular socially established group, such as class or caste. The use of this type of reference is common but not universal. In all societies the actual ascription of statuses to the individual is controlled by a series of these reference points which together serve to delimit the field of his future participation in the life of the group.

The division and ascription of statuses with relation to sex seems to be basic in all social systems. All societies prescribe different attitudes and activities to men and to women. Most of them try to rationalize these prescriptions in terms of the physiological differences between the sexes or their different roles in reproduction. However, a comparative study of the statuses ascribed to women and men in different cultures seems to show that while such factors may have served as a starting point for the development of a division the actual ascriptions are almost entirely determined by culture. Even the psychological characteristics ascribed to men and women in different societies vary so much that they can have little physiological basis. Our own idea of women as ministering angels contrasts sharply with the ingenuity of women as torturers among the Iroquois and the sadistic delight they took in the process. Even the last two generations have seen a sharp change in the psychological patterns for women in our own society. The delicate, fainting lady of the middle eighteen-hundreds is as extinct as the dodo.

When it comes to the ascription of occupations, which is after all an integral part of status, we find the differences in various societies even more marked. Arapesh women regularly carry heavier loads than men "because their heads are so much harder and stronger." In some societies women do most of the manual labor; in others, as in the Marquesas, even cooking, housekeeping, and baby-tending are proper male occupations, and women spend most of their time primping. Even the general rule that women's handicap through pregnancy and nursing indicates the more active occupations as male and the less active ones as female has many exceptions. Thus among the Tasmanians seal-hunting was women's work. They swam out to the seal rocks, stalked the animals, and clubbed them. Tasmanian women also hunted opossums, which required the climbing of large trees.

Although the actual ascription of occupations along sex lines is highly variable, the pattern of sex division is constant. There are very few societies in which every important activity has not been definitely assigned to men or to women. Even when the two sexes cooperate in a particular occupation, the field of each is usually clearly delimited. Thus in Madagascar rice culture the men make the seed beds and terraces and prepare the fields for transplanting. The women do the work of transplanting, which is hard and backbreaking. The women weed the crop, but the men harvest it. The women then carry it to the threshing floors, where the men thresh it while the women winnow it. Lastly, the women pound the grain in mortars and cook it. . . .

The use of age as a reference point for establishing status is as universal as the use of sex. All societies recognize three age groupings as a minimum: child, adult, and old. Certain societies have emphasized age as a basis for assigning status and have greatly amplified the divisions. Thus in certain African tribes the whole male population is divided into units composed of those born in the same years or within two- or three-year intervals. However, such extreme attention to age is unusual, and we need not discuss it here.

The physical differences between child and adult are easily recognizable, and passage from childhood to maturity is marked by physiological events which make it possible to date it exactly for girls and a few weeks or months for boys. However, the physical passage from childhood to maturity does not necessarily coincide with the social transfer of the individual from one category to the other. Thus in our own society both men and women remain legally children until long after they are physically adult. In most societies this difference between the physical and social transfer is more clearly marked than in our own. The child becomes a man not when he is physically mature but when he is formally recognized as a man by his society. This recognition is almost always given ceremonial expression in what are technically known as puberty rites. The most important element in these rites is not the determination of physical maturity but that of social maturity. Whether a boy is able to breed is less vital to his society than whether he is able to do a man's work and has a man's knowledge. Actually, most puberty ceremonies include tests of the boy's learning and fortitude, and if the aspirants are unable to pass these they are left in the child status until they can. For those who pass the tests, the ceremonies usually culminate in the transfer to them of certain secrets which the men guard from women and children.

The passage of individuals from adult to aged is harder to perceive. There is no clear physiological line for men, while even women may retain their full physical vigor and their ability to carry on all the activities of the adult status for several years after the menopause. The social transfer of men from the adult to the aged group is given ceremonial recognition in a few cultures, as when a father formally surrenders his official position and titles to his son, but such recognition is rare. As for women, there appears to be no society in which the menopause is given ceremonial recognition, although there are a few societies in which it does alter the individual's status. Thus Comanche women, after the menopause, were released from their disabilities with regard to the supernatural. They could handle sacred objects, obtain power through dreams and practise as shamans, all things forbidden to women of bearing age.

The general tendency for societies to emphasize the individual's first change in age status and largely ignore the second is no doubt due in part to the difficulty of determining the onset of old age. However, there are also psychological factors involved. The boy or girl is usually anxious to grow up, and this eagerness is heightened by the exclusion of children from certain activities and knowledge. Also, society welcomes new additions to the most active division of the group, that which contributes most to its perpetuation and well-being. Conversely, the individual who enjoys the thought of growing old is atypical in all societies. Even when age brings respect and a new measure of influence, it means the relinquishment of much that is pleasant. We can see among ourselves that the aging usually refuse to recognize the change until long after it has happened.

In the case of age, as in that of sex, the biological factors involved appear to be secondary to the cultural ones in determining the content of status. There are certain activities which cannot be ascribed to children because children either lack the necessary strength or have not had time to acquire the necessary technical skills. However, the attitudes between parent and child and the importance given to the child in the family structure vary enormously from one culture to another. The status of the child among our Puritan ancestors, where he was seen and not heard and ate at the second table, represents one extreme. At the other might be placed the status of the eldest son of a Polynesian chief. All the *mana* (supernatural power) of the royal line converged upon such a child. He was socially superior to his own father and mother, and any attempt to discipline him would have been little short of sacrilege. I once visited the hereditary chief of a Marquesan tribe and found the whole family camping uncomfortably in their own front yard, although they had a good house built

on European lines. Their eldest son, aged nine, had had a dispute with his father a few days before and had tabooed the house by naming it after his head. The family had thus been compelled to move out and could not use it again until he relented and lifted the taboo. As he could use the house himself and eat anywhere in the village, he was getting along quite well and seemed to enjoy the situation thoroughly.

The statuses ascribed to the old in various societies vary even more than those ascribed to children. In some cases they are relieved of all heavy labor and can settle back comfortably to live off their children. In others they perform most of the hard and monotonous tasks which do not require great physical strength, such as the gathering of firewood. In many societies the old women, in particular, take over most of the care of the younger children, leaving the younger women free to enjoy themselves. In some places the old are treated with consideration and respect; in others they are considered a useless incumbrance and removed as soon as they are incapable of heavy labor. In most societies their advice is sought even when little attention is paid to their wishes. This custom has a sound practical basis, for the individual who contrives to live to old age in an uncivilized group has usually been a person of ability and his memory constitutes a sort of reference library to which one can turn for help under all sorts of circumstances.

. . .

Before passing on, it might be well to mention still another social status which is closely related to the foregoing. This is the status of the dead. We do not think of the dead as still members of the community, and many societies follow us in this, but there are others in which death is simply another transfer, comparable to that from child to adult. When a man dies, he does not leave his society; he merely surrenders one set of rights and duties and assumes another. Thus a Tanala clan has two sections which are equally real to its members, the living and the dead. In spite of rather half-hearted attempts by the living to explain to the dead that they are dead and to discourage their return, they remain an integral part of the clan. They must be informed of all important events, invited to all clan ceremonies, and remembered at every meal. In return they allow themselves to be consulted, take an active and helpful interest in the affairs of the community, and act as highly efficient guardians of the group's mores. They carry over into their new status the conservatism characteristic of the aged, and their invisible presence and constant watchfulness does more than anything else to ensure the good behavior of the living and to discourage innovations. In a neighboring tribe there are even individual statuses among the dead which are open to achievement. Old Betsileo men and women will often promise that, after their deaths, they will give the living specific forms of help in return for specified offerings. After the death of one of these individuals, a monument will be erected and people will come to pray and make offerings there. If the new ghost performs his functions successfully, his worship may grow into a cult and may even have a priest. If he fails in their performance, he is soon forgotten.

Biological relationships are used to determine some statuses in all societies. The mere fact of birth immediately brings the individual within the scope of a whole series of social patterns which relate him to his parents, either real or ascribed, his brothers and sisters, and his parents' relatives. The biological basis for the ascription of these family statuses is likely to blind us to the fact that the physiological factors which may influence their content are almost exactly the same as those affecting the content of sex and age statuses. While there is a special relationship between the young child and its mother, based on the child's dependence on nursing, even this is soon broken off. After the second year any adult woman can do anything for the child that its mother can do, while any adult male can assume the complete role of the father at any time after the child is conceived. Similarly, the physiological factors which might affect the statuses of uncle and nephew, uncle and niece, or brother and sister are identical with those affecting the relations of persons in different age or sex groupings. This lack of physiological de-terminants may be responsible in part for the extraordinarily wide range of variation in the contents of the statuses ascribed on the basis of biological relationship in various societies.

Actually, the statuses associated with even such a close biological relationship as that of brother and sister are surprisingly varied. In some societies the two are close intimates. In others they avoid each other carefully and cannot even speak to each other except in the presence of a third party who relays the questions and answers. In some systems the eldest child ranks the others regardless of sex and must be respected and obeyed by them. In others the question of dominance is left to be settled by the children themselves, while in still others the youngest child ranks all those who preceded him. Practically every possible arrangement is represented in one society or another, suggesting that we have here a free field for variation, one in which one arrangement will work quite as well as another. The same sort of wide variation is found in the context of all the other statuses based on blood relationship with the exception of those relating to mother and child, and even here there is a fair degree of variation. There are a number of societies in which there is a more or less conscious attempt to break up the child's habits of dependence upon the mother and to alienate the child from her in order to bring it into closer association with its father's relatives. The child is taught that its mother really is not a member of the family, and hostility between mother and child is encouraged.

Not only do the statuses assigned by different societies to persons standing in the same blood relationships vary markedly, but there is also a high degree of variation in the sorts of blood relationship which are recognized and used as reference points for the assignment of status. Some societies, like our own, tend to recognize only close relatives and to be vague as to the reciprocal rights and duties of any relationship more remote than first cousin. Others select the line of the mother or the father and utilize relationships in this line to remote degrees while ignoring all but the closest relationships in the other line. In a very few cases relationship in both lines is recognized to remote degree, with a consequent assignment of status. Where this is the case the status based on relationship may actually include a whole tribe and determine the mutual rights and duties of all its members. Thus in certain Australian groups recognized blood relationships are extended to include not only the whole tribe but numerous individuals in other tribes as well. It is said that when a stranger visits such a tribe the old men investigate his genealogy until they find some point in common with one of the genealogies within their own group. When such a point of contact has been established, they can determine the relationship of the newcomer to all the various members of their own group and assign him a series of statuses which immediately fit him into the social body. If they are unable to find such a common point of relationship, they usually kill the stranger simply because they do not know what else to do with him. They have no reference points other than blood relationships by which statuses might be assigned to him.

There is another type of biologically conditioned relationship which is recognized in practically all societies. This is the relationship arising from the more or less continuous sexual association of individuals, i.e., marriage. The real importance of such associations lies in their continuity, in social recognition, and in the new series of blood relationships to which they give rise through the offspring which they produce. Casual or temporary sexual associations usually receive only a negative recognition from society, being ignored when not actually reprehended. Patterns may be developed to govern the behavior of individuals in such casual associations, but these patterns are usually extremely limited in their scope. They only affect the individuals who are directly involved and do not establish new statuses for the members of the families to which the contracting parties belong. Marriage, on the other hand, always establishes a series of such statuses. Thus the parents of a man and his mistress do not become parties to any reciprocal pattern of rights and duties, while the parents of a man and his wife always do become parties to such a pattern.

While relationships arising from sexual association are intrinsically different from those deriving from blood relationships, the two types have become interrelated in all societies. Blood relationships are everywhere used as reference points for delimiting the group of individuals within which marriage relationships may be contracted. This regulation is usually of a negative sort, certain blood relatives being prohibited from marrying but at the same time permitted freedom of choice among individuals not standing in these relationships. However, there are a fair number of societies in which such regulations assume a positive aspect. In such societies a man is not only forbidden to marry certain female relatives, such as his mother or sister, but is also enjoined to marry within a particular group of female relatives, as his mother's brother's or father's sister's daughters. In some cases these prescriptions are so strong that a man may have no alternatives except to marry a particular woman or remain a bachelor.

. . .

The bulk of the ascribed statuses in all social systems are parceled out to individuals on the basis of sex, age, and family relationships. However, there are many societies in which purely social factors are also used as a basis of ascription. There seems to be a general tendency for societies to divide their component individuals into a series of groups or categories and to ascribe to such categories differing degrees of social importance. Such divisions may originate in many different ways. They may grow out of individual differences in technical skill or other abilities, as in the case of craft groups or the aristocracies of certain Indian tribes, membership in which was determined by the individual's war record. They may also originate through the conscious formation of some social unit, such as the first college fraternity or the first business men's club, which is usually followed by the formation of a series of similar units organized upon nearly the same lines. Lastly, such divisions may originate through the subjugation of one society by another society, with the subsequent fusion of both into a single functional unit, as in the case of Old World aristocracies deriving from conquest. Even when the social divisions originate in individual differences of ability, there seems to be a strong tendency for such divisions to become hereditary. The members of a socially favored division try to transmit the advantages they have gained to their offspring and at the same time to prevent the entry into the division of individuals from lower divisions. In many cases these tendencies result in the organization of the society into a series of hereditary classes or castes. Such hereditary units are always used as reference points for the ascription of status.

The factor of social class or caste rarely if ever replaces the factors of sex, age, and biological relationship in the determination of status. Rather, it supplements these, defining the roles of individuals still more clearly. Where the class system is strong, each class becomes almost a society in itself. It will have a series of sex, age, and relationship statuses which are peculiar to its members. These will differ from the statuses of other classes even when both are determined by the same biological factors.

Not only is the commoner debarred from the occupation of aristocratic statuses, but the aristocrat is similarly debarred from the occupation of common statuses. It may be mentioned in passing that this arrangement is not always entirely to the advantage of the members of the upper class. During the nineteenth century the aristocratic prohibition against engaging in trade condemned many aristocrats to genteel poverty.

THE ROLE-SET:
PROBLEMS IN SOCIOLOGICAL THEORY

Robert K. Merton

THE PROBLEMATICS OF THE ROLE-SET

However much they may differ in other respects, contemporary sociological theorists are largely at one in adopting the premise that social statuses and social roles comprise major building blocks of social structure. This has been the case, since the influential writings of Ralph Linton on the subject, a generation ago. By status, and T. H. Marshall has indicated the great diversity of meanings attached to this term since the time of Maine, Linton meant a position in a social system involving designated rights and obligations; by role, the behaviour oriented to these patterned expectations of others. In these terms, status and roles become concepts serving to connect culturally defined expectations with the patterned conduct and relationships which make up a social

Reprinted by permission of the author and of Routledge & Kegan Paul from the *British Journal of Sociology*, Vol. 8 (1957), pp. 110–113.

structure. Linton went on to state the long recognized and basic fact that each person in society inevitably occupies multiple statuses and that each of these statuses has an associated role.

It is at this point that I find it useful to depart from Linton's conception. The difference is initially a small one, some might say so small as not to deserve notice, but it involves a shift in the angle of vision which leads, I believe, to successively greater differences of a fundamental kind. Unlike Linton, I begin with the premise that each social status involves not a single associated role, but an array of roles. This basic feature of social structure can be registered by the distinctive but not formidable term, role-set. To repeat, then, by role-set I mean that complement of role-relationships in which persons are involved by virtue of occupying a particular social status. Thus, in our current studies of medical schools, we have begun with the view that the status of medical student entails not only the role of a student *vis-à-vis* his teachers, but also an array of other roles relating him diversely to other students, physicians, nurses, social workers, medical technicians, and the like. Again, the status of school teacher in the United States has its distinctive role-set, in which are found pupils, colleagues, the school principal and superintendant, the Board of Education, professional associations, and, on occasion, local patriotic organizations.

It should be made plain that the role-set differs from what sociologists have long described as 'multiple roles.' By established usage, the term multiple role refers not to the complex of roles associated with a single social status, but with the various social statuses (often in differing institutional spheres) in which people find themselves—for illustration, the statuses of physician, husband, father, professor, church elder, Conservative Party member and army captain. (This complement of distinct statuses of a person, each of these in turn having its own role-set, I would designate as a status-set. This concept gives rise to its own range of analytical problems which cannot be considered here.)

The notion of the role-set reminds us, in the unlikely event that we need to be reminded of this obstinate fact, that even the seemingly simple social structure is fairly complex. All societies face the functional problem of articulating the components of numerous role-sets, the functional problem of managing somehow to organize these so that an appreciable degree of social regularity obtains, sufficient to enable most people most of the time to go about their business of social life, without encountering extreme conflict in their role-sets as the normal, rather than the exceptional, state of affairs.

If this relatively simple idea of role-set has any theoretical worth, it should at the least generate distinctive problems for sociological theory, which come to our attention only from the perspective afforded by this idea, or by one like it. This the notion of role-set does. It raises the general problem of identifying the social mechanisms which serve to articulate the expectations of those in the role-set so that the occupant of a status is confronted with less conflict than would

obtain if these mechanisms were not at work. It is to these social mechanisms that I would devote the rest of this discussion.

Before doing so, I should like to recapitulate the argument thus far. We depart from the simple idea, unlike that which has been rather widely assumed, that a single status in society involves, not a single role, but an array of associated rules, relating the status-occupant to diverse others. Secondly, we note that this structural fact, expressed in the term role-set, gives rise to distinctive analytical problems and to corresponding questions for empirical inquiry. The basic problem, which I deal with here, is that of identifying social mechanisms, that is, processes having designated effects for designated parts of the social structure, which serve to articulate the role-set more nearly than would be the case, if these mechanisms did not operate. Third, unlike the problems centred upon the notion of 'multiple roles', this one is concerned with social arrangements integrating the expectations of those in the role-set; it is not primarily concerned with the familiar problem of how the occupant of a status manages to cope with the many, and sometimes conflicting, demands made of him. It is thus a problem of social structure, not an exercise in the no doubt important but different problem of how individuals happen to deal with the complex structures of relations in which they find themselves. Finally, by way of setting the analytical problem, the logic of analysis exhibited in this case is developed wholly in terms of the elements of social structure, rather than in terms of providing concrete historical description of a social system.

All this presupposes, of course, that there is always a *potential* for differing and sometimes conflicting expectations of the conduct appropriate to a status-occupant among those in the role-set. The basic source of this potential for conflict, I suggest—and here we are at one with theorists as disparate as Marx and Spencer, Simmel and Parsons—is that the members of a role-set are, to some degree, apt to hold social positions differing from that of the occupant of the status in question. To the extent that they are diversely located in the social structure, they are apt to have interests and sentiments, values and moral expectations differing from those of the status-occupant himself. This, after all, is one of the principal assumptions of Marxist theory, as it is of all sociological theory: social differentiation generates distinct interests among those variously located in the structure of the society. To continue with one of our examples: the members of a school board are often in social and economic strata which differ greatly from that of the school teacher; and their interests, values and expectations are consequently apt to differ, to some extent, from those of the teacher. The teacher may thus become subject to conflicting role-expectations among such members of his role-set as professional colleagues, influential members of the school board, and, say, the Americanism Committee of the American Legion. What is an educational essential for the one may be judged as an education frill, or as downright subversion, by the other. These disparate and contradictory evaluations by members of the role-set greatly complicate the task of coping with them all. The familiar case of the teacher may be taken as paradigmatic. What holds conspicuously for this one status holds, in varying degree, for the occupants of all other statuses who are structurally related, through their role-set, to others who themselves occupy diverse positions in society.

• • •

STRUCTURE, NETWORK, PATTERN AND ROLE

S. F. Nadel

We begin with the most general definition of 'structure' which underlies the use of the term in all other disciplines. There structure is a property of empirical data—of objects, events or series of events—something they exhibit or prove to possess on observation or analysis; and the data are said to exhibit structure inasmuch as they exhibit a definable articulation, an ordered arrangement of parts. Indicating articulation or arrangement, that is, formal characteristics, structure may be contrasted with *function* (meaning by this term, briefly, adequacy in regard to some stipulated effectiveness) and with *content, material* or *qualitative character*. The former contrast is too familiar to need illustration; the latter has a wide application in psychology, linguistics, and logic.

It should be noted in passing that in two instances at least 'social structure' is explicitly

Reprinted with the permission of The Macmillan Company from *The Theory of Social Structure* by S. F. Nadel. Copyright 1957 by The Free Press, Pp. 7–19. Also published by Routledge & Kegan Paul, Ltd., London.

denied to have the character here envisaged, that is, to be a feature of 'empirical reality.' This view, expressed by Lévi-Strauss and Leach, will be discussed later (see p. 149). For the sake of completeness, we should add a third dichotomy to the two mentioned, i.e. *structure* and *process;* but this point, too, may at this stage be disregarded.

While the separation of structure from function implies a divergence of viewpoint and interest, the separation of structure from content, material, and qualitative character implies a move to a higher level of abstraction. For when describing structure we abstract relational features from the totality of the perceived data, ignoring all that is not 'order' or 'arrangement'; in brief, we define the positions relative to one another of the component parts. Thus I can describe the structure of a tetrahedron without mentioning whether it is a crystal, a wooden block, or a soup cube; I can describe the arrangement of a fugue or sonata without making any musical noises myself; and I can describe a syntactic order without referring to the phonetic material or semantic content of the words so ordered.

This has an important consequence, namely that structures can be transposed irrespective of the concrete data manifesting it [sic.]; differently expressed, the parts composing any structure can vary widely in their concrete character without changing the identity of the structure. Our definition should thus be rephrased as follows: structure indicates an ordered arrangement of parts, which can be treated as transposable, being relatively invariant, while the parts themselves are variable. This definition, incidentally, fully corresponds to the one logicians would apply in their field: there too one speaks of an 'identical structure' in the case of any 'abstract set' which 'may have more than one concrete representation,' the latter being potentially 'extremely unlike in material content.' (Cohen and Nagel 1947: 29).

Now to translate all this into the language appropriate to the analysis of societies. There is an immediate difficulty; for it is by no means easy to say precisely what a 'society' is. But whatever we may wish to include in a sophisticated definition of society, certain things are clear and can be stated quite simply. To begin with, societies are made up of people; societies have boundaries, people either belonging to them or not; and people belong to a society in virtue of rules under which they stand and which impose on them regular, determinate ways of acting towards and in regard to one another. Conceivably, in theory, there might be as many such ways of acting as there are situations in which people meet, practically an infinite number. But we are here speaking of ways of acting governed by rules and hence in some measure stereotyped (or rendered 'determinate'). And of the ways of acting so understood it is true to say that they are finite and always less numerous than the possible combinations of people: which means that the same ways of acting are repetitive in the population. We need only add that these ways of acting are repetitive also in the sense that they apply to changing or successive populations.

Let me expand this a little. For 'determinate ways of acting towards or in regard to one another' we usually say 'relationships,' and we indicate that they follow from rules by calling them 'institutionalized' or 'social' (as against 'private' or 'personal') relationships. We identify the mutual ways of acting of individuals as 'relationships' only when the former exhibit some consistency and constancy, since without these attributes they would merely be single or disjointed acts. But what is constant or consistent is not really the concrete behaviour, with its specific quality or content. If it were so, the individuals involved in any relationship would have to act vis-à-vis one another always in precisely the same manner. Now we may disregard that inevitable variability which comes into play when actions, even though intended to be identical, are repeated on different occasions and in varying circumstances. There remain a few approximations to the kind of relationship which would produce the same uniform behaviour throughout. They are exemplified in relationships which are strictly utilitarian and revolve upon a single purpose, such as the relationship between fellow workers, between shopkeeper and customer, perhaps between teacher and pupil.

Most relationships, however, lack this simple constancy or uniformity. Rather, the concrete behaviour occurring in them will always be diversified and more or less widely variable, intentionally changing with the circumstances; it will be constant or consistent only in its general character, that is, in its capacity to indicate a certain type of mutuality or linkage. We may still say of persons in a given relationship that they act towards each other 'always in the same manner'; but 'manner' should be in the plural, and 'the same' understood very broadly. It is in virtue of this general character or broad 'sameness' that we regard a whole series of genuinely varying ways of acting as adding up to a single ('constant,' 'consistent') relationship. Conversely, any relationship thus identified (and, incidentally, named as aptly as is possible) is understood to signify such a whole series subsumed in it.

Thus we take 'friendship' to be evidenced by a variety of mutual ways of acting, perhaps visible on different occasions, such as help in economic or other crises, mutual advice on various matters, efforts to be together, certain emotional responses. A 'respect relationship' will imply manners of greeting, a particular choice of language, advice sought and given, services offered and expected, etc. The parent-child relationship similarly includes actions exacting respect, behaviour indicative of love and care, and acts of a disciplinary or punitive kind. To say it again, the large majority of social relationships are of this inclusive and serial type (which Gluckman calls 'multiplex') (1954: 19). Differently expressed, each relationship has a whole range of 'concrete representations,' implying them all. Thus, in identifying any relationship we already *abstract* from the qualitatively varying modes of behaviour an invariant relational aspect—the linkage between people they signify.

This can be shown symbolically by indicating the diverse *modes* of behaviour by small letters (a to n), the *condition* 'towards' or 'acting towards' by the sign ':', and the implictness of the modes of behaviour in the relationship by the logical sign for *implication*, '⊃'; we further indicate the fact that a relationship rests not on a single 'way of acting' but a whole range or series by the mathematical symbol for 'series,' Σ. Thus, when we say of any two persons A and B that they stand in a particular relationship r which, for the sake of simplicity, we will assume to be a strictly symmetrical one, we mean that

(1)   A r B, if
      A (a, b, c . . . n): B, and *vice versa;*
      $r \supset \Sigma a \ldots n.$

Firth holds very similar views on the process whereby we identify social relationships, or 'infer' them from some observed sequence of acts: 'We see sufficient elements of likeness to allow us to attribute identity, to abstract and generalize into a type of social relation' (1951b: 21). Let us note, however, that this abstraction and generalization does not go very far. We still need to distinguish relationships or types of relationships qualitatively, by their content of aims, emotions, etc. It is thus that we speak of friendship as against love or loyalty, separate respect from reverence or servitude, or distinguish between relationships having an economic, political, religious or perhaps purely emotive significance.

It is clear, on the other hand, that all relationships, through the linkage or mutuality they signify, serve to 'position,' 'order' or 'arrange' the human material of societies. And considering what we said before about the repetitiveness of relationships in the population, it follows that they do satisfy the criterion of invariance implicit in the concept of structure. They do so in the sense that every relationship has its several 'concrete representations' also in the widely varying individuals who may, at any time, be linked or positioned in the stated fashion.

But relationships are not irregularly repetitive, and the individuals acting in them not variable at random. (We may ignore relationships occurring fortuitously, for example, owing to sympathies or antipathies which happen to affect people: they do not concern us to any great extent since social enquiry is *ex hypothesi* about regularities, not accidents.) Rather, the recurrence of relationships is once more circumscribed by rules, the same set of rules which determines the 'ways of acting' of people towards one another. It is part of these rules that they also specify the type of individuals—any individual satisfying certain conditions or placed in certain circumstances—who can or must act in particular relationships. Expressed more simply, individuals become actors in relationships in virtue of some brief; which brief is obviously as invariant as the relationships that hinge on it. And instead of speaking of individuals 'being actors in virtue of some brief,' we usually speak of individuals enacting *roles.*

This will become clearer a little later. At the moment only one further thing needs saying. Though relationships and roles (more precisely, relationships in virtue of roles) 'arrange' and 'order' the human beings who make up the society, the collection of existing relationships must itself be an orderly one; at least, it must be so if the ordered arrangement of human beings is indeed a total arrangement, running through the whole society. Think of a piece of polyphonic music: any two tones in it are positioned relative to one another by the intervals they describe; but the total design or structure of the piece clearly lies not in the mere presence and collection of all these intervals but in the order in which they appear. Though this analogy has drawbacks, it illustrates the point I wish to make if for intervals we read relationships and for musical structure, social structure.

Oddly enough, this question has rarely been raised, as a question. Most writers on social structure seem content to indicate that it is composed, in some unspecified manner, of persons standing in relationships or of the sum-total of these. Only Lévi-Strauss goes further, insisting that the mere 'ensemble' of existing relationships does not yet amount to 'structure' (see above, p. 5). Like myself, he thus stipulates a further 'order,' over and above the one implicit in the relationships, and interrelating the latter. Let us note that this is not merely a two-level hierarchy of, say, first-order relations (linking and arranging persons) and second-order relations (doing the same with relationships). We are dealing here with differences in kind; the orderliness *of* a plurality of relationships differs radically from the ordering of a plurality of individuals *through* relationship. And whatever the precise nature of the former, we can see that it must correspond to something like an overall system, network or pattern.

We may break off at this point. We now have all the terms needed for a definition of social structure, and we may put it this way: We arrive at the structure of a society through abstracting from the concrete population and its behaviour the pattern or network (or 'system') of relationships obtaining 'between actors in their capacity of playing roles relative to one another' (Parsons 1949: 34).

Though this and similar definitions are basically correct (and must be so if our reasoning has been correct) they conceal serious methodological difficulties; for a satisfactory theory of social structure on this basis presupposes an adequate theory of roles, and none has yet been ad-

vanced in any systematic fashion. As a next step, therefore, I propose to make this attempt. But a few comments are still needed to complete this preliminary discourse.

(i) First, let me stress that the phrase 'playing roles relative to one another' in our definition of social structure does not merely mean 'playing roles vis-à-vis one another'; that is, we are not restricting social structure to face-to-face relationships or situations. This viewpoint hardly needs justifying. I mention it only because in using the conventional phraseology (or one not too clumsy) one is apt to give the impression of considering primarily face-to-face situations. Relationships other than face-to-face do pose certain special technical problems such as appropriate machineries of communication. But the reliance, on the part of the society, on face-to-face relationships equally involved technical difficulties, now concerning facilities for the necessary physical propinquity of the actors. I shall disregard both questions, which refer to the prerequisite conditions of social structures rather than to social structure as such.

(ii) It might seem that the approach here proposed, starting from the concepts of roles and role-playing actors, must miss a whole province or aspect of social structure, namely that formed by the ordered arrangements of sub-groups and similar subdivisions of society. We may take it for granted that any society does contain within it a number of smaller and simpler replicas of itself, which we conventionally call sections, segments, sub-groups etc. Their presence and arrangement clearly represents as much an 'articulation' as does the division of society into role-playing actors. Which seems to suggest that our definition of social structure is incomplete and that, in order to make it complete, we have to mention not only relationships between actors or persons but also the interrelations between sub-groups. But this juxtaposition is deceptive in spite of the near-coincidence of the terms 'relationship' and 'interrelation.' The latter (applied to groups) is not a counterpart or parallel of the former (applied to persons), as even a cursory glance will show; for while the relationship of persons implies interaction between them, behaviour of one towards or in regard to the other, groups of which we say that they are interrelated do not interact or behave as such, collectively, save in relatively few, special cases. Rather we must look at the situation in a different way.

Sub-groups, like that widest group the 'society at large,' are made up of people in determinate, stable relationships. And any group is characterized by the kinds of relationships that occur between the people in question, holding them together. Now inasmuch as sub-groups are discrete entities, bounded units, at least certain of these characteristic relationships must be equally bounded, that is, they must come to an end somewhere, their cessation demarcating the boundaries of the group. From this point of view, then, we might describe sub-groups as areas of bounded relationships. But inasmuch as they are also subdivisions of a wider collectivity and not isolated, self-sufficient units, the bounded relationships must themselves be interrelated. In other words, they must exhibit or fit into the overall network or pattern we spoke of before. The interrelation of sub-groups is therefore only a special case of the relatedness or 'orderliness' of relationships, and our definition of social structure both covers it and will logically lead us to it.

For the sake of completeness I ought to add this further remark, if only in parenthesis. In a somewhat different frame of reference the bounded unity of groups (and of society at large) can be demonstrated more simply by the criterion of *co-activity,* i.e. by indicating the particular co-ordinated activity (or activities) which would hold between all persons in the human aggregate claimed to constitute a group. This is the criterion I in fact adopted in a previous study (1951: 186). But though satisfactory in that context, the criterion is less so than in the present one. For it is clear that a single, equally embracing co-activity cannot always be translated into a single, equally embracing, relationship. This is feasible only if either the co-activity involves no differentiation in the position of the participants (so that ArB equals BrC . . . *ad inf.*), or the relationship considered is of a highly general kind (e.g. the 'fellowship' of fellow tribesmen or citizens, the 'kinship' of a group based on descent). But usually the former condition will be inapplicable or the latter too uninformative, and the embracing co-activity will need to be broken up into a series of distinct relationships in accordance with the different parts played by the participants. Thus, from the present viewpoint, directed as it is upon relationships, the more devious definition of group unity quoted above proves the only possible one.

(iii) I must now explain that the two terms, 'network' and 'pattern,' are not meant as synonyms. Rather, they are intended to indicate two different types or perhaps levels of overall structuring with which we shall meet throughout this discussion but for which, frankly, I have not been able to find very satisfactory terms. The best way I can describe them is by saying that one type of structuring is abstracted from *interactions,* the other from *distributions.* The latter may in turn apply to a variety of things—to concrete populations, to persons in their roles, as well as to relationships and sub-groups. The terms 'network' and 'pattern' are meant to indicate this distinction primarily in regard to relationships.

Thus I shall mean by 'pattern' any orderly distribution of relationships exclusively on the grounds of their similarity and dissimilarity. It is best exemplified (there are other, less clear-cut examples) by societies of the type Durkheim calls 'segmental,' i.e. societies characterized by the repetition of like aggregates in them,' the 'aggregates' being, for instance, clans, lineages, age sets or social strata (1949: 175). Let me explain this more fully. Since any group or sub-group consists of an area of bounded relationships it follows that, if the sub-groups are repetitive, the relationships characterizing them will be distributed in a similarly repetitive manner. That is to say, the relationships will occur within each of the like units (or 'aggregates') but not outside or between them, disappearing or being replaced by different relationships at the group boundaries. Think of the particular fellowship linking age mates and age mates only; of the economic and ritual collaboration valid within (but not without) descent groups; or of the intercourse on an equal footing restricted to members of the same social stratum. We can visualize this discontinuous but repetitive distribution by representing the clusters of identical relationships (r) in the sub-groups, as against the relationships occurring at their boundaries (Br), in some such fashion:

$$\begin{bmatrix} rrr \\ rrr \\ rrr \end{bmatrix} Br \begin{bmatrix} rrr \\ rrr \\ rrr \end{bmatrix} Br \begin{bmatrix} rrr \\ rrr \\ rrr \end{bmatrix}$$

I suggest, then, that such distributive arrangements warrant special recognition, and that 'pattern' is an apt description. At the same time I do not propose to deal with them specifically in the subsequent discussion. Rather, I shall treat them as an unproblematic and relatively elementary aspect of social structure. They are unproblematic because there really is nothing further to be said about these patterns once we have described the repetitive distribution in question. And they are relatively elementary because a distributive order is the simplest kind of order, involving a very low level of abstraction. But we most note this. The distributive pattern never stands by itself; for if the respective subdivisions are in fact such, i.e. *components* of a society, then they must also be linked by certain interactions and by interrelations based on these: else they would not add up to one society (in which there must be behaviour 'towards and in regard to one another'). Thus the 'pattern' will go together with a 'network,' and it is from the combination of the two that genuine problems will arise, the sort of problems we have in mind when we talk about the interdependence of group segments, about 'social symbiosis,' or about the cohesion and integration of any 'society at large'.

By 'network,' on the other hand, I mean the interlocking or relationships whereby the interactions implicit in one determine those occurring in others. Firth has recently commented on the fondness of anthropologists for metaphors like 'network,' though he concedes the usefulness of this 'image' which allows us to visualize the relations between persons as 'links' and 'lines' (1954: 4). Obviously, the network talked about

by anthropologists is only a metaphor. But it has been used very effectively also by others, e.g. by physicists, engineers and neurophysiologists. They speak, for example, of communication networks or of the networks of nerve cells and paths. Let me stress that I am using the term in a very similar, technical sense. For I do not merely wish to indicate the 'links' between persons; this is adequately done by the word relationship. Rather, I wish to indicate the further linkage of the links themselves and the important consequence that, what happens so-to-speak between one pair of 'knots,' must affect what happens between other adjacent ones. It is in order to illustrate this interrelatedness or interlocking of the relationships (each a "link' between two 'knots'), that we require an additional term, and 'network' seems the most appropriate.

To mention another recent use of this metaphor. Barnes employs it to illustrate a particular kind of 'social field,' constituted by relationships which spread out indefinitely rather than close in, as it were, and hence do not 'give rise to enduring social groups.' This spreading-out follows roughly the schema ArB, BrC, CrD . . . , though any one person may have relationships with several other persons and the 'other persons' may conceivably also maintain relations among themselves. A paradigm is friendship, each person seeing 'himself as at the centre of a collection of friends,' who in turn have further friends and may or may not be friends with each other (1954: 43–4). This picture comes close to the one I have in mind, though it represents a special and simpler case. For Barnes's 'network' does not predicate more than that certain relationships interlock through persons participating in more than one relationship; I visualize a situation in which this interlocking also bears on 'what happens' in the relationships and hence on their effective interdependence. For Barnes, the important thing is the dispersal of the relationships, and the open-ended character of the network; for me, its coherence and closure, that is, its equivalence with a 'system.'

(iv) Let me, in conclusion, say a little more about 'distributive patterns,' more precisely about one particular type. It occurs when a society is so constituted that it contains a fixed number of subdivisions, of whatever kind. The fixed number only indicates the high degree of constancy characterizing the 'pattern'; and examples are of course familiar—societies having a moiety system, or six phratries (like the Zuni), four castes (like classical India), or so-and-so many age grades.

We might add that similar fixed numerical arrangements may apply also to the actors expected to fill particular roles or, more generally, to the population composing classes of people or sub-groups in the society. A club or association with a fixed membership and, perhaps, one President, two Vice-Presidents, and three Members of Council, is a simple illustration. More sophisticated examples will be found in Simmel, who paid special attention to this aspect of social structure, considering it highly relevant (Wolff 1950: 105 ff). Recently, from a somewhat different point of view, Lévi-Strauss has touched upon the same issue. He has in mind not a numerical arrangement fixed, i.e. kept invariant, by explicit social rules, but one exhibiting a purely statistical (and approximate) invariance (1953: 534–5). This would be the case, if I may choose my own examples, where we find that the size of clans varies round a mean number, which is maintained by fission (if clans grow too large) or fusion (if they grow too small); or again, we might find that the ruling class in a stratified society always approximates to, say, ten per cent of the population.

Now what is sociologically relevant in such numerical arrangements, whether they apply to persons in roles, to the population of sub-groups or to the number of the sub-groups themselves, is not the distributive pattern as such. Once more, considered by itself, it represents an unproblematic and elementary form of structuring. It becomes interesting and important only through its implication of interdependence between the persons or sections so numbered, that is, when it goes together with some differentiation and interlocking of their respective 'ways of acting' and hence with a 'network' of relationships. Thus the numbered set of phratries or castes may be so conceived that each has specific duties, secular or ritual, towards all others; a dual segmentation of the society, perhaps even the presence of two Vice-Presidents in an association, may serve to canalize and balance opposition; and the invariant population of clans or ruling classes may represent the optimum size for the particular activities assigned to these segments. Here we have a whole range of significant problems, and problems still in need of further study. They concern the extent to which these and similar forms of interdependence and integration depend on particular numerical arrangements or, conversely, the extent to which the numerical invariance facilitates (or the opposite) aimed-at possibilities of interaction. But these are essentially questions of adequacy, of the appropriateness of means to ends, that is, of *function,* and hence beyond the scope of this discussion.

ROLE AND INTERACTION

Erving Goffman

THE FRAMEWORK

A social establishment is any place surrounded by fixed barriers to perception in which a par-

From *Presentation of Self in Everyday Life* by Erving Goffman. Copyright © 1959 by Erving Goffman. Reprinted by permission of Doubleday & Company, Inc. Pp. 238–242, 252–255. Also published by Penguin Books Ltd., London.

ticular kind of activity regularly takes place. I have suggested that any social establishment may be studied profitably from the point of view of impression management. Within the walls of a social establishment we find a team of performers who cooperate to present to an audience a given definition of the situation. This will include the conception of own team and of audience and assumptions concerning the ethos that is to be maintained by rules of politeness and decorum. We often find a division into back region, where the performance of a routine is prepared, and front region, where the performance is presented. Access to these regions is controlled in order to prevent the audience from seeing backstage and to prevent outsiders from coming into a performance that is not addressed to them. Among members of the team we find that familiarity prevails, solidarity is likely to develop, and that secrets that could give the show away are shared and kept. A tacit agreement is maintained between performers and audience to act as if a given degree of opposition and of accord existed between them. Typically, but not always, agreement is stressed and opposition is underplayed. The resulting working consensus tends to be contradicted by the attitude toward the audience which the performers express in the absence of the audience and by carefully controlled communication out of character conveyed by the performers while the audience is present. We find that discrepant roles develop: some of the individuals who are apparently teammates, or audience, or outsiders acquire information about the performance and relations to the team which are not apparent and which complicate the problem of putting on a show. Sometimes disruptions occur through unmeant gestures, faux pas, and scenes, thus discrediting or contradicting the definition of the situation that is being maintained. The mythology of the team will dwell upon these disruptive events. We find that performers, audience, and outsiders all utilize techniques for saving the show, whether by avoiding likely disruptions or by correcting for unavoided ones, or by making it possible for others to do so. To ensure that these techniques will be employed, the team will tend to select members who are loyal, disciplined, and circumspect, and to select an audience that is tactful.

These features and elements, then, comprise the framework I claim to be characteristic of much social interaction as it occurs in natural settings in our Anglo-American society. This framework is formal and abstract in the sense that it can be applied to any social establishment; it is not, however, merely a static classification. The framework bears upon dynamic issues created by the motivation to sustain a definition of the situation that has been projected before others.

THE ANALYTICAL CONTEXT

The report has been chiefly concerned with social establishments as relatively closed systems. It has been assumed that the relation of one establishment to others is itself an intelligible area of study and ought to be treated analytically as part of a different order of fact—the order of institutional integration. It might be well here to try to place the perspective taken in this report in the context of other perspectives which seem to be the ones currently employed, implicitly or explicitly, in the study of social establishments as closed systems. Four such perspectives may be tentatively suggested.

An establishment may be viewed "technically," in terms of its efficiency and inefficiency as an intentionally organized system of activity for the achievement of predefined objectives. An establishment may be viewed "politically," in terms of the actions which each participant (or class of participants) can demand of other participants, the kinds of deprivations and indulgences which can be meted out in order to enforce these demands, and the kinds of social controls which guide this exercise of command and use of sanctions. An establishment may be viewed "structurally," in terms of the horizontal and vertical status divisions and the kinds of social relations which relate these several groupings to one another. Finally, an establishment may be viewed "culturally," in terms of the moral values which influence activity in the establishment—values pertaining to fashions, customs, and matters of taste, to politeness and decorum, to ultimate ends and normative restrictions on means, etc. It is to be noted that all the facts that can be discovered about an establishment are relevant to each of the four perspectives but that each perspective gives its own priority and order to these facts.

It seems to me that the dramaturgical approach may constitute a fifth perspective, to be added to the technical, political, structural, and cultural perspectives.[1] The dramaturgical perspective, like each of the other four, can be employed as the end-point of analysis, as a final way of ordering facts. This would lead us to describe the techniques of impression management employed in a given establishment, the principal problems of impression management in the establishment, and the identity and interrelationships of the several performance teams which operate in the establishment. But, as with the facts utilized in each of the other perspectives, the facts specifically pertaining to impression management also play a part in the matters that are a concern in all the other perspectives. It may be useful to illustrate this briefly.

The technical and dramaturgical perspectives intersect most clearly, perhaps, in regard to standards of work. Important for both perspectives is the fact that one set of individuals will be concerned with testing the unapparent characteristics and qualities of the work-accomplishments of another set of individuals, and this other set will be concerned with giving the impression that their work embodies these hidden attributes. The political and dramaturgical perspectives intersect clearly in regard to the capacities of one individual to direct the activity of another. For one thing, if an individual is to direct others, he will often find it useful to keep strategic secrets from them. Further, if one individual attempts to direct the activity of others by means of example, enlightenment, persuasion, exchange, manipulation, authority, threat, punishment, or coercion, it will be necessary, regardless of his power position, to convey effectively what he wants done, what he is prepared to do to get it done and what he will do if it is not done. Power of any kind must be clothed in effective means of displaying it, and will have different effects depending upon how it is drama-

[1] Compare the position taken by Oswald Hall in regard to possible perspectives for the study of closed systems in his "Methods and Techniques of Research in Human Relations" (April, 1952), reported in E. C. Hughes *et al.*, *Cases on Field Work* (forthcoming).

tized. (Of course, the capacity to convey effectively a definition of the situation may be of little use if one is not in a position to give example, exchange, punishment, etc.) Thus the most objective form of naked power, i.e., physical coercion, is often neither objective nor naked but rather functions as a display for persuading the audience; it is often a means of communication, not merely a means of action. The structural and dramaturgical perspectives seem to intersect most clearly in regard to social distance. The image that one status grouping is able to maintain in the eyes of an audience of other status groupings will depend upon the performers' capacity to restrict communicative contact with the audience. The cultural and dramaturgical perspectives intersect most clearly in regard to the maintenance of moral standards. The cultural values of an establishment will determine in detail how the participants are to feel about many matters and at the same time establish a framework of appearances that must be maintained, whether or not there is feeling behind the appearances.

. . .

STAGING AND THE SELF

The general notion that we make a presentation of ourselves to others is hardly novel; what ought to be stressed in conclusion is that the very structure of the self can be seen in terms of how we arrange for such performances in our Anglo-American society.

In this report, the individual was divided by implication into two basic parts: he was viewed as a *performer*, a harried fabricator of impressions involved in the all-too-human task of staging a performance; he was viewed as a *character*, a figure, typically a fine one, whose spirit, strength, and other sterling qualities the performance was designed to evoke. The attributes of a performer and the attributes of a character are of a different order, quite basically so, yet both sets have their meaning in terms of the show that must go on.

First, character. In our society the character one performs and one's self are somewhat equated, and this self-as-character is usually seen as something housed within the body of its possessor, especially the upper parts thereof, being a nodule, somehow, in the psychobiology of personality. I suggest that this view is an implied part of what we are all trying to present, but provides, just because of this, a bad analysis of the presentation. In this report the performed self was seen as some kind of image, usually creditable, which the individual on stage and in character effectively attempts to induce others to hold in regard to him. While this image is entertained *concerning* the individual, so that a self is imputed to him, this self itself does not derive from its possessor, but from the whole scene of his action, being generated by that attribute of local events which renders them interpretable by witnesses. A correctly staged and performed scene leads the audience to impute a self to a performed character, but this imputation—this self—is a *product* of a scene that comes off, and is not a *cause* of it. The self, then, as a performed character, is not an organic thing that has a specific location, whose fundamental fate is to be born, to mature, and to die; it is a dramatic effect arising diffusely from a scene that is presented, and the characteristic issue, the crucial concern, is whether it will be credited or discredited.

In analyzing the self then we are drawn from its possessor, from the person who will profit or lose most by it, for he and his body merely provide the peg on which something of collaborative manufacture will be hung for a time. And the means for producing and maintaining selves do not reside inside the peg; in fact these means are often bolted down in social establishments. There will be a back region with its tools for shaping the body, and a front region with its fixed props. There will be a team of persons whose activity on stage in conjunction with available props will constitute the scene from which the performed character's self will emerge, and another team, the audience, whose interpretive activity will be necessary for this emergence. The self is a product of all of these arrangements, and in all of its parts bears the marks of this genesis.

The whole machinery of self-production is cumbersome, of course, and sometimes breaks down, exposing its separate components: back region control; team collusion; audience tact; and so forth. But, well oiled, impressions will flow from it fast enough to put us in the grips of one of our types of reality—the performance will come off and the firm self accorded each performed character will appear to emanate intrinsically from its performer.

Let us turn now from the individual as character performed to the individual as performer. He has a capacity to learn, this being exercised in the task of training for a part. He is given to having fantasies and dreams, some that pleasurably unfold a triumphant performance, others full of anxiety and dread that nervously deal with vital discreditings in a public front region. He often manifests a gregarious desire for teammates and audiences, a tactful considerateness for their concerns; and he has a capacity for deeply felt shame, leading him to minimize the chances he takes of exposure.

These attributes of the individual *qua* performer are not merely a depicted effect of particular performances; they are psychobiological in nature, and yet they seem to arise out of intimate interaction with the contingencies of staging performances.

And now a final comment. In developing the conceptual framework employed in this report, some language of the stage was used. I spoke of performers and audiences; of routine and parts; of performances coming off or falling flat; of cues, stage settings and backstage; of dramaturgical needs, dramaturgical skills, and dramaturgical strategies. Now it should be admitted that this attempt to press a mere analogy so far was in part a rhetoric and a maneuver.

The claim that all the world's a stage is sufficiently commonplace for readers to be familiar with its limitations and tolerant of its presentation, knowing that at any time they will easily be able to demonstrate to themselves that it is not to be taken too seriously. An action staged in a theater is a relatively contrived illusion and an admitted one; unlike ordinary life, nothing real or actual can happen to the performed characters—although at another level of course something real and actual can happen to the reputation of performers *qua* professionals whose everyday job is to put on theatrical performances.

And so here the language and mask of the stage will be dropped. Scaffolds, after all, are to build other things with, and should be erected with an eye to taking them down. This report is not concerned with aspects of theater that creep into everyday life. It is concerned with the structure of social encounters—the structure of those entities in social life that come into being whenever persons enter one another's immediate physical presence. The key factor in this structure is the maintenance of a single definition of the situation, this definition having to be ex-

pressed, and this expression sustained in the face of a multitude of potential disruptions.

A character staged in a theater is not in some ways real, nor does it have the same kind of real consequences as does the thoroughly contrived character performed by a confidence man; but the *successful* staging of either of these types of false figures involves use of *real* techniques—the same techniques by which everyday persons sustain their real social situations. Those who conduct face to face interaction on a theater's stage must meet the key requirement of real situations; they must expressively sustain a definition of the situation: but this they do in circumstances that have facilitated their developing an apt terminology for the interactional tasks that all of us share.

RETHINKING 'STATUS' AND 'ROLE': TOWARD A GENERAL MODEL OF THE CULTURAL ORGANIZATION OF SOCIAL RELATIONSHIPS

Ward H. Goodenough

INTRODUCTORY COMMENT

This examination of the concepts 'status' and 'role' arises from my concern with a problem in ethnographic description. It is the problem of developing methods for processing the data of field observation and informant interview so as to enhance the rigor with which we arrive at statements of a society's culture or system of norms such that they make social events within that society intelligible in the way that they are intelligible to its members. My thinking about this problem has been inspired largely by structural linguistics, a discipline that has achieved a high degree of rigor in formulating descriptive statements of the normative aspects of speech behavior. I have found it useful to look upon the

From Michael Banton (ed.), *The Relevance of Models for Social Anthropology* (London: Tavistock, 1965), pp. 1–20. Reprinted by permission.

cultural content of social relationships as containing (among other things) 'vocabularies' of different kinds of forms and a 'syntax' or set of rules for their composition into (and interpretation as) meaningful sequences of social events.

This orientation was explicit in my account of the social organization of Truk (Goodenough, 1951). Out of it developed my later work with 'componential analysis' in what might be called descriptive or structural semantics (Goodenough, 1956a, 1957), representing an approach to constructing valid models of the categorical aspects of social norms. Here, I shall elaborate another analytical method that was first suggested in my Truk report, one aimed at a grammatical aspect of normative behavior. Hopefully it will enable us to make systematic and exhaustive descriptions of the cultural domain embraced by the expressions 'status' and 'role.'

THE POINT OF DEPARTURE

Ralph Linton (1936, pp. 113–114) defined statuses as 'the polar positions . . . in patterns of reciprocal behavior.' A polar position, he said, consists of 'a collection of rights and duties'; and a role is the dynamic aspect of status, the putting into effect of its rights and duties.

Unfortunately, Linton went on to discuss statuses not as collections of rights and duties but as categories or kinds of person. All writers who do not treat status as synonymous with social rank do much the same thing, including Merton (1957b, pp. 368–370) in his important refinement of Linton's formulation. All alike treat a social category together with its attached rights and duties as an indivisible unit of analysis, which they label a 'status' or 'position' in a social relationship. This lumping together of independent phenomena, each with organizations of their own, accounts, I think, for our apparent inability to exploit the status-role concepts to our satisfaction in social and cultural analysis. For example, my brother is my brother, whether he honors his obligations as such or not. A policeman's conduct in office may lead to social events that formally remove him from office, but it does not determine in any direct way whether he is a policeman or not. Other social transactions determine what his social category or identity actually is. Furthermore, there are legislative transactions that can serve to alter the rights and duties that attach to the category policeman in its dealings with other categories without the defining characteristics of the category being in any way altered. What makes him legally and formally a policeman need not have been affected.

These considerations have led me to break with established sociological practice. I shall consistently treat statuses as combinations of right and duty only. I shall emphasize their conceptual autonomy from social 'positions' in a categorical sense by referring to the latter as *social identities*. I would, for example, speak of ascribed and achieved identities where Linton (1936, p. 115) speaks of 'ascribed' and 'achieved' statuses. In accordance with Linton's original

definition, then, the formal properties of statuses involve (1) what legal theorists call rights, duties, privileges, powers, liabilities, and immunities (Hoebel, 1954, pp. 48–49) and (2) the ordered ways in which these are distributed in what I shall call *identity relationships*.

RIGHTS AND DUTIES

Rights and their duty counterparts serve to define boundaries within which the parties to social relationships are expected to confine their behavior. Privileges relate to the areas of option within these boundaries. For example, when I am invited out to dinner, it is my hostess's right that I wear a necktie; to wear one is my duty. It is also her right that its decoration be within the bounds of decency. But she has no right as to how it shall be decorated otherwise; it is my privilege to decide this without reference to her wishes. For status analysis, the boundaries (the rights and duties) command our attention and not the domain of idiosyncratic freedom (privileges). As for powers, they and their liability counterparts stem from privileges, while immunities result from rights and the observance of duties. None of them needs to be treated as a feature of status relationships that requires analysis independent of the analysis of rights and duties.

As used in jurisprudence, rights and duties are two sides of the same coin. In any relationship A's rights over B are the things he can demand of B; these same things are what B owes A, B's duties in the relationship. Therefore, whenever we isolate a right or a duty, we isolate its duty or right counterpart at the same time.

A great deal of social learning in any society is learning one's duties to others, both of commission and omission, and the situations in which they are owed. They are matters that informants can talk about readily; they have words and phrases for them. The methods of descriptive semantics (componential analysis), referred to above, should provide a suitable means for describing the actual content of specific rights and duties with considerable rigor. But even without this, once we have established the existence of a duty for which our informants have a word or expression in their language, we can explore its distribution in identity relationships without our necessarily having its exact content clearly defined. The informant knows what he is talking about, if we as investigators do not.

SOCIAL IDENTITIES

A social identity is an aspect of self that makes a difference in how one's rights and duties distribute to specific others. Any aspect of self whose alteration entails no change in how people's rights and duties are mutually distributed, although it affects their emotional orientations to one another and the way they choose to exercise their privileges, has to do with personal identity but not with social identity. The utility of this distinction is clear when we consider the father-son relationship in our own society. The status of the social identity 'father' in this relationship is delimited by the duties he owes his son and the things he can demand of him. Within the boundaries set by his rights and duties it is his privilege to conduct himself as he will. How he does this is a matter of personal style. We assess the father as a person on the basis of how he consistently exercises his privileges and on the degree to which he oversteps his status boundaries with brutal behavior or economic neglect. But as long as he remains within the boundaries, his personal identity as a stern or indulgent parent has no effect on what are his rights and duties in this or any other relationship to which he may be party.

Every individual has a number of different social identities. What his rights and duties are varies according to the identities he may appropriately assume in a given interaction. If John Doe is both my employer and my subordinate in the National Guard, then the duties I owe him depend on whether I assume the identity of employee or of company commander in dealing with him. We tend to think of duties as things we owe to individual alters, but in reality we owe them to their social identities. In the army, what we *owe* a salute is 'the uniform and not the man.'

Furthermore, what duties are owed depends on ego's and alter's identities taken together and not on the identity of either one alone, as Merton (1957b, p. 369) has observed. In our society, for example, a physician's rights and duties differ considerably depending on whether he is dealing with another physician, a nurse, a patient, or the community and its official representatives. If a status is a collection of rights and duties, then the social identity we label 'physician' occupies a different status in each of these identity relationships. Failure to take account of the identities of alters and to speak in general terms of the status of a chief or employer has been responsible for much of the apparent lack of utility of the status-role concepts.

Another source of difficulty has been a tendency for many analysts to think of the parties to status relationships as individual human beings. This mistake invites us to overlook the identity of the alter in those relationships where the alter is a group and not an individual. Obviously, communities, tribes, and nations become parties to status relationships when they make treaties with one another and when they enter into contracts with individuals and subgroups within their memberships. Criminal law, as it is usually defined, concerns the duties that individuals and corporations owe the communities of which they are members. Animals, inanimate objects, and purely imaginary beings may also possess rights and/or owe duties.

IDENTITY SELECTION

As Linton (1936, p. 115) aptly observed, some identities are 'ascribed' and some 'achieved.' He was talking about how one comes to possess a particular social identity as a matter of social fact. How is it that one comes to *be* a professor or a married man, for example? Everyone has many more identities, however, than he can assume at one time in a given interaction. He must select from among his various identities those in which to present himself.

As regards some identities, of course, there is no choice. Having reached a certain age, I have a duty as a member of my society to present myself as an adult and as a man in all social interactions to which I may be party. However, I am under no obligation to present myself as professor of anthropology in all interactions. Quite the contrary.

Several considerations govern the selection of identities.

An obvious consideration is an individual's (or group's) qualifications for selecting the identity. Does he in fact possess it? He may masquerade as a policeman, for example, donning the symbols that inform others of such an identity, and yet not be one. People often pretend to social identities for which they are not personally qualified, but such pretence is usually regarded as a serious breach of one's duties to fellow-members of one's peace group, duties that attach to one's identity as a member of a human community.

Another consideration is the occasion of an interaction. For any society there is a limited number of culturally recognized types of activity. The legitimate purposes of any activity provide the culturally recognized reasons for interactions, and they in turn define occasions. The same individuals select different identities in which to deal with one another depending on the occasion. For example, I may call upon someone who is in fact both my physician and my personal friend because I wish to be treated for an illness or because I wish to invite him to dinner. The purpose that specifies the occasion for the interaction determines whether I assume the identity of 'patient' or 'personal friend' in approaching him.

The setting, as distinct from the occasion, might also seem to be an obvious consideration in identity selection. For example, the same individual may or may not assume the identity of chairman of a meeting depending on what other persons are present, but here we are really dealing with the factor of qualifications for assuming an identity, already mentioned. Or again, when I invite my physician friend to dinner, how I approach him depends on whether or not one of his patients is a witness to the transaction, but this is not so much a matter of identity selection as it is a matter of choosing among alternative ways of honoring one's duties and exercising one's privileges. I suspect that settings are more likely to affect how one conducts oneself in the same identity relationship than to govern the selection of identities, but this is a matter requiring empirical investigation.

An important consideration is that, for any identity assumed by one party, there are only a limited number of matching identities available to the other party. If two people enter an interaction each assuming an identity that does not match the one assumed by the other, they fail to establish a relationship. The result is ungrammatical, and there is social confusion analogous to the semantic confusion that results from story-completion games in which no one is allowed to know anything but the last word that his predecessor in the game has written down. We take care to employ various signs by which to communicate the identities we wish to assume, so that others may assume matching ones and we can interact with mutual understanding. Any pair of matching identities constitutes an *identity relationship*.

It is noteworthy that different identities vary as to the number of identity relationships that are grammatically possible for them within a culture. But in all cases the number appears to be quite limited. Thus in my culture the identity relationships 'physician-physician,' 'physician-nurse,' 'physician-patient' are grammatical, but there is no such thing as a 'physician-wife' relationship or a 'physician-employee' relationship. The physician must operate in the identity 'husband' with his wife and in the identity 'employer' with his employees.

Finally, we must consider that the parties to a social relationship do not ordinarily deal with one another in terms of only one identity-relationship at a time. The elderly male physician does not deal with a young female nurse in the same way that a young male physician does, and neither deals with her as a female physician does. In other words, identities such as old, adult, young adult, man, and woman are as relevant as are the identities physician and nurse. Some identities are relevant to all social interactions. In my culture, for example, I must always present myself to others as an adult and as a male. This means that I am ineligible for any identity that is incompatible with being adult and male. Among the various identities that I do possess and that are compatible with these two, not all are compatible with one another, nor are they always mutually exclusive as to the occasions for which they are appropriate. The result is that for any occasion I must select several identities at once, and they must be ones that can be brought together to make a grammatically possible composite identity. In order to avoid confusion I shall reserve the term identity for anything about the self that makes a difference in social relationships, as defined earlier. The composite of several identities selected as appropriate to a given interaction constitutes the selector's *social persona* in the interaction (c.f. Goffman 1959: 252).

The selection of identities in composing social relationships, then, is not unlike the selection of words in composing sentences in that it must conform to syntactic principles governing (1) the arrangement of social identities with one another in identity relationships, (2) the association of identities with occasions or activities, and (3) the compatibility of identities as features of a coherent social persona.

IDENTITY RELATIONSHIPS AND STATUS RELATIONSHIPS

For each culturally possible identity relationship there is a specific allocation of rights and duties. The duties that ego's identity owes alter's identity define ego's duty-status and alter's right-status. Conversely, ego's right-status and alter's duty-status are defined by the duties that alter's identity owes ego's identity. As we shall see, one cannot deduce alter's duties from a knowledge of only ego's, except when both identities in a relationship are the same. In two separate identity relationships, ego may have the same duty-status and different right-statuses or the same right-status and different duty-statuses. When we examine the distributions of rights and duties among a society's identity relationships, we must look at every relationship twice and observe how the rights and duties are allocated from the point of view of each participating identity independently.

Every pair of reciprocal duty-statuses (or corresponding right-statuses) constitutes a *status relationship*. As we shall see, the same status relationships may be found to obtain in quite different identity relationships. We have already observed that the same identity may be in different status relationships according to the different identity relationships into which it can enter. These observations demonstrate that the structure of a society's status relationships must be analyzed and described in different terms from those that describe the structure of its identity relationships. A culturally ordered system of *social relationships,* then, is composed (among other things) of identity relationships, status relationships, and the ways in which they are mutually distributed.

THE ANALYSIS OF STATUSES

How duties distribute in the identity relationships in which people participate is a function of at least several independent considerations. For any identity relationship in which we participate in our society, for example, we must ask ourselves how much (if any) deference we owe? How much (if any) cordiality, reverence, and display of affection? How much sexual distance must we maintain? How much emotional independence? These are only some of the considerations that are relevant for the allocation of rights and duties among us. Each one of them presumably represents a single dimension of status difference in our culture's organization of status relationships. If this is so, then the several duties that in different combinations indicate socially significant differences along one such dimension will be mutually distributed in identity relationships according to the patterns of a "Guttman scale" (Guttman, 1944, 1950; Goodenough, 1944).

For purposes of illustration here, I shall confine discussion to the simplest scale pattern. Suppose that the duties expressing lowest degree of deference are most widely distributed in identity relationships; suppose that the duties expressing the next higher degree of deference are next most widely distributed and only in relationships in which duties expressing the lowest degree are also owed; and suppose that duties expressing the highest degree of deference are distributed in the fewest relationships, and in all of them duties expressing lesser degrees of deference are also owed. With such successively inclusive distributions, both the social identities for every identity-relationship in which they occur and the duties expressive of deference can be ranked simultaneously against each other in a special type of matrix table known as a 'scalogram' (Guttman, 1950; Suchman, 1950). Our ability so to rank them is the empirical test that the duties in question are distributed in accordance with a scale pattern and that they are indeed functions of one consideration or status dimension.

We anticipate, therefore, that analysis of scales will provide a means whereby we can empirically determine what duties are functions of the same dimension and at the same time discover the minimum number of dimensions needed to account for the distribution of all culturally defined duties in a system of social relationships. As a result of such analysis, all the duties would be sorted into several distinct sets. The duties in each set would form a scale, but those in different sets would not.

Table 1 presents a hypothetical example of a scalogram such as one might obtain for one set of duties. Each distinctive combination of duties represents a different status on the status dimension represented. Identity relationships are grouped and ranked according to the combinations of duties owed by the ego-identity to the alter-identity in each, so that every identity relationship appears twice in the scalogram according to which of the two social identities in it is the ego-identity and which the alter-identity. Duties that have identical distributions and that do not, therefore, discriminate status differences on the scale are grouped into duty clusters.

The scale in *Table 1* shows the distribution of duties for one person as ego in all the identity relationships in which he participates. Indeed,

the procedure for gathering data for this kind of analysis requires that the informant be held constant, since there is no guarantee that different individuals have exactly the same conceptual organizations of status relationships. Data gathering and analysis must be done over again, independently, for each informant. The degree to which the resulting organization of status relationships coincide indicates the degree of consensus among informants as to their expectations in social relationships.

Because status scales are worked out separately for each informant, they tend to be 'perfect' scales, in which no item is distributed in a way that is inconsistent at any point with the distributions of other items in the pattern of a scale. This makes the use of Guttman-scaling techniques much less complicated in the analysis of status relationships than is the case in attitude and opinion surveys, where many informants are asked the same set of questions relating to a single object and their different responses are plotted so as to rank the informants and the specific answers to the questions against each other simultaneously. Since different informants do not share the same cognitive organization of the subject under study in all respects, perfect scales cannot be obtained. Here, however, we are looking at how identity relationships and duties are simultaneously ranked against one another in the mind of one informant as revealed by the distribution of his answers. Under such circumstances almost perfect scales may reasonably be expected.

AN EXAMPLE FROM TRUK

A scale from an informant on Truk (Goodenough, 1951, p. 113), reproduced in *Table 2*, provides a concrete example of a series of duties whose distributions are functions of a single status dimension. The duties are:

(a)   to use the greeting *fääjiro* when encountering alter;
(b)   to avoid being physically higher than later in alter's presence, and therefore to crouch or crawl if alter is seated;
(c)   to avoid initiating direct interaction with alter, to interact with him only at his pleasure;

(d)   to honor any request that alter can make of ego if alter insists;

(e)   to avoid speaking harshly to alter or taking him personally to task for actions;

(f)   to avoid using 'fight talk' to alter or directly assaulting him regardless of provocation.

Each scale type in *Table 2* corresponds to a status. Under scale type 7 are all those relationships in which none of these duties is owed (in which ego is in duty-status 7 to alter), and under scale type 1 are those relationships in which all the duties are owed (in which ego is in duty-status 1 to alter).

The reason ego owes the four duties that mark statuses 1–4 is because he is not supposed to 'be above' alter. The seven scale combinations of

Table 1.   Hypothetical Status Scale

STATUS (SCALE) TYPE	RELATIONSHIP EGO'S IDENTITY	ALTER'S IDENTITY	SPECIFIC ALTER	DUTIES AND DUTY CLUSTERS I (1)	II (2)	III (3)	III (4)	IV (5)	V (6)	V (7)	VI (8)
1	A	X	a	Y	Y	Y	Y	Y	Y	Y	Y
	A	X	b	Y	Y	Y	Y	Y	Y	Y	Y
2	B	Y	c	Y	Y	Y	Y	Y	Y	Y	N
	B	Y	d	Y	Y	Y	Y	Y	Y	Y	N
	C	Z	o	Y	Y	Y	Y	Y	Y	Y	N
3	D	W	b	Y	Y	Y	Y	Y	N	N	N
	D	W	f	Y	Y	Y	Y	Y	N	N	N
4	D	Z	g	Y	Y	Y	Y	N	N	N	N
	E	G	h	Y	Y	Y	Y	N	N	N	N
	E	G	i	Y	Y	Y	Y	N	N	N	N
5	F	R	j	Y	Y	N	N	N	N	N	N
	R	F	k	Y	Y	N	N	N	N	N	N
	G	E	l	Y	Y	N	N	N	N	N	N
6	H	H	f	Y	N	N	N	N	N	N	N
	H	H	m	Y	N	N	N	N	N	N	N
	X	A	n	Y	N	N	N	N	N	N	N
	Y	B	o	Y	N	N	N	N	N	N	N
	I	N	p	Y	N	N	N	N	N	N	N
7	K	J	q	N	N	N	N	N	N	N	N
	J	K	r	N	N	N	N	N	N	N	N
	Z	C	s	N	N	N	N	N	N	N	N
	Z	D	t	N	N	N	N	N	N	N	N
	W	D	u	N	N	N	N	N	N	N	N
	M	I	v	N	N	N	N	N	N	N	N
	N	I	w	N	N	N	N	N	N	N	N
	I	M	m	N	N	N	N	N	N	N	N

KEY: Under 'relationship' capital letters represent specific social identities. The small letters represent specific alters. In the duty columns, Y indicates that the duty is owed by ego's identity to alter's identity, and N indicates that it is not owed. Alters b, f, and m appear in more than one identity relationship with ego. The entire scale is from the point of view of a single informant as ego.

Table 2. Duty Scale of 'Setting Oneself Above Another' in Truk

SCALE TYPE	RELATIONSHIP IN WHICH DUTY OWED	MUST SAY FÄÄJIRO	MUST CRAWL	MUST AVOID	MUST OBEY	MUST NOT SCOLD	MUST NOT FIGHT
1	Non-kinsman to chief	Yes	Yes	Yes	Yes	Yes	Yes
	Non-kinsman to *jitag*	Yes	Yes	Yes	Yes	Yes	Yes
2	Man to female *neji*	No	Yes	Yes	Yes	Yes	Yes
	Man to Wi's *mwääni*	No	Yes	Yes	Yes	Yes	Yes
	Woman to So of *mwääni*	No	Yes	No(?)	Yes	Yes	Yes
	Woman to *mwääni*	No	Yes	Yes	Yes	Yes	Yes
	Woman to So of Hu's older *pwiij*	No	Yes	Yes	Yes	Yes	Yes
	Woman to Wi of *mwääni*	No	Yes	Yes	Yes	Yes	Yes
3	Man to older *pwiij*	No	No	Yes	Yes	Yes	Yes
	Woman to older *pwiij*	No	No	Yes	Yes	Yes	Yes
4	Man to male *neji*	No	No	No	Yes	Yes	Yes
	Man to Wi of older *pwiij*	No	No	No	Yes	Yes	Yes
	Woman to Da of *mwääni*	No	No	No	Yes	Yes	Yes
	Woman to Da of Hu's *pwiij*	No	No	No	Yes	Yes	Yes
	Woman to So of Hu's younger *pwiij*	No	No	No	Yes	Yes	Yes
	Woman to Da of Hu's *feefinej*	No	No	No	Yes	Yes	Yes
	Woman to So of Hu's *feefinej*	No	No	No	Yes	Yes	Yes
	Woman to Hu of older *pwiij*	No	No	No	Yes	Yes	Yes
	Woman to Da's Hu	No	No	No	Yes	Yes	Yes
	Woman to So's Wi	No	No	No	Yes	Yes	Yes
5	Man to younger *pwiij*	No	No	No	No	Yes	Yes
	Man to Wi's older *pwiij*	No	No	No	No	Yes	Yes
	Woman to younger *pwiij*	No	No	No	No	Yes	Yes
	Woman to So of *pwiij*	No	No	No	No	Yes	Yes
	Woman to Hu's older *pwiij*	No	No	No	No	Yes	Yes
6	Man to Wi of younger *pwiij*	No	No	No	No	No	Yes
	Woman to own So	No	No	No	No	No	Yes
	Woman to Hu's younger *pwiij*	No	No	No	No	No	Yes
7	Man to *semej*	No	No	No	No	No	No
	Man to *jinej*	No	No	No	No	No	No
	Man to *feefinej*	No	No	No	No	No	No
	Man to Hu of *feefinej*	No	No	No	No	No	No
	Man to Wi	No	No	No	No	No	No
	Man to Wi's younger *pwiij*	No	No	No	No	No	No
	Woman to *semej*	No	No	No	No	No	No
	Woman to *jinej*	No	No	No	No	No	No
	Woman to own Da	No	No	No	No	No	No
	Woman to Da of *pwiij*	No	No	No	No	No	No
	Woman to Hu	No	No	No	No	No	No
	Woman to Hu of younger *pwiij*	No	No	No	No	No	No
	Woman to Hu's *feefinej*	No	No	No	No	No	No

KEY: Abbreviations are: Da, daughter; Hu, husband; So, son; and Wi, wife. The Trukese terms designate categories of kin. English kin terms are used only to subdivide the Trukese kinship categories when behavioral distinctions are made within them.

NOTE: Adapted from Goodenough, 1951, p. 113.

Table 3.   Status Scale of Sexual Distance in Truk

STATUS OR SCALE TYPE	EGO IN RELATION TO ALTER	AVOIDANCE DUTIES				
		SLEEP IN SAME HOUSE	BE SEEN IN COMPANY	SEE BREASTS EXPOSED	HAVE INTER-COURSE	JOKE SEXUALLY IN PUBLIC
1	Man with *feefinej*	F	F	F	F	F
2	Man with female *neji* (except Da of Wi's *mwääni*)	A	A	F	F	F
3	Man with Da of Wi's *mwääni*	A	A	D	F	F
4	Man with consanguineal *jinej*	A	A	A	F	F
5	Man with affinal *jinej*	A	A	A	D	D
6	Man with Wi	A	A	A	A	D
7	Man with *pwynywej* (other than Wi)	A	A	A	A	A

KEY: Abbreviations used are: A, allowed; D, disapproved; F, forbidden; Da, daughter; Wi, wife. The Trukese terms designate categories of kin.

NOTE: Adapted from Goodenough, 1951, p. 117.

duty express the degree to which ego is or is not forbidden from being above alter. The dimension in question seems best characterized as one of deference.

This scale illustrated that knowledge of ego's duty-status and alter's corresponding right-status does not allow one to deduce ego's right-status and alter's duty-status in an identity relationship. In the relationships 'brother'—'sister' (man to *feefinej* and woman to *mwääni*) and husband—wife (man to Wi and woman to Hu), both brother and husband are in duty-status 7 on the scale and sister and wife are in right-status 7. But brother is in right-status and sister in duty-status 2, whereas husband is in right-status and wife in duty-status 7.

COMPOSITE STATUSES

Another dimension on which status distinctions are made in Truk is that of sexual distance. The duty scale for this dimension is shown in *Table 3* as it pertains to male-female kin relationships (it has not been worked out exhaustively for all identity relationships). Obviously, whenever any Trukese man and woman interact, the identities in terms of which they compose their behavior call for mutual placement simultaneously on both the deference and sexual distance scales—in two different status

systems at the same time. In any relationship, therefore, it appears that the duties owed are functions not of one but of several status dimensions at once. Indeed, in every identity relationship in which a person participates he has a duty-status and a right-status on every status dimension in his culture's system of social relationships. The particular combination of duty-statuses occupied by an identity on all these dimensions at once in a given identity relationship is its composite duty-status (its Duty-Status with a capital D and S) in that relationship.

A complete analysis of a system of social relationships should permit us to construct a table in which every column (A, B, C, D . . . N) represents a status dimension and each number in a given column represents a status (scale combination of duties) on that dimension, as shown in *Table 4*. From such a table we could write the formula for every possible composite duty-status (e.g. A3-B1-C6-D7 . . . N2). We could compile an inventory of all possible identity relationships and after each one give the formulae for the composite duty-statuses (or right-statuses) of each identity in the relationship. This would provide a corpus of materials on which further analysis of cultural structure could then be undertaken.

Table 4.   Hypothetical Table of all Status Dimensions

DIMENSIONS	A	B	C	D	.	.	N
	1	1	1	1	.	.	1
Numbered	2	2	2	2	.	.	2
statuses	3	3	3	3	.	.	3
for each	4		4	4	.	.	4
dimension	5		5	5	.	.	5
			6	6	.	.	6
			7	7			

For one thing, we could see how identity relationships group into classes according to similarities of their reciprocal composite duty-statuses. We could do the same thing for each dimension separately and see the extent to which the same identity relationship bunch in the same classes from dimension to dimension. Cross-cultural differences in the organization of such syntactic classes could then be systematically explored.

For another thing, with the table in *Table 4* in mind, we are in a position to anticipate what I am certain research will show to be an interesting feature of the cultural organization of behavior, one that is responsible for a great deal of its apparent complexity. This has to do with the compatibility of the duties on different status dimensions for ready synthesis in a composite duty-status. Suppose, for example, that in terms of the possibilities in *Table 4*, the composite duty-status of identity X in relation to identity Y is A4-B2-C1-D1 . . . N4, and that the nature of one of the duties defining status B2 is such that honoring it precludes the possibility of honoring one of the duties in status C1. Some accommodation will have to be made in one of three possible ways: (1) one of the duties will have to be dropped in favor of the other; (2) one or both duties will have to be capable of being honored in more than one way, with allowance for the selection of compatible alternative modes of behavior; (3) both duties may be replaced by a distinctive third one that is simultaneously an alternative for both.

For example, it is my duty on certain occasions to rise when a lady enters the room. It often happens that I am for one reason or another

unable to do so, in which case I have the alternative duty to ask pardon for not rising. Here are two distinctive ways of honoring the same duty with a clear order of preference (it is wrong for me to ask pardon for not rising if I am clearly able to rise).

It is obvious that problems of this kind must arise frequently in composing actual behavior, especially when we consider that interactions often involve not a single identity relationship but several at once, for on many occasions the social personae of the participant actors are likely to consist of more than one relevant identity. Interactions involving more than two actors create even further possibilities of conflict among duties. In any social system, therefore, we can anticipate that there will be orderly procedures for handling conflicts of this kind, procedures that can be stated in the form of rules not unlike the rules of *sandhi* and vowel harmony in some languages.

ROLES

From the combinations in *Table 4*, we can readily describe all the composite duty-statuses and right-statuses for a given identity in all the identity relationships that are grammatically possible for it. The aggregate of its composite statuses may be said to constitute the identity's *role* in a sense a little less comprehensive than but otherwise close to Nadel's (1957) use of the term. It would be equivalent to a comprehensive 'role-set' in Merton's (1957b, p. 369) terms.

When we compare identities according to their respective roles, as thus defined, some identities will obviously be found to net more privileges (fewer duties) and/or more rights in all their identity relationships taken together than others. That is, the roles of some identities will have greater possibilities for gratification than the roles of others; some roles will allow more freedom of choice in action generally than others; and some will be more and some less cramping to particular personal styles of operation. Thus, different identities may be said to have different functions in the social system as a whole and to enjoy different value accordingly. Just how they differ, and how these differences relate to informants' evaluations of them, can be precisely described in relation to the sets of formulae that characterize the several composite statuses possible for each.

FEASIBILITY OF THE METHOD

To map out a social system in this way may be possible in theory, but is it not too time-consuming and tedious for investigator and informant alike? Certainly, collecting data of this kind is tedious. Nevertheless, Mahar (1959) was able to get a purity-pollution or ritual distance scale from eighteen different informants in Khalapur, India, with very satisfactory results, neatly solving the difficult problem of empirically determining local caste rankings and the degree of cross-caste agreement in these rankings. Her experience, added to my own from Truk, is encouraging.

But, we may ask, in any society we study, are there not so many duties, so many status dimensions, and so many identity relationships as to render the possibility of ever doing a complete analysis impracticable, however successful we may be in ferreting out a few scales? I do not think so. We are dealing with things that people manage to learn in the normal course of their lives without the benefit of systematic data collection and analysis. They are not likely, therefore, to be so complicated as to defy analysis.

On this point, findings in the psychology of cognition are highly suggestive. George Miller (1956) has called attention to impressive evidence that the human capacity to make judgements about where to class stimuli on unidimensional scales is severly limited. The greatest number of discriminations that can be made consistently on one dimension seems to be about seven (plus or minus two). In every interaction, on the basis of what he can observe of alter's behavior, ego has to make a judgement about where alter is putting him on every status scale, a judgement, that is, about the composite right-status that alter is ascribing to him in the relationship as alter perceives it. Ego may make these judgements for each dimension separately, but for any one dimension, the number of statuses about which he can make accurate judgments presumably will not exceed about seven. We expect, therefore, that no matter how many

duties may fit into the same scale, the number of distinctive distribution combinations (scale types) they will show will be within this limit for any one status dimension. This means that when there are more than six duties in a set forming a scale, some will have identical distributions, producing duty clusters on the scale, as shown in *Table 1*. Seven is in fact the number of statuses I obtained for each of the two status scales from Truk (*Tables 2* and *3*). Mahar (1959), moreover, found that of the thirteen actions whose distributions were clearly a function of ritual distance, some had to be treated as equivalent, so that she could derive only seven scale types from them for the purpose of scoring status differences.

Proceeding from dimension to dimension, ego may make several successive judgements in assessing what composite status alter is ascribing to him. But even this procedure must become cognitively difficult and cumbersome if many status dimensions are involved.

Finally, as complicatedly variable as human behavior seems to be, we must remember that the analysis outlined here is concerned only with duties (or rights). Many specific acts, I have suggested, are no more than different expressions of the same duty, like allomorphs of a morpheme in language. In this event their selection reflects syntactic rules of composition that are themselves ordered according to a limited number of principles. Much other variation in behavior reflects differences in behavioral styles, differences in the ways actors choose to elect their free options and exercise their privileges. Such variations need not concern us in deriving the formal properties of status systems.

These reasons lead me confidently to predict that the number of status dimensions in any system of social relationships will prove to be severely limited and that the number of statuses that are culturally discriminated on each dimension will prove to be in the neighbourhood of seven or less.

DUTY SCALES AS INSTRUMENTS OF SOCIAL ANALYSIS

So far I have presented a method for constructing models of how specific cultures have organized social relationships. I have also considered the feasibility of the method. But crucial questions remain: What can we do with the models once we have constructed them? Are they just an intellectual game? Or do they enable us to understand things about behavior that eluded us before? Answer to these questions is provided by the duty scales from Truk.

Scaling duties allows us to see the circumstances under which a breach of duty will be regarded as more or less serious. We would assume from *Table 2* that failure to honor a request would be least serious in Truk if alter were in right-status 4, the status in which this is the severest duty owed. It would be most serious if alter were in right-status 1, and there would be in-between degrees of seriousness if alter were in right-status 2 or 3. It is also possible that in those relationships in which a duty is the severest one owed, there is variation in the force of the obligation, its breach being forbidden in some instances and only disapproved in others. This is what we find in the second scale obtained from Truk (*Table 3*), one having to do with degrees of sexual distance (Goodenough, 1951, p. 117). If all four instances of 'disapproved' (D) in the scale were changed to 'forbidden' (F), eliminating this refinement, statuses 2 and 3 would merge, as would 4 and 5, and the total number of statuses discriminated on the dimension of sexual distance would be reduced from seven to five.

In every interaction, moreover, a Trukese ego has to decide to what extent he is forbidden from 'being above' alter and what is the appropriate cut-off point of his obligation on the duty scale shown in *Table 2*. If he wishes to flatter alter, he may act as if he were rendering one more duty than he feels is in fact required; and if he wishes to insult alter, he may render him one duty less. He must also decide what duties alter owes him and assess alter's behavior as proper, flattering, or insulting. The number of scale positions by which alter's behavior appears inappropriate measures the apparent degree of flattery or insult.

With this in mind, let us consider the occasion I encountered when an irate father struck his married daughter (right-status 2), to whom he owed all duties but the greeting *fääjiro*. Informants explained that he was angry, or he would not have done such a thing. Indeed, the fact that he was six points down the seven-point scale was a measure of how very angry he was. His daughter, it happened, was a self-centered and disagreeable young woman, whose petulant behavior had been getting on her kinsmen's nerves for some time. A good, hard jolt was just what she deserved. Being struck by her brother or husband, who were under no obligation not to strike her, would have had little dramatic impact. That her father struck her, however, the last man in the world who should, this was something she could not dismiss lightly. What provoked the incident was her indulgence in an early morning tirade against her husband whom she suspected of having just come from an amorous visit to her lineage sister next door. It is a Trukese man's privilege to sleep with his wife's lineage sisters (he is in duty-status 7 to them in *Table 3*), and men and women are not supposed to show any feelings of jealousy when this privilege is exercised. Her shrieking outburst against her husband, therefore, was another example of the 'spoiled child' behavior that made her unpleasant to live with. Witnesses seemed to relish her undoing as full of what we would call 'poetic justice.' I could not possibly have understood why they did so, if I had not already worked out the status scale of 'being above' another. Nor would I have been able to anticipate the feelings of shocked horror that people would have exhibited had the same act been performed in other circumstances. Indeed, relations between one informant and his older brother had been severely strained for about a year, because the former had violated his duties and told off his older brother (right-status 4) when the latter had exercised his privilege and struck their much older sister (right-status 7) in displeasure over some small thing she had done.

Methods that allow us objectively to measure such things as anger, insult, flattery, and the gravity of offenses, and that help us to appreciate the poetic justice of events in alien cultural contexts, such methods, I submit, are not exercises in sterile formalism. They promise to be powerful analytical tools. They encourage me to great optimism about the possibility of developing considerable precision in the science of social behavior.

SELECTED READINGS

Banton, Michael
1965 *Roles, an introduction to the study of social relations*. London: Tavistock.

Blumer, Herbert
1962 Society as symbolic interaction. In A. Rose (ed.), *Human behavior and social processes*. Boston: Houghton Mifflin.

Coser, Lewis A., and Bernard Rosenburg (eds.)
1964 *Sociological theory*. New York: Macmillan, chs. III, VIII.

Freed, Stanley A. and Ruth S. Freed
1971 A technique for studying role behavior. *Ethnology*, 10: 107–121.

Goffman, Erving
1959 *The presentation of self in everyday life*. Garden City, N.Y.: Doubleday.

Goodenough, Ward H.
1965 Rethinking status and role. In M. Banton (ed.), The relevance of models for social anthropology. *Association of Social Anthropologists of the Commonwealth, Monograph*, No. 1. London: Tavistock.

Homans, George
1958 Social behavior as exchange. *American Journal of Sociology*, 63: 597–606.

Linton, Ralph
1936 *The study of man*. New York: Appleton–Century–Crofts, ch. VIII, pp. 113–130.

Merton, Robert
1957a The role set: Problems in sociological theory. *British Journal of Sociology*, 8: 110–118.
———— 1957b *Social theory and social structure*. New York: Free Press.

Nadel, Siegfried
1957 *The theory of social structure*. New York: Free Press.

Rose, Arnold M. (ed.)
1962 Introduction to *Introduction to human behavior and social processes*. Boston: Houghton-Mifflin, pp. 3–19.

Sacks, Harvey
1963 Sociological description. *Berkeley Journal of Sociology*, 8: 1–16.

Sarbin, Theodore
1954 Role theory. In G. Lindzey (ed.), *Handbook of social psychology*. Reading, Mass.: Addison-Wesley, pp. 223 ff.

Schutz, Alfred
1964 *Collected papers II: Studies in social theory*. The Hague: Nijhoff.

XIV

INCEST TABOOS:
ORIGINS AND FUNCTIONS

Incest taboos—as well as the related phenomena of exogamy, the presence of the family, and the nature of intrafamilial roles—have, for a long time, interested anthropologists. Incest taboos prohibit sexual relationships between (classes of) persons because of their preexisting kinship relationships. Most authors have assumed that the range of incest prohibitions is the same as those of exogamy, that is, prohibitions on marriage between certain categories of kinsman. There are exceptions where sexual, but not permanent marital, relationships are allowed (e.g., Malinowski, 1927a; Fortes, 1949a; Goody, 1956), but these are rare.

Our fascination with the incest taboo stems from its universality as well as the great stress that the majority of societies places on it. Its universality and importance have led many writers to assume that the taboo plays the same functional role in all societies and, even more tenuously, that its original motivations can be equated with those that account for its maintainance. It should be reiterated that institutions of incest and exogamy are the reverse of the existence of "the family" (see chapter XV), that is, some solidary group within which mating is prohibited (cf. Murdock, 1949, in Chapter XV).

While incest taboos and exogamous prohibitions are universal, the ranges of their applications vary considerably from society to society —from the minimum prohibitions covering only parent-child matings in Egypt under the Roman Empire (Zeff, 1968), to moiety exogamy wherein half of the whole society is forbidden to the other half, to the extremes of caste endogamy in India where only a very small proportion of the whole society is available for choice of sexual mates. In the case of India, however, kinship is not the primary consideration. The range is generally most pronounced for the rules that concern the most distant kinsman; mating within the nuclear family (Pa-Ch, Br-Si), however, is very rarely allowed.

The earliest writers (e.g., Bachofen, Morgan, etc.) believed that there were primitive societies that did not have incest taboos or exogamous rules. They saw and explained the origin of these rules as an adaptive mechanism in their evolutionary schemes, one that allowed for the demarcation of more solidary corporate groups (e.g., gentes, clans) and for higher levels of political organization and, consequently, "success" in terms of survival of the fittest. The origins and functions of these taboos were therefore, in the opinion of these writers, political-adaptive acts (cf. Tylor, 1889; Lévi-Strauss, 1949).

Another common kind of explanation of the origins and functions of these phenomena lies in the assertion that those who are socialized together do not desire to mate with each other (cf. Westermark, 1891). The applicability of this type of explanation is limited because it does not account for the variability of incest taboos, the vehemence with which they have to be maintained, the high incidence of incest in various societies and groups, and such practises as the Chinese *sim-pua* (adopted sister marriage) (Wolf, 1968).

Another version of the "adaptive" explanation of incest taboos involves the assertion that sexual behavior is aggressive, dangerous, and likely to lead to competitive rivalries and role confusion if practised within such a small group as the family, for which smooth cooperation in its many diverse functions is essential. For instance, it is proposed that a son mating with his mother would make him a rival of his father and hence upset the hierarchy of authority in the family. This is of course related to Freud's story (see Chapter III) concerning a supposed origin of the incest taboo. This explanation can be partly refuted for the reasons outlined in the preceding paragraph.

Such sociological explanations are not totally satisfactory and, therefore, biological explanations have also been presented. The most common is the folk notion that "inbreeding" is physically bad and must therefore be avoided. Although statistically this might be true for certain populations having deleterious recessive genes, it, again, does not explain the variability of the range of taboos nor the high incidence of their breech with few observed ill consequences. Furthermore the statistically observable frequency of misfortunes is unlikely to be apparent to nonliterate populations unless they are able to perceive subliminal statistical trends and act upon them.

A more sophisticated type of biological explanation is put forward by Slater. ("Ecological Factors in the Origin of Incest," 1959.) It supposes that the eco-biosocial circumstances of early man precluded the possibility of much incest and, consequently, the practise of mating out became institutionalized. This, of course, does not satisfactorily explain why the taboo persisted or why it is given so much importance in most societies. Delving further into man's biosocial past, Aberle *et al* (1963) (see this chapter) compare the mating behavior of primates and higher animals in general. Their findings show that the matricentered nuclear family is the widest group within any species that prevents mating, and that, therefore, neither animal "instincts" nor "imprinting" are able to explain the human phenomenon. This was one of the first examples of the use of the growing ethological approach in anthropology. This approach examines animal and human behavioral systems and compares behavior across species.

The various functions of incest taboos and rules of exogamy are probably multiple and more complex than the considerations presented here. (See Fox, 1967: 54–76.) Few have examined the *folk* classifications of "sexual crimes" as thoroughly as Goody (1956). Whatever the total picture, it is probable that the general relaxation of sexual restrictions, as shown by recent court decisions in Sweden, indicates that the former necessities and motivations have lessened. This relaxation may even make it possible for us to see, more clearly, the relationships between instinct, socialization, alliance, and the incest taboo.

THE DEFINITION AND PROHIBITION OF INCEST

Leslie A. White

Again and again in the world's history, savage tribes must have had plainly before their minds the simple practical alternative between marrying-out and being killed out.

—*E. B. Tylor*

The subject of incest has a strange fascination for man. He was preoccupied with it long before he developed the art of writing. We find incestuous episodes in the mythologies of countless peoples. And in advanced cultures, from Sophocles to Eugene O'Neill, incest has been one of the most popular of all literary themes. Men seem never to tire of it but continue to find it ever fresh and absorbing. Incest must indeed be reckoned as one of man's major interests in life.

Yet, despite this intense and perennial concern, it is a fact that incest is but little understood even today. Men of science have been obliged all too often to admit that they are baffled and to declare that it is too mysterious, too obscure, to yield to rational interpretation, at least for the present.

One of the more common explanations of the universal prohibition of incest is that it is instinctive. Thus Robert H. Lowie (1920:15), a distinguished anthropologist, once accepted "Hobhouse's view that the sentiment is instinctive." To "explain" an element of behavior by saying that it is "instinctive" contributes little to our understanding of it as a rule. Sometimes it merely conceals our ignorance with a verbal curtain of pseudo-knowledge. To say that prohibitions against incest are "instinctive" is of course to declare that there is a natural, inborn and innate feeling of revulsion towards unions with close relatives. But if this were the case,

why should societies enact strict laws to prevent them? Why should they legislate against something that everyone already wishes passionately to avoid? Do not, as a matter of fact, the stringent and worldwide prohibitions indicate a universal and powerful desire for sexual unions with one's relatives? There are further objections to the instinct theory. Some societies regard marriage with a first cousin as incestuous while others do not. Are we to assume that the instinct varies from tribe to tribe? Certainly when we consider our own legal definitions of incest, which vary from state to state, to claim that a biological instinct can recognize boundary lines is somewhat grotesque. In some societies it is incestuous to marry a parallel cousin (a child of your father's brother or of your mother's sister) but it is permissible, and may even be mandatory, to marry a cross cousin (a child of your father's sister or of your mother's brother). We cannot see how "instinct" can account for this, either; in fact, we cannot see how instinct can distinguish a cross cousin from a parallel cousin. It is usually incestuous to marry a clansman even though no genealogical connection whatever can be discovered with him, whereas marriage with a close relative in *another* clan may be permissible. Plainly, the instinct theory does not help us at all, and it is not easy to find a scientist to defend it today.

Another theory, championed generations ago by Lewis H. Morgan and others, and not without defenders today, is that incest was defined and prohibited because inbreeding causes biological degeneration (1877). This theory is so plausible as to seem self-evident, but it is wrong for all that. In the first place, inbreeding as such does not cause degeneration; the testimony of biolo-gists is conclusive on this point. To be sure, inbreeding intensifies the inheritance of traits, good or bad. If the offspring of a union of brother and sister are inferior it is because the parents were of inferior stock, not because they were brother and sister. But superior traits as well as inferior ones can be intensified by in-breeding, and plant and animal breeders fre-quently resort to this device to improve their strains. If the children of brother-sister or father-daughter unions in our own society are frequently feeble-minded or otherwise inferior it is because feeble-minded individuals are more likely to break the powerful incest tabu than are normal men and women and hence more likely to beget degenerate offspring. But in societies where brother-sister marriages are permitted or required, at least within the ruling family, as in ancient Egypt, aboriginal Hawaii and Incaic Peru, we may find excellence. Cleopatra was the offspring of brother-sister marriages continued through several generations and she was "not only handsome, vigorous, intellectual, but also prolific . . . as perfect a specimen of the human race as could be found in any age or class of society (Mahaffy, 1915: 1).

But there is still another objection to the de-generation theory as a means of accounting for the origin of prohibitions against incest. A num-ber of competent ethnographers have claimed that certain tribes are quite ignorant of the nature of the biological process of reproduction, specifically, that they are unaware of the rela-tionship between sexual intercourse and preg-nancy. Or, they may believe that coitus is prerequisite to pregnancy but not the cause of it. B. Malinowski, for example, claims that the Tro-braind Islanders denied that copulation has any-thing to do with pregnancy, not only among human beings but among the lower animals as well. This thesis of ignorance of the facts of life among primitive peoples has been challenged by other ethnologists, and I am not prepared to adjudicate the dispute. But it may be pointed out that such ignorance should not be very surpris-

ing. Once a fact becomes well known there is a tendency to regard it as self-evident. But the relationship between coitus and pregnancy, a condition that would not be discovered until weeks or even a few months later, is anything but obvious. Furthermore, pregnancy does not always follow intercourse. And knowing primi-tive man's penchant for explaining so many things, the phenomena of life and death espe-cially, in terms of supernatural forces or agents, we should not be surprised to find some tribes even today who do not understand the physi-ology of paternity.

At any rate, there must have been a time at which such understanding was not possessed by any members of the human race. We have no reason to believe that apes have *any* appreciation of these facts, and it must have taken man a long time to acquire it. There are reasons, how-ever, as we shall show later on, for believing that incest tabus appeared in the very earliest stage of human social evolution, in all probability prior to an understanding of paternity. The rea-son for the prohibition of inbreeding could not therefore have been a desire to prevent deteri-oration of stock if the connection between copu-lation and the birth of children was not understood.

This thesis receives additional support from a consideration of the kinship systems of many primitive peoples. In these systems a person calls many of his collateral relatives "brother" and "sister," namely, his parallel cousins of several degrees for example, and the children of his mother's and father's parallel cousins, also of several degrees. Marriage between individuals who call each other "brother" and "sister" is strictly prohibited by the incest tabu, even though they be cousins of the third or fourth degree. But marriage with a *first cross cousin* may be permitted and often is required. Now these people may not understand the biology of conception and pregnancy, but they know which woman bore each child. Thus we see that the marriage rules disregard the degree of biological relationship so far as preventing inbreeding is concerned; they may prohibit marriage with a fourth parallel cousin who is called "brother" or "sister," but permit or require marriage with a first cross cousin who is called "cousin." Obviously, the kinship terms express sociological rather than biological relationships. Obvious also is the fact that the incest tabus follow the pattern of social ties rather than those of blood.

But suppose that inbreeding did produce inferior offspring, are we to suppose that ignorant, magic-ridden savages could have established this correlation without rather refined statistical techniques? How could they have isolated the factor of inbreeding from numerous others such as genetics, nutrition, illnesses of mother and infant, etc., without some sort of medical criteria and measurements—even though crude—and without the rudiments of statistics?

Finally, if we should grant that inbreeding does produce degeneracy, and that primitive peoples were able to recognize this fact, why did they prohibit marriage with a parallel cousin while allowing or even requiring union with a cross cousin? Both are equally close biologically. Or, why was marriage with a clansman prohibited even though the blood tie was so remote that it could not be established genealogically with the data available to memory, while marriage with a non-clansman was permitted even though he was a close blood relative? Obviously the degeneracy theory is as weak as the instinct hypothesis, although it may be more engaging intellectually.

Sigmund Freud's theory is ingenious and appealing—in a dramatic sort of way at least. Proceeding from Darwin's conjectures concerning the primal social state of man, based upon what was then known about anthropoid apes, and utilizing W. Robertson Smith's studies of totemism and sacrifice, Freud developed the following thesis: in the earliest stage of human society, people lived in small groups each of which was dominated by a powerful male, the Father. This individual monopolized all females in the group, daughters as well as mothers. As the young males grew up and became sexually mature, the Father drove them away to keep them from sharing his females with him. [See Chapter III.]

"One day," says Freud, "the expelled brothers joined forces, slew and ate the father, and thus put an end to the father horde. Together they dared and accomplished what would have remained impossible for them singly." But they did not divide their Father's women among themselves as they had planned. Now that he was dead their hatred and aggressiveness disappeared, and their love and respect for him came to the fore. As a consequence, they determined to give him in death the submission and obedience they had refused in life. They made therefore a solemn pact to touch none of their Father's women and to seek mates elsewhere. This pledge was passed on from one generation to the next: you must have nothing to do with the women of your father's household, i.e., of your own group, but must seek other mates. In this way the incest tabu and the institution of exogamy came into being.

This part of *Totem and Taboo* is great drama and not without value as an interpretation of powerful psychological forces, just as *Hamlet* is great drama in the same sense. But as ethnology, Freud's theory would still be inadequate even if this much were verifiable. It does not even attempt to account for the many and varied forms of incest prohibition.

It is not our purpose here to survey and criticize all of the many theories that have been advanced in the past to account for the definition and prohibition of incest. We may however briefly notice two others before we leave the subject, namely, those of E. Westermarck and Emile Durkheim.

Westermarck's thesis that "the fundamental cause of the exogamous prohibitions seems to be the remarkable absence of erotic feelings between persons living very closely together from childhood, leading to a positive feeling of averson when the act if thought of," (Westermarck, 1921, Table of Contents for Ch. 20.) is not in accord with the facts in the first place and would still be inadequate if it were. Propinquity does not annihilate sexual desire, and if it did there would be no need for stringent prohibitions. Secondly, incest tabus are frequently in force between persons not living in close association.

Durkheim attempts to explain the prohibition of incest as a part of his general theory of totemism. The savage knew intuitively, Durkheim reasoned (1898: 50 ff), that blood is a vital fluid or principle. To shed the blood of one's own totemic group would be a great sin or crime. Since blood would be shed in the initial act of intercourse, a man must eschew all women of his own totem. Thus the tabu against incest and rules of exogamy came into being. This theory is wholly inadequate ethnologically. Tabus against incest are much more widespread than totemism; the former are virtually universal, the latter is far from being so. And the theory does not even attempt to explain the many diverse forms of the definition and prohibition of incest.

In view of repeated attempts and as many failures to account for the origin of definitions of incest and of rules regulating its prohibition, is it any wonder than many scholars, surveying decades of fruitless theories, have become discouraged and have come to feel that the problem is still too difficult to yield to scientific interpretation?

In the same work in which he presented his theory, but some pages earlier, Freud said: "Still, in the end, one is compelled to subscribe to Frazer's resigned statement, namely, that we do not know the origin of incest dread and do not even know how to guess at it." [1]

Ralph Linton treats of the subject as follows:

> The causes which underlie such limitations on marriage, technically known as incest regulations, are very imperfectly understood. Since these regulations are of universal occurrence, it seems safe to assume that their causes are everywhere present, but biological factors can be ruled out at once. Close inbreeding is not necessarily injurious . . . Neither are purely social explanations of incest regulations altogether satisfactory, since the forms which these regulations assume are extremely varied. . . . It seems possible that there are certain psychological factors involved, but these can hardly be strong enough or constant enough to account for the institutionalization of incest

regulations. . . . They have probably originated from a combination of all these factors . . . (1936: 125–26).

In other words, *somewhere* in the man-culture situation lie the causes of incest regulations, but where they are and why and how they are exercised are matters too obscure for description or explanation.

The late Alexander Goldenweiser, a prominent disciple of Franz Boas, never discovered the secret of incest. In *Early Civilization* he spoke of certain tabus that "are everywhere reinforced by the so-called 'horror of incest,' an emotional reaction of somewhat mysterious origin." (1922: 242). Fifteen years later, in *Anthropology*, his last major work, he could go no further than to repeat these identical words (*idem*, 1937: 303).

The sociologists have little to offer. Kimball Young, for example, disavows instinct as the source of incest prohibitions, but he advances no further explanation than to assert that "the taboo is a rather constant and expected result arising from the very nature of the social interaction between parents and children and among the children themselves" (1942: 406) which is virtually equivalent to no explanation at all.

The late Clark Wissler, one of the foremost anthropologists of our day, observes:

> . . . . so far as we can see, the only facts sufficiently well established to serve as a starting point are that anti-incest responses of some kind are universal among mankind. As to why these are universal, we are no nearer a solution than before (1929: 145).

These are discouraging words indeed. "Anti-incest responses" help us no more than "an instinctive horror" of incest. But in the phrase "we are no nearer a solution [now] than before," we may find a clue to a way out of the dilemma. Perhaps these theorists have been on the wrong track. Science has found itself on the wrong track countless times during its relatively brief career so far. So many, in fact, that many of the important achievements of science consist, not in the discovery of some new fact or principle, but in erecting signs which read "Blind alley.

---

[1] Freud, 1931, p. 217. Frazer's statement was: "Thus the ultimate origin of exogamy and with it the law of incest—since exogamy was devised to prevent incest—remains a problem nearly as dark as ever." (*Totemism and Exogamy*, Vol. I, p. 165.)

Do not enter!" Phrenology was one of these blind alleys. But until it has been explored, how can one know whether a passage is a blind alley or a corridor leading to a new world? Once it has been found to be a blind alley, however, other scientists need not and should not waste their time exploring it again. Perhaps we are confronted by blind alleys in the various theories of incest and exogamy that we have just surveyed. Wissler's admission that "we are no nearer a solution [now] than before" would lead us to think so.

Fortunately we are not in the situation of a mariner who has lost his bearings and who must try to recover his true course. We do not need to seek a new path in the hope of finding an adequate solution of the problem of incest. The solution has already been found, and that long ago.

Confusion in this field of ethnological theory has been due to circumstances such as we have just described. Theorists who have sought biological or psychological explanations of incest tabus have been on the wrong track; they have only led us into blind alleys. Those who have sought a culturological explanation have succeeded fully and well. The culturological point of view is younger and less widely known than the psychological or even the sociological. Although it was set forth simply and adequately by the great English anthropologist, E. B. Tylor, as early as 1871, in the first chapter of *Primitive Culture*—which was significantly enough entitled "The Science of Culture"—it has not become widely known or appreciated among social scientists, even among cultural anthropologists. There are some who recognize in the new science of culture only a mystical, fatalistic metaphysic that should be shunned like the Devil. So habituated to psychological interpretations are many students of human behavior that they are unable to rise to the level of culturological interpretation. Thus, Goldenweiser looked to psychology for ethnological salvation (1937: 303). "It seems hardly fair to doubt that psychoanalysis will ultimately furnish a satisfactory psychological interpretation of this 'horror of incest'." Professor William F. Ogburn observes that:

Incest taboos and marriage regulations may be quite fully described historically and culturally, yet there is something decidedly strange about incest and about marriage prohibitions. One's curiosity is not satisfied by the cultural facts (1923:175).

And even men like Lowie and Wissler, who have done excellent work along culturological lines in other areas, have relapsed to the psychological level when confronted with the problem of incest. Thus Lowie once declared that "it is not the function of the ethnologist but of the biologist and psychologist to explain why man has so deep-rooted a horror of incest (1920: 15). And Wissler is inclined to turn over all problems of cultural origins to the psychologist, leaving to the anthropologist the study of traits after they have been launched upon their cultural careers.

The science of culture has, as we have already indicated, long ago given us an adequate explanation of incest prohibitions. We find it set forth simply and succinctly in an essay by E. B. Tylor published in 1888 [1889]: "On a Method of Investigating the Development of Institutions, Applied to the Laws of Marriage and Descent:"

Exogamy, enabling a growing tribe to keep itself compact by constant unions between its spreading clans, enables it to overmatch any number of small intermarrying groups, isolated and helpless. Again and again in the world's history, savage tribes must have had plainly before their minds the simple practical alternative between marrying-out and being killed out (1888: 267).

The origin of incest tabus greatly antedates clan organization, but a sure clue to an understanding of incest prohibitions and exogamy is given by Tylor nevertheless: primitive people were confronted with a choice between "marrying-out and being killed out." The argument may be set forth as follows:

Man, like all other animal species, is engaged in a struggle for existence. Cooperation, mutual aid, may become valuable means of carrying on this struggle at many points. A number of individuals working together can do many things more efficiently and effectively than the same individuals working singly. And a cooperative group can do certain things that lone individuals cannot do at all. Mutual aid makes life more secure for both individual and group. One might expect, therefore, that in the struggle for security and survival every effort would be made to foster cooperation and to secure its benefits.

Among the lower primates there is little co-operation. To be sure, in very simple operations one ape may coordinate his efforts with those of another. But their cooperation is limited and rudimentary because the means of communication are crude and limited; cooperation requires communication. Monkeys and apes can communicate with one another by means of signs—vocal utterances or gestures—but the range of ideas that can be communicated in this way is very narrow indeed. Only articulate speech can make extensive and versatile exchange of ideas possible, and this is lacking among anthropoids. Such a simple form of cooperation as "you go around the house that way while I go around the other way, meeting you on the far side," is beyond the reach of the great apes. With the advent of articulate speech, however, the possibilities of communication became virtually unlimited. We can readily see its significance for social organization in general and for incest and exogamy in particular.

One might get the impression from some psychologists, the Freudians especially, perhaps, that the incestuous wish is itself instinctive, that somehow a person "just naturally" focuses his sexual desires upon a *relative* rather than upon a *non*-relative, and among relatives, upon the closer rather than the remoter degrees of consanguinity. This view is quite as unwarranted as the theory of an "instinctive horror" of incest; an inclination toward sexual union with close relatives is no more instinctive than the social regulations devised to prevent it. A child has sexual hunger as well as food hunger. And he fixes his sex hunger upon certain individuals as he does his food hunger upon certain edible substances. He finds sexual satisfaction in persons close to him because they *are* close to him, not because they are his relatives, but that is another matter. As a consequence of proximity and satis-

faction the child fixates his sexual desires upon his immediate associates, his parents and his siblings, just as he fixates his food hungers upon familiar foods that have given satisfaction. He thus comes to have definite orientations and firm attachments in the realm of sex as in the field of nutrition. There is thus no mystery about incestuous desire; it is merely the formation and fixation of definite channels of experience and satisfaction.

We find therefore, even in sub-human primate families, a strong inclination toward inbreeding; one strives to obtain sexual satisfaction from a close associate. This tendency is carried over into human society. But here it is incompatible with the cooperative way of life that articulate speech makes possible. In the basic activities of subsistence, and defense against enemies, cooperation becomes important because life is made more secure thereby. Other factors being constant, the tribe that exploits most fully the possibilities of mutual aid will have the best chance to survive. In times of crisis, cooperation may become a matter of life or death. In providing food and maintaining an effective defense against foreign foes, cooperation becomes all-important.

But would primordial man be obliged to construct a cooperative organization for subsistence and defense from the very beginning, or could he build upon a foundation already in existence? In the evolutionary process, whether it be social or biological, we almost always find the new growing out of, or based upon, the old. And such was the case here; the new cooperative organization for food and defense was built upon a structure already present: the family. After all, virtually everyone belonged to one family or another, and the identification of the cooperative group with the sex-based family or another, and the identification of the cooperative group with the sex-based family would mean that the benefits of mutual aid would be shared by all. When, therefore, certain species of anthropoids acquired articulate speech and became human beings, a new element, an *economic* factor, was introduced into an institution which had up to now rested solely upon sexual attraction between male and female. We are, of course, using the term *economic* in a rather broad sense here to include safety as well as subsistence. The human primate family had now become a corporation with nutritive and protective functions as well as sexual and incidentally reproductive functions. And life was made more secure as a consequence.

But a regime of cooperation confined to the members of a family would be correspondingly limited in its benefits. If cooperation is advantageous *within* family groups, why not between families as well? The problem was not to extend the scope of mutual aid.

In the primate order, as we have seen, the social relationships between mates, parents and children, and among siblings antedates articulate speech and cooperation. They are strong as well as primary. And, just as the earliest cooperative group was built upon these social ties, so would a subsequent extension of mutual aid have to reckon with them. At this point we run squarely against the tendency to mate with an intimate associate. Cooperation *between* families cannot be established if parent marries child; and brother, sister. A way must be found to overcome this centripetal tendency with a centrifugal force. This way was found in the definition and prohibition of incest. If persons were forbidden to marry their parents or siblings they would be compelled to marry into some other family group—or remain celibate, which is contrary to the nature of primates. The leap was taken; a way was found to unite families with one another, and social evolution as a *human* affair was launched upon its career. It would be difficult to exaggerate the significance of this step. Unless some way had been found to establish strong and enduring social ties between families, social evolution could have gone no further on the human level than among the anthropoids.

With the definition and prohibition of incest, *families* became units in the cooperative process as well as individuals. Marriages came to be contracts first between families, later between even larger groups. The individual lost much of his initiative in courtship and choice of mates, for it was now a group affair. Among many primitive peoples a youth may not even be acquainted with his bride before marriage; in some cases he may not even have seen her. Children may be betrothed in childhood or infancy—or even before they are born. To be sure, there are tribes where one can become acquainted or even intimate with his spouse before marriage, but the group character of the contract is there nevertheless. And in our own society today a marriage is still an alliance between families to a very considerable extent. Many a man has expostulated, "But I am marrying *her*, not her family!" only to discover his lack of realism later.

The widespread institutions of levirate and sororate are explainable by this theory also. In the levirate a man marries the wife or wives of his deceased brother. When a man customarily married the unwed sister of his deceased wife the practice is called sororate. In both cases the group character of marriage is manifest. Each group of consanguinei supplies a member of the other group with a spouse. If the spouse dies, the relatives of the deceased must supply another to take his or her place. The alliance between families is important and must be continued; even death cannot part them.

The equally widespread institutions of bride-price and dowry likewise find their significance in the prohibition of incest to establish cooperation between family groups. The incest tabu necessitates marriage *between* family groups. But it cannot guarantee a continuation of the mutual aid arrangement thus established. This is where bride-price and dowry come in: they are devices for making permanent the marriage tie that the prohibition of incest has established. When a family or a group of relatives has received articles of value as bride-price or dowry, they distribute them as a rule among their various members. Should the marriage tie be broken or dissolved, they may have to return the wealth received at the time of the marriage. This is almost certain to be the case if it can be shown that the spouse whose relatives were the recipients of the bride-price or dowry was at fault. It very often happens that the relatives are reluctant to return the wealth if indeed they still have it. If it has already been consumed they will have to dig into their own pockets. It may already be earmarked for the marriage of one of their own group. In any event, the return of dowry or bride-price would be an inconvenience or a derivation. Consequently they are likely to take a keen interest in the marriage and to try to prevent their own relative from doing anything to disrupt it.

According to our theory the prohibition of incest has at bottom an economic motivation—not that primitive peoples were *aware* of this motive, however, for they were not. Rules of exogamy originated as crystallizations of processes of a *social system* rather than as products of individual psyches. Inbreeding was prohibited and marriage between groups was made compulsory in order to obtain the maximum benefits of cooperation. If this theory be sound, we should find marriage and the family in primitive society wearing a definite economic aspect. This is, in fact, precisely what we do find. Let us turn for summary statements to two leading authorities in social anthropology. Robert H. Lowie writes as follows:

> Marriage, as we cannot too often or too vehemently insist, is only to a limited extent based on sexual considerations. The primary motive, so far as the individual mates are concerned, is precisely the founding of a self-sufficient economic aggregate. A Kai (of New Guinea) does not marry because of desires he can readily gratify outside of wedlock without assuming any responsibilities; he marries because he needs a woman to make pots and to cook his meals, to manufacture nets and weed his plantations, in return for which he provides the household with game and fish and builds the dwelling (1920: 65–66).

And A. R. Radcliffe-Brown makes similar observations concerning the aborigines of Australia:

> The important function of the family is that it provides for the feeding and bringing up of the children. It is based on the cooperation of man and wife, the former providing the flesh food and the latter the vegetable food, so that quite apart

from the question of children a man without a wife is in an unsatisfactory position since he has no one to supply him regularly with vegetable food, to provide his firewood and so on. This economic aspect of the family is a most important one . . . I believe that in the minds of the natives themselves this aspect of marriage, i.e., its relation to subsistence, is of greatly more importance than the fact that man and wife are sexual partners (1930: 435).

Turning to the colonial period in America we find the economic character of the family equally pronounced. According to William F. Ogburn:

> In colonial times in America the family was a very important economic organization. Not infrequently it produced substantially all that it consumed, with the exception of such things as metal tools, utensils, salt and certain luxuries. The home was, in short, a factory. Civilization was based on a domestic system of production of which the family was the center.
>
> The economic power of the family produced certain corresponding social conditions. In marrying, a man sought not only a mate and companion but a business partner. Husband and wife each had specialized skills and contributed definite services to the partnership. Children were regarded, as the laws of the time showed, not only as objects of affection but as productive agents. The age of marriage, the birth rate and the attitude toward divorce were all affected by the fact that the home was an economic institution. Divorce or separation not only broke a personal relationship but a business one as well (1933: 661–2).

And in our own society today, the economic basis of marriage and the family is made clear by suits for breach of promise and alienation of affections in which the law takes a very materialistic, even monetary, view of love and romance. Suits for non-support, alimony, property settlements upon divorce, the financial obligations between parents and children, and so on, exhibit further the economic function of the family. Marriage for many women today means a greater economic return for unskilled labor than could be obtained in any other occupation. It is interesting to note, in this connection, that Freud who, according to popular belief, "attributes everything to sex," nevertheless declares that "the motivating force of human society is fundamentally economic." (Freud, 1920: 269).

The notion that marriage is an institution brought into being to provide individuals with a means of satisfying their sex hunger is naive and anthropocentric. Marriage *does* provide an avenue of sexual exercise and satisfaction, to be sure. But it was not sexual desire that produced the institution. Rather it was the exigencies of a social system that was striving to make full use of its resources for cooperative endeavor. Marriage, as an institution, finds its explanation in terms of socio-cultural process rather than individual psychology. In primitive society there was frequently ample means of sexual exercise outside of wedlock. And in our own society the great extent of prostitution, the high incidence of venereal disease as an index of promiscuity, as well as other evidence, show that the exercise of sexual functions is not confined to one's own spouse by any means. As a matter of fact, marriage very often restricts the scope of one's sexual activity. Indeed, monogamy ideally considered is the next thing to celibacy.

Nor is love the basis of marriage and the family, however fondly this notion may be cherished. No culture could afford to use such a fickle and ephemeral sentiment as love as the basis of an important institution. Love is here today but it may be gone tomorrow. But economic needs are with us always. Absence of love is not sufficient grounds for divorce. Indeed, one may despise and loathe, hate and fear one's mate and still be unable to obtain a divorce. At least one state in the Union will grant no divorce at all. And certain religious faiths take the same position. Marriage and the family are society's first and fundamental way of making provision for the economic needs of the individual. And it was the definition and prohibition of incest that initiated this whole course of social development.

But to return to the definitions and prohibitions themselves. These vary, as we saw at the outset, from culture to culture. The variations are to be explained in terms of the specific circumstances under which cooperation is to take place. One set of circumstances will require one definition of incest and one form of marriage; another set will require different customs. The habitat and the technological adjustment to it, the mode of subsistence, circumstances of defense and offense, division of labor between the sexes, and degree of cultural development, are factors which condition the definition of incest and the formulation of rules to prohibit it. No people known to modern science customarily permits marriage between parent and child. Brother-sister marriage has been restricted to the ruling families of a few advanced cultures, such as those of ancient Egypt, Hawaii and the Inca of Peru. But this is not "royal incest" as Reo Fortune calls it, (1932b: 622) or "sanctioned incest" to use Kimball Young's phrase (1942: 406). Incest is by definition something criminal and prohibited. These marriages between siblings of royal families were not only not prohibited; they were required. They are examples of endogamy, as the prohibition of brother-sister marriages are examples of exogamy. Solidarity is a source of strength and effective action in society, as cooperation is a way of achieving security. And endogamy promotes solidarity as exogamy fosters size and strength of mutual aid groups.

In view of the fact that a sure clue to the reason for the origin of prohibitions of incest was set forth by Tylor as early as 1888, it is rather remarkable that we should find anthropologists and sociologists today who juggle with "anti-incest responses" and who look to psychoanalysis for ultimate understanding. As a matter of fact, we find the reasons for exogamy set forth by Saint Augustine in The City of God (Bk. XV), more than 1400 years before Tylor:

> For it is very reasonable and just that men, among whom concord is honorable and useful, should be bound together by various relationships, and that one man should not himself sustain many relationships, but that the various relationships should be distributed among several, and should thus serve to bind together the greatest number in the same social interests. 'Father' and 'father-in-law' are the names of two relationships. When, therefore, a

man has one person for his father, another for his father-in-law, friendship extends itself to a larger number.

He comments upon the fact that Adam was both father and father-in-law to his sons and daughters:

> So too Eve his wife was both mother and mother-in-law to her children. . . . while had there been two women, one the mother, the other the mother-in-law, the family affection would have had a wider field. Then the sister herself by becoming a wife sustained in her single person two relationships which, had they been distributed among individuals, one being sister, and another being wife, the family tie would have embraced a greater number of persons.

Saint Augustine does not, in these passages at least, make explicit the advantages in security of life which would accrue to the group as a consequence of exogamy. But he makes it quite clear that community of social interest and "greater number of persons" in the group are the reasons for the prohibition of incest.

If an understanding of incest and exogamy is as old in social philosophy as Saint Augustine and as early in anthropological science as Tylor, why is it that the subject is still so obscure and so little understood among scholars today? We have already suggested the answer: a preference for psychological rather than culturological explanations. Anthropomorphism is an inveterate habit in human thought. To explain institutions in terms of psychology—of wish, desire, aversion, imagination, fear, etc.—has long been popular. Explanations of human behavior in terms of psychological determinants preceded therefore explanations in terms of cultural determinants. But culturological problems cannot be solved by psychology. Preoccupation with psychological explanations has not only kept many scholars from finding the answer; it has prevented them from recognizing the solution when it has been reached by the science of culture. The sociological explanation, such as Kimball Young's "social interaction," is no better. As a scientific explanation it is not only inadequate; it is empty and meaningless. The sociologist's fixation upon "social interaction" keeps him, too, from appreciating a scientific interpretation of culture as a distinct class of phenomena. Even men who have made notable contributions to culturology, such as Kroeber, Lowie, and Wissler, have failed to see the significance of Tylor's early discussion of exogamy. The following incident is remarkable and revealing. A. L. Kroeber and T. T. Waterman reprinted Tylor's essay, "On the Method of Investigating the Development of Institutions," in the *Source Book in Anthropology* in 1920. But in a subsequent edition, (*Ibid.*, 1931.) they cut the article down to conserve space, and omitted this highly significant passage!

Important contributions to science are sometimes made "before their time," that is, before the general level of scientific advance has reached a point where widespread appreciation becomes possible. There was really very little that was novel in the work of Darwin; most if not all of the ideas and facts had been presented before. But the broad front of the cultural process of biologic thought had not advanced sufficiently prior to 1859 to make a general acceptance of this point of view possible. So it is with the problem of incest. An adequate explanation has been extant for decades. But, because the problem is a culturological one, and because the science of culture is still so young and so few scholars even today are able to grasp and appreciate its nature and scope, an understanding of incest and its prohibitions is still very limited. As culturology develops and matures, however, this understanding as well as that of a host of other suprapsychological problems will become commonplace.

We do not wish to minimize the extent of this understanding today. Despite the ignorance and confusion of many scholars, there is a considerable number who do understand incest tabus. Thus Reo Fortune states that (1932b: 620)

> A separation of affinal relationship from consanguineous relationship assures a wider recognition of social obligation, . . . Any incestuous alliance between two persons within a single consanguineous group is in so far a withdrawal of their consanguineous group from

the alliance and so endangers the group's survival.

Malinowski, too, has illuminated the problem of incest tabus. Instead of emphasizing, however, the positive values that would accrue from alliances formed as a consequence of compulsory exogamy, he dwells upon the disruption and discord that the unrestricted exercise of sexual appetites would introduce into a small group of relatives or close associates. He writes:

> The sexual impulse is in general a very upsetting and socially disruptive force, [it] cannot enter into a previously existing sentiment without producing a revolutionary change in it. Sexual interest is therefore incompatible with any family relationship, whether parental or between brothers and sisters. . . . If erotic passion were allowed to invade the precincts of the home it would not merely establish jealousies and competitive elements and disorganize the family but it would also subvert the most fundamental bonds of kinship on which the further development of all social relations is based . . . A society which allowed incest could not develop a stable family; it would therefore be deprived of the strongest foundations for kinship, and this is a primitive community would mean absence of social order (1930: 630).

B. Z. Seligman expresses somewhat similar views—as well as others that are less discerning (1929: 243–244, 247, 268–269). A good statement on the nature and genesis of incest tabus is tucked away in a footnote in a recent monograph by John Gillin (1936: 93). William I. Thomas sees clearly the reasons for prohibitions of incest: "The horror of incest is thus plainly of social derivation" (1937: 197).

And Freud, apart from his drama of patricide, comes close to an understanding of incest tabus and exogamy. He says:

> The incest prohibition, had . . . a strong practical foundation. Sexual need does not unite men; it separates them. . . . Thus there was nothing left for the brothers [after they had killed their father], if they wanted to live together, but to erect the incest prohibition (1931: 250–1).

In another work he observes that:

> The observance of this [incest] barrier is above all a demand of cultural society, which must guard against the absorption by the family of those interests which it needs for the production of higher social units. Society, therefore, uses all means to loosen those family ties in every individual . . . (1938: 616–17).

The cultural function, if not the genesis, of incest tabus and of rules of exogamy seems to be very clearly seen and appreciated here. It is interesting to note, too, that Freud holds substantially the same view of the relationship between restrictions upon sexual gratification and social evolution that has been set forth earlier in this essay. One of the principal themes of *Civilization and Its Discontents* (1930) is "the extent to which civilization is built up on renunciation of instinctual gratifications. . . . This 'cultural privation' dominates the whole field of social relations between human beings" (p. 63). He sees that "the first result of culture was that a larger number of human beings could live together in common" (p. 68); that "one of culture's principal endeavors is to cement men and women together in larger units" (p. 72). Thus, although he proceeds from different premises, Freud comes to essentially the same conclusions as ours.

There is, then, considerable understanding of incest and exogamy extant in the literature today. Yet, in a comparatively recent review of the whole problem a prominent anthropologist, John M. Cooper, has concluded that "the desire to multiply the social bonds [has] in all probability not been [an] important factor" in the origin of incest prohibitions (1932: 20). How far he is from an understanding of the problem is indicated by the two "chief factors" which he cites: "(a) sex callousness, resulting from early and intimate association . . . ; (b) the distinctly social purpose of preserving standards of sex decency within the family and kinship circle." The first factor is contrary to fact; intimacy fosters incest rather than callousness. The second explains nothing at all: what are standards of sex decency, why do they vary from tribe to tribe, and why is it necessary to preserve them?

The culturological theory of incest receives support from a comparison of primitive cultures with our own. The crime of incest is punished with greater severity in primitive societies than in our own, as Reo Fortune (1932b: 620) has observed. Among the former the penalty of death is quite common; in our society punishment seldom exceeds ten years imprisonment and is often much less. The reason for this difference is not far to seek. In primitive societies, personal and kinship ties between individuals and families were more important than they are in highly developed cultures. The small mutual-aid group was a tremendously important social unit in the struggle for security. The very survival of the group depended to a considerable extent upon alliances formed by exogamy. In advanced cultures the situation is different. Society is no longer based upon kinship ties, but upon property relationships and territorial distinctions. The political state has replaced the tribe and clan. Occupational groups and economic organization also become important bases of social life. The importance of exogamy is thus much diminished and the penalties for incest become less severe. It is not to be expected, however, that restrictions upon inbreeding will ever be removed entirely. Kinship is still an important, though relatively less important, feature of our social organization and will probably remain so indefinitely. Rules of exogamy and endogamy will therefore continue to be needed to regulate and order this aspect of our social life.

In the various interpretations, both sound and unsound, of the definition and prohibition of incest we have a neat example of a contrast between psychological explanations on the one hand and culturological explanations on the other. The problem simply does not yield to psychological solution. On the contrary, the evidence, both clinical and ethnographic, indicates that the desire to form sexual unions with an intimate associate is both powerful and widespread. Indeed, Freud opines that "the prohibition against incestuous object-choice [was] perhaps the most maiming wound ever inflicted . . . on the erotic life of man." (1930: 74). Psychology discloses an "incestuous wish" therefore, not a motive for its prevention. The problem yields very readily, however, to culturological interpretation. Man, as an animal species, lives in groups as well as individually. Relationships between individuals in the human species are determined by the *culture* of the group—that is, by the ideas, sentiments, tools, techniques, and behavior patterns, that are dependent upon the use of symbols and which are handed down from one generation to another by means of this same faculty. These culture traits constitute a continuum, a stream of interacting elements. In this interacting process, new combinations and syntheses are formed, some traits become obsolete and drop out of the stream, some new ones enter it. The stream of culture thus flows, changes, grows and develops in accordance with laws of its own. Human behavior is but the reaction of the organism man to this stream of culture. Human behavior—in the mass, or of a typical member of a group—is therefore culturally determined. A people has an aversion to drinking cow's milk, avoids mothers-in-law, believes that exercise promotes health, practices divination or vaccination, eats roasted worms or grasshoppers, etc., because their culture contains trait-stimuli that evoke such responses. These traits cannot be accounted for psychologically.

And so it is with the definition and prohibition of incest. From psychology we learn that the human animal tends to unite sexually with someone close to him. The institution of exogamy is not only *not* explained by citing this tendency; it is contrary to it. But when we turn to the cultures that determine the relations between members of a group and regulate their social intercourse we readily find the reason for the definition of incest and the origin of exogamy. The struggle for existence is as vigorous in the human species as elsewhere. Life is made more secure, for group as well as individual, by cooperation. Articulate speech makes cooperation possible, extensive, and varied in human society. Incest was defined and exogamous rules were formulated in order to make cooperation compulsory and extensive, to the end that life be made more secure. These institutions were created by *social* systems, not by *neuro-sensory-muscular-glandular* systems. They were syntheses of culture elements formed within the interactive stream of culture traits. Variations of definition and prohibition of incest are due to the great variety of situations. In one situation, in our organization of culture traits—technological, social, philosophic, etc.—we will find one type of definition of incest and one set of rules of exogamy; in a different situation we find another definition and other rules. Incest and exogamy are thus defined in terms of the mode of life of a people—by the mode of subsistence, the means and circumstances of offense and defense, the means of communication and transportation, customs of residence, knowledge, techniques of thought, etc. And the mode of life, in all its aspects, technological, sociological, and philosophical, is culturally determined.

ECOLOGICAL FACTORS IN THE ORIGIN OF INCEST

Mariam Kreiselman Slater

INTRODUCTION

The universality of the incest taboo and/or exogamy is almost as puzzling a phenomenon today as it was at the dawn of anthropology. Although the latest attempts to account for it are satisfactory in some respects, they seem to be at variance with widely accepted developments in general anthropological theory, chiefly with interaction theory (Chapple and Arensberg 1940; Homans 1950; Homans and Schneider 1955; Polanyi, Arensberg and Pearson 1957).

In an attempt to align current theory and hypothesis, I suggest here a new approach to the origin of exogamy. The procedure used could be considered an exercise in the derivation of an hypothesis from theory, or simply the exploration of some implications of interaction principles in a purely speculative area where they have not yet been applied.

Juxtaposed with this methodology is another line of research—human ecology. The level of analysis within this dual orientation is neither psychological nor culturological but, in the broadest American sense, anthropological. That is, I

Reproduced by permission of the author and the American Anthropological Association from *American Anthropologist*, Vol. 61, 1959, pp. 1042–1043, 1048–1058.

do not hold human biology constant, but consider it a variable affected by changing techno-environmental contexts.

Not only the search but even the need for new questions about exogamy seems to be obscured by a number of philosophical presuppositions in the work of current authors, some even contrary to the principles of evolution. Perhaps certain assumptions have gone unnoticed because recent theories account adequately for certain stages of the problem, but not, I believe, the initial ones. My point of departure, therefore, must be a summary and critique of current opinion, for which I have selected the following representative anthropologists: Leslie White (1949); Brenda Z. Seligman (1950); and Claude Lévi-Strauss (1949, 1956).

THE PROBLEM

First it is necessary to make a brief statement about the cross-cultural data, the general problem, and the clarification of terms. To be concise, let us say that all societies have patterned some form of marriage, and in doing so, usually forbid an individual to mate with his parents, siblings, or children. These proscriptions may extend beyond the nuclear group. The following statement qualifies the above generalizations: No society ever permits an individual to mate with *all* members of his or her family of orientation or procreation.

The problem, of course, is to explain why this model is universal. The manner in which societies regulate restrictions on sexual intercourse and the formation of marriage ties has been described variously as "incest prohibition," "exogamy," and "incest taboo."

In the semantic juggling of these sometimes overlapping concepts, most students recognize three basic distinctions. First, there are differences between rules qua rules and those accompanied by behavior connoted by the word taboo. Secondly, some of the rules or attitudes pertain exclusively to the nuclear family, and some extend beyond. And finally, there are distinctions between norms governing sexual relations and those regulating marriage.

. . .

Early hominids did not mate out because of expediency, sentiment, or an accident that gave them a chance to survive. They did not mate out to form bonds of mutual aid or because of cultural prohibitions. On the contrary, the cooperative bonds as well as the prohibitions must have been consequences of their having already mated out because of structural necessity.

My hypothesis is, then, that a certain kind of group even mating at random, both incestuously and otherwise, would form extra-nuclear child-rearing ties with sufficient frequency (a tenet of interaction theory) as to be the only possible focus for elaboration once culture emerged. Random mating, of course, could not long persist among cultural animals, for where there is culture there is regularity. But such patterning or structuring must have a beginning and must make use of what exists. To repeat, marriage patterns must have been based on behavioral interaction that is statistically likely to have occurred among animals of a certain kind before they developed any cultural biases.

To prove the hypothesis, one would have to find an animal that had to seek individuals other than parents, children, or siblings for mates. An animal would be so compelled only if his kin were not of the proper ages for mating. Then one would have to demonstrate that the earliest hominid patterns arose from such a background. If these conditions were met, all variations of the ethnographic record pertaining to rules and taboos would be as explicable as any other cultural elaboration.

The reason why the ideal solution has not been considered self-evident is that in most contemporary cultures—as among lower animals—incestuous groups could function as long and as well as many others in terms of vital statistics. However, the very simplest technologies and subsistence ecologies involve biological factors not immediately apparent. It is in societies which approach this simplicity that one finds hints of that structural necessity which theory demands to have been the basis for the earliest form of human society.

The structural necessity that determines nuclear exogamy is complex, involving birth, fertility, and maturation rates as well as life expectancy and birth order. Let us first consider nonhuman primates and reconstruct some hypothetical vital statistics to demonstrate in a new sense how certain animals would have to mate out or die out. (Note that Tylor did not refer to marrying out or "dying out," but to marrying out or "being killed out." He did not assume natural death, but death as the result of actions of other people or the effects of a hostile environment if people did not band together.)

Let us imagine that the life span of a species is four years. Puberty occurs at the age of three years, after 75 percent of the life span has passed. The female produces only one offspring per birth, and the gestation period is three months. The progeny must be nursed for two months, whereupon the mother becomes pregnant again and three months later bears her second child. After the second child has nursed for two months and can fend for itself, the mother becomes pregnant again, but within two months she is dead, and thus no individual can give birth to more than two offspring in her lifetime. Furthermore, each child has a 50 percent chance of reaching the age of reproduction.

By the time the first child reached puberty, the parents would have been dead for about two years, thus preventing any parent-child incest. Even if sexual play occurred between adult and small child, sexual intercourse could not occur in the case of the immature male. At any rate, the species could not be continued through parent-child matings.

Let us now see whether the siblings, the F_1 generation, could continue the species, assuming that both live and are of opposite sex, a possibility realized in only one out of every five families. If two siblings mated, the female could produce only one offspring instead of her potential two, due to the five-month age differential between siblings. Thus, to continue the species, the single grandchild would have to mate out. Furthermore, as we have seen, in 80 percent of families any member of the F_1 generation would have to breed out or die childless. Even in families with two opposite-sexed siblings, the probability of incest if further minimized by the fact that the older child has already lived half of his or her sexually mature months before the younger reaches puberty. The chances are that this individual would already have mated out or left home before the other sibling comes of age.

Similar results would occur if the life span of a species is 20 years, if the female can give birth only every fourth year, and if each sex reaches the age of reproduction at 15, considering the gestation period to be one year. No mother could have more than two children, and the second child would have to be self-sufficient at the age of one. By the time the first child reached puberty, the parents would have been dead for 10 years. If the first child is female, she could conceive a child by her brother only in her next to last year of life. Again the F_3 generation would have to mate out. Finally, we see that a family with two children could occur only if the parent couple are closer age mates than intrafamily mating allows, except in the case of twins.

If the same age of puberty prevailed, but we raise the life expectancy to 27 and the fertility rate to one birth every five years, the following would occur:

Again, parent-child matings would be impossible. But the female would be able to bear three children in her life. If the first child were female

and the second male, the former could produce only two children by him. She could bear a third child only if the third sibling were male. In other words, any two children of oposite sex born in succession could produce only two children, thus causing the noncontinuance of the family as in the first case. Only rarely would the birth order permit a woman to have the three children she was capable of bearing.

It would be possible to extrapolate known human life cycles and approach the assumed vital statistics of some creature intermediate between the first hominid and his nearest precursor. But instead of postulating detailed patterns of a form whose fossil remains are unknown and whose habits are perhaps unknowable, let us examine only those hints available in the life of primitive contemporaries. Surprisingly, the more primitive the ecology, the more closely we approach the hypothetical ideal. So close do we approach it that we call the next heading "evidence" for the hypothesis that theory demands.

EVIDENCE

Ludwik Krzywicki, in his book *Primitive Society and Its Vital Statistics* (1935), has made a thorough search of the literature that underscores the following points necessary for our thesis: Relatively speaking, the life of the most primitive people is short, few children reach maturity, and the reproductive period is reduced. He quotes Spencer and Gillen on the subject of the Australian woman: "By the time she is 25 or, at most 30, she is completely passée, and at 40 is a veritable hag. . . . There are probably few who live beyond the age of 50" (Krzywicki 1935: 120). Of 25 of these women studied, 16 percent were under 12 at the birth of their first child, and 16 percent over 16, with an average age of 14. The average period of child-bearing is 15 years (Krzywicki 1935: 129), and the mother is usually barren by the age of thirty-five. No woman gives birth to more than five children, and from 40 to 50 percent of them die within a few months.

As among most hunters and gatherers, one finds in Australia a long suckling period, although this is not a nutritional necessity if the environment is a lush one providing easily digestible food. I have not found any material on the relation of suckling periods to exigencies of the ecology. I can only deal with existing practices, assuming some relation to necessity if there is a high correlation of long suckling and unfavorable ecologies.

According to Krzywicki, among the Australians each child is nursed from two to four years. If the mother dies within this period, the child too is likely to die. If a confinement occurs before three years have passed, the new child is killed or else it would die for lack of mother's milk. Such are the conditions of life in Australia whose surplus is sufficient for polygyny to be possible.

Even so primitive a contemporary as the Australians have an ecology vastly more developed than at the beginning of culture. They possess stone celts; their dart thrower is probably no earlier than the Würm glaciation. But even allowing for the greater ease of food getting among them, their vital statistics suggest corroborative evidence for our hypothesis. Under harder conditions, there must have been even fewer children born, and they had even shorter lives.

In the stationary population of the Andamans, where food is more abundant, Krzywicki reports (1935: 147) that each woman raises from three to four children. The Bushmen raise only two or three of their children, nursing each for three years and killing later infants. Only 50 percent of the Fuegians' average of four children reach maturity. One woman had 18 children, but all died except three. In Alaska the Eskimo have only one or two living children; on Bering Strait, from two to three (Krzywicki 1935: 151).

In *The Role of the Aged in Primitive Society*, Leo Simmons (1945) produces similar samplings and figures. "Between the thirtieth and fortieth years, in the case of men, and even earlier in the case of women," he quotes from Im Thurm's report on the Arawak, ". . . . the body, except the stomach, shrinks, the fat disappears and the skin hangs in hideous folds." Jenks describes the Igorot as getting old at thirty, their muscles losing form by forty-five. Howorth in Mongolia notes that the women are middle-aged at thirty.

On the whole, Simmons concludes, only 3 percent of primitive people reach sixty-five. And long before this they have passed the age of reproduction, for old age sets in between the ages of thirty and forty-five. Although reproduction may be possible despite the appearance of old age, the time of death shortens the period of child-rearing.

According to Todd, (1927: 481–496), the mean age of death in West Africa was 30, and more than half the Tasmanians were dead at twenty-five. Of 600 Indians at Pecos between the years 1800 and 1938, only sixty reached the age of sixty-five. In general, he says, 15 percent of deaths of primitive people between the ages of 20 and 39 are due to childbirth. He places the difference in peaks of mortality between primitives and moderns at thirty years.

Not only is the child-rearing cycle shortened by the early onset of senescence or death among primitive, but the human animal under all conditions does not as a rule begin to reproduce until relatively late. Neither ovulation nor spermatogenesis occurs before puberty (Henshaw 1953: 572), a stage marked in the female by the menarche. The onset of menstruation is the same on the average throughout the world, occuring at the age of 15; the lowest average reported is that among the Spanish-Maya at 12.81 years of age; the highest, among the Spanish from Austria, at 16.98 (Hooton 1947: 251). But puberty in women does not always coincide with the beginning of fertility, for: ". . . The first few years after the menses appear as a period of relative sterility" (Ford 1945: 22).

In modern Europe, the menopause occurs between the ages of 45 and 50; the male usually is fertile until after 50 (Hooton 1947: 266). And post-Neolithic man has a longer breeding period and is more prolific also because he possesses foods that render long suckling unnecessary. Depending on the culture and ecology, weaning takes place at any time from six months to twelve years (Ford 1945: 78; Hooton 1947: 259). However, modern man is weaned on the average at 18 months; primitive man on the average at 2 or 3 years (Hooton 1947). This difference lowers the birth rate among primitives because ovulation occurs only rarely during lactation. The technical reason for this is that "purified lactogenic hormone will induce functional activity of corpora lutea, which secrete progesterone, which in turn inhibits pituitary release of lutinizing hormone" (Henshaw 1953). It takes a theoretical minimum of 280 days after the first menstural flow following weaning the birth of a new baby (Hooton 1947: 255).

From the above data we have made two charts illustrating the degree of incompatibility between incestuous unions and child-rearing units in a society where the vital statistics conform to probable models. Among the vital statistics, there are five significant variables: age at menarche; length of sterile period; duration of suckling; onset of menopause; age at death. Although men can produce more children in a given time than women, this does not alter the situation. It is pointless to draw a chart for every possible combination of factors. In Chart 1 we take average conditions. Chart 2 shows the ages when the variables are the lowest points of the range.

In both of these cases, one sees the relative ages of one mother and her children. Since half of any woman's offspring are likely to die, each child has an equal chance of life or death. The relative ages of the siblings or half-siblings, then, depend on the time of death in relation to the order of birth. The relation of sex to order of birth is also an influence on mating patterns, and the chance of being male or female in any one case is of course equal.

We are led by the scant available literature to believe that on the average each woman bears five children within fifteen years of reproductive life. The number of children reaching maturity depends on all the variables mentioned.

In interpreting these charts as opposed to the imaginary life cycles outlines previously, not only vital statistics but another factor must be taken into consideration; i.e., the sexual division of labor, which is a given in all known human societies and totally absent among all other living primates. The sexual division of labor influences breeding patterns, but we cannot reconstruct the phylogenetic appearance of the phenomenon. Regarding this factor, we cannot extrapolate from human to protohominid society.

In the earliest human societies (possessing the simplest inventory of exploitative techniques), we know that no significant surplus is possible, whatever the environment—whether warm eolithic prairies and softwood forests, the woolly mammoth's habitat, or an interglacial environment like that of today. With no surplus, developmental laws assure us that there could have been no more than a sexual division of labor. It is also probable that this much division of labor was necessary. We are familiar with some Eskimo groups whose adults cannot survive without mates, or children without both parents. This is a special case, but Lévi-Strauss says that among primitives in general: "there are no bachelors, simply for the reason that they could not survive" (1956: 269). Furthermore, "The number of males and females in any random grouping is approximately the same with a normal balance of about 110 to 100 to the advantage of either sex" (1956: 267). Since polygyny is unlikely with such an ecology, men and women are approximately equally paired off at any given time, even if there is a continual succession of different mates.

Among the first hominids, food gathering was probably more insecure than it is among most of the simplest cultures observed by anthropologists in the ethnographic present. As Childe says, primitive contemporaries are more like Mesolithic than Paleolithic peoples; that is, their life is more settled and there is a larger surplus (Childe 1956: 97). According to Sauer, certain types of vegetation could not even have appeared until population pressure produced man's wanderings, which precipitated changes in his habitat (1947: 7–20). Even after they existed, millennia later, many items could not have been incorporated into the diet before fire. Nor could people use hard seeds before grinding. Sauer points out that there were probably no specialized hunters until the Solutrean period, and these were limited to the arctic and plains regions. Children must have depended for a long time on only their mother's milk, and the effects

Chart 1. Age in Years

Mother	19	20	21	22	23	24	25	26	27	28	29	30	31	32	33	34	35	36	37	38	39	40	41	42	43	44	45	46	47	48	49
1st child	1	2	3	4	5	6	7	8	9	10	11	12	13	14	15	16	17	18	19	20	21	22	23	24	25	26	27	28	29	30	31
2nd child					1	2	3	4	5	6	7	8	9	10	11	12	13	14	15	16	17	18	19	20	21	22	23	24	25	26	27
3rd child									1	2	3	4	5	6	7	8	9	10	11	12	13	14	15	16	17	18	19	20	21	22	23
4th child													1	2	3	4	5	6	7	8	9	10	11	12	13	14	15	16	17	18	19
5th child																	1	2	3	4	5	6	7	8	9	10	11	12	13	14	15
6th child																					1	2	3	4	5	6	7	8	9	10	11

Age at menarche—15 years.   Length of sterile period—2 years.   Duration of suckling—3 years.

Chart 2. Age in Years

Mother	15	16	17	18	19	20	21	22	23	24	25	26	27	28	29	30	31	32	33	34	35	36	37	38	39	40	41	42	43	44	45
1st child	1	2	3	4	5	6	7	8	9	10	11	12	13	14	15	16	17	18	19	20	21	22	23	24	25	26	27	28	29	30	31
2nd child				1	2	3	4	5	6	7	8	9	10	11	12	13	14	15	16	17	18	19	20	21	22	23	24	25	26	27	28
3rd child							1	2	3	4	5	6	7	8	9	10	11	12	13	14	15	16	17	18	19	20	21	22	23	24	25
4th child										1	2	3	4	5	6	7	8	9	10	11	12	13	14	15	16	17	18	19	20	21	22
5th child													1	2	3	4	5	6	7	8	9	10	11	12	13	14	15	16	17	18	19
6th child																1	2	3	4	5	6	7	8	9	10	11	12	13	14	15	16

Age at menarche—13 years.   Sterile period—none.   Duration of suckling—2 years.

of this practice are important in reducing the birth rate, as we have indicated. The density of these primitive sedentaries, although greater than that of modern gatherers, did not exceed one or several to a square mile (Sauer 1947: 19). Such a human group is something like Steward's patrilineal band, and an increase of total population in the band is impossible (Steward 1955: 126). We mention these details to show that until migration and expansion occur, the possibility of surplus is at a minimum. And if primordial groups could not have risen above the lowest ecological balance, this balance has specific sequelae. Only relatively stable pairs rather than lone individuals can rear children to maturity.

The effects of such patterning are considered below in a discussion of the interactions of individuals represented in the charts.

Mother-Son

Working with Chart 1, assuming the mother's menopause or death at 35, only one of her five possible children could be the father of any of his mother's children. This could occur if the first child is a male and if he lives to maturity. He would then be the father of his mother's fifth child. However, if the first child dies between weaning and puberty, the second child, if alive and male, could not produce a child with his mother, for the last child she can have would already be three years old when he reaches puberty. Only if the first child dies within the first year could the second child impregnate his mother; again, it is only one among her children who could do so. If death occurs before the age of 35, none of her children could father a child; if before 33, none could be a mate.

We see, then, that the chances of mother-son-child-rearing units are at a minimum, reduced by the probabilities of the sex and viability of the first child and by the age of death. Even under the most favorable conditions, a son could father only one child by his mother, and her death or old age would follow soon after. For all but the beginning of his reproductive life, the son would seek sexual partners elsewhere and be bound to outside child-rearing units of longer duration.

In Chart 2, where the reproductive cycle begins earlier and the conditions enable a mother to be more prolific, the mother has already had her fifth and probably last child, if we go by averages, by the time the first child reaches puberty, setting puberty in both sexes back to the age of 13 instead of fifteen. With the maximum of viable offspring, the mother is still suckling her fifth child when her first son reaches puberty. If he remains with his mother for the first two years of his reproductive life and if she has a statistically improbable sixth child, he can be its father. If some of her children die between her first living child and her last, the son could also father the fifth child. If her death occurs at 35, she could have a seventh child, but if she dies at 30, she would not have a sixth child. Again, the second child reaches puberty close to the onset of the mother's old age or death. And for an even longer period of his life than the first son, he would have to find mates elsewhere.

Father-Daughter

Again, the early death of the parent group would make the frequency of father-daughter matings low, but they would be more frequent than mother-son unions from the view of producing rather than rearing offspring because the death of the father would not interfere with suckling the infant. In Chart 1, we see that the fifth child is likely to die because the mother cannot nurse it for three years. This reduces the chances of having three generations of intrafamily matings. If a boy mates with his mother, the offspring would be this fifth child whose death prevents its father from mating in turn with it. Only very rarely could a male produce offspring by his mother and her daughter. He cannot even mate with the age-mates of such a child for a very long period of time. Again, the greatest number of breeding years of a woman cannot be with her aged father. In Chart 1 a father is 16; in Chart 2, 14, when his daughter is a year old. By the time, in

Chart 1, she is 17 and could conceive her first child, her father or any of his age mates would be 33, with little if any life expectancy. By the time, in Chart 2, that she is 13 and could conceive her first child, her father would be twenty-seven. He could provide for her for perhaps six years, during the suckling periods of her first two children, before death occurred. In none of these cases are we considering death at 25, which occurs with some frequency, according to our data. In such cases, there could be no parent-child incest whatever.

At best, any relationship between a person of the F_1 with a member of the F_2 generation, when the life span is from 25 to 35, and when puberty starts from 13 to 16, is extremely short-lived. Even if a marriage rule fostered such matings where they were possible, the rest of the members of the F_2 generation would have to seek mates elsewhere as would the incestuous siblings for most of their breeding life, for they cannot survive without mates, to the extent that there is a sexual division of labor. (To the extent that this whole mating picture depends on the sexual division of labor, a cultural phenomenon, it might indicate the emergence of culture before vital statistics evolved so divergently from those of the prehominids.)

Brother-Sister

In Chart 1, assuming that all the offspring live to maturity, and assuming that the first two adjacent siblings are of opposite sex, the second a male, by the time the male reaches puberty his sister will already have a suckling child. If the first child is the male, his sister will not be able to bear his child until he has already had at least six breeding years behind him. During these six years, chances are that because of the division of labor, he will already be tied to providing for another woman or series of them. Such are the conditions with only four years' difference in age.

With a difference of eight years, as between the first and third siblings, there is half the chance of establishing an intrafamily child-rearing-and-labor unit. The possibility of relations between the first and sixth child are even

more remote than parent-first-child unions, for there is a twenty-year gap between their ages. If the first and third children live, with a pre-weaning death of the intervening sibling, there is at least a six-year gap between the oldest and next oldest children. Even in the case of twins, the chances of incest are one divided by all the other eligible potential mates in the society.

If there are one female and four males, the population would increase only as if there were one pair. Nor would the one female be able to product the maximum number of children if she were the first or last child, unless outside mates entered. If the children are preponderantly female, the children of those without exclusive male partners would die.

In all diadal interactions mentioned, most sex-and-labor units would be outside the family. The probability of the occurrence of incestuous unions, as we have shown, is the lowest for mother-son relationships. Next in order of frequency is father-daughter and the highest probable frequency is between siblings. Interestingly, these frequencies are mirrored in the ethnographic record of the incidence of positively sanctioned incest relations.

SUMMARY AND CONCLUSION

Lévi-Strauss, as we quoted earlier, thinks the reason human organisms first began mating outside the family was that incest prohibitions existed, for he believes that animal life knows no rule in mating and procreation. But animal mating follows whatever "rules" its biological statistics reveal. Animals that are not born in litters, that must be suckled for about three years (instead of the chimpanzee's 18–21 months), that do not reach maturity for a decade and a half (unlike the macaque at three and a half the chimp at eight years and eleven months [Hooton 1947: 251]), and animals that die after some 25 or 35 years—such animals would almost always mate outside the family for most of their breeding life. The reason, we maintain, is that these animals are born in families that break up with the relatively early death of the parent couple. Among the siblings or half-siblings, the mating system is weighted in the direction of out-breeding because of the age distribution and the 50 percent chance of the birth order yielding two like-sexed adjacent siblings. Additional weights are offered by the fact that any child has only at most a 50 percent chance of surviving the first few months.

In short, under the most primitive conditions, where there is only a sexual division of labor, the probability of producing and rearing children is proportionate to the parity in ages of the parents. Most intrafamily breeding units, as we have seen are always impossible: those between the mother and four of her five children; those between the father and three or perhaps four of his daughters; those between the oldest and youngest of six children. Even when parent-child breeding units are possible, they would last only long enough to produce the female parent's last child and the daughter's first child or two. Even with age and viability permitting, parent-child unions could occur only if the oldest child happened to be of the right sex. Most of the siblings most of the time would be bound to outside mates.

It is, I suggest, around such patterns of interaction that all marriage rules crystallized, almost all of them showing an absence of sanctioned intranuclear matings. When in time cultures produced sufficient surplus or in other ways changed their ecology to the extent of shifting the balance in vital statistics, they either created rules permitting some incest (e.g., Egyptian royalty) or established prohibitions against it. I also suggest as probable that the earliest hominids were able to commit incest even less frequently, perhaps not at all.

I have taken several steps in advancing my suggestions. First, I emphasized the inadequacy, in my opinion, of present hypotheses to account for the origin of certain universal mating patterns, although they explain later stages in the development of the culture complex. Then I offered the only type of substitute hypothesis compatible with the theory that value follows action. This new hypothesis contains, so to speak, a Copernican twist: Cooperative bonds were determined by mating patterns, not vice versa. And these mating patterns were ecologically determined: in brief, by the time the children are of an age to mate, their parents would most likely be dead. There was nuclear exogamy. Eventually, changing ecology made it possible to change the institutions that had become enmeshed with it.

Next I tried to see what hints could be found in current societies to support these inferences, and found evidence for the frequency postulate of interaction theory: In the simplest ecologies, most of the people most of the time mate out, not in order to survive, but in order to mate at all.

A thorough re-examination of the ethnographic data in the light of this theory would be interesting, since a brief glance yielded the following three cases that may now be put in perspective.

Hoebel reports that the Plains Indians think incest neither a crime nor a sin, but impossible. The Comanche cannot recall any case of incest, nor can they conceive of a public reaction to it (1949:195) which indicates that they have no taboo, but simply an absence of incest.

Among the Tallensi, according to Meyer Fortes, father-daughter and brother-sister incest are "shameful, but not subject to supernatural penalties" (1936:246). But the idea of incest with one's mother, he reports, if suggested by the anthropologist, produces nothing but an incredulous laugh. It is said to be unthinkable in view of the fact that an adult male's mother is always an old woman.

Sex relations between old and young people, it may be objected, seem frequent enough in primitive societies where, for example, a nephew marries his classificatory father's sister or his mother's brother's wife. However, in one society where these intergenerational marriages were studied, the Tikopia, Firth shows that the partners are about the same age. ". . . Rivers' suggestion," says Firth, "that marriages which are anomalous in terms of kinship status of the parties who unite are necessarily between persons of disparate age as well is not borne out" (1936:267). He continues: "The marriage of people of approximately the same age but of disparate kinship grades tends to level out . . . discrepancies in terminology."

THE INCEST TABOO AND THE
MATING PATTERNS OF ANIMALS

David F. Aberle, Daniel R. Miller, Urie Bronfenbrenner,
David M. Schneider, Eckhard H. Hess, and James N. Spuhler

We have noted a new wave of interest in the theoretical and empirical study of the incest taboo. This is manifested by Slater's (1959) paper and by three papers on the subject at the American Anthropological Association Annual Meetings in 1961: Margaret Mead, "A Re-Examination of the Problem of Incest," Peter J. Wilson, "Incest—A Case Study," and Melvin Ember, "The Incest Taboo and the Nuclear Family." We have felt moved by this activity to present the results of a work group which met in the Spring of 1956 at the Center for Advanced Study in the Behavioral Sciences at Stanford, to consider the problem of the origins of the incest taboo.

The group consisted of the authors and the late Alfred L. Kroeber. After several months of work, the seven members of the group presented a mutually acceptable theoretical formulation at a seminar for Fellows at the Center. We hoped to move on to a well-documented publication, but this has proved impossible. We have been handicapped by our dispersion over several universities and have hitherto been hesitant to publish because we wished to assemble more materials on the limitations of inbreeding in animals and to construct various models of the population genetics of small, inbred groups. Although we have abandoned hope of more ample publication, we believe that the current interest in theories of incest justifies the publication of a schematic statement of the approach we developed in 1956. A few minor changes or elaborations of the 1956 seminar are specifically noted.

The incest taboo in any society consists of a set of prohibitions which outlaw heterosexual relationships between various categories of kinsmen. Almost always, it includes prohibitions on sexual relations between brother and sister, father and daughter, mother and son. Invariably, where any prohibitions are present, other, non-primary relatives are tabooed as well. There are rare cases where the taboos seem to have been abandoned. In the main, these involve very small groups in some way or other isolated from other populations to a degree which makes it impossible to maintain the taboo if the group is to reproduce at all. There are other cases where sexual relations between brother and sister or father and daughter are permitted or prescribed for special categories (e.g. chiefs, kings), or under special circumstances (e.g. ritual). It must be emphasized, however, that in the very societies where these sexual relations are permitted to some people, or under the circumstances, they are forbidden to the bulk of people and under most circumstances. Incest prohibitions are not always obeyed, but we will not attempt here to discuss rates, causes, or consequencies of transgressions.

Most theories about the incest taboo attempt to account for its origin and persistence, but especially for the origin and persistence of the taboo on sexual relationships within the nuclear family. (Here and elsewhere, the phrase "Sexual relationships within the nuclear family" will refer to sexual relationships between brother and sister, father and daughter, and mother and son. The phrase "familial incest taboo" will refer to the prohibition of these relationships.) It is hard to provide satisfactory support for any theory which attempts to account for a universal phenomenon. (Thus far, almost no theory of the origin of the incest taboo which has any currency has attempted to utilize the exceptions to universality noted above to account for origins. For all prac-

Reproduced by permission of the senior author and the American Anthropological Association from *American Anthropologist*, Vol. 65, 1963, pp. 253–264.

tical purposes, virtually all theories treat the familial taboo as a universal in discussing origins. Fortune [1932b] is an exception.) With a little ingenuity, virtually any universal phenomenon can be explained by, or be used to explain the existence of, any other universal phenomenon in the realm under discussion. There are no criteria save aesthetics and logical consistency for choosing among theories, since there is no possibility of demonstrating that A varies with B, if both A and B are universally and invariably present. Furthermore, most of the theories about the incest taboo provide a demonstration that in one or another sense it is adaptive, and thereby often confuse the question of origin and the question of persistence. It is not logically admissible to assert that a phenomenon has come to exist because it is adaptive: that men grew noses because they support spectacles. It can be said only that if something comes into existence which has superior adaptive potential, it is likely to be perpetuated or to spread. The question of the cause of its origin, however, remains unsolved.

Our concern, then, was to account for the origin of the incest taboo, and to find a range of phenomena such that the familial incest taboo need not be treated as a universal. This range of phenomena was the mating behavior of humans and certain other animals. Before this mating behavior is discussed, it is necessary to outline some of the theories respecting the origin and persistence of the incest taboo.

(1) *The inbreeding theory.* This theory asserts that the mating of close kin produces bad results, such as abnormal, enfeebled, or insufficiently numerous offspring. The incest taboo is therefore adaptive because it limits inbreeding, and arose on that account [Westermarck (1894: 352–53; 1929: 36–37); Muller (1913) provides information on beliefs of this sort; Morgan (1907: 69) seems to view inbreeding as deleterious, but assumes a prior stage when inbreeding did occur—hence inbreeding was not for Morgan an intolerable state of affairs.]

(2) *The socialization theory.* This theory asserts that the regulation and control of erotic impulses is an indispensable element in socialization—that it serves to maintain the growing child's motivation to accept the roles that he is taught. These roles include extra-familial and society-wide roles as well as those in the nuclear family. Since societies must be larger than a single nuclear family to be viable, and since non-familial roles are different from family roles, these roles in the wider society must be learned by the child. In order for this learning to occur, the socializing agent must control but not directly gratify the child's erotic impulses. Therefore it is necessary that these impulses be frustrated and directed outside the nuclear family. The incest taboo does this (Parsons (1954; Parsons and Bales 1955: 187–258).

(3) *The family theory.* This theory asserts that unregulated sexual competition is disruptive for any group, that the family is a crucial group, and that the incest taboo originated because it served this function. Freud, one of the proponents of this theory, made a vigorous effort to imagine the series of events which could have led from promiscuity and unregulated, lethal competition, to the final promulgation of nuclear family taboos (Freud 1950 [1918]; Malinowski 1927a; Malinowski 1931: 630; Seligman 1929, 1950).

(4) *The social and cultural system theory.* This theory asserts that, left to their own devices, human beings would prefer to mate within the family, but that the advantages of a wider group for mutual aid, collective economic security, internal peace, offense and defense, and of a wider group for the sharing of cultural innovations, make family and supra-family exogamy highly adaptive as a device for joining families or larger kinship groups. These advantages would be marked in any kinship-based society but were crucial in early human history. This is so because the first ordered human group to emerge was the family, and the incest taboo and exogamy permitted a society built on existing materials: these devices linked families by bonds developed within the family—the ties of parents and children and of siblings. Because of the strong tendency to mate within the family, the familial incest taboos were necessary to insure exogamy (Tylor 1888: 267; Fortune 1932b; White 1949, 1959: 69–116; Murdock 1949: 284–

313). The general theory of the social advantages of exogamy for a culture-bearing animal is to be found in all these writers; the theoretical sequence of development from anthropoid to human social organization is White's (1959); Murdock has stressed the importance of the spread of cultural innovations through marriage ties between families. Fortune has utilized lapses of the taboo among chiefs and kings to support his argument.

(5) *The indifference or revulsion theory.* According to this theory, the incest taboo is either a formal expression of the sexual indifference of kinsmen toward each other, or a formal expression of an instinctive horror of sexual relations among kinsmen. It is principally identified with Edward Westermarck (1894: 352–53, and 1929: 36–37).

(6) *The demographic theory.* This theory holds that for early man, the short life-span, small number of offspring to reach maturity, spacing of those offspring, and random sex ratio made intra-familial inbreeding a virtual demographic impossibility. Hence very early man bred out by necessity. Later, when technological improvements made for larger families and longer life, and intra-familial mating became possible, the already existing pattern of familial exogamy was given normative backing through the creation of the familial incest taboo. This taboo sustained a practice advantageous from the point of view of group cooperation. This theory, presented by Slater (1959), was not considered by the 1956 work group.

We omit various theories which center on the role of religious or mystical ideas in determining the specific prohibition on incest, such as those of Durkheim (1898) and Raglan (1933). We do not explicitly consider the numerous composit theories, most of which combine various elements from theories 1–4 to arrive at their conclusions.

We will now discuss various criticisms that have been, or might be directed at each of the six theories. The criticisms themselves are of three types. (1) The adaptive value claimed by the theory for the incest taboo may be rejected. (2) The adaptive value claimed by the theory for the incest taboo may be accepted, but the possibility that the adaptive quality gave rise to the taboo may be disputed. (3) The adaptive value claimed by the theory may be accepted, but the necessity to achieve this result through the incest taboo may be denied.

The inbreeding theory in its simplest form has been rejected for decades because it was thought to be wrong. In its pre-genetic form the inbreeding theory asserted that inbreeding caused a weakening or deterioration of the stock. The facts of genetics provided a simple corrective to this notion. It was found that inbreeding could not produce "deterioration" but could only bring to expression what was already present in the stock, by producing offspring homozygous for some recessive character. Therefore, it was argued, if deleterious recessives were present, they would also receive full expression. Thus the disadvantages of inbreeding were offset by the advantages.

This simple corrective, however, does not stand up in the face of new information from the field of population genetics (cf. Lerner 1958; Morton 1961; both of which appeared after the 1956 argument had been developed). First, it has become clear the ratio of deleterious and lethal recessive genes to selectively advantageous genes is very high indeed. This results from the random character of mutation. Second, as we move from (biologically defined) second cousin matings to first cousin matings to parent-child or sibling matings, both the models of population genetics and the experimental and observational evidence from animals indicate that the reduction of heterozygocity increases rapidly, and hence that the percentage of individuals homozygous for lethal or deleterious recessive genes also rises sharply. The same is true, of course, for adaptive recessive forms. Provided that the species in question can stand the loss of many offspring, close inbreeding can provide a superior strain—superior either from the point of view of adaptation to the environment or from the point of view of a human being practicing the selective breeding of some plant or animal domesticate. But where births are widely spaced, where the animal produces few offsprings at a time, or only one, and where the animal reaches reproductive maturity only slowly, the closely inbred population may not be able to stand either culling or natural selection. The abortions, still births, animals incapable of surviving to reproduce maturity, and the animals whose breeding period or capacity to rear their young is drastically shortened, through the inheritance of homozygous, disadvantageous recessive genes, may so reduce the total effective breeding population as to make its survival impossible, or as to result in its expulsion from its niche by an expanding, neighboring population. Close inbreeding of rats is possible over many generations; with chickens the process becomes more difficult; with cattle it seems to be impossible. Thus, in the perspective of population genetics, close inbreeding of an animal like man has definite biological disadvantages, and these disadvantages are far more evident as respects the mating of primary relatives than as respects other matings. Hence the biological advantages of the familial incest taboo cannot be ignored. (Ember, 1961, parallels this argument.)

It is difficult to see, however, how primitive man would come to understand the connection between familial inbreeding and low net reproductive rate or the production of monstrosities. We will return to this point.

It is often argued, however, that since many simple societies regard the marriage of first cross-cousins as highly desirable, the incest taboo by no means eliminates fairly close inbreeding. In this connection we must stress the fact that the familial incest taboo is virtually universal, and that familial inbreeding shows far more effects from the point of view of population genetics than cousin inbreeding.

The socialization theory is difficult to deal with. Fundamentally, it rests on psychoanalytic hypotheses of fixation and regression which have not yet been fully demonstrated. For this reason we will not attempt to discuss it further here.

The family theory has certain empirical difficulties. It rests on the supposed acute conflict that would arise out of sexual rivalries between father and son over mother and sister, between

mother and daughter over father and brother, between brothers over sisters, and sisters over brothers. Yet father and son, mother and daughter, brother and brother, sister and sister do in fact share sexual partners in a number of societies. With polyandry, father and son sometimes share the same wife (but not the son's mother), or brothers share the same wife (but not their sister). With polygyny, mother and daughter sometimes share the same husband (but not the daughter's father), or sisters share the same husband (but not their brother); there are a large number of instances of institutionalized sharing of sexual favors outside the marital bond, as well.

These objections to the family theory do not lead to the conclusion that the family could tolerate *unregulated* intra-familial sexual relations. There is ample evidence that sexual competition is disruptive. But there would seem to be two solutions to the problem of maintaining order within the family, rather than one. The first solution is, of course, the interdiction of sexual relations except for the parents: the familial incest taboo. The second, however, is the institutionalization of sexual access in the family. This would define the time, place, and rate of access of each member of the family to every other. This institutionalization could not be a complete solution for all families. In some families there would be no male offspring, and in others no female. Cohabitation with the parent of opposite sex would temporarily solve this problem, but since children normally outlive their parents, the solution would be only temporary. Nevertheless, it would be possible to adopt this sort of institutionalization as the primary pattern, with secondary alternatives available. Thus, societies with other preferential, or even prescribed mating patterns, must ordinarily afford alternatives to these patterns, or redefine the groups suitable for prescribed alliances over time.

The family theory has one distinctive advantage. It is easy to see how human groups might evolve rules to deal with immediate and obvious potential sources of disruption of social life. If indeed jealousy threatened the integrity of the family, it is possible to conceive of the development of norms to cope with this. And the incest prohibitions of any society constitute a set of conscious norms.

The social and cultural system theory, especially in its evolutionary form, as stated by White, does not raise serious empirical difficulties. It is clear that the advantages postulated by White exist, and that, given a tendency to choose the most easily available mates, a complete prohibition on familial sexual relations is the simplest device for forcing ties between families. His theory seems to assert that because this shift was advantageous, it came into being. Yet, like the family theory, this theory requires a movement in opposition to certain strong trends. It requires the elimination of some younger members from the family, in spite of emotional attachments, and entrusting these members to groups where stable relationships do not yet exist. It also requires that primitive men understand the advantages of the exchange —or else must assume that familial exogamy and the familial taboo arose as a chance "mutation" and survived because of their adaptive character.

The indifference theory has both logical and empirical difficulties. It is hard to see why what is naturally repugnant should be tabooed, and the evidence for sexual attraction among kinsmen is quite adequate for rejecting the theory. We mention it only for the sake of completeness.

The demographic theory makes certain assumptions about the life-span, breeding period, etc., of very early man. If these assumptions are correct, most of the rest of what is said in this presentation is irrelevant and unnecessary. But if any of its assumptions about age of maturity or spacing of births or length of breeding period can subsequently be shown to be wrong, this theory would also face difficulties. It serves to remind us of the number of implicit or explicit assumptions about the time and conditions of the emergence of the incest taboo which are made in the case of each theory. Slater assumes a cooperative group and normal breeding population larger than the family; White and our

work group assume a situation where family cooperative relationships have become reasonably firm, whereas inter-family relationships are fluctuating and unstable. Either approach, and various others, make assumptions about the biology and social life of our ancestors, which cannot be fully validated at present. More primatological and archaeological data may still make it possible to choose more carefully among these assumptions.

Thus far, for all of these theories except the demographic and the socialization theories, there are either empirical objections as regards their validity, or logical difficulties in understanding how the function that the taboo supposedly fulfills would have led to institutionalization of the taboo, or both. It should be noted that the empirical objections do not apply to the inbreeding theory or to the social and cultural system theory: in each case it seems fair to say that the advantages postulated would have resulted from the familial taboo, and that, for primitive man, it is hard to see what other device might have been an effective alternative.

In order to broaden the range of phenomena to be considered, let us now turn to the realm of animal behavior. We will here restrict the term "animal" to birds and non-human mammals. There is a wide range of behavior as regards inbreeding among mammals. At one end of the spectrum there is no restriction on matings except opportunity. At the other end, there is no intra-familial mating whatever, except for the parental pair. (An animal family will be defined as a relatively stable grouping of two generations of animals, of both sexes, including at least one sexual partnership, and smaller than a band of animals.) The most spectacular limitation on familial inbreeding is found in the case of the Canada Goose and the Graylag Goose. The behavior of the Canada Goose will be described here, based on observations by Eckhard H. Hess.

The young geese hatch in the spring. The following spring, they are not sexually mature, but are driven away from the family group while the parents rear the new brood. When the new brood is a few months old, the young from the previous year's brood rejoin the family group. During the next spring, the parents again drive off the older broods while they rear the current brood, and the older brood again join the family group a few months later. Hence, quite a large family develops. In the third year, the goslings from the first brood are sexually mature. They mate with individuals from other families. They will not mate with siblings or with the opposite-sex parent. The newly formed pairs may join either family or orientation, making one of the families even larger, or they may start their own family groups. Thus, in the Canada Goose, parents and children tend to remain in the same larger group after the young mature. These ties are very stable. Indeed, mating tends to be for life.

Experimental work on the Canada Goose indicates that this fastidious behavior is the result of sexual imprinting. It is necessary to emphasize that the reaction persists without external sanctions. The luckless breeder who takes a male and a female from the same brood to raise geese is doomed to disappointment: the pair will not mate even if no other partners are available. If, however, two members of the same brood are separated before hatching occurs and are subsequently re-introduced to each other, having been raised in different families, they may become mates.

There is no evidence to suggest that asexual imprinting occurs among mammals. There, the principal mechanism limiting inbreeding in animal groups with families—where there is such a mechanism—seems to take the form of competition between the parent and its same-sex child, when this child approaches or reaches sexual maturity. The older animal's superior size and strength normally result in the expulsion of the young animal from the family, so that it is forced to mate elsewhere. In the course of time, an older animal becomes enfeebled and may be overcome, so that some intra-familial mating will occur, but on a statistical basis this mechanism of intergenerational competition does ensure a large amount of outbreeding. It is particularly effective where most births are single births, so

that two siblings of opposite sex rarely become sexually mature at the same time. The beaver seems to expel its sexually mature young and this may be true of the gibbon.

Among animals with apparent complete promiscuity may be mentioned the rat, the spider monkey, and the macaque. (By promiscuity we refer to patterns which result in the animal's mating indifferently with siblings, parents, or others. Since there are more "others," promiscuity involves a preponderance of outbreeding, as regards primary relatives. Promiscuity need not imply truly random mating. Size, strength, age, etc., always result in some departure from randomness, if only in the ordering of the sequence of copulatory partnerships.)

Sexual behavior among animals, as has been said, varies from complete elimination of familial inbreeding. Under what circumstances is elimination of familial inbreeding likely to occur? It would seem that, on a cross-species basis, restriction of inbreeding, whether by competition or by asexual imprinting, is found among the larger, longer-lived, slower-maturing, and more intelligent animals. On a cross-species basis, these are also relatively late evolutionary products. Those species which limit inbreeding are among those which form families, although not all species that form families limit inbreeding. It would appear that a certain level of intelligence and length of life are necessary for animals to form stable attachments—that otherwise they will breed with kin or non-kin indifferently. When stable attachments are combined with familial groupings, however, they give rise to the potentiality for close inbreeding. Thus, there seems to be an empirical tendency for barriers against close inbreeding to be found where close inbreeding would otherwise be most likely to occur. Finally, it should be mentioned that among birds, asexual imprinting is particularly common in species which have both stable families and larger than familial groupings—a feature which we have not tried to account for.

We will now bring the animal and human data into juxtaposition and define the range of mating behavior which we will attempt to explain. Some animals have no barriers which prevent parent-child, brother-sister matings. Some animals have barriers which reduce or prevent such matings. Humans drastically limit such matings through the familial incest taboo. Thus human beings share with some animals a limitation on familial inbreeding, even though the mechanism of limitation differs from those of all animal species. Only humans have any limitations on mate choice beyond the nuclear family: in no human society is the incest taboo limited to the nuclear family, whatever its range of variation may be.

Let us first consider these facts in the light of the genetic theory. It has been suggested that close inbreeding might not be deleterious to animals which mature quickly and have numerous offspring. It is in such cases that promiscuity is most likely, and promiscuity itself tends to reduce inbreeding, on a purely statistical basis. So even here, close inbreeding is unlikely. Where intensive inbreeding is most likely to occur, barriers are common. The more intelligent, slower-maturing animals living in family groups, where stable attachments are likely, and human beings, who also live in family groups where stable attachments are likely, manifest patterns which limit familial inbreeding: asexual imprinting, intergenerational competition, and the familial incest taboo. We suggest that with the emergence of culture, if not before, relatively stable family groupings in the human evolutionary line required some limitation on familial inbreeding. From this inference, alone, however, one cannot predict the familial incest taboo.

Asexual imprinting would be an equally effective mechanism—but it does not seem to occur in man, the apes, the monkeys, or even in more remote mammalian species. It is plausible to assume that this adaptive device was simply not available—not a part of the genetic equipment of man's ancestors or relatives. Intergenerational competition, however, would seem, at first blush, to be a feasible alternative. Competing with others to get and to keep mates is a widespread mammalian pattern, though not a universal one. Nothing is required to bend it in the service of limiting inbreeding except that it be directed to maturing members of the family as well as to outsiders—and this does not represent a change in pattern, but merely the preservation of the mechanism as family life develops.

If, for any reason, a gap develops between the point at which the young animal is sexually mature and the point at which it is capable of fending for itself, expulsion becomes an unsuitable mechanism. There is such a gap in all known human groups—or at least in no known human group does the onset of sexual maturity coincide with full assumption of adult economic and social responsibilities. Even where marriage occurs at a very early age—indeed, especially where it does—the youthful marital partner, or pair, remains under the direction of senior members of the kingroup. In early human or protohuman society, a gap of even a year between sexual maturity and the capacity to operate independently would create problems for a family unit which used intergenerational competition and expulsion to limit inbreeding. If expulsion continued, the young would be exposed to dangers—unless they could find acceptance in another group, which would presuppose no intergenerational competition in the other group. If expulsion were abandoned, the family unit would be exposed both to an increase of the impetus toward inbreeding and to unregulated sexual competition within the familial unit. A gap between sexual maturity and full capacity could occur either through changes of maturational pattern or through the development of culture and the consequent need for time to transmit cultural information, information about the local scene, etc., or both. The incest taboo is a cultural phenomenon, and we must therefore assume that it emerged concomitantly with, or subsequent to, the beginnings of culture. We cannot, however, be certain whether the gap between sexual maturity and full performance was a matter of culture, physical maturation, or both.

What we seek is a situation which will result in the normative definition of the nuclear incest taboo. If, as can safely be assumed, unregulated sexuality is incompatible with a stable family unit, and if expulsion of the sexually maturing human animal is not possible, then the problem of maintaining order within the family posed by sexual competition would have to be solved. As has been said, two solutions are possible: institutionalized sexual access within the family, or the familial incest taboo. Either solves the competitive problem. Either is within the scope of a human animal with language and limited culture. The problem of order within the nuclear family would also be observable as a pressing problem, on a day-to-day basis, and the sources of the problem in sexual competition would be equally evident. Either mechanism might be adopted: regulation of sex, or its elimination from the family. But whereas either mechanism would solve the problem of order, only one mechanism, the familial taboo, would solve the genetic problem. Hence that group, or those groups of human beings which adopted a taboo on intra-familial mating would have an advantage both over those groups which could not solve the problem of order and over those groups which solved the problem by institutionalized intra-familial sexual activity, thereby encouraging close inbreeding. Hence, over time, only the familial incest taboo could survive, because of its superior selective advantages.

We suggest, then, that man, along with certain other animals, is particularly vulnerable to deleterious effects arising out of close and continuous inbreeding, and that he shares with these animals the characteristic of having a mechanism which limits or prevents inbreeding within the family. We suggest that this problem may have been the underlying cause for the development of the familial incest taboo, since man shares a limitation on familial inbreeding with other animals which are not cultural, which socialize their young far less elaborately than do humans, which do not have to educate them for role systems in a wider cultural order, and which do not have to cope with the problem of ordering the relationships of a number of potential sexual competitors in the same family. This suggestion of a common core shared by the various devices of animals and humans which limit familial inbreeding has the advantage of theoretical parsimony. It is also open to partial test, since there are a large number of studies of animals which could be carried

out to demonstrate whether the variation we suggest on the basis of somewhat piecemeal evidence in fact occur. But the human device, the familial incest taboo, is unique to humans, and is both required by and made possible by culture. The incest taboo requires symbols, but it becomes significant only when expulsion from the family is impossible: a state of affairs largely, though perhaps not wholly dependent on the existence of a corpus of cultural tradition which must be fully transmitted for adequate functioning as an adult to occur.

The familial taboo has, of course, the *de facto* result of linking families, as well as of solving the problem of order within the family and the genetic problem. The stable attachments between individuals long associated in family units which make intra-familial mating so potent a possibility also create ties of interest and sentiment between members of an original family or procreation as they disperse. The advantages of ties between families have been clearly pointed out by Tylor, White, Fortune, and others: an enlarged circle of cooperation, sharing, offense, and defense. These advantages, in turn, generate the last phenomenon to be accounted for: the fact that in no animal group are there restrictions on inbreeding except for the family unit, whereas in no human group are incest taboos limited to the nuclear family. Once the familial taboo is in existence, extensions of the taboo to other categories of kin become a simple evolutionary step. Whether this step is made by stimulus generalization, planning, aesthetic reactions, or whatever, its adaptive value is such as to perpetuate the extensions, which increase the circle of cooperation still further.

Extensions of the incest taboo beyond the family sometimes involve permitted, preferential, or theoretically prescribed matings between first cousins. Hence the extensions may involve no further genetic advantage. Once again, we must point out that the results of familial inbreeding are genetically far more deleterious than those of first cousin matings.

Among animals, in the absence of symbolling, it is still conceivable that further restrictions on inbreeding might occur—e.g., through severe intergenerational sexual competition within a band, or through asexual imprinting such that the young would accept no members of the local group as mates. Such instances are, however, unknown. The genetic advantages of such a step would be considerably less than those of preventing familial inbreeding, and in the absence of culture the social advantages would also appear to be slight. This is so because cooperation in animals is limited in scope.

We might briefly query why a mechanism particularly suitable for maintaining the social and biological integrity of kinship-based societies is maintained not only in these societies but in complex societies as well. First, not the problem of order within the family remains important, and the familial taboo, though not the only possible device for solving this problem, is the existing and well-institutionalized device. Second, for the bulk of pre-industrial complex societies, the functions of the incest taboo in its extended form remain important at the community level. There, the regulation of affairs is not impersonal and legal. On the contrary, the world remains divided into kinsmen, consanguine allies, and neutral or hostile groups. The nexus of social life and cooperation continues to be based on kinship to a significant degree, until societies with well-developed market economies appear. In just these societies, the scope of the incest taboo narrows, until in our own society its legal definition is often limited to primary relatives, secondary relatives, and the spouses of certain primary and secondary relatives. It is in such societies that participation on a relatively impersonal basis in a social system of considerable scope becomes significant, and it may be that under these circumstances the significance of the familial incest taboo in socializing individuals toward participation in this larger orbit increases. It is probable that if the nuclear family were to be dissolved, and to be supplanted by collective, non-kinship forms of life, the incest taboo would dissolve with it, provided that these new forms made close inbreeding statistically a rare phenomenon.

In sum, we propose that the adoption of the familial incest taboo was adaptive primarily because of the genetic results of close inbreeding, and that man's familial taboo is to be considered part of the class of devices which limit familial inbreeding among intelligent, slow-maturing animals which bear few offspring at a time and which live in family units. The selection of the taboo, however, we hypothesize, occurred through efforts to solve the problem of sexual competition within the family in a cultural animal with an organized family life. Among the available mechanisms, the incest taboo solved this problem and the genetic problem. Other alternatives solved only one of these problems. Hence it had high selective value. We suggest that it might not have come into being as a response to needs for cooperation between families, but that, once it existed, it did promote this cooperation, which had an adaptive function of little significance for animals. Finally, the familial taboo could be extended, by a simple evolutionary step, to a wider group of kinsmen, with great selective advantages. To date, some combination of the various advantages imputed to the nuclear and more extended incest taboos has resulted in their perpetutation, even in post-industrial societies organized as states. The taboo in some form or other is likely to survive so long as the family remains a significant part of the social order.

SELECTED READINGS

Aberle, David, Daniel R. Miller, Urie Bronfenbrenner, David M. Schneider, Eckhart H. Hess, and James N. Spuhler
1963 The incest taboo and the mating patterns of animals, *American Anthropologist*, 65: 253–264.
Durkheim, Emile
1898 La prohibition de l'incest et ses origines. *L'Année Sociologique*, 1: 1–70.
Fortune, Reo F.
1932b Incest. *Encyclopedia of Social Sciences*, 7: 620–622.
Fox, Robin
1962 Sibling incest. *British Journal of Sociology*, 13: 128–150.
—1967 Incest. In *Kinship and Marriage*. London: Penguin, pp. 54–76.

Freud, Sigmund
1918 *Totem and taboo.* New York: Vintage, 1946.
Goody, Jack
1956 A comparative approach to incest and adultery. *British Journal of Sociology,* 7: 286–304.
Lévi-Strauss, Claude
1949 *Les structures élémentaires de la parenté.* Paris: Press Universitaires de France.
Malinowski, Bronislaw
1927a *Sex and repression in savage society.* London: Routledge & Kegan Paul for International Library of Psychology, Philosophy, and Scientific Method.
Murdock, George P.
1949 *Social structure.* New York: Macmillan, chs. IX–XI, pp. 260–322.
Parsons, Talcott
1954 The incest taboo. *British Journal of Sociology,* 5: 102–115.
Seligman, Brenda Z.
1950 The problem of incest and exogamy: A restatement. *American Anthropologist,* 52: 305–316.

Slater, Mariam K.
1959 Ecological factors in the origin of incest. *American Anthropologist,* 61: 1042–1058.
Tylor, Edward B.
1888–1889 On a method of investigating the development of institutions applied to laws of marriage and descent. *Journal of the Royal Anthropological Institute,* 18: 245–272.
Washburn, Sherwood L. (ed.)
1961 The social life of early man. *Wenner-Gren Publication,* No. 31.
White, Leslie A.
1948b The definition and prohibition of incest. *American Anthropologist,* 50: 416–434.
Wolf, Arthur P.
1968 Adopt a daughter-in-law, marry a sister: A Chinese solution to the problem of the incest taboo. *American Anthropologist,* 70: 864–874.
Zeff, Andrew
1968 An enquiry into the regulation of incest. Unpublished M.A. thesis. University of California, Los Angeles.

XV

THE FAMILY AND MARRIAGE

Assertions of the universality of the nuclear family and, consequently, the institution of marriage, have been accepted by most anthropologists since, at least, Westermark's time (1891). These assertions, which include the basically bilateral nature of all kinship systems, have been made by Malinowski (1913, 1930), Radcliffe-Brown (1914), Kroeber (1917 a and b), Lowie (1920), and many others. Murdock, in his monumental comparative work (*Social Structure*, 1949) on the nature of kinship structures, asserted these universalities after examining the extensive materials in the Human Relations Area Files. These assertions imply, of course, the equally universal extent of the incest taboo (see Chapter XIV) and the presence of minimum rules of exogamy. Therefore, apart from its other functions, the nuclear family can be seen as the minimum unit within which sexual mating is only allowed in the husband-wife role and is forbidden to all other possible dyads.

Murdock, in looking for exceptions to these general assertions, mentioned the case of the Nayar but, from sources available at that time, concluded that it did not provide incontrovertible contradiction (1949: 3). Gough, who published two papers ("Changing Kinship Usages in the Setting of Political and Economic Change among the Nayars of Malabar," 1952; "Female Initiation Rites on the Malabar Coast," 1955b) based upon her field work among the Nayar, contributed to the argument concerning the universality of marriage and the nuclear family. For comparative purposes, anthropolo-

gists had tried to arrive at a satisfactory definition of marriage (*Notes and Queries,* 1951), but this became difficult in the case of the Nuer because they allow certain marriages between women (Evans-Pritchard, 1951b: 108–109). Leach, in a general article on the subject (*Polyandry, Inheritance, and the Definition of Marriage,* 1955), used the Nayar case as an example of a society without marriage in the traditional sense and therefore without the institution of the nuclear family. Gough replied ("The Nayars and the Definition of Marriage," 1959) by reconsidering her Nayar data. The Nayar, a subcaste in South India, had traditionally "married" (*tali*) children before puberty. After the ceremony, however, the *tali* tie was "cut" and the two mates had hardly anything to do with each other. Women were allowed to take in "lovers" after dark, but otherwise lived in the households of their brothers in this matrilineal sub-society. Men might have one or more women that they "visited," but had no responsibilities towards the rearing of the resulting children, though they might have to admit to paternity. Gough concludes that the few obligations between the couples joined by *tali*, such as funeral obligations, are sufficient to classify the *tali* system within the marriage category, even though she does not make a case for the nuclear family. A similar, though less extreme, case for the existence of Mo-MoBr-child household units has also been made for the Minangkabau. (See Josselin de Jong, 1951).

Anthropologists have had relatively little to

say on those factors that account for the (lack of) stability of marriages, whereas, for instance, sociologists have done a great deal of work in this area, concerning their own societies. Resurfacing through Evans-Pritchard's (1951b) account of Nuer kinship was the idea that one of the major functions of bride-price is the insurance of the stability of marriage. The reasoning behind this theory is that—in lineage societies—the man's family pays a bride-price in exchange for the rights to a woman's economic output and fertility; the greater the bride-price, the more complete is the transfer of rights over her from her natal family to that of her husband; the dissolution of a marriage, requiring the return of bride-price, is less likely to occur if the bride-price is large and has been redistributed among many members of the wife's family. The ensuing arguments (Schneider, 1953b; Gluckman, 1953; Leach, 1953; Gluckman, 1954; Watson, 1954; Leach, 1954a) did much to open up the subject of marriage stability,

to consider exactly what is meant by stability, and to stimulate cross-cultural comparisons with respect to the accuracy of the hypothesis concerning the bride-price.

Nevertheless the study of differential marriage stability within one *particular* society has remained relatively neglected (compared with such emphases in our own society). Cohen, who worked among the Kanuri near Lake Chad, was stimulated, by their very high divorce rate, to investigate the phenomenon (1961). *Within* Kanuri society, Cohen concludes that the amount of bridewealth paid does not correlate with frequency of divorce because this rate is determined by such factors as socioeconomic status, other alliances established, and the previous divorce record of the woman. However, as a generalization applying to more than one society, the Evans-Pritchard-Gluckman hypothesis is not thereby controverted.

THE NUCLEAR FAMILY

George Peter Murdock

The family is a social group characterized by commons residence, economic cooperation, and reproduction. It includes adults of both sexes, at least two of whom maintain a socially approved sexual relationship, and one or more children, own or adopted, of the sexually cohabiting adults. The family is to be distinguished from marriage, which is a complex of customs centering upon the relationship between a sexually associating pair of adults within the family. Marriage defines the manner of establishing and terminating such a relationship, the normative behavior and reciprocal obligations within it, and the locally accepted restrictions upon its personnel.

Used alone, the term "family" is ambiguous. The layman and even the social scientist often apply it undiscriminatingly to several social groups which, despite functional similarities, exhibit important points of difference. These must be laid bare by analysis before the term can be used in rigorous scientific discourse.

Three distinct types of family organization emerge from our survey of 250 representative human societies. The first and most basic, called herewith the *nuclear family*, consists typically of a married man and woman with their offspring, although in individual cases one or more additional persons may reside with them. The nuclear family will be more familiar to the reader as the type of family recognized to the exclusion of all others by our own society. Among the majority of the peoples of the earth, however, nuclear families are combined, like atoms in a molecule, into larger aggregates. These composite forms of the family fall into two types, which differ in the principles by which the constituent nuclear families are affiliated. A *polygamous* [1] *family* consists of two or more nuclear families affiliated by plural marriages, i.e., by having one married parent in common. Under polygyny, for instance, one man plays the role of husband and father in several nuclear families and thereby units them into a larger familial group. An *extended family* consists of two or more nuclear families affiliated through an extension of the parent-child relationship rather than of the husband-wife relationship, i.e., by joining the nuclear family of a married adult to that of his parents. The patrilocal extended family, often called the patriarchal family, furnishes an excellent example. It embraces, typically, an older man, his wife or wives, his unmarried children, his married sons, and the wives and children of the latter. Three generations, including the nuclear families of father and sons, live under a single roof or in a cluster of adjacent dwellings.

Of the 192 societies of our sample for which sufficient information is available, 47 have normally only the nuclear family, 53 have polygamous but not extended families, and 92 possess some form of the extended family. The present chapter will concern itself exclusively with the nuclear family. The composite forms of family organization will receive special attention in Chapter 2.

The nuclear family is a universal human social grouping. Either as the sole prevailing form of the family or as the basic unit from which more complex familial forms are compounded, it exists as a distinct and strongly functional group in every known society. No exception, at least, has come to light in the 250 representative cultures surveyed for the present study, which thus corroborates the conclusion of Lowie (1920:66–7):

---

[1] The terms "polygamy" and "polygamous" will be used throughout this work in their recognized technical sense as referring to any form of plural marriage; "polygyny" will be employed for the marriage of one man to two or more women, and "polyandry" for the marriage of one woman to two or more men.

It does not matter whether marital relations are permanent or temporary; whether there is polygyny or polyandry or sexual license; whether conditions are complicated by the addition of members not included in *our* family circle: the one fact stands out beyond all others that everywhere the husband, wife, and immature children constitute a unit apart from the remainder of the community.

The view of Linton (1936:153) that the nuclear family plays "an insignificant role in the lives of many societies" receives no support from our data. In no case have we found a reliable ethnographer denying either the existence or the importance of this elemental social group. Linton mentions the Nayar of India as a society which excluded the husband and father from the family, but he cites no authorities, and the sources consulted by ourselves for this tribe do not substantiate his statement. Whatever larger familial forms may exist, and to whatever extent the greater unit may assume some of the burdens of the lesser, the nuclear family is always recognizable and always has its distinctive and vital functions—sexual, economic, reproductive, and educational—which will shortly be considered in detail. It is usually spatially as well as socially distinct. Even under polygyny a separate apartment or dwelling is commonly reserved for each wife and her children.

The reasons for its universality do not become fully apparent when the nuclear family is viewed merely as a social group. Only when it is analyzed into its constitutent relationships, and these are examined individually as well as collectively, does one gain an adequate conception of the family's many-sided utility and thus of its inevitability. A social group arises when a series of interpersonal relationships, which may be defined as sets of reciprocally adjusted habitual responses, binds a number of participant individuals collectively to one another. In the nuclear family, for example, the clustered relationships are eight in number: husband-wife, father-son, father-daughter, mother-son, mother-daughter, brother-brother, sister-sister, and brother-sister. The members of each interacting pair are linked to one another both directly through reciprocally reinforcing behavior and indirectly through the relationships of each to every other member of the family. Any factor which strengthens the tie between one member and a second, also operates indirectly to bind the former to a third member with whom the second maintains a close relationship. An explanation of the social utility of the nuclear family, and thus of its universality, must consequently be sought not alone in its functions as a collectivity but also in the services and satisfactions of the relationships between its constituent members.

The relationship between father and mother in the nuclear family is solidified by the sexual privilege which all societies accord to married spouses. As a powerful impulse, often pressing individuals to behavior disruptive of the cooperative relationships upon which human social life rests, sex cannot safely be left without restraints. All known societies, consequently, have sought to brings its expression under control by surrounding it with restrictions of various kinds. On the other hand, regulation must not be carried to excess or the society will suffer through resultant personality maladjustments or through insufficient reproduction to maintain its population. All peoples have faced the problem of reconciling the need of control with the opposing need of expression, and all have solved it by culturally defining a series of sexual taboos and permissions. These checks and balances differ widely from culture to culture, but without exception a large measure of sexual liberty is everywhere granted to the married parents in the nuclear family. Husband and wife must adhere to sexual etiquette and must, as a rule, observe certain periodic restrictions such as taboos upon intercourse during menstruation, pregnancy, and lactation, but normal sex gratification is never permanently denied to them.

This sexual privilege should not be taken for granted. On the contrary, in view of the almost limitless diversity of human cultures in so many respects, it should be considered genuinely astonishing that some society somewhere has not forbidden sexual access to married partners, confining them, for example, to economic cooperation and allowing each a sexual outlet in some other relationship. As a matter of fact, one of the societies of our sample, the Banaro of New Guinea, shows a remote approach to such an arrangement. In this tribe a groom is not permitted to approach his young wife until she has borne him a child by a special sib-friend of his father. Certain peasant communities in Eastern Europe are reported to follow a somewhat analogous custom. A father arranges a marriage for his immature son with an adult woman, with whom he lives and raises children until the son is old enough to assume his marital rights. These exceptional cases are especially interesting since they associate sexual rights, not with the husband-wife relationship established by marriage, but with the father-mother relationship established by the foundation of a family.

As a means of expressing and reducing a powerful basic drive, as well as of gratifying various acquired or cultural appetites, sexual intercourse strongly reinforces the responses which precede it. These by their very nature are largely social, and include cooperative acts which must, like courtship, be regarded as instrumental responses. Sex thus tends to strengthen all the reciprocal habits which characterize the interaction of married parents, and indirectly to bind each into the mesh of family relationship in which the other is involved.

To regard sex as the sole factor, or even as the most important one, that brings a man and a woman together in marriage and binds them into the family structure would, however, be a serious error. If all cultures, like our own, prohibited and penalized sexual intercourse except in the marital relationship, such an assumption might seem reasonable. But this is emphatically not the case. Among those of our 250 societies for which information is available, 65 allow unmarried and unrelated persons complete freedom in sexual matters, and 20 others give qualified consent, while only 54 forbid or disapprove premarital liaisons between non-relatives, and many of these allow sex relations between specified relatives such as cross-cousins. Where premarital license prevails, sex certainly cannot be alleged as the primary force driving people into matrimony.

Nor can it be maintained that, even after marriage, sex operates exclusively to reinforce the matrimonial relationship. To be sure, sexual intercourse between a married man and an unrelated woman married to another is forbidden in 126 of our sample societies, and is freely or conditionally allowed in only 24. These figures, however, give an exaggerated impression of the prevalence of cultural restraints against extramarital sexuality, for affairs are often permitted between particular relatives though forbidden with non-relatives. Thus in a majority of the societies in our sample for which information is available a married man may legitimately carry on an affair with one or more of his female relatives, including a sister-in-law in 41 instances. Such evidence demonstrates conclusively that sexual gratification is by no means always confined to the marital relationship, even in theory. If it can reinforce other relationships as well, as it commonly does, it cannot be regarded as peculiarly conducive to marriage or as alone accountable for the stability of the most crucial relationship in the omnipresent family institution.

In the light of facts like the above, the attribution of marriage primarily to the factor of sex must be recognized as reflecting a bias derived from our own very aberrant sexual customs. The authors who have taken this position have frequently fallen into the further error of deriving human marriage from mating phenomena among the lower animals. These fallacies were first exposed by Lippert (1886–7) and have been recognized by a number of subsequent authorities.

In view of the frequency with which sexual relations are permitted outside of marriage, it would seem the part of scientific caution to assume merely that sex is an important but not the exclusive factor in maintaining the marital relationship within the nuclear family, and to look elsewhere for auxiliary support. One such source is found in economic cooperation, based upon a division of labor by sex. Since cooperation, like sexual association, is most readily and satisfactorily achieved by persons who habitually reside together, the two activities, each deriving from a basic biological need, are quite compat-

ible. Indeed, the gratifications from each serve admirably to reinforce the other.

By virtue of their primary sex differences, a man and a woman make an exceptionally efficient cooperating unit. Man, with his superior physical strength, can better undertake the more strenuous tasks, such as lumbering, mining, quarrying, land clearance, and housebuilding. Not handicapped, as is woman, by the physiological burdens of pregnancy and nursing, he can range farther afield to hunt, to fish, to herd, and to trade. Woman is at no disadvantage, however, in lighter tasks which can be performed in or near the home, e.g., the gathering of vegetable products, the fetching of water, the preparation of food, and the manufacture of clothing and utensils. All known human societies have developed specialization and cooperation between the sexes roughly along this biologically determined line of cleavage. It is unnecessary to invoke innate psychological differences to account for the division of labor by sex; the indisputable differences in reproductive functions suffice to lay out the broad lines of cleavage. New tasks, as they arise, are assigned to one sphere of activities or to the other, in accordance with convenience and precedent. Habituation to different occupations in adulthood and early sex typing in childhood may well explain the observable differences in sex temperament, instead of *vice versa*.

The advantages inherent in a division of labor by sex presumably account for its universality. Through concentration and practice each partner acquires special skill at his particular tasks. Complementary parts can be learned for an activity requiring joint effort. If two tasks must be performed at the same time but in different places, both may be undertaken and the products shared. The labors of each partner provide insurance to the other. The man, perhaps, returns from a day of hunting, chilled, unsuccessful, and with his clothing soiled and torn, to find warmth before a fire which he could not have maintained, to eat food gathered and cooked by the woman instead of going hungry, and to receive fresh garments for the morrow, prepared, mended, or laundered by her hands. Or perhaps the woman has found no vegetable food, or lacks clay for pottery or skins for making clothes, obtainable only at a distance from the dwelling, which she cannot leave because her children require care; the man in his ramblings after game can readily supply her wants. Moreover, if either is injured or ill, the other can nurse him back to health. These and similar rewarding experiences, repeated daily, would suffice of themselves to cement the union. When the powerful reinforcement of sex is added, the partnership of man and woman becomes inevitable.

Sexual unions without economic cooperation are common, and there are relationships between men and women involving a division of labor without sexual gratification, e.g., between brother and sister, master and maidservant, or employer and secretary, but marriage exists only when the economic and the sexual are united into one relationship, and this combination occurs only in marriage. Marriage, thus defined, is found in every known human society. In all of them, moreover, it involves residential cohabitation, and in all of them it forms the basis of the nuclear family. Genuine cultural universals are exceedingly rare. It is all the more striking, therefore, that we here find several of them not only omnipresent but everywhere linked to one another in the same fashion.

Economic cooperation not only binds husband to wife; it also strengthens the various relationships between parents and children within the nuclear family. Here, of course, a division of labor according to age, rather than sex, comes into play. What the child receives in these relationships is obvious; nearly his every gratification depends upon his parents. But the gains are by no means one-sided. In most societies, children by the age of six or seven are able to perform chores which afford their parents considerable relief and help, and long before they attain adulthood and marriageability they become economic assets of definite importance. One need only think here of the utility of boys to their fathers and of girls to their mothers on the typical European or American farm. Moreover, children represent, as it were, a sort of investment or insurance policy; dividends, though deferred for a few years, are eventually paid generously in the form of economic aid, of support in old age, and even, sometimes, of cash returns, as where a bride-price is received for a daughter when she married.

Siblings are similarly bound to one another through the care and help given by an elder to a younger, through cooperation in childhood games which imitate the activities of adults, and through mutual economic assistance as they grow older. Thus through reciprocal material services sons and daughters are bound to fathers and mothers and to one another, and the entire family group is given firm economic support.

Sexual cohabitation leads inevitably to the birth of offspring. These must be nursed, tended, and reared to physical and social maturity if the parents are to reap the afore-mentioned advantages. Even if the burdens of reproduction and child care outweigh the selfish gains to the parents, the society as a whole has so heavy a stake in the maintenance of its numbers, as a source of strength and security, that it will insist that parents fulfill these obligations. Abortion, infanticide, and neglect, unless confined within safe limits, threaten the entire community and arouse its members to apply severe social sanctions to the recalcitrant parents. Fear is thus added to self-interest as a motive for the rearing of children. Parental love, based on various derivative satisfactions, cannot be ignored as a further motive; it is certainly no more mysterious than the affection lavished by many people on burdensome animal pets, which are able to give far less in return. Individual and social advantages thus operate in a variety of ways to strengthen the reproductive aspects of the parent-child relationships within the nuclear family.

The most basic of these relationships, of course, is that between mother and child, since this is grounded in the physiological facts of pregnancy and lactation and is apparently supported by a special innate reinforcing mechanism, the mother's pleasure or tension release in suckling her infant. The father becomes involved in the care of the child less directly, through the sharing of tasks with the mother. Older children, too, frequently assume partial charge of their younger siblings as a chore suited to their age. The entire family thus comes to participate in child care, and is further unified throughout this cooperation.

No less important than the physical care of offspring, and probably more difficult, is their social rearing. The young human animal must acquire an immense amount of traditional knowledge and skill, and must learn to subject his inborn impulses to the many disciplines prescribed by his culture, before he can assume his place as an adult member of his society. The burden of education and socialization everywhere falls primarily upon the nuclear family, and the task is, in general, more equally distributed than is that of physical care. The father must participate as fully as the mother because, owing to the division of labor by sex, he alone is capable of training the sons in the division of labor by sex, he alone is capable of training the sons in the activities and disciplines of adult males. Older siblings, too, play an important role, imparting knowledge and discipline through daily interaction in work and play. Perhaps more than any other single factor, collective responsibility for education and socialization welds the various relationships of the family firmly together.

In the nuclear family or its constituent relationships we thus see assembled four functions fundamental to human social life—the sexual, the economic, the reproductive, and the educational. Without provision for the first and third, society would become extinct, for the second, life itself would cease; for the fourth, culture would come to an end. The immense social utility of the nuclear family and the basic reason for its universality thus begin to emerge in strong relief.

Agencies or relationships outside of the family may, to be sure, share in the fulfillment of any of these functions, but they never supplant the family. There are, as we have seen, societies which permit sexual gratification in other relationships, but none which deny it to married spouses. There may be extraordinary expansion in economic specialization, as in modern industrial civilization, but the division of labor between man and wife still persists. There may, in exceptional cases, be little social disapproval of childbirth out of wedlock, and relatives, servants, nurses, or pediatricians may assist in child care, but the primary responsibility for bearing and rearing children ever remains with the family. Finally, grandparents, schools, or secret initiatory societies may assist in the educational process, but parents universally retain the principal role in teaching and discipline. No society, in short, has succeeded in finding an adequate substitute for the nuclear family, to which it might transfer these functions. It is highly doubtful whether any society ever will succeed in such an attempt, utopian proposals for the abolition of the family to the contrary notwithstanding.

The above-mentioned functions are by no means the only ones performed by the nuclear family. As a firm social constellation, it frequently, but not universally, draws to itself various other functions. Thus it is often the center of religious worship, with the father as family priest. It may be the primary unit in land holding, vengeance, or recreation. Social status may depend more upon family position than upon individual achievement. And so on. These additional functions, where they occur, bring increased strength to the family, though they do not explain it.

Like the community, the nuclear family is found in sub-human societies, although here the father is less typically a member and, where he is, usually less firmly attached. But man's closest animal relatives possess, at best, only a rudimentary division of labor by sex, and they seem to lack culture altogether. The universal participation of the father in the human family would thus seem to depend mainly upon economic specialization and the development of a body of traditional lore to be transmitted from one generation to the next. Since both are products of cultural evolution—indeed, amongst the earliest of such—the human family cannot be explained on an instinctive or hereditary basis.

This universal social structure, produced through cultural evolution in every human society as presumably the only feasible adjustment to a series of basic needs, forms a crucial part of the environment in which every individual grows to maturity. The social conditions of learning during the early formative years of life, as well as the innate psychological mechanism of learning, are thus essentially the same for all mankind. For an understanding of the behavior acquired under such conditions the participation of the social scientist would seem as essential as that of the psychologist. It is highly probably, for instance, that many of the personality manifestations studied by depth psychology are rooted in a combination of psychological and social-cultural constants. Thus the "Oedipus complex" of Freud seems comprehensible only as a set of characteristic behavioral adjustments made during childhood in the face of a situation recurrently presented by the nuclear family.

Perhaps the most striking effect of family structure upon individual behavior is to be observed in the phenomenon of incest taboos. The essential facts, however, must be stated at this point, since an understanding of them is absolutely crucial to the further analysis of social structure. Despite an extraordinary variability and seeming arbitrariness in the incidence of incest taboos in different societies, they invariably apply to every cross-sex relationship within the nuclear family save that between married spouses. In no known society is it conventional or even permissible for father and daughter, mother and son, or brother and sister to have sexual intercourse or to marry. Despite the tendency of ethnographers to report marriage rules far more fully than regulations governing premarital and postmarital incest, the evidence from our 250 societies, presented in Table 1, is conclusive.

The few apparent exceptions, in each instance too partial to appear in the table, are neverthe-less illuminating, and all those encountered will therefore be mentioned. Certain high Azande nobles are permitted to wed their own daughters, and brother-sister marriages were preferred in the old Hawaiian aristocracy and in the Inca royal family. In none of these instances, however, could the general population contract incestuous unions, for these were a symbol and prerogative of exalted status. Among the Dobuans, intercourse with the mother is not seriously regarded if the father is dead; it is considered a private sin rather than a public offense. The Balinese of Indonesia permit twin brothers and sisters to marry on the ground that they have already been unduly intimate in their mother's womb. Among the Thonga of Africa an important hunter, preparatory to a great hunt, may have sex relations with his daughter—a heinous act under other circumstances. By their special circumstances or exceptional character these cases serve rather to emphasize than to disprove the universality of intra-family incest taboos.

The first consequence of these taboos is that they make the nuclear family discontinuous over time and confine it to two generations. If brother-sister marriages were usual, for example, a family would normally consist of married grandparents, their sons and daughters married to one another, the children of the latter, and even the progeny of incestuous unions among these. The family, like the community, the clan, and many other social groups, would be permanent, new births ever filling the gaps caused by deaths. Incest taboos completely alter this situation. They compel each child to seek in another family for a spouse with whom to establish a marital relationship. In consequence thereof, every normal adult in every human society belongs to at

Table 1

RELATIVE (OF MAN)	PREMARITAL INTERCOURSE		POSTMARITAL INTERCOURSE		MARRIAGE	
	FORBIDDEN	PERMITTED	FORBIDDEN	PERMITTED	FORBIDDEN	PERMITTED
Mother	76	0	74	0	184	0
Sister	109	0	106	0	237	0
Daughter	—	—	81	0	198	0

least two nuclear families—a *family of orientation* in which he was born and reared, and which includes his father, mother, brothers, and sisters, and a *family of procreation* which he establishes by his marriage and which includes his husband or wife, his sons, and his daughters.

THE NAYARS AND THE DEFINITION OF MARRIAGE

Kathleen Gough

The problem of a satisfactory definition of marriage has vexed anthropologists for decades and has been raised, but not solved, several times in recent years. Over time it became clear that cohabitation, ritual recognition, definition of sexual rights or stipulation of domestic services each had too limited a distribution to serve as a criterion for all the unions anthropologists intuitively felt compelled to call 'marriage.' For good reason therefore the *Notes and Queries* definition of 1951 makes no reference to any of these: 'Marriage is a union between a man and a woman such that children born to the woman are recognized legitimate offspring of both parents.'

Admirably concise though it is, this definition too raises problems in a number of societies. The Nuer institution of woman-marriage-to-a-woman would be a case in point. Here, both parties to the union are women yet, as Evans-Pritchard (1951b, pp. 108–9) has shown, the legal provisions of the union are strictly comparable to those of simple legal marriage between a man and a woman. Few therefore would question Evans-Pritchard's logic in calling this union a marriage.

The *Notes and Queries* definition contains two criteria: that marriage is a union between one man and one woman, and that it establishes the legitimacy of children. Nuer woman-marriage does not conform to the first criterion but it does to the second. At this point the problem

Reprinted by permission of the Royal Anthropological Institute of Great Britain and Ireland from the *Journal of the Royal Anthropological Institute,* Vol. 89 (1959), pp. 23–24.

therefore becomes: is a definition feasible which would insist only on the second criterion, that of legitimizing children?

In Europe, Dr. Edmund Leach initiated the most recent chapter in this discussion (Leach 1955), and rather than review its whole history it is pertinent for me to take up the argument where he and others have left it. In effect, Dr. Leach answered 'no' to the question posed above. He argued not only against the vagueness of the phrase 'legitimate offspring' but also against any use of potential legal paternity as a universal criterion of marriage. He concluded in fact that no definition could be found which would apply to all the institutions which ethnographers commonly refer to as marriage. Instead he named ten classes of rights which frequently occur in connection with what we loosely term marriage, added that 'one might perhaps considerably extend this list,' and seemed to conclude that since no single one of these rights is invariably established by marriage in every known society, we ought to feel free to call 'marriage' any institution which fulfils any one or more of the selected criteria.

There is, surely, a quite simple logical flaw in this argument. For it would mean in effect that every ethnographer might extend at will Dr. Leach's list of marital rights, and in short define marriage in any way he pleased. This may be legitimate in describing a single society. But I would argue that for purposes of cross-cultural comparison, we do need a single, parsimonious definition, simply in order to isolate the phenomenon we wish to study.

In support of his argument against using the legitimizing of children as a universal criterion of marriage, Dr. Leach cited the Nayar case. On the basis of two of my papers on the Nayars (Gouch 1952, 1955a), he stated that the Nayars traditionally had 'no marriage in the strict (i.e. *Notes and Queries*) sense of the term but only a "relationship of perpetual affinity" between linked lineages (Gough 1955a). The woman's children, however they might be begotten, were simply recruits to the woman's own matrilineage.' He stated further, 'The notion of fatherhood is lacking. The child uses a term of address meaning "lord" or "leader" towards *all* its mother's lovers, but the use of this term does not carry with it any connotation of paternity, either legal or biological. On the other hand the notion of affinity is present, as evidence by the fact that a woman must observe pollution at her ritual husband's death (Gough 1955a).' Later Dr. Leach concludes that 'among the matrilineal matrilocal Nayar, as we have seen, right J (to establish a socially significant "relationship of affinity" between the husband and his wife's brothers) is the only marriage characteristic that is present at all' (Leach 1955, p. 183).

This paper has two objectives. It will begin by analyzing traditional Nayar marital institutions and thereby showing that in fact the notion of fatherhood is not lacking and that marriage does serve to establish the legitimacy of children. My analysis will, I hope, not only dispose of a misinterpretation on Dr. Leach's part, but will in general clarify what has always proved a crucial but difficult borderline case for theorists of kinship. The paper will conclude with a new definition of marriage which will again make the status of children born to various types of union critical for decisions as to which of these unions constitute marriage. The ultimate aim is not of course to re-define marriage in a dogmatic way to suit a particular case, for definitions are tools of classification and not aims of research. The aim is to show that there *is* a common element not only in the institutions anthropologists have confidently labelled 'marriage' by the *Notes and Queries* definition, but also in some unusual cases to which that definition does not apply. Whether we call the element 'marriage' does not much matter provided it is made explicit, but it would probably be convenient to do so.

NAYAR MARRIAGE IN CENTRAL KERALA

This account will refer to Nayars in the former kingdoms of Calicut, Walluvanad, and Cochin in the centre of the Malabar Coast or Kerala. In the northernmost kingdoms (Kolattunad, Kottayam) and probably also in the southernmost kingdom of Travancore, Nayar residence appears to have been avunculocal even before the period of British rule, marriage was optionally polygynous but not polyandrous, and individual men appear to have had definite rights in and obligations to their children. Full information is not available for these northernmost and southernmost kingdoms in the pre-British period. But it seems probable that in the northern kingdoms at least, even the *Notes and Queries* definition of marriage was applicable to the Nayars. It was certainly applicable in the latter half of the nineteenth century for which I have accounts from informants.

My account of marriage in the central kingdoms is a reconstruction of a state of affairs which appears to have been general before 1792 when the British assumed government of the Coast. As I have shown elsewhere (Gough 1952) Nayar kinship was slowly modified in the nineteenth century and more rapidly in the twentieth. But in remote villages the traditional institutions persisted until towards the end of the nineteenth century and were remembered by a few of my older informants. Their reports are not contradicted and are substantially corroborated by writings of Arab and European travellers of the fifteenth to eighteenth centuries.

In this account I shall use the terms 'marriage,' 'husband' and 'wife' without definition. My reasons for doing so will appear later.

In each of the three central kingdoms the Nayar caste was divided into a number of ranked subdivisions characterized by different political functions. Chiefs of these were (a) the royal lineage, (b) the lineages of chiefs of districts, (c) the lineages of Nayar village headmen and (d) several sub-castes of commoner Nayars.

Each of these last either served one of the categories (a) to (c) or else served patrilineal landlord families of Nambudiri Brahmans. I shall deal first with the commoner Nayars of category (d).

There were present in each village some four to seven exogamous matrilineages of a single subcaste of commoner Nayars. These owed allegiance to the family of the head of the village, which might be a patrilineal Nambudiri family, a Nayar village headman's matrilineage, a branch of the lineage of the chief of the district, or a branch of the royal lineage. The commoners held land on a hereditary feudal-type tenure from the headman's lineage and, in turn, had authority over the village's lower castes of cultivators, artisans, and agricultural serfs. Each retainer lineage tended to comprise some four to eight property-owning units which I call property-groups. The property-group formed a segment of the total lineage and was usually composed of a group of brothers and sisters together with the children and daughters' children of the sisters. The members owned or leased property in common, lived in one house, and were under the legal guardianship of the oldest male (*kāranavan*) of the group. Both the property-group and the lineage were called *taravād*.

Nayar men trained as professional soldiers in village gymnasia, and for part of each year they tended to be absent from the village in wars against neighbouring kingdoms or for military exercises at the capitals. Only the *kāranavan*, the women and the children of the property-group remained permanently in their ancestral homes.

The Nayars of one village or of two adjacent villages formed a neighbourhood group (*kara* or *tara*) of some six to ten lineages. Each lineage was linked by hereditary ties of ceremonial co-operation with two or three other lineages of the neighborhood. These linkages were reciprocal but not exclusive, so that a chain of relationships linked all the lineages of the neighbourhood. The lineages linked to one's own were called *enangar;* the total neighbourhood group, the *enangu*. At least one man and one woman of each linked lineage must be invited to the house of a

property-group for the life-crisis rites of its members. Its linked lineages were also concerned if some member of a lineage committed a breach of the religious law of the caste. It was their duty at once to break off relations with the offending lineage and to call a neighbourhood group as a whole to the offending lineage and were special guardians of its morality. Sometimes in small neighbourhoods the commoner Nayar lineages were all *enangar* to each other, but in larger neighbourhoods this was not feasible, for the heads of property-groups would have had too many ceremonial obligations to fulfil.

The linked lineages played their most important role at the pre-puberty marriage rites (*tālikettukalyānam*) of girls (Gough 1955b). At a convenient time every few years, a lineage held a grand ceremony at which all girls who had not attained puberty, aged about seven to twelve, were on one day ritually married by men drawn from their linked lineages. The ritual bridegrooms were selected in advance on the advice of the village astrologer at a meeting of the neighbourhood assembly. On the day fixed they came in procession to the oldest ancestral house of the host lineage. There, after various ceremonies, each tied a gold ornament (*tāli*) round the neck of his ritual bride. The girls had for three days previously been secluded in an inner room of the house and caused to observe taboos as if they had menstruated. After the *tāli*-tying each couple was secluded in private for three days. I was told that traditionally, if the girl was nearing puberty, sexual relations might take place. This custom began to be omitted in the late nineteenth century, but from some of the literature it appears to have been essential in the sixteenth and seventeenth centuries. At the end of the period of seclusion each couple was purified from the pollution of cohabitation by a ritual bath. In Calicut and Walluvanad each couple in public then tore in two the loin-cloth previously worn by the girl during the 'cohabitation' period, as a token of separation. This rite appears to have been omitted in Cochin. In all three kingdoms, however, the ritual husbands left the house after the four days of ceremonies and had no further obligations to their brides.

A bride in turn had only one further obligation to her ritual husband: at his death, she and all her children, by whatever biological father, must observe death-pollution for him. Death pollution was otherwise observed only for matrilineal kin. In Cochin, even if their mother's ritual husband never visited his wife again, her children must refer to him by the kinship term *appan*. Children in the lower, patrilineal castes of this area used this word to refer to the legal father, who was presumed also to be the biological father. In Walluvanad and Calicut I did not hear of this verbal usage and do not know by what term, if any, Nayar children referred to their mother's ritual husband.

The pre-puberty *tāli*-rite was essential for a girl. If she menstruated before it had been performed, she should in theory be expelled from her lineage and caste. In fact, however, my informants told me that in such a case the girl's family would conceal the fact of her maturity until after the rite had been performed. But it was a grave sin to do so and one which would never be publicly admitted.

The *tāli*-rite marked various changes in the social position of a girl. First, it brought her to social maturity. She was now thought to be at least ritually endowed with sexual and procreative functions and was thenceforward accorded the status of a woman. After the rite people addresed her in public by the respectful title *amma* meaning 'mother,' and she might take part in the rites of adult women. Second, after the *tāli*-rite a girl must observe all the rules of etiquette associated with incest prohibitions in relation to men of her lineage. She might not touch them, might not sit in their presence, might not speak first to them and might not be alone in a room with one of them. Third, after the *tāli*-rite and as soon as she becomes old enough (i.e. shortly before or after puberty), a girl received as visiting husbands a number of men of her sub-caste from outside her lineage, usually not necessarily from her neighbourhood. In addition she might be visited by any Nayar of the higher sub-castes of village headmen, chiefs or royalty, or by a Nambudiri Brahman. All of them relationships were called *sambandham*. Among commoner Nayar women, however, the great majority of unions were with men of commoner sub-caste.

Relations between any Nayar women and a man of *lower* Nayar sub-caste, or between any Nayar woman and a man of one of the lower, non-Nayar castes, were strictly prohibited. If a woman was found guilty of such a relationship her lineage's *enangar* carried the matter to the neighbourhood assembly. This temporarily excommunicated the woman's property-group until justice had been done. In the nineteenth century and early this century the property-group was re-accepted into caste only after its *kāranavan* had dismissed the woman from her household and caste, never to return. In pre-British times a woman so dismissed became the property of the king or chief and might be sold into slavery with foreign traders. Alternatively, however, the men of her property-group had the right, sometimes exercised, to kill both the woman and her lover and thus preserve the good name of their lineage.

After the ritual marriage the bridegroom need have no further contact with his ritual wife. If both parties were willing, however, he might enter into a sexual relationship with his ritual bride about the time of her puberty. But he had no priority over other men of the neighborhood group. There is some uncertainty as to the number of visiting husbands a woman might have at one time. Writers of the sixteenth and seventeenth centuries report that a woman usually had some three to eight regular husbands but might receive other men of her own or a higher caste at will. Hamilton in 1727 stated that a woman might have as husbands 'twelve but no more at one time' (Hamilton 1727 I, p. 310). As late as 1807 Buchanan reported that Nayar women vied with each other as to the number of lovers they could obtain (Buchanan 1807 I, p. 411). A few of my older informants could remember women who had had three of four current husbands, although plural unions were being frowned upon and had almost died out by the end of the last century. There appears to have been no limit to the number of wives of appropriate sub-caste whom a Nayar might visit concurrently. It seems, therefore, that a woman customarily had a small but not a fixed number of husbands from within her neighbourhood, that relationships with these men might be of long standing, but that the woman was also free to receive casual visitors of appropriate sub-caste who passed through her neighbourhood in the course of military operations.

A husband visited his wife after supper at night and left before breakfast next morning. He placed his weapons at the door of his wife's room and if others came later they were free to sleep on the verandah of the woman's house. Either party to a union might terminate it at any time without formality. A passing guest recompensed a woman with a small cash gift at each visit. But a more regular husband from within the neighbourhood had certain customary obligations. At the start of the union it was common although not essential for him to present the woman with a cloth of the kind worn as a skirt. Later he was expected to make small personal gifts to her at the three main festivals of the year. These gifts included a loin-cloth, betel-leaves and arecanuts for chewing, hair-oil and bathing-oil, and certain vegetables. Failure on the part of a husband to make such a gift was a tacit sign that he had ended the relationship. Most important, however, when a woman became pregnant it was essential for one or more men of appropriate sub-caste to acknowledge probable paternity. This they did by providing a fee of a cloth and some vegetables to the low caste midwife who attended the woman in childbirth. If no man of suitable caste would consent to make this gift, it was assumed that the woman had had relations with a man of lower caste or with a Christian or a Muslim. She must then be either expelled from her lineage and caste or killed by her matrilineal kinsmen. I am uncertain of the precise fate of the child in such a case, but there is no doubt at all that he could not be accepted as a member of his lineage and caste. I do not know whether he was killed or became a slave; almost certainly, he must have shared the fate of his mother. Even as late as 1949, over a hundred and fifty years after the establishment of British rule, a Nayar girl who became pregnant before the modern marriage ceremony was regarded as acting within the canons of traditional religious law if she could simply find a Nayar of suitable sub-caste to pay her delivery expenses. But if no Nayar would consent to this she ran the danger of total ostracism, with her child, by the village community. I heard of several cases in which such a girl was driven from her home by her *kāranvan* at the command of the sub-caste assembly. Her natal kinsmen then performed funeral rites for her as if she had died. In each case the girl took refuge in a town before or shortly after her child was born.

Although he made regular gifts to her at festivals, in no sense of the term did a man maintain his wife. Her food and regular clothing she obtained from her matrilineal group. The gifts of a woman's husbands were personal luxuries which pertained to her role as a sexual partner—extra clothing, articles of toilet, betel, and areca-nut the giving of which is associated with courtship, and the expenses of the actual delivery, not, be it noted, of the maintenance of either mother or child. The gifts continued to be made at festivals only while the relationship lasted. No man had obligations to a wife of the past.

In these circumstances the exact biological fatherhood of a child was often uncertain, although, of course, paternity was presumed to lie with the man or among the men who had paid the delivery expenses. But even when biological paternity was known with reasonable certainty, the genitor had no economic, social, legal, or ritual rights in nor obligations to his children after he had once paid the fees of their births. Their guardianship, care and discipline were entirely the concern of their matrilineal kinsfolk headed by their *kāranavan*. All the children of a woman called all her current husbands by the Sanskrit word *acchan* meaning 'lord.' They did not extend kinship terms at all to the matrilineal kin of these men. Neither the wife nor her children observed pollution at the death of a visiting husband who was not also the ritual husband of the wife.

In most matrilineal systems with settled agriculture and localized matrilineal groups, durable links are provided between these groups by the interpersonal relationships of marriage, affinity and fatherhood. The husbands, affines, fathers, and patrilateral kin of members of the matrilineal group have customary obligations to and rights in them which over time serve to mitigate conflicts between the separate matrilineal groups. The Nayars had no such durable institutionalized interpersonal links. This does not mean that men did not sometimes form strong emotional attachments to particular wives and their children. My information indicates that they did. I know for example that if a man showed particular fondness for a wife, his wife's matrilineal kin were likely to suspect the husband's matrilineal kin of hiring sorcerers against them. For the husband's matrilineal kin would be likely to fear that the husband might secretly convey to his wife gifts and cash which belong rightfully to his matrilineal kin. This suspicion was especially rife if the husband was a *kāranavan* who controlled extensive property. Informal emotional attachments did therefore exist between individuals of different lineages. But what I wish to indicate is that among the Nayars, these interpersonal affinal and patrilineal links were not invested with customary legal, economic, or ceremonial functions of a kind which would periodically bring members of different lineages together in mandatory forms of co-operation. Four special kinship terms did apparently exist for use in relation to affines acquired through the *sambandham* relationship, although, as I have said, there were no patrilateral terms for kin other than the mother's husbands. All men and women currently engaged in *sambandham* unions with members of ego's property group, and all members of the property-groups of these individuals, were collectively referred to as *bandhukkal* ('joined ones'). A current wife of ego's mother's brother was addressed and referred to as *ammāyi*, and a wife of the elder brother as *jyeshtati amma* (lit. 'elder-sister-mother'). Finally, the own brother and the *sambandham* husband of a woman employed the reciprocal term *aliyan* to refer to each other but used no term of address. All the current *bandhukkal* of a property-group were invited to household feasts, but as individual affines they had no ceremonial or economic obligations and were not obliged to attend. As rep-

resentatives of *enangar* lineages, however, some of these same individuals might be obliged to attend feasts and to fulfil ceremonial obligations as *enangar*. But as particular affines they had no obligations. In place therefore, of institutionalized interpersonal patrilateral and affinal links, the Nayars had the hereditary institution of linked lineages. Whether or not, at a particular time, sexual relationships existed between individuals of linked lineages, the linked lineages must fulfil their obligations at household ceremonies and give neighbourly help in such emergencies as birth and death. In the patrilineal and double unilineal castes of Kerala precisely the same obligations are fulfilled by the matrilateral kin and affines of individual members of the patrilineal group. The linked lineages of the Nayars must therefore, I think, be regarded as having a relationship of 'perpetual affinity,' which carried the more formal functions of affinity and persisted through the making and breaking of individual sexual ties.

In view of these facts, it is convenient to mention here that Dr. Leach's statement that Nayar marriage served 'to establish a socially significant relationship between the husband and his wife's brothers' is not, strictly speaking, correct. The *sambandham* union did not establish 'a socially significant relationship' between brothers-in-law, for in spite of the reciprocal kinship term these persons had no institutionalized obligations to one another by virtue of the particular *sambandham* tie. Further, the *tāli*-rite did not *establish* a relationship between the ritual husband and the brothers of his ritual bride. The ceremony set up no special obligations between these persons; it was merely that their lineages were, hereditarily, *enangar*, both before and after any particular *tāli*-rite. What the rite did *establish* was a ritual relationship between the *tāli*-tier and his ritual bride, and, as I shall try to show later, a relationship of group-marriage between the bride and all men of her sub-caste outside her lineage. But a particular *tāli*-rite in no way modified the hereditary relationships between male *enangar*. It is for this reason that I call the *enangar* relationship one of 'perpetual affinity' *between lineages*, which, though it carried the ceremonial functions of affinity, persisted irrespective of particular *sambandhams* and *tāli*-rites.

The Nayars of this area were thus highly unusual. For they had a kinship system in which the elementary family of father, mother and children was not institutionalized as a legal, productive, distributive, residential, socializing or consumption unit. Until recent years, some writers have thought that at least as a unit for some degree of co-operation in economic production and distribution, the elementary family was universal. This view has been put forward most forcibly by Murdock (Murdock 1949, chapter I). Radcliffe-Brown, however, was one of the earliest (1950: 73 ff.) anthropologists to observe that if the written accounts of the Nayars were accurate, the elementary family was not institutionalized among them. My research corroborates his findings.

I turn briefly to marital institutions among the higher Nayar sub-castes of village headmen, district chiefs, and royalty. At various times during the pre-British period these lineages were accorded political office and set themselves up as of high ritual rank than the commoner Nayars. The ritual ranking between these major aristocratic sub-divisions was farily stable, but the mutual ranking of lineages within each sub-division was in dispute. Most village headmen acknowledged the ritual superiority of district chiefs, and most chiefs, of the royal lineages. But some village headmen disputed among themselves for ritual precedence and so did many chiefs. As a result, each of these aristocratic lineages tended to set itself up as a separate sub-caste, acknowledging ritual superiors and inferiors but acknowledging no peers. In the course of time, moreover, following the vicissitudes of political fortune, such lineages could rise or fall in the ritual hierarchy. It was in these lineages therefore that hypergamous unions became most highly institutionalized, for most of these lineages refused to exchange spouses on equal terms. Instead, most of them married all their women upwards and all their men downwards. Women of village headman's lineages entered *sambandham* unions with chiefly, royal, or Nambudiri

Brahman men. Men of these lineages had unions with commoner Nayar women. Chiefly women had unions with royals or Nambudiris; chiefly men, with the women of village headmen's or commoner Nayar lineages, Royal women for the most part had unions with Nambudiri Brahmans of the highest rank. A few, especially in Calicut, however, had unions with men of older and ritually higher ranking royal lineages which had through conquest become politically subordinate to their own. Among Nambudiri Brahmans, only eldest sons were permitted to marry Nambudiri women and beget children for their own families. Younger sons of Nambudiri households might have *sambandham* unions with Nayar women of any sub-caste.

In all these hypergamous unions the visiting husband owed the same periodic gifts to his wife as in the case of equal unions between persons of the same commoner sub-caste. The husband in a hypergamous union was also held responsible for payment of delivery expenses at the birth of a child to his wife. Hypergamous unions differed from 'equal' unions in that in the former, the husband, being of higher ritual rank, might not eat in the house of his wife. The husband was also prohibited from touching his wife, her children, or her other kinsfolk during the daytime while he was in a state of ritual purity. Finally, although children called their mother's higher caste husband by the term *acchan* plus the caste title, Nayars as a whole were not permitted to use affinal terms toward the Nambudiri husbands of their womenfolk, nor did Nambudiris address or refer to their Nayar wives' brothers as affines. Nayars insist however that that a *sambandham* union with a Nambudiri Brahman was of the same character as a *sambandham* union with a Nayar of equal sub-caste. It seems that from the legal point of view we must also judge it to be so, since the Brahman husband, like the Nayar, was responsible for payments at the birth of a child to his Nayar wife. During my field work, the three Nambudiri Brahmans whom I was able to question closely on this subject told me that from *their* point of view only marriage to a Nambudiri woman with Vedic rites could be regarded as true marriage and that *sam-*

bandham unions with Nayar women were a kind of concubinage. There seems to me no reason why we should not regard these latter unions as concubinage from the point of view of the Nayars. This seems to me, in fact, the only possible interpretation, since the Brahmans are patrilineal and the child of a Brahman-Nayar union is not legitimized into the Brahman caste. The contrast from the Brahman point of view appears most sharply in the case of an eldest son, who may marry one or more Nambudiri women with Vedic rites and may also have liaisons with one or more Nayar women. The Brahman wife's children are or course fully legitimized into the Brahman caste from birth. But the Nayar wife and her children traditionally had no rights of patrilineal descent or inheritance whatsoever, might not enter the kitchen of the Brahman house and might not touch its inhabitants.

Consistently with the difference in direction of *sambandham* unions, the *enangar* institution in these aristocratic Nayar lineages differed somewhat from that in the commoner sub-castes. In general, an aristocratic Nayar lineage had as *enangar* two or more lineages of a sub-caste higher than itself from which its women were wont to draw husbands in the *sambandham* relationship. The linked lineage relationship was in these cases not reciprocal. A chiefly lineage might act as *enangar* for the lineages of one or two village headmen, but had as its own *enangar* one or two chiefly or royal lineages of higher rank than itself. Nambudiri Brahman lineages acted as *enangar* for the highest ranks of chiefs and royalty. In this case too the aristocratic Nayar lineage had of course no reciprocal ritual obligations towards the Brahman families with which it was linked. The functions of these aristocratic *enangar* were, as far as I can detect, the same as in the case of commoner Nayars. In particular, men of the higher ranking *enangar* lineages tied the *tāli* at the pre-puberty marriage of aristocratic girls—appropriately, for it was from these and other such higher ranking lineages that the girls would later draw visiting husbands. Plural unions were customary in these aristocratic lineages as among commoner Nayars. Obviously, however, the choice of husbands became more and more restricted as one ascended the scale of ranked sub-castes, and at the top of the Nayar hierarchy it was restricted to Nambudiri Brahmans.

I turn now to my interpretation of Nayar marital institutions. To accomplish this it is necessary to classify the rights and obligations obtaining between 'spouses' and between 'fathers' and their 'children.' These fall into two categories: those of the *tāli*-rite and those of the *sambandham* union. In relations between spouses of the *tāli*-rite, the important rights are those of the woman. The ritual husband had, it is true, apparently at one time the right to deflower his bride. But the accounts of many writers indicate that this right was not eagerly sought, that in fact it was viewed with repugnance and performed with reluctance. The ritual husband also had the right that his ritual wife should mourn his death. But we may assume that this right had more significance for the wife than for the husband, for it was not attended by offerings to the departed spirit. These could be performed only by matrilineal kin. The ritual bride's rights were complementary to her husband's, but for her they were of supreme importance. She had, first, the right to *have* a ritual husband of her own of a superior sub-caste before she attained maturity. Her life depended on this, for if she was not ritually married before puberty she was liable to excommunication and might possibly be put to death. She held this claim against her sub-caste as a whole exclusive of her lineage, or (in the case of aristocratic lineages) against a higher sub-caste. This group must, through the institution of the linked lineages, provide her with a ritual husband of correct rank and thus bring her to maturity in honour instead of in shame. It was the duty of her lineage kinsmen to see to it that some representative from their linked lineages fulfilled this right. The ritual wife's second right was that of observing pollution at the death of her ritual husband. I interpret this as a mark of proof that she had once been married in the correct manner and that this ritual relationship had retained significance for *her* throughout her ritual husband's life.

The *tāli*-tier had no rights in his ritual wife's

children except that they should observe pollution at his death. From the child's point of view, however, his mother's ritual husband must have been a figure of great symbolic significance. For a child whose mother had no ritual husband could not acquire membership in his caste and lineage at all. The birth of a child before his mother's *tāli*-rite was absolutely forbidden and, in the nature of the case, can scarcely ever have happened. If it did occur, mother and child must certainly have been expelled and were most probably killed. The child's observance of pollution for his mother's ritual husband—like the use of the kinship term *appan* in Cochin—was a formal recognition that, for ritual purposes, he had been 'fathered' by a man of appropriate caste.

Turning to the *sambandham* union, it seems clear that the husband had no exclusive rights to his wife. He had only, in common with other men, sexual privileges which the wife might withdraw at any time. Again it is the wife's rights which are important. The wife had the right to gifts from her husband at festivals, gifts of little economic value but of high prestige value, for they established her as a woman well-favoured by men. But most significant was the woman's right to have her delivery expenses paid by one or more husbands of appropriate caste, that is, to have it openly acknowledged that her child had as biological father a man of required ritual rank. Her matrilineal kinsmen could if necessary press for the fulfilment of this right in a public assembly of the neighbourhood: in cases of doubtful paternity any man who had been currently visiting the woman could be forced by the assembly to pay her delivery expenses. But if no man of appropriate rank could be cited as potential father, woman and child were expelled from their lineage and caste.

The *sambandham* father had no rights in his wife's children. Here again, however, the child had one right in his possible biological fathers: that one or more of them should pay the expenses associated with his birth, and thus entitle him to enter the world as a member of his lineage and caste.

It is clear therefore that although the elementary family of one father, one mother and their children was not institutionalized as a legal, residential, or economic unit, and although individual men had no significant rights in their particular wives or children, the Nayars did institutionalize the concepts of marriage and of paternity, and gave ritual and legal recognition to both. It is here that I must contradict Dr. Leach's interpretation of the situation, for it is not true that 'the notion of fatherhood is lacking' nor is it true that 'a woman's children, however they might be begotten, were simply recruits to the woman's matrilineage' (Leach 1955, p. 183). For unless his mother was ritually married by a man of appropriate caste and, unless his biological paternity was vouched for by one or more men of appropriate caste, a child could never enter his caste or lineage at all. As I pointed out in both the papers quoted by Dr. Leach, the Nayars were aware of the physiological function of the male in procreation and attached significance to it, for they expected a child to look like his genitor. Like all the higher Hindu castes of India, they based their belief in the moral rightness of the caste system in part upon a racist ideology which involved the inheritance of physical, intellectual, and moral qualities by a child from both of its natural parents, and which held that the higher castes were, by virtue of their heredity, superior to the lower castes. It was ostensibly for this reason that the Nayars forbade with horror sexual contacts between a Nayar woman and a man of lower caste, and that they expelled or put to death women guilty of such contacts. This racist ideology also provided a motive for hypergamous unions, for Nayars of aristocratic lineages boasted of the superior qualities they derived from royal and Brahmanical fatherhood.

Moreover, although individual men had no significant customary rights in their wives and children, marriage and paternity were probably significant factors in political integration. For hypergamous unions bound together the higher sub-castes of the political and religious hierarchies. Multiple sexual ties, as well as the *enangar* relationship, linked office-bearing lineages to each other and to their retainers in a complicated manner. And Nayar men phrased their loyalty to higher ranking military leaders, rulers, and Brahmans in terms of a debt owed to benevolent paternal figures whose forebears had collectively fathered them and whose blood they were proud to share. The generalized concept of fatherhood thus commanded the Nayar soldier's allegiance to his wider caste unit, to the rulers of his village, chiefdom, and kingdom and to his religious authorities. It was associated with tender loyalty and with fortitude in war.

I cannot entirely blame Dr. Leach for underestimating the significance of Nayar paternity on the basis of his reading of my earlier papers. For in those papers I was concerned to emphasize the lack of rights of individual men in their spouses and children. It is true that in 1952 I wrote: 'Marriage . . . was the slenderest of ties, while as a social concept fatherhood scarcely existed' (Gough 1952, p. 73). I had not then realized the fundamental necessity to a Nayar of having both a ritual and a biological father of appropriate caste. Moreover I myself confused the issue by referring to the *sambandham* partners as 'husbands' and 'wives' in my first paper (Gough 1952) and as 'lovers' and 'mistresses' in my second (Gough 1955a). For it was not until some time after I read Dr. Leach's paper that I decided to classify Nayar unions unequivocally as marriage and arrived at a definition which would include the Nayar case. In my own defence I must, however, note that in my paper of 1955 I mentioned that children must observe death pollution for their mother's ritual husband, and that in Cochin they used the kinship term *appan* for this ritual father. In both papers quoted by Dr. Leach, finally, I noted that sexual relations were forbidden between a Nayar woman and a man of lower caste or sub-caste, and that the current *sambandham* husbands of a woman must pay her delivery expenses.

I regard Nayar unions as a form of marriage for two reasons. One is that although plural unions were customary, mating was not promiscuous. Sexual relations were forbidden between members of the same lineage on pain of death. It was also forbidden for two men of the same property-group wittingly to have relations with one woman, or for two women of the same property-group to have relations with one man. (This rule of course automatically excluded relations between a man and his biological daughter). Further, relations were absolutely prohibited between a Nayar woman and a man of lower sub-caste or caste. These prohibitions are directly connected with my second and more important reason for regarding these unions as marriage, namely that the concept of legally established paternity *was* of fundamental significance in establishing a child as a member of his lineage and caste.

Granted that Nayar unions constituted a form of marriage, we must I think classify them as a clear case of group-marriage. This was the interpretation to which I inclined in 1952 (Gough 1952, p. 73) and it is, I now think, the only interpretation which makes sense of the descriptive material I have presented. The *tāli*-rite, as I see it, initiated for each individual Nayar girl a state of marriage to a collectivity of men of appropriate caste. First, the rite ceremonially endowed the girl with sexual and procreative functions. (The mock menstrual seclusion before the rite is relevant to this, as is the actual defloration.) Second, the woman's natal kinsmen surrendered the newly acquired rights in her sexuality, though not in her procreative functions, to a male representative from outside her lineage. This appears in that rules of etiquette associated with incest prohibitions came into force from this date. Third, rights in the woman's sexuality were received by her *enangan* as representative of the men of his sub-caste as a whole. This appears in that the individual *enangan*, as a special sexual partner, was dismissed at the end of the ceremonies and might approach the woman again only as one among a series of equal husbands. In the commoner sub-castes the *enangan* was of the same sub-caste as the woman, and through him as representative sexual rights in the woman were conferred on all men of her sub-caste as a collectivity. They were also in fact extended to any man of higher sub-caste who might favour her with his attentions. In aristocratic lineages the ritual husband was of a sub-caste higher than the woman's, and through him, as representative, sexual rights in the woman were conferred upon all men of higher sub-caste as a collectivity. Fourth, the *tāli*-rite, by providing the woman with a ritual husband who (in my view) symbolized all the men of his sub-caste with whom the woman might later have relationships, also provided her children with a ritual father who symbolized the correctness of their paternity. The children acknowledged their debt to him by mourning at his death.

The later *sambandham* unions, by this interpretation, involved the claiming of sexual privileges by men all of whom were potential husbands by virtue of their membership in a sub-caste. The husbands had, however, no individually exclusive rights and could be dismissed at the woman's wish. Their duties as members of their caste were to provide the woman and her lineage with children and to acknowledge their potential biological paternity through birth-payments which legitimized the woman's child.

THE DEFINITION OF MARRIAGE

I have called the Nayar unions marriage because they involved the concept of legal paternity. It is clear however that such a form of group marriage will not fit the *Notes and Queries* definition of 'a union between *a* man and *a* woman such that children born to the woman are recognized legitimate offspring of both parents' (my italics). For legitimacy in the case of the Nayar child required both a ritual father and a 'legalized genitor' of appropriate rank, and indeed a child might have more than one 'legal genitor' if two or more men had jointly paid the expenses of his birth.

As a tentative move toward a new definition which will have cross-cultural validity and will fit the Nayar and several other unusual cases, I suggest the following: 'Marriage is a relationship established between a woman and one or more other persons, which provides that a child born to the woman under circumstances not prohibited by the rules of the relationship, is accorded full birth-status rights common to normal members of his society or social stratum.'

A few footnotes to this definition may help to vindicate its inevitably clumsy phraseology. 'One or more persons' (in place of 'a man') will bring into the definition both group-marriage of the Nayar type and also true fraternal polyandry. It also brings within the definition such unusual types as woman-marriage-to-a-woman. 'Under circumstances not prohibited by the rules of the relationship' would bring into the definition various problematic cases. It is possible for example that there are patrilineal societies in which a husband may legally repudiate a child illicitly begotten upon his wife by another man, without divorcing the wife herself. In this case the previous establishment of the marriage would *not* ensure full birth-status rights to the child, for the rules of the marriage relationship would have been broken through the circumstances which led to his birth. 'Full birth-status rights common to all normal members . . .' is a compressed reference to all the social relationships, property-rights, etc. which a child acquires at birth by virtue of his legitimacy, whether through the father or through the mother. For patrilineal societies the phrase 'full birth-status rights' will include the rights which a child acquires in his *pater* as a person and in his *pater's* group. It will include, that is to say, the legitimization of fatherhood, or, more precisely, of 'father-sonhood.' The phrase is, however, broader than any concept of specific rights in a particular father. It will therefore take care of a case like the Nayar in which all rights are acquired *through* the mother but in which a relationship must be established between the mother and one or more other persons in order for these matrilineal rights to be ratified. Such a process may be called the legitimization of motherhood, or more precisely of 'mother-sonhood.' Moreover 'full birth-status rights' is, I think, not only broader but more precise than 'recognized legitimate offspring', to the vagueness of which Dr. Leach took exception. The inclusion of 'society or social stratum' makes allowances for class or caste systems in which birth-status rights vary between strata. The case of the Nayars, who are a matrilineal caste in a predominantly patrilineal society, is an obvious example of this.

It should also perhaps be pointed out that this definition does not state that full birth-status rights cannot be acquired by a child except through the marriage of its mother, but only that marriage provides for the acquisition of these rights. The definition does not therefore exclude societies like the Nuer in which a man may legitimize the child of an unmarried woman upon payment of a legitimization fee, without becoming married to the mother (Evans-Pritchard 1951b, pp. 21, 26).

Prince Peter has objected to the *Notes and Queries* definition and, by implication, to any definition which would make the legitimization of children through the mother's relationship to another party the distinctive characteristic of marriage (1956, 46). His reason for objecting is that in some societies like the Toda, 'marriage and legitimacy of the children can be looked upon as two different and separate concepts, and it may be necessary to go through a ceremony of legitimization of the offspring (the Toda *pursütpimi* ceremony) in order to establish who is the legal father, because marriage rites are insufficient in themselves to do this.'

However, it seems from Rivers' account that precisely what distinguishes the Toda institution which Prince Peter translates as 'marriage' (*mokh-vatt*) from that which the translates as 'concubinage' (*mokhthoditi*) (1957, 35), is that a 'husband' holds the right to legitimize some or all of his 'wife's' children by the *pursütpimi* ceremony, it seems, by virtue of arranged marriage to an infant or through payment of cattle to a former husband or to a group of former husbands of the wife. The Toda marriage union at its inception does therefore provide that a child born to the woman (under circumstances not prohibited by the rules of the relationship) *must be* legitimized before his birth; the *pursütpimi* ceremony confirms his legitimacy by attaching him to a particular father and giving him rights in the father's patrilineal group. In

the Toda case again therefore the concept of legal paternity is *the* distinguishing characteristic of marriage, even though the individual husband, because of polyandry, may be permitted to legitimize only some and not all of the children born to his wife. The Toda case therefore fits my definition (See Fischer, 1956) whether we regard the *pursütpimi* ceremony as the final one of a sequence of marriage rites, or as a legitimizing act which, under circumstances not prohibited by the rules of the relationship, one or another of the woman's husband is legally obliged to fulfil.

I do not argue that all societies must necessarily be found to have marriage by my definition. There may yet turn out to be whole societies —or more probably whole social strata—in which children acquire no birth-status rights except through their mother, by the simple fact of birth. It is possible for example that some slave populations do not have marriage in this sense of the term. What I do wish to suggest however is that for most if not all the societies for which we now have information, including the Nayar, marriage as I have defined it is a significant relationship, distinguished by the people themselves from all other kinds of relationships. My definition should therefore enable us to isolate marriage as a cross-cultural phenomenon, and from there to proceed to the more exciting task: that of investigating the differential circumstances under which marriage becomes invested with various other kinds of rights and obligations. Some of the most important of these Dr. Leach has already listed for us.

SELECTED READINGS

Cohen, Ronald
  1961 Marriage instability in Nigeria. *American Anthropologist*, 63: 1246–1248.
Evans-Pritchard, Edward Evan
  1934 The social character of bridewealth. *Man*, 34: 194.
—1951b *Kinship and marriage among the Nuer*. London: Oxford University Press.
Fallers, Lloyd
  1957 Some determinants of marriage instability in Busoga. *Africa*, 27: 106–121.

Gluckman, Max

1950 Kinship and marriage among the Lozi . . . and Zulu. . . . In A. R. Radcliffe-Brown and C. D. Forde (eds.), *African systems of kinship and marriage*. London: Oxford University Press for the International African Institute, pp. 166–206.

——— 1953 Bridewealth and the stability of marriage. *Man*, 53: 141–142.

Gough, Kathleen

1952 Changing kinship usages in the setting of political and economic change among the Nayars of Malabar. *Journal of the Royal Anthropological Institute*, 82: 71–88.

——— 1959 The Nayars and the definition of marriage. *Journal of the Royal Anthropological Institute*, 89: 23–34.

Leach, Edmund R.

1950a Social science research in Sarawak. *Colonial Research Studies*, London: Colonial Office. No. 1.

——— 1953 Bridewealth and the stability of marriage. *Man*, 53: 179–180.

———1954a Bridewealth and the stability of marriage. *Man*, 54: 173.

——— 1955 Polyandry, inheritance and the definition of marriage. *Man*, 55, pp. 182–186.

——— 1957b Aspects of bridewealth and marriage stability among the Kachin and Lakher. *Man*, 57: 59.

Malinowski, Bronislaw

1913 *The family among the Australian aborigines*. London: University of London Press for the International African Institute.

Murdock, George P.

1949 *Social structure*. New York: Macmillan, chs. I, II, pp. 1–40.

Prince Peter of Greece and Denmark

1957 For a new definition of marriage. *Man*, 57: 35.

Radcliffe-Brown, Alfred R. and C. Daryll Forde (eds.)

1950 *African systems of kinship and marriage*. London: Oxford University Press for the International African Institute.

Schneider, David M.

1953b A note on bridewealth and the stability of marriage. *Man*, 53: 55–57.

Schneider, David M., and Kathleen Gough (eds.)

1961 Introduction to *Matrilineal kinship*. Berkeley: University of California Press.

Spiro, Melford E.

1954 Is the family universal? *American Anthropologist*, 56: 839–846. Reprinted in P. Bohannan and J. Middleton (eds.), *Marriage, family and residence*. New York: The Natural History Press, 1968a.

Westermarck, Edward A.

1891 *The history of human marriage*. New York: Allerton. Also reprinted 1894, 1921.

XVI

KINSHIP IN CONTEMPORARY SOCIETIES

For the purposes of this chapter we will restrict ourselves to case studies of a small sample of societies that might be called "complex." Our choices reflect an ethnocentric bias toward Western industrialized societies. The kinship systems of contemporary complex non-Western societies have been the subject of some studies but, because of limitations of space and focus, we must refer the reader to works of other experts on such areas as India (e.g., Karvé, 1956; Lewis, 1958; Mandelbaum, 1959), China (e.g., Fei, 1949; Freedman, 1958, 1966, 1970; Fried, 1953; Yang, 1965), and other "peasant societies" (cf., Potter, Diaz, and Foster, 1967).

Thus delimited, the subject of this chapter narrows down to include those societies from which anthropologists usually come, as well as some from Latin America. The last two essays presented concern contemporary kinship institutions under the influences of urbanization. They illustrate how many of the functions traditionally performed by these institutions are being taken over by, or interwoven with, non-kinship relationships and institutions.

For many decades the idea of studying one's own society was antithetical to some of the basic values of anthropologists, such as the "objectivity" of the outside observer, the use of comparisons, the insights gained by studying simpler societies, and so on. It was not until recently that anthropologists started to study the kinship and social structure of Western societies in any detail. Sociologists had, of course, conducted numerous studies of our "family" system, but

their methods differed from those of anthropologists in two major respects: sociologists tended to concentrate on the individual and dyadic relationships in smaller groups and, secondly, were more problem oriented than anthropologists and, hence, tended to concentrate on social pathology rather than normative behavior.

One earlier anthropological study of a "Western" society was the account of the rural Irish by Arensburg and Kimball (1940), but even this did not conflict essentially with the values mentioned above, for the "natives" were still "foreigners," and the system was "simple" and lent itself to comparisons with "primitive" societies more easily than with "complex" ones. Some results of this study have already been mentioned in Chapter X. During World War II little anthropological research was carried out, except for those efforts applied to the war itself. Talcott Parsons, a leading American sociologist, attempted to analyze the structure of American kinship in terms of role theory (1943). After World War II the number of anthropologists as well as of their studies increased—both within and outside of Western industrial areas. Again, some of the research was directed only obliquely towards our complex society (e.g., the earlier studies of French Canadian culture and society conducted by Miner [1939], Hughes [1946], and Garigue [1956].)

Raymond Firth, while trying to train English graduate students without sending them to do field work abroad, began a "traditional anthropological" study of kinship in South London

(1956). Without focusing on the special problems of personal adjustment, Firth's study was able to demonstrate the importance of non-nuclear family kinsmen to a far greater degree than were the works of sociologists. Other studies of English family and kinship and their relation to the wider society were made by Young and Willmott (1957), Curle (1952), and, perhaps most importantly, Bott (1957).

Bott, trained in Chicago but doing her research in London, concentrated on both the nuclear family relations and the extended kin network in 24 "normal" urban families. Her main finding was that the kind of conjugal relationship between husbands and wives is a function of the type of social network that each has outside the nuclear family. Generally speaking, the greater the solidarity of the non-family network, the greater the division of labor and sex role differences of the husband and wife. The non-nuclear family social network is generally expressed as male peer groups, for example, work groups or club friends for the men, and mother-sister extended matrilateral kin and female friends for the woman. As we might expect, it was found that the strict division of labor and the tight non-nuclear family network are found more among lower-class couples, and that the loose non-family network, involving more equalitarian, companionate marriages, is found in middle-class families.

Outstanding among the students of the kinship system in Western industrial society is David M. Schneider, who did his original field work on Yap (1953c). While working with the distinguished sociologist George Homans, Schneider initiated a study of American kinship as experienced by the rather non-random, middle-class population represented in the Harvard student body (1955). In studying the American kinship system through the terminology of both address and reference used and known by their informants, Schneider and Homans were able to demonstrate three of the phenomena that characterize American (and other Western industrialized) kinship and to differentiate such systems from those of typical "primitive" peoples. These include: the great variability and

uncertainty as to the range of the system, the great variability in terminology of both address and reference for the members of the system, and the overwhelming concentration on members of the nuclear family. Schneider and Homans were able to show that the variability expresses not the unimportance of the kinship system in America but, rather, the personalism of the roles ("individualism") with which, it is supposed, older Americans view younger Americans. For example, older people generally use names rather than kin categories for the younger relatives, whereas the younger members of the family are more likely to use kin terms. On these and other grounds, Schneider and Homans were able to show quite convincingly that, in this society, kinship has retained its "pure scope" and "embodies in clear and communicable form the essence of the dominant values of the whole culture . . . discharging those functions universal to kinship systems . . ." This is so, moreover, in spite of the fact that kinship and kinship groups are no longer the major axes around which politics, religion, and macroeconomics revolve. On his own, Schneider later undertook further studies of the American kinship system (1965b, 1968). In his last monograph, based upon extensive field work done in Chicago, Schneider expresses his definition of the kinship system as a system of symbols and elucidates the nature and meaning of such symbols (blood, in-law, step, family) in American society. This most recent study of American kinship was undertaken in cooperation with Raymond Firth who did a parallel study among a comparable group in London (1970). A comparative study of American and English kinship should be forthcoming.

Further studies on various aspects of such kinship systems have once more brought to light the problem of the nature of the kin group in bilaterally organized societies—the so-called "kindred" (Mitchell, 1963). (See also Chapter X in this reader.) During the past two decades, the relationship between our knowledge of primitive society and our knowledge of kinship in our own society has been reversed; it is possible to say that we have as good, if not better, data on the nature of kinship, at least for middle-class North American and English society, as we have for any other society in the world. Anthropological interest in the social organization of complex societies has been growing rapidly and, with respect to our subject, has been expanding in at least two directions. First, increasing numbers of studies are being done on normative kinship (as opposed to pathological) in all the classes and ethnic groups within our own society and in other societies of the Western industrialized world. Kinship patterns in such complex societies are spreading along with industrialization to other areas, such as Japan, parts of Africa, India, and urban Latin America, and studies are being formulated and carried out along these lines.

In a slightly different direction we are increasing our anthropological study of non-kin relationships in complex societies—particularly those relationships that take the place of kinship and perform functions of kinship in the majority of those societies that we have studied previously. Such institutions include various forms of friendship (Wolf, 1964; Davila, 1970), *com-padrazgo*, patron-client relationships, personalized employer-employee relationships, "primary groups," and so on. Anthropologists still tend to neglect those relationships in complex industrial society that are unfamiliar in our traditional work. However, this is changing as we are being made aware of the necessity for anthropological (as opposed to sociological, psychological, and legal) studies of, for example, lawyer-client relationships, social worker-welfare client relationships, government-client relationships, and union-management relationships, and so on. Even more than these specialized kinds of relationships, we should be aware of the larger social structures of modern industrialized society that have been almost completely neglected in the work of anthropologists. An increasing proportion of the world's population lives in these kinds of societies and performs within these kinds of relationships, and anthropologists are quickly finding that their romantic traditions are leading down an ever-narrower path as the majority still tends to ignore "most of the world" (cf. Mangin, 1963).

KINSHIP TERMINOLOGY AND THE AMERICAN KINSHIP SYSTEM

David M. Schneider and George C. Homans

TERMINOLOGY, THE KINSHIP SYSTEM AND AMERICAN CULTURE

We have suggested that the use of alternate terms for kinsmen in the American terminological system might vary with their classifying aspects or their role-designating aspects or both. What in fact happens is that variation is greatest along the dimension of role designation and least with respect to classification. Further, in the few places where there are alternate modes

Reproduced by permission of the authors and the American Anthropological Association from *American Anthropologist*, Vol. 57, 1955, pp. 1203–1208.

of classification, the basic scheme of Eskimo type is almost never transgressed.

One important implication of these data is that there is a single, basic pattern of kinship structure *within* which, but not across which, wide degrees of latitude for variation occur. That is, the American people do not show a wide variety of descent systems, a wide variety of kin group types, or a wide variety of terminological types, but a single, basic form—bilateral descent, strongly emphasized nuclear family, and a distinct but secondarily important kindred. But within this framework there is considerable latitude for variation, and the variation is in terms of roles and relationships, not in terms of the basic kin-groups or kinsmen.

To make this point in another way, it might be said that the American ideal of "unity in diversity" might better be phrased, in the kinship system at least, as "diversity centering on a basic unity."

A second implication of these data is further specification of what is already well known and widely commented on, and that is the central importance of the nuclear family in the kinship system. It is, after all, one of only two kin groups in the system, and the evidence suggests that the other, the loose, amorphous kindred, tends to vary in importance from time to time in the life-history of any given nuclear family, from region to region, from class to class, and from ethnic group to ethnic group. In some groups it looms large; in others, it is held to a bare minimum. Upward mobile persons keep only shallow ties with members of their kindred, if they keep them at all; downward mobile persons may be neglected by their kindred; members of spatially static occupation groups can but need not, and so on.

The features reflecting the central importance of the nuclear family as against the kindred are many. First there is elaborate role-differentiation within the nuclear families of orientation and procreation and a much lower level of differentiation outside these groups. This situation is comparable to the high degree of internal differentiation found in lineage systems in the "own lineage" group as against the minimal differentiation within more distant groups such as in matrilineal systems, father's matrilineage and mother's father's matrilineage. Second, there are those few alternate terms that present alternate modes of classification.

With only one exception, those alternate terms which vary in their classifying aspect occur either *within* the nuclear family or *outside* it, but the nuclear family line is never crossed. Thus the terms "parents" and its reciprocal "the children" or "the kids" makes a unit of Mo and Fa vis-à-vis the internally undifferentiated unit of So and Da. Here, in addition to the alternates for Fa and Mo, there is the additional alternate

which groups them together into one unit. Similarly, and of more than passing interest, are the terms "old man" and "old woman" applied to Hu and Fa, Wi and Mo, respectively, and the term "father" or "dad" for both Hu and Fa, the term "mother" or "mom" for both Mo and Wi. It is our impression that the classes and the regions where "old man" and "old woman" refer to Hu-Fa and Wi-Mo, respectively, are not the same as the class or regions where "father" or "dad" and "mother" or "mom" group Hu-Fa and Wi-Mo, respectively. The fact that these occur in very different subgroups of the population suggests that a very general and basic process is at work and not merely class or regional styling. But the point of primary concern here is that this alternate mode of classification again is confined within the nuclear family and does not cut across that line.

It should be noted that, in the group we interviewed, neither of these two patterns for the grouping of Fa-Hu and Mo-Wife was at all common. Informants suggested that spouse is only called by a parental term in the presence of children, or at least after children come on the scene. We have too few cases of this sort to provide anything like a secure ground for generalization, but our impression is that in some cases the designation of the spouse by a parental term preceded the presence of children, and in some cases occurred among couples of sufficiently advanced age so that the prospect of children might be taken as unlikely and among couples whose children were full grown and far away.

It is interesting, too, that when one spouse uses a parental term for the other, the other does not reciprocate with a child term; that is, when husband is called "father," wife is not called "daughter"—this despite the frequent comment that one of the classic reefs on which marital relations may founder or, conversely, thrive is the psychological identification of the spouse with the parent of opposite sex. It is noteworthy that we did not discover a single terminological symbol of this phychological relationship, unless it be argued that, when husband calls wife "mother," she acts as mother to him, and he reciprocates by alternating his roles between father and son. We did not delve deeply enough to discover evidence either for or against this view.

Outside the nuclear family, the alternates are of a somewhat different sort. Where "parents," "the children," "old man," "old woman," "dad," and "mom" combine two otherwise differentiated genealogical categories, the alternate modes of classification outside the nuclear family tend toward what might be called "gross grouping," taking in a wide swath of genealogically distinct categories. The term "cousin" applied to cousins of each and every remove is one such term. Another is the appearance of such designations as "the Ohio Browns," "the bunch from Maine," "the Joneses," "the drunken Smiths." The one possible exception to the generalization that alternate modes of classification do not cut across the nuclear family is the designation "father's family" or "mother's side." Some informants were concerned to point out that, when they said "father's family" or "mother's family," they did not include father or mother but only their relatives. But other informants either implied or stipulated that father along with all his kinsmen were or were not held in high esteem, low esteem, or at any rate lumped together in some fashion by such terms.

We may now return to the problem of variation within the framework of bilateral kinship and emphasized nuclear family. The question is whether the variation is random or determinate.

The variation occurs along two distinct dimensions. One is variation from subgroup to subgroup within the American population, the subgroups being regional, ethnic, class, age-group, sex group, etc. One sample was too small and unsystematically selected to show what we suspect to be the case—that this kind of variation is asociated with what Florence Kluckhohn has called "variant value patterns."

The other kind of variation is in the forms any individual employs within a given relationship—what we call the use of alternate terms. As one informant said, "I usually call my father 'pop,' but if I want something from him I say, 'Dad, may I take the car tonight?'"

One of the determinants of the latter form of variation is the degree to which personal qualities or individualistic values are emphasized. We have already noted that the use of personal names reflects the value of personal qualities or the special value of the individual. We now want to say something about the over-all social arrangements within which this value may be more or less stressed.

Generally speaking, kinship terms are employed primarily when the person spoken to is senior in age or generation, but first names are employed between age and generation equals or when the speaker is senior in age or generation to the person addressed or referred to. Thus Fa calls So by the latter's first name, but the So usually uses some kinship term for Fa. Br calls Br or Si by first name, but BrCh usually calls FaBr by a designation involving a kinship term —"Uncle Bill," for instance.

As Linton noted, American culture is oriented about achieved rather than ascribed status, and parents are concerned that their children achieve some appropriate status. Ascribed status as a family member is insufficient to carry most people through life. If status is to be achieved, it has to be achieved, according to American values, on the merits of the person, his qualities and accomplishments as a person that meet value standards that Parsons has called "universalistic." Hence to go and do the things that need to be done to achieve something, he must be relatively free of any encumbering bonds of kinship, and he must be motivated to do so. It is as part of this wider context, we suspect, that the older generation uses personal names rather than kinship terms toward the younger generation. Again, we repeat, this does not mean that the young person is freed from all kinship obligations. It only stresses personal qualities within the definition of his kinship role. It stressed the unique qualities of a person as he himself will have to stress his own initiative, his own inventiveness, if he is to achieve anything on his own.

On the other hand, there are two problems from the point of view of the younger generation. On the one hand, their view of the older generation is in part that the latter have achieved; they have arrived, so to speak. This is seen especially clearly in the usages of pre-school children. In their view, almost all adults are mothers or fathers, depending on sex, if they are not otherwise designated as aunts, uncles, or grandparents. In a suburban housing project with the high birthrate characteristic of such units, where practically every family has at least one and usually more children, it was customary for all adults to be known teknonymously as "Johnny's daddy" or "Margaret's mother," etc. Here, one of the authors encountered a young man of about four engaged in a hopeless struggle with a knotted shoelace. The author did not know this child, and the child did not know the author. The child looked up and called out, "Somebody's daddy! Please fix my shoelace." Similarly, children of this age have difficulty comprehending the possibility that a woman might have any other status than mother. In this same housing project it was repeatedly noted that small children would ask adult men to, "Go ask your mother if you can come out and make a snowman with us." For the younger generation, there is an entirely imaginary quality of stability to the older generation: they are set, while the young are to make their way onward, upward, around, and past their elders. Hence their designation by kinship terms, that is, by terms that stress their status and their apparently eternal roles, is entirely appropriate.

On the other hand, the tasks of socialization and the responsibilities of parents all too often require that they act accordingly to the long view of "what we want our child to be." They must exercise some discipline, however much or little they like, and this exercise must be stated in moral and rational terms and not as the product of transient states of mood or momentary emotions. In the nature of the case it is impossible to discipline an equal. The asymmetrical distribution of authority and the knowledge of right and wrong must be made clear as part of the institutionalized definitions of the respective roles. There is thus a problem for the older generation, of maintaining the generational stratification or, as adults sometimes put it, of "keeping children in their place." When parent and child each uses first name, they tend to view

one another as equals. Informants whose children used first names for them and informants who themselves used their parents' first names constantly indicated that the problem of maintaining the separation of status and blocking the tendency toward treating each other as equals was especially prominent. Parents always have the problem of dealing with children who, at certain ages, insist that, "If you can do it, why can't I?" But where first names are used reciprocally, we find that this problem is especially acute and especially difficult to handle. This is not to imply that *only because* first names are used is the relationship difficult; rather, the self-reciprocal use of first names reflects the definition of the relationship as one which tends toward equality.

The use of kinship terms from junior to senior is thus an affirmation of the authority and superordination of the elder and, equally, of the junior's view of the static position of the elder, which the junior is to equal or surpass. The use of first name from senior to junior thus affirms the elder's view of the junior as "up and coming" and emphasizes the qualities of junior as a unique person, an individual in his own right.

It is worth noting, in this connection, the very narrow range of kinship in America and the very narrow limits within which it is extended. In part this is probably connected with the high value placed on the individual but in part it is probably tied equally closely to the fact that the dominant social values center on achievement and not on ascription. The wider the range of extensions, the narrower the possibilities for achievement.

We have heard the view expressed that American kinship is "pushed to the wall" and "distorted by nonkinship considerations and values from outside the kinship system." By this is meant, of course, that kinship has a narrow range not only in the sense that there are only a few kinsmen compared with an enormous number of nonkinsmen with whom ego interacts but also in the sense that considerations of kinship are confined to only a small portion of the total activities which ego enters into. Occupational achievement is supposed to be outside the realm of kinship, and, where other societies view nepotism as an ideal, we treat it under certain circumstances as a crime.

We have no basic quarrel with this view, except that it is not the most useful formulation from which to work. The kinship system occupies a unique place in any culture, since it is almost always the context within which most socialization takes place. If the dominant values of a culture are to be transmitted and if the culture is to continue beyond the lifespan of any individual, then new recruits to the society must be taught that culture. The dominant values of the total culture must find expression in the kinship system, and they must be so expressed that they can be conveyed to children. This means, for one thing, that those values must be distilled and simplified. The first social system in which an individual acts is the reduced system of kinship. If he learns the lessons of kinship, he can go on. Kinship must therefore teach him more than the limited scope of pure kinship; *it must teach him the fundamentals of his whole culture.*

In a sense the whole complex of kinship relations is informed by the system of which those relations are a part. The kinship system as a whole is therefore a socialization device, a "child-training practice," if you will, which looms considerably larger than any given child-training practice like weaning or toilet training or aggression control. Weaning and toilet training, to use two well-worn examples, are aspects of the kinship relation between mother and child, take their shape from this larger context, and therefore may be treated as expressions of it. Where it may be difficult to place an exact socialization value on weaning as such, it is much less difficult to discover the socialization values of a whole kinship system.

Far from being "pushed to the wall" and "distorted by values from outside kinship," the American kinship system embodies in clear and communicable form the essence of the dominant values of the whole culture even while it manages to discharge those functions universal to kinship systems, those social functions which are prerequisite to the maintenance of any social and cultural system.

THE NATURE OF ENGLISH KINSHIP

Raymond Firth

The anthropologist approaching the problems of kinship in a Western society might pose his preliminary questions in some such form as this: Are there significant differences between at least some sectors of Western society and some primitive societies? If, as might seem likely, Western kinship is less formal and less noticeable in the social field, is extra-familial kinship important at all in Western society? If kin relations, and in particular extra-familial kin relations, do have social importance, are there sufficient regularities in the behaviour to allow one to speak of a

From Raymond Firth, *Two Studies of Kinship in East London* (London: Athlone, 1956), pp. 13, 16–21. Reprinted by permission.

kinship system? If so, then what is the nature of this system?

. . .

The English kinship system has come to be described as a bilateral one in view of the relative lack of differentiation in kinship behaviour between mother's and father's kin, apart from transmission of the father's surname to legitimate children. But the term bilateral when applied to kin groups has come to have two meanings. One is to the set of kin who orient their behaviour to a particular person, Ego, and who trace their relationship to him through his father or his mother as the case may be. This set of persons may constitute a group in virtue of their assembly and common operations in respect of Ego on particular occasions. But they constitute a group of personal orientation. Moreover, they are frequently a group only in a theoretical or ideal sense, since they may never actually assemble as a whole. They are in a sense a group of potential mobilisation. They may have no actual corporate existence. Again, their boundaries are relatively undefined. There come points at which it is difficult to say whether there are or are not more persons who should be included in the bilateral kin or Ego. Again, even when it is known that certain persons belong genealogically to this group, there may be uncertainty as to whether they regard themselves as in any active sense members of it. So much is this the case that the term group is often denied to this bilateral set of kin. If used at all it is apt to be restricted to those kin who fairly constantly orient social activity to Ego. Furthermore, the group lacks the principle of continuity. Actual continuity indeed may be preserved to the degree that the relations and responsibilities accepted in regard to Ego are regarded as operative also in the case of Ego's children. In this sense, the sporadic and occasional character often attributed to such kin sets may be empirically false; there may in fact be some continuity of relationship from one generation to another. On the other hand, the increasing remoteness of genealogical connection tends to give good reason for an increasing remoteness of social connection. Here, proximity of residence and childhood familiarity may play a great part in the maintenance of kin ties. For example, children of Ego's father's father's brother's sons may be reckoned as close patrilineal kin and this relationship may continue without evident diminution to their respective offspring. Such continuity may be stimulated by the absence of siblings for Ego.

It is in this way that the conversion of bilateralism into multilineality occurs. Continuance of the connection through either mother or father or both into the next generation and the process of cousin assimilation into a sibling position means that the original duplex field of selection has now become multiplied to provide four, eight or more sets of kin who can be referred to.

What is difficult, however, is to ascribe the term descent to this process. In one sense Ego is a member of the set of persons oriented towards him. But this membership is of a different kind than that of the unit ordinarily described as a descent group. By descent is implied the limitation and recognition of the continuity of kin ties for certain social purposes (in particular, membership of continuing named groups) and the accent is on the notion of continuity. In many of the societies studied by anthropologists, these continuing named groups are unilineal in descent principle. Membership of them must be traced genealogically, but the genealogical tie may be through either mother or father, or indeed in some cases through either a male or female more remote ancestor. Such is the type of descent group, corporate in its activities, which has been described as bilateral (or ambilateral).

Different societies vary in the amount of selectivity allowed in claiming and receiving membership. In some, such as the Maori, a person may effectively claim membership of both his father's and his mother's groups, the effective operation of his claim in terms of land and status rights, for example, depending largely upon his residential situation. Ultimately, without any validation by residence, his claim becomes extinguished. (This is what I have termed the ambilateral type.) In others again, choice seems to be more rigid and the person is allowed to belong to one or other of his mother's or father's groups but not both (for this type the term utrolateral has been proposed). (Freeman 1955:8)

In all these cases, there are, empirically, kin groups of a continuing kind operating multiple social functions (excluding rights over land). But they are not operating unilineally. These form a bilateral kin group in the second sense.

The question is, to what category do the kin groups in the English system belong? As mentioned later, the first term to describe them is patrinominal because of the use of the father's name in transmission of membership.[1] As also described later, the kin relation with the mother is extremely strong. But it does not appear as a formal defining principle and hence does not entitle the system to be termed matrilateral. Whatever term is chosen to designate the system will depend upon the emphasis seen in it by the investigator.

It would seem that the English system has three recognisable types of groups. One is the elementary family which for social convenience is referred to patrinominally. The second is an extension of this, usually in three-generation form with incorporation of affines in the form of children's spouses. Again, for social convenience this is commonly referred to, patrinominally, in terms of the original father. In such cases, some grandchildren, offspring of daughters, are included matrinominally in virtue of the attachment of their mother to her original family, but this represents incorporation only on limited occasions and for limited purposes, as Christmas dinner or a birthday celebration. For other occasions, as for example at school, these daughter's children are known patrinominally. The patrinominally extended family is then only a partially operative, and not a completely regular, social unit. It may well be that for these assemblages and for other contacts between members of this group it is the original mother who is the focus, the enduring tie. But it should be noted that for naming purposes the group is usually called by her husband's surname.

Finally, there is the type of group which assembles at a wedding or funeral and in which may be represented most of the patrinominal kin groups which have traceable genealogical relation to Ego. This is assembled on a bilateral basis. But in this it is similar to kin groups all over the world.

[1] It has been argued that it might be termed matrinominal since the child always takes the mother's surname. If the mother is married, she bears her husband's surname, if she is unmarried the child takes her surname. But the normal adoption of the husband's surname by the wife renders the term patrinominal for the descent principle appropriate.

The upshot then is that in the English kinship system no single emphasis seems to be outstanding enough to give its quality to the system as a whole. There is some patrilineal bias expressed in particular through the naming system and through some occupational preferences. There is in the ordinary social field a strong matrilineal bias with particular emotional significance. If a single term is felt necessary it is probably best to adopt the suggestion of W. H. R. Rivers and to refer to the English kinship system as a familial system, bearing in mind, *inter alia*, the lack of descent groups of depth.

So far I have discussed mainly kinship structure. What of the content of kin relations? Mention has already been made of the marked lack of economic co-operation with kin in daily life. Compared with the working of a primitive community, the occupational diversity in a Western industrialised society bars easy kinship relations in the field of production. This means that kinship, if it is to operate, must do other things to give body to the relationships.

In many primitive societies, part of this body is given by ritual. In the nineteenth century it might have been said that for certain sections of British society some kinship content was to be found in the ritual field. The custom whereby the younger son might enter the Church and receive a family living is marginal to the problem. But the reciprocal moral and ritual support between family observances and those of the Church was important in many social spheres. This now operates to a much less degree. But kin group relations would still seem to be fairly intimately linked with ritual relations in some circles, say in those of the conventional Nonconformist or orthodox Jewish families. Judaism, for instance, has been rightly called a family religion, but it could also be termed a kin-group religion since the emphasis is not simply upon the elementary family but upon the quasi-kinship of the congregation. Moreover, certain kin associations, as in the nomination of Cohen and Levi in the reading of excerpts from the Law, rest putatively upon descent and kinship recognition in traditional terms. However, in British society at large the importance of the ritual factor in kinship is probably slight.

The significance of kin ties outside the elementary family in contemporary British society lies primarily in the positive social contacts in visiting, in recreation, in exchange of news and advice, in attendance on ceremonial occasions and at crises of life, and in the moral obligations that frequently attach to such contacts.

Kinship recognition and relations are important as a part of social living in general rather than as components of specific economic, political, or ritual aspects of institutions.

The problems arising may be further expressed in this way. What, under British conditions, is the importance of kin outside the elementary family? What is the character of recognition, the structure and organisation of their relationships? Can significant patterns be seen in the apparent maze of interpersonal relations in complex urban conditions where each individual is apparently following his own wishes—significant, that is, for the anthropologist in his frame of reference as a student of comparative social behaviour? In urban conditions, it is generally assumed that there is a marked tendency for individuals and the elementary families in which they are set to live and operate in comparative isolation. This seems to be not merely an inference from empirical observation of the kinds of relationships which people have in an urban environment. It also seems to involve emotional and aesthetic, even moral elements, with the implication that such isolation (if it exists) is repugnant to good living and to be deplored. There is also the set of interpretations which links this notion of isolation with the development of particular kinds or facets of personality and character.[2] Precise in-

formation is thus desirable about the definition of the kinship universe of an individual and of the elementary family, and of the social use made of it. (Indices of definition of the kinship universe are discussed later.)

The reputed isolation of an individual or elementary family is thought to be due not merely to the general demands, occupational and other, of large-scale social life in modern conditions. It is thought to be specifically related to the severance of ties from kinsfolk by geographical dispersion. The degree of propinquity of members of the elementary family to their kin outside the immediate household may, therefore, be important as a diagnostic feature in the interpretation of kinship recognition and inter-relationship. In every society, an individual needs recognition and support from others in his activities. In modern Western society, he gets it from the members of his elementary family, from his friends, from members of work groups, recreational groups, etc. But is may be argued that not only an individual but also a social unit, such as an elementary family, needs recognition and support. Here, too, it gets this from friends, from associations which it enters into as a group, e.g. a church, a sports club, etc. But one important field for recognition and support of the family's activities is that of its kin. In some primitive societies, as in tribal Australia or in Tikopia, every personal contact with a member of the community must be with a kinsman. In others, some choice between kin and non-kin is possible, though there is always some kin base. But the degree of selectivity in contemporary Western society allows not merely of choice between kin, or between kin and non-kin, but also rejection of kin altogether. This is largely true also of the modern African or Asian living in cities, though there may be some difference of degree. But if one assumes that in modern urban life relations with people who live close to one are much more attenuated than they are in rural life—in the urban situation one may not even know one's next-door neighbour at all—then one

[2] Three categories of phenomena may be seen under the general head of 'isolation': (a) residential separation; (b) separation from others as regards services and contacts; (c) a psychological, objective feeling of deprivation, better termed loneliness. These three categories are by no means always coincident. Indeed, physical and social isolation may not necessarily imply loneliness at all, but positive preference for separation. We are concerned here primarily with the relation between residential and social separation, i.e. (a) and (b) and not directly with (c) at all.

might put forward a hypothesis. In rural English life, an elementary family is supported by its kin primarily because they are *de facto* in close geographical proximity; and this, even in the rural scene, implies co-operation. In urban English life, on the other hand, an elementary family tends to be supported by its kin because of the lack of full neighbour relations. But experience suggests that such a hypothesis is not likely to be borne out. The general patterns of industrial living have penetrated modern Western rural society far further than is often thought. For instance, in a remote Dorset village, a young man who had grown up there, but been away for a while, said rather ruefully that he did not know the people who were living two doors from him. Even in a country village the neighbour relations have far more of the impersonal quality often attributed solely to urban living than is commonly realised. I have referred to such a hypothesis, even though it may be unacceptable, in order to emphasise the relation between nearness or separation of residence and maintenance or obliteration of kin relations. Any investigation of kinship in an urban environment soon brings out the great degree of variation in relations with kin. The reasons for this are complex, and their force in various types of kin situation is not entirely clear. But among the correlates of the varying recognition and maintenance of kin ties would appear to be the following: residential accessibility; common economic interests, as in occupation, or in property-holding; composition of household; composition of elementary family, especially as regards that of the sibling group; the biological range of persons available for kin recognition; the existence of key personalities in the kin field, to take the initiative in kin contacts; and the phase of development in which any given family finds itself. Through these combinations of circumstances runs the element of personal selection, leading again to the question of what regularities can be discerned.

FAMILY AND SOCIAL NETWORK: SUMMARY AND GENERAL DISCUSSION

Elizabeth Bott

An attempt has been made in this book to analyse several types of variation—variation in conjugal roles, in network-connectedness, in behaviour towards kin, and in concepts of class and norms of conjugal roles. I should like now to summarize the analysis and to discuss some of the problems that have arisen in the research.

Variation in the performance of conjugal roles has been discussed in terms of the extent to which husband and wife carried out their activities and tasks separately and independently of each other. Some couples had considerable segregation between them in their conjugal role-

Reprinted from Elizabeth Bott, *Family and Social Network* (London: Tavistock, 1957), pp. 216–219. Reprinted by permission.

relationship. Such couples had a clear differentiation of tasks and a considerable number of separate, individual interests and activities. At the other extreme were couples who had as little segregation as possible between them in their conjugal role-relationship. Such husbands and wives expected to carry out many activities together with a minimum of task differentiation and separation of interests. There were many degrees of variation between these two extremes. In Chapter III it has been suggested that one set of factors affecting these variations in degree of conjugal segregation is the pattern of relationships maintained by the members of the family with external people and the relationships of these external people with one another.

The immediate social environment of an urban family consists of a network rather than an organized group. A network is a social configuration in which some, but not all, of the component external units maintain relationships with one another. The external units do not make up a larger social whole. They are not surrounded by a common boundary.

In all societies elementary families have a network of social relationships. But in many small-scale societies with a simple division of labour, elementary families are also contained within organized groups that control many aspects of their daily activities. Urban families are not completely encapsulated by organized groups in this way. As individuals, members of the family may belong to organized groups. As a family, some aspects of their activities may be controlled by a doctor, by a church, by a local borough council and other government bodies. But there is no organized group that regulates all aspects of a family's life, informal activities as well as formal. Urban families are not isolated since members maintain many relationships with individuals and groups outside the family. But they are more 'individuated' than families in relatively small, closed communities. Many of the individuals and groups to which an urban family is related are not linked up with one another, so that although each external individual or group may control some aspect of familial activity, social control of the family as a whole is dispersed among several agencies. This means that each family has a relatively large measure of privacy and of freedom to regulate its own affairs.

The networks of urban families vary in degree of connectedness, namely in the extent to which the people with whom the family maintains relationships carry on relationships with one another. These variations in network-connectedness are particularly evident in informal relationships between friends, neighbours, and relatives. Such differences in connectedness are associated with differences in degree of segregation of conjugal roles. The degree of segregation in the role-relationship of husband and wife varies directly with the connectedness of the family's social network. Four sets of families have been described in Chapter III, and the relationship between the connectedness of their networks and the degree of their conjugal role segregation has been discussed.

It has been suggested that if husband and wife come to marriage with close-knit networks, and if conditions are such that this pattern of relationships can be continued, the marriage is superimposed on the previous relationships and each partner continues to be drawn into activities with outside people. Each gets some emotional satisfaction from these external relationships and demands correspondingly less of the spouse. Rigid segregation of conjugal roles is possible because each partner can get help from people outside. But if husband and wife come to marriage with loose-knit networks, or if their networks become loose-knit after marriage, they must seek in each other some of the emotional satisfaction and help with familial tasks that couples in close-knit networks can get from outsiders. Joint organization becomes more necessary for the success of the family as an enterprise.

It seems to me that many clinical workers, doctors, and family research workers take it for granted that joint organization is the natural and normal form for familial behaviour to take. Advice based on this assumption must be rather bewildering to families in close-knit networks, as Michael Young has suggested (1956). And behaviour that might correctly be interpreted as overdependent or defensively authoritarian in families with loose-knit networks should be interpreted differently if it occurs in families with close-knit networks. I do not mean to say that such behaviour should be accepted as 'normal' in the clinical sense simply because it is culturally acceptable to certain types of family, but I think that one should be prepared to see whether it has different psychological meanings and effects for the people concerned.

I do not believe it is sufficient to explain variations in conjugal segregation as cultural or subcultural differences. To say that people behave differently or have different expectations because they belong to different cultures amounts to no more than saying that they behave differently because they behave differently—or that cultures are different because they are different. It is for this reason that I do not think it would be illuminating to attribute differences in conjugal segregation to social class differences even if the correlation were high. This is only a first stage of analysis, a preliminary classification on a descriptive level. It is essential to push the analysis further, to find out what factors in social class are relevant to conjugal segregation and how they actually produce an effect on the internal role structure of families.

AMERICAN KINSHIP: A CULTURAL ACCOUNT

David M. Schneider

RELATIVES

I.

What the anthropologist calls kinsmen are called "relatives," "folks," "kinfolk," "people," or "family" by Americans; the possessive pronoun may precede these terms. In different regions and dialects various words may be used, but people from different parts of the country generally understand each other and share the same fundamental definitions even when they do not use the same names for the same cultural categories. I will use the American term "relative" as the very rough equivalent for the anthropologist's term "kinsman," but this is a very rough translation indeed.

The explicit definition which Americans readily provide is that a relative is a person who is related by blood or by marriage. Those related by marriage may be called "in-laws." But the word relative can also be used by Americans in a more restricted sense for blood relatives alone and used in direct opposition to relative by marriage. Thus it may be said, "No, she is not a relative; my wife is an in-law." Or it may equally properly be said, "Yes, she is a relative; she is my wife."

One can begin to discover what a relative is in American culture by considering those terms which are the names for the kinds of relatives—among other things—and which mark the scheme for their classification.

American kinship terms can be divided into two groups. The first group can be called the *basic* terms, the second, *derivative* terms. Derivative terms are made up of a basic term plus a modifier.[1] "Cousin" is an example of a basic term, "second" a particular modifier. "Second cousin" is an example of a derivative term. "Father" is another example of a basic term, "in-law" a modifier. "Father-in-law" is an example of a derivative term.

The basic terms are "father," "mother," "brother," "sister," "son," "daughter," "uncle," "aunt," "nephew," "niece," "cousin," "husband," and "wife." The modifiers are "step-" "-in-law," "foster," "great," "grand," "first," "second," etc., "once," "twice," etc., "removed," "half," and "ex-." The "removed" modifier is reserved to "cousin." The "half" modifier is reserved to "brother" and "sister." The "ex-" modifier is reserved to relatives by marriage. "Great" only modifies "father," "mother," "son," and "daughter" when they have first been modified by "grand," as in "great grandfather." "Great" and "grand" do not modify "cousin," "brother," "sis-

---

[1] I take this distinction between basic and derivative terms from W. H. Goodenough, "Yankee Kinship Terminology: A Problem in Componential Analysis," in E. A. Hammel (ed.) "Formal Semantic Analysis," *American Anthropologist*, 67: 5, Part 2 (1965), 259–87.

ter," "husband," or "wife." Otherwise modifiers can be used with any basic term.[2]

The modifiers in this system form two different sets with two different functions. One set of modifiers distinguishes true or blood relatives from those who are not. These are the "step-," "-in-law," and "foster" modifiers along with the "half" modifier which specifies less than a full blood sibling. Thus "father" is a blood relative, "foster brother" is not. "Daughter" is a blood relative, "step-daughter" is not.

The other set of modifiers define the range of the terms as infinite. These are the "great," "grand," "removed," "first," etc., and "ex-" modifiers. That is, the range or extent of the terms is without limit.

There are, therefore, two different kinds of modifiers. One kind, the *restrictive,* sharply divides blood relatives from those in comparable positions who are not blood relatives. The other kind of modifier, the *unrestrictive,* simply states the unrestricted or unlimited range of certain relatives.

One more important point should be noted about the modifiers. The unrestrictive modifiers mark distance, and they mark it in two ways. The first is by degrees of distance. Thus "first cousin" is closer than "second cousin," "uncle" closer than "great uncle," "great uncle" closer than "great great uncle," and so on. The second way of marking distance is on a simple "in/out"

[2] Compare W. H. Goodenough, *op. cit.* For the difference between his view and mine, see footnote, p. 99, below. It should also be noted that I do not offer this as a definitive or exhaustive list of American kinship terms. "Parent," "child," "sibling," "ancestor," "ancestress," "descendant," "pa," "pappy," "pop," "papa," "ma," "mammy," "mom," "mama," and so forth could all be considered as candidates for such a list, along with terms like "old man," "old woman," "old lady," "governor," and so forth. It is really not possible to assume that there is a finite lexicon or vocabulary of kinship terms without first providing a clear definition of just what a kinship term is and whether this definition is imposed on the data for analytic purposes or whether it is a definition inherent in the culture itself. Since I am not undertaking an analysis of either kinship terms or of terms for kinsmen here, I will reserve these questions for another time. My aim here is simply to use some terms which have kinship meanings as these are defined in American culture, as a way to begin to discover what the American cultural definition of a relative is.

basis. Husband is "in," ex-husband is "out." (But note that "first," "second," etc., as modifiers of "husband" and "wife" do not mark closeness but only succession in time.)

This structure states a substantial part of the definition of what is and what is not a relative. The first criterion, blood or marriage, is central. The two kinds of modifiers are united in their functions; one protects the integrity of the closest blood relatives. The other places relatives in calibrated degrees of distance if they are blood relatives, but either "in" or "out" if they are relatives by marriage.

II.

If a relative is a person related "by blood," what does this mean in American culture?

The blood relationship, as it is defined in American kinship, is formulated in concrete, biogenetic terms. Conception follows a single act of sexual intercourse between a man, as genitor, and a woman, as genetrix. At conception, one-half of the biogenetic substance of which the child is made is contributed by the genetrix, and one-half by the genitor. Thus each person has 100 per cent of this material, but 50 per cent comes from his mother and 50 per cent from his father at the time of his conception, and thereby is his "by birth."

Although a child takes part of the mother's makeup and part of the father's, neither mother nor father shares that makeup with each other. Since a woman is not "made up of" biogenetic material from her husband, she is not his blood relative. But she is the blood relative of her child precisely because the mother and child are both "made up of," in part, the very same material. So, too, are the father and child.

It is believed, in American kinship, that both mother and father give substantially the same kinds and amounts of material to the child, and that the child's whole biogenetic identity or any part of it comes half from the mother, half from the father. It is not believed that the father provides the bone, the mother the flesh, for instance, or that the father provides the intelligence, the mother the appearance.

In American cultural conception, kinship is

defined as biogenetic. This definition says that kinship is whatever the biogenetic relationship is. If science discovers new facts about biogenetic relationship, then that is what kinship is and was all along, although it may not have been known at the time.

Hence the real, true, verifiable facts of nature are what the cultural formulation is. And the real, true, objective facts of science (these are the facts of nature too, of course) are that each parent provides one-half of his child's biogenetic constitution.[3]

The relationship which is "real" or "true" or "blood" or "by birth" can never be severed, whatever its legal position. Legal rights may be lost, but the blood relationship cannot be lost. It is culturally defined as being an objective fact of nature, of fundamental significance and capable of having profound effects, and its nature cannot be terminated or changed. It follows that it is never possible to have an ex-father or an ex-mother, an ex-sister or an ex-brother, an ex-son or an ex-daughter. An ex-husband or ex-wife is possible, and so is an ex-mother-in-law. But an ex-mother is not.

It is significant that one may disown a son or a daughter, or one may try to disinherit a child (within the limits set by the laws of the various states). The relationship between parent and child, or between siblings, may be such that the two never see each other, never mention each other's name, never communicate in any way, each acting as if unaware of the other's existence. But to those directly concerned, as to all others who know the facts, the two remain parent and child or sibling to each other. Nothing

[3] The cultural premise is that the real, true, objective facts of nature about biogenetic relationships are what kinship "is." But it does not follow that every fact of nature as established by science will automatically and unquestioningly be accepted or assimilated as part of the nature of nature. People may simply deny that a finding of science is true and therefore not accept it as a part of what kinship "is." By the same token, some items in some people's inventories of the real, true, objective facts of nature may be those which scientific authority has long ago shown to be false and untrue but which these Americans nevertheless insist are true. But this should not obscure my point here, which is simply that the cultural definition is that kinship is the biogenetic facts of nature.

can really terminate or change the biological relationship which exists between them, and so they remain blood relatives. It is this which makes them parent and child or sibling to each other in American culture.

Two blood relatives are "related" by the fact that they share in some degree the stuff of a particular heredity. Each has a portion of the natural, genetic substance. Their kinship consists in this common possession. If they need to prove their kinship, or to explain it to someone, they may name the intervening blood relatives and locate the ascendent whose blood they have in common. It is said that they can trace their blood *through* certain relatives, that they have "Smith blood in their veins." But their kinship to each other does not depend on intervening relatives, but only on the fact that each has some of the heredity that the other has and both got theirs from a single source.

Because blood is a "thing" and because it is subdivided with each reproductive step away from a given ancestor, the precise degree to which two persons share common heredity can be calculated, and "distance" can thus be stated in specific quantitative terms.

The unalterable nature of the blood relationship has one more aspect of significance. A blood relationship is a relationship of identity. People who are blood relatives share a common identity, they believe. This is expressed as "being of the same flesh and blood." It is a belief in common biological constitution, and aspects like temperament, build, physiognomy, and habits are noted as signs of this shared biological makeup, this special identity of relatives with each other. Children are said to look like their parents, or to "take after" one or another parent or grandparent; these are confirming signs of the common biological identity. A parent, particularly a mother, may speak of a child as "a part of me."

In sum, the definition of a relative as someone related by blood or marriage is quite explicit in American culture. People speak of it in just those terms, and do so readily when asked. The conception of a child occurs during an act of sexual intercourse, at which time one-half of the biogenetic substance of which the child is formed is contributed by the father, its genitor, and one-half by the mother, its genetrix. The blood relationship is thus a relationship of substance, of shared biogenetic material. The degree to which such material is shared can be measured and is called *distance*. The fact that the relationship of blood cannot be ended or altered and that it is a state of almost mystical commonality and identity is also quite explicit in American culture.

III.

"Relative by marriage" is defined with reference to "relative by blood" in American kinship. The fundamental element which defines a relative by blood is, of course, blood, a substance, a material thing. Its constitution is whatever it is that really is in nature. It is a natural entity. It endures; it cannot be terminated.

Marriage is not a material thing in the same sense as biogenetic heredity is. It is not a "natural thing" in the sense of a material object found in nature. As a state of affairs it is, of course, natural; it has natural concomitants or aspects, but it is not in itself a natural object. It is terminable by death or divorce.

Therefore, where blood is both material and natural, marriage is neither. Where blood endures, marriage is terminable. And since there is no such "thing" as blood of which marriage consists, and since there is no such material which exists free in nature, persons related by marriage are not related "in nature."

If relatives "by marriage" are not related "in nature," how are they related?

Consider the step-, -in-law, and foster relatives. The fundamental fact about these relatives is that they have the role of close relatives without, as informants put it, being "real or blood relatives." A step-mother is a mother who is not a "real" mother, but the person who is now the father's wife. A father-in-law is a father who is not Ego's own father, but his spouse's father. And a foster son is not one's own or real son, but someone whom one is caring for as a son.

It is possible to describe a foster-child's *relationship* to his foster parents, or a step-child's *relationship* (and this is the word which informants themselves use) to his step-parent. This is, in its main outline, a parent-child relationship

in the sense that it is a pattern for how interpersonal relations should proceed.

The natural and material basis for the relationship is absent, but relatives of this kind have a relationship in the sense of following a pattern for behavior, a code for conduct.

The classic tragedy of a step-child in Western European folklore, Cinderella for instance, states exactly the nature and also the problem of this relationship. A woman's relationship to her own child is one in which she has an abiding love and loyalty for it; her relationship to her husband's child by his earlier marriage is one in which that child is someone else's child, not hers. What she does for her step-child she does because of her husband's claim on her. Hence, if her husband does not protect his child, she may be cruel to it and favor her own child. This is seen as tragic because a child should have a mother who will mother it, and the parent-child relationship is quite distinct from the blood-tie which underlies it. The cruel step-mother of folklore should rise above the literal definition of her relationship to her step-child, and have the kind of *relationship* —affection, concern, care, and so forth—which a mother has for a child.

When a person is related to a blood relative he is related first by common biogenetic heredity, a *natural substance*, and second, by a *relationship*, a pattern for behavior or a code for conduct. The spouse, on one hand, and the step-, -in-law, and foster- relatives, on the other hand, are related by a *relationship* alone; there is no natural substance aspect to the relationship.

The distinctive feature which defines the order of blood relatives, then, is blood, a natural substance; blood relatives are thus "related by nature." This, I suggest, is a special instance of *the natural order* of things in American culture. The natural order is the way things are in nature. It consists in objects found free in nature. It is "the facts of life" as they really exist.

The feature which alone distinguishes relatives by marriage is their relationship, their pattern for behavior, the code for their conduct. I suggest, this is a special instance of the other general order in American culture, the *order of law*. The order of law is imposed by man and consists of rules and regulations, customs and traditions. It is law in its special sense, where a foster-parent who fails to care properly for a child can be brought to court, and it is law in its most general sense: law and order, custom, the rule of order, the government of action by morality and the self-restraint of human reason. It is a relationship in the sense of being a code or pattern for how action should proceed.

All of the step-, -in-law, and foster relatives fall under the order of law. It is in this sense that a mother-in-law is not a "real" or "true" mother—not a genetrix, that is—but is in the relationship of mother–child to her child's spouse. It is in this sense that a step-mother is not a "real" mother, not the genetrix, but in in a mother–child relationship to her husband's child. The crux of the Cinderella story is precisely that where the "real mother" is related to her child both by law and by nature, the step-mother lacks the "natural" basis for the relationship, and lacking this natural substance she "feels" no love except toward her "own" child and is thus able to cruelly exploit the child related to her *in law* alone.

If there is a relationship in law without a relationship in nature, as in the case of the spouse, step-, -in-law, and foster relatives, can there be a relationship in nature without a relationship in law? Indeed there can and there is. What is called a "natural child" is an example. He is a child born out of wedlock, a child, that is, whose mother and father are not married. He is a "natural child" because in his case his relationship to his parents is by nature alone and not by law as well; he is an "illegitimate" child. Similarly, the "real mother" of a child adopted in infancy, whether legitimate or not, is a relative in nature alone and not in law, and so is the genitor of such a child. Although the child is adopted and has every right and every duty of the blood child, in American belief it remains related to its "true" mother and father, its genitor and genetrix, in nature though not in law.

IV.

In sum, the cultural universe of relatives in American kinship is constructed of elements from two major cultural orders, the *order of nature* and the *order of law*. Relatives in *nature*

share heredity. Relatives *in law* are bound only by law or custom, by the code for conduct, by the pattern for behavior. They are relatives by virtue of their *relationship*, not their biogenetic attributes.

Three classes of relatives are constructed from these two elements. First there is the special class of relatives in nature alone. This class contains the natural or illegitimate child, the genitor or genetrix who is not the adoptive father or mother, and so on. The second class consists of relatives in law alone. This class may be called "by marriage" or it may be called "in law." It contains the husband and wife, the step-, -in-law, foster-, and other such relatives. The third class consists in relatives in nature *and* in law. This class of relatives is called "blood relatives" and contains the "father . . . daughter," "uncle . . . grandaughter," "cousin," sets, and so on.

The second and third classes of relatives can each be divided into two subclasses. The second

Table I

RELATIVES	NATURE	LAW
(1) In Nature	+	−
(A) Natural child, illegitimate child, natural mother, natural father, etc.		
(2) In Law	−	+
(A) Husband, wife.		
(B) Step-, -in-law, foster, etc.*		
(3) By Blood	+	+
(A) Father, mother, brother, sister, son, daughter.		
(B) Uncle, aunt, nephew, niece, grandfather, grandmother, grandson, granddaughter, cousin, first cousin, etc., great grandfather, etc., great grandson, etc.		

* This category includes relatives for whom there are no kinship terms in the usual sense but who can nevertheless properly be counted as, or considered to be, relatives by marriage or in-law. This category of kin, therefore, contains kin without kinship terms. As will be clear from Chapter Five below, the cousin's spouse, the spouse of the nephew or niece of Ego's own spouse, as well as others can occur in this category in American kinship. This follows from the different application of alternate norms *within* the framework set by these categories, and may (or may not) entail the use of alternate kinship terms as well. These points will be developed in Chapter Five.

class, relatives in law alone, consists of the subclass of husband and wife and the remainder, a subclass which contains the step-, -in-law, and foster- relatives and those for which there are no special lexemes. Husband and wife take basic kinship terms; the others take derivative terms. Husband and wife are the only relatives in law on a par with the closest blood relatives (the "father . . . daughter" set). Father and mother are properly also husband and wife. Finally, husband and wife are the only true relatives "by marriage" in one sense of marriage, namely, that sexual relationship between a man and a woman.

The third class also consists of two subclasses. The first consists of the "father . . . daughter" set of relatives, the second of those relatives who take the "uncle . . . granddaughter" and "cousin" terms. The modifier functions symbolize the difference between these subclasses:

the first subclass is marked by the restrictive modifiers, the second by the unrestrictive modifiers. That is, the "father . . . daughter" subclass is sharply restricted and distinguished from other kinds or degrees of "father," "mother," etc., while the "uncle . . . granddaughter" and "cousin" sets are infinitely expandable, but each expansion adds a degree of distance. Table I represents this summary.

I have put this summary in terms of the different classes or categories of relatives in American kinship. Yet these categories are built out of two elements, *relationship as natural substance* and *relationship as code for conduct.* Each of these elements derives from or is a special instance of the two major orders which American culture posits the world to be made up of, the *order of nature,* and the *order of law.*

COMPADRAZGO: FICTIVE KINSHIP IN LATIN AMERICA

Mario Dávila

In this paper, I will discuss the differences in form and function of a fictive kinship relationship, *compadrazgo,* in Latin American "peasant" communities, and will attempt to present a possible explanation for these differences. The reader will become aware that the majority of the ethnographic data which will be discussed is from villages in Mexico and Central America. This limitation, and the emphasis on compadrazgo in rural communities, is imposed for the most part by the lack of data on this mechanism from other areas or from the urban sectors of Latin America. However, the limitation is also partially self imposed. The area dealt with is one of the centers of contact, conquest, and merging of Iberian culture with the high Indian cultures. Both the nature of the rural community and the differences between "Indian" and "mestizo"

Unpublished manuscript, University of California, Berkeley, 1970. Reproduced by permission of the author.

communities are central elements in my analysis.

Compadrazgo is the Latin American form of ritual godparenthood, the ceremonial relationship established through the ritual of Catholic baptism. This ritual involves a triad of relationships between the three individuals involved: child, parent, and sponsor. Besides the relationship between the parent and child, which is formed within the boundaries of the nuclear family, this ritual establishes two new relationships: between the sponsor and the child and between the sponsor and the child's parents.

Compadrazgo (co-parenthood), as opposed to *padrinazgo* (godparenthood), is the more appropriate term for the Latin American form of Catholic godparenthood since it emphasizes the relationship established between the parent and the sponsor. The ethnographic data from Latin American rural communities indicates quite clearly that for the peasant as well as for the anthropologist attempting an analysis of peasant social structure, this particular relationship is as important, and in most cases more important, as the relationship which is established between the sponsor and the child, Church dogma is the contrary. This is borne out by the fact in many of the communities which have been reported on, relationships are established between adults in which the same fictive kin term, *compadre*, is used and in which the same type of obligations associated with compadrazgo through baptism are incurred by the individuals, but in which a non-human object or event replaces the child as the third point in the triad.

COMPADRAZGO AS FICTIVE KIN

In their discussion of compadrazgo, Mintz and Wolf (1950) note that there are three central elements in the ritual of Catholic baptism: the notion of spiritual rebirth, of sponsorship, and of a spiritual affinity established between the participants. In Catholic theology, baptism is the "rebirth" of the individual as a member of the Christian community. An analogy is drawn between the sponsor's special role in the ritual, and the parent's role (as defined by Catholic theology) at conception, and between the sponsor's obligation for the spiritual well-being of the child and the parent's, for the child's physical well-being. This creates the basis for the notion of spiritual affinity between the sponsor and the child. As the early Church practice of having the parents stand as sponsors for their own children disappeared and a new set of individuals were brought into the ceremonial relationship, the spiritual affinity between sponsor and child and the co-responsibility for the child was the basis for a feeling of affinity between the parent and the sponsor. This spiritual affinity between the individuals involved in the ritual was in turn the basis for the formation of fictive kinship relationships.

This notion of spiritual kinship is borne out in the terms for the positions in the triad and in the behavior appropriate to each dyad. The analogy between the parent-child and the sponsor-child dyad is quite clear. The Spanish terms for father and mother are *padre* and *madre;* for

godfather and godmother, *padrino* and *madrina.* For son and daughter, they are *hijo* and *hija;* for godson and goddaughter, *ahijado and ahijada.* The dyad is assymetrical, the relationship is hierarchical. As in the ideal parent-child relationship, the child is supposed to show absolute respect and obedience towards his padrino; the latter is supposed to provide moral advice and counsel for his ahijado, and physical and economic help if necessary. A frequently mentioned ideal obligation is that the padrino is expected to adopt his ahijado should he be orphaned. It is doubtful, however, whether this is done with any frequency.

It is more difficult to draw an analogy between the parent-sponsor dyad and a "model" in the kinship network. In this case, the dyad is reciprocal and symetrical. Both sponsor and parent· use the term *compadre,* or co-parent, in addressing each other, and the obligations and expectations are essentially equal in form and quantity. Relations between compadres are marked by extreme formality and respect:

> Behavior between new compadres becomes more formal. If previously they addressed each other with the familiar second person "tu," now they use the third person formal "Usted." Simultaneously they abandon the use of personal names and address each other as compadre. The compadre relationship is in theory considered to be the most sacred form of human ties. (Foster, 1961: 1178)

Besides respect, compadres are ideally supposed to assist one another in any way possible, according to Foster (*ibid.*), "whatever the personal sacrifices and inconvenience may be."

Finally, he notes that the complex of relationships created by compadrazgo "is much like the family in that it has religious sanction, shares the same incest prohibitions, and once established is indissoluble."

We are concerned, then, with a mechanism for the formation of special, essentially dyadic relationships primarily, though not exclusively, through the Catholic ritual of baptism. But, while the institution of compadrazgo conforms to the general description presented above, there are significant differences in the various components of the ritual and in the nature of the resulting relationships. In the next section, I will present some of the differences described in the ethnographies.

DIFFERENTIAL FORMS OF LATIN AMERICAN COMPADRAZGO

Though there are many variations in some of the minor aspects of the ritual, the differences we are concerned with involve 1) the mechanisms for creating ritual kinship ties, 2) the choosing of compadres, and 3) the nature and importance of the established relation.

Mechanisms for ritual kinship formation

Baptism is the principle ritual through which compadrazgo relationships are created. But the ethnographic material describes a number of alternate methods by which it is possible to extend one's compadrazgo relations to many individuals. In fact, Foster (1953:7) notes that the most important distinction between compadrazgo in Spain and Spanish America is that in Spanish America a great premium is usually placed on bringing together a large number of individuals into the relationship.

Extension of compadrazgo relationships can occur in two ways: by increasing the number of individuals with whom relations are established at any one particular ritual, and increasing the number of events at which a sponsor is required.

The Council of Trent (1545–63AD) limited the ritual kinship relationship to the baptizing priest, the child, the child's parents and the child's sponsors, putting an end to spiritual fraternity and to spiritual relationships between the sponsors themselves. In fact, however, the blanketing in of relatives of the actual participants still occurs in many communities. In Yalalág, in Oaxaca, all living, ascending relatives of both the sponsor and the parent are regarded as being in the compadrazgo unit. (Fuente, 1949:168). In Pascua, a Yaqui migrant settlement outside Tuscon, the grandparents of the ahijados become compadres of the padrino. Also, all the sponsors of any individual, regardless of their types, are considered compadres of one another. (Spicer, 1940:94). In Chinautla, in Guatemala, all members of the two families linked by compadrazgo

are involved in the ritual relationship. One of Riena's informants stated that his madrina's children were his brother and sister, though he recognized that they were different from his biological sibs. Reina also notes that marriage among such godsibs is considered incest. (1966:233).

A second mode of extension is to increase the number of events for which sponsors are required. According to Foster (1953), more than twenty occasions have been described for Latin America. Gillin lists 14 for Moche a Peruvian Coastal Town (1947:105); Parsons, 8 for Mitla in Oaxaca (1936:68–69); Spicer 7 in Pascua (op. cit.: 96–99), "while 4 to 6 are common in many places." Other Catholic sacramental rites besides baptism are the principle occasions, and of these, marriage is the most important, occurring in Moche (Gillin, op. cit.: 111), Mitla (Parsons, op. cit.: 69), Pascua (Spicer, op. cit.: 99), Chan Kom in the Yucatan (Redfield and Villa, 1934:99–100; Tzintzuntzan in Michoacan (Foster, 1948:263), Yalalág (Fuente, 1949), Tusik in Quintano Roo (Villa, 1945:90). Sponsors are choosen for confirmation in Moche (Gillin, op. cit.: 110), Mitla (Parsons, op. cit.: 68), Pascua (Spicer, op. cit.: 91), Chinautla (Reina, op. cit.: 229), and Tzintzuntzan (Foster, op. cit.: 263). Sponsors are also selected for first communion in Mitla and Tzintzuntzan.

Other events which are not religious ones, such as haircutting and nail clipping may also be used as events which require sponsors. An interesting adaptation of compadrazgo is reported by Redfield and Villa in Chan Kom. Here, the pagan ritual of hetzmek has been merged with Christian baptism, and the god-parents of baptism serve as the "godparents" in the hetzmek ritual (1934:144) Another ritual which is utilized is the ear piercing ceremony for male children in Moche (Gillin, op. cit.: 185).

Besides events which center on a child, the sponsorship of non-human objects is also frequent. The principle event of this type is the housewarming reported in Moche (Gillin, op. cit.: 111), and Mitla (Parsons, op. cit.: 69).

The possible proliferation of godparents is so great that the relationships can be forgotten or meaningless after the event has taken place.

However, there seems to be a difference of degree of importance of these relationships. Baptismal sponsorship and the relationship between the actual sponsor and the parent seem to be the most significant.

Choosing a sponsor

In this section we are concerned with how choices for sponsors are made, including who might be choosen. One difference is the attitude toward making a choice. In Dzitas (Redfield, 1941: 222), the choice is generally made only a short time before baptism, and there seems to be relative indifference to the matter. In Tusik (*ibid.:* 221), the choice is made as soon as pregnancy is known. In San Antonio Palapo (Redfield, 1945: 86), the decision is made in consultation with the four grandparents.

As for who is chosen, there seem to be few rules for preferential choice. In fact, the point that compadrazgo, as opposed to the kinship system, allows the individual freedom of choice in establishing dyads is often cited as one of the reasons for its importance in peasant communities. Generally speaking, choices are made among those who are not already blood relatives of the parent. That is, the individual does not usually choose someone with whom he already has a kin or kin-like relationship. Beals in Cheran (1946: 103) and Foster in Tzintzuntzan (1948: 263) note that blood relatives may be chosen, but that this is generally a matter of expediency among poor families, since it is not necessary to observe the formalities among relatives in these communities. For Yalalag, Fuente notes that the wealthier or socially higher families become so pressed to serve as godparents that they have come in some cases to take compadres only among relatives as a means of avoiding exploitation. (*op. cit.:* 171). The most notable exception which occurs, however, is in the Yucatan, in Tusik, and to a lesser degree in Chan Kom. In Tusik, among the X-Cacal, the paternal grandparents, if they are alive, *must* be chosen as sponsors (Villa, 1945: 90). In Chan Kom, grandparents are also desirable as sponsors, though it is not *required* that they be chosen, as in Tusik. (Redfield and Villa, 1934: 99).

As for horizontal *vs.* vertical choices with respect to socio-economic status, Foster notes that vertical choices occur with much greater frequency in Latin America than in Spain. In a quantative sense, however, the majority of relationships in America are established between people of more or less the same socio-economic level. (1953: 9). The choice of sponsors from a superior socio-economic level is reported for Moche (Gillin, *op. cit.:* 107), San Jose, Puerto Rico (Mintz and Wolf, 1950: 362), Yalalag (Fuente, *op. cit.:* 172), Peguche (Parsons, 1945: 44) and Tzintzuntzan (Foster, 1963: 1283).

Formalities, usually gift exchange, at the time of petitioning are reported by Spicer for Pascua (*op. cit.:* 96). Gifts are exchanged after acceptance in Tzintzuntzan (Foster, 1948: 262) and San Antonio Palapo (Redfield, 1945: 90–91).

Few ethnographies mention rejection of a request to serve as sponsor, perhaps because it is so rare. Being asked to serve as compadre is a great honor, and can only be excused for "urgent reasons." In Yalalág, however, Fuente notes refusal is actually made because of a feeling of imposition.

The compadrazgo relationship

Foster has stated that compadrazgo is considered to be the most sacred of human ties in the peasant community. Most ethnographers agree that it is one of the central elements in the social structure of their communities. The respect and formality associated with compadrazgo are reported for most of the communities discussed above. Another feature of the relationship, the reciprocal nature of the obligations incurred is also considered a central element. However, in view of the fact that vertical choices are made in some of the communities discussed, one would expect that the nature of obligations and expectations would be changed in these cases. This point will be discussed in greater detail later.

Compadrazgo and syncretism

One approach to the differences evidenced in the Latin American form of compadrazgo was to isolate and examine possible indigenous Indian elements and to look for parallels in pre-Conquest culture which differentially merged with the Spanish godparenthood.

Data of an ethnographic nature on pre-Conquest societies give evidence of baptismal ceremonies, ceremonial sponsorship, and ritualized "friendships." Sahagun's description of an Aztec baptismal ceremony bears considerable similarity to the Christian rite. (1932: 1.6, chap. 37). According to Landa, the baptismal ceremony of the Maya of Yucatan was so like the Catholic ritual that "Some of our Spaniards have taken occasion to persuade themselves and believe that in times past some of the apostles or successors to them passed over the West Indies and that ultimately those Indians were preached to." (1941: 227). Rojas Gonzales stresses the parallel in the use of water in baptismal ceremonies. The role that native priests and shaman play in both ceremonies facilitated the transfer to ceremonies officiated by Catholic priests.

Landa's account of Mayan baptism notes that sponsors were chosen to take the child to the temple. Sahagun notes that sponsors were also chosen by the Aztecs for the ear-piercing ceremonies, and we have mentioned their use in the *hetzmek* ritual reported by Redfield for Chan Kom. Unfortunately, there is little information on the nature of the relationships established through participation in these rituals. Paul has suggested that there may be a basis for the compadrazgo relationship (compadre-compadre) in the various kinds of formal, ritualized friendships or "blood brotherhood" among native peoples. These friendships involve ritual sanctions, mutual respect and mutual aid. (1942: 85).

An examination of the material on parallels and survivals from pre-Conquest cultures does not provide satisfactory explanations for the differences in forms of compadrazgo, particularly those which we are concerned about in this paper. The data which are available are inadequate; it is drawn mostly from a description of ceremonies in centers of high cultures and does not provide much information on local variation, and there is some question of its accuracy. As for the material on survivals, it is generally highly localized and "almost ancedotal in nature." (Erasmus, 1950: 48).

Nor does an examination of godparenthood in Spain provide satisfactory explanations. Though Foster feels that the godparenthood system de-scribed by Steward for Acala (1954: 107–10) probably represents the system which was the antecedent for Latin American godparenthood (1960: 107–108), he still notes some very fundamental differences. Basically, Spanish godparenthood is a means of reenforcing existing ties, particularly family ties. Only in the case of baptism is the compadre relationship ever recognized as establishing a bond which otherwise would not exist. The number of godparents, compadres, and ahijados which an individual will have accumulated in his life time is generally small, and not much emphasis is placed on numbers as an advantage. Finally, the bond between child and sponsor is a particularly important one, the bonds established between them are primary ones. (1953: 7).

A more satisfactory explanation of the mechanism is provided by an examination of the differences in function. Actually, compadrazgo's principle function is the formation of alliances. We are concerned with the types of alliances formed and their relation to other elements of the rural society.

In his comparative article on compadrazgo and cofradia, Foster states his investigative hypothesis as follows (1953: 1), "In all societies there is a minimal co-operating group which is necessary for the functioning of every day life." The size of the group is a function of the natural environment, the "social" enviroment, the type of economy, the type of technology, etc. Dyadic alliances, such as are generally formed through compadrazgo, are one type of group; polyadic alliances, such as corporate families, corporate "communities," voluntary associations, are another.

DYADIC AND POLYADIC ALLIANCES AND COMPADRAZGO

Foster feels that one of the reasons that compadrazgo was so readily accepted was its similarity to pre-existing native forms . . . "above all the native kinship systems disrupted by Spanish contact."

Ethnographic data makes it clear that before the conquest, Indian society was marked by much more widespread clan, lineage and extended family relationships than today. Membership in such a group automatically aligned each individual with a much larger "in-group" than was possible with the restricted bilateral family. Through compadrazgo it was possible to recapture some of the security that was lost with the destruction of the old forms. (Foster, 1953, 23).

But if this is the case, and if clans are essentially polyadic, corporate groups, then why is it that compadrazgo characteristically forms dyadic relationships? What is involved here is not so much the replacement of blood kin ties with fictive kin ties, but the replacement of polyadic alliances with dyadic ones in rural MesoAmerican communities. This is best illustrated by examining the decline of the extended family as a significant factor in MesoAmerican peasant social structure.

There is considerable evidence for the existence of clans and lineages in Meso America (Cf. Beals, 1932; Foster, 1949; Eggan, 1934; Guiteras, 1947). One of the principle functions of these corporate groups seems to have been control over means of production, specifically, land, Mendieta y Nuñez states that the land holding village was a characteristic of both Central Mexican and Mayan societies. Among those of the Central region, these villages were composed of patrilineally organized clan-like groups, the *capulli*, each of which controlled distinct parts of the village lands. (Mendieta y Nuñez, 1959: 6–7) Among the Maya, control of the land was much more firmly vested in the community group. Medieta y Nuñez suggests that this was due to Mayan swidden technology. Thus, the individual right's to plots were overridden by the community's need to have some land available at all times (*ibid.*: 11–12).

Certainly the devastation of Indian society and the depopulation which took place during the 16th century (cf. Diffie, 1945: 179–80; Cook and Simpson, 1948) wrecked havoc on the existing family groups. But more central to the decline of these groups was the imposition of a centralized, administrative state organization, and the institution of individual ownership of land. Throughout the rise and fall of the various Indian empires on the central plateau, the land holding villages retained considerable independence and autonomy. Even the Aztec (Mexica) empire was never a centralized state, and the principal obligations of the village was the payment of tribute to Tenochtitlan. Having met this, they were allowed to continue traditional patterns. Central authority, never very great among the Maya, was even less at the time of the Conquest, the last centralized government at Mayapan having collapsed in 1441 and given way to petty, feuding tribal kings. (Morley, 1956: 98–99).

The Spanish Conquest resulted in the establishment of a centralized state, and this state absorbed most of the functions which extended kin groups had previously performed for the individual. It provided him with protection from encroachment by other groups, it performed certain "necessary" rituals, it provided for the socialization of his children, etc. The joint responsibility of the corporate group for the actions of its members for the actions of the individual members as a means of social control was also absorbed by the state. The functions that were left to the kin group find no special enhancement in the size of the co-operating group.

The corporate group's control over land and labor was destroyed by the legal institution of individual ownership of land and the alienability of land. This was often simply an intermediate step to the actual alienation of land from the indigenous population by the Spanish. Even where individuals managed to retain land, and, after the 1910–20 revolution with the distribution of ejido land on a individual basis, there was no need for a co-operating group beyond the immediate nuclear family, as Wolf demonstrates (1966: 65–73).

Neither the power of the state nor the alienation of land from the indigenous population occured simultaneously or uniformly over all parts of MesoAmerica. One finds a more effective state control and a more extensive alienation of land in the central plateau and in other regions, such as the Valley of Oaxaca, where the land is most suitable to plantation agriculture, with both factors diminishing as you move into the more isolated highlands of Chiapas-Guatemala and the inhospitable Yucatán plateau. One would therefore expect to find a differential decrease in the importance of extended family. Indeed, this is

the case. In Cheran (Beals, *op. cit.*) and Tzintzuntzan (Foster, 1948) in Michoacan, in Tepoz-
tlan (Redfield, 1930; Lewis, 1951) in the Valley
of Morelos, and Mitla (Parsons, 1936) in the
Valley of Oaxaca, one finds the extended kin
group to be lacking, and blood kin relationships
beyond the nuclear family are of little significance. In Tzintzuntzan, the nuclear family is not
only the ideal but also the most common household grouping, and the extended family is "non-
corporate, highly informal, and rarely consisting
of more than three generations." (Foster, 1961:
1179–80).

At the other end of the continuum we find relatively isolated communities such as Tusik (Villa,
1945) in Quinitano Roo, and Oxchuc (Villa, 1946)
and Cancuc (Guiteras, *op. cit.*) in the Chiapan
highlands. Tusik is one of a number of settlements of the subtribe X-Cacal. The subtribe-
community orientation is strong, the land is held
in common by the tribe, and the principle political subunit is the military company, to which
each married man belongs, membership being
inherited through the male line. (Villa, 1945: 94).
In Axchuc and Cancuc, Tzeltal communities in
the Chiapan highlands which have remained
relatively isolated and hostile towards outsiders,
are still strong and functioning.

There is also an inverse differential development of dyadic alliances, particularly as in compadrazgo. In the first group, Foster notes that
"we find a godparent system which is almost an
ideal type." (1953: 24). In Tusik, we find compadrazgo operating to strengthen the existing
kinship-community bonds. Sponsor choice is pre-
determined by custom: if either paternal grandparent is alive, they must be chosen as sponsors.
If they are both dead, chiefs or other officials of
the military company to which the father belongs
is preferred. In Cancuc, Guiteras Holmes notes
that compadrazgo plays a completely insignificant role. The villagers know of the system, and
a few individuals have been baptised, but "the
people of Cancuc do not like to baptise. There are
no *compadres*, . . . , in Cancuc, 'aqui ninguno
quiere (Here no one wants to).' " (1947: 1–17).
In Oxchuc, Villa notes that "the tie of compadrazgo has little importance. Occasionally it is

established in a casual fashion, taking advantage
of the presence of any friend who wishes to sponsor the child at baptism . . . (there are) few
occasions in which the relations between godparent and godchild appear to have any significance. (1946).

Chinautla (Reina, *op. cit.*) in Guatemala,
would seem to pose a problem, in that it would
seem from Reina's description that corporateness
and polyadic alliances are still important features
of the social system—i.e., in the workings of the
cofradia system and in the fact that extension
along blood lines occurs with respect to the ritual
relationship established through compadrazgo, so
that in effect, it is a union of two corporate
groups, to some extent. However, with regard to
the extended family, he notes:

> The individual seems to stand alone among a
> potential web of relatives. Remarks like "because
> he is my blood relative, we co-operate," are the
> rare exceptions . . . Under ordinary conditions,
> indifference, apathy, and antagonism towards
> relatives of any age frequently appear. (228)

Reina feels that what is taking place is a
change in land tenure patterns, and that this is
affecting the relationships within the extended
family. The extended family is the ideal resident
unit, even though only 35% of the households
conform to this pattern, and historical documents as well as the memories of present residents indicate that in the past a family's land
was under the management of the head of the
extended family. The present trend, however, is
toward more individually owned property:

> Most families in Chinautla are tied to the land
> —either through ownership, leasing/borrowing,
> or by labor. The ownership of a patch of land of
> any size or quality is greatly desired, now simply
> for security, now in the hope that more may be
> acquired or a trade made. (p. 41)
> Since the desire for land is so intense and since
> parents, not waiting for death, often hand over
> their land when they themselves can no longer
> work it, strife and everlasting disputes within
> the family over inheritance are common. (There
> is no set pattern, the decision as to who inherits
> and how much is totally up to the individual

when he makes out his will.) Reflected in this disagreement is a certain amount of loosening of the ties of the extended family. (p. 42)

Whether this breakdown in the corporate family structure will effect other spheres is difficult to say. Certainly the corporate bonding achieved through extension of ritual relationships long blood lines will be altered.

Another community which seems unusual is Pascua (Spicer, *op. cit.*). The residents of Pascua are for the most part landless wage earners. They depend almost entirely on ties outside the community for subsistence, but this subsistence is terms of cash, not payment in kind. Pascua can hardly be said to exhibit the same kind of physical isolation that Cancuc or Tusik do. Yet, in a very real sense, Pascua seems to have a high degree of social isolation. Although economic bonds are almost exclusively with outside sources of income, in most other respects, the community seems to be well integrated and relatively homogenous in the sense that it is a "self-contained class." It seems to exhibit a high degree of corporateness in a community sense, and compadrazgo plays an integral part in achieving and maintaining this corporateness. Spicer describes (1940: 90–99) the compadrazgo system as being an "all-pervasive network of relationships which take into its web every person in the village." It will be remembered that Pascua is one of the communities in which mechanisms for extension of compadrazgo relationships is significant. Spicer describes seven different types of occasions which allow for the formation of compadrazgo relationships. In addition, a blanketing of non-participants occurs. The grandparents of the compadres also become part of the relationship. Also, Pascua exhibits a unique pattern for Latin America in that all the sponsors of an individual become compadres to one another. These two patterns of extension suggest the formation of polyadic rather than dyadic groups.

In general, then, the patterning of alliances along polyadic lines affects and shapes the mechanisms of compadrazgo. In Tusik, it provides reenforcement for an already existant kin based corporate group. In Pascua, it provides the mechanism for the creation and maintenance of a less well defined "community" corporate group. In both cases a hostile social, cultural and ecological environment makes it impossible for the individual to stand alone: In Pascua, the individual does not control the land which is the basis of his subsistence, nor does he have means of obtaining it. In Tusik, the nature of the technology makes individual control of the land impractical and community control imperative. The peasant has dealt with the problem of "selective pressures" (Wolf, 1966: 78) by developing mechanisms for sharing in times of need through communal responsibility and aid.

In the communities in Central Mexico, the peasant has faced the problem in much the same manner, that is by establishing mechanisms for sharing resources in time of need, not through communal action, but through the development of a selective network of dyadic ties with *himself* as the center nexus. Dyads provide more manipulability than polyadic relationships. He exercises greater freedom in choosing whether to initiate, continue, or terminate a particular relationship. His freedom of action in the matter rests to a large part on the fact that he controls the means of production at least as far as his own needs are concerned, and in times of dire emergency, even if he is unable to meet any of his obligations, he can still depend on his own resources.

Chinautla represents a community which is undergoing a transition. Unfortunately, Riena does not discuss how changes in land tenure patterns and the weakening of corporate family bonds is affecting compadrazgo bonds.

SOCIAL MOBILITY AND COMPADRAZGO

A second significant feature of godparent choice is whether choices are made within the same socio-economic class or across socio-economic class lines. Mintz and Wolf (1950) analyze data from five different communities, and come to the decision that such a patterning will be determined by the amount of social mobility, real or perceived, is available to the individual in a given situation. Although they discount the possibility of isolatedness or homogeneity being the sole factors in patterning horizontal *vs.* vertical choice, in Tusik and in Pascua, isolation—in the one case because of physical barriers and in the other, social ones—and the homogeneity of each society—the one a classless tribe, the other a self-contained mono-class—almost axiomatically affect the amount of perceived mobility.

In Moche (Gillin, *op. cit.*) we find a society in transition from an Indian group to a more mestizo community. Steward notes that "(the village) lands . . . are now owned individually, and they are being alienated through sale and litigation. It is on a cash rather than subsistence basis economically . . . Many Mocheros even work outside their community for wages, and some are in professions . . . Formal aspects of native social organization have disappeared, and contacts with the outside world are increasing" ("Foreword" by Julian Steward).

Moche is marked by "an absence of spontaneous community organization and solidarity." (p. 104) With regard to the extended family, Gillin notes that,

> Although an individual's blood relatives beyond the immediate family are recognized as such, they are not recognized, either by the individuals involved or by others, as a group with internal functional organization of with recognized status relations vis-à-vis other groups. Extended families or kinship groups are not among the constituent units of Moche society. (p. 101)

Given our previous discussion, one would expect that comprazgo would function to form dyadic alliances, and indeed this is the case:

> Although adults, by entering such a system of *compadrazgo*, form a group of compadres, it must be recognized that this is not an organized group with status in the society as a whole. The relationships are phrased in terms of social connections between individual statuses and the individuals who occupy them. Although the child might be considered the symbol of the group, there is no leadership, no group activity, no right or obligation to the group as a whole, and no internal organization. Furthermore, there is no word in use in Moche referring to groups of this sort as discrete functioning entities, occupying a

place in the social organization. In short, there are no symbolic, representational, or actional patterns in the Moche culture which would lead us to see these aggregates as status groups. (pp. 109–110)

Compadrazgo bonds are used to provide security, but on an individual basis, as in Tzintzuntzan, rather than on a corporate basis, as in Pascua. The tendency to form compadrazgo relationships is carried to extremes in Moche; Gillin lists fourteen possible occasions.

There are no true social classes in Moche as such, though differentiations are made along lines of 1) wealth, 2) differences in residence, i.e., town, *compiña* (countryside, rural), and *playa* (beach, residence of landless fishermen), and 3) between Mocheros and *forasteros* (Creoles who have settled in Moche but who are considered outsiders by the Indian peoples. *ibid.*, p. 113). Also, prestige is accrued through individual effort rather than through group affiliation, notably through the accumulation of wealth (provided it is combined with agreeable habits), and the ability to read and to acquire "influence" with the powers that be is becoming an important prestige giving characteristic. This would suggest that though there are no clear socio-economic class lines as such, there is a perceived mobility within the system. One would then expect that compadrazgo choices would show a great deal of vertical patterning and this is borne out,

> From the point of view of the parents it is desirable to chooose godparents who are financially responsible, if not rich, and also persons who have influence and prestiful social connections. The real function of godparents is to broaden, and if possible, increase the social and economic resources of the child and the parent and by the same token to lower the anxieties of the parents on this score. (*ibid.*, 107–108)

In Tzintzuntzan, Foster also found an increasing number of vertically patterned alliances, which he called patron-client relationships. Compadrazgo played a major role in the formation of these relationships. He notes that although some patron-client relationships were formed with individuals of higher status within the village, a large number were being formed with outsiders who were in a position to provide aid. The asymmetrical nature of these bonds was recognized and no attempt was made to hide it. Relations continued to be formal and reinforced by reciprocal exchange. But while the client compadre continued to use *Usted* in address, the patron very often used *tu*. Likewise, different kinds of goods and services were exchanged. "It is, in fact, the ability to offer one's partner something distinct from that which he offers that makes the system worthwhile." (Foster, 1963, 1967).

Not all dyads are vertical, the vast majority, in fact are horizontal (Foster, 1948, 1961). Nor are all vertical alliances strictly dyadic. In situations marked by strong class differentiation and very limited mobility, or with insurmountable barriers such as those of race, cross class ties may serve to bind the members of the community together in a very loose sort of group corporateness. This may be what is taking place in the formation of Indio-Landino bonds in Chinautla, though Riena does not make this point clear. It appears to be the case in San Jose, Puerto Rico (Mintz and Wolf, 1950) in the formation of ties through compadrazgo between large landowners and small landowners and peones.

CONCLUSIONS

Differences in form in the compadrazgo mechanism reflect differences in function. Differences in function are related to several factors which are themselves functionally related. The major factors would appear to be 1) the peasant's relation to the means of production, principally land, 2) his dependence on corporate group structures such as the extended kin group or the "community," and 3) the degree of freedom the individual perceives he has to effect a change in his socio-economic position.

Generally speaking, where the individual excercises little control over the means of production, where corporateness is stressed, and where the individual does not perceive opportuni-ties for mobility, compadrazgo mechanisms function so as to create and support polyadic alliances. Where such societies are internally homogenous, choices will be horizontal, almost axiomatically. Where such societies evidence stable internal stratification, sponsor choices will tend to be vertical.

Where the individual does exercise considerable control over his own land, and where corporate groups such as the extended family are not significant, then dyadic alliances will tend to form. Where the perceived degree of freedom of mobility is small, such as in a relatively homogenous peasant community, then choices will tend to be horizontal. Where the degree of freedom is made greater by changes within the village itself or accessibility to people in superior positions outside the village, then choices will tend to be vertical ones.

The communities discussed in the analysis seem to represent extremes in terms of the factors discussed above—Tusik, Pascua, the Chiapas/Guatemala Mayan groups (Oxchuc, Cancuc, Chinautla) at one end; Moche, Tzintzuntzan, Cheran, etc., at the other. Certainly the choice of extremes facilitated the analysis. But they are important extremes in that they represent two models which have been advanced for the understanding of Meso-American peasant social organization. The first group seem to typify Wolf's "closed, corporate" peasant community (1955, 1966:83-89). Though they lack some of the individual characteristics, they demonstrate more or less the same type of organization vis-à-vis the relationship of the peasant to the land, his dependency on group corporateness, and his relative isolation from the greater society. The cargo system of the Chiapan Maya (Nash, 1958; Cancian, 1965) and the cofradia in Chinautla function as leveling mechanisms on the one had, and on the other, they re-enforce group solidarity.

The villages at the other extreme are or are rapidly becoming *"mestizo*-ized" as they are drawn into closer contact with the greater society. They fit Foster's model of a peasant society which is highly individualized, organized chiefly by dyadic alliances, and dominated by an awareness of their own relative deprivation vis-à-vis this greater society. (Foster, 1961, 1963, 1965).

Both types typify certain peasant communities. What they demonstrate, and what I hope this paper has demonstrated, is the adaptiveness of the rural agriculturalist, commonly called "peasant." The variations in compadrazgo illustrate the adaptation of a cultural mechanism to the needs of a given situation.

URBANISATION CASE HISTORY IN PERU

William Mangin

There have been big cities in Peru for at least five hundred years and they have grown largely through migration from the hinterland. The tremendous population growth in Peru, together with the centralization of social, political, economic and cultural rewards in Lima, the capital city, has led to recent intensified migration from the provinces to Lima. It is safe to say that at least a million of Lima's two million people were born outside the city. The increase in the numbers of migrants to the city and the subsequent dramatic resettlement of many of them in 'unaided self-help' squatter settlements, 'barriadas' on the banks of the Rimac River and on hillsides surrounding the city, have drawn considerable attention locally and abroad, and for the first time have made many Peruvians aware of the situation. The city has probably grown in the past in much the same way, but the magnitude and the visibility of the recent influx make it seem to be a new phenomenon. The migrants come from practically all regions and all social classes and ethnic groupings in the country.

The composite case-history presented overleaf illustrates some of the human problems encountered in migration to the city and locating and housing a family in a squatter settlement. The couple referred to as Blas and Carmen do exist and their story of moving to the barriada is true.

Some of the details of slum life and house con-struction in the barriada were drawn from the experiences of other migrants in Lima.

• • •

Fortunato Quispe, a Quechua-speaking Indian from an hacienda in the mountains of Peru, contracted himself out to a coastal sugar plantation for a year's work in order to earn some cash for a religious festival.

After a year on the coast he took a wife and settled down on the plantation leaving his mountain home for good. He and his wife had seven children. When their oldest, Blas, was 18, he found himself with no job, no possibility of schooling, and under pressure from his father to leave and get a job. The small two-room adobe company house was hardly big enough for the parents and the seven children and the sugar company was mechanizing the plantation even as its resident population expanded rapidly. Blas, who had spoken mainly Quechua as a child, was, at 18, fully at home in Spanish. He had visited Lima, the capital city, twice, was an avid radio and movie fan and considered the life of the plantation town dull.

Six months after his eighteenth birthday he and his friend, Antonio, took a truck to the Lima valley and took a bus from the edge of the valley to the city. Having been there before, they knew how to get to the house of an uncle of Antonio's near the wholesale market district. The uncle had heard via the grapevine that they might come. He was renting a three-room house on a crowded alley for his own family of seven, and his maid

Reprinted from *Architectural Design*, Vol. 38, No. 8 (1963), pp. 366–370 by permission of the author.

and her child slept in the small kitchen. He was only able to put them up for one night. They moved into a cheap hotel and pension near the market, and through Antonio's uncle were recruited for a provincial club, Sons of Paucartambo, the native mountain district of Antonio's and Blas' father. Much of their social activity is still with members of the club, and their first orientation to life in Lima was from club members.

Antonio went to work for his uncle, and Blas, who had been robbed of all his clothing from the hotel, took a job as a waiter and clean-up man in a modest boarding house catering to medical and engineering students. He worked six-and-a-half days a week in the pension, taking Thursday nights and Sunday afternoons off. During his first year he saved a little money. He impregnated a maid from a neighbouring house, Carmen, and agreed to marry her sometime. Meanwhile, they rented a two-room, one-storey adobe house in a large lot not far from the boarding house. The lot was packed solidly with similar houses and the walks between them were about five feet wide. They had filthy, constantly clogged common baths and water taps for every ten houses and the rent was high. They paid extra for electricity and for practically non-existent city services.

Through a relative of one of the students Blas got a better job as a waiter in a rather expensive restaurant. In spite of the distance and the extra money spent for transportation it paid to take the job. With the arrival of a second child plus a boost in their rent, they found themselves short of money even though Blas' job was quite a good one for a person of his background.

Carmen, Blas' common law wife, had come to Lima at the age of fourteen from the southern highland province of Ayacucho. She had been sent by her mother and step-father to work as a servant in the house of a Lima dentist, who was also a land-owner in Ayacucho, and Carmen was to receive no pay. The dentist promised to 'educate' her but, in fact, she was not only not allowed to go to school but was rarely allowed outside the house. During her third year with the dentist's family her mother, who had left her

stepfather in Ayacucho, rescued her from the dentist's house after a terrible row. Her mother then found a maid's job for Carmen where she was paid. Carmen worked in several private houses the next few years and loaned a large part of her earnings to her mother. Blas was her first serious suitor. Previously she had had little experience with men and when Blas asked her to come and live with him after she became pregnant, she was surprised and pleased.

In her own crowded house with Blas and their son she was happier than she had been since her early childhood with her grandmother. Although her work was hard, it was nothing like the work she had done in the houses in Lima. They were poor but Blas had steady work and they ate better than she had in any of her previous homes. Her infrequent arguments with Blas were usually over money. He had once hit her when she had loaned some of the rent money to her mother, but, on the whole, she considered herself well-treated and relatively lucky in comparison with many of her neighbours.

She did not have too much to do with her neighbours, mostly longer-time residents of Lima than she, and she was afraid of the Negroes in the area, having been frightened as a child in the mountains by stories of Negro monsters who ate children. She found herself being drawn into arguments over petty complaints about children trespassing, dogs barking and messing the sidewalk, husband's relative success or failure, mountain Indian traits as opposed to coastal Mestizo traits, etc. She was mainly occupied with her son and her new baby daughter, and the constant arguing annoyed Blas more than it did Carmen. Blas had also been disturbed by the crowded conditions. There was no place for the children to play and the petty bickering over jurisdiction of the small sidewalk was a constant irritant. Thievery was rampant and he had even lost some of his clothes since they had to hang the washing outside above the alley. In Lima's damp climate, it often takes several days to dry clothes even partially.

He had been thinking of moving and, although Carmen was settled into a more or less satisfactory routine, she was interested as well. They carried on for another year and another child without taking any action. When their landlord told them that he was planning to clear the lot and build a cinema within six months, they decided to move. A colleague of Blas' in the restaurant had spoken to him about a group to which he belonged. The members were organizing an invasion of state land to build houses and they wanted fifty families. The group had been meeting irregularly for about a year and when Blas was invited they had forty of the fifty they sought.

The waiter's group came mainly from the same central highland region and their spokesman and leader was a bank employee who was also a functionary of the bank employees' union. The other major faction was a group of career army enlisted men, including several members of a band that plays at state functions, who were stationed near the proposed invasion site. About half of the group had been recruited as Blas was. Blas himself recruited a neighbour and another family from the Sons of Paucartambo, to which he still belonged.

They met a few times with never more than fifteen men present. They were encouraged by the fact that the government seemed to be tolerating squatter invasions. Several earlier invasion attempts had been blocked by the police and in many barriadas people had been beaten, some shot, and a few killed. The recent attitude, in 1954, seemed tolerant, but under a dictatorship, or under any government, the law is apt to be administered whimsically and their planned invasion was illegal. Another factor pointing to haste was the loss of seven of their families who had found housing some other way. Blas was one of those suggesting that they move fast because his eviction date was not far off.

Many barriada invasions had been arranged for the eve of a religious or national holiday. Their invasion site was near the area used once a year, in June, for a grand popular folk-music festival, so they decided to wait until that was over. The next holiday was the Independence Day vacation, July 28th, 29th, 30th; so they picked the night of the 27th. It would give them a holiday to provide a patriotic aura as well as three days off from work to consolidate their position. They thought of naming their settlement after the dictator's popular wife, but, after taking into account the vicissitudes of current politics, they decided to write to her about their pitiful plight, but to name the place after a former general-dictator, long dead, who freed the slaves.

A letter was drawn up for mailing to the dictator's wife and for presentation to the press. The letter stressed equally their respect for the government and their abandonment by the government. They had no hesitation about wringing the most out of the clichés concerning their status as humble, abandoned, lost, helpless and disillusioned but always patriotic servants of the fatherland.

During the last month word was passed from the active meeting-goers, still never more than 20 or 25, to the others and preparations were made. Each family bought its own straw mats and poles for the house and small groups made arrangements for trucks and taxis. Each household was asked to get a Peruvian flag or make one of paper. No two remember the details of the invasion the same way, but about thirty of the expected forty-five families did invade during the night. A newspaper photographer was notified by the invaders and he arrived about the time the houses were being finished. The members had discussed previously what lots they would take, and how the streets were to be laid out and there was very little squabbling during the first day. By early morning when the police arrived there were at least thirty one-room straw houses flying Peruvian flags and the principal streets were outlined with stones.

The police told them they would have to leave. A picture and story appeared in two papers and by the 30th of July about twenty or thirty more families had come, including some of the old members. A few with the help of friends and relatives and, in at least one case, paid workers, had built brick walls around their lots. These families and a few other early arrivals, most of whom are still in the barriada in 1963, proudly refer to themselves as the original invaders and tend to exaggerate the opposition they faced.

They were told to leave several times but no-one forced them. A resident, not one of the original invaders, was killed by the police in 1960 during an attempt to build a school on government land. The unfavourable publicity caused the government to desist and the residents cut a lot out of the hillside and built a school.

Blas and Carmen picked a lot about fifteen by thirty metres on the gradual slope of the hill on the principal street. The lot was somewhat larger than most subsequent lots, an advantage of being an original invader.

Blas and some friends quickly expanded the simple invasion one-room house to a three-room straw mat house and they outlined the lot with stones. He worked hard on Sundays and some nights, sometimes alone, sometimes with friends from the barriada or from outside. He soon managed to get a brick wall six-and-a-half feet high round his property.

Many of the residents of barriadas hurry to erect the walls around their lots and then take anywhere from one year to five or ten to finish the house. After about a year of working on the lot and making his 'plan,' Blas decided to contract a 'specialist' to help him put up walls for four rooms. He paid for the materials brought by the 'specialist' and helped out on the job. When the walls were done he roofed the rooms with cane, bricked up the windows and put in cement floors. With his first pay cheque, after finishing paying for the walls, Blas made a down payment on a large, elaborate cedar door costing about $45. With the installation of the door and wooden windows they finally felt like home-owners. They even talked of getting formally married.

About two years later, after a particularly damp winter during which his children were frequently sick, he decided to hire another 'specialist' to help him put on a concrete roof. He hired a neighbour who had put on other roofs and he found out that the first 'specialist' had sold him faulty cement and had also erected the walls in such a way that it would be difficult to put on a roof. It took considerable money, time and energy to rectify the mistakes and put on the roof, but when it was done it was a good job

and strong enough to support a second floor some day. Meanwhile a straw mat room has been erected on the roof and Blas helps out with the houses of friends and neighbours against the day he will ask them to help with his second floor.

Skilled bricklayers and concreters abound in barriadas and the bulk of the construction in these places is cheaper than on contracted houses. Much of it is done through informal mutual aid arrangements and when contractors are hired they are generally very closely supervised. There is considerable cheating by contractors on materials and many of the specialists hired for roofing and electrical and plumbing installations are not competent. Transport of materials is often expensive but the personal concern of the builder often results in lower prices at purchase. Some barriadas have electricity from the central power plant and public water; the one in this story does not. The front room/shop combination they have in their house is not only fairly common in barriadas but throughout the provincial area of Peru.

Their principal room fronts on the street and doubles as a shop which Carmen and the oldest children tend. Blas is still a waiter and they now have five children. The saving on rent and the income from the shop make them considerably more prosperous than before, but, in spite of their spectacular view of the bright lights of the centre of Lima some twenty minutes away, Carmen has never seen the Plaza San Martin and has passed through the central business district on the bus only a few times. She has never been inside the restaurant where Blas works. She gets along with most of her neighbours and has the company and assistance of a fifteen-year-old half-sister deposited with her by her mother.

Blas and Carmen have a television set which runs on electricity bought from a private motor owner and they are helping to pay for it by charging their neighbours a small amount to watch. It also brings some business to the store.

Carmen and Blas bemoan the lack of sewage disposal, running water and regular electricity in the barriada and they complain about the dust from the unpaved streets.

They are also critical of the ramshackle auxiliary bus which serves them, but, on the whole, they are not dissatisfied with their situation. They own a house which is adequate, Blas has steady work, their oldest children are in school, and Blas has been on the elected committee that runs barriada affairs and feels that he has some say in local government. Since local elections are unknown in Peru the barriadas' unofficial elections are unique. The committee passes judgement on requests from new applicants to settle in the barriada and cut new lots out of the hillside. They also decide on requests to sell or rent. Renting is against the rules of the association. Another important function is presenting petitions and requests to various government ministries for assistance. Until 1960 barriada residents had no legal basis for their ownership of lots. Any recognition by the government in the form of assistance or even taxation was an assuring sign. In 1960 the congress passed a law saying, in effect, that what could not be changed might as well be made legal, and residents of barriadas are to be given their lots. As of 1963 new land titles had been given out by the government, but the people have been buying and selling for years with home-made titles.

The committees are also concerned with internal order. Barriadas are ordinarily quiet places composed mainly of hard-working family groups, but the public image is one of violence, immorality, sloth, crime and revolutionary left-wing politics. Barriada residents are quite sensitive about this and the committees try to screen out potential trouble makers and control those present. They also try to get as much publicity as possible for the productive work done by barriada people.

The experience of this couple is probably happier than that of the average family but is certainly well within the 'typical' range. They feel, in comparison to people like themselves and in terms of their own aspirations, that they have done well. When asked what they would do if they required a large sum of money, they both answer in terms of improving their present property and educating their children. There is some resentment of the children, and Blas beats the oldest boy for not doing well in school, and all five children are bedwetters, but they give the impression of a happy family and, although Carmen cried during several interviews, they smile frequently and seem to be getting along. Carmen speaks some Quechua with her neighbours and her half-sister, and has actually improved her Quechua since coming to the barriada. Spanish is the principal language, however, and neither she nor Blas have any strong interest in their children learning Quechua.

The children themselves learn some Quechua but they speak Spanish with their peers, and in a group of children it is difficult to distinguish those of recently arrived near-Indian migrants from those of the most *Criollo* coastal families. There is a certain amount of antagonism among the adult barriada dwellers over race, cultural difference, politics, and place of origin. The children, however, are strikingly similar in attitude and have very little of the mountain Indian about them.

The situation of Blas and Carmen is similar to that of many others. They have some friends, some relatives and some income, but they could be ruined by a loss of job or any chronic illness of Blas, and they are aware of it. If there is a potentially disruptive factor in their lives it is that the high aspirations they have for their children are vastly unrealistic. They are sacrificing and plan to sacrifice more for the education of the children, but they overrate the probable results. They say they want the children to be professionals, doctors, teachers, people with comfortable lives, and in this they are similar to most interviewed barriada families. But it is highly unlikely that they will be, unless there are monumental and rapid changes in Peru.

When the children come to this realization they may fulfil the presently paranoid prophecy of many middle and upper class Peruvians who see the barriada population as rebellious and revolutionary.

SELECTED READINGS

Anshen, Ruth (ed.)
  1949 *The family*. New York: Harper & Row.

Arensburg, Conrad M., and Solon T. Kimball
1940 *Family and community in Ireland*. Gloucester, Mass.: Peter Smith.

Bernard, Jessie
1966 *Marriage and the family among Negroes*. Englewood Cliffs, N.J.: Prentice-Hall.

Bonnerjea, Biren
1930 The Hindu family. *Primitive Man*, v: III: 3–19.

Bott, Elizabeth
1957 *Family and social network*. London: Tavistock.

Chao, Hsi-Lin
1930 The Chinese family. *Primitive Man*, v: III: 19–22.

Cumming, Elaine, and David M. Schneider
1961 Sibling solidarity: A property of American kinship. *American Anthropologist*, 63: 498–507.

Dávila, Mario
1970 Campadrazgo: Fictive kinship in Latin America. (Unpublished manuscript, University of California, Berkeley.)

Fei, Hsiao-t'ung
1949 *Earthbound China*. London: Routledge & Kegan Paul.

Firth, Raymond W.
1956 Two studies of kinship in East London. *London School of Economics Monographs in Social Anthropology*, No. 15. London: Athlone.

Firth, Raymond W., J. Hubert, and A. Forge.
1970 *Families and their relatives*. London: Routledge & Kegan Paul.

Freed, Stanley A.
1963 Fictive kinship in a North Indian village. *Ethnology*, 2: 86–103.

Freedman, Maurice
1958 Lineage organization in southeastern China. *London School of Economics Monographs in Social Anthropology*, No. 18. London: Athlone.
——— 1966 Chinese lineage and society: Fukien and Kwangtung. *London School of Economics Monographs in Social Anthropology*, No. 33. London: Athlone.

Freedman, Maurice (ed.)
1970 *Family and kinship in Chinese society*. Stanford: Stanford University Press.

Fried, Morton H.
1953 *The fabric of Chinese society*. New York: Praeger.

Friedl, Ernestine
1959 The role of kinship in the transmission of the national culture of Greece. *American Anthropologist*, 61: 30–38.

Friedrich, Paul
1964 Semantic structure and social structure: An instance from Russian. In W. Goodenough (ed.), *Explorations in cultural anthropology*. N.Y.: McGraw-Hill.

Garigue, Phillip
1956 French Canadian kinship and urban life. *American Anthropologist*, 58: 1090–1101.

Goodenough, Ward H.
1965 Yankee kinship terminology: A problem in componential analysis. In E. A. Hammel (ed.), *Formal semantic analysis*. *American Anthropologist*, 67: 5 (Part 2): 259–287. Special Publication.

Hammel, Eugene A.
1968b *Alternative social structures and ritual relations in the Balkans*. Englewood Cliffs, N.J.: Prentice-Hall.
——— 1969a Economic change, social mobility and kinship in Serbia. *Southwestern Journal of Anthropology*, 25: 188–197.

Hsu Francis L. K.
1948 *Under the ancestor's shadow*. New York: Columbia University Press.

Hughes, Everett C.
1946 *French Canada in transition*. Chicago: University of Chicago Press.

Karvé, Irawati
1953 Kinship organization in India. *Deccan College Monograph*, No. 11. Poona.

Lambert, Richard D.
1962 The impact of urban society upon village life. In R. Turner (ed.), *India's urban future*. Berkeley: University of California Press.

Lewis, Oscar T.
1958 *Village life in northern India*. Urbana: University of Illinois Press.
——— 1966 *La vida: A Puerto Rican family*. New York: Random House.

Mandelbaum, David G.
1959 The family in India. In R. Anshen (ed.), *The family: Its function and destiny*. New York: Harper & Row.

Mangin, William
1963 Urbanisation case history in Peru. *Architectural Design*, 38: 366–370.

Miner, Horace
1939 *St. Denis: A French Canadian parish*. Chicago: University of Chicago Press.

Parsons, Talcott
1943 The kinship system of the contemporary United States. *American Anthropologist*, 45: 22–38.

Potter, Jack, May Diaz, and George Foster (eds.)
1967 *Peasant society: A reader.* Boston: Little, Brown.

Schneider, David M.
1965b American kinship terms and terms for kinsmen: A critique of Goodenough's componential analysis of Yankee kinship terminology. In E. A. Hammel (ed.), Formal semantic analysis. *American Anthropologist,* 67:5 (Part 2):288–308. Special Publication.

———— 1967 *American kinship: A cultural account.* Englewood Cliffs, N.J.: Prentice-Hall.

Schneider, David M., and George Homans
1955 Kinship terminology and the American kinship system. *American Anthropologist,* 57:1194–1208.

Wiser, William H. and Charlotte V.
1963 *Behind mud walls 1930–1960.* Berkeley: University of California Press.

Wolf, Eric
1965 Kinship, friendship and patron-client relations in complex societies. In M. Banton (ed.), The social anthropology of complex societies. *Association of Social Anthropologists of the Commonwealth Monographs,* No. 4, pp. 1–18. London: Tavistock.

Yang, Ch'ing-k'un
1965 *Chinese Communist society: Family and village.* Cambridge: M.I.T. Press.

ABBREVIATIONS OF
THE NAMES OF PUBLISHERS
AND PUBLICATIONS

A.A.	American Anthropologist
A.A.A.	American Anthropological Association
A.J.S.	American Journal of Sociology
A.S.A.	Association of Social Anthropologists of the Commonwealth
B.A.E.	Bureau of American Ethnology
B.J.S.	British Journal of Sociology
I.A.I.	International African Institute
I.C.A.	International Congress of Americanists, Proceedings of
J.A.F.	Journal of American Folklore
J.R.A.I.	Journal of the Royal Anthropological Institute
L.S.E.	London School of Economics
N.C.R.C.	Northern Coordination and Research Centre
S.J.A.	Southwestern Journal of Anthropology
U.C.P.A.A.E	University of California Publications in Archeology, Anthropology and Ethnology

BIBLIOGRAPHY

This bibliography includes references cited by the authors of the selections in the text. All publication dates are given as cited by the authors. In a few cases, incorrect dates were cited. These have been enclosed in parentheses, and correct dates, where available, have been included in the entry. An asterisk following a reference indicates that *complete* bibliographic information is given in the cross-reference.

Aberle, D., D. R. Miller, U. Bronfenbrenner, D. M. Schneider, E. H. Hess, and I. N. Spuhler
1963   The incest taboo and the mating patterns of animals. *A.A.*, 65: 253–264.

Ackerknecht, E. H.
1954   On the comparative method in anthropology. In R. F. Spencer (ed.), 1954.*

Adam, F.
1952   *The clans, septs and regiments of the Scottish highlands.* 4th ed. Revised by Sir T. Innes of Learney. Edinburgh: W. and A. K. Johnston.

Adam, L.
1948   Virilocal and uxorilocal. *Man,* 48: 12.

Aginsky, B. W.
1935a   Kinship systems and forms of marriage. *A. A.,* Memoir 45.
——— 1935b   The mechanics of kinship. *A.A.,* 37: 450–457.

Alpert, H.
1961   *Emile Durkheim and his sociology.* New York: Russell & Russell.

Anshen, R. (ed.)
1949   *The family.* New York: Harper & Row.

Arensberg, C. M., and S. T. Kimball
1940   *Family and community in Ireland.* Gloucester, Mass.: Peter Smith. Reprinted in 1961.

Aristotle
(1934)   Nichomachean ethics VIII. In *The Nichomachean ethics of Aristotle.* j. 1155a, 32. London: J. M. Dent, New York: Dutton.

Atkins, J. R.
1954   Some observations on the concept of "role" in social science. (Unpublished M.A. thesis, University of Pennsylvania.)

Atkinson, J. J.
1903   Primal law. In A. Lang (ed.), *Social origins.* London, New York: Longmans, Green, pp. 209–294.

Ayoub, M.
1959   Parallel cousin marriage and endogamy. *S.J.A.,* 15:266–275.

Bachofen, J. J.
1861   *Das Mutterecht.* Stuttgart: Krais & Hoffman.

Banton, M.
1965   *Roles, an introduction to the study of social relations.* London: Tavistock.

Barić, L.
1967   Levels of change in Yugoslav kinship. In M. Friedman (ed.), *Social organization.* London: Cass.

Barnes, J. A.
1949   Measures of divorce frequency in simple societies. *Royal Anthropological Institute,* 79.
——— 1951   Marriage in a changing society: A study in structural change among the Fort Jameson Ngoni. *Rhodes-Livingston Paper,* No. 20. Cape Town: Oxford University Press.
——— 1954   Class and committee in a Norwegian island parish. *Human Relations,* 7.

Barth, F.
1961   *The Nomads of South Persia.* New York: Humanities Press.
——— 1966   Models of social organization. *Royal Anthropological Institute Occasional Paper,* No. 33.

Barton, R. F.
1919   Ifugao law. *U.C.P.A.A.E.,* XV: 1–127.

Beaglehole, E., and P. Beaglehole
1938   Ethnology of Pukapuka. *Bernice P. Bishop Museum Bulletin,* No. 150. Honolulu.

Beals, R.
1932   Unilateral organizations in Mexico. *A.A.,* 34: 467–475.
——— 1946   Cheran: A sierra Tarascan village. *Smithsonian Institute of Social Anthropology Publication,* No. 2.
——— 1951   Urbanism, urbanization and acculturation. *A.A.,* 53: 1–10.

Bellah, R. N.
1952   *Apache kinship systems.* Cambridge: Harvard University Press.

Benedict, R.
1923   The concept of the guardian spirit in North America. *A.A.,* Memoir 29.

———1934   *Patterns of culture.* Boston: Houghton Mifflin.

——— 1948   Anthropology and the humanities. *A.A.,* 50: 585–593.

Bennett, W. C.
1953   Area archeology. *A.A.,* 55: 5–16.

Berliner, J. S.
1962   The feet of the natives are large: An essay on anthropology by an economist. *Current Anthropology,* 3; 1 (February): 47–77.

Bernard, J.
1966   *Marriage and the family among Negroes.* Englewood Cliffs, N.J.: Prentice-Hall.

Berreman, G. D.
1963   Behind many masks: Ethnography and impression management in a Himalayan village. *Society for Applied Anthropology Monograph,* No. 4. Ithaca, New York.

——— 1966   Anemic and emetic analyses in social anthropology. *A.A.,* 68: 346–354.

Bloomfield, L.
1933   *Language.* New York: Holt, Rinehart & Winston.

Blumer, H.
1962   Society as symbolic interaction. A. Rose (ed.), 1962, pp. 179–192.*

Boas, F.
1896   The limitations of the comparative method in anthropology. *Science,* 4: 901–908.

——— 1908   (ed.), Handbook of American Indian languages. *Bureau of American Ethnology Bulletin,* No. 40, 1911. Part I.

——— 1920   The social organization of the Kwakiutl. *A.A.,* 22: 111–126.

——— 1922   Das Verwandtschaftssystem der Vandau. *Zeitschrift fur Ethnologie,* 54: 41–51.

——— 1927   Primitive art. *Instittutet for Sammenlignende Kulturforskning,* Series B, No. VIII. Oslo: A. A. Schehoug & Co.

——— 1937   (ed.), *General anthropology.* Lexington, Mass.: Raytheon/Heath.

——— 1940   *Race, language and culture.* New York: Macmillan.

Bohannan, L.
1949   Dahomean marriage: A reevaluation. *Africa,* 19; 4: 273–287.

——— 1951   A comparative study of social differentiation in a primitive society. (Ph.D. dissertation, Oxford University.)

Bohannan, L., and P. J. Bohannan
1953   The Tiv of Central Nigeria. *Ethnographic survey of Africa: Western Africa.* Part VIII. London: I.A.I.

Bohannan, P. J.
1951   Political and economic aspects of land tenure and settlement patterns among the Tiv of Central Nigeria. (Ph.D. dissertation, Oxford University.)

——— 1954   The migration and expansion of the Tiv. *Africa,* 24: 2–16.

——— 1957   An alternate residence classification. *A.A.,* 59: 126–131.

Bohannan, P. J., and J. Middleton (eds.)
1968a   *Marriage, family and residence.* New York: Natural History Press.

——— 1968b   *Kinship and social organization.* New York: Natural History Press.

Bonnerjea, B.
1930   The Hindu family. *Primitive Man,* v; III: 3–19.

Bott, E.
1957   *Family and social network.* London: Tavistock.

Bowers, A. W.
1948   A history of the Mandan and Hidatsa. (Ph.D. dissertation, University of Chicago, Department of Anthropology.)

——— 1950   *Mandan social and ceremonial organization.* Chicago: University of Chicago Press.

——— 1965   *Hidatsa social and ceremonial organization.* Washington, D.C.: U.S. Government Printing Office.

Briffault, R.
1927   *The mothers.* New York: Macmillan.

Brinton, D. G.
1885   The Lenape and their legends. *Library of Aboriginal American Authors,* No. 5. Philadelphia: the author.

Brown, G. G., and J. H. Barnett
1942   Social organization and social structure. *A.A.,* 44: 30–36.

Bruner, E. M.
1953   Assimilation among Fort Berthold Indians. *The American Indian,* 6: 21–29.

——— 1955   Two processes of change in Mandan-Hidatsa kinship terminology. *A.A.,* 57: 840–850.

Buchanan, F.
1807   *A journey from Madras through Mysore, Canara and Malabar.* 3 vols. London: Cadell & Davies.

Buchler, I. R., and H. A. Selby
1968   *Kinship and social organization.* New York: Macmillan.

Burling, R.
1964   Cognition and componential analysis: God's truth or hocus pocus? *A.A.*, 66: 20–28
——— 1965   Burmese kinship terminology. In E. A. Hammel (ed.), 1965, pp. 106–117.*

Busia, K. A.
1951   *The position of the chief in the modern political system of Ashanti.* London, New York: Oxford University Press, for the I.A.I.

Cancian, F.
1965   *Economics and prestige in a Maya community.* Stanford: Stanford University Press.

Carr-Saunders, A. M., and D. C. Jones
1927   *A survey of the social structure of England and Wales as illustrated by statistics.* London: Oxford University Press.

Carruthers, D.
1914   *Unknown Mongolia: A record of travel and exploration in Northwest Mongolia and Dzungaria.* 2 vols. Philadelphia: Lippincott.

Chao, H-L.
1930   The Chinese family. *Primitive Man,* v; III: 19–22.

Chapple, E. D., and E. M. Arensberg
1940   Measuring human relations. *Genetic Psychology Monograph,* No. 22.

Childe, V. G.
1956   The new stone age. In H. L. Shapiro (ed.), *Man, culture and society.* New York: Oxford University Press.

Clarke, E.
1957   *My mother who fathered me.* London: Allen & Unwin.

Cohen, M. R., and E. Nagel
1947   *An introduction to logic and scientific method.* New York: Harcourt Brace Jovanovich.

Cohen, R.
1959   The structure of Kanuri society. (Ph.D. dissertation, University of Wisconsin.) Library of Congress, mic. 60–986.
——— 1961   Marriage instability in Nigeria. *A.A.,* 63: 1246–1248.

Cohen, Y.
1961   Patterns of friendship. In Cohen (ed.), *Social structure and personality: A casebook.* New York: Holt, Rinehart & Winston, pp. 351–386.
——— 1961   A hypothesis for the genetic basis of the universality of the incest taboo and its relation to kinship organization. Paper delivered at the annual meetings of the A.A.A.S., Section H. Symposium on Cross-species incest behavior. Denver, December 30. Mimeo.

Collingwood, R. G.
1946   *The idea of history.* Oxford: Clarendon.

Colson, E.
1951   Residence and village stability among the Plateau Tonga. *Rhodes-Livingston Journal,* 12: 41–67.

Colson, E., and M. Gluckman (eds.)
1951   *Seven tribes of British Central Africa.* London: Oxford University Press, for the Rhodes-Livingston Institute of Northern Rhodesia. Reprinted with minor corrections by Manchester University Press in Manchester and New York, 1959.

Comte, A.
1831   *Préliminaires généraux.* Reprinted in *Cours de Philosophie Positive.* Vol. I. Comte, 1864.
——— 1864   *Cours de Philosophie Positive.* Paris: J. B. Bailliére. New York: Bailliére Brothers.

Conklin, H. C.
1955   Hanunóo color categories. *S.J.A.,* 11 : 339–344.
——— 1962a   Lexicographical treatment of folk taxonomies. In F. W. Householder and S. Saporta (eds.), *Problems in lexicography. Indiana University Research Center in Anthropology, Folklore, and Linguistics Publication,* No. 21. Supplement to *International Journal of American Linguistics.*
——— 1962b   Comment on ethnographic study of cognitive systems. In T. Gladwin and W. C. Sturtevant (eds.), *Anthropology and human behavior.* Washington, D.C.: Anthropological Society of Washington.

Cook, S. F., and L. B. Simpson
1948   The population of Central Mexico in the sixteenth century. *Ibero-Americana,* 31.

Cooper, J. M.
1932   Incest prohibitions in primitive culture. *Primitive Man,* 5: 1–20.

Coser, L. A., and B. Rosenburg (eds.)
1964   *Sociological theory.* New York: Macmillan.

Coult, A. D.
1964   Role allocation, position structuring and ambilineal descent. *A.A.,* 66: 29–40.

Cumming, E. E., and D. M. Schneider
1961   Sibling solidarity: A property of American kinship. *A.A.,* 63: 498–507.

Curle, A.
1952   Kinship structure in an English village. *Man,* 52: 68–69.

Czaplicka, M. A.
1914   *Aboriginal Siberia: A study in social anthropology.* Oxford: Clarendon.

D'Andrade, R.
1965   Trait psychology and componential analysis. In E. A. Hammel (ed.), 1965, pp. 215–218.*

Davenport, W.
1959   Nonunilinear descent and descent groups. *A.A.,* 61: 557–572.

Davila, M.
1971   Compadrazgo: Fictive kinship in Latin America. In N. H. H. Graburn (ed.), *Reader in kinship and social structure.* New York: Harper & Row.

Davis, K., and W. L. Warner
1937   The structural analysis of kinship. *A.A.,* 39: 291–313.

Deacon, A. B. [C. H. Wedgwood (ed.)]
1929   Notes on some islands of the New Hebrides. *J.R.A.I.,* 59: 461–515.

Delbruck, B.
1890   *Die indogermanischer Verwandtschafts-namen.* Leipzig.

Dixon, R. B.
1928   *The building of cultures.* New York: Scribner's.

Dozier, E. P.
1951   Resistance to acculturation and assimilation in an Indian pueblo. *A.A.,* 53: 56–66.

Dry, P. D. L.
1950   The social structure of a Hausa village. (B.Sc. dissertation, Oxford University.)

Dumont, L.
1953   Dravidian kinship terminology as an expression of marriage. *Man,* 53: 54.
——— 1957   *Hierarchy and marriage alliance in south Indian kinship.* London: Royal Anthropological Institute.
——— 1961   Descent, filiation and affinity. *Man,* 61: 11.
——— 1966   Descent or intermarriage? A relational view of Australian section systems. *S.J.A.,* 22: 231–250.
——— 1968   Marriage alliance. In *International encyclopedia of social sciences.* New York: Macmillan and Free Press, pp. 19–23.

Durkheim, E.
1893   *La division du travail social.* Paris: Alcan. Later translated by G. Simpson as *The division of labor in society.* New York: Free Press, 1948. (Also reprinted 1948, 1949.)
——— 1895   *Les règles de la méthode sociologique.* Paris (publisher unknown). Later translated by S. Solovay and J. Mueller as *The rules of the sociological method.* G. E. G. Catlin (ed.) New York: Free Press, 1951.
——— 1897   *Le suicide.* Paris (publisher unknown). Later translated by J. Spaulding and G. Simpson as *Suicide.* New York: Free Press, 1951.
——— 1898   La prohibition de l'incest et ses origines. *L'Année Sociologique,* 1: 1–70.
——— 1912   *Les formes élémentaires de la vie religieuse.* Paris: Presses Universitaires. Later translated by J. W. Swain as *The elementary forms of religious life.* London: Allen & Unwin, 1926. New York: Free Press, 1954.

Ebeling, F.
1960   *Linguistic units.* The Hague: Mouton.

Edwards, J.
1932   The Choctaw Indians in the middle of the nineteenth century. *Chronicles of Oklahoma,* 10. Oklahoma City.

Eggan, F.
1934   Maya kinship system and cross-cousin marriage. *A.A.,* 36: 188–202.
——— 1937a   The Cheyenne and Arapaho kinship system. In F. Eggan, 1937c.*
——— 1937b   Historical changes in the Choctaw kinship system. *A.A.,* 39: 34–52.
——— 1937c   (ed.), *Social anthropology of the North American tribes.* Chicago: University of Chicago Press. (2nd ed. 1955.)
——— 1941   Some aspects of culture change in the northern Philippines. *A.A.,* 43: 11–18.
——— 1949   The Hopi and the lineage principle. In M. Fortes (ed.), 1949c.*
——— 1950   *The social organization of the Western Pueblos.* Chicago: University of Chicago Press.
——— 1952   The ethnological cultures and their archaeological backgrounds. In J. B. Griffin (ed.), *Archaeology of the eastern United States.* Chicago: University of Chicago Press.
——— 1954   Social anthropology and the method of controlled comparison. *A.A.,* 56: 743–763.
——— 1955   Social anthropology: Methods and results. In F. Eggan (ed.), *Social anthropology of the North American tribes.* 2nd ed., pp. 485–551.
——— 1956   Review of Homans and Schneider, 1955. *American Sociological Review,* 21: 402–403.
——— 1960   Lewis Henry Morgan in kinship perspective. In G. E. Dole and R. Y. Carneiro (eds.), *Essays in the science of culture in honor of Leslie*

White. New York: Thomas Y. Crowell, pp. 179–201.

—— 1961 Introduction to R. H. Lowie, *Primitive society* (1920). New York: Harper Torchbook, pp. vii–xii.

—— 1966 *The American Indian: Perspectives for the study of social change.* Chicago: Aldine.

Eggan, F., and W. Lloyd Warner
1956 A. R. Radcliffe-Brown (Obituary). *A.A.,* 58: 544–547.

Elwin, V.
1947 *The Muria and their Ghotul.* London: Oxford University Press.

Ember, M.
1961 The incest taboo and the nuclear family. Paper read at the Annual Meetings of the American Anthropological Association, Philadelphia, November 16–19.

Emory, K. P.
1956 Personal communication (to William Davenport).

Engels, F.
1884 *Der Urpsrung des Eigentums, der Familie und des Staates.* Zurich (publisher unknown). Translated as *Origin of the family, private property and the state.* New York: International Publishers, 1942.

Erasmus, C.
1950 The compadre system in Latin America. (Research problem as part of Ph.D. qualifying examination. University of California, Berkeley, Anthropology Library.)

Evans-Pritchard, E. E.
1929 The study of kinship in primitive societies. *Man,* 29: 190–195, note 148.

—— 1932 The nature of kinship extensions. *Man,* 32: 12–15, note 7.

—— 1933–1935 The Nuer: Tribe and clan. *Sudan Notes and Records,* vol. XVI, part I, vol. XVII, part I. Khartoum.

—— 1934 The social character of bridewealth. *Man,* 34: 194.

—— 1937 *Witchcraft, oracles and magic among the Azande.* London: Oxford University Press.

—— 1940a *The Nuer.* London: Oxford University Press.

—— 1940b The political system of the Nuer. In M. Fortes and E. E. Evans-Pritchard (eds.), 1940.*

—— 1948 The divine kingship of the Shilluk of the Nilotic Sudan. Given in 1948 as The Frazer Lecture. Compiled with other essays in E. E.

Evans-Pritchard, *Essays in social anthropology.* London: Faber & Faber, 1962.

—— 1949a Nuer rules of exogamy and incest. In M. Fortes (ed.), *Social structure: Essays presented to Radcliffe-Brown.* Oxford: Clarendon.

—— 1949b *The Sanusi of Cyrenaica.* Oxford: Clarendon.

—— 1951a *Social anthropology.* London: Cohen & West.

—— 1951b *Kinship and marriage among the Nuer.* London: Oxford University Press.

—— 1963 *The comparative method in social anthropology.* London: Athlone.

Fallaize, E. N.
1913 Family. In J. Hastings (ed.), *Encyclopedia of religion and ethics.* New York: Scribner's.

Fallers, L.
1957 Some determinants of marriage instability in Busoga. *Africa,* 27: 106–121.

Fei, H.-T.
1949 *Earthbound China.* London: Routledge & Kegan Paul.

—— 1953 *China's gentry.* Chicago: University of Chicago Press.

Firth, R.
1929 *The primitive economics of the New Zealand Maori.* New York: Dutton.

—— 1930 General observations upon the classificatory system of relationships. *J.R.A.I.,* 60: 266–268.

—— 1936 *We, the Tikopia.* London: Allen & Unwin. Abridged ed.; New York: Beacon Paperbacks, 1963.

—— 1951a Contemporary British social anthropology. *A. A.,* 53: 474–489.

—— 1951b *Elements of social organization.* London: Watts. New York: Beacon paperbacks, 1963.

—— 1954 Social organization and social change. *J.R.A.I.,* 84: 1–20.

—— 1956 Two studies of kinship in East London. *L. S. E. Monographs in Social Anthropology,* No. 15. London: Athlone.

—— 1957a (ed.), *Man and culture* (the work of Malinowski). London: Routledge & Kegan Paul. New York: Harper Torchbook, 1964.

—— 1957b A note on descent groups in Polynesia. *Man,* 57: 4–8.

—— 1959 *Social change in the Tikopia.* London: Allen & Unwin.

—— 1963 Bilateral descent groups: An operational viewpoint. In I. Schapera (ed.), *Studies in kinship and marriage. R.A.I.,* Paper 16, pp. 22–37.

Firth, R., J. Hubert, and A. Forge
1970 *Families and their relatives.* London: Routledge & Kegan Paul.

Fischer, H. T.
1935 De aanverwantschap bij enige volken van de Nederlands-Indische Archipel. *Mensch en naatschappij* (Amsterdam), 11: 285–297, 365–378.

—— 1936 Het asymmetrisch cross-cousin-*nuwelik* in Nederlandsch Indië. *Tijdschrift voor Indische Taal-, Land-, en Volkenkunde,* 76: 359–372.

—— 1952 *Inleiding tot de culturele anthropologie van Indonesie.* Haarlem: De Erven F. Bohn.

—— 1956 For a new definition of marriage. *Man,* 56: 82.

Fischer, J. L.
1958 The classification of residence in censuses. *A.A.,* 60: 508–517.

Fison, L., and A. W. Howitt
1880 *Kamilaroi and Kurnai.*

Fletcher, A.
1904 *The Hako: A Pawnee ceremony.* Twenty-second Annual Report, Bureau of American Ethnology, Washington, D.C.

Ford, C. S.
1945 A comparative study of human reproduction. *Yale University Publications in Anthropology,* No. 32.

Forde, C. D.
1938 Fission and accretion in the patrilineal clans of a semi-Bantu community, *J.R.A.I.,* 68: 311–338.

—— 1939 Kinship in Umor: Double unilateral organization in a semi-Bantu society. *A.A.,* 41: 523–553.

—— 1941 Marriage and the family among the Yako in southeast Nigeria. *L.S.E. Monographs in Social Anthropology,* No. 5. London: Athlone.

—— 1947 The anthropological approach in social science. *The Advancement of Science,* 4; 15: 213–224. Reprinted in M. H. Fried, *Readings in anthropology.* New York: Thomas Y. Crowell, 1959.

—— 1950a Anthropology science and history. *Man,* 50; 254: 155–156.

—— 1950b Double descent among the Yakö. In A. R. Radcliffe-Brown and C. D. Forde (eds.), 1950.*

—— 1950c Ward organization among the Yakö. In *Africa,* 20; 4: 267–289.

—— 1951a The integration of anthropological studies. *J.R.A.I.,* 78: 1–10.

—— 1951b The Yoruba-speaking peoples of southwestern Nigeria. In *Ethnographic survey of Africa: Western Africa.* Part IV. London: I.A.I.

Forde, C. D., and G. I. Jones
1950 The Ibo and Ibibio-speaking peoples of southeastern Nigeria. In *Ethnographic survey of Africa: Western Africa.* Part III, Vol. 1. London: I.A.I.

Fortes, M.
1936 Kinship, incest and exogamy of the northern territories of the Gold Coast. In L. H. D. Buxton (ed.), *Custom is king.* London: Hutchinson.

—— 1940 The political systems of the Tallensi of the northern territory of the Gold Coast. In M. Fortes and E. E. Evans-Pritchard (eds.), 1940.*

—— 1945 *The dynamics of clanship among the Tallensi.* London: Oxford University Press.

—— 1949a *The web of kinship among the Tallensi.* London: Oxford University Press.

—— 1949b Time and social structure: An Ashanti case study. In M. Fortes (ed.), 1949c.*

—— (ed.) 1949c *Social structure: Essays presented to Radcliffe-Brown.* Oxford: Clarendon Press.

—— 1950 Kinship and marriage among the Ashanti. In A. R. Radcliffe-Brown and C. D. Forde (eds.), 1950.*

—— 1953a Analysis and description in social anthropology. *Advancement in Science,* No. 38, p. 190–210. London.

—— 1953b *Social anthropology at Cambridge since 1900.* Cambridge: Cambridge University Press.

—— 1953c The structure of unilineal descent groups. *A.A.,* 55: 17–41.

—— 1957 Malinowski and the study of kinship. In R. Firth (ed.), 1957a.*

—— 1959 Descent, filiation and affinity. *Man,* 59: 193–197, 206–212.

—— 1963 The "submerged descent line" in Ashanti. In I. Schapera (ed.), *Studies in kinship and marriage. R.A.I. Paper,* No. 16, pp. 58–67.

—— 1969 *Kinship and the social order: The legacy of Lewis Henry Morgan.* Chicago: Aldine.

Fortes, M., and E. E. Evans-Pritchard (eds.)
1940 *African political systems.* London, New York: Oxford University Press, for the I.A.I.

Fortune, R. F.
1932a *The sorcerers of Dobu.* New York: Dutton. Dutton paperback, 1963.

—— 1932b Incest. *Encyclopedia of Social Sciences,* 7: 620–622.

——— 1933   A note on some forms of kinship structure. In *Oceania*, 4: 1–9.

Foster, G. M.

1948   Tzintzuntzan: Empire's children. *Smithsonian Institute of Social Anthropology Publication*, No. 6.

——— 1949   Sierra Popoluca kinship terminology and its wider implications. *S.J.A.*, 5; 4: 330–344.

——— 1953   Cofradia and compadrazgo in Spain and Spanish America. *S.J.A.*, 9: 1–28.

——— 1960   Culture and conquest: America's Spanish heritage. *Viking Fund Publication in Anthropology*, No. 27.

——— 1961   The dyadic contract: A model for social structure in a Mexican village. *A.A.*, 63: 1173–1192.

——— 1963   The dyadic contract in Tzintzuntzan. II: Patron-client relationships. *A.A.*, 65: 1280–1294.

——— 1965   Peasant society and the image of limited good. *A.A.*, 67: 293–315.

——— 1967   *Tzintzuntzan: Mexican peasants in a changing world*. Boston: Atlantic-Little, Brown.

Fox, R.

1962   Sibling incest. *British Journal of Sociology*, 13: 128–150.

——— 1967   *Kinship and marriage*. London: Penguin.

Frake, C. O.

1961   The diagnosis of disease among the Subanun of Mindanao. *A.A.*, 63: 113–132.

——— 1962   The ethnographic study of cognitive systems. In T. Gladwin and W. C. Sturtevant (eds.), *Anthropology and human behavior*. Washington, D.C.: Anthropological Society of Washington.

——— 1964   Further discussion of Burling. *A.A.*, 66: 119.

Frazer, Sir J. G.

1890   *The golden bough* (1911–1915. 3rd ed. 12 vols.) London: Macmillan, 1st ed., vol. 1.

——— 1910   *Totemism and exogamy*. 4 vols. London: Macmillan.

Freed, S. A.

1960   Changing Washo kinship. *Anthropological Records*, 14: 6. Berkeley: University of California Press.

——— 1963   Fictive kinship in a North Indian village. *Ethnology*, 2: 86–103.

Freedman, M.

1958   *Lineage organization in southeastern China*. *L.S.E. Monographs in Social Anthropology*, No. 18. London: Athlone.

——— 1966   *Chinese lineage and society: Fukien and Kwangtung*. *L.S.E. Monographs in Social Anthropology*, No. 33. London: Athlone.

——— 1970   (ed.), *Family and kinship in Chinese society*. Stanford: Stanford University Press.

Freeman, J. D.

1955   Iban agriculture. *Colonial Research Studies*, No. 18. London: Colonial Office.

——— 1957   *The family of the Iban of Borneo. Report of the Department of Anthropology and Sociology*. Canberra: Australian National University.

——— 1958   The family system of the Iban of Borneo. In J. Goody (ed.), The developmental cycle in domestic groups. *Cambridge Papers in Social Anthropology*, No. 1. Cambridge: Cambridge University Press, pp. 15–52.

——— 1961   On the concept of the kindred. *J.R.A.I.*, 91: 192–220. Reprinted in P. J. Bohannan and J. Middleton (eds.), 1968a, pp. 255–272.*

Freud, S.

1918   *Totem and taboo*. Later translated by A. A. Brill. New York: Moffat, Yard & Co. New York: Vintage, 1946. (Also reprinted 1931, 1950.)

——— 1920   *General introduction to psychoanalysis*. New York.

——— 1930   *Civilization and its discontents*. New York.

——— 1938   Contributions to the theory of sex. In *The basic writings of Sigmund Freud*. New York: Modern Library.

Fried, M. H.

1953   *The fabric of Chinese society*. New York: Praeger.

——— 1960   On the evolution of social stratification and the state. In S. Diamond (ed.), *Culture in history*. New York: Columbia University Press, for Brandeis University, pp. 713–731.

Friedl, E.

1959   The role of kinship in the transmission of the national culture of Greece. *A.A.*, 61: 30–38.

Friedrich, P.

1964   Semantic structure and social structure: An instance from Russian. In W. Goodenough (ed.), *Explorations in cultural anthropology*. New York: McGraw-Hill, pp. 111–130.

Fuente, J. de la

1949   Yalalag: Una villa Zapoteca serrana. *Museo Nacional de Antropologia, Serie Cientifico*, No. 1. Mexico.

Fustel de Coulanges, N. D.

1864   *The ancient city*. Later translated by W. Small. New York: Doubleday Anchor.

Galbraith, J. K.
1955   *Economics and the art of controversy.* New Brunswick: Rutgers University Press.

Galton, H.
1957   The Indo-European kinship terminology. *Zeitschrift fur ethnologie,* 82 (September): 121–138.

Garigue, P.
1956   French Canadian kinship and urban life. *A.A.,* 58: 1090–1101.

Gearing, F.
1958   The structural poses of 18th-century Cherokee villages. *A.A.,* 60: 1148–1157.

Geertz, C.
1959   Form and variation in Balinese village structure. *A.A.,* 61: 991–1012.

Gellner, E.
1958   Time and theory in social anthropology. *Mind, Quarterly Review of Psychology and Philosophy,* 67: 182–202.

Geoghegan, W.
1970   Information processing systems in culture. In P. Kay (ed.), *Explorations in mathematical anthropology.* Cambridge: M.I.T. Press.

Gifford, E. W.
1916   Miwok moieties. *U.C.P.A.A.E.,* 12: 4: 139–194.
———   1922   California kinship terminologies. *U.C.P.A.A.E.,* 18: 155–219.
———   1929   Tongan society. *Bernice P. Bishop Museum Bulletin,* No. 61. Honolulu.

Gilbert, W. H., Jr.
1934   Eastern Cherokee social organization. (Ph.D. dissertation, University of Chicago.) Reprinted (in part?) in F. Eggan (ed.), 1937c.*

Gillin, J.
1936   The Barama River Caribs of British Guiana. *Papers of the Peabody Museum of American Archeology and Ethnology, Harvard University,* 14: 2.
———   1947   Moche: A Peruvian coastal community. *Smithsonian Institute of Social Anthropology Publication,* No. 3.

Gluckman, M.
1949   Malinowski's sociological theories. *Rhodes-Livingston Paper,* No. 16. London: Oxford University Press. One essay, Malinowski's "functional" analysis of social change, was previously published in *Africa,* 27 (1947): 103–121.
———   1950   Kinship and marriage among the Lozi of Northern Rhodesia and the Zulu of Natal. In A. R. Radcliffe-Brown and C. D. Forde (eds.), 1950.*

———   1951   The Lozi of Barotseland in northwestern Rhodesia. In E. Colson and M. Gluckman (eds.), 1951.*
———   1953   Bridewealth and the stability of marriage. *Man,* 53: 141–142.
———   (1954)   *The judicial process among the Barotse of Northern Rhodesia.* New York: Free Press, 1955.

Gluckman, M., and E. Colson (eds.)
1951   See Colson and Gluckman, 1951.

Goffman, E.
1959   *The presentation of self in everyday life.* New York: Doubleday Anchor.
———   1961   *Encounters: Two studies in the sociology of interaction.* Indianapolis: Bobbs-Merrill.
———   1967   *Interaction ritual.* Chicago: Aldine.

Goldenweiser, A. A.
1910   Totemism: An analytical study. *J.A.F.,* 23: 1–115.
———   1922   *Early civilization.* New York: Knopf.
———   1937   *Anthropology.* New York: Crofts.

Goldstein, K.
1951   *Der aufbau des organismus.* French translation, Paris. English translation, New York, 1939.

Goode, W.
1966   Industrialization and family change. In B. F. Hoselitz and W. E. Moore (eds.), *Industrialization and society.* The Hague: UNESCO.

Goodenough, W. H.
1944   A technique for scale analysis. *Educational and Psychological Measurement,* 4: 179–190.
———   1951   Property, kin and community on Truk. *Yale University Publications in Anthropology,* No. 46.
———   1955   A problem in Malayo-Polynesian social organization. *A.A.,* 57: 71–83.
———   1956a   Componential analysis and the study of meaning. *Language,* 32: 195–216.
———   1956b   Residence rules. *S.J.A.,* 12: 22–37.
———   1957   Cultural anthropology and linguistics. *Georgetown University Series on Language and Linguistics,* No. 9, pp. 167–173.
———   1962   Kindred and hamlet in Lalakai. *Ethnology,* 1: 5–12.
———   (ed.)   1964   *Explorations in cultural anthropology.* New York: McGraw-Hill.
———   1965a   Rethinking status and role. In M. Banton (ed.), *The relevance of models for social anthropology. A.S.A. Monographs,* No. 1. London: Tavistock, pp. 1–24.

——— 1965b Yankee kinship terminology: A problem in componential analysis. In E. A. Hammel (ed.), 1965, pp. 259–287.*

Goody, J.
1956 A comparative approach to incest and adultery. *B.J.S.*, 7: 286–304.

——— 1958 (ed.), The developmental cycle in domestic groups. *Cambridge Papers in Social Anthropology*, No. 1. Cambridge: Cambridge University Press.

——— 1959 The mother's brother and sister's son in West Africa. *J.R.A.I.*, 89: 61–87.

——— 1961 The classification of double descent systems. *Current Anthropology*, 2 (February): 3–25.

Gough, E. K.
1950 Kinship among the Nayar of the Malabar coast of India. (Ph.D. dissertation, Cambridge University.)

——— 1952 Changing kinship usages in the setting of political and economic change among the Nayars of Malabar. *J.R.A.I.*, 82: 71–88.

——— 1955a The traditional lineage and kinship system of the Nayars. (Unpublished manuscript in the Haddon Library, Cambridge.)

——— 1955b Female initiation rites on the Malabar Coast. *J.R.A.I.*, 85: 45–80.

——— 1959 The Nayars and the definition of marriage. *J.R.A.I.*, 89: 23–34.

Graburn, N. H. H.
1964 *Taqagmiut Eskimo kinship terminology.* N.C.R.C. –64–1. Ottawa: Dept. of Northern Affairs and National Resources.

——— 1971 Naskapi family and kinship. In F. Eggan and A. Spoehr (eds.), *Anthropological studies in comparison, social structure and change.* Chicago: University of Chicago Press. (In press.)

Greenberg, J. H.
1954 Concerning inferences from linguistic to non-linguistic data. In H. Hoijer (ed.), *Language in culture.* Chicago: University of Chicago Press, pp. 3–19.

Grey, Sir G.
1841 *Journals of two expeditions in northwestern and western Australia.* London: Boone.

Grigson, W.
1949 *The Maria Gonds of Bastar.* London: Oxford University Press.

Grinnell, G. B.
1902 Social organization of the Cheyennes. *I.C.A.*, 13: 135–146.

Gross, N., W. S. Mason, and A. W. McEachern
1958 *Explorations in role analysis: Studies of the school superintendency role* New York: Wiley.

Guiteras Holmes, C.
1947 Clanes y sistema de parentesco en Cancuc. *Acta America*, 5: 1–17.

Guttman, L.
1944 A basis for scaling qualitative data. *American Sociological Review*, 9: 139–150.

——— 1950 The basis for scalogram analysis. In *Studies in social psychology in World War II.* Vol. 4. *Measurement and prediction.* Princeton: Princeton University Press, pp. 60–90.

Haar, B. ter
1946 *Beginselen en stelsel van het adatrecht.* Gronginen-Batavia.

——— 1948 *Adat law in Indonesia.* In E. A. Hoebel and A. A. Schiller (trans. and eds.). New York: Institute of Pacific Relations.

Hall, O.
1952 Methods and techniques of research in human relations. In E. C. Hughes et al. (eds.), *Cases on field work.*

Hallowell, A. I.
1926 Recent changes in the kinship terminology of the St. Francis Abenaki. *Proceedings of the I.C.A.* Vol 2. Rome, 1928, pp. 97–145.

——— 1928 Was cross-cousin marriage formerly practiced by the North-Central Algonkian? *Proceedings of the I.C.A.* New York, 1930, pp. 519–544.

——— 1950 Personality structure and the evolution of man. *A.A.*, 52: 159–173.

——— 1953 Culture, personality and society. In A. L. Kroeber et al. (eds.), 1953.*

Hamilton, A.
1727 *A new account of the East Indies.* 2 vols. Edinburgh.

Hammel, E. A.
1964 Further comments on componential analysis. *A.A.*, 66: 1167–1171.

——— 1965 (ed.), Introduction to *Formal semantic analysis. A.A.*, 67: 5 (Part 2). Special Publication.

——— 1966 Nacrt ispitivanja drustvene pokretljivosti i njejog uticaja na medjulicne odnose. *Sociologija*, 8; 3: 105–120.

——— 1968a Anthropological explanations: Style in discourse. *S.J.A.*, 24; 2: 155–169.

——— 1968b *Alternative social structures and ritual relations in the Balkans.* Englewood Cliffs, N.J.: Prentice-Hall.

——— 1969a Economic change, social mobility and kinship in Serbia. *S.J.A.*, 25: 188–197.

——— 1969b *The pink yoyo: Occupational mobility in Belgrade ca. 1915–1965.* Berkeley: University of California Press, for the Institute of International Studies.

Hammond, J. L., and B. Hammond
1911 *The village labourer,* Vol. 1. London: Guild. London: Longmans, Green, 1948.

Hanson, O.
1913 *The Kachins, their customs and traditions.* Rangoon: ABM Press.

Harris, M.
1968 *The rise of anthropological theory: A history of theories of culture.* New York: Thomas Y. Crowell.

Hart, C. M.
1950 Review of Lévi-Strauss, 1949. *A.A.,* 53: 392.

Held, G. J.
1953 Review of P. E. de Josselin de Jong, 1951. *Bijdragen tot de Taal-, Landen Volkenkunde,* 109: p. 109. The Hague.

Henshaw, P. S.
1953 Physiologic control of fertility. *Science,* 117; 3048: 572–582.

Herskovits, M.
1924 A preliminary consideration of the culture areas of Africa. *A.A.,* 26: 50–63.
——— 1930 The culture areas of Africa. *Africa,* 3: 59–77.
——— 1938 *Dahomey, an ancient West African kingdom.* New York: J. J. Augustin.
——— 1944 Review of Evans-Pritchard, 1940. *A.A.,* 46: 396–400.
——— 1948 *Man and his works: The science of cultural anthropology.* Part VI. *Cultural dynamics.* New York: Knopf. (Author reprinted 1950.)
——— 1954 Some problems of method in ethnography. In R. F. Spencer (ed.), 1954.*

Hocart, A. M.
1937 Kinship systems. *Anthropos,* 32: 545–551. Reprinted in *The life-giving myth.* London: Methuen, 1952.

Hoebel, E. A.
1949 *Man in the primitive world.* New York: McGraw-Hill.
——— 1954 *The law of primitive man.* Cambridge: Harvard University Press.

Hogbin, H. I.
1930 The study of kinship in primitive societies. *Man,* 30; 69: 114–115.
——— 1934 *Law and order in Polynesia: A study of primitive legal institutions.* London: Christophers.

Homans, G. C.
1950 *The human group.* New York: Harcourt Brace Jovanovich.
——— 1958 Social behavior as exchange. *A.J.S.,* 63: 597–606.
——— 1965 Anxiety and ritual: The theories of Malinowski and Radcliffe-Brown. In W. Lessa and E. Vogt (eds.), *Reader in comparative religion.* 2nd ed. New York: Harper & Row, pp. 123–138.

Homans, G. C., and D. M. Schneider
1955 *Marriage, authority and final causes: A study of unilateral cross-cousin marriage.* New York: Free Press.

Hooton, E. A.
1947 *Up from the ape.* New York: Macmillan.

Householder, F. W.
1952 Review of methods in structural linguistics by Zellig S. Harris. *International Journal of American Linguistics,* 18: 260–268.

Howells, W. W.
1952 The study of anthropology. *A.A.,* 54: 1–7.

Hsu, F. L. K.
1948 *Under the ancestor's shadow: Chinese culture and personality.* New York: Columbia University Press.

Hubbell, L.
1966 Non-unilineal kinship studies. (Unpublished manuscript, University of California, Berkeley.)

Hughes, E. C.
(1946) *French Canada in transition.* Toronto: W. J. Gage (copyright, 1943).

Hunter, M.
1936 *Reaction to conquest.* London, New York: Oxford University Press, for the I.A.I.

Hymes, D. M.
1964 Discussion of Burling's paper. *A.A.,* 66: 116–119.

Jakobson, H.
1959 Boas' view of grammatical meaning. *A.A.,* Memoir 89: 139–145.

Jakobson, R.
1957 *Shifters, verbal categories and the Russian verb.* Harvard University: Russian Language Project.

Jones, E.
1925 Mother-right and the sexual ignorance of savages. *International Journal of Psychoanalysis,* 6; 2: 109–130.

Jones, L. F.
1914 *A study of the Thlingets of Alaska.* New York, Chicago: Henry H. Revell.

Josselin de Jong, J. P. E. de
1951 *Minangkabau and Negri Sembilan: Socio-political structure in Indonesia.* Leiden: E. J. Brill.
——— 1952 *Lévi-Strauss' theory on kinship and marriage.* Museum voor Volkekunde, Nedelelingen 10. Leiden: E. J. Brill.

Junod, H.
1913 *The life of a South African tribe.* 2 vols. London: D. Nutt.

Kardiner, A., and E. Preble
1961 *They studied man.* New York: World.

Karvé, I.
1953 *Kinship organisation in India. Deccan College Monograph Series,* No. 11. Poona.

Kay, P.
1966 Comment on Colby's ethnographic semantics: A preliminary survey. *Current Anthropology,* 7; 1: 20–23.

Keuning, J.
1948 *Verwantschapsrecht en volksordening, huwelijksrecht en erfrecht, in het Koeriagebied van Tapanoeli.* Leiden.

Kirschoff, P.
1932 Verwandschaftsbezeichnungen und Verwandtenheirat. *Zeitschrift für Ethnologie,* 64: 41–72.

Kluckhohn, C.
1944 Navaho witchcraft. *Papers of the Peabody Museum of American Archeology and Ethnology, Harvard University,* 22: 2.
——— 1949 The Ramah project. *Papers of the Peabody Museum of American Archeology and Ethnology, Harvard University,* 40: 1.
——— 1954 Southeastern studies of culture and personality. *A.A.,* 56: 685–697.

Kobben, A. J.
1952 New ways of presenting an old idea: The statistical method in social anthropology. *J.R.A.I.,* 82: 89.

Kohler, J.
1897 Zur Urgeschichte der Ehe. (On the origin of marriage.) *Zeitschrift fur vergleichende Rechtswissenschaft,* 12: 187–353. Stuttgart.

Kroeber, A. L.
1909 Classificatory systems of relationship. *J.R.A.I.,* 39: 77–84. Reprinted in P. J. Bohannan and J. Middleton (eds.), 1968b, pp. 19–28.*
——— 1917a California kinship systems. *U.C.P.A.-A.E.,* 12; 9: 340–396.
——— 1917b Zuni kin and clan. *American Museum of Natural History Anthropological Papers,* 19: 39–204.

——— 1917c The matrilineate again. *A.A.,* 19: 571–579.
———1920 Review of *Primitive society* (R. H. Lowie). *A.A.,* 22: 377–381.
——— 1933 Process in the Chinese kinship system. *A.A.,* 35: 151–157.
——— 1935 History and science in anthropology. *A.A.,* 37: 539–569.
——— 1938 Basic and secondary patterns of social structure. *J.R.A.I.,* 68: 299–310.
——— 1939 *Cultural and natural areas of native North America.* Berkeley: University of California Press.
——— 1944 *Configurations of culture growth.* Berkeley and Los Angeles: University of California Press.
——— 1948 *Anthropology.* New York: Harcourt Brace Jovanovich.
——— 1952 *The nature of culture.* Chicago: University of Chicago Press.
——— 1953 Introduction and concluding review. In S. Tax et al. (eds.), 1953.*
——— 1954 Critical summary and commentary. In R. F. Spencer (ed.), 1954.*

Kroeber, A. L., et al. (eds.)
1953 *Anthropology today: An encyclopedic inventory.* Chicago: University of Chicago Press.

Kroeber, A. L., and C. Kluckhohn
1952 Culture, a critical review of concepts and definitions. *Papers of the Peabody Museum of American Archeology and Ethnology, Harvard University,* 47: 50.

Kroeber, A. L., and T. T. Waterman
1920 *Sourcebook in anthropology.* Berkeley: University of California Press. New York: Harcourt Brace Jovanovich, 1931.

Krzywicki, L.
1935 *Primitive society and its vital statistics.* New York: Macmillan.

Kuper, H.
1947 *An African aristocracy.* London, New York: Oxford University Press, for the I.A.I. Reprinted with new preface, 1961.

Labouret, H.
1929 La parenté à plaisanteries en Afrique Occidentale. *Africa,* 2: 244.

Lafitau, J. F.
1721 *Moeurs des sauvages Ameriquains.* Paris: Saugrain l'ainé (1724).

Laguna, F. de
1952   Some dynamic forces in Tlingit society. *S.J.A.* 8: 1–12.

Lambert, B.
1966   Ambilineal descent groups in the north Gilbert Islands. *A.A.,* 68: 641–664.

Lambert, R. D.
1962   The impact of urban society upon village life. In R. Turner (ed.), *India's urban future.* Berkeley: University of California Press.

Landa, D. de
1941   Relaciones de las cosas de Yucatan. English translation, in A. M. Tozzer (ed.), *Papers of the Peabody Museum of American Archeology and Ethnology, Harvard University.* Vol. 18.

Lane, R. B.
1963   Patrilateral cross-cousin marriage. *Ethnology,* 1: 467–499.

Lawrence, P.
1955   Land tenure among the Garia. *Australian National University Social Science Monographs,* No. 4. Canberra, Australian National Museum.

Lawrence, W. E.
1937   Alternating generation in Australia. In G. P. Murdock (ed.), *Studies in the science of society.* New Haven: Yale University Press.

Lawrence, W. E., and G. P. Murdock
1949   Murngin Social Organization. *A.A.,* 51: 58–65.

Leach, E. R.
1945   Jinghpaw kinship terminology. *J.R.A.I.,* 75: 59–72. Reprinted in E. R. Leach, 1962, 28–53.*

———— 1947   Cultural change, with special reference to the hill tribes of Burma and Assam. (Ph.D. dissertation, University of London.)

———— 1950a   Social science research in Sarawak. *Colonial Research Studies,* No. 1 London: Colonial Office.

———— 1950b   Review of *Social structure* (G. P. Murdock, 1949). *Man,* 50: 169.

———— 1951   The structural implications of matrilateral cross-cousin marriage. *J.R.A.I,* 81: 23–55. Reprinted in E. R. Leach, 1962, pp. 54–104.

———— 1953   Bridewealth and the stability of marriage. *Man,* 53: 179–180.

———— 1954a   Bridewealth and the stability of marriage. *Man,* 54: 173.

———— 1954b   *Political systems of highland Burma.* Cambridge: Harvard University Press.

———— 1955   Polyandry, inheritance and the definition of marriage. *Man,* 55: 182–186. Reprinted in P. J. Bohannan and J. Middleton, 1968a, pp. 73–84.*

———— 1957a   The epistomological background to Malinowski's empiricism. In R. Firth (ed.), 1957a, pp. 119–138.*

———— 1957b   Aspects of bridewealth and marriage stability among the Kachin and Lakher. *Man,* 57: 59.

———— 1958   Concerning Trobriand clans and the kinship catagory *tabu.* In J. Goody (ed.), 1958, pp. 120–145.*

———— 1961   *Pul Eliya, a village in Ceylon.* Cambridge: Cambridge University Press.

———— 1962   *Rethinking anthropology.* London: Athlone.

Lederer, J.
1672   *Discoveries.* London: Samuel Heyrick.

Lerner, I. M.
1958   *The genetic basis of selection.* New York: Wiley.

Lesser, A.
1929   Kinship origins in the light of some distributions. *A.A.,* 31: 710–730.

———— 1930   Some aspects of Siouan kinship. *Proceedings of the I.C.A.,* 23: 563–571.

———— 1935   Functionalism in social anthropology. *A.A.,* 37: 385–402.

Lévi-Strauss, C.
1943   The social use of kinship terms among Brazilian Indians. *A.A.,* 45: 398–409.

———— 1949   *Les structures élémentaires de la parenté.* Paris: Presses Universitaires de France.

———— 1951   Language and the analysis of social laws. *A.A.,* 53: 155–163.

———— 1953   Social structure. In A. L. Kroeber et al. (eds.), 1953.*

———— 1955a   The structural study of myth. *J.A.F.,* 68: 428–444.

———— 1955b   *Tristes tropiques.* Paris: Librairie Plon.

———— 1956   The family. In H. L. Shapiro (ed.), *Man, culture and society.* New York: Oxford University Press.

———— 1962   (1966) *The savage mind.* Chicago: University of Chicago Press.

———— 1963a   *Totemism.* Translated by R. Needham. Boston: Beacon.

———— 1963b   *Structural anthropology.* New York: Basic Books.

———— 1966   The future of kinship studies. *Proceedings of the R.A.I.* (1965): 13–22.

———— 1969a   *The elementary structures of kinship.* (*Les structures élémentaires de la parenté.*) Translated by J. H. Bell and I. R. von Sturmer; R. Needham (ed.). Boston: Beacon.

———— 1969b *The raw and the cooked.* Translated by J. and D. Weightman. New York: Harper & Row.

Lewis, O.

1958 *Village life in northern India.* Urbana: University of Illinois Press.

———— 1966 *La vida: A Puerto Rican family.* New York: Random House.

Linton, R.

1936 *The study of man.* New York: Appleton-Century-Crofts.

———— 1945 *The cultural background of personality.* New York: Appleton-Century-Crofts.

Linton, R., M. Herskovits, and R. Redfield

1935 Memorandum on the study of acculturation. *Man,* 35: 145–148. Also in *A.A.,* 38(1936): 149–152, and *Africa,* 9(1936): 114–118.

Lippert, J.

1886–1887 *Kulturgeschichte der Menschheit in ihrem organischen Aufbau.* 2 vols. Stuttgart.

Lounsbury, F. G.

1956 A semantic analysis of Pawnee kinship usage. *Language,* 32: 158–194.

———— 1962 Review of Needham, 1962. *A.A.,* 64: 1302–1311.

———— 1964a The Omaha and Crow kinship terminologies. In W. H. Goodenough (ed.), *Explorations in cultural anthropology.* New York: McGraw-Hill.

———— 1964b The structural analysis of kinship semantics. In H. G. Hunt (ed.), *Proceedings of the Ninth International Congress of Linguists.* The Hague: Mouton, pp. 1073–1092.

———— 1965 Another view of Trobriand kinship categories. In E. A. Hammel (ed.), 1965, pp. 142–187.*

Lowie, R. H.

1912a Social life of the Crow Indians. *American Museum of Natural History—Annual Proceedings,* 9: pt. 2.

———— 1912b Some problems in the ethnology of the Crow and village Indians. *A.A.,* 14: 60–71.

———— 1914 Social organization. *A.J.S.,* 20: 68–97.

———— 1915 Exogamy and the classificatory systems of relationship. *A.A.,* 17: 223–239.

———— 1916 Historical and sociological interpretations of kinship terminologies. In F. W. Hodge (ed.), *Holmes Anniversary Volume.* Washington, D.C.: Bryan, pp. 293–300.

———— 1917a *Culture and ethnology.* New York: Holt, Rinehart & Winston.

———— 1917b Notes on the social organization and customs of the Mandan, Hidatsa and Crow Indians.

American Museum of Natural History—Annual Proceedings, 21: 1–99.

———— 1917c Review of Rivers, 1914c, 1915 a and b. *A.A.,* 19: 269–272.

———— 1919 The matrilineal complex. *U.C.P.A.A.E.,* 16: 29–45.

———— 1920 *Primitive society.* New York: Liveright. New York: Harper Torchbook, 1961.

———— 1928 A note on relationship terminologies. *A.A.,* 30: 263–268.

———— 1929 Relationship terms. *Encyclopedia Britannica.* 14th ed. 19: 84–86.

———— 1930 Omaha and Crow kinship terminologies. (A paper presented at the I.C.A.)

———— 1933 Queries. *A.A.,* 35: 288–296.

———— 1934a Some moot problems in social organization. *A.A.,* 36: 321–330.

———— 1934b Omaha and Crow kinship terminologies. *Proceedings of the I.C.A.,* 24: 102–108.

———— (1936) Introduction. In W. L. Warner (ed.), 1937, pp. xiii–xvi.*

———— 1937 *The history of ethnological theory.* New York: Holt, Rinehart & Winston.

———— 1948 *Social organization.* New York: Holt, Rinehart & Winston.

———— 1949 Social and political organization of the tropical forest and marginal tribes. *Handbook of South American Indians,* 5: 313–350.

———— 1953 Ethnography, cultural and social anthropology. *A.A.,* 55: 527–534.

———— 1955 Lewis Henry Morgan in historical perspective. In E. A. Hoebel (ed.), *Readings in anthropology.* New York: McGraw-Hill.

———— 1956 Review of Homans and Schneider, 1955. *A.A.,* 58: 1144.

———— 1959 *Robert H. Lowie, ethnologist.* Berkeley: University of California Press.

Lubbock, Sir J.

1871 On the development of relationships. *J.R.A.I.,* 1: 1–29.

Mahaffy, J. P.

1915 Cleopatra VI. *Journal of Egyptian Archeology,* 2.

Mahar, P. M.

1959 A multiple scaling technique for caste ranking. *Man in India,* 39: 127–147.

Maine, Sir H.

1861 *Ancient law, its connection with early society.* London: Oxford University Press. Boston: Beacon paperback, 1963.

Malinowski, B.

1913 *The family among the Australian aborigines.* London: University of London Press. New York: Schocken paperbacks, 1963.

———— 1922 Argonauts of the western Pacific. *Studies in Economics and Political Science,* No. 25. London.

———— 1923 The psychology of sex and the foundations of kinship in primitive societies. *Psyche,* 4(October): 98–128.

———— 1926 *Crime and custom in savage society.* London, New York: Routledge & Kegan Paul, for the International Library of Psychology, Philosophy and Scientific Method.

———— 1927a *Sex and repression in savage society.* London: Routledge & Kegan Paul, for the International Library of Psychology, Philosophy and Scientific Method.

———— 1927b The father in primitive psychology. *Psyche Miniatures,* No. 8. London.

———— 1929a *The sexual life of savages in North-Western Melanesia.* London: Routledge & Kegan Paul. New York: Liveright.

———— 1929b. Kinship. *Encyclopedia Britannica.* 14th ed.

———— 1929c Marriage. *Encyclopedia Britannica.* 14th ed.

———— 1930 Kinship. *Man,* 30; 2: 19–29.

———— 1931 Culture. *Encyclopedia of the Social Sciences,* 4: 621–646.

———— 1932a *The sexual life of savages.* 3rd ed. London: Routledge & Kegan Paul.

———— 1932b Introduction. In R. F. Fortune (ed.), 1932a, pp. xv–xxxii.*

———— 1936 Preface. In R. Firth (ed.), 1936, pp. vii–xi.*

———— 1944 *A scientific theory of culture (and other essays).* Chapel Hill: University of North Carolina Press.

———— 1945 *The dynamics of culture change.* P. Kaberry (ed.). New Haven: Yale University Press.

Manchen-Helfen, O.
1931 *Reise ins asiatische Tuwa.* Berlin: Der Büchevkreis.

Mandelbaum, D. G.
1959 The family in India. In R. Anshen (ed.), 1949, pp. 167–187.*

Mangin, W.
1963 Urbanisation case history in Peru. *Architectural Design,* 38 (August): 366–370.

Marx, K.
1969 Pre-capitalist economic formations. In Eric J. Hobsbawn (ed.), New York: New World Paperbacks. Original edition appeared in 1857.

Matthews, W.
1904 On the Navaho clan. *A.A.,* 6: 758.

Mauss, M.
1925 *Essai sur le don. L'Année Sociologique,* n.s., 1: 30–186. Paris. Later translated by I. Cunnison as *The Gift.* London: Cohen & West, 1947. New York: Free Press, 1954.

Maybury-Lewis, D.
1965 Durkheim on relationship systems. *Journal for the Scientific Study of Religion,* 4: 253–260.

Mayer, P.
1949 The lineage principle in Gusii society. *I.A.I.,* Memorandum XXIV.

McConnel, U. H.
1939–1940 Social organization of the tribes of Cape York Peninsula, North Queensland. *Oceania,* 10: 54–72, 434–455.

McGee, W. J.
1896 The beginning of marriage. *A.A.,* 9: 371–383.

McIlwraith, T. F.
1948 *The Bella Coola Indians.* 2 vols. Toronto: University of Toronto Press.

McLennan, J. F.
1865 *Primitive marriage.* Edinburgh: A. C. Black.

Mead, G. H.
1934 *Mind, self, and society.* Chicago: University of Chicago Press.

Mead, M.
1961 A re-examination of the problem of incest. Paper read at the Annual Meetings of the American Anthropological Association, Philadelphia, November 16–19.

Mendieta y Nuñez, L.
1959 *El problema agrario de Mexico.* 7th ed. Mexico.

Merton, R. K.
1949 *Social theory and social structure.* New York: Free Press.

———— 1957a The role-set: Problems in sociological theory. *B.J.S.,* 8: 110–118.

———— 1957b *Social theory and social structure.* Rev. and enlarged ed. New York: Free Press.

Miller, G. A.
1956 The magical number seven, plus or minus two: Some limits on our capacity for processing information. *Psychological Review,* 63: 81–97.

Mills, C. W.
1959 *The sociological imagination.* New York: Grove Press.

Miner, H.
1939 *St. Denis: A French Canadian parish.* Chicago: University of Chicago Press.

Mintz, S., and E. R. Wolf
1950 An analysis of ritual co-parenthood (compadrazgo). *S.J.A.,* 6: 341–368.

Mitchell, J. C.
1950 Social organization of the Yao of Southern Nyasaland (Unpublished Ph.D. dissertation, Oxford University.
————— 1956 *The Yao village.* Manchester: University of Manchester Press.
————— 1969 (ed.), *Social networks in urban situations.* Manchester: University of Manchester Press.

Mitchell, W.
1963 Theoretical problems in the concept of kindred. *A.A.,* 65: 343–354.

Montesquieu, Charles Louis de Secondat, Baron de la Brède et de
1750 *De l'esprit des lois.* Later translated by Thomas Nugent. London: G. Bell, 1878.

Mooney, J.
1896 The ghost-dance religion and the Sioux outbreak of 1890. In *U.S. Bureau of American Ethnology, fourteenth annual report . . . 1892–1893.* Washington: U.S. Bureau of American Ethnology.
————— 1907 The Cheyenne Indians. *American Anthropological Association Memoirs,* I: 6.

Moore, W. E.
1964 *Social change.* Englewood Cliffs, N.J.: Prentice-Hall.

Morgan, L. H.
1851 *League of the ho-de-no-sau-nee, or Iroquois.* New York: Dodd, Mead, 1851, 1901. Reprinted by New Haven: Human relations area files, 1954.
————— 1870 *Systems of consanguinity and affinity of the human family.* (1871.) Washington, D.C.: Smithsonian Contributions to Knowledge No. 17.
————— 1877 *Ancient society.* New York: Holt, Rinehart & Winston. (Author reprinted 1907.)

Morley, S. G.
1956 *The ancient Maya.* Stanford: Stanford University Press.

Morris, C.
1946 *Signs, language and behavior.* Englewood Cliffs, N. J.: Prentice-Hall.

Morton, N. E.
1961 Morbidity of children from consanguineous marriages. In A. G. Steinberg (ed.), *Progress in medical genetics.* New York: Grune & Stratton.

Muller, H. F.
1913 A chronological note on the physiological ex-

planation of the prohibition of incest. In *Journal of Religious Psychology,* 6: 294–295.

Murdock, G. P.
1934 Kinship and social behavior among the Haida. *A.A.,* 36: 355–385.
————— 1943 B. Malinowski (Obituary). *A.A.,* 45: 441–451.
————— 1947a *Our primitive contemporaries.* 2nd ed. New York: Macmillan.
————— 1947b Bifurcate merging: A test of five theories. *A.A.,* 49:56–63.
————— 1949 *Social structure.* New York: Macmillan.
————— 1951 Forward. In W. H. Goodenough, 1951, pp. 5–8.*
————— 1955 Changing emphases in social structure. *S.J.A.,* 11: 361–370.
————— 1959 Evolution of social organization. In *Evolution and anthropology.* Washington, D.C.: Anthropological Society of Washington.
————— 1960 Cognatic forms of social organization. In G. P. Murdock (ed.), *Social structure of Southeast Asia.* Chicago: Quadrangle, pp. 1–14.

Murphy, R. F.
1956 Matrilocality and patrilocality in Mundurucú society. *A.A.,* 58: 414–433.
————— 1960 *Headhunter's heritage: Social and economic change among the Mundurucú Indians.* Berkeley: University of California Press.

Nadel, S. F.
1940 The Kede: A riverian state in northern Nigeria. In M. Fortes and E. E. Evans-Pritchard (eds.), 1940, pp. 195–196.*
————— 1943 *Black Byzantium.* London: Oxford University Press.
————— 1945 Notes on Beni Amer society. *Sudan Notes and Records,* 26: 16–17.
————— 1950 Dual descent in the Nuba hills. In A. A. Radcliffe-Brown and C. D. Forde (eds.), 1950, pp. 333–359.*
————— 1951 *The foundations of social anthropology.* London: Cohen & West.
————— 1952 Witchcraft in four African societies: An essay in comparison. *A.A.,* 54: 18–29.
————— 1957 *The theory of social structure.* New York: Free Press.

Nash, M.
1958 Political relations in Guatemala. *Social and Economic Studies,* 7:65–75.

Needham, R.
1956a Review of Homans and Schneider, 1955. *A.J.S.,* 62: 107–108.

———— 1956b A note on kinship and marriage on Pantara. *Bijdragen tot de Taal-, Land- en Volkenkunde*, 112: 285–290. The Hague.

———— 1957 Circulating connubium in Eastern Sumba: A literary analysis. *Bijdragen tot de Taal-, Land- en Volkenkunde*, 113: 168–178. The Hague.

———— 1958a A structural analysis of Purum society. *A.A.*, 60: 75–101.

———— 1958b The formal analysis of prescriptive patrilateral cross-cousin marriage. *S.J.A.*, 14: 199–219.

———— 1960 A structural analysis of Aimol society. *Bijdragen tot de Taal-, Land-, en Volkenkunde*, 116: 81–108.

———— 1961 Notes on the analysis of asymmetric alliance, *Bijdragen tot de Taal-, Land-, en Volkenkunde*, 117: 93–117.

———— 1962 *Structure and sentiment: A test case in social anthropology.* Chicago: University of Chicago Press.

Nett, B. R.
1952 Historical changes in the Osage kinship system. *S.J.A.*, 8; 2: 164–81.

Nicholas, R.
1964 Review of Needham, 1962. *Man*, 64: 71.

Nimuendaju, C.
1942 *The Serente.* Translated by Robert H. Lowie. In *Publications of the Frederick Webb Hodge Anniversary Publication Fund.* Vol. 4. Los Angeles: Southwest Museum.

no author
1951 *Notes and queries in anthropology.* 6th ed. London: R.A.I., for the British Association for the Advancement of Science.

Ogburn, W. F.
1922 *Social change.* New York: Viking.

———— 1933 The family and its functions. In *Recent social trends in the United States.* New York.

Opler, M. E.
1937a An outline of Chiracahua Apache social organization. In F. Eggan, 1937c, pp. 173–242.*

———— 1937b Apache data concerning the relations of kinship terminology to social classification. *A.A.*, 39: 201–212.

Parsons, E. C.
1924 Tewa kin, clan and moiety. *A.A.*, 26: 333–339.

———— 1936 *Mitla: Town of souls.* Chicago: University of Chicago Press.

———— 1945 *Peguche.* Chicago: University of Chicago Press.

Parsons, T.
1943 The kinship system of the contemporary United States. *A.A.*, 45: 22–38.

———— 1949 *Essays in sociological theory: Pure and applied.* New York: Free Press.

———— 1954 The incest taboo. *B.J.S.*, 5: 102–115.

———— 1957 Malinowski and the theory of social systems. In R. Firth, 1957a, pp. 53–70.

Parsons, T., and R. F. Bales
1955 *Family, socialization and interaction process.* Glencoe: Free Press.

Paul, B. D.
1942 Ritual kinship: With special reference to godparenthood in Middle America. (Unpublished Ph.D. dissertation, University of Chicago.)

Paulme, D.
1939 Parenté à plaisanteries et alliance par le Sang en Afrique Occidentale. *Africa*, 12: 433–444.

Pedler, F. J.
1940 Joking relationships in East Africa. *Africa*, 13; 2: 170–173.

Pehrson, R. N.
1954 Bilateral kin groupings as a structural type. *Journal of East Asiatic Studies*, 3: 199–202.

———— 1957 *The bilateral network of social relations in Könkämä Lapp district.* Bloomington: Indiana University Publication, Slavic and East European Series. Vol. 5.

Peters, E. L.
1951 The sociology of the Bedouin of Cyrenaica. (Unpublished Ph.D. dissertation, Oxford University.)

Phillpotts, B. S.
1913 *Kindred and clan in the Middle Ages and after.* Cambridge: Cambridge University Press.

Pitt-Rivers, J.
1954 *The people of the Sierra.* New York: Criterion Books.

Polyani, K., C. M. Arensberg, and H. W. Pearson
1957 *Trade and market in the early empires.* New York: Free Press.

Pospisil, L.
1957 Field notes on the Nunamiut Eskimo, Alaska. (Unpublished.)

———— 1960 The Kapauku Papuans and their kinship organization. *Oceania*, 30: 188–205.

———— 1964 Law and societal structure among the Nunamiut Eskimo. W. H. Goodenough (ed.), *Explorations in cultural anthropology.* New York: McGraw-Hill, 1964, pp. 395–432.

Potter, J., M. Diaz, and G. Foster (eds.)
1967 *Peasant society: A reader.* Boston: Atlantic-Little, Brown.

Prince Peter of Greece and Denmark
1957 For a new definition of marriage. *Man,* 57: 35.
———— 1963 *A study of polyandry.* The Hague: Mouton.

Radcliffe-Brown, A. R.
1913 Three tribes of western Australia. *J.R.A.I.,* 43: 143–194.
———— 1914 Review of Malinowski, 1913. *Man,* 14: 16.
———— 1922 *The Andaman islanders.* Cambridge: Cambridge University Press. New York: Free Press, 1948.
———— 1923 The methods of ethnology and social anthropology. *South African Journal of Science,* 20: 124–147. Reprinted in M. N. Srinivas (ed.), *Method in social anthropology: Selected essays.* Chicago: University of Chicago Press, 1958.
———— 1924 The mother's brother in South Africa. *South African Journal of Science,* 21: 542–555. (Reprinted in Radcliffe-Brown 1952c, 15–31.*)
———— 1929a A further note on Ambryn. Man, 29: 35.
———— 1929b Bilateral descent. *Man,* 29, note 157.
———— 1930 The social organization of Australian tribes. *Oceania,* 1: 34–63. Reprinted as The social organization of Australian tribes. *Oceania Monographs,* No. 1, 1931.
———— 1931 The present position of anthropological studies. Anthropology Proceedings, Section H, Association for the Advancement of Science. London.
———— 1935a On the concept of function in social science (reply to Lesser, 1935). *A.A.,* 37: 394–402. Reprinted in A. R. Radcliffe-Brown 1952c, pp. 178–187.*
———— 1935b Patrilineal and matrilineal succession. *Iowa Law Review,* 20: 286–303. Reprinted in A. R. Radcliffe-Brown, 1952c, pp. 32–48.*
———— 1935c Kinship terminologies in California. *A.A.,* 37: 530–535.
———— 1940a On social structure. *J.R.A.I.,* 70: 1–22. Reprinted in A. R. Radcliffe-Brown, 1952c, pp. 188–204.*
———— 1940b Preface to M. Fortes and E. E. Evans-Pritchard (eds.), 1940.*
———— 1940c On joking relationships. *Africa,* 13: 195–210. Reprinted in A. R. Radcliffe-Brown, 1952c, pp. 90 ff.*

———— 1941 The study of kinship systems. *J.R.A.I.,* 70, 1–18. Reprinted in A. R. Radcliffe-Brown, 1952c, pp. 49–89.*
———— 1944 *A natural science of society.* New York: Free Press. (Reprinted 1948.)
———— 1945 Religion and society. *J.R.A.I.,* 75: 1 (Henry Myers lecture).
———— 1949 A further note on joking relationships. *Africa,* 19: 133–140. Also in A. R. Radcliffe-Brown, 1952c, pp. 105 ff.*
———— 1950 Introduction. In A. R. Radcliffe-Brown and C. D. Forde (eds.), 1950, pp. 1–85.*
———— 1951a Murngin social organization. *A.A.,* 53: 37–55.
———— 1951b The comparative method in social anthropology. *J.R.A.I.,* 81: 15–22.
———— 1952a Historical note on British social anthropology. *A.A.,* 54: 275–277.
———— 1952b Social anthropology, past and present. *Man,* 52: 13–14.
———— 1952c *Structure and function in primitive society.* London: Cohen & West. (Contains Radcliffe-Brown 1924, 1933a, 1933b, 1935a, 1935b, 1940a, 1941, plus a valuable introduction.)

Radcliffe-Brown, A. R., and C. D. Forde (eds.)
1950 *African systems of kinship and marriage.* London: Oxford University Press, for the I.A.I.

Raglan, F. R. S.
1933 *Jocasta's crime.* London: Methuen.

Rattray, R. S.
1929 *Ashanti law and constitution.* Oxford: Oxford University Press.

Redfield, R.
1930 *Tepoztlán, a Mexican village.* Chicago: University of Chicago Press. (Reprinted 1949.)
———— 1937 Introduction. In F. Eggan (ed.), 1937c.*
———— 1941 *The folk culture of Yucatan.* Chicago: University of Chicago Press.
———— 1945 Notes on San Juan Palopo. *Microfilm collection of manuscripts on Middle American cultural anthropology,* No. 4. Chicago: University of Chicago Library.
———— 1953 Relations of anthropology to the social sciences and to the humanities. In A. L. Kroeber et al. (eds.), 1953.*

Redfield, R., R. Linton, and M. Herskovits
1936 Memorandum on the study of acculturation. *A.A.,* 38: 149–152. Also in *Man,* 35: 145–148, and *Africa,* 9: 114–118.

Redfield, R., and A. V. Rojas
1934 Cham Kom: A Mayan village. *Carnegie Institute Publication,* No. 448. Washington, D.C.

Reina, R.
1966   *Law of the saints*. New York: Bobbs-Merrill.
Richards, A. I.
1936   Mother right in central Africa. In E. E. Evans-Pritchard, R. Firth, B. Malinowski, and I. Schapera (eds.), *Essays presented to C. G. Seligman*. London: Paul, Trench & Trubner.
———— 1939   *Land, labour, and diet in Northern Rhodesia*. London: Oxford University Press.
———— 1940   The political system of the Bemba. In M. Fortes and E. E. Evans-Pritchard (eds.), 1940.*
———— 1950   Some types of family structure amongst the central Bantu. In A. R. Radcliffe-Brown and C. D. Forde (eds.), 1950.*
———— 1952   Review of Lévi-Strauss, 1949. *Man*, 52: 12–13.
Richardson, J., and A. L. Kroeber
1940   Three centuries of women's dress fashions: A quantitative analysis. *Anthropology Records*, No. 2. Berkeley: University of California Press.
Rivers, W. H. R.
1900   A geneological method of collecting social and vital statistics. *J.R.A.I.*, 30: 74–82.
———— 1906   *The Todas*. London: Macmillan.
———— 1907   On the origin of the classificatory system of relationships. In N. W. Thomas (ed.), *Anthropological essays presented to E. B. Tylor*. London: Oxford University Press.
———— 1910   The geneological method of anthropological enquiry. *Sociological Review*, 3: 1.
———— 1911   The ethnological analysis of culture. (Presidential address to the Anthropological Section of the British Association for the Advancement of Science, London.) Printed in *Science*, 34: 385–397.
———— 1914a   *Kinship and social organization*. London: Constable. Reprinted, with commentaries by R. Firth and D. Schneider. London: Athlone, 1968, and New York: Humanities Press, 1968.
———— 1914b   *The history of Melanesian society*. 2 vols. Cambridge: Cambridge University Press.
———— 1914c   Kin, kinship. In *Hastings encyclopedia of religion and ethics*. Vol. 7. New York: Scribner's, pp. 700–707.
———— 1915a   Marriage, introductory and primitive. In *Hastings encyclopedia of religion and ethics*. Vol. 8, pp. 423–432.
———— 1915b   Mother-right. In *Hastings encyclopedia of religion and ethics*. Vol. 8, pp. 851–859.
———— 1924   *Social organization*. London: Kegan Paul, Trench, Trubner.
———— 1926   *Psychology and ethnology*. London: Kegan Paul, Trench, Trubner.

Romney, A. K., and R. D'Andrade
1964   Cognitive aspects of English kin terms. *A.A.*, 66: 3 (Part 2): 146–170.
Rose, A. (ed.)
1962   Introduction to *Human behavior and social processes*. Boston: Houghton Mifflin, pp. 3–19.
Rowe, J. H.
1965   The Renaissance foundations of anthropology. *A.A.*, 67: 1–20.
Russell, R. V.
1916   *Tribes and castes of the central provinces of India*. 4 vols. London.

Sacks, H.
1963   Sociological description. *Berkeley Journal of Sociology*, 8: 1–16.
Sahagun, B. de
1932   *Historia de las cosas de Nuevo Espana*. 5 vols. Madrid: Francisco de Paso.
Sahlins, M. D.
1958   *Social stratification in Polynesia*. Seattle: University of Washington Press.
———— 1961   The segmentary lineage: An organization of predatory expansion. *A.A.*, 63: 322–345.
———— 1962   *Moahla: Culture and nature on a Fijian island*. Ann Arbor: University of Michigan Press.
Sahlins, M. D., and E. R. Service (eds.)
1960   *Evolution and culture*. Ann Arbor: University of Michigan Press.
Sapir, E.
1909   *Wishram texts*. Publications of the American Ethnological Society. Vol. 2. Leyden.
———— 1913   A note on reciprocal terms of relationship in America. *A.A.*, 15: 132–138.
———— 1916a   Terms of relationship and the levirate. *A.A.*, 18: 327–337.
———— 1916b   Time perspective in aboriginal American culture: A study in method. *Memoir 90, Geological Survey of Canada. Anthropological series*, No. 13. Ottawa: King's Printer.
———— 1921   *Language*. New York: Harcourt Brace Jovanovich. Reprinted in New York: Harvest Book, 1949.
Sarbin, T.
1954   Role theory. In G. Lindzey (ed.), *Handbook of social psychology*. Reading, Mass.: Addison-Wesley, ch. VI, pp. 223 ff.
Sauer, C. O.
1947   Early relations of man to plants. *Geographical Review*, 37: 1–25.

Schapera, I.
1950 Kinship and marriage among the Tswana. In A. R. Radcliffe-Brown and C. D. Forde, 1950.*
—— 1953 Some comments on the comparative method in social anthropology. *A.A.*, 55: 353–362.

Scheffler, H.
1964 Descent concepts and descent groups: The Maori case. *Journal of the Polynesian Society*, 73: 126–133.
—— 1970 The elementary structure of kinship, by C. Lévi-Strauss: A review article. *A.A.*, 72: 251–268.

Schmitt, K., and I. O. Schmitt
n.d. *Wichita kinship: Past and present.* Norman, Okla.: University Book Exchange.

Schneider, D. M.
1953a Review of *Kinship and marriage among the Nuer* by E. E. Evans-Pritchard, *A.A.*, 55: 582–584.
—— 1953b A note on bridewealth and the stability of marriage. *Man*, 53: 55–57.
—— 1953c Yap kinship terminology and kinship groups. *A.A.*, 55: 21–36.
—— 1961 The distinctive features of matrilineal descent groups. In D. Schneider and E. K. Gough (eds.), *Matrilineal kinship*. Berkeley: University of California Press.
—— 1965a Some muddles in the models: Or, how the system really works. In M. Banton (ed.), *The relevance of models for social anthropology. Association of Social Anthropologists of the Commonwealth Monographs*, No. 1. London: Tavistock.
—— 1965b American kin terms and terms for kinsmen. In E. A. Hammel (ed.), 1965, pp. 288–308.*
—— 1967 *American kinship: A cultural account.* Englewood Cliffs, N.J.: Prentice-Hall.

Schneider, D. M., and E. E. Gough (eds.)
1961 Introduction to *Matrilineal kinship*. Berkeley and Los Angeles: University of California Press.

Schneider, D. M., and G. C. Homans
1955 Kinship terminology and the American kinship system. *A.A.*, 57: 1194–1208.

Schneider, D. M., and J. M. Roberts
1956 *Zuni kin terms.* Notebook No. 3. Lincoln: University of Nebraska, Laboratory of Anthropology.

Schutz, A.
1964 *Collected papers II: Studies in social theory.* New York: Nijhoff.

Seligman, B. Z.
1928 Asymmetry in descent, with special reference to Pentacost *J.R.A.I.*, 58: 533–558.

—— 1929 Incest and descent. *J.R.A.I.*, 59: 231–272.
—— 1950 The problem of incest and exogamy: A restatement. *A.A.*, 52: 305–316.

Seligman, C. G., and B. Z. Seligman
1932 *Pagan tribes of the Nilotic Sudan.* London: Routledge & Kegan Paul.

Service, E. R.
1960 Kinship terminology and evolution. *A.A.*, 62: 747–763.
—— 1962 *Primitive social organization: An evolutionary perspective.* New York: Random House.

Sharp, L.
1934 The social organization of the Yir-Yoront tribe, Cape York Peninsula. *Oceania*, 4: 404–431; 5: 19–42.

Simmons, L.
1945 *The role of the aged in primitive society.* New Haven: Yale University Press.

Singer, M. B.
1953 Summary of comments and discussion of Shapera, 1953. *A.A.*, 55: 362–366.

Slater, M.
1959 Ecological factors in the origin of incest. *A.A.*, 61: 1042–1058.

Smith, E. W.
1935 Africa: What do we know of it? *J.R.A.I.*, 65: 1–81.

Smith, E., and A. Dale
1920 *The Ila-speaking people of northern Rhodesia.* London: Macmillan.

Smith, R. T.
1956 The Negro family in British Guiana. London: Routledge & Kegan Paul.

Smith, W. R.
1885 *Kinship and marriage in early Arabia.* Cambridge: Cambridge University Press.
—— 1907 *Lecture on the religion of the Semites.* London: Adam & Charles Black.

Sousberghe, L. de
1955 *Structures de parenté et d'alliance d'après les formules pende.* Brussels: Academic Royale des Sciences Coloniale.

Speck, F. G.
1909 Ethnology of the Yuchi Indians. *Anthropological Publications, University Museum, University of Pennsylvania*, 1: 1–154.

Spencer, H.
1910 *Scientific essays.* London, New York: Appleton-Century-Crofts.

Spencer, R. F. (ed.)
1954 *Method and perspective in anthropology. Papers in honor of Wilson D. Wallis.* Minneapolis: University of Minneapolis Press.

Spicer, E. H.
1940   *Pascua: A Yacqui village in Arizona.* Chicago: University of Chicago Press.

Spier, L.
1925   The distribution of kinship systems in North America. *University of Washington Publications in Anthropology,* 1; 2: 69–88.

——— 1929   Problems arising from the cultural position of the Havusupai. *A.A.,* 31:213–222.

Spiro, M. E.
1954   Is the family universal? *A.A.,* 56: 839–846. Reprinted in P. J. Bohannan and J. Middleton, 1968a, pp. 221–236.*

Spoehr, A.
1947   Changing kinship systems. *Chicago Field Museum of Natural History Publication 583, Anthropological Series,* 33: 151–235.

——— 1950   Observations on the study of kinship. *A.A.,* 52: 1–15.

Srinivas, M. N. (ed.)
1958   *Method in social anthropology: Essays by Radcliffe-Brown.* Chicago: University of Chicago Press. (Contains Radcliffe-Brown 1923, and other valuable essays.)

Stark, C. N.
1889   *The primitive family.* London: Routledge & Kegan Paul.

Steward, J.
1954   *People of the Sierra.* Chicago: University of Chicago Press.

——— 1955   *Theory of culture change.* Urbana: University of Illinois Press.

Strong, W. D.
1929   Cross-cousin marriage and the culture of the northeast Algonkian. *A.A.,* 31: 277–288.

Suchman, E. A.
1950   The scalogram board technique for scale analysis. In *Studies in social psychology in World War II.* Vol. 4. *Measurement and prediction.* Princeton: Princeton University Press, pp. 91–121.

Swanton, J. R.
1905   The social organization of American tribes. *A.A.,* 7: 663–673.

——— 1917   Some anthropological misconceptions, *A.A.,* 19: 459–470.

——— 1918–19   Tlingit. *Smithsonian Institute. Bureau of American Ethnology Bulletin,* No. 40.

——— 1928   *Social organization and social usages of the Indians of the Creek confederacy. 42nd Annual Report.* Washington, D.C.: Bureau of American Ethnology.

——— 1931   *Source materials for the social and ceremonial life of the Choctaw Indians. Bulletin 103.* Washington, D.C.: Bureau of American Ethnology.

Tax, S.
1937a   Some problems of social organization. In F. Eggan (ed.), 1937c, pp. 3–34.*

——— 1937b   The social organization of the Fox Indians. In F. Eggan (ed.), 1937b, pp. 243–284.*

——— 1937c   From Lafitau to Radcliffe-Brown. In F. Eggan (ed.), 1937c.*

——— 1941   World view and social relations in Guatamala. *A.A.,* 43: 27–42.

Tax, S., et al. (eds.)
1953   *An appraisal of anthropology today.* Chicago: University of Chicago Press.

Thomas, W. I.
1937   *Primitive behavior.* New York: McGraw-Hill.

Thurnwald, R.
1921   *Die Gemeinde der Bánaro.* Stuttgart: Ferdinand Enke.

Thurston, E.
1909   *Caste and tribes of southern India.* 7 vols. Madras.

Todd, T. W.
1927   Skeletal records of mortality. *Scientific Monthly,* 24: 481–496.

Tomasevich, J.
1963   *Peasants, politics and economic change in Yugoslavia.* Stanford: Stanford University Press.

Tönnies, F.
1887   *Gemeinshaft und Gesellschaft.* Leipzig. Translated by C. P. Loomis as *Community and society.* East Lansing: Michigan State University Press, 1957.

Tylor, E. B.
1865   *Researches into the early history of mankind.* London: J. Murray.

——— 1871   *Primitive culture.* London: J. Murray.

——— 1881   *Anthropology: An introduction to the study of man and civilization.* New York: Appleton-Century-Crofts.

———1889   On a method of investigating the development of institutions; applied to laws of marriage and descent. *J.R.A.I.,* 18: 245–272.

Unwin, J. D.
1929   The classification system of relationship (letter). *Man,* 29: 164.

Villa Rojas, A.
1945   The Maya of east central Quintano Roo. *Carnegie Institute Publication No. 559.* Washington, D.C.: Carnegie Institute.
—— 1946   Notas sobre la ethnografia de los Indios Tzeltals de Uxchuc, Chiapas, Mexico. *Microfilm Collection of Manuscripts on Middle American Cultural Anthropology,* No. 7, Chicago, University of Chicago Library.

Von Neumann, J., and O. Morgenstern
1944   *Theory of games and economic behavior.* 2nd ed. Princeton: Princeton University Press, 1947.

Waitz, T.
1860–77   *Anthropologie der naturvoelker.* 6 vols. Leipzig: F. Fleischer.

Wake, C. S.
1879   The primitive human family. *J.R.A.I.,* 9: 3–19.

Wallace, A. F. C.
1961a   *Culture and personality.* New York: Random House.
—— 1961b   On being just complicated enough. In *Proceedings of the National Academy of Sciences,* 47: 458–464.
—— 1962   Culture and cognition. *Science,* 135: 351–357.
—— 1965   The problems of psychological validity of componential analysis. In E. A. Hammel (ed.), 1965, pp. 229–248.*

Wallace, A., and J. Atkins
1960   The meaning of kinship terms. *A.A.,* 62: 58–80.

Warner, W. L.
1930   Morphology and functions of the Australian Murngin-type of kinship. *A.A.,* 32: 207–256.
—— 1931   Idem *A.A.,* 33: 172–198.
—— 1933   The kinship morphology of 41 north Australian tribes. *A.A.,* 35: 63–86.
—— 1937   *A black civilization.* New York: Harper & Row. Reprinted in Harper Torchbook edition, 1964.

Washburn, S. L. (ed.)
1961   *The social life of early man.* New York: Wenner-Gren Foundation. (*Viking Fund Publication in Anthropology,* No. 31.)

Watson, W.
1954   Bridewealth and the stability of marriage. *Man,* 54: 67–68.

Weber, M.
1925   *Wirtschaft und Gesellschaft.* Tubingen: J. C. B. Mohr.

—— 1947   *The theory of social and economic organization.* Translated by A. R. Hudson and T. Parsons. New York: Free Press.

Westermark, E.
1891   *History of human marriage.* London: Macmillan. 5th ed., 1921. (Also reprinted 1894.)
—— 1929   *Marriage.* New York: Jonathan Cape & Harrison Smith.

White, L. A.
1948a   Lewis Henry Morgan: Pioneer in the theory of social evolution. In H. E. Barnes (ed.), *An introduction to the history of sociology.* Chicago: University of Chicago Press, pp. 138–154.
—— 1948b   The definition and prohibition of incest. *A.A.,* 50: 416–434.
—— 1949   *The science of culture.* New York: Farrar, Straus & Giroux.
—— 1959   *The evolution of culture.* New York: McGraw-Hill.
—— 1966   The social organization of ethnological theory. In *Rice University Studies,* 52: 4. (*Monograph in Cultural Anthropology.*) Houston: Rice University Press.

Wilson, M.
1950   Nyakyusa kinship. In A. R. Radcliffe-Brown and C. D. Forde (eds.), 1950.*
—— 1951a   Nyakyusa age-villages. *J.R.A.I.,* 79: 21–25.
—— 1951b   *Good company: A study of Nyakyusa age villages.* London: Oxford University Press.

Wilson, P. J.
1961   Incest: A case study. (Paper read at the Annual Meetings of the *A.A.A.,* Philadelphia, November 16–19.)

Wiser, W. H., and C. V. Wiser
1963   *Behind mud walls, 1930–1960.* Berkeley: University of California Press.

Wissler, C.
1914   Material cultures of the North American Indian. *A.A.,* 16: 501 ff.
—— 1922   *The American Indian.* 2nd ed. New York, Oxford: Oxford University Press.
—— 1926   *The relation of nature to man in aboriginal America.* New York, London: Oxford University Press.
—— 1929   *An introduction to social anthropology.* New York: Holt, Rinehart & Winston.

Wolf, A. P.
1968   Adopt a daughter-in-law, marry a sister: A Chinese solution to the problem of the incest taboo. *A.A.,* 70: 864–876.

Wolf, E. R.
1955   Types of Latin American peasantry: A preliminary discussion. *A.A.*, 57: 452–471.
——— 1965 Kinship, friendship and patron-client relations in complex societies. In M. Banton (ed.), *The social anthropology of complex societies. A.S.A.,* No. 4. London: Tavistock, pp. 1–18.
——— 1966 *Peasants.* Englewood Cliffs, N.J.: Prentice-Hall.

Wolff, K. H. (ed.)
1950   *The sociology of Georg Simmel.* New York: Free Press.

Wolfram, E. M. S.
1956   The explanation of prohibitions and preferences of marriage between kin. Unpublished Ph.D. dissertation, Oxford University.

Wouden, F. A. E. van
1935   *Sociale structuurtypen in Groote Oost.* Leiden: Ginsberg.
——— 1956. *Locale groepen en dubbele afstamming in Kodi, West Sumba. Bijdragen tot de Taal-, Land- en Volkenkunde,* 112: 204–246. The Hague.

Yakovlev, E. K.
1900   Etnograficheski obzor inorodcheskogo naseleniya dolini yuzhnovo Yeniseya. *Opisaniye Minussinskovo Musea.* Vol. 4. Minussinsk.

Yalman, N.
1962   The structure of the Sinhalese kindred: A re-examination of the Dravidian terminology. *A.A.,* 64: 548–575.

Yang, C. K.
1965   *Chinese Communist society: Family and village.* Cambridge: M.I.T. Press.

Young, K.
1942   *Sociology, a study of society and culture.* New York: American Book.

Young, M., and P. Willmott
1957   *Family and kinship in east London.* London: Routledge & Kegan Paul.

Zborowski, M., and E. Herzog
1952   *Life is with people.* New York: International Universities Press.

ATHAPASKANS

ALGONKIANS

IRISH

ENGLISH

INCA

LIST OF TRIBAL AND GEOGRAPHICAL NAMES

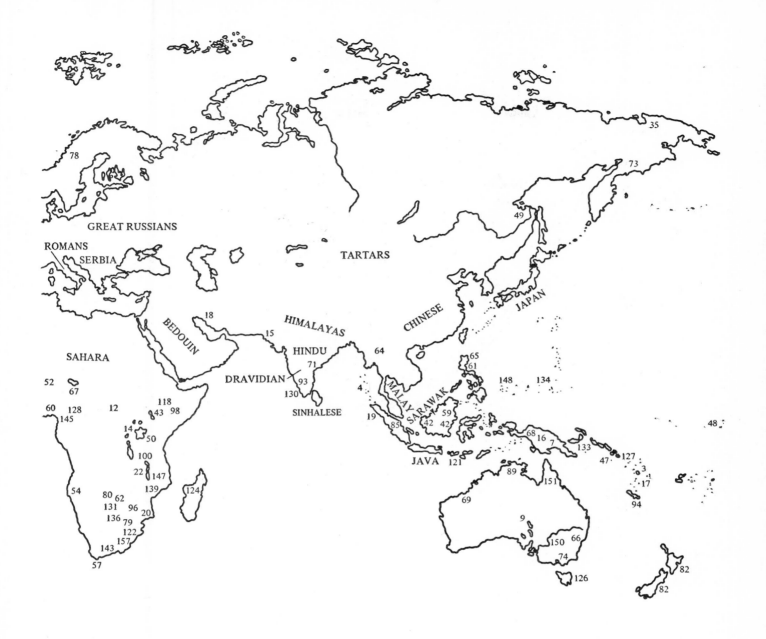

GREAT RUSSIANS

ROMANS
SERBIA

TARTARS

BEDOUIN

HIMALAYAS

CHINESE

JAPAN

SAHARA

HINDU

71

DRAVIDIAN

93

64

130

SINHALESE

MALAY

SARAWAK

JAVA

81. Mandan
82. Maori
83. Maya
84. Menomini
85. Minangkabau
86. Miwok
87. Moche
88. Mundurucu
89. Murngin
90. Naskapi
91. Natchez
92. Navaho
93. Nayar
94. New Caledonia
95. Nez Percé
96. Ngoni (Shona)

97. Nootka
98. Nuer
99. Nupe
100. Nyakyusa
101. Omaha
102. Osage
103. Paiute
104. Papago
105. Pascua
106. Pawnee
107. Peguche
108. Pima
109. Pomo
110. Pueblos
111. Pukapuka
112. Purum

113. Quechua
114. Salish
115. Samoans
116. Seneca
117. Serente
118. Shilluk
119. Shoshone
120. Siriono
121. Sumba
122. Swazi
123. Tallensi
124. Tanala
125. Tarascan
126. Tasmanians
127. Tikopia
128. Tiv

129. Tlingit
130. Toda
131. Tonga
132. Tongans
133. Trobriands (inc. Dobu)
134. Truk
135. Tsimshian
136. Tswana (Bechuana)
137. Tzintzuntzan
138. Tzeltal
139. VaNdau
140. Washo
141. Winnebago
142. Wishram
143. Xhosa
144. Yahgan

145. Yako (Ekoi)
146. Yana (Yahi)
147. Yao
148. Yap
149. Yaqui
150. Yaralde
151. Yir Yoront
152. Yokuts-Mono
153. Yoruba
154. Yuchi
155. Yurok
156. Zapotec
157. Zulu
158. Zuni